Development of Economic Analysis

Sixth Edition

D0217519

Development of Economic Analysis has been instrumental in introducing a generation of students to the history of economic thought. Beginning with the ancients, Ingrid Hahne Rima charts the development of economics from its establishment as an analytical discipline in the eighteenth century, through the classicism of Ricardo and Malthus, the socialism of Marx, and the explicitly scientific approaches of Walras and Marshall.

The later chapters exhibit the influence of these various traditions in the twentieth century: primarily the theories of Keynes, but also the thinking of institutionalists, the Chicago School and the emergence of econometrics.

Rima is unapologetic in her insistence that studying the history of economic thought *matters* and that economics is a discipline of competing paradigms. This edition has been fully revised and updated and includes:

- chronologies of the key dates in the development of economics

- the inclusion of extracts from original texts

- a clear examination of how the study of the history of economic thought impinges upon modern thinking

This classic, comprehensive and accessible text boasts a host of features, including charts, questions, and a glossary of key terms. It will prove to be an invaluable guide to students seeking to understand the development of economic analysis.

Ingrid Hahne Rima is Professor of Economics at Temple University, Pennsylvania

Development of Economic Analysis

Sixth Edition

Ingrid Hahne Rima

London and New York

First published 1967 by Richard D. Irwin, Inc.

New editions published 1972, 1978, 1986, 1991

Fifth edition published 1996
by Routledge
11 New Fetter Lane, London EC4P 4EE

Simultaneously published in the USA and Canada
by Routledge
29 West 35th Street, New York, NY 10001

Sixth edition 2001

Reprinted 2002

Routledge is an imprint of the Taylor & Francis Group

© 1967, 1972, 1978, 1986, 1991, 1996, 2001 Ingrid Hahne Rima

Typeset in Times by RefineCatch Limited, Bungay, Suffolk
Printed and bound in Great Britain by
TJ International Ltd, Padstow, Cornwall

All rights reserved. No part of this book may be reprinted or
reproduced or utilised in any form or by any electronic,
mechanical, or other means, now known or hereafter
invented, including photocopying and recording, or in any
information storage or retrieval system, without permission in
writing from the publishers.

British Library Cataloguing in Publication Data
A catalogue record for this book is available from the British Library

Library of Congress Cataloging in Publication Data
Rima, Ingrid Hahne
     Development of economic analysis / Ingrid Hahne Rima. – 6th ed.
        p.   cm.
     Includes bibliographical references and index.
        1. Economics – History.   I. Title.
     HB75 .R46   2000   00–038255
     330′.09 – dc21

ISBN 0–415–23296–1 (hbk)
ISBN 0–415–23297–X (pbk)

For Philip – of course!

Contents

Contents

Preface to the sixth edition

When the first edition of *Development of Economic Analysis* was published in 1967, economists had already established their discipline as 'scientific,' in the mathematical style in which they presented their arguments, which were quite explicitly modeled to become joined to quantitative research. That the new style of economic discussion and communication leaned in this direction was partly a reflection of the influx of mathematicians, physicists and engineers into the profession. It also reflected the shift of focus in the allocation of research funds during the Great Depression, by such well-endowed organizations as the Rockefeller Foundation, toward 'scientific' endeavors. Thus, by the late 1960s the discursive non-mathematical style of textbooks in the history of economic thought made them appear outmoded compared with the increasingly formal presentations in other textbooks that had, by then, become focused on micro- or macroeconomic analysis.

Because there was still a substantial interest in the history of economics, the idea of writing a text that would focus on the development of the analytical tools of economics seemed to offer a vehicle for narrowing the distance between books in economic theory and the traditional book in the history of thought. Accordingly, the first chapter of *Development of Economic Analysis* posed the question: 'Why was the emergence of economic analysis delayed until the latter part of the eighteenth century, when economic ideas can be traced to the philosophical, legal, religious, ethical and political writings of the scholars of antiquity?' Thus, the chapters that followed were designed to present the emergence of economics as a discipline that was becoming increasingly 'scientific,' partly in consequence of its greater reliance on the tools and perspective of the natural sciences, and because it focused less on the value judgments that characterized the discipline before the days of 'logical positivism.' Lamentably, the preference that professional economists now have for the language of mathematics and empirical testing is, in no small measure, responsible for the present relative neglect of the history of economic ideas, economic history, and institutionally oriented courses in contemporary graduate and undergraduate programs in economics. On the positive side, the history of econometrics and its relation to economic theory has become an important new research area for historians of economic thought. It was for this reason that the fifth edition incorporated a new chapter that articulated the emergence of econometrics as the 'sister discipline' of economics.

The chief concern of the sixth edition is to bring the study of the history of economic theory and method into the twenty-first century. The discipline of economics has undergone changes, some of which are subtle, when compared with the state of economics in 1967, when the history of economic thought was a requirement for students in economics at doctoral, masters, and baccalaureate levels. It was also a recommended and popular course among non-majors. This requirement has been substantially eliminated, because it is widely believed that study time is better spent in mastering mathematics for economists and econometrics. It thus seems essential to rethink how the history of economic thought might best be presented to recapture the interest of readers who have either been misled into thinking that the historical aspects of their discipline are an unnecessary frill that will not add much to their expertise if they are, or plan to become, professional economists; or even that the history of economic thought is not particularly useful for an educated person who is simply seeking to understand how the economic world functions.

One vehicle for reviving student interest in the history of economics is to provide a more enlightened perspective about the role of what might be termed 'numeracy' in the development of economics. The conventional wisdom that reliance on mathematics and quantitative techniques is largely the province of modern economists is quite misguided. The growth of knowledge throughout human history has required numeracy to measure, quantify and lend precision to its concepts and ideas. The growth of knowledge about the behavior of the economy is no exception. It is simply that historians of economic thought have been quite tardy in integrating the role of numeracy into their expositions of the development of analytical economics, while those who were mathematically trained had little reason to educate them. The present edition seeks to correct that omission by emphasizing the parallel emergence of numeracy in economics on a textbook level.

User response to the *Issues–Answers* format for incorporating selections from the original source readings that comprise the Masterworks of the history of economics has been so positive that this feature is carried over into this edition, with several additions that relate specifically to numeracy. These are introduced within the context of the many controversial issues to which those who shaped economics gave their attention. This format offers the double advantage of providing easy access to original source readings while re-enforcing reader appreciation of the intensely practical concerns of our intellectual forebears as problem solvers. The differing 'answers' that they offered also make it manifestly clear that intellectual controversy has been a characteristic of economic inquiry from its earliest days.

Many students are acquiring a fairly sophisticated level of mathematical and econometric training, even as undergraduates. However, because mathematics is not a 'discovery tool' in economics, the language of mathematics will not be substituted for English in this text. Not only would it add little that is substantive, but it no doubt would preclude other readers (and among undergraduates they are probably the majority) who have limited mathematical training, but who are nevertheless ready to address the 'big questions' of the twenty-first century. One of these is, assuredly, the policy question of the appropriate balance between individual and public responsibility in promoting human welfare. While the primary concern of this revision is to offer a systematic account of the development of the body of knowledge that comprises economic theory and the methods (deduction versus empiricism) by which knowledge is to be discovered and given expression, whether in words or numbers, it would be inappropriate to overlook completely the fact that numeracy often has had a policy dimension that warrants examination as part of the history of economic theory and method.

The introduction of numeracy lends itself comfortably to retaining the division of the subject matter of the book into six parts. Some numerical concepts and techniques can be traced to antiquity, and are thus part of the 'pre-classical' period that specifically influenced economic thought. Others accompanied the revival of trade from the fifteenth century onwards, and proliferated as part of the contributions of the French and British political arithmeticians of the seventeenth and early eighteenth centuries. Their contributions constitute what might be termed the 'first stage' of numeracy in economics, yet they are a little appreciated part of the contributions to the 'pre-classical' period, which is the subject matter of Part I of this book.

Adam Smith's *Wealth of Nations* laid an important part of the groundwork for the classical tradition, but his lack of enthusiasm for political arithmetic brought an early end to the first stage of numeracy in economics. The thinkers who followed Adam Smith thus relied on the deductive method rather than empiricism to establish the principles of the Classical tradition. Part II explores the major themes of Classicism in terms of the specific contributions of Smith, Malthus, Say, Ricardo, John Stuart Mill and Senior. The chapter titles are intended to convey the specific topic areas of their contributions.

Part III, 'The Critics of Classicism,' focuses on the writings of an extremely diverse group of nineteenth-century writers. Besides including Karl Marx's alternative analytical system, the best known among these are the 'first generation' marginalists – Jevons, Menger, and Walras. The German and English historical schools, and the English socialists, were also part of the dissent against the classical tradition. Several who worked in England were part of the new movement 'to collect, arrange and compare facts' relating to economic activities, events, and outcomes, and present them in numerical form, which laid the foundation for the new science of statistics. Their mission culminated in the establishment of the Statistical Section of the British Association for the Advancement of Science (subsequently Section F) in 1833, and the Statistical Society of London (later the Royal Statistical Society) in 1834. Within a few short years, proponents of the science of fact-gathering undertook to infer behavioral generalizations or economic 'laws' from their data as a basis for mounting public policies to gain compliance with standards of moral conduct that would promote the greatest good for the greatest number. Especially in the work of W. Stanley Jevons, this perspective led to the identification of mathematical expressions of economic behavior and the view that, when supplemented by the empirical science of statistics, economics might gradually be erected into an exact science.

Part IV, 'The Neoclassical Tradition,' begins with the eclectic efforts of Alfred Marshall to join marginalist techniques and thinking to the classical tradition. His promotion of the use of diagrams as part of his effort to make economics 'scientific' at long last fully appreciated the possibilities recognized as long ago as René Decartes' *Geometria* (1637), that the diagrams used in mathematics, meteorology, and engineering could become models for those drawn by political economists. While Marshall was skeptical that 'statistical treatment alone can give us definitions and precision of thought' (Book V, Chap XII, p. 461), it is he who led economists to posit that money can serve as a basis for measuring human behavioral motives. His technique has made economics unique among the social sciences with respect to quantification.

Marshall's oral and written tradition was refined and embellished by his students and colleagues, as well as by American scholars who came under their influence. These developments are part of the stunning intellectual breakthroughs that were achieved during the period George Shackle so colorfully called 'the years of high theory.' These years were also characterized by the dissenting voices of the institutionalists, the theoretical socialists, and John Maynard Keynes, whose intent was nothing less than to generate an intellectual revolution. The issues of their dissent are examined in the three chapters that comprise Part V; these also set the stage for the concluding Part VI, 'Beyond High Theory,' which undertakes to provide a historical guide to contemporary theory. Chapter 22, which introduces Part VI, interprets econometrics as playing a key role in shaping not only contemporary economics, but in defining critical areas of controversy and dissent. These topics are more fully articulated in Chapters 23–25, which examine the competing paradigms of contemporary economics within the framework of their historical traditions.

As in previous editions, the division of the subject matter is intended to accommodate the preferences of individual users in tailoring their course content. For users who prefer a firm delineation between the history of economic thought and contemporary economics, Parts I through IV comprise a substantially traditional course. Their focus is on the development of neoclassical economics up to approximately 1945. The overview at the beginning of each part facilitates omission of certain chapters, if necessary, without sacrificing continuity. For users who also wish to examine criticisms of mainstream thinking during the same period, Institutionalist, Socialist, and Keynesian contributions are given extended treatment in Part V.

Part VI is intended for those who wish to examine the continuum of ideas that links contemporary theory with the history of thought. It is written to capture the perspective that the majority of the economics profession now strives to emulate the hard sciences in establishing mathematically modeled propositions of 'pure' theory to be tested by means of econometric techniques. This 'mainstream' approach to economics constitutes the professional core of the PhD degree in economics at virtually all of the graduate schools in the United States, the United Kingdom, Canada, Australia and Western Europe. With the professionalization of economics via an international community of scholars who stay in close touch via journals, associations, society conferences, fax, e-mail and the internet, the similarities among their programs are often greater than their differences. Nevertheless, there is also a strong expression of dissent, especially among American and British economists who categorically reject what each terms 'the mainstream.' The time when most members of the economics profession were in essential agreement about the propositions they accepted and the way in which they communicated their beliefs, and the extent (limited, if any) of their support of public policies, is long passed. Thus, in the closing decades of the twentieth century economic inquiry reflected a competition among different paradigms: institutionalism, the 'new left' variant of Marxian theory, and a rebirth of the Austrian school transplanted (so to speak) via Vienna and the London School of Economics to Chicago and numerous 'Ivy League' institutions.

There are also at least two variants of post-Keynesian economics developed by individuals in the United States, the United Kingdom (in particular at Cambridge), Canada, and to a lesser extent, Australia. Their teaching and research relates to themes they consider consistent with the economics of J. M. Keynes and his *The General Theory of Employment, Interest and Money* (1936). However, those who identify themselves as post-Keynesian are far from agreement in their interpretation of what precisely it means to be a post-Keynesian. Thus, it is an important part of this revision to articulate the nature of their dissent.

For users who are attracted to Part VI, but do not have time to use the entire text, I offer the following outline for a one-semester course. Assign Chapters 1 and 2; proceed to Part II Overview and Chapters 4, 5, and 9. Continue with Part III, assigning the Overview and Chapter 12. These chapters examine the essentials of the classical tradition and the subsequent dissent from it. The Overview and Chapters 14 of Part IV provide the essentials of the neoclassical tradition as it developed between 1890 and 1945. The Overview of Part V and Chapters 19 and 21 provide an equivalent treatment of the dissent from neoclassicism during the same period. These four chapters provide sufficient background to enable a reasonably advanced undergraduate to understand the chapters that comprise Part VI. This selection of these chapters is somewhat more technical than an equivalent

number selected from the earlier part of the book, but it provides an effective semester course in which the history of economics is linked to the theory of the contemporary mainstream. Except for Marx, Veblen, and Keynes, the critics of the mainstream are accorded little space in textbooks on the history of economics. Yet, dissent now reflects an increasingly important part of contemporary writings in economics. It thus seems appropriate to conclude this volume with a sufficiently detailed survey of writings directed against the mainstream theorizing and its methods, to provide at least some understanding of the possible future direction of economics.

A substantial number of historians of economic thought share my appreciation of the role which numeracy has played in the development of economics. Among those who have particularly contributed to the specific topics that have been integrated into the present edition, I especially wish to thank, in alphabetical order, S. Ambirajan, Bradley W. Bateman, Randall Bausor, John B. Davis, Robert W. Dimand, M. H. I. Dore, Robert S. Goldfarb, Shaun Hargreaves Heap, James P. Henderson, Sherryl D. Kasper, Donald W. Katzner, Jinbang Kim, Judy L. Klein, Philip A. Klein, Sandra J. Peart, Robert E. Prasch, John Smithin, Vincent J. Tarascio, Yanis Varoufakis, Murray Wolfson, and Nancy Wulwick. Our conversations helped clarify my own ideas about the role of numeracy in economics, and their written contributions to my edited volume *Measurement, Quantification and Economic Analysis* have clearly established that reliance on mathematics and quantitative tools is by no means the special province of contemporary economists. Mark Perlman has also incorporated this theme into his research and has, over the years, generously shared his ideas with me in our many conversations. Robin Rowley and Ronald Bodkin have also contributed to my appreciation of numeracy, especially as it relates to the role of econometrics and contemporary macroeconomics. They have also offered very useful suggestions on several other chapters; I am grateful for the time they took to comment on earlier manuscript drafts. Special thanks are also due to Luis José Cardozo who published a lengthy review of the fifth edition in *The European History of Economic Thought* Journal. Some of his thoughtful suggestions are incorporated into this edition.

A substantial intellectual debt in the preparation of this edition is to my many colleagues in the History of Economics Society, whose academic candor and warm friendship provided a rare and positive stimulus to my efforts. Several anonymous reviews were also important in helping me to think more carefully about accommodating readers with different levels of background who are studying in different English speaking countries. They were incredibly useful, and are gratefully acknowledged, as is the important preparatory task for which Miss Heidi Bagtazo took responsibility. Finally, I wish to thank my editor, Mr. Robert Langham, for his creative ideas relating to a more modern format for my volume, and Mr. Goober Fox for keeping me on schedule when my professorial instincts to linger might have delayed the process. Mr. Peter Waterhouse provided outstanding assistance in finalizing the manuscript's text, and Mr. Martin Hargreaves provided superlative indexing. Their attention to detail is greatly appreciated. All of their efforts were coordinated with incredible skill by my husband Philip, without whose comparative advantage in program management this volume would have been considerably delayed.

Development of Economic Analysis

Part I

Preclassical Economics

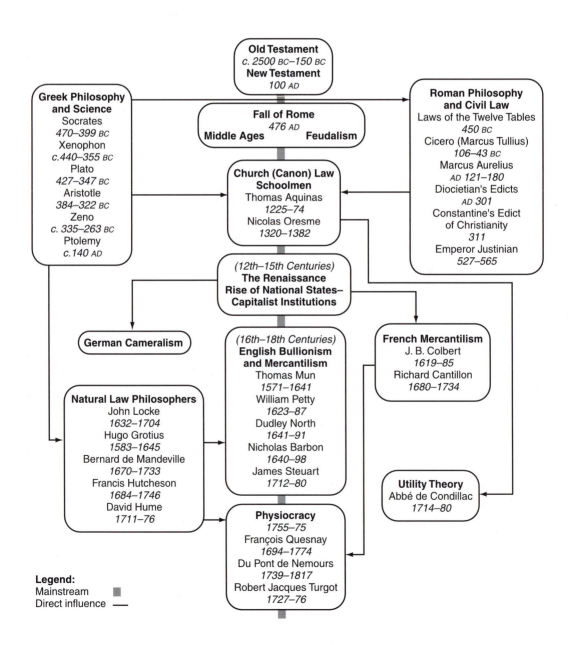

Old Testament
c. 2500 BC–150 BC
New Testament
100 AD

Greek Philosophy and Science
Socrates
470–399 BC
Xenophon
c.440–355 BC
Plato
427–347 BC
Aristotle
384–322 BC
Zeno
c. 335–263 BC
Ptolemy
c.140 AD

Fall of Rome
476 AD
Middle Ages   **Feudalism**

Roman Philosophy and Civil Law
Laws of the Twelve Tables
450 BC
Cicero (Marcus Tullius)
106–43 BC
Marcus Aurelius
AD 121–180
Diocietian's Edicts
AD 301
Constantine's Edict of Christianity
311
Emperor Justinian
527–565

Church (Canon) Law Schoolmen
Thomas Aquinas
1225–74
Nicolas Oresme
1320–1382

(12th–15th Centuries)
The Renaissance Rise of National States– Capitalist Institutions

German Cameralism

(16th–18th Centuries)
English Bullionism and Mercantilism
Thomas Mun
1571–1641
William Petty
1623–87
Dudley North
1641–91
Nicholas Barbon
1640–98
James Steuart
1712–80

French Mercantilism
J. B. Colbert
1619–85
Richard Cantillon
1680–1734

Natural Law Philosophers
John Locke
1632–1704
Hugo Grotius
1583–1645
Bernard de Mandeville
1670–1733
Francis Hutcheson
1684–1746
David Hume
1711–76

Utility Theory
Abbé de Condillac
1714–80

Physiocracy
1755–75
François Quesnay
1694–1774
Du Pont de Nemours
1739–1817
Robert Jacques Turgot
1727–76

Legend:
Mainstream
Direct influence ——

Key dates

c.369–370 BC	Plato	The Republic
c.355 BC	Xenophon	The Ways and Means to Increase the Revenues of Athens
c.300 BC	Aristotle	Politics, The Nicomachean Ethics
c.AD 1269–1272	Thomas Aquinas	Summa Theologica
c.1360	Nicholas Oresme	Tractatus de origine natura jure, et mutationibus monetarum
1613	Antonio Serra	Breve trattato delle cause che possono far abbondare li regni d'oro et d'argento, dove non sono miniere con applicazione al Regno di Napoli (A Brief Treatise on the Causes Which Can Make Gold and Silver Plentiful in Kingdoms Where There Are No Mines)
1664	Thomas Mun	England's Treasure by Forraign Trade
1690	Josiah Child	Discourse about Trade
1690	Sir William Petty	Political Arithmetick
1692	Dudley North	Discourse upon Trade
1696	Nicholas Barbon	A Discourse concerning making the New Money Lighter
1714	Bernard de Mandeville	The Fable of the Bees: or Private Vices, Publick Benefits
1752	David Hume	Political Discourses
1755	Richard Cantillon	Essai sur la nature du commerce en général
1767	James Steuart	An Inquiry into the Principles of Political Oeconomy

Why study the history of economic analysis in the twenty-first century?

If time is the most valuable resource each of us has, why should anyone, other than a history buff, allocate several hours a week for a semester, or even two, to become acquainted with the ideas of thinkers long dead? One of the most insightful answers to this question came from John Maynard Keynes who once wrote 'Practical men, who believe themselves to be quite exempt from any intellectual influences, are usually the slaves of some defunct economist.'[1]

Keynes's observation is even more pertinent today than in the mid-1930s because there is less agreement among economists and political philosophers about the merits of the puzzle solving capabilities of their respective approaches. Economics has become more professionalized than it was in his day, and many of its practitioners have acquired a level of mathematical and quantitative competence that rivals that of some natural scientists. The technical approach of these practitioners is now the hallmark of economic research, and the body of 'neoclassical' generalizations they teach their students is the most fruitful approach for studying market behavior and its driving influence in developed free enterprise economies.

It is thus something of an irony that the grand claims made for economics as a science of rigor and relevance were so quickly challenged following the pinnacle of its 1970s' repute. High on the list of problems for which contemporary economists are unable to provide agreed-upon theoretical explanations and policy agendas are: how to provide employment for all who are willing to work at the currently prevailing level of wages and prices; how to check inflation without creating unemployment, how to reduce the federal deficit without raising taxes; how to achieve economic growth without further environmental pollution; and how to promote international trade with stable exchange rates. These problems are further complicated by the competition for markets that has emerged worldwide as older industrial economies encounter the productive potential of the 'newly emerged' industrial economies of Asia and Eastern Europe.

Many of these economies have long histories of state management to which the principles of capitalist economies do not apply. The problems confronted suggest that not only economists, but thinking non-professionals everywhere, will gain a better understanding of the material world around them if they are familiar, not only with modern day neoclassical principles, but also with other economic paradigms which focus on different questions and offer alternative explanatory hypotheses about economic phenomena. A chief difference between economics and the natural sciences is that, in the latter, the discovery of a 'new' theory offering a 'solution' to a puzzle that defies explanation under the prevailing paradigm causes the older theory to be discarded. The classic example is the so-called 'Copernican revolution' which resulted in the replacement of the Ptolemaic theory that the Earth is the center of the universe. The counter argument by the Polish astronomer Nicolaus Copernicus (1473–1543), that the Earth is but one planet among many that revolve around the sun, destroyed forever the old Egyptian belief. The case is fundamentally different in economics than it is in the natural sciences. Alternative economic paradigms have not merely survived from the seventeenth, eighteenth and nineteenth centuries, but have become refined and modernized and, together with similarly modernized versions of Keynes's doctrines, stand as challenges to the neoclassical or 'mainstream' paradigm.

One can, of course, study contemporary economic issues and problems without any paradigmatic perspective other than the conventional wisdom of neoclassical theory. Indeed, this is the content of the core courses of contemporary economic programs. Yet, even if one is persuaded that neoclassical principles do indeed offer the most robust and sophisticated hypotheses articulated up until now to explain how modern economies function and progress, it needs to be recognized that neoclassical principles are themselves the product of considerable intellectual change and challenge. The neoclassicism that rules today reflects the intellectual marriage of the classical tradition that preceded it and the traditions of general equilibrium analysis, marginalism and the challenges they confronted from Marxism and historicism. Familiarity with only contemporary economic theory, without any historical understanding of how it came to be, is thus likely to be relatively unsophisticated. The principles of modern economics rest, in large part, on historical conceptions about what the issues of economics are and what are the methods by which answers shall be sought. Economics has become a science of multiple paradigms whose competing claims to validity comprise the basis for contemporary controversy.

While the history of economics is worth studying for its own sake, a more positive reason for studying it as the problems of the twenty-first century emerge is surely to understand what are the questions that economists ought to ask, and by what methods shall they seek to answer them. It is not an exaggeration to say that economics did not exist as a separate field of study prior the eighteenth century. Even in advanced ancient civilizations, such as those achieved by the Greeks and Romans,

inquiry into economic matters was quite a minor aspect of intellectual effort. Yet the inquiries of many pre-eighteenth century writers are so profound, and continue to have so great an impact on the way in which human beings conceive of their relationship to one another and their environment, that they are remembered as part of the intellectual heritage of Western civilization.

An overview of preclassical economics

The writings of Aristotle, Plato, Socrates, Aurelieus, Oresme, and Aquinas are among the masterworks of human knowledge bequeathed by the ancients. While the inquiries of the ancients into economic questions are unsystematic, and in most cases little more than moral pronouncements, it is also the case that even those thinkers who, like Aristotle, had a desire for knowledge for its own sake were most concerned about the solution of practical problems. The philosophical studies of the ancient Greeks and Romans were undertaken in the context of particular issues and problems. It was they who taught us to seek solutions for practical problems, including those that arise in our complex present-day material environment. The modern word *economics* has its origin in the Greek word *oikonomia*, which means the art of household management. In studying the nature of this art, Aristotle undertook to examine what is probably the first economic issue to have been subjected to formal inquiry: what sort of wealth-getting activity is necessary and honorable for humans to undertake? While Aristotle's was an ethical and moral question, it was answered by means of reasoned inquiry. That one of the areas about which knowledge should be sought concerns human relationships as they relate to the material environment was a major intellectual departure for which we are indebted to early Greek thinkers like Aristotle.

Roman and medieval thinkers also adopted a problem-solving perspective, particularly about practical applications in jurisprudence and animal husbandry. Their concern was with solving specific problems and answering specific questions, many of which related to the material environment. Their intellectual legacy is pre-scientific and pre-classical in the sense that it does not represent a body of general principles about economic matters, but observations and prescriptions relating to the good life or good citizenship embedded in writings concerned chiefly with religion, ethics, politics, or law. Even inquiries made during the vital era known as the *Renaissance* failed to produce anything in the way of systematic principles or analysis, and so these were substantially delayed until seventeenth century mercantilist thought.

The development of quantifying concepts and techniques has accompanied the growth of knowledge throughout human history. In earliest times, their principal use was rooted in such practical undertakings as the building of roads, dams, and canals, in particular by the Romans, and magnificent burial sites, such as the pyramids of Egypt. The ancient Greeks, as philosophers and geometers, were generally less interested in the practical application of numeracy. Socrates, on the other hand (according to Plato), even though he was not interested in quantification *per se*, seems to have anticipated the expectations of many contemporary economists about the potential power of quantification as a learning tool when he said 'the arts of measuring and numbering and weighing come to the rescue of human understanding, and the apparent greater or less, or more or heavier, no longer have mastery over us, but give way

before calculation and measure and weight.'[2] Given the present-day reliance by economists on mathematics and on econometrics as the sister discipline of economics, the study of the development of economic analysis is quite appropriately extended to include reliance on what may broadly be called 'numeracy,' as it came to be used during different historical stages of inquiry into economic phenomena.[3]

A quantified or numerical variable is one whose values are expressed as numbers which measure a particular property or characteristic using a specific ordinal, cardinal, or ratio scale. By contrast, a non-quantified or qualitative variable is one whose values do not lend themselves to numerical expression. We will use the term 'numeracy' as a convenient 'catch-all' for all the techniques that have been used by political economists, and subsequently by economists, to enumerate, measure, and quantify, ranging from simple arithmetic to contemporary econometric techniques.

The revival of trade from the fifteenth century onwards gave an impetus to financial techniques such as double entry bookkeeping and bills of exchange. These coincided with the era of *mercantilism*, which was characterized by strong national economies that pursued commercial activity as an instrument of statecraft. Mercantilism's chief goal was to increase the political power and wealth of nation-states with respect to one another. Mercantilistic goals directed economic activity and thought in England, France, and northern Europe from the sixteenth century well into the eighteenth century. Some theoretical ideas, and also what may be termed 'the first stage' of numeracy, date from this time.

The transition period of the mid seventeenth to the mid eighteenth centuries was thus a time that was animated by many inquiring minds, and was a period of great economic vitality during which a substantial middle class engaged in industry and trade came into power, particularly in England, but also in France and Holland. These economic developments were accompanied by an attitude of increasing liberality: people began to believe that greater freedom from governmental restrictions would be advantageous to themselves as well as to the economy. Economics had not yet become established as a separate discipline, perhaps because there was so much theological and political controversy and such great interest in the natural sciences. However the ground from which the classical tradition subsequently germinated was being prepared. The three chapters that follow examine the highlights of preclassical economics and their legacy as masterworks in economics.

Notes

1 Keynes, J. M., *The General Theory of Employment, Interest and Money*, New York: Harcourt Brace and Company, 1936, p. 383. Donald A. Walker offers a contemporary retrospective relating to the many present-day concerns for which past economic doctrine is not merely relevant, but essential to sophisticated understanding. See his 'Relevance for present economic theory of economic theory written in the past' in *Journal of the History of Economic Thought*, 21(1), March 1999.

2 Plato, *The Dialogues*, Translated by B. Jowett, *Great Books of the Western World*, vol.7, p. 431; Chicago: Encyclopedia Britannica, 1952.

3 The parallel development of economic theory and reliance on tools of numeracy to measure, quantify and lend greater precision to its concepts and relationships is examined in Rima, I. H. (ed) *Measurement, Quantification and Economic Analysis: Numeracy in Economics* (London: Routledge, 1995).

Chapter 1

Early masterworks as sources of economic thought

Not until the eighteenth century did speculation about economic phenomena begin to emerge as economic analysis rather than as economic thought. The reasons why economics did not exist as a separate subject in this preanalytic stage offer a useful departure point for studying the historical development of economic analysis. There is much to be learned about the history of economics by examining the reasons why the focus of intellectual inquiry was on politics, ethics, philosophy, and theology but not on economics *qua* economics. Yet the ancients left a legacy of masterworks, two of which will be examined in this chapter. Aristotle, in his book *Politics*, posed the question of whether there is a difference between the art of acquisition, which is a necessary part of the management of the household, and the wealth-getting activities of commerce. The answer he gave distinguished between two sorts of wealth getting activities in which households may engage; that which is 'necessary and honorable' and that which is 'unnatural.' Aristotle's observational experience led him to value private ownership of property as most conducive to the preservation and the improvement of its productive powers.

While Aristotle's teaching started from his acceptance of the Ptolemaic tradition of studying the reality of ideas, his approach was to divide reality into the several separate subjects of physics, biology, ethics, and politics, each of which he studied from observable facts. He classified them with such scrupulous care that, with the rediscovery of his works in the Middle Ages, he became revered as a 'master of those who know' from actual and concrete observations, thus laying down the rules for the empirically based world of knowledge. Centuries later, during the Italian Renaissance, the churchman Thomas Aquinas posed a series of questions related to acts of cheating and other improper behaviors that sometimes arise in buying and selling. There is much to be learned by exploring why the context in which Aristotle, Aquinas, and others who wrote before the eighteenth century impeded the development of analytical economics. Despite the non-analytical character of thinking about economic phenomena, the use of thought forms that express ideas, relationships, and the characteristics of objects, and sometimes persons, in terms of numbers and measures, satisfied an intellectual need, even in ancient times.

Politics as economic thought

Greek thinkers believed that a good life is the purpose of existence, and that it is best achieved within the city-state (*polis*). To a

Greek, the city-state was not merely a legal structure; it was a way of life to which is connected every aspect of daily existence. Individuals derived their importance from their relation as citizens to the state on which they depend, and to whose welfare they can contribute. It is the state, rather than the individual, that is omnipotent. Thus, the attention of Greek thinkers was primarily absorbed by political theory, although the theory of the city-state embraced more than politics in the narrow sense. It encompasses, at one and the same time, ethics, sociology, economics, and political science.

The absorption of Greek thinkers with the origin and functioning of the ideal state and, for Plato (though not for Aristotle), the subordination of the individual to the state, had the effect of limiting the development of economic thought. Consider, for example, the contribution of the Greek historian Xenophon (*c.* 431–*c.* 352 BC). His work *On the Means of Improving the Revenue of the State of Athens* begins with a description of the natural advantages of Athens as a commercial center attractive to foreigners. Foreigners were welcomed as a lucrative source of revenue because, as outsiders, they were subject to tax levies from which others were exempt. In similar vein, merchants and shipowners were regarded as superior citizens because they brought wealth to the city. Thus, Xenophon recommended various measures to the state to encourage merchant activity in Athens. He also urged increased production of silver because he thought this metal would never lose its value.

These recommendations are noteworthy from our point of view because they reflect the preoccupation with the importance of the state that dominated ancient Greek thought. Plato, especially, believed that human happiness can be achieved only within the city-state. Thus, the search for the good life was at one and the same time the search for the ideal state. While the emphasis on the state as an instrument to achieve socially optimal results is not incompatible with what has come to be called *social economics*, it does preclude the emergence of economics as a body of theory that seeks to explain how socially optimal results can be achieved in the absence of a central authority that directs the allocation of resources.

Philosophy as economic thought

After the disintegration of the Greek city-states and the emergence of the empires of Alexander and later of Rome, the belief that individuals as citizens are inseparable from the self-sufficient city-state was replaced by new schools of thought which separated the good life for persons from the good state as a political entity. Thus began the divorce of politics from ethics and an appreciation of the individual as a person rather than a social being who is a part of the whole.

Greek philosophy was introduced into the Roman world through Stoicism, which became the most influential of the post-Aristotelian schools. Although first conceived by Zeno (*c.* 335–263 BC), the philosophy of Stoicism received its most profound expression in the *Meditations* of the Roman emperor Marcus Aurelius (AD 121–180). According to the Stoics, the universe is systematic and rational, being governed by the all-pervading law of nature. Wise individuals live according to nature; reason guides their conduct so that their actions conform to the dictates of natural necessity. 'Be satisfied with your business and learn to love what you were bred to do, and as to the remainder of your life, be entirely resigned, and let the gods do their pleasure with your body and soul.' This is the essence of the stoic philosophy. It is clearly not conducive to improvements in the production or distribution of wealth, and thus did not encourage individuals to think about improving their material well-being. On the contrary, the belief that happiness is achieved by conforming to the inevitability of destiny or of fate suggests a perspective similar to the belief of Arab-Islamic scholars in *kismet*. It is probably the case that the intellectual values of the Middle Ages of Western Europe cannot be fully understood without the background influence of Islam.

There is disagreement between two major history of economic thought scholars, Karl Pribram and Joseph Schumpeter, concerning the contributions of Arabic thinkers. Whereas Schumpeter disputes that Islamic scholars made substantive contributions (Schumpeter, 1954, Chapter 2, p. 12), Pribram recognizes the influence on the scholastics, not only of Aristotle, but also 'the treatises in which Arabian philosophy interpreted Aristotle's work in light of their own reasonings' (Pribram 1983, p. 4). Modern scholars increasingly accept Pribram's interpretation as expressed in his posthumously published work.

Ethics as economic thought

Economics did not emerge as a separate field of inquiry until the satisfaction of material needs became a desirable goal of human activity. The thousands of years during which the pursuit of wealth was regarded with disdain could scarcely have produced a systematic body of principles to explain acquisition. A negative attitude toward wealth among the ancient peoples is perhaps most clearly in evidence in the thinking of the Hindus and Chinese, although it is typical of Oriental thought in general. Oriental philosophy regards a state of mind in which material

wants are negligible as essential to happiness. It accepts poverty with fatalistic passivity and views wealth with indifference. Oriental philosophy was less conducive to both economic progress and the development of economic thought than the philosophy that originated in Europe.

The ancient Hebrews, while considerably less ascetic than the oriental philosophers, also believed that happiness is not dependent on wealth and that the pursuit of riches would lead to sin. The lives of these people were circumscribed by the rules of conduct set forth in the commands of Moses and the prophets. These rules minutely regulated every phase of human existence, guiding individuals in their relationships with one another as well as in their personal lives. The rules were detailed and complex and also extended to the economic aspects of life. For example, charging interest to fellow Hebrews for the use of money or goods was strictly forbidden as usury. The term 'usury' refers here, not to an excessive interest rate, which is its present-day meaning, but to any interest charge. Since loans were made primarily for charitable reasons, the Old Testament proscription against the taking of usury introduced a moral standard into economic behavior. There are many other directives of an economic nature in the Old Testament, such as the rules concerning the restitution of property, the remission of debt, and the production and harvesting of agricultural output. Many of these rules commemorate events of religious significance, such as the seventh day in the story of the creation. These are typical of the economic aspects of the Mosaic law and are of interest to us because they demonstrate that a separate science of wealth is incompatible with adherence to a religious and philosophical code that completely dictates economic behavior. The religious significance of the seventh day illustrates an early recognition of the need to measure the passage of time.

Even Greece, with its highly developed culture, did not produce a separate body of economic thought. This is not because the Greeks were disdainful of material goods. On the contrary, Plato and Aristotle believed that a minimum amount of wealth is essential to the good life. According to Aristotle, the household (*oikos*) exists for the purpose of satisfying natural wants by producing useful commodities or acquiring them by exchange for consumption. Thus, retail trade, which is exchange for the purpose of making money, is unnatural, as are all commercial activities for the acquisition of coin. The most unnatural among these is to demand interest for a loan, for money is intended only as a medium of exchange. Usury, which is its use to beget money, is a perversion of its proper function. Aristotle's *Politics* endures as a masterwork of economics because it shaped the thinking of successive generations about the distinction between natural and unnatural economic activities and forms of wealth.

Issues and Answers from the Masterworks 1.1

Issue
When is it honorable for individuals to engage in wealth-getting activities?

Aristotle's answer
From *Politics* (*c.* 300 BC) Book I Chapters 3, 4, 8, 9, 10.

Politics, **Chapter 3**
Seeing then that the state is made up of households, before speaking of the state we must speak of the management of the household. The parts of household management correspond to the persons who compose the household, and a complete household consists of slaves and freemen . . . And there is another element of a household, the so-called art of getting wealth, which, according to some, is identical with household management, according to others, a principal part of it; the nature of this art will also have to be considered by us . . .

Politics, **Chapter 4**
Property is a part of the household, and the art of acquiring property is a part of the art of managing the household; for no man can live well, or indeed live at all, unless he be provided with necessaries. And as in the arts which have a definite sphere the workers must have their own proper instruments for the accomplishment of their work, so it is in the management of a household. Now instruments are of various sorts; some are living, others lifeless; in the rudder, the pilot of a ship has a lifeless, in the look-out man, a living instrument; for in the arts the servant is a kind of instrument. Thus, too, a possession is an instrument for maintaining life. And so, in the arrangement of the family, a slave is a living possession, and property a number of such instruments; and the servant is himself an instrument which takes precedence of all other instruments.

Politics, **Chapter 8**
Of the art of acquisition then there is one kind which by nature is a part of the management of a household, in so far as the art of household management must either find ready to hand, or itself

provide, such things necessary to life, and useful for the community of the family or state, as can be stored. They are the elements of true riches; for the amount of property which is needed for a good life is not unlimited, although Solon in one of his poems says that

'No bound to riches has been fixed for man'

But there is a boundary fixed, just as there is in the other arts; for the instruments of any art are never unlimited, either in number or size, and riches may be defined as a number of instruments to be used in a household or in a state. And so we see that there is a natural art of acquisition which is practiced by managers of households and by statesmen, and what is the reason of this.

Politics, Chapter 9

There is another variety of the art of acquisition which is commonly and rightly called an art of wealth-getting, and has in fact suggested the notion that riches and property have no limit. Being nearly connected with the preceding, it is often identified with it. But though they are not very different, neither are they the same. The kind already described is given by nature, the other is gained by experience and art.

Let us begin our discussion of the question with the following considerations:

Of everything which we possess there are two uses: both belong to the thing as such, but not in the same manner, for one is the proper, and the other the improper or secondary use of it. For example, a shoe is used for wear, and is used for exchange; both are uses of the shoe. He who gives a shoe in exchange for money or food to him who wants one, does indeed use the shoe as a shoe, but this is not its proper or primary purpose, for a shoe is not made to be an object of barter. The same may be said of all possessions, for the art of exchange extends to all of them, and it arises at first from what is natural, from the circumstance that some have too little, others too much. Hence we may infer that retail trade is not a natural part of the art of getting wealth; had it been so, men would have ceased to exchange when they had enough. In the first community, indeed, which is the family, this art is obviously of no use, but it begins to be useful when the society increases. For the members of the family originally had all things in common; later, when the family divided into parts, the parts shared in many things, and different parts in different things, which they had to give in exchange for what they wanted, a kind of barter which is still practiced among barbarous nations who exchange with one another the necessaries of life and nothing more; giving and receiving wine, for example, in exchange for corn, and the like. This sort of barter is not part of the wealth-getting art and is not contrary to nature, but is needed for the satisfaction of men's natural wants. The other or more complex form of exchange grew, as might have been inferred, out of the simpler. When the inhabitants of one country became more dependent on those of another, and they imported what they needed, and exported what they had too much of, money necessarily came into use. For the various necessaries of life are not easily carried about, and hence men agreed to employ in their dealings with each other something which was intrinsically useful and easily applicable to the purposes of life, for example, iron, silver, and the like. Of this the value was at first measured simply by size and weight, but in the process of time they put a stamp upon it, to save the trouble of weighing and to mark the value.

When the use of coin had once been discovered, out of the barter of necessary articles arose the other art of wealth-getting, namely, retail trade; which was at first probably a simple matter, but became more complicated as soon as men learned by experience whence and by what exchanges the greatest profit might be made. Originating in the use of coin, the art of getting wealth is generally thought to be chiefly concerned with it, and to be the art which produces riches and wealth; having to consider how they may be accumulated. Indeed, riches are assumed by many to be only a quantity of coin, because the arts of getting wealth and retail trade are concerned with coin. Others maintain that coined money is a mere sham, a thing not natural, but conventional only, because, if the users substitute another commodity for it, it is worthless, and because it is not useful as a means to any of the necessities of life, and, indeed, he who is rich in coin may often be in want of necessary food. But how can that be wealth of which a man may have a great abundance and yet perish with hunger, like Midas in the fable, whose insatiable prayer turned everything that was set before him into gold?

Hence men seek after a better notion of riches and of the art of getting wealth than the mere acquisition of coin, and they are right. For natural riches and the natural art of wealth-getting are a different thing; in their true form they are part of the management of a household; whereas retail trade is the art of producing wealth, not in every way, but by exchange. And it is thought to be concerned with coin; for coin is the unit of exchange and the measure or limit of it. And there is no bound to the riches which spring from this art of wealth-getting. As in the art of medicine there is no limit to the pursuit of health, and as in the other arts there is no limit to the pursuit of their several ends, for they aim at accomplishing their ends to the uttermost (but of the means there is a limit, for the end is always the limit), so, too, in this art of wealth-getting there is no limit of the end, which is riches of the spurious kind, and the acquisition of wealth. But the art of wealth-getting which consists in household management, on the other hand, has a limit; the unlimited acquisition of wealth is not its business. And, therefore, in one point of view, all riches must have a limit; nevertheless, as a matter of fact, we find the opposite to be the case; for all getters of wealth increase their hoard of coin without limit. The source of the confusion is the near connection between the two kinds of wealth-getting; in either, the instrument is the same, although the use is different, and so they pass into one another; for each is a use of the same property, but with a difference; accumulation is the end in the one case, but there is a further end in the other. Hence some persons are led to believe that getting wealth is the object of household management, and the whole idea of their lives is that they ought either to increase their money without limit, or at any rate not to lose it. The origin of this disposition in men is that they are intent upon living only, and not upon living well; and, as their desires are unlimited, they also desire that the means of gratifying them should be without limit. Those who do aim at a good life seek the means of obtaining bodily pleasures; and, since the enjoyment of these appears to depend on property, they are absorbed in getting wealth: and so there arises the second species of wealth-getting.

Politics, **Chapter 10**

There are two sorts of wealth-getting, as I have said; one is a part of household management, the other is retail trade; the former necessary and honorable, while that which consists in exchange is justly censured; for it is unnatural, and a mode by which men gain from one another. The most hated sort, and worth the greatest reason, is usury, which makes a gain out of money itself, and not from the natural object of it. For money was intended to be used in exchange, but not to increase at interest. And this term interest, which means the birth of money from money, is applied to the breeding of money because the offspring resembles the parent. Wherefore of all modes of getting wealth this is the most unnatural.

Source: *Aristotle's* Politics (Jowett translation), Oxford: Clarendon Press (1885).

Summing up: Aristotle's key point

Aristotle addressed, for the first time in recorded human history, the issue 'when is it honourable for individuals to engage in wealth-getting activities?' In his view, there is a difference between the art of acquisition, which is a necessary part of the management of the household, and the wealth-getting activities of retail trade. Retail trade and usury are unnatural, for their purpose is the acquisition of coin (i.e. money), which is 'not useful as a means to any of the necessities of life.' The issue Aristotle posed was a major intellectual departure in the sense that it clearly established that economic questions are often also ethical and moral questions.

Church doctrine as economic thought

Christianity was but one religion among many during the Roman era, and its followers were often victims of persecution. It was not until the fourth century that emperor Constantine declared Christianity the official religion of the empire. Father Augustine's (354–439) *The City of God*, written during this early Christian era, taught that humans belong to two kingdoms – the kingdom of man and the kingdom of God. Unlike earthly kingdoms, the kingdom of God will endure forever to reward those who follow its teachings with life everlasting. He attributed the fall of Rome to the barbarians to conflicts between the City of God and the City of Man.

The long interval between the fall of Rome (AD 426) and the fall of Constantinople to the Turks in 1453 is generally known as the 'Dark' or Middle Ages. For roughly 1000 years of human existence the barbarians who invaded from the north imperiled civilized society. Two institutions provided relief: feudalism and the Christian church. Feudal lords provided law and order on the landed estates or manors, and their rule ensured that everyone, freemen included, had a place in society and a function to perform. Custom perpetuated these arrangements from generation to generation until, approximately, the twelfth century. By then, the revival of trade and the emergence of town life lured freemen, as well as serfs, away from the manors. These developments encouraged individuals to acquire material goods by engaging in money-making activities that included commerce and money lending. Church scholars, among them Thomas Aquinas (1225–74) and Nicholas Oresme (1320–82) who viewed these pursuits as compromising peoples' spiritual lives, added to the conflicts about which Augustine wrote. They undertook to resolve these moral problems by trying to reconcile the scholarship of the ancients with their own Christian theology. They studied the rediscovered works of the Greeks, especially Aristotle and Claudius Ptolemy, that had been lost when Rome fell.

Ptolemy was the greatest of the Greco-Roman astronomers who lived during the second century. He is known for his complex mathematical system that accounts for the motion of the stars and planets (known as wandering stars), based on the widely held belief that the earth is at rest at the center of the universe. The churchmen adopted Ptolemy's model and added their own interpretation that the universe is a hierarchy leading to God. God's creatures occupy Earth, which is at the center between Heaven above and Hell below. Thus, the studies of the *Schoolmen – or Scholastics*, as these church scholars are sometimes called – succeeded in their task of joining the Ptolemaic conception of the universe to Christian theology.

Their interpretations of Aristotle's ethics

undoubtedly also reflects the treatises of Arabian philosophers with whom they were familiar, and which they also used as a basis for interpreting Aristotle's work, and to reconcile his ethics with their own positions. The Churchmen considered avarice or lust for earthly things as one among the seven deadly sins; only those economic activities that maintain individuals in the rank order into which God has placed them were regarded as proper. Within this framework, society was seen as an integrated whole in which God, nature, and man each had a preordained place. The good life required that each class – farmer, artisan, priest, and nobleman – perform its proper work according to the laws by which God and nature would preserve the class structure.

Readers acquainted with Chaucer's *Canterbury Tales* will, perhaps, remember the words of the Parson, who observes, 'God has ordained that some folk should be more high in estate and in degree, and some folk more low, and that everyone should be served in his estate and in his degree.' By putting these words into the Parson's mouth, Chaucer achieves a synthesis of philosophy and theology – the essence of medieval thought.

The view of the Churchmen, like Aristotle's before them, was that it is essential that human affairs be conducted in accordance with the principles of distributive and commutative justice. *Distributive justice is* concerned with the criteria for allocating honors, income, and wealth to particular persons or classes. *Commutative justice* (from *commutates* or transaction) is concerned with equity, or fairness, in transactions among individuals. From Thomas's perspective, which reflected the influence of Roman civil law, it is necessary to determine whether an action that is not unlawful may, nevertheless, be sinful. While modern economists are not interested in matters such as these, the *Summa Theologica* survives as a masterwork of economics because it confronts the coexistence of ethical and economic questions in human behavior as a seminal issue.

Issues and Answers from the Masterworks 1.2

Issue
Are the civil contracts governing individual relationships also consistent with a higher natural law? Specifically, is it lawful to sell a thing for more than it is worth? What are the obligations of buyers and sellers with regard to transactions? Is it a sin to take usury for economics?

Aquinas's answer
From *Summa Theologica* (1269–90), Part 11, Questions 77 and 78.

Question 77. Of cheating, which is committed in buying and selling
We must now consider those sins which relate to voluntary commutations. First, we shall consider cheating, which is committed in buying and selling; secondly, we shall consider usury, which occurs in loans. In connection with the other voluntary commutations no special kind of sin is to be found distinct from rapine and theft.

Under the first head there are four points of inquiry: (1) Of unjust sales as regards the price; namely, whether it is lawful to sell a thing for more than its worth? (2) Of unjust sales on the part of the thing sold. (3) Whether the seller is bound to reveal a fault in the thing sold? (4) Whether it is lawful in trading to sell a thing at a higher price than was paid for it?

Source: *Summa Theologica* (AD 1269–90), translated by the Fathers of the English Dominican Province (London: Washborne, 1911), pp. 1513–14; 1518–19.

First article: Whether it is lawful to sell a thing for more than its worth?

We proceed thus to the First Article:

Objection 1. It would seem that it is lawful to sell a thing for more than its worth. In the commutations of human life, civil laws determine that which is just. Now according to these laws it is just for buyer and seller to deceive one another (Cod., IV, xliv, *De Rescind. Vend. 8,* 15); and this occurs by the seller selling a thing for more than its worth, and the buyer buying a thing for less than its worth. Therefore it is lawful to sell a thing for more than its worth.

Objection 2. Further, that which is common to all would seem to be natural and not sinful. Now Augustine relates that the saying of a certain jester was accepted by all. You *wish to buy for a song and to sell at a premium,* which agrees with the saying of Prov. xx. *14, It is naught, it is naught, saith every buyer: and when he is gone away, then he will boast.* Therefore it is lawful to sell a thing for more than its worth.

Objection 3. Further, it does not seem unlawful if that which honesty demands be done by mutual agreement. Now, according to the Philosopher (*Ethics*, viii, 13), in the friendship which is based on utility, the amount of the recompense for a favor received should depend on the utility accruing to the receiver; and this utility sometimes is worth more than the thing given, for instance if the receiver be in great need of that thing, whether for the purpose of avoiding a danger, or of deriving some particular benefit. Therefore, in contracts of buying and selling, it is lawful to give a thing in return for more than its worth.

On the contrary, it is written (Matth. vii, 12): *All things . . . whatsoever you would that men should do to you, do you also to them.* But no man wishes to buy a thing for more than its worth. Therefore no man should sell a thing to another man for more than its worth . . .

It is altogether sinful to have recourse to deceit in order to sell a thing for more than its just price, because this is to deceive one's neighbor so as to injure him. Hence Tully says (*De Offic. iii*, 15): *Contracts should be entirely free from double-dealing: the seller must not impose upon the bidder, nor the buyer upon one that bids against him*.

But, apart from fraud, we may speak of buying and selling in two ways. First, as considered in themselves, and from this point of view, buying and selling seem to be established for the common advantage of both parties, one of whom requires that which belongs to the other and vice versa, as the Philosopher states (*Polit. i*, 3). Now whatever is established for the common advantage, should not be more of a burden to one party than to another, and consequently all contracts between them should observe equality of thing and thing. Again, the quality of a thing that comes into human use is measured by the price given for it, for which purpose money was invented, as stated in *Ethic. v*, 5. Therefore, if either the price exceeds the quantity of the thing's worth or, conversely, the thing exceeds the price, there is no longer the equality of justice; and consequently, to sell a thing for more than its worth, or to buy it for less than its worth, is in itself unjust and unlawful.

Secondly we may speak of buying and selling, considered as accidentally tending to the advantage of one party, and to the disadvantage of the other; for instance, when a man has great need of a certain thing, while another man will suffer if he be without it. In such a case the just price will depend not only on the thing sold, but on the loss which the sale brings on the seller. And thus it will be lawful to sell a thing for more than it is worth in itself, though the price paid be not more than it is worth to the owner. Yet if the one man derive a great advantage by becoming possessed of the other man's property, and the seller be not at a loss through being without that thing, the latter ought not to raise the price, because the advantage accruing to the buyer, is not due to the seller, but to a circumstance affecting the buyer. Now no man should sell what is not his, though he may charge for the loss he suffers.

On the other hand if a man find that he derives great advantage from something he has bought, he may, of his own accord, pay the seller something over and above; and this pertains to his honesty.

Reply Objection 1. As stated above (I-II, Q. 96, A. 2) human law is given to the people among whom there are many lacking virtue, and it is not given to the virtuous alone. Hence human law was unable to forbid all that is contrary to virtue. Accordingly, if without employing deceit the seller disposes of his goods for more than their worth, or the buyer obtain them for less than their worth, the law looks upon this as licit, and provides no punishment for so doing, unless the excess be too great, because then even human law demands restitution to be made, for instance if a man be deceived in regard to more than half the amount of the just price of a thing.

On the other hand the Divine law leaves nothing unpunished that is contrary to virtue. I add this condition, because the just price of things is not fixed with mathematical precision, but depends on a kind of estimate, so that a slight addition or subtraction would not seem to destroy the equality of justice.

Question 78. Of the sin of usury

We must now consider the sin of usury, which is committed in loans; and under this head there are four points of inquiry: (1) Whether it is a sin to take money as a price for money lent, which is to receive usury? (2) Whether it is lawful to lend money for any other kind of consideration, by way of payment for the loan? (3) Whether a man is bound to restore just gains derived from money taken in usury? (4) Whether it is lawful to borrow money under a condition of usury?

First article: Whether it is a sin to take usury for money lent?

We proceed thus to the First Article:

Objection 1. It would seem that it is not a sin to take usury for money lent. For no man sins through following the example of Christ. But Our Lord said of Himself (Luke xix, 23): *At My coming I might have exacted it*, i.e. the money lent, *with* usury. Therefore it is not a sin to take usury for lending money.

Objection 2. Further, according to Ps. xviii, *8, The law of the Lord is unspotted*, because, to wit, it forbids sin. Now usury of a kind is allowed in the Divine law, according to Deut. xxiii, 19, 20. *Thou shalt not fenerate to thy brother money, nor corn, nor any other thing, but to the stranger*; nay more, it is even promised as a reward for the observance of the Law, according to Deut. xxviii, 12; *Thou shalt fenerate to many nations, and shalt not borrow of any one*. Therefore it is not a sin to take usury.

Objection 3. Further, in human affairs justice is determined by civil laws. Now civil law allows usury to be taken. Therefore it seems to be lawful.

Objection 4. Further, the counsels are not binding under sin. But, among other counsels we find (Luke vi, 35): *Lend, hoping for nothing thereby.* Therefore it is not a sin to take usury . . .

It is written (Exod. xxii: 25), *If thou lend money to any of thy people that is poor, that dwelleth with thee, thou shalt not be hard upon them as an extortioner, nor oppress them with usuries* . . .

To take usury for money lent is unjust in itself, because this is to sell what does not exist, and this evidently leads to inequality which is contrary to justice.

In order to make this evident, we must observe that there are certain things the use of which consists in their consumption; thus we consume wine when we use it for drink, and we consume wheat when we use it for food. Accordingly, if a man wanted to sell wine separately from the use of the wine, he would be selling the same thing twice, or he would be selling what does not exist, wherefore he would evidently commit a sin of injustice. In like manner, he commits an injustice who lends wine or wheat, and asks for double payment, viz. one, the return of the thing in equal measure, the other, the price of the use, which is called usury.

Now money, according to the Philosopher (*Ethic. v*, 5; *Polit. i*, 3) was invented chiefly for the purpose of exchange; and consequently the proper and principal use of money is its consumption or alienation whereby it is sunk in exchange. Hence it is by its very nature unlawful to take payment for the use of money lent, which payment is known as usury; and just as a man is bound to restore other ill-gotten goods, so is he bound to restore the money which he has taken in usury.

Reply Objection 1. In this passage usury must be taken figuratively for the increase of spiritual goods which God exacts from us, for He wishes us ever to advance in the goods which we receive from Him; and this is for our own profit not for His.

Reply Objection 2. The Jews were forbidden to take usury from their brethren, i.e. from other Jews. They were permitted, however, to take usury from foreigners, not as though it were lawful, but in order to avoid a greater evil, lest, to wit, through avarice . . . Where we find it promised to them as a reward, *Thou shalt fenerate to many nations*, etc, fenerating is to taken in a broad sense for lending, as in Ecclus. xxix, 10, where we read: *Many have refused to fenerate, not out of wickedness*, i.e. they would not lend. Accordingly, the Jews are promised in reward an abundance of wealth, so that they would be able to lend to others . . .

Reply Objection 3. Human laws leave certain things unpunished, on account of the condition of those who are imperfect, and who would be deprived of many advantages, if all sins were strictly forbidden and punishments appointed for them. Wherefore human law has permitted usury, not that it looks upon usury as harmonizing with justice, but lest the advantage of many should be hindered. Hence it is that in civil law it is stated that *those things according to natural reason and civil law which are consumed by being used, do not admit of usufruct*, and that *the senate did not (nor could it) appoint a usufruct to such things, but established a quasi-usufruct*, namely by permitting usury. Moreover, the Philosopher, led by natural reason, says that to *make money by usury is exceedingly unnatural*.

Reply Objection 4. A man is not always bound to lend, and for this reason it is placed among the counsels. Yet it is a matter of precept not to seek profit by lending; although it may be called a matter of counsel in comparison with the maxims of the Pharisees, who deemed some kinds of usury to be lawful, just as love of one's enemies is a matter of counsel. Or again, He speaks here not of the hope of usurious gain, but of the hope which is put in man. For we ought not to lend or do any good deed through hope in man, but only through hope in God.

Source: *Summa Theologica* (AD 1269–90). Translated by the Fathers of the English Dominican Province (London: Washborne, 1811), pp. 1513–14, 1518–19.

Summing up: Aquinas's key points

The questions to which Aquinas gave his attention in the *Summa Theologica* were intended to provide guidance for Christian behavior under circumstances that arose as a result of expanding commercial activities. These led him to examine the civil law in the light of Christian teaching and the then recently rediscovered works of Aristotle. Aquinas's studies had their basis in theology or, more precisely, Christian ethics. In contrast with modern economics, which seeks to explain economic phenomena, Aquinas and the Schoolmen sought to lay down rules of conduct for Christian behavior and salvation. Among these conduct rules, none are of greater importance than those that relate to cheating, either in the sale of goods or the lending of money. There are specific transgressions that Aquinas identifies as examples of cheating: selling a thing for more than it is worth, failing to reveal a fault in an item that is being sold, and selling an item at a higher price than was paid for it. His object was to establish a standard for commutative justice to guide people in their dealings with one another.

The moral necessity for justice applies also to monetary transactions. Since Aquinas, like Aristotle, saw money only as a medium of exchange, he condemns most interest charges on loans as usury and as unjust, even though he entertained the possibility that such a charge is permissible if there is a delay in repayment or if there is restitution of stolen money. The latter exception subsequently provided a basis for rationalizing the legitimacy of all interest payments.

The scholastics' insistence on ethics as a basis for reaching conclusions about issues that relate to the material world gives them relevance beyond their use as an instrument for teaching Christian precepts. Yet the intellectual focus of church scholars precluded the development of a systematic body of economic analysis, such as that which developed from the mid-eighteenth century onward into modern times. The interest to medieval scholars in economic questions was peripheral to their interest in theology and philosophy, just as for the ancient Greeks, it was peripheral to philosophy and politics.

Concluding comments

Every society must establish priorities among the material desires of its citizens, for scarcity of resources universally imposes the necessity of choice. The common characteristic of all societies before the eighteenth century is that decisions about the priority of wants and the allocation of resources to satisfy them were dictated by central authority and reinforced by custom. How well a particular group or individual could fare relative to others depended on one's status in the social hierarchy, and this status reflected the importance attached to one's function by society. Soldiers, scholars, priests, artisans, farmers, and tradespeople have performed their functions from time immemorial, but different societies have accorded them varying degrees of status. The source of authority and the criteria according to which wants were given priority differed from one ancient society to another. But there was an essential similarity: the prime mover of economic activity was compounded of custom and command, and was a reflection of the prevailing philosophical or theological standard for social and moral well-being. Economic decision making was, thus, outside the scope of individual action and individual acquisition. Taking interest (or usury) was especially censured. This framework was incompatible with the development of economics in the modern sense. Why resources are allocated as they are, required no special explanation. It was, simply, a matter of law or tradition. Ancient Greek, Jewish, and Roman philosophers, law givers, and priests were concerned with explaining misfortune, which was sometimes economic, and prescribing proper human behavior as part of their teaching about ethics, religion, and politics. Natural phenomena and mathematics were also of interest to them. But there was neither opportunity nor necessity to explain economic events or behavior because, in ancient societies, decision making about economic activities was outside the scope of individual action. In addition, these societies were not yet oriented to thinking in terms of the ever-expanding abundance of physical goods that later technical skills, organization, and capital accumulation were to make possible. Consuming units – among them household estates such as the Greek *oikos*, the Roman *latifundium*, and the feudal manor – were typically self-sustaining. The goods that society required were produced according to time-honored methods and distributed for consumption

according to custom or the regulations of the ruling authority This method of want satisfaction left little need for economic explanation. Tradition and law explained virtually everything. Thus, it was not until the eighteenth century that speculation about economic phenomena began to develop as economic analysis rather than as economic thought.

Questions for discussion and further research

1 How is economic analysis different from economic thought? What characteristics of early societies (e.g. Greek, Judaic, Roman, Egyptian) inhibited the development of analytical economics?

2 How does the excerpt from Aristotle's *Politics*, reprinted above, substantiate the point that early scholars addressed economic questions within the context of larger concerns? What specific issue does Aristotle address in the selection above? Do his insights have any contemporary relevance?

3 What are the major economic questions that Thomas Aquinas addressed in *Summa Theologica*? How does this work reflect the influence of Aristotle on philosophy and how does it relate to the theological concerns of church scholars?

4 Is it appropriate to describe the *Summa Theologica* as an early contribution to economic analysis? Why or why not?

Notes for further reading

The New Palgrave Dictionary of Economics (hereafter *The New Palgrave*), edited by John Eatwell, Murray Milgate, and Peter Newman (London and New York: Macmillan and Stockton Press, 1989), has already become the most valuable general reference for seasoned economics scholars and students alike on topics relating to economics and its history. Among the entries relating specifically to this chapter are M. I. Finley on Aristotle, vol. 1, pp. 112–13; Barry Gordon on St. Thomas Aquinas, vol. 3, pp. 754–55; N. E. Simmonds on Natural Law, vol. 3, pp. 602–3; Henry W. Spiegel on Xenophon, vol. 4, pp. 935–36; and P. R. Stein on Jurisprudence, vol. 1, pp. 1037–39.

General references

Of special note, Wesley Mitchell's *Types of Economic Theory: From Mercantilism to Institutionalism*, Vols I and II, with an introduction by Joseph Dorfman, New York: Augustus Kelley, 1967, 1969, is a classic contribution by one of the founders of institutional economics.

Mark Perlman and Charles R. McCann, Jr. are the authors of *The Pillars of Economic Understanding,* Ann Arbor MI: University of Michigan Press, 1998. Theirs is the most recent among interpretations of the history of economic thought in the grand tradition of Schumpeter, Mitchell and Pribram by American scholars.

The magnum opus of the late Joseph Schumpeter, *History of Economic Analysis* (1954), is the most comprehensive and sophisticated treatise by a European scholar. A more recent posthumously published contribution, also conceived on a grand scale, is Karl Pribram's *A History of Economic Reasoning*, Baltimore: Johns Hopkins University Press, 1983.

There are also numerous textbooks on the history of economic thought that can serve as useful collateral reading either because they include contributions of a less theoretical nature than those that are the focus of this book, or because they provide interpretations and examine the impact of economic ideas in a way that is precluded by the scope of this inquiry. Two books on contemporary economic analysis are also included in the list that follows because of their historical orientation; each is marked with an asterisk.

Bell, John E. *A History of Economic Thought* (New York: Ronald Press, 1953).

*Blaug, Mark. *Economic Theory in Retrospect*, Revised edn (Homewood, Ill.: Richard D. Irwin, 1968).

Bonar, James. *Philosophy and Political Economy*. 2nd edn (London: George Allen and Unwin, 1909).

Canterbery, E. Ray. *The Making of Economics*, Revised edn (Belmont, Calif.: Wadsworth, 1980).

Ekelund, Robert B., Jr., and Robert E. Hebert. *A History of Economic Theory and Method*. 3rd edn (New York: McGraw-Hill, 1990).

*Fellner, William, *The Emergence and Concern of Modern Economic Analysis* (New York: McGraw-Hill, 1960).

Ferguson, John M. *Landmarks of Economic Thought*. 2nd edn (New York: Longmans, Green, 1950).

Gide, Charles, and Rist, Charles. *A History of Economic Doctrine*. Translated by R. Richards. 7th edn (Boston: D.C. Heath, 1948).

Gray, Alexander. *The Development of Economic Doctrine* (New York: Longmans, Green, 1933).

Gruchy, Allan G. *Modern Economic Thought: The American Contribution* (New York: Prentice-Hall, 1947).

Haney, Lewis H. *History of Economic Thought*. 4th edn (New York: Macmillan, 1949).

Heibroner, Robert. *The Worldly Philosophers* (New York: Simon & Schuster, 1953).

Heimann, Eduard. *History of Economic Doctrine* (New York: Oxford University Press, 1964).

Homan, Paul T. *Contemporary Thought* (New York: Harper & Row, 1928).

Hutchison, Terrence W. *A Review of Economic Doctrines. 1870–1929* (Oxford: Clarendon Press, 1953).

Landreth, Harry, and David Collander. *History of Economic Theory* (Boston: Houghton Mifflin, 1989).

Lekachman, Robert. *A History of Economic Ideas* (New York: Harper & Row, 1959).

Lekachman, Robert, (ed.) *The Varieties of Economics*, 2 vols (New York: Harcourt Brace Jovanovich, 1962).

Pribram, Karl. *A History of Economic Reasoning* (Baltimore, Md.: Johns Hopkins University Press, 1983) (published posthumously).

Rogin, Leo. *The Meaning and Validity of Economic Theory* (New York: Harper & Row, 1956).

Roll, Eric. *A History of Economic Thought*. 3rd edn (Englewood Cliffs, NJ: Prentice-Hall, 1956).

Schumpeter, Joseph A. *A History of Economic*

Analysis (New York: Oxford University Press, 1954).

Schumpeter, Joseph A. *Economic Doctrine and Method.* Translated by R. Aris (New York: University Press, 1967).

Seligman, Ben. *Main Currents in Modern Economics* (New York: Free Press, 1962).

Taylor, Overton. *A History of Economic Thought* (New York: McGraw-Hill, 1960).

Whittaker, Edmund. *Schools and Streams of Economic Thought* (Chicago: Rand McNally, 1960).

Zweig, Ferdynand. *Economic Ideas: A Study in Historical Perspective* (Englewood Cliffs, NJ: Prentice-Hall, 1950).

There are also several collections of readings from original sources and essays on economic thought or about the works of specific contributors with which the reader will find it useful to be acquainted.

Abbot, Leonard D., (ed.) *Masterworks of Economics* (Garden City, NY: Doubleday Publishing, 1949).

Ghazanfar, S. M., 'Scholastic economics and Arab scholars: the "Great Gap" thesis reconsidered,' in *Diogenes: International Review of Humane Sciences.* (Paris: International Council for Philosophy and Humanistic Studies, No. 154, 1991).

Gheritity, James A., (ed.) *Economic Thought: A Historical Anthology* (New York: Random House, 1965).

Keynes, John Maynard. *Essays in Biography.* Revised edn (London: Rupert Hart-Davis, 1951).

Lowry, S. Todd, *The Archeology of Economic Ideas: The Classical Greek Tradition* (Durham, NC: Duke University Press, 1987).

Monroe, Arthur E., (ed.) *Early Economic Thought* (Cambridge, Mass.: Harvard University Press, 1924).

Newman, Philip, Arthur Gayer, and Milton Spencer (eds) *Source Readings in Economic Thought* (New York: W. W. Norton, 1954).

Patterson, S. Howard (ed.) *Readings in the History of Economic Thought* (New York: McGraw-Hill, 1932).

Rima, I. H., (ed.) *Readings in the History of Economic Theory* (New York: Holt, Rinehart & Winston, 1970).

Robbins, Lionel. *A History of Economic Thought,*

edited by S. Medema and W. Samuels (Princeton, NJ: Princeton University Press), Lectures 1–3, pp. 5–26.

Schumpeter, Joseph A. *Ten Great Economists* (London: Oxford University Press, 1951).

Spengler, Joseph J., and W. Allen, (eds) *Essays in Economic Thought: Aristotle to Marshall* (Chicago: Rand McNally, 1960).

Spiegel, William H., (ed.) *The Development of Economic Thought* (New York: John Wiley & Sons, 1952).

Viner, Jacob. *The Long View and the Short* (New York: Free Press, 1958).

Wilson, George W. (ed.) *Classics of Economic Theory* (Bloomington: Indiana University Press, 1964).

Selected references and suggestions for further reading

Aquinas, Thomas. *Summa Theologica.* Translated by Fathers of the Dominican Province. (London: Washborne, 1811).

Aristotle. *The Works of Aristotle.* Edited by W. D. Ross, 12 vols (Oxford: Clarendon Press, 1908–52).

Bonar, James. *Philosophy and Political Economy.* 2nd edn (London: George Allen and Unwin, 1909).

Lowry, S. Todd. *The Archaeology of Economic Ideas* (Durham, NC: Duke University Press, 1987).

Plato. *The Republic.* Translated by R. W. Sterling and W. C. Scott (New York: Norton, 1985).

Plato. *Theaetetus.* Translated by John McDowell (Oxford: Clarendon Press, 1973).

Tawney, R. H. *Religion and the Rise of Capitalism* (New York: Penguin Books, 1947).

Weber, Max. *Protestant Ethic and the Spirit of Capitalism.* Translated by Talcott Parsons (New York: Scribner, 1948).

Weisskopf, Walter A. *The Psychology of Economics* (Chicago: The University of Chicago Press, 1955).

Worland, Stephen. *Scholasticism and Welfare Economics* (South Bend, Ind.: University of Notre Dame Press, 1967).

Xenophon. *Memorabilia and Oeconomicus.* Translated by E. C. Marchant (New York: G. P. Putnam & Sons, 1923).

Chapter 2

The origins of analytical economics

· ·

Introduction

The dawning of the Renaissance unleashed the forces that were ultimately to provide the climate for the development of economics as a separate discipline. Historians are not in complete agreement as to the exact time span during which the many and complex forces that were to destroy feudal economic, political, social, and religious life were at work. Usually, the beginning of the Renaissance is placed at the time of the fall of Constantinople in 1453, although many of the events of the eleventh and twelfth centuries heralded the changes that reached fuller development in later centuries.

The precise dating of the Renaissance as a momentous time in human history is considerably less important than recognizing the tremendous, although gradual, changes taking place in every aspect of human life. From an economic and social point of view, it was a period during which commerce revived, new forms of wealth emerged, and a town life dominated by an entirely new social class came into existence. Intellectually, it was a time of skepticism, increasing secularization, and a corresponding decline in the authority of the church in Rome. Politically, it was a period of emerging nation-states that rivaled one another to acquire stocks of gold, whether by exploratory expeditions to the New World, conquest, or pursuing export trade. Thus, mercantile or business interests became aligned with the sovereign to pursue policies that promised success in the acquisition of national treasure. The era of mercantilism or statecraft was the product of their symbiosis. It gave rise to an important new issue: specifically, can the wealth-getting activities of the merchant also enrich the sovereign and promote the economic gain of the nation? The answer of the merchant, whose chief spokesperson was Thomas Mun (1571–1641), an officer of the powerful East India Company, was a resounding affirmative. This chapter examines the post-Renaissance changes that indirectly helped stimulate economic inquiry.

Such changes as the decline of the manorial system, the emergence of a wage-earning class of persons, the Protestant Reformation, the Copernican revolution, and political Nationalism all played a critical role in paving the way for the rise of capitalism and the market system. Since it is the functioning of the market system that economics as a discipline undertakes to explain, the many evolutionary changes that led to its development indirectly served to stimulate economic inquiry.

Stimuli to economic inquiry

The decline of the manorial system: the end of feudalism

The power vacuum created by the fall of the Roman empire was filled by feudal lords who provided law and order on their manors, as their landed estates are known. Each manor constituted a self-sufficient economic, social, and political unit that functioned according to the orders of the lord who held the most exalted position by virtue of his ownership of the land and everything on it. His position was reinforced by tradition and, in reciprocity for his power, he was pledged to protect the lives of the serfs and freemen of his domain who, in turn, had the obligation to serve in the lord's army. More than any other economic phenomenon the disintegration of the manorial system heralded the Renaissance and the dawn of modern times.

The decline of feudalism was gradual and, if we view the experience of Europe as a whole, extended over several centuries. Yet, the most dramatic feature of the Renaissance was the decline of the manorial system, for it signaled the end of feudalism. While the specific causes of its decline are exceedingly complex, the expansion of trade was a major force. Two great commercial movements took place in Europe between the eleventh and sixteenth centuries; one centered around the Mediterranean and Adriatic Seas, the other on the northern shores of Europe that were accessible via the North and Baltic Seas. Trade was conducted from the Arab world, both before and after the crusades, through Russia to Poland to the Baltic area and northward to central Europe and even Scandinavia. The transmission of techniques and instruments of commerce, in long use in the Arab world, was developed along with evolving commercial relationships. The institution

of written contracts (*commendas*) which establishes the financial and managerial responsibilities between partners has been documented from the fifteenth century. The *commenda* and other partnership contracts were indigenous to the Arab world, and spread to Latin Europe through the influence and writings of Arab scholars, jurists and merchants.[1] Arab coins and the spirit of entrepreneurship were not unfamiliar in a medieval Europe centered around the Mediterranean and Adriatic.

The heartland of continental Europe was still slumbering in the unchanging institutions of feudalism until the population migration that accompanied the crusades brought commercial activity from Constantinople to the interior of the continent, introducing new and exotic commodities from the East. This encouraged the regional specialization of production that the accident of natural resource distribution and the growth of population made possible in Northern Europe. By the eleventh century Flanders was so heavily populated that it began to concentrate on the production of cloth, which it exported for raw materials and food. Wool from England and fish from Denmark and southern Sweden became the staples of interregional trade, which was centered in Flanders.[2] Great international fairs developed in places located at road or river junctions. Champagne, a small principality near Paris where roads from Flanders, Italy, France, and Germany converged, became the most famous of several commercial oases to which merchants brought their wares.

The institutions that were to become an integral part of capitalism flourished together with the commercial activities of medieval Europe. Italy – or more specifically, Venice – is the birthplace of the financial institutions of capitalism. Besides her several important industries – among them the glass industry which flourishes and is famous to this day – and her extensive commercial trade, Venice had financial institutions for dealing in bills of exchange, conducting credit transactions, and writing maritime insurance. The Florentines also excelled in banking; London's Lombard Street is a modern reminder of the place of the Lombards in the early history of banking. The Medici family also specialized in facilitating foreign exchange, that is, exchanging the currencies of one locale for that of another. This activity was the natural outgrowth of the expansion of trade and the medieval fairs. Because these attracted merchants with different currencies from all over Europe, money changers provided facilities for conversion at some standard rate. Bills of exchange were used in long-distance trade because they reduced the need to ship gold and silver. Thus, in their banking activities, the merchant bankers of the late medieval period pioneered the use of debt as a money substitute – a factor that became an essential feature of modern banking activity.

Another by-product of the expansion of trade was that it established an economic base for city life, which was virtually destroyed with the disintegration of the Roman Empire. Originally, the feudal lords claimed jurisdiction over the towns adjacent to their lands, but the commercial activities of the towns were inconsistent with the restrictions inherent in feudal relationships. As a result, it was not uncommon for a town to purchase a charter granting political freedom from the feudal lords. The status of the townspeople was uniquely different from the servitude of most of the rural population, the majority of whom were not free. The legal sanction to individual freedom provided by the town charters was an additional factor that contributed to the destruction of feudal

institutions and their mode of economic behavior. Feudal lords were reduced to collecting revenues from the townspeople in exchange for political freedom; townspeople directed their attentions to nurturing their economic gain through trade.[3]

The merchant traders formed voluntary associations, known as guilds, and often banded together in overland caravans to better ensure the safety of both merchandise and traders. Various regional guilds joined to form national guilds, and larger organizations of merchants in free German cities were known as Hansas. National guilds became typical in England, whereas Hansas developed and flourished in areas like Germany, which lacked a strong central government even into modern times. The Hanseatic League was the most powerful and famous of all. It served as a proxy for central government from the late Middle Ages until the political unification of Germany, while at the same time facilitating trade between the various regions of Europe.

During the latter part of the thirteenth century, north European trade shifted from its early center of Champagne, to Bruges, Antwerp, and Amsterdam. This change marked the transition from the traveling to the sedentary merchant as the chief participant in long-distance trade. It was accompanied by important developments in both business and market organization and in operating techniques. In particular, the bourse replaced the fair as a selling organization. The fairs of earlier eras had offered varying grades and types of merchandise sold by individual craftsmen. The bourses facilitated the sale and purchase of items that lent themselves to sufficient physical standardization that the actual goods did not need to be physically present. The institution of the bourse operated under conditions approximating those of pure competition, offering homogeneous commodities along with access to free markets. From the sixteenth century to the present day this is symbolized by the inscription 'Open to the merchants of all nations.'

Emergence of a wage class: the putting-out system

Europe's population growth and natural resource endowments, coupled with improved techniques of production, facilitated both the expansion of production and the extension of markets. Growing markets made it possible for workers to specialize in particular products and acquire skills as artisans. Specialization, and the division of labor which tends to accompany it, resulted in production for market rather than the more primitive form of production for self-consumption that was typical of the manor. The medieval handicraft industry is thus an intermediate step toward industrialization.

During the most advanced stage of the handicraft system, craft-workers contracted their outputs to merchants and thereby divorced themselves from the final consumer. At a still later stage, which developed as the market became further extended, merchants contracted for output directly with workers, who now worked for wages instead of functioning as independents. The merchants frequently provided tools as well as raw materials, and collected and sold the finished product. This system, which is known as the putting-out, or *domestic*, system, served as the intermediary step in the development of the factory system out of the more primitive handicraft system, and marks the beginning of the first permanent wage-earning class.

No wage class existed under the medieval craft system – apprentices typically became journeymen, who developed their skills and became masters themselves. Under the putting-out system, capital became a factor completely separate from labor, typically provided by rural folk working out of their own cottages. Thus, by the fourteenth century, the extension of the market was the primary force leading to the decline of the medieval handicraft system just as the expansion of trade was a primary force in destroying the manorial system two centuries earlier.

New political concepts: the state and natural law

Further stimulus to economic inquiry came from changing political developments and ideas. The Reformation was a major source of such political developments. Europe became torn by religious dissension as Protestants and Catholics fought for supremacy. The principal beneficiary of this struggle was absolute monarchy. In the interpretation offered by the great sixteenth-century political theorist Thomas Hobbes (1588–1679) only the monarch, i.e. a strong central authority which he idealized as *Leviathan* (1651), has the power to create a sufficiently powerful social order to curb the base natural tendencies of humans to be perpetually in a state of war. As monarchy replaced feudal relationships, so taxation superseded personal service as a means of supporting the state. The emergence of national governments, and the necessarily associated need to find ways to enhance their revenues, marks the beginning of modern political economy. This was the era of mercantilism, during which economic decision making was not yet liberated from the state, and economics remained in its pre-analytic phase. The subsequent divorce of economics from politics required the development of the concepts of the natural order and the natural law. These concepts became the vehicle for the political and economic liberalism of the Physiocrats John Locke and Adam Smith in the eighteenth century. Both derive from the Stoic philosophy, which eventually passed into Roman legal conceptions through the writings of Marcus Tullius Cicero (106–43 BC). According to Roman jurists, natural law is not only universal and immutable but is also the foundation of the state, since it existed before the founding of any state. Thus, the state is 'an assemblage of men associated in consent to law.' This Roman concept is different from the Greek view of the state as the outgrowth of 'natural necessity.'

Roman thinkers thus contributed two ideas that were profoundly to affect future political and economic thought: first, the idea of universal law; second, the idea of the state being based on mutual consent. These two ideas provided the foundation for the conception of individual rights, without which modern capitalism would not have evolved. While Roman thinkers contributed little as far as the development of economic thought is concerned, it is Roman law, with its emphasis on private property and freedom of contract, that constitutes the basis for the legal doctrines and institutions of capitalism. These were given new expression during the seventeenth century. Individuals challenged the uncompromising authority of the monarch who claimed to rule by divine right, for such authority was in conflict with the whole conception of an autonomous individual subject only to his or her own conscience and the dictates of 'right reason.' This seventeenth century conception of natural law was conceived by the Dutch jurist Hugo Grotius.

Grotius's secularized version of natural law was especially significant in regard to defining the natural rights that reason demonstrates as belonging to individuals by virtue of their

humanity. These are the inalienable rights that cannot be abrogated by law and which John Locke (1632–1704) later formulated as the 'right to life, liberty and property.' The rising commercial classes were quick to embrace this philosophy, for it reflected their own growing aspirations. As a result of their enhanced economic status during the period of mercantilism, they eventually challenged privileges based on birth and social position. They believed in the rights of individuals to own property and the fruits of their own labor; to speak, to write, to assemble, and to worship as they chose; to have the right to fair trial and freedom from arbitrary imprisonment and cruel or unusual punishment. Thus, the same burgher class that supported the absolutism of the Tudors in England during the sixteenth century led the Glorious Revolution which culminated in establishing the supremacy of Parliament in the seventeenth century. This protest against the unlimited power of the sovereign marked the first victory of liberalism over absolutism – a victory later echoed in the American Revolution for independence from Britain in 1776 and the French Revolution of 1789.

The Protestant ethic: individualism and accumulation

As the preceding discussion suggests, by the end of the fifteenth century, only the last vestiges of a rural feudalistic economy remained. Many islands of capitalism flourished in both northern and southern Europe and were on the verge of expanding over European economic life as a whole. Only one essential prerequisite of capitalism was absent: an ethical standard that was compatible with accumulation. The teachings of such churchmen as Saints Augustine (AD 396–430) and Aquinas (1225–74) were negative toward activities undertaken to pursue wealth and thus were difficult to reconcile with the need to accumulate. If capitalistic production was to continue its growth, an entirely new ideology was required to give moral sanction to acquisitive behavior. This sanction came within the framework of a wholly new intellectual climate.

The philosophical and political transition, which precedes the theorists of the sixteenth century and the evolution of economic relationships that would later emerge with the development of capitalism, is apparent in the very different perspective about the 'faith versus reason' debate. These became encapsulated in the 'common-sense' views of anti-Catholic (low church) thinkers. The directly challenging view of Thomas Hobbes is perhaps the most important among the non-clerical exponents of the view that knowledge is the product of observation not faith. This was to stimulate the birth not only of modern philosophy and the Protestant Reformation but also of modern science.

Essentially, these developments have a common origin, which is the thesis that human reason, as distinct from divine revelation, is sufficient to discover truth. This thesis destroyed the link forged by the Scholastics of the Middle Ages between faith and reason, and thus between theology and philosophy. To Aquinas, knowledge was the product not only of reason (philosophy) but also of revelation (theology). As in the Arabic sources with which the churchmen were undoubtedly familiar, all branches of learning (logic, ethics, politics, and economics) were welded together into one great whole through theology. The union between philosophy and theology was, however, far from permanent, and over a period of centuries, it was challenged even from within the church itself.[4]

The consequence of the eventual divorce between reason and faith was a secularism and a religious skepticism that was to characterize intellectual activity from the fifteenth through the seventeenth centuries. In essence, this intellectual revolution asserted the primacy of the individual as capable of reason and possessed of an individual will. These principles became fundamental to the spiritual revolution inherent in the Protestant Reformation, which Martin Luther provoked with his sixteenth-century attack on the misuse of indulgences, the worship of images and relics, and the necessity for the faithful to call upon the Mother of God and the saints for their salvation. To Luther, humans are autonomous individuals created in the image of God and therefore inherently good, but individually responsible for their salvation. The idea of a 'masterless' man possessing an individual will and therefore power to think and discover truth gave the people of the Renaissance feelings of self-worth and importance in the scheme of things that would have been inconceivable in the Middle Ages.

While Luther's interpretation of Christian teachings was not particularly sympathetic to industry and trade, the reform movements of John Calvin, John Knox, and the Puritans in the same century were much more so. Indeed, they adopted such strongly favorable attitudes toward acquisition by useful labor and the judicious and prudent use of wealth that their views have been described as the Protestant ethic, which launched and encouraged the development of capitalism in northern Europe. This thesis was advanced in the nineteenth century by Max Weber, the German sociologist and economist, in *The Protestant Ethic and the Spirit of Capitalism*.

Weber's hypothesis, of course, does not necessarily tell the whole story, for the fact that northern Europe and England were geographically well located for trade and had a climate and resources conducive to industry was undoubtedly also a factor in their industrial development. Nevertheless, Protestantism was congenial to the development of personal attributes that encouraged business activity. In this sense, the Reformation contributed toward capitalist development and economic thought.[5]

Protestantism considers acquisition a virtue rather than a sin and, instead of merchants being considered un-Christian because of their activities for profit, they came to be regarded as pillars of the church and the community. Their pursuit of gain, unrelated to material needs and the virtue of frugality, became as integral a part of Protestant ethic as the autonomy of the individual. Joined with the notion of the dignity and moral worth of work, Protestant emphasis on frugality served the capitalistic system well, for it stimulated thrift and capital accumulation.

Modern science

The new intellectualism brought with it a quest for new knowledge, new techniques for its acquisition, and new bases for its evaluation. The studies of the Polish astronomer Nicolaus Copernicus (1473–1543), which noted that the actual movements of the planets. Mercury and Venus did not coincide with the predictions of Ptolemy's system, led him to hypothesize that the Earth rotates on an axis of its own and orbits the sun, as do the other planets.

While Copernicus's theory, that the spheres of the universe were sun-centered, was denounced by the Church as contrary to scripture, it nevertheless served to drive another wedge (besides those of Hobbes and Luther) between faith and reason. Thus, the Copernican revolution became important for the history of natural science and, eventually, for economics. Together with the later studies of the German, Johannes Kepler (1571–1630) and the Italian, Galileo Galilei (1564–1642), Copernicus precipitated an intellectual revolution that was to alter completely our conception of the universe. Galileo, whose experiments represented a breakthrough into the behavior of the physical universe, also looked through his telescope and, upon identifying the mountainous surface of the moon, surmised that 'Heaven' was no more 'perfect' than earth. He observed the satellites orbiting Jupiter and concluded that these are heavenly spheres that orbit neither the Sun nor the Earth. His studies brought him into conflict with the church, which threatened him with excommunication until he retracted his heretical beliefs.

Not much later, in Germany, Kepler noted that the planets orbited earth in an elliptical, rather than a circular, motion. His observations, like those Galileo made at the Tower of Pisa concerning falling bodies, proclaimed the existence of laws governing the behavior of heavenly bodies. These special cases were ultimately encompassed in the mechanics of Isaac Newton (1642–1727), whose death came only four years after the birth of Adam Smith in 1723. Smith was later to describe the Newtonian system as 'the greatest discovery ever made by man.'[6]

Newton saw the entire universe as governed by a small number of mathematical laws – in particular his celebrated inverse-square law of gravitation. Even though the universe is not mechanically perfect, making it necessary for God to intervene from time to time to take care of planetary perturbations, Newton's emphasis on the usefulness of mathematics and experimentation established the rhetoric and tone of modern science.

Another aspect of the development of science that took place during the century of the Enlightenment deserves notice. Once it was recognized that the physical universe obeys certain laws that can be discovered by experimentation and observation, it was only a matter of time before it was asked whether the same principles might not also be applied to society to discover the laws that govern social phenomena. Just as Newton sought to discover the regularities governing the behavior of the physical universe and give them expression in a system of natural laws, the Physiocrats of France, John Locke (1632–1704), and the Scottish moral philosophers, among them David Hume (1711–76), Francis Hutcheson (1684–1746), and his most eminent pupil, Adam Smith (1723–90), sought to identify the natural laws ruling the behavior of society. Developments in the natural sciences, physics, and, in particular, astronomy, were thus influential in establishing the point of view and methodology for studying the behavior of the economic system.

Statecraft as economics

The growth of religious and political freedom was paralleled by greater economic freedom, which gave rise to new economic problems and phenomena requiring explanation. Some headway was made during the period of mercantilism in the development of economic concepts and tools of analysis. Mercantilist thinkers, particularly in the early period, were practitioners dedicated to improving their own fortunes and those of their nation in the struggle against other states for supremacy. The ultimate test of the strong state was its ability to wage war, make conquests, and hold colonial areas. These national objectives presented problems different from those encountered during the Middle Ages. The lord of the manor recruited soldiers and materials for warfare from his own domain.

However, the modern state needed money to acquire the sinews of war. It depended on an army of mercenaries employed by the sovereign. The essence of mercantilism, therefore, was statecraft (*Staatsbildung*); thus, economic policy became a primary instrument to promote the simultaneous development and growth of the economy and the state.

The revival of trade during the Renaissance and the emergence of a money economy had already cemented the association between money and wealth. While the accumulation of precious metals was common in the ancient world and during the Middle Ages, England and the countries of Western Europe pursued the acquisition of gold as a matter of national policy well into the eighteenth century. Spain had an advantage over rivals because colonizing ventures in the New World provided direct access to gold. France and England were largely unsuccessful in their gold-seeking expeditions and had to devise other ways to increase their stocks of the precious metals. Thus, they directed their attention to policies designed to promote a favorable balance of payments, the presumption being that if they sold more to foreigners than they bought, the surplus would return to them in gold. They also encouraged the growth of population and regulated production, giving special attention to the growth and manufacture of exportable commodities and those that would promote domestic self-sufficiency.

Sources of early mercantilist thought

A tract entitled *A Brief Treatise on the Causes Which Can Make Gold and Silver Plentiful in Kingdoms Where There Are No Mines*, written by an Italian merchant, Antonio Serra, in 1613, is generally regarded as the earliest written exposition of mercantilistic thought.

The final systematic presentation of mercantilistic doctrines was Sir James Steuart's *Inquiry into the Principles of Political Economy*, published in 1767. The ideas and policy recommendations to which the label *mercantilistic* has been given may be extracted from the large volume of tracts, pamphlets, and articles that appeared between those dates. Examination of this literature, however, reveals such a diversity of ideas and recommendations that to describe them simply as mercantilistic tends to obscure and minimize their differences.

A considerable portion of the seventeenth-century English writing came from the merchants, who naturally identified wealth with precious metals. While their funds were used to buy raw materials, tools, and labor, their businesses required the restoration of capital funds to monetary form through the sale of goods. Since domestic trade was widely viewed as merely circulating existing stocks of money, they especially prized foreign trade. Here, they looked to the state to facilitate their efforts by controlling the relationship of imports and exports, regulating interest rates and exchange rates, and chartering joint-stock trading companies, such as the British East India Company and the Merchant Adventurers, both of which had monopoly privileges.

A unity of interest between the state and the merchants evolved, because the accumulation of treasure was a primary aim of the sovereign while its acquisition depended on the foreign trade balance. Insofar as a heterogeneous group of writers may be said to have a chief spokesman, Thomas Mun (1571–1641) is generally regarded as most representative of the English mercantile interests of his day. That he was also the most influential appears evident from Adam Smith's famous critique of mercantilism in *The Wealth of Nations*.

Smith discusses the nature and shortcomings of mercantilism almost exclusively in terms of Mun's *England's Treasure by Foreign Trade*, even though Sir James Steuart's *Inquiry into the Principles of Political Economy* had been published and other writers had produced a large number of papers, pamphlets, essays, and tracts.

Mun was a successful merchant, a director of the East India Company, and a member of the Board of Trade. He wrote 'A discourse of trade from England into the East Indies' (1621) to clear the East India Company (after the loss of a company vessel carrying a gold shipment) of the bullionists' charge that its export of specie was contrary to the best interests of the country. The 'Discourse' was so obviously a special interest plea that it is much less impressive than his later work, *England's Treasure by Foreign Trade*, which was published posthumously by his son.

The arguments of such English exponents of mercantilism as Gerard De Malynes, Dudley Diggs, and Thomas Mun, reflect wide differences in their ideas and policy recommendations, although they were all spokespersons for the business interests of their day. The flow of ideas from merchant authors, together with those of the philosophers, government officials, and scientists who also turned their attention to economic matters, resulted in a heterogeneous body of literature. It is no easy task, therefore, to set forth mercantilistic doctrines. We can examine the leading ideas on foreign trade, money and interest, and labor and production, yet our efforts will not yield a homogeneous body of thought. Nevertheless, several important analytical concepts of monetary and international trade theory can be traced to mercantilist writings. Chief among these are the *balance of trade* and the generalization that later became known as *the quantity theory of money*.

The balance of trade and the acquisition of wealth

The concept of the balance of trade is the most important tool of economic analysis developed by mercantilist writers. In modern terminology, the term *balance of trade* includes only merchandise imports and exports, whereas the *balance of payments* includes, in addition, invisible exports and imports, long-term and short-term capital, and gold. Merchandise and invisible exports, exports of monetary metals, and transfers of claims on the domestic economy to the rest of the world are designated as plus items in the balance of payments. Commodity and invisible imports, imports of monetary metals and acquisitions of claims *vis-à-vis* the rest of the world, set up an outward flow of foreign exchange to other countries and are negative items in the balance of payments.

If a country has a surplus of commodity and invisible imports, this will be balanced by an outward movement of specie, new foreign debts, or diminished foreign assets. Conversely, an excess of merchandise and invisible exports will be offset by an inflow of gold or the acquisition of claims on the rest of the world. It is in this sense that the balance of payments, which is nothing more than an accounting statement of a country's foreign transactions, must always be in balance. Bullionist, mercantilist, and cameralist writers argued that a nation should strive for a favorable balance of trade as a matter of national policy. They expected an excess of merchandise and invisible exports relative to imports to be offset either by a flow of gold or by foreign credits. Since the primary concern was the acquisition of treasure, they advocated policies that would insure gold imports to compensate for a surplus in the balance of trade.

Mun emphasized that it is the relationship between aggregate imports and exports that is crucial for the nation's treasure, not the relationship between specific imports and exports. He was also well aware of the significance of invisible items of trade as a source of additional foreign credits, for he says: 'The value of our exportations may be much advanced when we perform it ourselves in our own Ships, for then we get not only the price of our wares as they are worth here, but also the Merchants gains, the charges of ensurance and freight to carry them beyond the seas.'[7] In order to cultivate a favorable balance, he urges that the country should strive for self-sufficiency to diminish its imports and practice frugality to have more available for export. The consumption of luxuries is also to be discouraged, if necessary, by import duties high enough to discourage consumption of foreign goods in England.

The most controversial matter pursued by Mun concerned the export of specie as a means to increase England's treasure. It was this issue that brought him into conflict with the bullionists, who advocated complete prohibition of gold exports. The essence of his argument was that, when gold is used in trade to acquire goods that are subsequently re-exported at advantageous prices, even more gold will be returned to England than was originally sent out. To keep gold in the kingdom does not multiply wealth; on the contrary, it will raise prices and diminish exports.

Profitable export trade served two purposes. It enriched the merchant as well as the sovereign. When it became apparent that expeditions, such as those financed by Ferdinand and Isabella of Spain and Elizabeth of England, were often not successful in discovering gold, the rising commercial, or mercantilist, classes promoted the idea that gold could be made to flow into their country by means of a favorable balance of trade. The mercantilists urged their sovereign to promote a menu of activities that, in the language of Thomas Mun, would serve to 'increase our Wealth and Treasure.' The relevance of trade to statecraft is nowhere expressed with greater vigor or clarity than in his *England's Treasure by Foreign Trade* (1664). Mun details the various measures to be followed. The most controversial among them is whether gold used in trade to purchase luxury goods, like spices, tea, and silk, for resale could ultimately bring back an even greater quantity of gold than had originally been exported. If the answer is affirmative, the place of merchants in the hierarchy of persons that contribute to the well-being of the nation is greatly enhanced. This side issue concerning the positive contribution of merchants to national well-being is not unimportant in a business-oriented society. This consideration adds relevance to *England's Treasure by Foreign Trade* as a masterwork of economics.

Issues and Answers from the Masterworks 2.1

Issue

Do the wealth-getting activities of individual businessmen also contribute to strengthening their nation's economic and political power while it enriches them personally?

Mun's answer

From *England's Treasure by Foreign Trade* (1664), Parts I, II, and III.

The Means to Enrich This Kingdom, and to Increase Our Treasure

Although a Kingdom may be enriched by gifts received, or by purchase taken from some other Nations, yet these are things uncertain and of small consideration when they happen. The ordinary means therefore to increase our wealth and treasure is by *Foreign Trade*, wherein we must ever observe this rule; to sell more to strangers yearly than we consume of theirs in value. For suppose that when this Kingdom is plentifully served with the Cloth, Lead, Tin, Iron, Fish and other native commodities, we do yearly export the overplus to foreign Countries to the value of twenty two hundred thousand pounds; by which means we are enabled beyond the Seas to buy and bring in foreign wares for our use and Consumptions, to the value of twenty hundred thousand pounds; By this order duly kept in our trading, we may rest assured that the Kingdom shall be enriched yearly two hundred thousand pounds, which must be brought to us in so much Treasure; because the part of our stock which is not returned to us in wares must necessarily be brought home in treasure . . .

It would be very beneficial to export money as well as wares, being done in trade only, it would increase our Treasure; but of this I write more largely in the next Chapter to prove it plainly . . .

The Exportation of Our Moneys in Trade of Merchandize is a Means to Increase Our Treasure

This Position is so contrary to the common opinion, that it will require many and strong arguments to prove it before it can be accepted of the Multitude, who bitterly exclaim when they see any monies carried out of the Realm; affirming thereupon that we have absolutely lost so much Treasure, and that this is an act directly against the long continued laws made and confirmed by the wisdom of this Kingdom in the High Court of Parliament, and that many places, nay *Spain* it self which is the Fountain of Money, forbids the exportation thereof, some cases only excepted. To all which I might answer, that *Venice, Florence, Genoa, the Low Countries* and divers other places permit it, their people applaud it, and find great benefit by it; but all this makes a noise and proves nothing, we must therefore come to those reasons which concern the business in question.

First, I will take that for granted which no man of judgment will deny, that we have no other means to get Treasure but by foreign trade, for Mines we have none which do afford it, and how this money is gotten in the managing of our said Trade I have already showed, that it is done by making our commodities which are exported yearly to over balance in value the foreign wares which we consume; so that it resteth only to show how our moneys may be added to our commodities, and being jointly exported may so much the more increase our Treasure.

We have already supposed our yearly consumptions of foreign wares to be for the value of twenty hundred thousand pounds, and our exportations to exceed that two hundred thousand pounds, which sum we have thereupon affirmed is brought to us in treasure to balance the account. But now if we add three hundred thousand pounds more in ready money unto our former exportations in wares, what profit can we have (will some men say) although by this means we should bring in so much ready money more than we did before, seeing that we have carried out the like value.

To this the answer is, that when we have prepared our exportations of wares, and sent out as much of every thing as we can spare or vent abroad: It is not therefore said that then we should add our money thereunto to fetch in the more money immediately, but rather first to enlarge our trade by enabling us to bring in more foreign wares, which being sent out again will in due time much increase our Treasure.

For although in this manner we do yearly multiply our importations to the maintenance of more Shipping and Mariners, improvement of His Majesty's Customs and other benefits: yet our consumption of those foreign wares is no more than it was before; so that all the said increase of commodities brought in by the means of our ready money sent out as is afore written, doth in the end become an exportation unto us of a far greater value than our said moneys . . . if those Nations which send out their monies do it because they have but few wares of their own, how come they then to have so much Treasure as we ever see in those places which suffer it freely to be exported at all times and by whomsoever? I answer, Even by trading with their Moneys; for by what other means can they get it, having no Mines of Gold or Silver?

Thus may we plainly see, that when this weighty business is duly considered in his end as all our humane actions ought well to be weighed, it is found much contrary to that which most men esteem thereof, because they search no further than the beginning of the work, which mis-informs their judgments, and leads them into error: For if we only behold the actions of the husband-man in the seed-time when he casteth away much good corn into the ground, we will rather account him a mad man than a husbandman: but when we consider his labours in the harvest which is the end of his endeavours, we find the worth and plentiful increase of his actions.

The Conclusion upon All That Hath Been Said, Concerning the Exportation or Importation of Treasure

The sum of all that hath been spoken, concerning the enriching of the Kingdom, and the increase of our treasure by commerce with strangers, is briefly thus. That it is a certain rule in our foreign trade, in those places where our commodities exported are overbalanced in value by foreign wares brought into this Realm, there our money is undervalued in exchange; and where the contrary of this is performed, there our money is overvalued. But let the Merchants exchange be at a high rate, or at a low rate, or at the *Par pro pari*, or put down altogether; Let Foreign Princes enhance their Coins, or debase their Standards, and let His Majesty do the like, or keep them constant as they now stand; Let foreign coins pass current here in all payments at higher rates than they are worth at the Mint; Let the Statute for employments by Strangers stand in force or be repealed; Let the mere Exchanger do his worst; Let Princes oppress, Lawyers extort, Usurers bite, Prodigals waste, and lastly let Merchants carry out what money they shall have occasion to use in traffic. Yet all these actions can work no other effects in the course of trade than is declared in this discourse. For so much Treasure only will be brought in or carried out of a Commonwealth, as the Foreign Trade doth over or under balance in value. And this must come to pass by a Necessity beyond all resistance. So that all other courses (which tend not to this end) whomsoever they may seem to force money into a Kingdom for a time, yet are they (in the end) not only fruitless but also hurtful: they are like to violent floods which bear down their banks, and suddenly remain dry again for want of waters.

Behold then the true form and worth of foreign Trade, which is, *The great Revenue of the King, the honour of the Kingdom, The Noble profession of the Merchant, The School of our Arts, The supply of our wants, The employment of our poor, The improvement of our Lands, The Nursery of our Mariners, The walls of the Kingdoms. The Means of our Treasure, the Sinews of our wars, The terror of our Enemies.* For all which great and weighty reasons, do so many well governed States highly countenance the profession, and carefully cherish the action, not only with policy to increase it, but also with power to protect it from all foreign energies: because they know it is a Principal in Reason of State to maintain and defend which doth Support them and their estates.

Source: *Early English Tracts on Commerce*, J. R. McCulloch (ed.)
(London: Political Economy Club, 1856).

Summing up: Mun's key point

Thomas Mun's essay *England's Treasure by Foreign Trade* (1664) reflects the influence of two major events in human history. One was the emergence, in England, of a work ethic as part of the Protestant Reformation. Contrary to prevailing Catholic doctrine, this ethic maintained that individual wealth-getting activities were not inherently sinful. The second event was the emergence of political nationalism, principally in England, Spain, France, and Holland as these nations competed with one another for wealth and power. Their competition provoked a major new issue. Might individual wealth-getting activity also contribute to enriching the nation and enhancing its political power? If the answer to this question is affirmative, what positive measures can government introduce that will simultaneously add to its wealth and power and also enrich its individual citizens? Aquinas and the churchmen deplored individual wealth-getting activities as sinful. The change of viewpoint that is evident in Mun's work reflects the dramatic change that had taken place between the destruction of the command society of the feudal manor and the era of mercantilism and statecraft that flourished between the fifteenth and eighteenth centuries.

The issue that Mun addressed about the advantage to England of 'trading with its money' has considerable contemporary relevance, for it points to early recognition of interdependence among the economies of the world through their trade balances, exchange rates, and capital movements. The larger issue of the role of trade in raising living standards was not the concern of the mercantilists. For them, the purpose of trade is to enrich the king and strengthen the nation politically. Their 'fear of goods' was rooted in the premise that the quest for gold, like the quest for territory, is a zero-sum game; that is, more for England is at the expense of Spain, Italy, and Holland, and vice versa.

Monetary analysis

Most mercantilists suspected a direct relationship between the quantity of money and the level of prices, maintaining that 'plenty of money in a Kingdom doth make the native commodities dearer.' The earliest theoretical analysis of the relationship between the quantity of money and inflationary price increases was made by the sixteenth century French political philosopher, Jean Bodin. He attributed the marked price rise experienced by Western Europe in his time primarily to the inflow of monetary metals from South America, thus emphasizing what is today treated as M (monetary means of payment) in our

modern equations of exchange. He also observed that monopolies, through their policies of restricting output, and large demands by consumers of luxury commodities, contributed to price increases. Thus, he was not unaware of the significance of what is today designated as T and V in the transactions version of the equation of exchange.[8]

Since few mercantilists favored inflation, their recommendations for a continuous accumulation of monetary metals via a favorable balance of trade appears contradictory. But this seeming contradiction of objectives is reconciled if changes in M affect T rather than P. Thus, mercantilists typically thought increases in the amount of money 'quicken trade' instead of producing an inflation of prices. Their advocacy of a favorable balance of trade, with its associated inflow of specie, was thereby rescued from a seeming contradiction of objectives.

This line of reasoning reflects an awareness that a growing volume of money and credit is essential to continued expansion of the physical volume of trade. Since the embryonic state of the credit system at that time precluded a well functioning system of note issue (demand deposit creation being a still later phase of banking development), mercantilist emphasis on the desirability of accumulating greater quantities of gold in order to expand the money supply is more comprehensible than it would be if the credit system had been better developed. They reasoned that an inflow of hard money would keep interest rates low, while the downward pressure on prices resulting from an inadequate supply of money would serve to dampen further expansion of economic activity.

Mercantilists seemed to sense the necessity of avoiding downward pressure on prices if commercial activity was to be expanded. Although they thought of these relationships in purely monetary terms, real factors, which they did not understand, are involved. Economic analysis is conducted in real terms when it views money as facilitating the process of exchange by serving as a unit of account but does not affect the relative commodity or factor prices or the level of economic activity in any way. A monetary analysis, on the other hand, regards money as capable of exerting an effect on the magnitudes of the economy.

Mercantilists overlooked the interaction between real and monetary factors when they failed to see that falling prices raise the real rate of interest, which impedes economic expansion. It is the value of a loan in terms of the goods and services it represents, rather than money rates as such, that affects the profitability of borrowing. If the price level is falling, the principal value of a loan is necessarily rising in real terms since the borrower contracts to repay a given number of dollars, which will purchase more goods and services at low prices than at higher prices. What the mercantilists failed to understand was that the reason an increased quantity of money is associated with a lower rate of interest is not simply due to the greater supply of funds thus available for borrowing, but because this is generally associated with an increase in real income. This is a relationship that the mercantilist monetary theory of interest overlooked. It was not until the writings of David Hume, Anne-Robert Jacques Turgot, and Richard Cantillon that real, as opposed to monetary, theories of interest began to evolve.

Mercantilist views on production and related matters

Preoccupation with the wealth and growth of the state and the acquisition of treasure set the stage for a number of corollary doctrines and policies intended to foster the achievement of these goals. The theory of production is of major importance, for the creation of the largest possible export surplus requires maximum utilization of the factors of production. Some viewed natural resources as the basis of wealth, while other writers regarded labor as a more important factor than natural resources. Lewes Roberts, for example, viewed the earth as 'the fountaine and mother of all riches,' while Sir William Petty said that 'labor is the father and active principle of wealth as land is the mother.' The policy counterpart of both viewpoints is to be found in measures to increase natural resources and the productivity of labor by discouraging idleness and introducing specialization. Even before Smith's celebrated description of the advantages of the division of labor in the manufacture of pins, Petty observed that 'cloth must be cheaper when one cards, another spins, another weaves, another draws, another dresses, another presses and packs, than when all the operations above were clumsily performed by the same hand.'

Mercantilistic writers distinguished between productive and unproductive labor in terms of its contribution to national opulence. Manufacturers and farmers were regarded as productive, although the warmest praise was, understandably, reserved for merchants. Retailers, the clergy, doctors, lawyers, and entertainers were generally regarded as unproductive. It was also urged that the government hold the number of unproductive people to a minimum in order to direct their labor to some more useful occupation. Mercantilistic ideas on production are part of their legacy from the Scholastics of the medieval period, who regarded wealth as evidence of God's bounty and production as the exploitation of this bounty by labor. Thus,

Thomas Hobbes wrote that 'plenty God usually either giveth freely, or for labor selleth to mankind.'[9] Emphasis on the appropriation of the natural or divine bounty by the efforts of human labor is to be found throughout British economic literature in the period before Adam Smith. Virtually without exception, it was urged that government must increase both the quantity and the utilization of natural wealth and labor. Thus, Mun advocated the growing of hemp, flax, cordage, and tobacco on wastelands, and the exploitation of fisheries in the North Sea, which are 'our own natural wealth and would cost nothing but labor.'[10] Similarly, Roger Coke proposed that idle workers be employed to reclaim wastelands.[11] Willful idleness was not to be tolerated, and there is an abundance of literature setting forth proposals to make England's population as productive as possible. This is the responsibility of government, for if people are idle, 'that is for want of being rightly governed.'[12]

Still another aspect of mercantilistic emphasis on the importance of labor in production is the encouragement of population growth, not for the sake of mere numbers, but to increase the size of the working force. Attention was frequently called to Holland, a very prosperous country that, although it had few resources, was enriched through the industry of its people; and to Spain, which was impoverished through its sparse population, although it was rich in colonial mines. Proposals to increase population by encouraging early marriage and immigration are so common to most of the English writers of this period that they cannot be specifically associated with the name of any one writer. It was generally accepted that a large population, by keeping wages close to subsistence levels, would not only reduce the cost of producing goods but would also discourage the idleness that might become associated with higher wage levels.

One of the most interesting bits of mercantilistic reasoning incorporating views on both labor and balance of payments is the argument that appeared in successive issues of the *British Merchant* regarding foreign-paid incomes.[13] Briefly, the line of reasoning pursued was that when goods were exported, foreigners, in effect, pay the wages of the workers employed in making them, whereas imports involve like payments to foreigners. The obvious duty of government would therefore be to minimize foreign imports in order to achieve a favorable balance of foreign-paid income. Bullion is the most desirable import because it *is* wealth, and also has little labor incorporated in it as compared with the manufactured commodities that England concentrated on exporting.

Many of the forces that contributed to the development of the modern nation-state also nurtured the development of a competitive market economy. In England, and also in the German states, the rise of various Protestant religious groups made a powerful contribution toward establishing that, for persons to engage in wealth-getting activities is appropriate and desirable and not inconsistent with their Protestant belief. Thus, the teachings of Protestant clerics were less hostile to the commercial interests that prospered along with the town life, especially when compared with the teachings of the Roman Churchmen, who denied them moral sanction. These clerics praised useful labor and considered acquisition and thrift as personal virtues that would contribute to man's salvation in the next world. They also contributed to the early success of the English handicraft trades, which supplied commodities for export as well as domestic use, by teaching the virtue of work.

Concluding remarks

During the era of mercantilism, economic behavior began to manifest itself through commercial, rather than exclusively household and other non-commercial, activities. Accordingly, mercantilist thinkers emphasized the importance of commerce and industry and the role of the state in promoting economic development and national wealth. They looked to the state to pursue policies that encouraged the growth of the labor force by natural increase and immigration, and fostered its employment-productive activities.

The possibility of increasing productivity by specialization was appreciated, but the role of invention in increasing labor productivity was still too infrequently observed to receive much attention. The importance of increasing efficiency in the use of land and other natural resources in order to reduce the cost of wage goods was also given considerable attention. All these measures were thought of as contributing to the maintenance of a favorable balance of trade, which served to increase the supply of precious metals and money. Money was thus viewed as playing an active role in economic development because, supposedly, it kept interest rates low and prevented unfavorable price movements.

The economic analysis that emerged in connection with these recommendations was crude and unsystematic by modern standards. The early mercantilists, especially, were practitioners rather than theorists, and their interest was in economic policy rather than in analysis. Much of their analysis was implicit in their discussions on policy, and even when given explicit formulation, it lacked the rigor that was to become associated with the inquiries of writers of the transition period. Even so, John Maynard Keynes, writing his 'Notes of Mercantilism' at the conclusion of

The General Theory of Employment, Interest and Money in 1936, credited the mercantilists with anticipating some of his thinking about the stimulating effect of low interest rates on investment. He credited them with awareness that the propensity to save tends to be high, relative to the inducement to invest. Insufficient investment is the likely cause, Keynes concluded, when an economy equilibrates at less than full employment. Modern governments rely on monetary management and public investment to stimulate employment when investment is insufficient, but these techniques were not yet developed during the mercantilistic era. Keynes thus regarded the mercantilist policy of encouraging inflation through gold inflows resulting from a favorable trade balance as the only available method to expand the money supply, thereby lowering interest rates and stimulating investment and employment.

Keynes appreciated mercantilist warnings against holding money idle and understood their reason for arguing that a favorable trade balance has employment-creating effects. However, the analogy between their views and his must not be carried too far; Keynes's own analysis related specifically to modern industrial economies.[14]

The mercantilist pursuit of precious metals has also recently been explained in the light of the unique liquidity problems then encountered by England in buying Baltic wheat and East Indian spices.[15] These were items for which the English were unable to pay with merchandise exports or services. In the absence of a fully developed international money market, there was only limited convertibility of sterling with other currencies; stocks of precious metals thus provided the only reliable means of paying for these highly prized imports. Mun's warning against the loss of specie that would result from 'not trading with our money' applies particularly to the type of trade carried on with the East Indies and the Baltic countries. Further gains could be gotten from stockpiling these goods and then exporting them again at advantageous prices.

During the seventeenth century, the English were particularly envious of the success that Holland had in augmenting its stocks of precious metals through trade, while also experiencing a stable or falling level of prices. Since conventional wisdom generally links inflation to increases in the money supply, the mercantilistic goal of augmenting the country's stock of gold would seem inherently inflationary. The Dutch experience, however, demonstrates that this is not necessarily the case. If the inflow of gold from favorable trade balances is accompanied by increased employment and production or, alternatively, is used to finance the stockpiling of commodities for re-export (which is known as *entrepôt* trade), it becomes possible to avoid increased domestic prices. Thus, the failure of mercantilist writers to recognize analytically the potentially inflationary effects of an influx of gold can be explained in terms of the unique nature of their East Indian and Balkan trade and the empirical fact that, under certain circumstances, falling prices can accompany large gold movements into a country.[16]

Notes

1 Ghazanfar, S. M., 'Scholastic economics and Arab scholars: the "Great Gap" thesis reconsidered', in *Diogenes: International Review of Humane Sciences*, Paris: International Council for Philosophy and Humanistic Studies, No. 154, 1991.

2 This former European country on the coast of the North Sea now comprises the Belgian provinces of East and West Flanders and part of northern France.

3 Historical events that contributed to the development of economic thought during the pre-classical period are put into perspective by W. J. Ashley in *An Introduction to English Economic History and Theory,* vol. 1, Part 1 (1888), Chapter 3, Part 11(1893), Chapter VI (New York: Augustus Kelley, 1969). This background is further examined by Karl Polanyi *et al.* in *Trade and Markets in Early Empires* (New York: Free Press, 1957). Chapter 5 is especially recommended.

4 Ghazanfar speculates that the scholastics probably feared that Arabic interpretations of Aristotle would eclipse the influence of Aquinas, which partly explains the paucity of citations to the work of Arab scholars in the writings of the Scholastics. Ghazanfar, S. M., 'Scholastic economics and Arab scholars: the "Great Gap" thesis reconsidered,' in *Diogenes: International Review of Humane Sciences*, Paris: International Council for Philosophy and Humanistic Studies, No. 154, 1991, pp. 130–34)

5 R. H. Tawney's *Religion and the Rise of Capitalism* (New York: Penguin Books, 1947) and Max Weber's *Protestant Ethic and the Spirit of Capitalism*, translated by Talcott Parsons (New York: Scribner, 1948), explore the relationship between religion and the rise of capitalism.

6 Adam Smith, 'An essay on the history of astronomy,' in *The Early Writing of Adam Smith.* edited by Ralph Lingren (New York: Augustus Kelly, 1967).

7 Thomas Mun, *England's Treasure by Foreign Trade* (London, 1664), in *Early English Tracts on Commerce*, edited by John R. McCulloch (Norwich: Jarrold and Sons, 1952), p. 129. This essay was published posthumously by his son. It is more highly regarded than his earlier 'A discourse of trade from England into the East Indies' (1621), written after a gold shipment by the British East India Company was lost at sea. The latter is generally viewed as a self-serving defense of the company of which he was an officer.

8 In the now familiar form introduced by Irving Fisher in 1930, the equation of exchange states that

$$MV = PT$$

In this equation, *M* designates the monetary means of payment available for conducting transactions in the economy, V designates the average number of times the units of payment change hands in a given period of time, P stands for the average level of prices, and T for the quantity of goods and services available to be purchased. The equation, as it stands, is nothing more than the truism that the monetary value of the goods and services paid for is equal to the monetary value of the goods and services sold. It becomes analytically useful only within the framework of a hypothesis about the behavior of elements in the equation. As a result of certain assumptions with respect to T and V, conventional wisdom now maintains that there is a direct causal relationship between the quantity of money and the general price level. It is argued that, other things being equal, the general price level varies directly with the quantity of money. Although they lacked the analytical framework that was later developed, this is a conclusion with which mercantilists were in accord.

9 Thomas Hobbes. *Leviathan* (London: Harmondsworth, 1651), Penguin p. 127.

10 Thomas Mun, *England's Treasure by Foreign Trade* (London, 1664). Reprinted in *Early English Tracts on Commerce*, edited by John R. McCulloch (Norwich: Jarrold and Sons, 1952), pp. 127, 130.

11 Roger Coke, A *Discourse of Trade* (London, 1670), pp. 16–17.

12 Attributed to Malachy Postlethwayt, in E. A. J. Johnson, *Predecessors of Adam Smith* (New York: Prentice-Hall, 1937), p. 287.

13 See E. A. J. Johnson. *Predecessors*, Chapter 15, for a complete description of these views.

14 A more recent reinterpretation of Mercantilist policy by B. Basinger, R. B. Eklund and R. D. Tolleson in 'Mercantilism as a rent seeking society' in *Towards a Theory of the Rent Seeking Society*, College Station TX: Texas A & M University Press, 1980, interprets mercantilist policy from the mainstream perspective of profit seeking behavior on the part of merchants engaged in the political process of aligning themselves with the interests of monarchy.

15 Gould, J. D. 'The trade crisis of the early 1620s and English economic thought,' *Journal of Economic History*, 15(2), (1955), pp. 121–32.

Glossary of terms and concepts

Economic literature is full of expressions and terms that serve almost as a shorthand to identify various economic relationships and phenomena. These are frequently of historical origin and have survived, though sometimes in altered form, beyond their initial context. Because at least some of the continuity between contemporary theory and older theoretical doctrines is reflected in concepts of this sort, it appears useful to identify these briefly at the end of the chapter in which they are first introduced, in order to build a familiarity to facilitate understanding of later theoretical developments.

Balance of payments
Summary of the monetary value of a country's transactions with the rest of the world, including merchandise, invisible exports and imports, capital movements, and gold.

Equation of exchange
$MV = PT$ expresses the identity between aggregate demand (MV) and aggregate supply (PT) in monetary terms.

Quantity theory of money
A hypothesis that relates changes in P, the general price level, to changes in M, the quantity of money, assuming that V velocity, and T, transactions, are given magnitudes in the short run.

Reprinted in *Readings in the History of Economic Theory*, edited by I. H. Rima (New York: Holt, Rinehart & Winston, 1970).

16 This hypothesis is also advanced by W. D. Grampp in his provocative article, 'Liberal elements in English mercantilism,' *Quarterly Journal of Economics*, 66 (November 1952). Grampp takes the position that the main objective of mercantilist policy was to achieve full employment rather than a favorable balance of trade *per se*.

Questions for discussion and further research

1 What do you infer from reading Thomas Mun's *England's Treasure by Foreign Trade* about the relationship between seventeenth century English nationalism and mercantilism?

2 It is sometimes said that mercantilists had 'a fear of goods.' 'What do you interpret this to mean and how is it reflected in the policy measures that Mun was recommending for England to follow?

3 Do you regard Mun's essay as a contribution to economic analysis?

Notes for further reading

From *The New Palgrave*

William Allen on mercantilism, vol. 3, pp. 445–49; S. Bauer on balance of trade, history of the theory, vol. 1, pp. 179–81; Mario I. Blejer and Jacob A. Frenkel on the monetary approach to the balance of payments, vol. 3, pp. 497–99; Walter Eltis on Thomas Mun, vol. 3, pp. 576–77, and on Sir James Steuart, vol. 4, pp. 494–97; A. C. Fix on Jean Bodin, vol. 1, p. 254; Milton Friedman on the quantity theory of money, vol. 4, pp. 3–19; Peter Groenewegen on Victor Riquetti Marquis de Mirabeau, vol. 3, p. 478, and on Antonio Serra, vol. 4, pp. 313–14; C. B. Macpherson on Thomas Hobbes, vol. 2, pp. 663–64; Lawrence H. Officer on Gerard de Malynes, vol. 3, p. 293; Alessandro Roncaglia on William Petty, vol. 3, pp. 853–55; Eugene Rotwein on David Hume, vol. 2, pp. 692–95; Karen I. Vaughn on John Locke, vol. 3, pp. 229–30; Douglas Vickers on Nicholas Barbon, vol. 1, p. 189, on Josiah Child, vol. 1, p. 418, and on Dudley North, vol. 3, p. 682; Vivian Walsh on Richard Cantillon, vol. 1, pp. 317–20.

Selected references and suggestions for further reading

Ashley, W. J. *An Introduction to English Economic History and Theory*, Vol. 1 (New York: Augustus Kelley, 1969).

Chalk, Alfred E. 'Natural law and the rise of economic individualism in England.' *Journal of Political Economy*, 59 (August, 1951), pp. 330–47.

Ecklund, R. B. and Tolleson, T. D. 'Economic regulation in mercantile England: Hecsher revisited.' *Economic Inquiry*, 18 (October, 1980).

Gould, J. D. 'The trade crisis of the early 1620s and English economic thought.' *Journal of Economic History*, 15 (1955), pp. 121–32. Reprinted in *Readings in the History of Economic Theory*, edited by I. H. Rima (New York: Hold, Rinehart & Winston, 1970).

Grampp, W. D. 'Liberal elements in English mercantilism.' *Quarterly Journal of Economics*, 66 (November, 1952).

Heckscher, Eli. *Mercantilism*. 2 vols. Translated by Mendel Shapiro (London: G. Allen, 1934).

Johnson, E. A. J. *Predecessors of Adam Smith* (New York: Prentice Hall, 1937).

Keynes, J. M. *The General Theory of Employment, Interest and Money*, chapter 22 (New York: Harcourt Brace, 1936).

Magnusson, L. *Mercantilism: The Shaping of Economic Language* (London: Routledge, 1891).

Magnusson, L. (ed.) *Mercantilist Economics* (Boston: Kluwer Academic Publishers, 1993).

Mun, Thomas. *England's Treasure by Foreign Trade* (London, 1664). Reprinted in *Early English Tracts on Commerce*, edited by J. R. McCulloch (Norwich: Jarrold and Sons, 1952).

Perrota, C. 'Early Spanish mercantilism: the first analysis of underdevelopment' in *Mercantilist Economics*, edited by L. Magnusson (Boston: Kluwer Academic, 1993).

Perrota, C. 'Is mercantilist theory of the favorable balance of trade really erroneous?' *History of Political Economy*, 23 (Summer, 1991), pp. 301–36.

Polanyi, Karl, *et al. Trade and Markets in Early Empires* (New York: Free Press, 1957).

Robbins, Lionel. Lectures 4 and 5, 'Pamphleteers', in *A History of Economic Thought*, edited by

S. Medema and W. Samuels (Princeton NJ: Princeton University Press, 1998), pp. 35–54.

Smith, Adam. 'An essay on the history of astronomy.' *Early Writings of Adam Smith*, edited by Ralph Lingren (New York: Augustus Kelley, 1967).

Tawney, R. H. *Religion and the Rise of Capitalism* (New York: Penguin Books, 1947).

Weber, Max. *Protestant Ethic and the Spirit of Capitalism.* Translated by Talcott Parsons (New York: Scribner, 1948).

Chapter 3

The transition to classical economics

···

The environment and leading contributors

Economic thought entered a transitional phase in the second half of the seventeenth century. During this phase, thinkers who were adverse to mercantilistic views displaced businessmen as the chief inquirers into economic questions. The methodological approach of deduction and the *laissez-faire* attitudes that would later characterize the writings of the classical era also began to appear. The newly emerging attitude was one of increasing liberality; people came to believe that greater freedom from governmental restrictions would be advantageous to themselves as well as to the economy. This attitude reflected the gradually evolving idea that the economic system is a self-generating autonomous mechanism that does not require management from above, but functions best when allowed to regulate itself. This proposition was made particularly explicit by the free-thinking David Hume. By committing himself to finding the basis for society and government outside scriptures and the church, he paved the way for separating the theory of economic behavior from moral philosophy. Following the interpretations of the Protestant natural-law theorists, the writers of the transition period tended to de-emphasize God's role in the operation of

worldly affairs. The Scholastic tradition of natural law philosophy had little influence on the English thinkers of the late seventeenth and early eighteenth centuries.

These liberal trends in economic thinking were joined to a hedonistic philosophy of material gain and enjoyment, as opposed to the medieval view of the virtue of self-denial. Bernard de Mandeville (1670–1733), a Dutchman who settled in England, gained considerable notoriety for himself as a satirist by advocating, in the context of an allegorical poem entitled 'The Grumbling Hive or Knaves Turn'd Honest,' that individual vice (i.e. self-interest) yields social benefits. His theme was further embellished in a second poem, 'The Fable of the Bees: or Private Vices, Publick Benefits'; Part I was published in 1714 and Part 11 in 1729. According to de Mandeville, spending is the life of the trade. Economic progress thrives under the stimulus of self-interest and higher levels of personal consumption. These views were particularly evident in England, whose growing middle class included many who were engaged in trade and industry.

While de Mandeville was, in other respects, still committed to mercantilist views (for example, his acceptance of the view of the utility of poverty), the paradox of public benefit, as the product of private vice rather than private virtue, was regarded as nothing short of scandalous when it was offered. The argument that purely egoistic individual impulses can generate a viable social order was ahead of the time and was influential in giving direction to the liberal thinking of the later eighteenth century economic thinking.

It is perhaps interesting to note that, like several other thinkers of the period, de Mandeville earned a medical degree (from the Dutch University of Leyden in 1691) and pursued a practice that specialized in 'Hypochondriack and hysterick.' However, most of the writers of the transition period were businessmen who, like Josiah Child (1630–99) and Nicholas Barbon (1637–98), were suited by experience to write about economic matters. Child was a merchant who sold supplies to the English navy and eventually became the largest single stockholder in the East India Company.[1] His most famous work is a pamphlet, *Brief Observations*, published in 1668, in which he undertook to prove that England could equal the prosperity of the Dutch by following policies that he believed to be the source of Holland's great wealth. He believed a low rate of interest to be the most important of these and strongly advocated that the then existing legal rate of interest be reduced.

Nicholas Barbon (1640–98) was also a businessman, although he too earned a medical degree, his from the University of Utrecht in 1661. His earliest business interest was in building, and he became prosperous as a result of the destruction of most of the city of London by the Great Fire. He was also astute enough to venture into mortgage banking, and he developed the first workable plan for writing fire insurance. His leading work is *Discourse on Trade* (1690), although he wrote many pamphlets on fire insurance, building, and banking.

Merchants were still not highly esteemed; indeed, while the social benefits of commerce had begun to be more appreciated than previously, there was such suspicion about their recommendations that merchant authors often preferred to write anonymously or wrote prefaces that denied that their policy would benefit them privately.[2] These denials notwithstanding, the fact is that private interests were seldom really subordinated to the public good, and public suspicion of merchant-supported proposals was more frequently justified than not. Their recommendations that the legal rate of interest and the bullion content of silver coins be reduced (the latter was done in 1696) provided reason for thinking that as business borrowers, they would also be beneficiaries. Nor was the argument that devaluation would make the country richer as convincing as it might have been were it not apparent that it would also benefit those who had hoarded bullion or old coins whose bullion content had not been reduced by clipping. As a banker, Barbon had this opportunity, although he pointed out that banks would also profit if coins were fewer and heavier, for 'nothing can be of greater advantage to banks than scarcity of money when men will be glad to take a bank note for want of it.'[3]

The policy recommendations offered by Barbon and Child were unsupported by any kind of economic analysis. Typically, they argued for their proposals on the grounds that they had worked well previously or because current policies were not producing satisfactory results. Another technique of argumentation was to refute the objections that others made against the policies they recommended. But there was no attempt to derive general principles on which the policies recommended must necessarily rest, if they were to work as claimed. It is plain, therefore, that before economics could make headway as a science, a deductive system, which derives its conclusions from a set of premises, was urgently needed. The only critique that can then be made against an analysis is that the premises are false or inappropriate, or that the reasoning is imperfect. Failing this, the conclusions are valid, irrespective of the personal interests of the author, for the conclusions are inherent in the premises. In short, economics required the methodology that the French philosopher René Descartes (1595–1650) had already introduced in his *Discourse on Method* in the mid seventeenth century to lay a foundation for natural science. Like his older contemporary Francis Bacon (1561–1626), Descartes was deeply concerned with the question of the method for obtaining real knowledge through the process of reason on the basis of what we know or infer with certainty.[4] He particularly valued the method of mathematics because it began with the simplest notions and then proceeded to inferences that could be derived from them. Thus he argued, notwithstanding his recognition of the role of experience in generating knowledge, that all scientific investigation begins from the simplest and most basic notions and then proceed logically to more complex truths.

The method followed by Sir Dudley North (1641–91) in his anonymously published pamphlet, *Discourse upon Trade* (1691), is essentially Cartesian, although he had no formal education. North came from a family that was fairly accomplished academically and which sent him to writing school from which he was apprenticed to a merchant with the Levant Company. According to the biography written by his brother Roger North, Dudley passed many of the next 20 years abroad, principally in Turkey, where he accumulated enough from

his various trading activities to return to England and a life of ease in his early 40s. He had also acquired such vast technical information about every aspect of trade that, in 1683, he was appointed Commissioner of Customs and later elected to Parliament. During this period North became increasingly aware that private and public interests frequently diverge and that it is necessary to separate the two when inquiring into economic matters. The method by which he thought this could be accomplished was later described by Roger North in the Preface to his brother's biography.[5] Because private interests might interfere with objective thinking in economic matters, he argued that it is essential that conclusions be 'built on clear and evident truths.' It is necessary to lay down incontrovertible premises and to reason from them to the conclusions they imply. Thus, Sir Dudley North's pamphlet, *Discourse upon Trade*, substantially marks the beginning of deductive analysis in economics. Unfortunately, this pamphlet made little impression and was soon forgotten. As was subsequently often the case in the history of economic thought, its rediscovery came too late to be of more than historical interest.[6]

The waning role of merchants as writers

The writings of two philosophers, John Locke (1632–1704) and David Hume (1711–66), along with William Petty (1623–87), and Richard Cantillon (1680–1734), mark a turning point in the development of economics because none of these were associated, even in a remote way, with the business world. John Locke, who was educated at Christ Church, Oxford, where he took a medical degree, became personal physician and later personal secretary and assistant to Lord

Ashley, the chancellor of the Exchequer. Thus, he practiced his profession only on a limited scale, but was brought into contact with practical matters of trade, such as the proposal concerning the reduction of the interest rate.[7] He drafted a reply to Child's *Brief Observations* in which he examined the effect that a reduction in the rate of interest would have from the standpoint of natural law. This led to his book *Some Considerations of the Consequences of Lowering of Interest and Raising the Value of Money*, which examined the nature and determination of interest, rent, and the value of land. His argument was that, from the standpoint of natural law, any statute contrary to the inexorable laws of nature is both inappropriate and unworkable. This principle led Locke to the conclusion that natural law, not laws made by humans, should determine interest rates and the value of coins.

Locke's approach to examining economic questions had profound implications for the development of economics. It suggested that society is governed by a body of laws in precisely the same way as the natural universe. Locke's work, therefore, helped establish the natural law perspective of later economic analysis. Whereas seventeenth-century writers typically addressed themselves directly to practical questions and policy proposals, the subsequent approach attempted to discover the principles of particular phenomena such as value, price, and interest in order to examine their underlying relevance to particular problems. Locke became so well versed in colonial problems that he was appointed, in 1673, as Secretary to the Council for Trade and Plantations. He returned to private life two years later and turned his attention to such works as the *Treatise of Civil Government* and the *Essay Concerning Human Understanding*, which established him as one of the great philosophers of his day.

The natural law perspective is also evident in the writings of David Hume, who is also among the transitional thinkers whose economic writings helped break the influence of mercantilistic principles. Although he was primarily a philosopher, Hume's *Political Discourses* (1752) includes numerous essays, including the important 'Of money,' 'Of interest,' 'Of commerce,' 'Of the balance of trade,' and 'Of the jealousy of trade,' which made significant contributions to theoretical economics.[8]

The significance of the contribution made by the Irish-born English financier Richard Cantillon (1680–1734) to economic theory is debatable. Judged in terms of content, it is probably not overgenerous to regard him as the co-founder, along with Adam Smith, of the classical school. However, if we judge, instead, on the basis of the impact he had in his own time, his role in the history of economic analysis is considerably less significant. His *Essay on the Nature of Commerce in General* was not published until 20 years after his death, and then it was forgotten until it was rediscovered and rescued from virtual oblivion by William Jevons in 1881.[9] The most significant impact of the essay was on the Physiocrats, particularly as regards their emphasis on land as the source of wealth. Victor Riquetti, Marquis de Mirabeau, had a copy, and several of the ideas developed in his *L'Ami de Homme* (1760) paralleled those introduced by Cantillon in his essay. During the heyday of commercial capitalism, the central problem was trade and the growth of merchant capital through profitable exchange. With the growth of industry, production rather than exchange became the central problem.

Political arithmetic: prelude to numeracy in economics

Sir William Petty (1623–87) who, like many educated men of his generation, was trained in medicine, made a pioneering contribution to reliance on numeracy in his important work *Political Arithmetick* (1690), which reaffirmed the foundational role of empiricism in the quest for knowledge. Before studying medicine in the Netherlands he served for a time in the Royal Navy and later became physician general to English troops serving in Ireland during the Civil War. Afterwards, he was commissioned to survey the lands that were to be distributed among Oliver Cromwell's soldiers. The experience familiarized him with land rents and taxes, and encouraged him to pioneer an empirical approach to economic inquiry. His observations and studies generated an impressive array of numbers concerning land, cattle, houses, shipping, gold, merchandise, and people as part of his first work *Treatise on Taxes and Contributions* (1662).

Petty's data can only be described as scanty, for they were based primarily on various tax office reports, mortality, marriage, and birth records which were, as he himself recognized, nothing more than 'a commin Knife and a Clout . . . instead of the many more helps which such a work requires.'[10] Accordingly, what he could not ascertain directly in terms of 'number, weight or measure,' he inferred on the basis of what he had already learned empirically. This was the essence of his method of 'political arithmetic.' His inferences depended on the Law of Large Numbers. For example, in the absence of a census, Petty undertakes to calculate London's population on the basis of the number of burials and the number of houses, which he reasons must bear some

relation to the population. The number of burials are, somewhat arbitrarily multiplied by 30, to be added to the number of houses which he multiplied by eight to arrive at London's aggregate population. The population of England is estimated as 11 times that of London, on the premise that London pays the 11th part of England's tax collection. While the chance of error that is inherent in his method is raised with each successive multiplicative procedure, Petty maintained that his computations are consistent with other accounts such as poll tax records.

Petty's intent was not simply to rework and describe reality in terms of numerical variables, but to use them as mental abstractions to understand relationships that can be useful as a basis for formulating policy. One of Petty's specific policy objectives was to formulate a program for taxing the rebellious Irish to limit the possibilities for a future uprising against the English. His *Treatise of Taxes and Contributions* thus marks the first stage in the development of numeracy as it relates to economics.[11] His method relied on illustrative rather than actual data to express premises and conclusions in hypothetical numerical terms. Thus, Petty was an early empiricist whose work, particularly in his *Treatise of Taxes and Contributions,* is also a contribution to economic theory and policy.

The changing concepts of the transition period

Classification of writers such as Petty, North, Locke, Hume, and Cantillon as mercantilists is somewhat arbitrary. All were mercantilists to some degree, although certain aspects of their thinking were closer to the ideas of Adam Smith and the Physiocrats, who wrote during the eighteenth century, than to those of their predecessors. Thus, they may be treated either as later or liberal mercantilists, or as forerunners of classicism and economic liberalism. While sufficient reason can be advanced for either treatment, the subject matter of economic inquiry was undergoing a change, and their thinking was transitional.

Although the Industrial Revolution was not yet under way, commercial capitalism was already evolving into industrial capitalism. Compared with its status in the previous century, manufacturing, as contrasted with agriculture, had grown in importance. New products and modes of production, new forms of enterprise and credit facilities had been developed. These changes were accompanied by the pauperization of numerous farmers, the decay of many agricultural areas, the impoverishment of many artisans, and considerable technological unemployment. During the heyday of commercial capitalism, the central problem was trade and the growth of merchant capital through profitable exchange. With the growth of industry, production rather than exchange became the central problem.

The most significant aspect of the transition period of the second half of the seventeenth century is that several key economic concepts came into use during this time. The most fundamental was in the meaning attached to the nature and source of wealth. The question of whether the taking of interest is proper, and the determination of its rate and the rent of the land, were also important. However, the most critical question of all related to the validity of the mercantilistic principle that a favorable trade balance is the permanent source of a nation's riches. During the transition period these ideas gave way to the more modern ones of the classical era.

The nature of wealth

The mercantilist concept that gold and silver are the wealth of a nation and that every effort should be made to preserve and augment the supply of precious metals was rapidly becoming outmoded during the transition period. Even merchants were becoming free of the bullion illusion. Nicholas Barbon was among the first to recognize that while gold and silver have characteristics that make them particularly satisfactory for coinage, there is no greater advantage to be derived from accumulating them rather than any other commodity. 'If there could be account taken of the balance of trade, I can't see where the advantage of it could be. For the reason that's given for it – that the overplus is paid in bullion and the nation grows so much richer . . . is altogether a mistake. For gold and silver are but commodities, and one sort of commodity is as good as another so be it of the same value.'[12]

Dudley North attacked another aspect of the mercantilist view of trade when he disassociated riches from gold and silver. Mercantilists viewed trade as being essentially like warfare; one nation gained what the other lost. North asserted, on the contrary, that trade is mutually advantageous, for no one will accept a smaller value in exchange for what is given up. Moreover, he asserted, it is not trade that most enriches the nation, but production, particularly of manufactured goods; 'he who is most diligent, and raiseth most Fruits or maketh most of Manufactory, will abound most in what others make or raise; and consequently be free from Want and enjoy most Conveniences, which is truly to be Rich, altho there were no such things as Gold, Silver or the like amongst them.'[13]

The mercantilist identification of wealth

with money and trade was also disputed by David Hume. His essay 'Of Money' asserted that money merely represents 'the real strength of the community,' which is 'men and commodities.'[14] Sir William Petty wrote even more persuasively about wealth than Hume when he maintained that the appropriate measure of the increase in England's power and wealth is evident by the abundance of its 'People, Buildings, Shipping, and the production of many useful commodities.' With the accession of James II in 1685, he again utilized political arithmetic to prove the political and economic superiority of England over France to the new king. His formulation of the question and the reply he generates is among the masterworks of economics.

Issues and Answers from the Masterworks 3.1

Issue
On what basis can it be established that the power and wealth of England has increased?

Petty's answer
From *Political Arithmetick* (1690), Chapter VI: That the Power and Wealth of England hath increased this last forty years.

It is not much to be doubted, but that the Territories under the King's Dominions have increased; Forasmuch as *New England*, *Virginia*, *Barbadoes*, and *Jamaica*, *Tangier*, and *Bombay*, have since that time, been either added to His Majesties Territories, or improved from a *Desart condition*, to abound with People, Buildings, Shipping, and the Production of many useful Commodities. And as for the Land of *England*, *Scotland*, and *Ireland*, as it is not less in quantity, than it was forty years since; so it is manifest that by reason of the Dreyning of *Fens*, watering of dry Grounds, improving of *Forrests*, and *Commons*, making of *Heathy* and *Barren Grounds*, to bear *Saint-foyne*, and *Clover grass;* meliorating, and multiplying several sorts of Fruits, and Garden-Stuffe, making some Rivers Navigable, etc. I say it is manifest, that the Land in its present Condition, is able to bear more Provision, and Commodities, than it was forty years ago.

Secondly, although the People in *England*, *Scotland*, and *Ireland*, which have extraordinarily perished by the Plague, and Sword, within this last forty years, do amount to about three hundred thousand, above what have dyed in the ordinary way; yet the ordinary increase by Generation of ten Millions, which doubles in two hundred years, as hath been shewn by the Observators upon the Bills of Mortality, may in forty years (which is a fifth part of the same time) have increased 1/5 part of the whole number, or two Millions. Where note by the way, that the accession of *Negroes* to the *American* Plantations (being all Men of great Labour and little Expence) is not inconsiderable; besides it is hoped that *New England*, where few or no Women are Barren, and most have many Children, and where People live long, and healthfully, hath produced an increase of as many People, as were destroyed in the late Tumults in *Ireland*.

As for *Housing*, the Streets of *London* itself speaks it, I conceive it is double in value in that City, to what it was forty years since; and for *Housing* in the Country, they have increased, at *Newcastle*, *Yarmouth*, *Norwich*, *Exeter*, *Portsmouth*, *Cowes*, *Dublin*, *Kingsaile*, *Londonderry*, and *Coleraine* in *Ireland*, far beyond the proportion of what I can learn have been dilapidated in other places. For in *Ireland* where the ruin was greatest, the *Housing* (taking all together) is now more valuable than forty years ago, nor is this to be doubted, since *Housing* is now more splendid, than in those days, and the number of Dwellers is increased, by near 51 part; as in the last Paragraph is set forth.

As for Shipping, his Majesties Navy is now triple, or quadruple, to what it was forty years since, and before the *Sovereign* was Built; the Shipping Trading to *Newcastle*, which are now about eighty thousand Tuns, could not be then above a quarter of that quantity. First, Because the City of *London* is doubled. 2. Because the use of Coals is also at least doubled, because they were heretofore seldom used in Chambers, as now they are, nor were there so many Bricks burned with them as of late, nor did the Country on both sides the *Thames*, make use of them as now. Besides there are employed in the *Guinny* and *American Trade*, above forty thousand Tun of Shipping *per annum*; which Trade in those days was inconsiderable. The quantity in Wines Imported was not near so much as now; and to be short, the Customs upon Imported, and Exported Commodities, did not then yield a third part of the present value: which shews that not only *Shipping*, but *Trade* it self hath increased, somewhat near that proportion.

As to Mony, the Interest thereof was within this fifty years, at 10 *per cent*, forty years ago, at 8 per cent, and now at *6 per cent*, no thanks to any Laws which have been made to that purpose, forasmuch as those who can give good security, may now have it at less: But the natural fall of Interest, is the effect of the increase of Money. Moreover if *rented Lands*, and *Houses*, have increased; and if *Trade* hath increased also, it is certain that mony which payeth those *Rents*, and driveth on *Trade*, must have increased also.

Lastly, I leave it to the consideration of all Observers, whether the number, and splendor of *Coaches, Equipage*, and *Houshold Furniture*, hath not increased, since that time; to say nothing of the Postage of Letters, which have increased from one to twenty, which argues the increase of Business, and Negotiation. I might add that his Majesties Revenue is near tripled, and therefore the means to pay, and bear the same, have increased also.

Source: *The Economic Writings of Sir William Petty*, vol. 1,
Charles Hall (ed.), (London, 1899).

Summing up: Petty's key points

In the post-Elizabethan age during which England's power *vis-à-vis* France and even Holland became a matter of concern to persons loyal to the King, a major theme of Petty's *Political Arithmetick* was to offer what he regarded as empirical proof based on his estimates of the growth of England's wealth over the last 40 years. His empirical prowess is very much in the tradition of the scientific method which he learned from Thomas Hobbes even before he undertook his medical training. Unlike the bullionists, and even Thomas Mun, he does not reckon England's increase of wealth in terms of gold, but in terms of the increase in arable lands to produce 'Provision(s) and Commodities,' increases in population and housing, the number of shipping vessels and their tonnage, coaches, and household furniture. He also considers the reduction in interest rates to 6 percent as compared to the 10 percent rate of 40 years ago, along with the increased volume of letters posted as evidence of the increase in England's wealth.

Petty's empirical skill is equally evidenced in his earlier Verbum Soprenta (1664) as supplemental to *Political Anatomy of Ireland* in which he generated an accounting of Ireland's national income which stands as a forerunner to the national income accounting procedure which became central to macro-economic empiricism in the twentieth century. His objective with respect to Ireland was to establish a factual basis on which the King could tax away as much Irish wealth as possible. Indeed, he felt it appropriate that England undertake whatever measures are necessary for the good of the Crown, even to the extent of relocating population from Ireland to England whether they wished it or not.[15]

The quantity theory

Although the notion that the level of economic activity is related to the supply of money was already common in mercantilist days, John Locke gave the principle, now known as the quantity theory of money, a more refined statement than it had been given previously. In particular, he pointed out 'the necessity of some proportion of money to trade,' although he recognized that it is hard to determine what that proportion should be. The quantity of money needed to carry on trade is hard to determine because it depends also on 'the quickness of its circulation[;] . . . to make some probable guess we are to consider how much money it is necessary to suppose must rest constantly in each man's hands as requisite to the carrying on of trade.' His recognition of the importance of velocity of circulation was the most sophisticated treatment of quantity theory that had yet been offered. Later writers formulated his ideas on the velocity of circulation and the volume of trade with greater precision, but Locke deserves credit for a greatly improved statement of the quantity theory of money. Unfortunately, however, he was led via his quantity theory of money to advocate the desirability of an export surplus. He thought this would be to England's advantage because it would cause an inflow of specie and enable her to sell at high prices, while buying cheaply from other countries that have low prices because they have less bullion.

The reverse specie flow mechanism

The most sophisticated rebuttal to Locke's argument and to the mercantilist view about the role of trade in promoting the nation's well-being came from David Hume. He disagreed with the old mercantilist dogma that the prosperity of other countries will permanently undermine England's domestic prosperity because it is achieved on the basis of English gold losses. The fallacy of this argument, which he criticized John Locke for holding, is exposed in the context of the issue, whether one nation is likely to impoverish others through trade, which is examined next.

Issues and Answers from the Masterworks 3.2

Issue
Is the prosperity that one nation gains from commerce a threat to that of its neighbors?

Hume's answer
From his essay 'Of the Jealousy of Trade' (1758).

Having endeavoured to remove one species of illfounded jealousy, which is so prevalent among commercial nations, it may not be amiss to mention another, which seems equally groundless. Nothing is more usual, among states which have made some advances in commerce, than to look on the progress of their neighbours with a suspicious eye, to consider all trading states as their rivals, and to suppose that it is impossible for any of them to flourish, but at their expence. In opposition to this narrow and malignant opinion, I will venture to assert, that the encrease of riches and commerce in any one nation, instead of hurting, commonly promotes the riches and commerce of all its neighbours; and that a state can scarcely carry its trade and industry very far, where all the surrounding states are buried in ignorance, sloth, and barbarism.

It is obvious, that the domestic industry of a people cannot be hurt by the greatest prosperity of their neighbours; and as this branch of commerce is undoubtedly the most important in any extensive kingdom, we are so far removed from all reason of jealousy. But I go farther, and observe, that where an open communication is preserved among nations, it is impossible but the domestic industry of every one must receive an encrease from the improvements of the others. Compare the situation of GREAT BRITAIN at present, with what it was two centuries ago. All the arts both of agriculture and manufactures were then extremely rude and imperfect. Every improvement, which we have since made, has arisen from our imitation of foreigners; and we ought so far to esteem it happy, that they had previously made advances in arts and ingenuity. But this intercourse is still upheld to our great advantage: Notwithstanding the advanced state of our manufactures, we daily adopt, in every art, the inventions and improvements of our neighbours. The commodity is first imported from abroad, to our great discontent, while we imagine that it drains us of our money: Afterwards, the art itself is gradually imported, to our visible advantage: Yet we continue still to repine, that our neighbours should possess any art, industry, and invention; forgetting that, had they not first instructed us, we should have been at present barbarians; and did they not still continue their instructions, the arts must fall into a state of languor, and lose that emulation and novelty, which contribute so much to their advancement.

The encrease of domestic industry lays the foundation of foreign commerce. Where a great number of commodities are raised and perfected for the home-market, there will always be found some which can be exported with advantage. But if our neighbours have no art or cultivation, they cannot take them; because they will have nothing to give in exchange. In this respect, states are in the same condition as individuals. A single man can scarcely be industrious, where all his fellow citizens are idle. The riches of the several members of a community contribute to encrease my riches, whatever profession I may follow. They consume the produce of my industry, and afford me the produce of theirs in return.

Nor need any state entertain apprehensions, that their neighbours will improve to such a degree in every art and manufacture, as to have no demand from them. Nature, by giving a diversity of geniuses, climates, and soils, to different nations, has secured their mutual intercourse and commerce, as long as they all remain industrious and civilized. Nay, the more the arts encrease in any state, the more will be its demands from its industrious neighbours. The inhabitants, having become opulent and skillful, desire to have every commodity in the utmost perfection; and as they have plenty of commodities to give in exchange, they make large importations from every foreign country. The industry of the nations, from whom they import, receives encouragement: Their own is also increased, by the sale of the commodities which they give in exchange.

But what if a nation has any staple commodity, such as the woolen manufacture is in ENGLAND? Must not the interfering of our neighbours in that manufacture be a loss to us? I answer, that, when any commodity is denominated the staple of a kingdom, it is supposed that this kingdom has some peculiar and natural advantages for raising the commodity; and if, notwithstanding these advantages, they lose such a manufacture they ought to blame their own idleness, or bad government, not the industry of their neighbours. It ought also to be considered, that, by the encrease of industry among the neighbouring nations, the consumption of every particular species of commodity is also encreased; and though foreign manufactures interfere with them in the market, the demand for their product may still continue, or even encrease. And should it diminish, ought the consequence to be esteemed so fatal? If the spirit of industry be preserved, it may easily be diverted from one branch to another; and the manufacturers of wool, for instance, be employed in linen, silk, iron, or any other commodities, for which there appears to be a demand. We need not apprehend, that all the objects of industry will be exhausted, or that our manufacturers, while they remain on an equal footing with those of our neighbours, will be in danger of wanting employment. The emulation among rival nations serves rather to keep industry alive in all of them: And any people is happier who possess a variety of manufacturers, than if they enjoyed one single great manufacturer, in which they are all employed. Their situation is less precarious; and they will feel less sensibly those revolutions and uncertainties, to which every particular branch of commerce will always be exposed.

The only commercial state, that ought to dread the improvements and industry of their neighhours, is such a one as the DUTCH, who enjoying no extent of land, nor possessing any number of native commodities, flourish only by their being the brokers, and factors, and carriers of others. Such a people may naturally apprehend, that, as soon as the neighbouring states come to know and pursue their interest, they will take into their own hands the management of their affairs, and deprive their brokers of that profit, which they formerly reaped from it. But though this consequence may naturally be dreaded, it is very long before it takes place; and by art and industry it may be warded off for many generations, if not wholly eluded. The advantage of superior stocks and correspondence is so great, that it is not easily overcome; and as all the transactions encrease by the encrease of industry in the neighbouring states, even a people whose commerce stands on this precarious basis, may at first reap a considerable profit from the flourishing condition of their neighbours. The DUTCH, having mortgaged all their revenues, make not such a figure in political transactions as formerly; but their commerce is surely equal to what it was of the last century, when they were reckoned among the great powers of EUROPE.

Were our narrow and malignant politics to meet with success, we should reduce all our neighbouring nations to the same state of sloth and ignorance that prevails in MOROCCO and the coast of BARBARY. But what would be the consequence? They could send us no commodities: They could take none from us: Our domestic commerce itself would languish for want to emulation, example and instruction: And we ourselves should soon fall into the same condition, to which we had reduced them. I shall therefore venture to acknowledge, that not only as a man, but as a BRITISH subject, I pray for the flourishing commerce of GERMANY, SPAIN, ITALY, and even FRANCE itself. I am at least certain, that, GREAT BRITAIN, and all those nations, would, flourish more, did their sovereigns and ministers' adopt such enlarged and benevolent sentiments towards each other.

Source: *The Philosophical Works of David Hume*, vol. 3, edited by T. H. Green *et al.*
(London: Longmans, Green, 1875).

Summing up: Hume's key points

Hume's pronouncement at the end of his essay 'Of the jealousy of trade' that international specialization is the basis of prosperity, and his remark, 'As a British subject, I pray for the flourishing commerce of Germany, Spain, Italy and even France itself,' challenged the very basis of the mercantilists' quest for a favorable balance of international payments as being inseparable from their commitment to the notion that a wealthy nation is one that abounds in gold. While their national policy directives were aimed at discouraging or even prohibiting (in the case of the bullionists) the exodus of gold to other countries, Hume's essay not only questioned that increased gold stocks can give a country a permanent benefit but also noted the fallacy of Locke's argument that a nation can continuously accumulate gold. His argument was that if a nation has a favorable balance, and therefore acquires gold, it will also experience a rise in its domestic price level. This will cause it to lose its export trade and stimulate imports for domestic use. Its stock of specie will always adjust to the actual needs of trade. Thus, 'a government has great reason to preserve with care its people and its manufactures. Its moneys it may safely trust to the course of human affairs.' In support of this proposition, his related essay 'Of money' links together the quantity theory of money and the price specie flow mechanism to explain the distribution of precious metals internationally. The essential parts of his argument are, first, that the quantity of money is the determinant of the price level; second, that the volume of exports and imports depends on relative price levels at home and abroad; and, third, that the difference in international balances of payments among nations must be paid in specie. The joining of the three preceding propositions yields a theory of a self-regulating system of international specie distribution that completely undermines the mercantilist case of pursuing gold as wealth. In the process, Hume's argument established the key components of classical monetary theory.[16] It also eventually bore fruit in the commercial treaty England concluded with France in 1786.

The Cantillon effect

An even more sophisticated rebuttal to the mercantilists' argument about a favorable balance of payments as the means by which a nation can continuously amass gold is attributable to Richard Cantillon. His rebuttal to the mercantilists started from the assumption that new mines are discovered, and proceeded to trace the spread of inflation that results from the additional purchasing power received by persons engaged in mining new gold. They are enabled to outbid others whose incomes are fixed, so the additional money causes higher prices to spread as gold is absorbed into the economy. Inflation will also alter the *structure* of prices in a way that reflects the source of the new injection of money and the relative demands for goods by those who receive it.

The concept of the differential impact of new money on the structure of prices is now known as the *Cantillon effect*. Unfortunately, as already noted above, it was not well known during his lifetime. Cantillon used it to compare the effect of an increase in specie that originates from an export surplus with that resulting from new mines or an expansion of paper currency. An increase in specie that originates from an export surplus is more likely to stimulate trade than new money originating from an expansion of paper currency or the discovery of new mines. New gold production,

55

without accompanying increases in output, is more likely to increase prices. Rising prices in any country will, quite naturally, cause people to expand their purchases from countries in which prices have not yet risen. The home market will therefore become depressed, and gold will leave the country to pay for foreign imports until eventually prices will again be low enough to induce domestic buyers to buy at home rather than abroad. He concluded, therefore, that no country benefits permanently from the discovery of precious metals.

Cantillon also noted that inflation can result from an increase in the supply of paper money as well as from metallic money. He thought that price increases resulting from increased paper money are likely to prove disastrous because paper, lacking an intrinsic value, is likely to be refused acceptance. This is precisely what happened in France following John Law's famous experiment with a paper currency in 1716. Cantillon refused to endorse that proposal when it was presented to him, predicting that it would have unfortunate results.

The propriety of interest and determination of its rate

The problem of interest, especially as regards the establishment of a legal rate, generated a large literature throughout the transition period. The earliest of these contributions, like Josiah Child's, contained virtually no theoretical analysis. Child was quite simply in favor of reducing the legal rate of interest in order to duplicate the advantages enjoyed by Dutch traders. He asserted it would make the country richer but offered no explanation for why he thought it would have this effect.

Petty's views on interest were also relatively unsophisticated but do offer a theoretical explanation that relates the interest rate to the rent that land can earn. He thought that if a lender can demand repayment of a loan at any time, he is not entitled to interest. But if money is lent for a fixed period of time, the lender is entitled to 'a compensation for this inconvenience which he admits against himself.' Then, anticipating the Physiocratic analysis of a century later, Petty maintained that if there is no doubt concerning the security of a loan, the interest it earns is equivalent to the 'Rent of so much Land as the money lent will buy.'[17] He also suggested that if the security of a loan is in doubt, 'a kind of ensurance must be interwoven with the simple natural interest.'[18] These observations led him to conclude that it is useless to try to fix interest rates by law.

Nicholas Barbon, who was also opposed to fixing interest rates by law, had a more sophisticated view of the relationship between interest and rent. Land is 'natural stock' and earns rent. Capital is 'wrought stock'; its return is the return to land. 'Interest is commonly-reckoned for money, because the money borrowed at interest is to be repaid in money. But this is a mistake, for paid for stock; the money borrowed is laid out to buy goods or pay for them before bought. No man takes up money at interest to lay it by him and lose the interest of it.[19]

The wrought stock to which Barbon referred consists of processed goods that merchants sell, as distinct from the unprocessed goods farmers sell exactly as nature produces them. Farmers hire land and pay rent to acquire natural stock; merchants acquire processed goods, or wrought stock, intended for sale. Dudley North had much the same idea when he talked to the 'stock lord,' who receives a return called interest for permitting others to use the property he has accumulated in the form of money.

Perhaps if Barbon's and North's inquiries had not been associated so specifically with the activities of the merchant, they would have formulated more clearly the principle of interest as the net yield on capital. But they did not conceive of stock or capital, as it is now called, as a separate factor of production that is entitled to a functional reward. Later, in the nineteenth century, wrought stock was plainly identified as a separate factor of production, distinct from labor and land, and entitled to a return equivalent to its net yield. But this is a much more advanced notion than either Barbon or North had of stock and its return.

Just as the seventeenth century concept of stock related generally to money rather than real capital goods, so interest was explained as a monetary rather than a real phenomenon. Thus, Locke wrote: 'That which most sensibly raises the rate of interest of money is when money is little in proportion to the trade of the country.'[20] North similarly applied price analysis to the explanation of interest rates. 'That as more Buyers than Sellers raiseth the price of a Commodity, so more Borrowers than Lenders, will raise Interest.'[21] David Hume also argued that the rate of interest depends on the demand and supply of borrowers and lenders. If there is 'a great demand for borrowing but little riches to supply that demand,' the rate of interest will be high. Viewing profits as interdependent with interest, he asserts that it is not the quantity of gold and silver that causes the interest rate to be high, but the volume of industry and commerce The commercial classes, especially, contribute to a reduction of the interest rate, for their frugality and rivalry for gain reduce not only profit but interest.

Rent and the value of land

Although the problem of interest was frequently approached from the standpoint of the rent of land, the problem of rent was also dealt with in connection with the value of land itself. How much, asked Petty, would rent-yielding land be worth? He was apparently unaware that the value of land is related to the rate of interest. Thus, instead of capitalizing on the return in terms of the rate of interest, he suggested that the purchase price that will be paid for land depends on the number of years a prospective purchaser and his immediate descendants are likely to enjoy the yield. In *The Treatise of Taxes*, he estimates that three generations of males may be expected to live concurrently for 21 years, and that the value of land is therefore equal to that number times its annual rent.

John Locke, however, was aware of the relationship between the price of land and the interest rate. He reasoned that the value of land depends on the income that can be derived from it, and that the value of land and its income bear the same relationship to each other as the principal of a loan bears to the interest it earns. The value of land (and other assets) is established by capitalizing its rental income in terms of the interest rate. Thus, given a certain rental income, the value of land will be raised if the interest rate in terms of which it is capitalized is lowered.

The value of commodities

The problem of the value of commodities was also beginning to concern the thinkers of the transition period although, for most, it was not yet a topic of inquiry. Petty's value theory must, for example, be extracted from his inquiry into the 'mysterious nature' of rent. Rent, he maintained, is the agricultural surplus that remains after the seed and the farmer's subsistence are deducted from the proceeds of the harvest. This view of rent as a differential surplus, which is price-determined rather than price-determining, anticipates by some 150 years the theory of rent that during the classical era, was to become associated with Thomas Malthus and David Ricardo. Petty thought that the value of an agricultural worker's product in excess of subsistence could be considered as rent. Since the value of laborers (i.e. their wages) was regarded as the cost of producing their subsistence, the monetary value of this product would be equal to the amount of gold that could be produced in the same labor time as that needed to produce the worker's food. Thus, if equivalent amounts of labor time are involved in producing different commodities, they would tend to have equal values in exchange for one another. Labor time, therefore, became the common denominator of all values for Petty, who thereby anticipated the development of the labor theory of value, which was subsequently associated with Adam Smith, David Ricardo, and Karl Marx.

Although Petty considered labor more important than land in creating value, he also struggled with the problem of attributing some part of value to land. He maintained that all things should be measured by 'two natural denominations, which is Land and Labor,' and regarded the establishment of a natural par between these two elements as a major problem of political economy. This would imply that rent is price-determining and that land and labor are joint determinants of value. Petty struggled with this difficulty time and again, but he was unable to resolve it.

Cantillon arrived at essentially the same explanation of value as Petty. He attributed value to the amount of labor and land required in production; the cost of labor and materials drawn from land were seen as determining the intrinsic value of commodities. The latter would, he thought, never vary. However, the market price will fluctuate above or below the intrinsic value, depending on the state of demand and supply. By demonstrating how increasing or decreasing demand will raise or lower the price of a commodity and thereby encourage or discourage production, Cantillon advanced an explanation of the nature and functioning of the price system as the automatic mechanism through which an otherwise unregulated economy regulates itself. This view of the self-regulatory nature of a price-directed economy was later to become the core of the classical and neoclassical systems of economics. Thus, Cantillon may be considered as an early classicist or, at least, as a forerunner of classical economic thinking.

Concluding remarks: how does a science develop?

The transition to classical economics provides some degree of insight and appreciation about the process by which a science, in this case economic science, advances. In the chapters that follow, this book undertakes to examine the unfolding of economic theories and their related concepts from the period of mercantilism to the present. It will be seen that each contribution emerged during a particular period in history and was associated with the events and political problems of the period as well as the ideology and philosophy of the writers who developed them. In particular, it is clear that contributions to political economy, from their earliest days, reflect two essentially different techniques or methodologies for arriving at the 'truths' they intended to establish. By the seventeenth century, the methodological conflict is clearly apparent in the Cartesian approach of Dudley North, as contrasted with the empirical approach of William Petty, which itself reaches back to the observational approach that Francis Bacon and Thomas Hobbes urged scientists to follow as they rejected the method of Scholasticism.

Are these associations a basis for explaining why particular theories emerged when they did? In the view of some historians of economic thought, they are. Thus, one interpretation of the development of economic thought has sought to understand the economic aspects of human life as an aspect of a broader societal experience.[22] Other historians explain the development of economic doctrines in terms of the philosophical preconceptions of their authors.[23] At least one historian of economic thought has advanced the hypothesis that particular theories were advanced in order to provide principles in support of policies their authors regarded as politically and socially appropriate.[24] This approach is indicative of a second basic dichotomy in the way political economists have envisioned their roles. While belief in the role of *laissez-faire* has been the most pervasive political philosophy, the opposing, Hobbsian, view that government is needed to keep order has been an ongoing challenge.

A more recent interpretation of the history of economics views its development as an example of a scientific advance in response to problems that the prevailing doctrine or 'paradigm' is unable to explain. Thomas Kuhn, a historian of science, advanced the hypothesis that the practitioners of a discipline (e.g. economists) are typically engaged in what he terms *normal science*.[25] Together with their colleagues, they direct attention toward problems their scientific community identifies as solvable in terms of the principles of their discipline. These principles constitute the core of ideas, or *paradigm*, that the community of scholars accepts as a basis for the research that constitutes the day-to-day activity of normal science.

According to Kuhn, the study of paradigms 'prepares the student for membership in the particular scientific community with which he will later practice.'[26] The problems selected and the rules for solving them are paradigm-directed. Such anomalies as occasionally appear are typically explained by qualifying or making relatively minor refinements in the principles that the scientific community accepts.

Minor paradigmatic changes will not suffice when a problem arises that cannot be solved within the prevailing framework. The outcome then is an intellectual crisis. In the natural sciences, such crises lead to scientific revolutions whose outcomes are the replacement of the existing paradigm by an alternative mode of puzzle solving. For example, when the Ptolemaic paradigm proved inadequate for explaining the behavior of the planets Mercury and Venus, the resulting intellectual crisis produced the Copernican revolution. In essence, this scientific revolution rejected the Ptolemaic paradigm and adopted the Copernican conception of the universe to guide the scientific community in its research.

The physical sciences have encountered numerous intellectual crises since the challenges precipitated by the studies of Copernicus, Kepler, and Newton. As a result, their paradigms were replaced by alternatives that later practitioners in physics, astronomy, chemistry, and other natural sciences, accepted as providing a superior framework for scientific inquiry.

Have there been similar scientific revolutions in economics? We will have occasion, when we encounter major challenges to theories prevailing at particular times in history, to inquire whether they represent revolutions in the Kuhnian sense. This is, of course, a far less ambitious undertaking than to explain (or, at least, try to explain) why economic thought emerged as it did. To explain the structure of scientific revolutions in economics is considerably beyond the scope of this book. Our objective is more precisely to examine the development of the concepts and tools of analysis that have evolved over time to explain economic phenomena. In this sense, the preclassical development of economics, which has been the concern of the present Part 1, is also *prescientific*.

Economics as a science dates from the work of François Quesnay (1694–1774), physician to the French royal family, whose understanding of the functioning of the economic system is said to have been inspired by the discovery by the English physician William Harvey of the human circulatory system.[27] Quesnay and his followers established the tradition of *Physiocracy*, whose chief concern was to explain and recommend tax changes and agrarian reform to improve the sagging economy of prerevolutionary France by restoring it to greater consistency with the 'rule of nature,' i.e. *laissez-faire*. Their work, which joined economic policy to economic analysis, identified general laws that were believed to govern the behavior of the social universe; this work marks the beginning of economics as a discipline. This beginning of formal economics also marks the beginning of the classical tradition of economics, which is examined in depth in Part II of this book.

Notes

1 An interesting account of the lives and works of some leading writers of this transitional period in the history of economic doctrine is given in William Letwin, *The Origins of Scientific Economics* (London: Methuen, 1963).

2 Josiah Child's *Discourse about Trade* (London, 1690), an anonymous re-publication of his earlier *Brief Observations*, is typical of efforts to conceal authorship. The preface was written by the publisher, who assured the reader that the writer was not a trader and that the manuscript came to him accidentally. Reprinted in J. R. McCulloch (ed.), *Early English Tracts on Commerce* (Norwich: Jarrold and Sons, 1952).

3 Nicholas Barbon, *A Discourse Concerning Coining the New Money Lighter, in Answer to Mr. Locke's Considerations about Raising the Value of Money* (London, 1696). Practices such as 'clipping' or 'sweating' reduced the bullion content of coins by heating them to clip or sweat their edges for metal fragments.

4 Descartes was writing at a time when the method of scholasticism (i.e. faith versus reason), which he rejected, was still dominant. In his autobiographical *Discourses* he explained how a dream led him to doubt all the truths he had ever learned. Ultimately he doubted even his own existence. The light dawned on him when he recognized himself as a thinking being. He summed up his famous experience in the phrase 'I think, therefore I am' ('Cogito, ergo sum'). Whatever is clear and distinct to man's reason and perception is true. Thus Descartes, or in its Latin version Cartesius, is the father of modern rationalism. The relevance of this to the development of economics as a scientific discipline is that it encapsulated the later view that economic principles are predicated on indisputable propositions that become the basis for deducing conclusions which are inherently 'true.'

5 Roger North, *The Life of the Honorable Sir Dudley North and of Dr. John North*, vol. 2 (London: George Bell, 1826), pp. 132 ff., 153–54, 180–82.

6 The work of Dudley and Roger North is revisited in a useful recent article by George D. Chomsky 'The bi-furcated economics of Sir Dudley North and Roger North: one holistic analytic engine,' *History of Political Economy*, 35 (Fall 1990, pp. 477–92).

7 Maurice Cranston, *John Locke* (New York: Macmillan, 1957).

8 The economic writings of Hume are available in Eugene Rotwein, *The Economic Writings of David Hume* (Edinburgh: Nelson, 1955).

9 This essay was originally written in English and translated into French by Cantillon to

make it available to a friend. It was reprinted in facsimile (1892) by G. H. Ellis for Harvard University and subsequently translated by Henry Higgs (New York: Macmillan, 1931).

10 Details of Petty's life are readily available in *The Economic Writings of Sir William Petty*, edited by Charles Henry Hull, 1899, vol. I (New York: A. M. Kelley, 1963–1964).

11 Ingrid H. Rima, 'The role of numeracy in the history of economic analysis,' *Journal of the History of Economic Thought*, 16 (Fall 1994).

12 Nicholas Barbon, *A Discourse Concerning Coining the New Money Lighter, in Answer to Mr. Locke's Considerations about Raising the Value of Money* (London, 1696).

13 Dudley North, 'A discourse concerning the abatement of interest,' in *Early English Tracts on Commerce*, edited by John R. McCulloch (Norwich: Jarrold and Sons, 1952) p. 516.

14 David Hume, 'Of money,' *Essays* (London: Longmans, Green, 1912), p. 319.

15 C. H. Hull (ed.), *Economic Writings of Sir William Petty*, 1899, vol. I (New York: A. M. Kelley, 1963–64), p. lxii.

16 Compare Jacob Viner's summary in *Studies in the Theory of International Trade* (New York: Harper and Row, 1937), p. 249.

17 *Economic Writings of Sir William Petty*, edited by Charles H. Hull, 1899, vol. I (New York: A. M. Kelley, 1963–1964), p. 48.

18 *Economic Writings of Sir William Petty*, edited by Charles H. Hull, 1899, vol. I (New York: A. M. Kelley, 1963–1964), p. 48.

19 Nicholas Barbon, *A Discourse Concerning Coining the New Money Lighter, in Answer to Mr. Locke's Considerations about Raising the Value of Money* (London, 1696).

20 From Locke's early manuscript on interest in William Letwin, *The Origins of Scientific Economics*, Appendix 5, p. 278.

21 Dudley North, 'A Discourse concerning the Abatement of Interest,' in John R. McCulloch, *Early English Tracts* (London: Methuen, 1963), p. 522.

22 W. Stark, *The History of Economics in its Relation to Social Development* (London: K. Paul, Trench, Truber, 1945), and Eric Roll, *A History of Economic Thought*, third edn (New York: Prentice-Hall, 1956), are among those who interpret the development of economic thought primarily as an attempt to understand and rationalize experience. The introductory chapter, entitled 'The Development of Economics as a Science,' in Joseph Schumpeter's *Economic Doctrine and Method* (Oxford University Press, 1967) is especially recommended for its clarity in distinguishing between the philosophical and practical roots of economics.

23 A classic example of a writer who has explained economic doctrine in terms of its philosophical foundations is James Bonar, *Philosophy and Political Economy*, second edn (London: George Allen and Unwin, 1909). Walter A. Weisskopf has given a psychological interpretation of the development of economic thought in *The Psychology of Economics* (Chicago: The University of Chicago Press, 1955).

24 This relationship has led at least one writer to advance the hypothesis that particular theories evolved in order to lend support to policies and programs that seemed politically and socially appropriate at particular times in history. See Leo Rogin, *The Meaning and Validity of Economic Theory* (New York: Harper & Row, 1956).

25 Thomas Kuhn, *The Structure of Scientific Revolutions* (Princeton, NJ: Princeton University Press, 1970).

26 Thomas Kuhn, *The Structure of Scientific Revolutions* (Princeton, NJ: Princeton University Press, 1970), p. 176.

27 Schumpeter (1954) defines science as 'tooled knowledge' which is characterized by the use of 'special techniques' and a 'command of facts unearthed by those techniques that are beyond the range of the mental habits and the factual knowledge of every day life' (Schumpeter, 1954, p. 7). While he interprets Greek economic thought as being consistent with his definition, his formal inquiry begins with Aquinas's *Summa Theologica*. Our classification, by contrast, recognizes that the Scholastic notion of 'just price' lends itself to being interpreted in the modern sense of 'normal competitive price,' but that their thinking also implies a *behavioral prescriptive*. It is for this reason that we think of the work of Church scholars, as it relates to economic concepts, as prescientific.

Glossary of terms and concepts

Cantillon effect
The effect of an injection of money on the structure of prices (as opposed to the level of prices) depending on its source and its impact on recipients.

Real analysis versus monetary analysis
A real analysis is one in which money has no influence on the relative factor and commodity prices or the level of economic activity. A monetary analysis is one in which money is not viewed as passive but exercises an independent influence (through mechanisms that differ from writer to writer) over the economic magnitudes.

Reverse specie flow mechanism
David Hume's principle concerning the return flow of specie that results when a country experiences a reduction in exports in consequence of a price level that is high relative to that of other countries.

Questions for discussion and further research

1 The second half of the seventeenth century was a period of increasing liberality in economic thinking. As a result, several key economic concepts date from this time. Identify what some of these are and how they reflect a change from the mercantilist thinking of the previous era.

2 On what grounds did David Hume argue that the prosperity of one nation does not diminish that of its neighbors?

3 What is the concern of Hume's price specie flow principle? How does it correct the earlier view that a nation can add indefinitely to its gold stocks and wealth by pursuing a favorable balance of payments?

4 What is the Cantillon effect and how does it supplement Hume's principle?

Notes for further reading

From *The New Palgrave*

S. Bauer on balance of trade, vol. 1, pp. 179–81; Milton Friedman on the quantity theory of money, vol. 4, pp. 3–19; Alessandro Roncaglia on William Petty, vol. 3, p. 682; N. Rosenberg on Bernard de Mandeville, vol. 3, pp. 297–98; Eugene Rotwein on David Hume, vol. 2, pp. 692–95; Karen I. Vaugh on John Locke, vol. 3, pp. 229–30; Douglas Vickers on Josiah Child, vol. 1, p. 418, and on Nicholas Barbon, vol. 1, p. 189 and Vivian Walsh on Richard Cantillon, vol. 1, pp. 317–20.

Selected references and suggestions for further reading

Blaug, Mark. *The Methodology of Economics, or How Economists Explain* (London: Cambridge University Press, 1980).

Bonar, James. *Philosophy and Political Economy*, second edn (London: George Allen and Unwin, 1909).

Childs, Joseph. *Discourse about Trade* (London, 1690).

Chomsky, George D. 'The bi-furcated economics of Sir Dudley North and Roger North: one holistic analytic engine.' *History of Political Economy*, 35 (Fall, 1990), pp. 477–92.

Hull, Henry, (ed). *The Economic Writings of Sir William Petty*, vol. 1 (New York: August M. Kelly, 1963).

Kuhn, T. S. *The Structure of Scientific Revolutions*. second edn (Chicago: The University of Chicago Press, 1970).

Letwin, William. *Origins of Scientific Economics* (London: Methuen, 1963).

Merton, Robert. *The Sociology of Science* (Chicago: The University of Chicago Press, 1973).

Misselden, Edward. *The Circle of Commerce*. In

Source Readings in Economic Thought, edited by Philip C. Newman, Arthur T. Gayer, and Milton H. Spencer (New York: Norton, 1954).

North, Dudley. 'A discourse concerning the abatement of interest,' in John R. McCulloch, *Early English Tracts* (London: Methuen, 1963).

North, Roger. *The Life of the Honorable Sir Dudley North and of Dr. John North*, vol. 2 (London: George Bell, 1826).

Petty, William. *The Economic Writings of Sir William Petty*. 2 vols. Edited by C. H. Hull (New York: A. M. Kelley, 1963).

Robbins, Lionel. Lecture 6, 'Sir William Petty'; Lecture 7, 'Child and Locke (Interest)', in *A History of Economic Thought*, edited by S. Medema and W. Samuels (Princeton, NJ: Princeton University Press, 1998), pp. 55–73.

Robbins, Lionel. Lecture 11, 'Locke and Hume on property – Hume on money'; Lecture 12, 'Hume on interest and trade – precursors of Adam Smith.' In *A History of Economic Thought*, edited by S. Medema and W. Samuels, (Princeton NJ: Princeton University Press, pp. 104–24).

Robertson, H. M. *Aspects of the Rise of Economic Individualism* (Cambridge: Cambridge University Press, 1933).

Rogin, Leo. *The Meaning and Validity of Economic Theory* (New York: Harper & Row, 1956).

Roll, Eric. *A History of Economic Thought*, third edn (New York: Prentice-Hall, 1956).

Rotwein, Eugene. *The Economic Writings of David Hume* (Edinburgh: Nelson, 1955).

Schumpeter, Joseph. *History of Economic Analysis*, edited by E. Boody (New York: Oxford University Press, 1954).

Stark, W. *The History of Economics in its Relation to Social Development* (London: K. Paul, Trench, Truber, 1945).

Vickers, Douglas. *Studies in the Theory of Money, 1690–1776* (Philadelphia: Chilton, 1959).

Viner, Jacob. *Studies in the Theory of International Trade* (New York: Harper, 1937).

Von Hornick, P. W. 'Austria over all if she only will.' In *Early Economic Thought*, edited by A. E. Monroe (Cambridge, MA: Harvard University Press, 1965).

Weisskopf, Walter A. *The Psychology of Economics* (Chicago: The University of Chicago Press, 1955).

Part II

Classical Economics

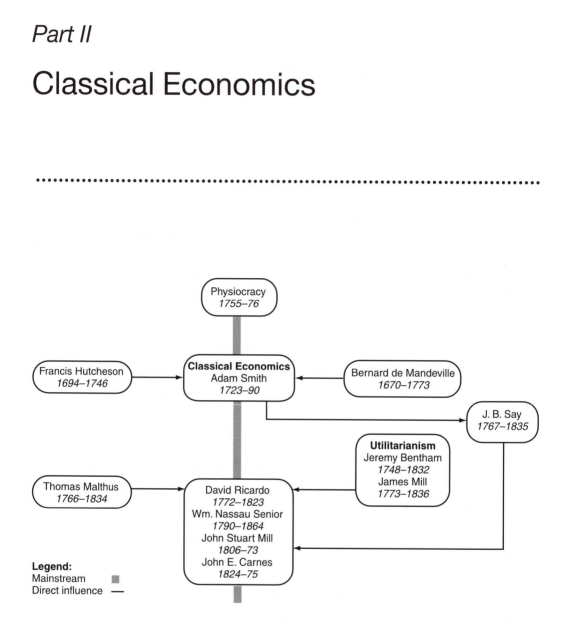

Key dates

1755	Richard Cantillon	Essai sur la nature du commerce en général
1758	François Quesnay	Tableau Économique
1759	Adam Smith	Theory of Moral Sentiments
1766	Anne-Robert Jacques Turgot	Reflections on the Formation and Distribution of Wealth
1776	Adam Smith	Wealth of Nations
1798	Thomas Malthus	An Essay on the Principle of Population
1803	Thomas Malthus	Revised edition of the Essay
1803	J. B. Say	Traité
1814	Thomas Malthus	Observations on the Effects of the Corn Laws
1815	David Ricardo	The Influence of a Low Price of Corn on the Profits of Stock
1817	David Ricardo	Principles of Political Economy and Taxation
1820	Thomas Malthus	Principles of Political Economy
1822	David Ricardo	On Protection to Agriculture
1823	David Ricardo	Plans for the Establishment of a National Bank
1836	William Nassau Senior	Outline of the Science of Political Economy
1848	John Stuart Mill	Principles of Political Economy
1869	W. T. Thornton	On Labor
1869	J. S. Mill	Review of Thornton's *On Labor* (Fortnightly Review)
1874	J. E. Cairnes	Some Leading Principles of Political Economy Newly Expounded

An overview of classical economics

An abundance of materials had been stored up by the middle of the eighteenth century out of which a new discipline, to be known as economics, would soon emerge. Greek philosophy was its ultimate source, but its beginnings are more precisely to be found in the emergence of modern science during the late Renaissance. The investigations and researches that culminated in the Newtonian system indirectly stimulated the rise of social science. The recognition that physical events obey certain laws made it reasonable to inquire whether there also are laws governing human events, and whether ways of improving the social environment might be prescribed on the basis of these principles. The Physiocrats scrutinized social processes with a view to discovering causation and a principle of regularity, just as Sir Isaac Newton (1632–1727) and other physical scientists had done before them with respect to natural phenomena. Their system of thought sought after the laws that govern the distribution of wealth, and France is quite appropriately regarded as the locale of the first school of theoretical economics and the beginning of a tradition of thought that has come to be called *classical*.

Yet the influence of Physiocracy was brief, lasting only for the short span of years, from 1758, the year François Quesnay's *Tableau Économique* was published, to 1776. In fact, 1776 was a fateful year for economics. The deposition of Anne-Robert Jacques Turgot as French minister of finance not only ended the influence of the Physiocrats as political reformers but also the intellectual influence of their system of thought. It was also the publication date of Adam Smith's *Wealth of Nations*, which shifted the scene of further development of the principles of what was to

become the classical tradition from France to England.

Appreciation of classical economics is facilitated by a preview of its several major themes and special points of view. Beginning with the Physiocrats, the phenomenon of economic growth became the classicists' central theme of inquiry. The growth theme also dominates Smith's *Wealth of Nations*. This theme is closely associated with the question of the way in which capitalist production generates a social surplus and the effect that the division of the surplus between capital accumulation and consumption has on the capacity of an economy to reproduce and continue to grow. The growth phenomenon was further explored by Thomas Malthus (1766–1834), David Ricardo (1772–1823), and John Stuart Mill (1806–73). These followers of Smith articulated their concern about economic growth to such related questions as the behaviour of population, the tendency toward diminishing returns, the principles of international trade, and the ultimate possible movement toward a stationary state.

In *The Wealth of Nations*, Smith also laid the foundation for the second major theme of classical economists, namely, their concern with the problem of exchange value and the role of the price mechanism in allocating labor and other resources among the sectors of the economy. His exposition of value in use and value in exchange posed the problem of the relationship between utility and cost of production in determining value. The so-called paradox of value, which his followers interpreted to mean that utility is relatively unimportant in explaining why commodities have value in exchange, is among the results of his inquiry. After Adam Smith, Thomas Malthus, David Ricardo, John Stuart Mill, and others who followed the tradition, offered value theories that emphasized the governing role of costs of production, as opposed to utility.

The problem of distribution, that is, the sharing of the nation's product among the three great social classes in the form of wages, profit, and rent, is the third major theme of the classical writers. Smith is the first to integrate the problem into his analysis, but it is Ricardo and John Stuart Mill who gave special focus to the question of income shares. The policy orientation of the classical school, whose members, from Smith to John Stuart Mill, were *political economists* rather than pure theorists, is particularly apparent in association with such questions as the Corn Law and the Poor Law, which relate to the distribution of income.

William Nassau Senior (1790–1864) was the only leading figure among members of the classical school who maintained that the concern of economics as a science is exclusively to deduce general laws about the behavior of the economic system and that the formulation of policy is outside its proper domain. The influence of his view is evident in the publication of books concerned with principles of economics rather than principles of political economy as the period associated with the establishment of the classical tradition came to an end.

The first writer to use the term *classical political economy* to investigate the real relations of production in a society in which property is privately owned appears to have been Karl Marx. If the core of classical analysis is perceived to be the theory of capital accumulation, then Marx is properly considered a classical economist. Like Smith and his English followers, Marx also sought to explain the long-run tendencies of the capitalistic system. However, Marx's interpretation of Smith's cost of production theory of value became articulated with his theory of exploitation and, thus, with what the perceived as a tendency of the capitalistic system toward ultimate destruction. A tradition has thus developed, which we will follow, to confine the designation *classical economics* to the work of the English successors of Adam Smith.

Chapter 4

Physiocracy: the beginning of analytical economics

••

Introduction

Origins and philosophy of Physiocracy

The reaction against the doctrines and restrictive practices of mercantilism was, if anything, more violent in France than in England. The French economy was basically agrarian and prospered little from the industry-stimulating measures introduced during the reign of Louis XIV by Jean Baptiste Colbert (1619–83), who served as minister of finance from 1661 until his death. Added to this, French wealth was drained by unsuccessful colonial wars and extravagant expenditures at court, both of which required high taxes to support them. The difficulty of assessing personal income and the exemption of the clergy and nobility from taxation burdened the commoner landowner and the peasant with substantially the whole revenue requirement. This situation so impoverished the rural classes that demands for reform became insistent until, at last, they culminated in 1789 with the French Revolution. However, before this great explosion, the Physiocrats presented an eloquent plea for 'revolution from above.'

Some of the observations and recommendations that were made later by the Physiocrats were anticipated in the writings of Pierre Boisguilbert (1646–1707) and Sébastien de Vauban (1633–1707). Both writers reacted against adverse conditions during the reign of Louis XIV. Understandably, they put their greatest emphasis on tax reforms and the abolition of export duties on grain. Boisguilbert, foreshadowing the Physiocrats, regarded land as the primary source of wealth and criticized mercantilist emphasis on precious metals. He viewed wealth as consisting of the supply of necessary and convenient things required to satisfy diverse human wants. The primary requisite for the creation of wealth, he maintained, is the elimination of artificial obstructions to natural harmony, such as tax abuses, customs duties, monopolistic guild practices, court extravagances, and large public debts. Vauban made tax reform his particular concern and proposed a single poll tax to replace all other direct taxes.

Unfortunately, the reforms proposed by Boisguilbert and Vauban brought them dishonor rather than praise. Their writings were suppressed; the absolute monarchy of the *ancien regime* tolerated little criticism. But their ideas survived nevertheless, and many were incorporated in reform efforts that came later with the Physiocrats. Pleas for reform and even programs for reform, such as the *Project for the Royal Tithe*, which Vauban offered in 1707, failed to catalyze change.

What was needed, in addition, was a philosophy and a systematic analysis to provide a rationale for reform by explaining the source of the ills that plagued the French economy. The Physiocrats, or *les economistes*, as they preferred to call themselves, were to supply these needs.

The Physiocratic system is primarily associated with François Quesnay (1694–1774), physician to Madame de Pompadour and later Louis XV. Partly as a result of his early experiences with farming and partly as a result of his belief in the primacy of nature, he interested himself in the plight of the French peasantry and its relationship to the ills of France. Quesnay directed his inquiries toward explaining the nature and creation of wealth, and the relationship that the mode of its circulation bears to the well-being of the economy. The inference was plain that something definite might be done to prevent the progressive diminution of the country's wealth, which had been taking place during the long and ill-fated reign of the Bourbon kings. The idea of reform was, of course, not new. What made the Physiocratic program unique was, first, that it was articulated with a theoretical system that purported to explain the creation, circulation, and reproduction of the nation's wealth, and, secondly, that it was based on the premise that the monarchy and the existing class structure would continue.

The term *physiocracy* came from the French word *Physiocrate*, first used by Du Pont de Nemours in 1776 after Quesnay's death. It means 'the rule of nature.' Quesnay accepted the idea that a divine providence has ordained the existence of a universal and inherently perfect natural order. Conformity to the laws of the natural order will ensure maximum happiness, whereas infringement of the fixed laws of nature will call forth correspondingly disastrous consequences.

Because humans are rational creatures created by a benevolent providence, they will tend to conform to a higher design in all activities. This philosophy suggests that it is both unnecessary and undesirable for governments to regulate. Legislation that conforms to nature is unnecessary, and that which is in conflict with nature is certain to fail; in the long run, the law of nature is supreme. This rationale is the basis for the famous maxim, *laissez-faire, laissez-passer* ('Let it be, let it go'), which was to figure so importantly in the subsequent development of economic theory. With it, the Physiocrats unavoidably invited comparison between France as it was under the absolute rule of a divine-right monarch, and the France that might have been under a system of perfect liberty.

So great was the discrepancy between the *ancien regime* and the ideal that it would appear that Physiocratic philosophy and doctrines heralded the French Revolution. It was not, however, the intention of the Physiocrats to alter the social status quo. On the contrary, the Physiocrats were enthusiastic supporters of monarchy and nobility. They interpreted the rule of nature as the absence of unnecessary legislation but not lawlessness. The function of the sovereign is to give expression to the divine wisdom that already rules the universe, and in so doing, he should be an absolute despot.

Contrary to the popular notion that the task of governing is extremely complicated, the Physiocrats maintained that, in practice, there would be relatively little for kings to do, for all reasonable persons would obey the rule of nature if only they were acquainted with it.[1] Enlightened individuals would recognize that the king is merely the instrument through which the laws of nature are carried out. The Physiocrats thus held the principle of political liberty in contempt because elected representatives cannot always link personal and group interests for the entire nation. Only the hereditary monarch, permanent and without self-interest, can harmonize the interest of all. It should be obvious, therefore, that the Physiocrats were not proponents of democratic self-government. Nor were they pleading for benevolent despotism. They wanted merely an enlightened despot, who recognized that the only road to happiness is to acquiesce to the rule of nature, which would bring about revolution from above.

Economic analysis

Philosophy and Quesnay's method

The work of Quesnay and his disciples marks the beginning of economics as a discipline. Using the process of abstraction, they were the first to seek out the existence of general laws according to which economic phenomena behave. By closing the gap between free will and natural law that had so long divided theology and science, they laid the groundwork for the systematic study of social phenomena. They were also the first after Sir William Petty to use hypothetical data in an economic model, which became known as the *Tableau Economique*, as a basis for formulating policy recommendations relating to agricultural reform and taxation.

Philosophers such as Descartes, Hobbes, and Hume had already argued that knowledge is achieved postnatally and that free will governs behavior. A society can become sick from abuses derived from human behavior. From this observation the Physiocrats addressed the question: whether laws regulating economic behavior can improve on the outcomes that are likely to follow if people were simply left to the guidance of nature.

This issue was provoked by the policy measures introduced by Jean Baptiste Colbert (1619–85), minister of finance under Louis XIV, in the hope of duplicating the success of English mercantilism. Although France was basically an agrarian economy, *Colbertism*, as the French system of mercantilism became known, directed resources out of agriculture into the production of luxury handicrafts such as porcelain, velvets, tapestry, and crystal. These were intended for consumption by French royals and aristocrats and for export to wealthy buyers elsewhere in Europe. Like England and Spain, France also imposed heavy tax burdens on the peasant class (nobles and clergy were tax-exempt) to finance colonizing expeditions to the New World. Eventually the agricultural sector stagnated for want of funds to replace the seed and livestock that was needed to continue production.

The Physiocrats attributed these ills directly to Colbert's policies of burdening agricultural activities while encouraging handicraft production and foreign trade, which they regarded as a misdirection of resources. They argued that workers are only capable of producing a *net product*, or surplus, in excess of their own subsistence when their efforts are applied to land-based production, principally farming and animal husbandry. Thinkers like François Quesnay (1694–1774), Du Pont de Nemours (1739–1817), and Victor Riqueti, Marquis de Mirabeau (1715–89) hoped to rescue the French economy from financial ruin by replacing Colbertism with Physiocracy, or 'the rule of nature.' They are the first group of thinkers whose ideas were, in general, so acceptable to all that most individual identities, with the exception of Quesnay, are lost in that group as a whole; thus they are the first economic thinkers to constitute a school of thought.

Anne-Robert Jacques Turgot (1727–81), although he rejected the Physiocratic tenet that land is the sole source of wealth, was, nevertheless, strongly sympathetic to their system of thought and, as a tax collector for the Limoge district, he had the opportunity to introduce tax reforms intended to achieve the Physiocratic objective of simplification.

Concepts

We are indebted to the Physiocrats for an analysis of production and wealth that, although imperfect, is greatly in advance of mercantilist views. In mercantilist thinking, it will be remembered, wealth consisted of treasure, and it was believed that only trade could make a nation prosperous. The Physiocrats maintained that wealth consists of goods that are produced with the aid of nature in industries such as farming, fishing, and mining. This line of thought is in advance of the mercantilist idea, even though the restriction of wealth to the output of the primary industries is unduly narrow.

Their belief that only land is the source of wealth led them to think that only labor engaged in primary occupations, farming in particular, is productive. They conceived of the economy as being composed of three classes: the proprietor (or landowner) class; the cultivator (or tenant farmer) class; and the artisan (or sterile) class. The nature of each of these classes and its role in the economy are to be understood and appraised in relation to what the Physiocrats called the *produit net*, or net product. A class is productive only if it is capable of producing a net product; that is, an output of greater value than its own subsistence requirements. The cultivator class, whose members are primarily tenant farmers renting land from the proprietors, are uniquely able to do this. They and others who work with the

land, such as miners, fishermen, and trappers, were thought to be the only ones capable of producing a net product because they have the advantage of being assisted by nature. Nature, as it were, labors along side of man and makes possible a net product that is a true surplus in excess of the subsistence requirements of labor.

The artisan class, on the other hand, which includes all those not belonging to the other two classes, produces no such surplus. Finished products produced by artisans, for example, have a value in excess of the raw materials they embody that is equivalent only to the labor expended in the transformation process. Therefore, there is no surplus associated with their efforts, and this is the reason why they are termed sterile or unproductive. While only the cultivators and others engaged in primary occupations are members of the productive class, it must be emphasized that it is nature, rather than their labor, that is the source of the surplus.

There is no agreement about the status of the proprietors in Quesnay's social classification. Quesnay himself was not entirely consistent in his earlier and later writings. In his earlier expositions, he regards proprietors as being sterile because they are not directly engaged in raw material production. This suggests that he thought of their rental incomes as being unearned. Later, he took the position that landowners are at least partly productive because they maintained the permanent improvements made on land and also performed the necessary functions of government. Mercier de la Rivière and Abbé Baudeau, two of Quesnay's more ardent followers, both took the position that the landlords are productive because they, or their forebears, bore the original cost of clearing and draining the land, and that these efforts gave them a claim to its fruits that took precedence over those of the present cultivators. In any event, the Physiocrats reasoned that in order to preserve the flow of the net product to the landlord, the cultivators, like the artisans, are entitled only to subsistence.[2]

The Physiocrats regarded the work of artisans as considerably more acceptable than that of those engaged in trade and finance, for those so engaged do add value to the raw materials they fabricate. Artisans have legitimate values to exchange against agricultural commodities. The incomes they receive are therefore earned and tend to equal the values they create. Their presence in the economy is also necessary for maintaining a *bon prix* ('good price') for farm commodities. Manufacturing industry, however, is desirable only if it does not diminish the agricultural market or inhibit the growth of agricultural capital.

Since the primary industries, agriculture in particular, are the source of the net product upon which the prosperity of the nation rests, agriculture would be specially encouraged in an ideally functioning economy. The number of persons engaged in trade and finance would be kept to an absolute minimum. The Physiocrats regarded the activities of tradespeople and financiers with disdain because they were merely engaged in exchanging the values created by others. They were thought to be incapable of producing any new values whatever. Some middlemen were, of course, regarded as necessary to the functioning of the economy, but Quesnay maintained retailers are present in far greater numbers than is required for the distribution of goods. Moreover, the large merchant capitalists are engaged in *trafic* ('trade') that is frequently speculative and directed toward a favorable balance of trade that will channel resources artificially into industry, to the consequent detriment of agriculture. The incomes merchants received were thus viewed as parasite incomes that could only represent a deduction from the net product. Since merchants themselves produce no values and since the farmers and artisans receive no more than their subsistence, in the Physiocratic view, tradespersons are necessarily supported out of the net product. This injury to the economy is compounded by the waste of much of their income on luxury commodities subsidized by the state or imported from abroad.

The *Tableau Économique*

François Quesnay devised an Economic Table (the *Tableau Économique*) to illustrate how the circulation of the net product produced by the cultivator class sustains the economy in a manner analogous to the life supporting function of the blood supply in the human body. Quesnay's *Tableau* simultaneously illustrated, by means of its quite remarkable structure, the production and circulation of goods throughout the economy and the associated monetary flows for an economy that is (to use contemporary language) in an equilibrium state. Quesnay understood that, analytically speaking, stationary state equilibrium is a logical starting point for examining the effect of a disturbance to the equilibrium condition represented in the *Tableau* on aggregate output. For Quesnay, the likely sources of disturbance are (a) a change in the proportion of incomes spent on agricultural output; (b) a change in the tax system; and (c) an increase in the price of food that would improve the rate of return in agriculture. The zigzag lines crossing over from one column to another, as in Figure 4.1, are intended to demonstrate the interdependence of economic classes that nourish and sustain one another by means of their expenditures.

The *Tableau Économique* is the first attempt to demonstrate the nature and achievement of equilibrium from a macroeconomic point of view. It depicts an economy assumed to be closed and stationary; that is, foreign trade is absent, and savings are equal to the replacement needs of capital. It is also assumed that there is private property in land, the owners receiving rent from the cultivators who supply their own capital and employ whatever wage labor they require. The analysis is limited to the agricultural sector of the economy but applies also to mining and fishing, and the net product, which is the focal point of the analysis, is explicitly the output of the agricultural sector. The sterile sector of the economy with its individual enterprises and financial organ-

izations is not analyzed, and all exchanges are inter-class exchanges rather than inter-individual exchanges. In short, the *Tableau* is designed to explain the manner in which the net product is created and circulated among the three classes of society and, ultimately, is reproduced the following year so that the system maintains itself.

Quesnay's table consists of three columns which are headed 'Expenditures by tenant farmers relative to land,' 'Expenditures by landowners from rent and revenue,' and 'Sterile expenditures by artisans and servants.' It is not entirely clear from the *Tableau* (or Figure 4.1) that the circulation of both goods and

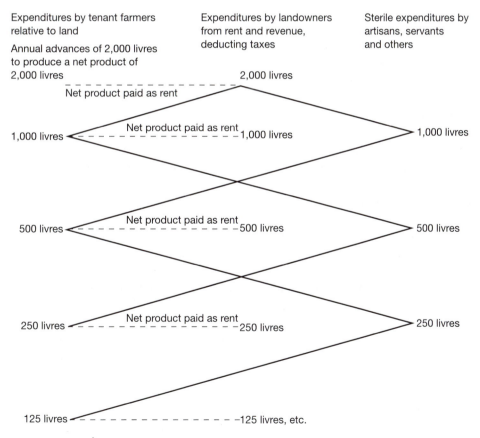

Figure 4.1 *Tableau Économique*

Source: Based on a presentation by Marquis de Mirabeau in *Éléments de la Philosophie Rurale*, 1767, Paris.

money is involved. It is, however, stated by Nicolas Baudeau, Quesnay's disciple, and implied in Quesnay's discussions that, at the end of the harvest, cultivators who lease land have the money stock as well as the economy's entire net product. The size of the net product reflects the capital investment (*advances annuelles*) made by those engaged in agriculture during the year. Quesnay assumes these investments produce a net product of 100 percent over and above the expenses of production, which are taken to include the tenant farmer's profit. Thus, if 2000 livres are invested, there will be a net product of 2000 livres available to be paid to the landowners as rent. The payment of rent by the tenant farmers is shown by dotted horizontal lines moving from the first column to the second. This initiates the circular flow of money and goods during the ensuing year.[3]

The rental incomes spent by the landowners are assumed to be directed in equal proportions toward the purchase of agricultural products and products made by the artisans and other members of the so-called sterile class. Lines moving outward from the center column to the left and to the right illustrate the expenditure streams by which purchasing power is circulated from the landowner class to the other two classes of society in return for the products they produce. By spending its revenue of 2000 livres equally on agricultural and non-agricultural products, the landowner class generates 1000 livres of income for the farmer and artisan classes, out of which they purchase their subsistence needs, raw materials, capital requirements, services of various kinds, and so forth.

Since the result of expenditures made on primary products, as represented by the flow of purchasing power to the column on the left, is quite different from that associated with the expenditures on manufactured products or services, these two expenditure streams must be examined separately. All expenditures directed toward production on the land, whether in agriculture, mining, fishing, or forestry, will yield a *net product*, which Quesnay assumes throughout to be 100 percent. Thus, a net product of 1000 livres is again created and, as shown by dotted horizontal lines moving from the first column to the second, is paid as rent to the landlords. This is the amount over and above the farmer's expenditures, including replacement of capital and profit. Actually, the income of the farmer in Quesnay's *Tableau* is equivalent to the management wage and interest on capital, rather than profit. Profit, in its modern conception, is thought of as a reward for the entrepreneurial function of risk bearing. The concept of the entrepreneur and the concept of profit as a distinct income share rewarding this function were introduced later by Jean Baptiste Say in the early nineteenth century.

Assuming once more that landlord revenues, which now amount to 1000 livres, are equally divided between purchases from the productive class and the sterile class, 500 livres will again be spent on products of the land. This investment will again yield a net product of 100 percent, or an additional 500 livres, which will flow to the landlords as rent. Each subsequent expenditure for the products of the productive sector will reproduce itself in the same way. It would, however, complicate the table unnecessarily to follow the expenditure of successive rental payments. The *Tableau* shown in Figure 4.1, therefore, only traces the circulation of the first 2000 livres.

Unlike expenditures made on primary products, landowner purchases from the artisan class do not add to the net product. Landowners are assumed to spend their revenue of 2000 livres equally on the products of the artisan class and on primary products. Thus, the artisan class is now also in receipt of 1000 livres, as shown on the right-hand side of the table. This amount represents all the expenditures that do not support farming and other extractive industries. It includes such items as interest payments, transportation costs, payments for foreign goods and services, and payments to domestics and others who provide services, including professionals, the military, and civil servants. Again, assuming an equal division of expenditures, one half of these receipts, or 500 livres, is spent on the products or the extractive industries. The other 500 livres are spent on the products and services of other members of the sterile class. Thus, one half of their revenues, as indicated by the diagonal lines moving to the left-hand side of the table, is used productively and so will generate a net product; the other half of their revenues is consumed unproductively and is therefore not conveyed to the left-hand side of the table.

All expenditures made by the landowners and artisans on products produced by the extractive industries are shown on the left-hand side of the table and thus assist in the creation of a net product. Conversely, if society increases its consumption of goods and services provided by the sterile classes, it will be at the expense of primary production, which causes a decline in annual advances and annual reproduction. The crucial factor in the Physiocratic view, insofar as the level of economic activity is concerned, is that the continuity of the circular flow be maintained by means of an appropriate pattern of consumption. It is not consumption, as such, that is required, but the kind of consumption that will cause a sufficient portion of national income to be spent on primary products. Thus, the Physiocrats conceived of the possibility that the prosperity of an entire

economy could become undermined by the excessive expenditures of the sterile class and by excessive consumption of their products. Clearly, the luxury expenditures of the nobles, especially when they were lavished on imported goods, were at issue, as were the disastrous and unpopular wars pursued by Louis XV.

The Physiocrats, their followers, and admirers considered that this demonstration of the circular flow of money and goods had great significance. Typical of the esteem in which the *Tableau* was held was the observation of Mirabeau that there have been three great inventions since the world began. The first is writing, the second is money, and the third is the economic table.[4]

It was hoped that actual data would eventually be collected to supplement the hypothetical quantities shown in the *Tableau*. These merely represented the relationships that Quesnay and other Physiocrats regarded as being ideal in the sense that they were consistent with reproducing the output of the system over successive production periods. Comparison of actual relationships with the ideal represented in the *Tableau* would then facilitate a diagnosis of the way in which actual processes of production and circulation differed from the ideal.

The Physiocrats were also concerned about the rate of savings. Unlike most thinkers who followed them, the Physiocrats did not consider savings to be desirable, regardless of their source in the economy or the uses to which they are put. They saw money as more than the 'wheel of circulation' Smith thought it to be. They were concerned with hoards and the impact these would have on the *bon prix* ('good price') of agricultural products and, therefore, on the net product. The manner of living pursued by the landowners, especially the king as the largest landholder, and the members of the sterile class, therefore determines not only the kind of economic activity conducted in the nation but also the level of national wealth. The moral of this observation is obvious, and it is the basis for Physiocratic concern about the proper distribution of nature's product among the classes of society.

Physiocratic proposals for reform

Tax reform

The real meaning of the *Tableau* emerges when its pure theory is articulated with Physiocratic proposals for reform. The essence of the theory and numerical examples that the *Tableau* intends to support and demonstrate is that only nature can produce a net product and that an ideal economy would maintain only those activities and practices that would not encroach upon its creation. Under Louis XIV, Louis XV, and Louis XVI, France was far from this ideal. It suffered a variety of tax abuses, trade impediments on a national as well as an international level, an unnecessarily large merchant class, an unsound agricultural organization, monopolized industrial enterprises, and an ever-expanding public debt associated with unsuccessful colonial wars and lavish court expenditures.

Proposals for tax reform had long been a central issue in France. In a predominantly agricultural country, it is obvious that the bulk of governmental revenues had to be derived from the land, especially in view of the difficulty of taxing less tangible forms of wealth. Tradition, however, exempted the clerical and lay nobility from the *taille*, as the land tax was known, thus shifting the bulk of the taxes to the 'third estate,' that is, to persons who were not members of the clergy or the aristocracy. The burden imposed thereby on the typically poor peasant eventually became intolerable, but what is more, the revenues collected fell so short of the needs of government that large-scale public loans from professional speculators and financiers were necessary. Many of these individuals further enriched themselves through the privilege of tax farming (paying a fixed sum for taxes collected and pocketing the difference) as well as farming out trading rights in certain commodities. Much of the fortune they accumulated tended to be drained into speculation at home or abroad, or hoarded. In either case, the Physiocrats believed these practices lessened the demand for agricultural commodities and contributed to the impoverishment of agriculture. These moneyed interests, however, became so essential to the sovereign that it was virtually impossible for such men as Richelieu, Colbert, and Turgot to introduce economy measures in the court.

The Physiocrats proposed not only that hereditary land tax exemptions be eliminated but also that the entire complex conglomeration of taxes currently levied be replaced by one single tax, the *impôt unique*, which all landholders would pay according to their respective shares of the net product. Needless to say, this proposal met violent opposition, not only because of the financial burden it would have imposed on those previously free from taxes, but also because it would have deprived them of a cherished symbol of class status.

The logic of the Physiocratic proposal for a single tax on the net product was clear and simple. They believed only land was capable of yielding a net product, or surplus, in excess of the subsistence requirements of those who labored on it. The supply price of laborers' services tended to be no more than the value they added to the product; consequently, workers were incapable of bearing taxes. Any taxes levied on them, reasoned the Physio-crats, come to rest ultimately on the only pos-sible source of payment, namely, the net product. We encounter here, in embryonic form, our modern theory of tax shifting, according to which, under certain circum-stances, taxes can be shifted forward to the purchasers of a product by being added to the price they pay, or shifted backward to the factors of production if it is possible to reduce the payments made to them.

The Physiocrats did not think of tax shift-ing in this modern sense, but rather associated it with the reduction of the net product that would take place if taxes were imposed on the members of the cultivator or sterile classes. They reasoned that if taxes were levied on the tenant farmers who cultivate the land, it would necessarily reduce their ability to finance the next crop. This would reduce the net product that would become available after the next harvest. In this way, the landowning class would come to bear the burden of the tax. In like manner, if the tax were imposed on artisans or other members of the sterile class, it would reduce their purchases from the cultivators, which would also diminish the net product. Thus, the Physiocrats reasoned it would be sounder and more economical to levy a tax on the net product in the first instance. It was suggested that this *impôt unique* would not need to absorb more than one third of the net product. They expected that if expenditures were curbed and the productivity of agriculture was increased, a levy of this size would be adequate to meet the revenue needs of the state. At least some progress toward the goal of a single tax was made by Turgot during his brief tenure between August 1774 and May 1776 as minis-ter of finance under Louis XVI. Many local duties were eliminated and a general land tax was established as a source of revenue.

The reorganization of agriculture

The improvement of agricultural productivity was regarded as fundamental to the success-ful functioning of the single-tax system, and the Physiocrats proposed to accomplish this by reorganizing agriculture on a more capital-istic basis. French agriculture was typically conducted on a small scale, each individual tenant farmer cultivating a small acreage with a minimum investment. Only by the introduc-tion of *grande culture* in place of the *petite culture* that prevailed could agricultural productivity be enhanced, thereby substan-tially increasing the net product. From the standpoint of the social and economic struc-ture, this proposal meant that if this Physio-cratic proposal were adopted, the relatively large number of small peasant farmers would be superseded by relatively few large-scale capitalistic farmers, who could introduce the more progressive methods of production that are practical only when conducted on a larger scale.

From the standpoint of its impact on productivity, the Physiocratic proposal for agricultural reorganization undoubtedly makes sound sense, but it should be obvious that a measure that promised to convert a major portion of the land-hungry peasantry into wage labor precluded popular support.

Trade

It has already been noted that the Physiocrats regarded the activities of traders as unproductive, because they thought trade merely involved the exchange of equal values. Their activities were therefore thought incapable of producing new wealth whether the exchange took place on a domestic level or internationally.

The difference between Physiocratic

reasoning about trade and that of the mer-cantilists should be immediately obvious. The latter held that trade is the only way to increase the wealth of a nation and that every effort should be made to secure a favorable balance. Under Colbert, trade in France was strictly regulated with precisely this end in view. Clearly, the Physiocrats were to find themselves in opposition to both the mercan-tilist and Colbertist points of view, for both were directed toward achieving a favorable balance of trade. In terms of Physiocratic thinking, the latter was not merely incapable of creating any new wealth; it actually tended to diminish wealth by reducing the demand for agricultural products.

How, then, can we explain the Physiocratic support of free trade? Is it not inconsistent with their position that commerce is unproductive? Present-day supporters of free trade, after all, do so on the grounds that it will enhance the wealth of the participating countries, not by increasing their gold hold-ings, but by securing them a greater quantity and better quality of goods and services than they could enjoy on the basis of their domestic production alone. But this is not the line of reasoning pursued by the Physiocrats, although theirs is the first free-trade position of note, and they are generally regarded as the first supporters of free trade. Their sup-port, it should be noted, focused chiefly on freedom to export grain, which was restricted, while the import of manufactured goods was encouraged. They viewed restrictive measures that deprived farmers of foreign markets as incompatible with maintaining the *bon prix* of agricultural products, which they thought essential to the growth of the *produit net*. Res-toration of domestic free trade in grain is among the important reforms Turgot accom-plished in his short career as finance minister. Unfortunately, his downfall in 1776 brought an end to this and other reforms he had tried to encapsulate in his 1776 edicts.

The usury question revisited

No one examined the moral and economic bases for the distribution of income and wealth among the cultivators, artisans, and proprietors more carefully than Anne-Robert Jacques Turgot (1727–81) who also served as a tax collector ((*intendent*) for the district of Limoges from 1761 to 1774). He conceived of cultivators and artisans as working class per-sons who are recompensed for their labor by wages that provide the equivalent of their subsistence requirements. The source of their wages is the net product of the land, which is also the source from which the incomes of all three classes are drawn. Turgot was thus concerned to ask whether the proprietor class should continue to draw rent from land, even after its members no longer work the soil.

While Turgot was not a fully committed disciple of Quesnay, in the sense of accepting all the views of Physiocracy, he did accept their ideal of the inherent sanctity of the nat-ural order, making it the basis for his argu-ment for civil laws that guarantee rent to the 'first cultivators' and their heirs.[5] Such pay-ments are properly due the proprietor class, even after they have ceased to work the land they own. His *Reflections on the Formation and Distribution of Wealth* (1766) was written 10 years before Adam Smith's *Wealth of Nations* and remains an important early statement of the right of private property and anticipated many of the themes that sub-sequently became embodied in classical eco-nomics. This work had its origin in a set of tutorial questions intended for the instruction of students studying under the Jesuit fathers. Among its themes are the following: the division of labor, the origin and use of money, the improvement of agriculture, the nature and employment of capital, interest on loans, and the rent of land. The latter two topics are of particular concern for they harken back to an issue that had already been addressed by the Schoolmen and, before them, by Aristotle.

Issues and Answers from the Masterworks 4.1

Issue
Is it proper to receive income in the form of interest or to require that interest be paid on a loan of money?

Turgot's answer
From *Reflections on the Formation and Distribution of Wealth*, Sections 19, and 29 to 34.

Of capitals in general, and of the revenue of money
There is another way of being rich, without labouring and without possessing lands, of which I have not yet spoken. It is necessary to explain its origin and its connection with the rest of the system of the distribution of riches in the society, of which I have just drawn the outline. This way consists of living upon what is called the revenue of one's money, or upon the interest one draws from money placed on loan.

Capitals being as necessary to all undertakings as labour and industry, the industrious man is ready to share the profits of his undertaking with the capitalist who furnishes him with the funds of which he has need. Since capitals are the indispensable foundation of every undertaking, since also money is a principal means for economising from small gains, amassing profits, and growing rich, those who, though they have industry and the love of labour, have no capitals or not enough for the undertakings they wish to embark on, have no difficulty in making up their minds to give up to the Possessors of capitals or money, who are willing to trust them with it, a portion of the profits they expect to gain over and above the return of their advances.

The loan upon interest: Nature of the loan. The Possessors of money balance the risk their capital may run if the enterprise does not succeed, with the advantage of enjoying a definite profit without labour; and they are influenced thereby to demand more or less profit or interest for their money, or to consent to lend it in return for the interest the Borrower offers them. Here, then, is another outlet open to the Possessor of money, lending on interest, or the trade in money. For one must not make a mistake; lending on interest is nothing in the world but a commercial transaction in which the Lender is a man who sells the use of his money and the Borrower a man who buys it; precisely as the Proprietor of an estate and his Farmer sell and buy respectively the use of a piece of land which is let out. This is what is perfectly expressed by the name the Latins gave to the interest of money placed on *loan*, *usura pecuniæ*, a word the French rendering of which has become hateful in consequence of the false ideas which have been formed as to the interest of money.

Errors of the Schoolmen refuted. It is for want of having looked at lending on interest in its true light that certain moralists, more rigid than enlightened, have endeavoured to make us regard it as a crime. The Scholastic theologians have concluded from the fact that money produces nothing by itself that it was unjust to demand interest for money placed on loan. Full of their prejudices, they have believed their doctrine was sanctioned by this passage of the Gospel:

Mutuum date, nihil inde sperantes. Those theologians who have adopted more reasonable principles on the subject of interest have had to endure the harshest reproaches from writers of the opposite party.

Nevertheless, it needs but little reflection to realise the frivolity of the pretexts which have been made use of to condemn the taking of interest. A loan is a reciprocal contract, free between the two parties, which they make only because it is advantageous to them. It is evident that, if the Lender finds it to his advantage to receive something as the hire of his money, the Borrower is equally interested in finding the money of which he stands in need; as is shown by his making up his mind to borrow and to pay the hire of the money: but on what principle can one imagine a crime in a contract which is advantageous to the two parties, with which both are content and which certainly does not injure anyone else. To say that the Lender takes advantage of the Borrower's need of money to demand interest for it is to talk as absurdly as if one should say that a Baker who demands money for the bread he sells takes advantage of the Purchaser's need of bread. If, in the latter case, the money is the equivalent of the bread the Purchaser receives, the money which the Borrower receives today is equally the equivalent of the capital and of the interest which he promises to return at the expiration of a certain time; for, in short, it is an advantage for the Borrower to have during this interval the money he stands in need of, and it is a disadvantage to the Lender to be deprived of it. This disadvantage is capable of being estimated, and it is estimated; the interest is the price of it. This price ought to be higher if the Lender runs a risk of losing his capital by the insolvency of the Borrower. The bargain, therefore, is perfectly equal on both sides, and consequently fair. Money considered as a physical substance, as a mass of metal, does not produce anything; but money employed in advances for enterprises in Agriculture, Manufacture, and Commerce procures a definite profit. With money one can purchase an estate, and thereby procure a revenue. The person, therefore, who lends his money does not merely give up the barren possession of that money; he deprives himself of the profit or of the revenue which he would have been able to procure by it; and the interest which indemnifies him for this privation cannot be regarded as unjust.

True foundation of the interest of money. A man, then, may let his money as properly as he may sell it; and the possessor of money may do either one or the other, not only because the money is the equivalent of a revenue and a means to procure a revenue, not only because the lender loses during the time of the loan the revenue he might have secured by it, not only because he risks his capital, not only because the borrower may employ it in advantageous purchases or in undertakings from which he will draw large profits: the Proprietor of money may properly draw the interest of it in accordance with a more general and more decisive principle. Even if all the foregoing were not the case, he would none the less have a right to require the interest of the loan, simply because his money is his own. Since it is his own, he is free to keep it; nothing makes it his duty to lend; if, then, he does lend, he may attach to his loan such a condition as he chooses. In this he does no wrong to the borrower, since the latter acquiesces in the condition, and has no sort of right to the sum lent. The profit that a man may obtain by the use of the money is doubtless one of the commonest motives influencing the borrower to borrow on interest; it is one of the sources of the ease he finds in paying this interest; but this is by no means what gives a right to the lender to require it; it is enough for him that his money is his own, and this right is inseparable from that of property.

There exists no truly disposable revenue in a State except the net produce of lands. We see, by what has been said, that the interest of money placed on loan is taken either from the revenue of lands or from the profits of undertakings in agriculture, industry or commerce. But as to these profits themselves, we have already shown that they were only a part of the produce of lands; that the produce of lands falls into two parts; that the one was set aside for the wages of the cultivator, for his profits, and for the return of his advances and the interest upon them; and that the other was the share of the proprietor, that is to say, the revenue the proprietor expended at his pleasure, and from which he contributed to the general expenses of the State. We have shown that all that the other classes of the Society receive is merely the wages and the profits that are paid either by the proprietor from his revenue, or by the agents of the productive class from the part which is set aside to satisfy their needs, for which they are obliged to purchase commodities from the industrial class. Whether these profits be distributed in wages to work-men, in profits to undertakers, or in interest upon advances, they do not change their nature, and do not increase the sum of the revenue produced by the productive class over and above the price of its labour, in which sum the industrial class participates only to the extent of the price of its labour.

The proposition, then, remains unshaken that there is no revenue save the net produce of lands, and that all other annual profit is either paid by the revenue, or forms part of the expenditure which serves to produce the revenue.

The land has also furnished the whole amount of moveable riches, or capitals, in existence, and these are formed only by part of its produce being saved every year. Not only does there not exist nor can there exist any other revenue than the net produce of lands, but it is also the land which has furnished all the capitals which make up the sum of all the advances of agriculture and commerce. It was that which offered without tillage the first rude advances which were indispensable for the earliest labours; all the rest is the accumulated fruit of the economy of the centuries that have followed one another since man began to cultivate the earth. This economiz-ing has doubtless taken place not only out of the revenues of the proprietors, but also out of the profits of all the members of the working classes. It is even generally true that, although the proprietors have a greater superfluity, they save less because, as they have more leisure, they have more desires and more passions; they regard themselves as more assured of their for-tunes; they think more about enjoying it agreeably than about increasing it: luxury is their inherit-ance. The wage-receiver, and especially the undertakers of the other classes, who receive profits proportionate to their advances, to their talent and to their activity, although they have no revenue properly so called, have yet a superfluity beyond their subsistence; and almost all of them, devoted as they are to their undertakings, occupied in increasing their fortunes, removed by their labour from expensive amusements and passions, save all their superfluity to invest it again in their business and so increase it. Most of the undertakers in agriculture borrow little, and scarcely any of them seek to make a profitable employment of anything but their own funds. The undertakers in other employments, who wish to make their fortunes stable, also try to get into the same position; and, unless they have great ability, those who carry on their enterprises upon borrowed funds run a great risk of failing. But, although capitals are partly formed by saving from the profits of the working classes, yet, as these profits always come from the earth, inasmuch as they are all paid, either from the revenue, or as part of the expenditure which serves to produce the revenue, it is evident that capitals come from the land just as much as the revenue does; or, rather, that they are nothing but the accumulation of the part of the values produced by the land that the proprietors of the revenue, or those who share it with them, can lay by every year without using it for the satisfaction of their wants.

Although money is the immediate subject of saving, and is, so to speak, the first material of capitals when they are being formed, specie forms but an almost inappreciable part of the sum total of capitals. We have seen that money plays scarcely any part in the sum total of existing capitals; but it plays a great part in the formation of capitals. In fact, almost all savings are made in nothing but money; it is in money that the revenues come to the proprietors, that the advances and the profits return to undertakers of every kind; it is, therefore, from money that they save, and the annual increase of capitals takes place in money: but none of the undertakers make any other use of it than to convert it *immediately* into the different kinds of effects upon which their undertaking depends; and thus this money returns to circulation, and the greater part of capitals exists only in effects of different kinds, as we have already explained above.

Turgot's linking of the process of production to the distribution of income among the three classes of society, anticipated the thinking of Adam Smith and the classical school. It also completes the theoretical foundation for Physiocratic proposals for reform.

Source: *Réflexions sur la formation des richesses*, Anne-Robert Turgot, English translation 1898 (London: Macmillan), Sections 19 and 29–34.

Summing up: Turgot's key point

In rejecting the Schoolmen's theological argument about the sterility of money and the impropriety of taking interest, Turgot makes the important distinction between money as a means of facilitating the exchange of goods for one another and money as capital which, when it is 'employed in advances for enterprises in Agriculture, Manufacture and Commerce procures a definite profit.' In this context profit is a return on productive investment that has an interest component for having made an 'advance' and also an entrepreneurial remuneration for risk and supervision. Turgot's vision of the economy as a user of capital in manufacturing activity, and not just in agriculture, fishing, and mining, which was Quesnay's conception, reflects an advance in understanding, for it leads readily to the principle of division of labor. It also leads to the notion of the 'lengthening of the time period of production,' which, as will be examined when the Austrian contribution is studied, is central to nineteenth century capital

and interest theory. Turgot's defense of the lender's right to earn interest on money is also a reflection of his strong laissez-faire position – a point of view that is also the essence of the policy stance of Adam Smith and the classical economists generally.

Concluding remarks

Turgot's *Reflections* quite clearly substantiate the concluding comment at the end of Part I that, in the closing years of the eighteenth century, the development of economics as a science was further advanced in France than it was in England. French theorists demonstrated conclusively that the economic process consists of a flow of goods and a flow of money income. Our modern concepts of gross national product and gross national income are based on the recognition of the fact that the total income earned in a given period of time is exactly equivalent to the value of the total product produced. Similarly, our concept of net national product is arrived at by making appropriate deductions from the gross national product. Only depreciation is deducted in the modern scheme of national income and product accounting, whereas Quesnay, deducting also the subsistence requirement (i.e. wages) of the cultivators, conceived of the net product as representing only the surplus available to the landlord as rent. However, the Physiocrats, no less than present-day national product estimators, had a concept designed to arrive at the net results of the economy's performance for a given period of time. It is perhaps unnecessary to add that they did not make quantitative estimates of the sort that are today compiled by the US Department of Commerce. However, it is important to recognize that Quesnay, his followers, and such predecessors as Bois Guilbert and Vauban, contributed to the first stage in the development of measurement and quantification techniques in economics. Their collection of quantitative information about the French economy, which later served as a basis for the single tax proposal, was valuable for its own sake, but is also reflective of the essentially quantitative aspects of early political economy in the service of policy.

We are also indebted to the Physiocrats for their demonstration of the nature and appearance of an economic surplus, a phenomenon that was subsequently to occupy the attentions of Adam Smith, David Ricardo, and Karl Marx. Clearly, in the history of production, society must pass beyond the stage of bare subsistence before a surplus of any kind is a possibility. Since the earliest and simplest civilizations are fundamentally agrarian, the first appearance of a surplus is likely to be in the agricultural sector. Such an economy is not likely to be an exchange economy, but rather one in which the use values created are directly appropriated.

Although the exchanges described in the *Tableau* are expressed in terms of money, it is the circulation of the use values in which the Physiocrats are interested. Thus, the problem of determining the exchange value, which was to become so important in the later development of economic thought, was virtually ignored by the Physiocrats. Their chief concern was to develop a systematic model of a self-sustaining economy. Inputs into the production process created outputs which, in farming and primary production, generally generated a surplus that provides inputs with which the economy 'reproduces' itself. In the subsequent development of economics, the Physiocratic vision of the economy as 'reproducing' itself came to be challenged by the alternative vision that the economy exhibits 'equilibrium' tendencies, which implies that the presence of 'disturbances' and 'disruptions' call forth corrective forces that restore equilibrium. The vision of an economy from the perspective of its reproductive capabilities derives from the life sciences such as biology and botany which reflect Quesnay's training as a physician and the interests of the Physiocrats in nature and its processes. On the other hand, the vision of an economy as an equilibrating mechanism has its modern origins in Newtonian physics, which became the prototype for Adam Smith's vision of the 'natural order.'[6]

The prices of the goods sold in the economy being represented in the *Tableau* are implicitly cost-of-production prices, which are a summation of the subsistence costs of those who participate in making goods available for sale. The subjective elements that affect the values and prices were not of interest to them. Turgot, whose thinking along these lines was considerably more advanced than that of his contemporaries, appreciated that there were many factors an individual would take into consideration in valuing a good. But it remained for Etienne de Condillac (1714–80) to present a more thorough-going consideration of value. He wrote: 'Value is not an attribute of matter, but represents our sense of its usefulness, and this utility is relative to our need. It grows or diminishes according as our need expands or contracts.'[7] This Jesuit philosopher-economist, who assisted Turgot during the riots of 1776 to restore free domestic trade in grain, realized that scarcity, which makes want satisfaction more difficult, and abundance, which makes it less difficult, cause exchange values to be greater or less, depending upon the quantities available relative to the demand for them. Thus, he not only established the psychological basis of value; he also anticipated what in the later French, English, and Austrian analysis became known as *final* or *marginal utility*; that is, the additional satisfaction associated with the last unit of a good acquired. However, it was to take approximately a hundred years before a similar approach found its way into English political economy.[8]

Turgot can also be credited with the discovery of the law of diminishing returns, and for providing a verbal statement of its operation in agriculture.[9]

He hypothesizes that equal increments of capital operating as a variable factor are applied to a given amount of land. It will yield a positive increase in output which implies that the marginal productivity of capital is positive. As the rate of capital to land increases so will output, which reaches a peak and then declines until it reaches zero. The total product of capital, which is the sum of the marginal products, is at a maximum when the marginal product declines to zero. It is thus clear that Turgot was describing what in the contemporary language of economists is a production function.[10]

It is interesting to note in this connection that, as crude as the Physiocratic concept of hoarding was, it is surprisingly suggestive of J. M. Keynes's writings during the 1930s, in which hoarding is related to a reduction in effective demand. The *Tableau* has also been hailed as 'a great turning point in the development of classical analysis.' Not only did it profoundly influence Karl Marx's model for explaining the requirements for a self sustaining capitalist system, 'in the twentieth century it [anticipated] the general equilibrium models of the classical type …'[11] Nobel prize winner Wassily Leontief has also recognized the *Tableau Economique* as an important precursor of his input–output anlaysis.[12]

Notes

1 An oft-repeated anecdote associated with this contention concerns the visit of the Physiocrat, Mercier de la Riviére, to Catherine the Great of Russia to advise her concerning reforms in government. He is purported to have told her that the wisest policy she could follow was simply to let things alone to take their own course, for nature would rule. It is said that she responded to his advice by wishing him a prompt goodbye.

2 The classification of artisans, domestic servants, merchants, financiers, and anyone else who is not a cultivator, as *sterile* is an unfortunate and inconsistent choice of terms, for it does not distinguish between those who are, within the framework of Physiocratic thinking, capable of producing their own subsistence and those who are not. Quesnay himself was not completely consistent, for in an unpublished article, 'Hommes,' he said that domestic servants may be indirectly productive if they free some of the energies of the agricultural classes. See Henry Higgs, *The Physiocrats* (New York: Macmillan, 1897), p. 127.

3 The livre is a former French money of account originally equal to a pound of silver. It was gradually reduced in value and replaced by the franc.

4 Henry Higgs, *The Physiocrats* (New York, Macmillan, 1857) p. 57. This work remains the classic reference. Charles Gide and Charles Rist add further background and insight in *A History of Economic Doctrines*, translated by R. Richards, seventh edn. (Boston: D. C. Heath, 1948), Chapter I. Ronald Meek, *Economics of Physiocracy, Essays and Translations* (Cambridge: Harvard University Press, 1962), includes a selection of Quesnay's writings and essays on various aspects of physiocracy. Two important contemporary interpretations of the Physiocratic contribution to the development of economics are Gianni Vaggi, *The Economics of François Quesnay* (Durham, NC: Duke University Press, 1987), and Steven Pressman, *Quesnay's Tableau Economique: A Critique and Assessment* (New York: A. M. Kelley, 1994.)

5 Ronald Meek, *Introduction to Turgot on Progress, Sociology and Economics* (Cambridge University Press, 1973), p. 311.

6 Vivian Walsh and Harvey Gram, *Classical and Neoclassical Theories of General Equilibrium* (New York and Oxford: Oxford University Press, 1980). Their chapter 2 examines Physiocracy as the first systematic model of a self-sustaining economy. This chapter is especially useful in its identification of the classical theme of surplus value prior to the Physiocratic model in the writings of Sir William Petty and Richard Cantillon.

7 Etienne de Condillac, *Le Commerce et le gouvernement* (Paris, 1776), p. 15.

8 *The Theory of Political Economy*, by William Jevons, was first published in 1871.

9 P. J. Lloyd, 'Elementary geometric/arithmetic series and early production theory,' *Journal of Political Economy*, 77, January/February 1969, pp. 21–34.

10 It results in positive first derivatives, positive then negative second derivatives, and positive cross-partial derivatives.

11 Vivian Walsh and Harvey Gram, *Classical and Neoclassical Theories of General Equilibrium* (New York and Oxford: Oxford University Press, 1980), chapter 2.

12 Wassily Leontief, *The Structure of the American Economy 1919–1929* (Cambridge: Harvard University Press, 1941), chapter 2.

Glossary of terms and concepts

Circular flow
The circulation of goods and money incomes throughout the economic system resulting from economic interdependency.

Law of markets (Say's law or Say's equality)
Aggregate demand is necessarily sufficient to clear the markets of the economy of the aggregate supply of all goods because the production process simultaneously creates goods and generates purchasing power. Equality between aggregate demand and supply requires that there be no interruption to the circular flow.

Produit net (net product)
The surplus produced by workers employed in the primary industries in excess of their own subsistence requirements.

Single tax
A single levy on the economic surplus yielded by land. Such a tax was originally recommended by the Physiocrats. Their recommendation was later revived in the nineteenth century by the American social reformer Henry George on the premise that its collection will not reduce production and that the amount collected will be adequate for revenue needs.

Tableau Économique
The economic table that depicts the circulation of the net product among the three classes of society and the return of the net product to the farmer that supports investment in agriculture.

Questions for discussion and further research

1 Compare the Physiocratic conception of the nature and source of wealth (based on your reading of Turgot's *Reflections)* with the

mercantilist's conception (based on your reading of Mun's *England's Treasure by Foreign Trade).*

2 The Physiocrats, among them Turgot, liked to call themselves the Economists. Do you consider this label appropriate? Why or why not? Did their system of thought contribute to the development of economics as a field of intellectual inquiry separate from philosophy, ethics, and theology?

3 On what basis did Turgot criticize and correct the Schoolmen on the question of the propriety of interest as a form of earnings? Does his argument have relevance for modern views about the right of private property?

4 Identify and explain key economic concepts that have become part of contemporary economics that are part of the Physiocratic legacy.

Notes for further reading

From *The New Palgrave*

The following selections are particularly useful in appreciating the Physiocrats' contribution as well as those of their predecessors: E. Castelot on *laissez-faire, laissez-passer,* history of the maxim, vol. 3, p. 116; Mason Gaffney on single tax, vol. 4, pp. 347–48; Giorgio Gilibert on circular flow, vol. 1, pp. 424–26; Peter Groenewegen on Pierre le Pesant Sieur de Boisguilbert, vol. 1, pp. 259–60, and on Pierre Samuel Dupont de Nemours, vol. 1, pp. 942–43; R. E Hébert on Jean-Baptiste Léon Say, vol. 4, p. 251; Thomas Sowell on Say's law, vol. 4, pp. 249–51; G. Vaggi on the Physiocrats, vol. 3,

pp. 869–75, on produit net, vol. 3, p. 1013, and on François Quesnay, vol. 4, pp. 22–29; and Paolo Varri on net product, vol. 3, pp. 637–38.

Selected references and suggestions for further reading

Beer, Max. *An Inquiry into Physiocracy* (New York: Russell & Russell, 1966 [1939]).

Cantillon, Richard. *Essai sur la nature de la commerce en général.* Edited by H. Higgs (London: Macmillan, 1931 [1755]).

Cole, C. W. *French Mercantilism 1683–1700* (New York: Columbia University Press, 1943).

Daire, Eugene. *Economistes financiers du 18ᵉ siécle* (Paris: Guillaumin, 1851).

Eltas, W. A. 'François Quesnay: a reinterpretation.' *Oxford Economic Papers*, 27 (July, November, 1975), pp. 167–200, 327–51.

Gide, Charles and Rist, Charles. *A History of Economic Doctrines*, second English edition (Boston: D. C. Heath and Co., 1949) Chapter 1, 'The Physiocrates,' pp. 21–68.

Groenewegen, P. D. *The Economics of A. R. J. Turgot* (The Hague: Martinus Nijhoff, 1977).

Higgs, Henry. *The Physiocrats* (New York: Macmillan, 1897).

Meek, Ronald. *Economics of Physiocracy, Essays and Translations* (Cambridge, Mass.: Harvard University Press, 1962).

Robbins, Lionel. Lectures 8 and 9, 'Cantillon – Physiocracy,' in *A History of Economic Thought*, edited by S. Medema and W. Samuels (Princeton, NJ: Princeton University Press, 1998) pp. 77–103.

Turgot, A. R. J. *Reflections on the Formation and Distribution of Wealth.* English edition, 1898 (London: Macmillan, 1911).

Vaggi, Gianni. *The Economics of François Quesnay* (Basingstoke, UK, and London: Macmillan, 1987).

Walsh, Vivian, and Harvey Gram. *Classical and Neoclassical Theories of General Equilibrium*, chapter 2 (New York and Oxford: Oxford University Press, 1980).

Chapter 5

Adam Smith: from moral philosophy to political economy

•••

Introduction

Life and times (1723–1790)

The Wealth of Nations (1776) is the second book in the trilogy planned, but never completed, by the Scottish moral philosopher Adam Smith. It was preceded by his *Lectures on Jurisprudence* (1766) which focused on the social aspects of economic behavior and the institutions that preceded the nascent industrial economy of the England of his own day. Even earlier, he examined the ethical values of life in *The Theory of Moral Sentiments* (1759). It was only following these important works that he turned his attention to subjects that today constitute the major concern of economic inquiry. He viewed *The Wealth of Nations* as a capstone to his work as a philosopher. He lectured at the University of Glasgow on the whole field of moral philosophy after the manner of his teacher Francis Hutcheson (1694–1746), who classified his subject into four branches: natural theology, ethics, jurisprudence, and political economy.

In turning his attention to examining the self-interested behavior of people engaged in market activity, Smith confronted the intellectual problem of reconciling the motive of self-love with the equally strong motive of sympathy for one's fellows. The issue, as Smith posed it, and the answer he offered in *The Theory of Moral Sentiments*, are examined in this chapter because they reflect, perhaps more clearly than any other masterwork of economics, the grounding of classical political economy in moral philosophy. The 'stages of social history' theme which Smith introduced in his *Lectures* is an equally important theme of classical economics. Its concern, which became the primary theme of the tradition that followed, was to examine the requisites for the 'advancement of riches' in the form of an increasing economic surplus that is essentially the theme pursued by the Physiocrats and, before them, by Sir William Petty.[1]

Like most great works, *The Wealth of Nations* is the product of the man and the times. With respect to the times, it may be observed that, during the last quarter of the eighteenth century, the English business scene was already dominated by the capitalist enterpriser who hired wage labor and frequently did business using the corporate form of organization. Agriculture was still the most important industry, and the rural classes were still well off. However, the technical strides being made, particularly in the textile and metalworking industries, were soon to call forth the Industrial Revolution. England had passed through its most extreme period of protectionism, and its foreign trade was making great forward progress as the huge trading companies of bygone decades gradually lost their privileges. Nevertheless, mercantilistic restraints were still numerous and onerous, especially with the colonies, and the psychological moment for dissent had now come. *The Wealth of Nations* is, first and foremost, an attack against the principles and practices of mercantilism.

The Wealth of Nations is not, as is sometimes erroneously contended, a plea for extending industrialization and advancing the interests of business owners. On the contrary, Smith directs some of his most biting criticisms against manufacturers and traders, reserving his sympathies for workers and his warmest plaudits for agriculture. It must also be remembered that the Industrial Revolution was still in its most embryonic stages. True, the spinning jenny and the water frame had already been invented to transform the textile industry, and James Watt had patented his steam engine in 1769, but their widespread practical application was still in the future. The wool and linen industries, which were among the largest, were still organized in domestic units rather than in factories. In short, the England of Smith's day was primarily commercial and agricultural rather than industrial. But it was not to take many more decades before the Industrial Revolution was to emerge.[2]

It was also a time of changing social and political relationships. Ideas of political liberalism had come to the forefront in England even before the French Revolution sounded the call of freedom elsewhere in Europe. Within this framework, economic theory was also acquiring new concepts and broadening its scope. Quesnay's *Tableau* offered a macroeconomic model of an interdependent economy using money to analyze the requirements for producing and maintaining a net product, or surplus. Turgot's *Reflections on the Formation and Distribution of Wealth*, written 10 years before Adam Smith's *Wealth of Nations*, anticipated such Smithian themes as the division of labor, the origin and use of money, the nature and employment of capital; and the question of interest of loans and revenue from land. However, despite the brilliance of these pioneering efforts, it was Smith's *Wealth of Nations* that became the first major work of classical political economy.

What was there about Smith that made his efforts more fruitful than those of several able contemporaries whose intellectual curiosity led them to explore along many of the same paths as he? It has often been suggested that there was nothing really unusual about Adam Smith, the boy or the man. He himself is said to have remarked: 'I am a beau in nothing but my own books.' He lived a rather uneventful life with his widowed mother, devoting himself largely to academic pursuits, although he also served as Commissioner of Customs in Edinburgh from 1778 until his death in 1790. Except for his sojourn in France as tutor to the young Duke of Buccleuch, which position brought him a lifetime pension, he traveled little. Even so, his natural talents, coupled with his educational experiences at Glasgow College and later at Balliol College, Oxford, his contacts with such associates as Francis Hutcheson, who was his teacher at Glasgow, David Hume, his friend of a lifetime, the Physiocrats whom he met during his travels in France, as well as the opportunity for firsthand observation in the expanding commercial metropolis of Glasgow, enabled him to produce the great creative work that is *The Wealth of Nations*.

The Theory of Moral Sentiments *(1759)*

Smith's theory of the social origin of moral judgments

The concern of moral philosophy, said Smith, is human happiness and well-being. Of this, the ancient moral philosophers were well aware, for they sought to examine 'the happiness and perfection of a man, considered not only as an individual but as a member of a family, of a state, and of a great society of mankind.'[3] This view was sharply different from that of the Middle Ages and the belief that happiness is inconsistent with virtue and that the only true virtue is self-denial. Although the material progress of the modern world rendered the medieval view of morality increasingly indefensible, Bernard de Mandeville's *Fable of the Bees, or Private Vices and Publick Benefits*, had already mocked the old view and dared to suggest that human vices, specifically the quest of luxuries and material gain, generate wealth.

The Fable attracted wide attention; most of Mandeville's contemporaries considered it worthy of a reply. Smith faulted his system of moral philosophy as 'wholly pernicious,' for it 'seems to take away altogether the distinction between vice and virtue.'[4] Where Mandeville appeared to be recommending anti-social behaviors for pursuing riches, Smith viewed this pursuit as merely one among many human desires. It is, in fact, tempered by the equally strong desire for the approbation of one's fellows. These desires, says Smith, are with us from the womb to the grave and operate in every sphere of our lives. 'It is not from the benevolence of the butcher, the brewer, or the baker that we expect our dinner, but from their regard to their own interest. We address ourselves not to their humanity, but to their self-love, and we talk to them not of our necessity, but of their advantages.'[5] Self-interest is thus seen as directing every aspect of human behavior and activity. In the economic sphere, it prompts the division of labor (an effect that Mandeville had also noted) and the accumulation of capital, which enhances productivity. In the field of justice, it operated, Smith believed, to promote a high degree of efficiency in the English courts which tried to hear as many cases as possible because they functioned on the basis of the fees they collected from parties who came before them.[6]

It was precisely the absence of the principle of self-interest that Smith found so deplorable with regard to English universities. His years at Oxford convinced him of the adverse effect on the quality of instruction where professors are paid without due regard for their own efforts. By contrast, the teachers of ancient Greece, who were compensated on the basis of the number of students they attracted, were much more efficient, in Smith's opinion, then the majority of those he encountered at Oxford. Self-interest, then, is the motive that naturally drives people, and impediments to its operation generally have an adverse effect. Moreover, this is precisely the motive that *ought* to prevail, for, says Smith, 'I have never known much good done by those who affected to trade for the public good.'[7]

Yet, this observation suggests a possible inconsistency on Smith's part in explaining human motivation and behavior, for his earlier work, *The Theory of Moral Sentiments*, begins with this observation: 'How selfish so ever man may be supposed, there are evidently some principles in his nature which interest him in the fortune of others and render their happiness necessary to him though he derive nothing from it except the pleasure of seeing it.' How can individuals extend sympathy to their fellow humans while also serving their self-interest? Can these seemingly inconsistent behaviors be reconciled in a socially beneficent way?

It is, says Smith, imagination that prompts even mean individuals to sacrifice their own interests, at times, to the greater interests of others, for imagination takes the place of experience and enables them to have an idea about the unpleasant sensations of another. Personal experience and introspective psychology thus underlie the growth of individual moral sentiments. If a person grew up in isolation without communication, these sentiments would be impossible to conceive, but 'bring him into society and he is immediately provided with the mirror that he wanted before.'[8] We see the world through our own senses; and because we desire, above all, the sympathy and approbation of our fellow humans, it is necessary for each of us to regard happiness, not in that degree in which it appears to the self, but in that degree in which it appears to people in general.

The end result is that a beneficent social order emerges as the unintended consequence of individual actions. This result is Smith's famous 'invisible hand' doctrine – which, in spite of its fame, is specifically mentioned only twice in Smith's works – once in *The Moral Sentiments* and again in Book IV of *The Wealth of Nations*. In *The Moral Sentiments*, Smith alludes to the invisible hand to explain why the 'natural selfishness' of rich landlords turns out not to be wholly pernicious:

In spite of their natural selfishness and rapacity, though they mean only their own conveniency, though the sole end which they propose from the labours of all the thousands whom they employ be the gratification of their own vain and insatiable desires, they divide with the poor the produce of all their improvements.

They are led by an invisible hand to make nearly the same distribution of the necessities of life which would have been made had the earth been divided into equal portions among all its inhabitants; and thus, without intending it, without making it, advance the interest of the society, and afford means to the multiplication of the species.[9]

In short, conscience and sympathy will always deter undesirable conduct in the economic sphere as in every other. Smith's belief in the morality of sympathy and the influence of social experience leads him to have faith in the role of liberty to direct human behavior for the social good as well as for individual benefit. This is the basis for his belief that the natural order is able to function well without the human direction the mercantilists undertook to give it.

The Wealth of Nations

Philosophical and psychological background

The theory of the social origin of moral judgments and standards is fundamental to the doctrine of the harmony of individual and national interests that pervades *The Wealth of Nations*. It appears reasonable, therefore, to interpret the doctrine of sympathy as developed in *The Theory of Moral Sentiments* as the conceptual antecedent of the doctrine of the natural order set forth in *The Wealth of Nations*.[10]

The philosophy on which Smith's economic principles are based is nowhere specifically mentioned in *The Wealth of Nations*. Yet it pervades his entire work to an even greater extent than the philosophy of the natural order colored the writings of the Physiocrats. Above all, Smith was dedicated to the 'simple system of natural liberty.' Standing at the center of his system are individuals who follow their own interests while promoting the welfare of society as a whole, for such is the nature of natural order. The Physiocrats also equated the existence of the natural order with the ideal society, but with a difference. For the Physiocrats, the natural order was to be discovered through the intellect and brought to fruition through enlightened despotism. For Smith, the existence of the natural order is a fact. It exists in spite of human interferences.

A variety of beneficent economic institutions are spontaneously generated within the framework of the natural order. Among them are the division of labor, the development of money, the growth of savings and the investment of capital, the development of foreign trade, and the adjustment of supply and demand to each other. These spring into existence as a result of natural human behavior and operate for the benefit of society as a whole.

Smith's psychology must likewise be culled out of his writings, as it is not specifically set forth. He does, however, appear to follow David Hartley, John Locke, and his good friend David Hume in regarding sensation as the source of ideas and knowledge.

Plan and scope

The Wealth of Nations is divided into an introduction, which sets forth the plan of the author, five books, and an appendix. The first book is 'Of the Causes of Improvement in the Productive Powers of Labour, and of the Order According to Which Its Produce Is Naturally Distributed among the Different Ranks of the People.' Book II is 'Of the Nature, Accumulation and Employment of Stock,' and Book III is 'Of the Different Progress of Opulence in Different Nations.' These three books are primarily a presenta-

tion of economic principles. Book IV, 'Of Systems of Political Economy,' and Book V, 'Of the Revenue of the Sovereign or Commonwealth,' take Smith into the area of political economy.

It is worth noting that *The Wealth of Nations* contains remarkably few references to the writings of other authors and that Smith was perhaps less scholarly in this regard than he might have been. He knew precisely, however, what to extract from other works and how to use it to make his final product in every way unique and peculiarly his own, although many individual ideas and even illustrations are not original to him. Smith is the first of the great eclectics who wove into a harmonious whole the more important ideas of predecessors and contemporaries alike. Some ideas even derived from thinkers with whom he was in disagreement, such as Bernard de Mandeville. The influence of Hutcheson and Hume is particularly in evidence; he also owed much to Turgot and the Physiocrats, especially Quesnay and such liberal mercantilists as North, Petty, Child, and Tucker. However, *The Wealth of Nations* effectively brought an end to political arithmetic as a policy instrument and, coincidentally, brought the first relatively brief stage of numeracy in the development of economic theory to a close.

Smith's disenchantment with the political arithmetic of his contemporaries was perhaps a matter of his own idiosyncrasies, for his personal library included the works of most leading practitioners, with the surprising exclusion of William Petty.[11] Indeed, he used some of their findings to support his own arguments. Thus, it may be inferred that his negative observation 'I have no great faith in political arithmetic' (*Wealth of Nations* IV, pp. 534) is less a reflection of their methods or findings than it is a reflection of the changing political environment and, more particularly, of the methodological perspective of the eighteenth century. In keeping with the natural order philosophy of the enlightenment, political economists from Smith onward relied on deductive logic to articulate the vision of an economy comprised of self-interested individuals whose actions are consistent with beneficial results for all participants.

Even today, *The Wealth of Nations* is an interesting book to read. Smith knew how to intersperse facts with illustrations and persuasive reasoning. The result is neither repetitious nor complicated in its logic but, rather, remarkably straightforward and simple. The attractiveness of the text greatly complicates the task of selecting among its many not-to-be-missed passages. Limitations of space dictate that we examine only two. The first relates to the issue of the nature and source of wealth. The second considers whether it is appropriate for capitalists to receive profits and landlords to receive rent if labor effort is the source of a commodity's value. The first issue offers important contrasts between the thinking of the mercantilists, the Physiocrats, and Smith. The second issue has become a perennial one, which each generation of economic thinkers undertakes to examine anew.

Issues and Answers from the Masterworks 5.1

Issue

What is the nature and source of wealth? How is it best augmented?

Smith's answer

From *An Inquiry into the Nature and Causes of the Wealth of Nations*, excerpts from the Introduction and Book 1.

Introduction

The annual labour of every nation is the fund which originally supplies it with all the necessaries and conveniences of life which it annually consumes, and which consist always either in the immediate produce of that labour, or in what is purchased with that produce from other nations.

According therefore, as this produce, or what is purchased with it, bears a greater or smaller proportion to the number of those who are to consume it, the nation will be better or worse supplied with all the necessaries and conveniences for which it has occasion.

But this proportion must in every nation be regulated by two different circumstances; first by the skill, dexterity, and judgment with which its labour is generally applied; and, secondly, by the proportion between the number of those who are employed in useful labour, and that of those who are not so employed. Whatever be the soil, climate, or extent of territory of any particular nation, the abundance or scantiness of its annual supply must, in that particular situation, depend upon those two circumstances ... Among civilized and thriving nations, on the contrary, though a great number of people do not labour at all, many of whom consume the produce of ten times, frequently of a hundred times more labour than the greater part of those who work; yet the great, that all are often abundantly supplied, and a workman, even of the lowest and poorest order, if he is frugal and industrious, may enjoy a greater share of the necessities and conveniencies of life than it is possible for any savage to acquire.

The causes of this improvement, in the productive powers of labour, and the order, according to which its produce is naturally distributed among the different ranks and conditions of men in the society, make the subject of the First Book of this Inquiry.

Book 1: Of the Causes of Improvement in the Productive Powers of Labour, and of the Order according to Which Its Produce Is Naturally Distributed among the Different Ranks of the People

Chapter 1: Of the division of labour

The greatest improvement in the productive powers of labour, and the greater part of the skill, dexterity, and judgment with which it is anywhere directed, or applied, seem to have been the effects of the division of labour.

The effects of the division of labour, in the general business of society, will be more easily understood, by considering in what manner it operates in some particular manufactures.

To take an example, therefore, from a very trifling manufacture; but one in which the division of labour has been very often taken notice of, the trade of the pin maker; a workman not educated to this business (which the division of labour has rendered a distinct trade), nor acquainted with the use of the machinery employed in it (to the invention of which the same division of labour has probably given occasion), could scarce, perhaps, with his utmost industry, make one pin in a day, and certainly could not make twenty. But in the way in which this business is now carried on, not only the whole work is a peculiar trade, but it is divided into a number of branches, of which the greater part are likewise peculiar trades. One man draws out the wire, another straightens it, a third cuts it, a fourth points it, a fifth grinds it at the top for receiving the head; to make the head requires two or three distinct operations; to put it on, is a peculiar business, to whiten the pins is another; it is even a trade by itself to put them into the paper; and the important business of making a pin is, in this manner, divided into about eighteen distinct operations, which, in some manufactories, are all performed by distinct hands, though in others the same man will sometimes perform two or three of them. I have seen a small manufactory of this kind where ten men only were employed, and where some of them consequently performed two or three distinct operations. But though they were very poor, and therefore but indifferently accommodated with the necessary machinery, they could, when they exerted themselves, make among them about twelve pounds of pins in a day. There are in a pound upwards of four thousand pins of a middling size. Those ten persons, therefore, could make among them upwards of forty-eight thousand pins in a day. Each person, therefore, making a tenth part of forty-eight thousand pins, might be considered as making four thousand eight hundred pins in a day. But if they had all wrought separately and independently, and without any of them having been educated to this peculiar business, they certainly could not each of them have made twenty, perhaps not one pin in a day; that is, certainly not the two hundred and fortieth, perhaps not the four thousand eight hundredth part of what they are at present capable of performing, in consequence of a proper division and combination of their different operations.

In every other art and manufacture, the effects of the division of labour are similar to what they are in this very trifling one; though, in many of them, the labour can neither be so much sub-divided, nor reduced to so great a simplicity of operation. The division of labour, however, so far as it can be introduced, occasions, in every art, a proportionable increase of the productive powers of labour. The separation of different trades and employments from one another, seems to have taken place, in consequence of this advantage. This separation too is generally carried furthest in those countries which enjoy the highest degree of industry and improvement; what is the work of one man, in a rude state of society, being generally that of several in an improved one. In every improved society, the farmer is generally nothing but a farmer; the manufacturer, nothing but a manufacturer. The labour too which is necessary to produce any one complete manufacture, is almost always divided among a great number of hands. How many different trades are employed in each branch of the linen and woollen manufactures, from the growers of the flax and the wool, to the bleachers and smoothers of the linen, or to the dyers and dressers of the cloth? The nature of agriculture, indeed, does not admit of so many subdivisions of labour, nor of so complete a separation of one business from another, as manufactures. It is impossible to separate so entirely, the business of the grazier from that of the corn farmer, as the trade of the carpenter is commonly separated from that of the smith. The spinner is almost always a distinct person from the weaver; but the ploughman, the harrower, the sower of the seed, and the reaper of the corn, are often the same. The occasions for those different sorts of labour returning with the different seasons of the year, it is impossible that one man should be constantly employed in any one of them.

This impossibility of making so complete and entire a separation of all the different branches of labour employed in agriculture, is perhaps the reason why the improvement of the productive powers of labour in this art, does not always keep pace with their improvement in manufactures. The most opulent nations, indeed, generally excel all their neighbours in agriculture as well as in manufactures; but they are commonly more distinguished by their superiority in the latter than in the former.

Source: Adam Smith, *An Inquiry into the Nature and Causes of the Wealth of Nations* (London: Everyman's Library, 1910).

Summing up: Smith's key points

A nation is well off in accordance with its supply of 'necessaries and conveniences' in relation to the number of its inhabitants. Goods, not gold, thus constitute the wealth of a nation. This Smithian point becomes abundantly clear in Book IV, which deals at length with mercantilism. Smith's chief focus thus parallels that of the Physiocrats, whose concern was the increase of the nation's net product. The primary difference between his conception of the nature and source of wealth and that of the Physiocrats is thus immediately brought into focus. It is not nature, but human effort, that makes commodities available. His emphasis on labor was not intended to deny the importance of either land or capital stock but rather to call attention to labor, as opposed to the forces of nature, as the prime mover of production. Without the cooperative efforts of labor, neither land nor capital would be able to bring forth anything. Division of labor enhances the dexterity of each worker, saves time by making it unnecessary to shift from one type of work to another, and also stimulates the invention of labor-saving devices. The result is a great increase in the quantity of work that a given number of people can perform. It is to the division of labor that Smith attributes the relatively high standards of living that prevailed during his day for even the lowest ranks of people and concludes 'that the accommodation of a European prince does not always so much exceed that of an industrious and frugal peasant as the accommodation of the latter exceeds that of many an African King.'[12]

Division of labor comes into existence

spontaneously without the necessity of human wisdom, planning, or intervention; it is the consequence of the 'propensity to truck, barter, and exchange one thing for another.'[13] This inclination to trade is found only in humans and is but one expression of self-interested behavior. Only by exchanging their surplus with others can persons acquire all the goods of which they have need; and in order to serve their own interests, they appeal to the self-interest of others.

It should also be noted that while his illustration of division of labor is drawn from a relatively small-scale operation, Smith was well aware that there were already some large-scale operations in Great Britain, chief among them the iron works at Carron in Scotland.[14]

Manufacturing generally lends itself better to division of labor than agriculture, and although the richest countries generally excel, compared with their neighbors, in agriculture as well as manufacturing, their superiority is usually greater in manufacturing. Everywhere, the practicality of engaging in division of labor is limited by the size of the market to be served.[15] Thus, Smith anticipates later discussions concerning the limits of what is today known as increasing returns to scale. He also observes that regions of relatively sparse population afford little opportunity to carry on division of labor, whereas well populated areas and those made easily accessible by good water and land transportation will be more likely to enjoy its advantages.

Productive and unproductive labor

Both the mercantilists and the Physiocrats employed the notion of productive and unproductive labor. For the former, the criterion of productivity was the degree to which the effort contributed to securing a favorable balance of trade, while the latter believed that only workers engaged in agriculture and the extractive industries were productive, in that they were assisted by nature, which alone is capable of creating a surplus. Unfortunately, Smith also thought in terms of productive and unproductive labor, and created considerable confusion with his distinction, not only as regards the discussion itself, but also as regards its compatibility with other parts of his theory.

In the third chapter of Book II, he observes that some labor realizes itself in a vendible commodity and is thus to be considered as productive, while certain other labor is unproductive in that it does not 'fix or realize itself in any particular subject ... which endures after that labour is past and for which an equal quantity of labour could afterwards be purchased.' The labor of domestic servants, entertainers, professionals, government servants, and others among 'the most respectable orders in the society' fall into this class.[16]

The foregoing distinction between productive and unproductive labor is also coupled with two other grounds on which the one type of labor is distinguished from the other. The first is the relationship of labor to the creation of value. Thus, he observes that productive labor 'adds to the value of the subject on which it is bestowed.'[17] The effort of labor engaged in manufacturing is in this class, while that of menial servants is not.

> Thus, the labourer of a manufacturer adds, generally, to the value of the materials that he works upon, that of his own maintenance and of his master's profit ... Though the manufacturer has his wages advanced to him by his master, he, in reality, costs him no expense, the value of those wages being generally restored, together with a profit, in the improved value of the subject upon which his labourer is bestowed.[18]

The notion of labor as the creator of a surplus is pursued in a somewhat different vein in Book IV, in which Smith analyzes the Physiocratic system. He begins with the observation that the labor of artisans and traders is not as productive as that of farmers because agricultural workers produce not only their own subsistence and profit on the stock of their employer but also rent for the landlord. Like the Physiocrats, Smith was persuaded that nature labors alongside farmers in agriculture to produce a surplus. His predilection for agriculture is equally apparent in Book II, which is devoted to the accumulation and employment of capital, and in which he insists that capital employed in agriculture is the most productive. 'The capital employed in agriculture, therefore, not only puts into motion a greater quantity of productive labour which it employs, it adds a much greater value to the annual produce of the land and labour of the country, to the real wealth and revenue of its inhabitants.'[19] It was on these grounds that Smith believed that a nation should give preference to agriculture and pursue other economic activities only as its increasing capital accumulation permits. He regarded manufacturing as the second most productive activity, followed by domestic trade. Foreign trade was identified as the least advantageous field for investment; it returned lower profits and was more difficult to supervise than capital invested at home.

Smith's distinction between productive and unproductive labor created confusion in at least three areas of economic thinking. First, his exclusion of services as part of the national product and the designation of the work of those who render them as unproductive labor were later recognized as incorrect. Second, his identification of revenues in excess of wages in manufacturing enterprises as a *surplus* blurred the difference between profit and interest. This was unfortunate because profit and interest are

functional returns rewarding two distinct activities, namely, the entrepreneurial function of risk bearing and management, and the lender's function of making funds available. The third area of confusion concerns the productive powers of land and its relationship to the appearance of rent. Like the Physiocrats, Smith believed there is something unique about the productive powers of land, which created an erroneous idea of the nature of rent and the circumstances under which it arises. However, unlike the Physiocrats, Smith recognized that profit is a separate form of surplus (i.e. as distinct from rent). Thus, profit and rent were both viewed by Smith as a source of saving and investment, whereas the Physiocrats regarded profit as a deduction from rent.

The most meaningful interpretation of Smith's distinction between productive and unproductive labor is in connection with saving and capital accumulation. It is clear from this third chapter in Book II, 'On the Accumulation of Capital or of Productive and Unproductive Labor,' that he is concerned with the effect of using savings for luxuries by those who are prodigal instead of channeling them to purchase fixed or circulating capital. He is, in effect, arguing that failure to use savings in this manner is an impediment to economic growth. This line of reasoning is somewhat obscured by his observation that 'what is annually saved is as regularly consumed as what is annually spent, and in nearly the same time too; but it is consumed by a different set of people.'[20] This seems to imply that it matters little whether income is used for consumption or saving because savings flow back into the income stream via investment. Hoarding is implicitly regarded as an exceptional occurrence in this context. Money is primarily desired as a medium of exchange and only seldom as a store of value. Thus, Smith did not seriously entertain the idea that hoarding could diminish the flow of income payments in the economy. On the contrary, he pictured the frugal individual as contributing to the public welfare because the savings are used to set productive labor into motion and to add to the stock of fixed capital. This view of the relationship of savings and investment anticipates the principle that subsequently became important in economic analysis as Say's law.

The theory of value and exchange

The origin and use of money

Smith's opening theme of production and economic growth is quickly set aside to explore a host of other matters that tend, particularly for the uninitiated reader, to detract from Smith's central concern with the problem of economic growth. The growth problem is not specifically addressed until it is examined from a historical point of view in Book III, as a prelude to issues related to mercantilism, which are examined in Book IV. The concerns of the first two books, however lay the microeconomic foundation for those that follow and, for the alert reader, ought not to obscure Smith's central theme of economic growth.

The use of money, like the division of labor, is viewed by Smith as a spontaneous development resulting from self-interested behavior. The use of money eliminates the inconvenience of barter situations. Thus, Smith tells us that 'in order to avoid the inconvenience of such situations, every prudent man in every period of society after the first establishment of the division of labour must naturally have endeavoured to manage his affairs in such a manner as to have at all times by him, besides the peculiar product of his own industry, a certain quality of some one commodity or other such as he imagined few people would be likely to refuse in exchange for the produce of their industry.'[21] Many different commodities, he observes, have served this purpose, but the precious metals seem particularly well suited to it. These observations are, of course, commonplace today, and every discussion since has been couched in almost identical terms.

Use value and exchange value

Having identified labor as the source of the wealth of nations, and the division of labor as the chief means of enhancing labor's effectiveness, Smith next addressed the issue of the relationship between the labor effort needed to produce a commodity and its value in exchange. The change of focus from the wealth of a nation to the worth of a commodity (a central question for Smith, who is, above all, a moral philosopher) leads him to distinguish between a commodity's *value in use* and *value in exchange.*

Smith's proposal at the close of Chapter 4, Book I, to examine the exchangeable value of commodities, introduced the issue now referred to as 'the paradox of value.' Why is it that things which have the greatest value in exchange have frequently little or no value in use? 'Nothing is more useful than water: but it will purchase scarce anything; scarce anything can be had in exchange for it, a diamond on the contrary has scarce any value in use; but a very great quantity of other goods may frequently be had in exchange for it.'[22] It is with these words that Smith *severs* the use value of a commodity from its exchange value on the premise that value in exchange is unrelated to value in use – what, in contemporary language, would be called *utility.*

Today's student of economics will probably

recognize several errors in the sentences just quoted. First, a commodity cannot possibly command other commodities in exchange unless it has value in use; only the ability to yield satisfaction to a user makes a commodity worth acquiring by giving up other goods or money. Smith's failure to recognize this rather obvious relationship was most significant for the future development of value theory, for it led to the attempt to explain exchange value without reference to utility. Some hundred years were to elapse before English political economy specifically took utility into consideration in explaining value.[23]

A further error in Smith's famous opening statement on value is his failure to recognize the significance of the relative scarcity of the commodity at the margin. It is clearly misleading to compare a single diamond to the total supply of water. If he had compared the utility of a single diamond with the utility of a single unit of water, he could not have been misled. It was not until it was recognized that it is the ratio of exchange between individual units that should be compared that the paradox of the diamond and water was resolved. A comparison of marginal units makes it perfectly plain that water commands little or nothing in exchange while a diamond commands a great deal because the supply of diamonds is so much smaller in relation to the intensity of the desire for them than is the case with water. It is surprising that Smith was unaware of this relationship, for it had been clearly pointed out by John Locke[24] and others.[25] Finally, Smith applied a personal moral standard in deciding that a diamond has no use value. The fact that one does not approve of the consumption of a particular commodity, or that its use may be harmful or even illegal, does not deprive the commodity of its utility. The mere fact that a commodity can command a price is sufficient evidence of its utility.

Having thus failed to consider utility, Smith turned his attention next in Chapters 5 through 7 of Book I, to the role of labor as a determinant of value. What is the basis for a commodity's value in exchange? Is its price some sort of labor equivalent, which Smith expresses as 'the toil and trouble of acquiring it' or, alternatively, as 'the real price of everything'?[26] Among the famous observations of Book I, Chapter VI, is the following:

> In that early and rude state of society which precedes both the accumulation of stock and the appropriation of land, the proportion between the quantities of labour necessary for acquiring different objects seems to be the only circumstance which can afford any rule for exchanging them for another ... It is natural that what is usually the produce of two day's or two hours' labour, should be worth double of what is usually the produce of one day's or one hour's labour.[27]

These statements imply Smith's acceptance of a *labor cost theory* in which labor is the cause or determinant of value. Yet, he also remarks that 'a commodity's value to those who possess it, and who want to exchange it for some new production, is precisely equal to the quantity of labour which it can entitle them to purchase or command.'[28] This statement expresses a *labor command theory of value*, according to which a commodity has a value equivalent to the labor it can command in exchange for itself either directly or indirectly in the form of some other commodity. When used in this sense, labor serves as a measure of value.

Several questions concerning these relationships may now be asked: first, if labor is the measure of value, why are values commonly expressed in money? Second, can labor not be both the cause and the measure of value – that is, can we not assign a value to a commodity in accordance with the amount of labor it contains and measure its worth in terms of some other commodity or group of commodities containing the same amount of labor? If this is possible, there is no incompatibility between the labor command theory and the labor cost theory. Finally, is it not possible that Smith intended the labor theory of value to apply only in 'that early and rude state of society' and considered that the cause of value after the appropriation of land and the accumulation of stock might not be labor alone? The latter two questions are especially pertinent in trying to understand Smith's theory of value.

In regard to the first question, Smith says that once barter ceases, it becomes 'natural' to exchange commodities for money rather than other commodities. Gold and silver are the most satisfactory monetary media, but they vary in value, like all other commodities, depending on the quantity of labor required to mine them. Corn (grain) also can be used to measure value, but it too will vary in value, depending on the quantity of labor required for its production.[29] He concludes, therefore, that labor is the only universal, as well as the only accurate, measure of value, or the only standard by which we can compare the values of different commodities at different times and places, in spite of the fact that values are commonly expressed in terms of money.[30]

Smith reasoned that commodities will have greater or less exchange value depending on the quantity and quality of the labor they contain. It does not matter, then, whether we speak of the value of the commodity or the value of the labor in it. Thus, Smith tells us in the beginning of the sixth chapter of Book I that, in 'the early and rude state of society' which antedates private property in land and the accumulation of capital, a commodity has value in accordance with the amount of labor congealed in it, and commodities containing equal amounts of labor will exchange equally for one another. The labor cost of a commodity is thus exactly equal to its labor command.

The only problem that Smith conceived to exist in this state had to do with the fact that equivalents of labor time are not automatically equivalents of labor content since some labor is more difficult, unpleasant, or dangerous, or requires more training, dexterity, or ingenuity. But this does not introduce a major difficulty, for such differences in the quality of labor will be reflected in different rewards. In the advanced state of society, allowances of this kind, for superior hardship and superior skill, are commonly made in the wages of the labourer; and something of the same kind must probably have taken place in its earliest and rudest period.[31] He took it for granted that the market process of wage-rate determination will automatically result in a wage commensurate with the labor performed by each worker and that wage differentials will be reflected in commodity values. The subject of wage differentials is thus introduced into the discussion of the value problem.

The matter of wage differentials is not pursued further until a later chapter, but it is already apparent that Smith believed the market sets commodity prices in accordance with the worth of the labor embodied in the commodities. Thus, he concluded that commodities would be exchanged for one another in accordance with their content of labor, the latter being the product of time, hardship, and ingenuity. 'If among a nation of hunters, for example. it usually costs twice the labour to kill a beaver which it does to kill a deer, one beaver should naturally exchange for or be worth two deer.'[32]

No problems of interpretation are involved with respect to Smith's discussion of the pre-capitalist era, which precedes land ownership and capital accumulation. The only factor of production is labor, and commodities are exchanged for one another in accordance with the labor they contain. In this state of things the whole product belongs to labor. There is neither landlord nor capitalist with whom it must be shared. Not until land becomes privately owned and the accumulation of capital has taken place does a share of the product go to the owner of stock and the landlord. The whole produce of labor does not then always belong to the laborer, but must be shared with the capitalist. Thus, the development of the economy beyond its original early and rude state has great significance not only for Smith's theory of value but for distribution theory and the issue of potential class conflict.

Issues and Answers from the Masterworks 5.2

Issue
If workers must share their produce with capitalists and landlords, does it follow that labor alone creates value only 'in that early and rude state of society'? Alternatively, if in an advanced society, workers must share their product with capitalists and landlords, is the worker being exploited?

Smith's answer
From *The Wealth of Nations*, Chapters VI and VII.

From Chapter VI: 'Of the Component Parts of the Price of Commodities'
In that early and rude state of society which precedes both the accumulation of stock and the appropriation of land, the proportion between the quantities of labour necessary for acquiring different objects seems to be the only circumstance which can afford any rule for exchanging them for one another. If among a nation of hunters, for example, it usually costs twice the labour to kill a beaver which it does to kill a deer, one beaver should naturally exchange for or be worth two deer. It is natural that what is usually the produce of two days or two hours labour, should be worth double of what is usually the produce of one day's or one hour's labour.

If the one species of labour should be more severe than the other, some allowance will naturally be made for this superior hardship; and the produce of one hour's labour in the one way may frequently exchange for that of two hours labour in the other.

Or if the one species of labour requires an uncommon degree of dexterity and ingenuity, the esteem which men have for such talents will naturally give a value to their produce, superior to what would be due to the time employed about it. Such talents can seldom be acquired but in consequence of long application, and the superior value of their produce, may frequently be no more than a reasonable compensation for the time and labour which must be spent in acquiring them. In the advanced state of society, allowances of this kind, for superior hardship and superior skill, are commonly made in the wages of labour; and something of the same kind must probably have taken place in its earliest and rudest period.

In this state of things, the whole produce of labour belongs to the labourer; and the quantity of labour commonly employed in acquiring or producing any commodity, is the only circumstance which can regulate the quantity of labour which it ought commonly to purchase, command, or exchange for.

As soon as stock has accumulated in the hands of particular persons, some of them will naturally employ it in setting to work industrious people, whom they will supply with materials and subsistence, in order to make a profit by the sale of their work, or by what their labour adds to the value of the materials. In exchanging the complete manufacture either for money, for labour, or for other goods, over and above what may be sufficient to pay the price of the materials, and the wages of the workmen, something must be given for the profits of the undertaker of the work who hazards his stock in this adventure. The value which the workmen add to the materials, therefore, resolves itself in this case into two parts, of which the one pays their wages, the other the profits of their employer upon the whole stock of materials and wages which he advanced. He could have no interest to employ them, unless he expected from the sale of their work something more than what was sufficient to replace his stock to him; and he could have no interest to employ a great stock rather than a small one, unless his profits were to bear some proportion to the extent of his stock.

The profits of stock, it may perhaps be thought, are only a different name for the wages of a particular sort of labour, the labour of inspection and direction. They are, however, altogether different, are regulated by quite different principles, and bear no proportion to the quantity, the hardship, or the ingenuity of this supposed labour of inspection and direction . . .

They are regulated altogether by the value of the stock employed, and are greater or smaller in proportion to the extent of this stock . . . In the price of commodities, therefore, the profits of stock constitute a component part altogether different from the wages of labour, and regulated by quite different principles.

As soon as the land of any country has all become private property, the landlords, like all other men, love to reap where they never sowed, and demand a rent even for its natural produce. The wood of the forest, the grass of the field, and all the natural fruits of the earth, which, when land was in common, cost the labourer only the trouble of gathering them, come, even to him, to have an additional price fixed upon them. He must give up to the landlord a portion of what his labour either collects or produces. This portion, or, what comes to the same thing, the price of this portion, constitutes the rent of land, and in the price of the greater part of commodities makes a third component part.

The real value of all the different component parts of price, it must be observed, is measured by the quantity of labour which they can, each of them, purchase or command. Labour measures the value not only of that part of price which resolves itself into labour, but of that which resolves itself into rent, and of that which resolves itself into profit.

In every society the price of every commodity finally resolves itself into some one or other, or all of those three parts; and in every improved society, all the three enter more or less, as component parts, into the price of the far greater part of commodities . . .

Chapter VII: 'Of the Natural and Market Price of Commodities'

There is in every society or neighbourhood an ordinary or average rate both of wages and profit in every different employment of labour and stock. This rate is naturally regulated, as I shall show hereafter, partly by the general circumstances of the society, their riches or poverty, their advancing, stationary, or declining condition; and partly by the particular nature of each employment.

There is likewise in every society or neighbourhood an ordinary or average rate of rent, which is regulated too, as I shall show hereafter, partly by the general circumstances of the society or neighbourhood in which the land is situated, and partly by the natural or improved fertility of the land.

These ordinary or average rates may be called the natural rates of wages, profit, and rent, at the time and place in which they commonly prevail. When the price of any commodity is neither more nor less than what is sufficient to pay the rent of the land, the wages of labour, and the profits of the stock employed in raising, preparing, and bringing it to market, according to their natural rates, the commodity is then sold for what may be called its natural price.

The commodity is then sold precisely for what it is worth, or for what it really costs the person who brings it to market; for though in common language what is called the prime cost of any commodity does not comprehend the profit of the person who is to sell it again, yet if he sells it at a price which does not allow him the ordinary rate of profit in his neighbourhood, he is evidently a loser by the trade; since by employing his stock in some other way he might have made that profit. His profit, besides, is his revenue, the proper fund of his subsistence. As, while he is preparing and bringing the goods to market, he advances to his workmen their wages, or their subsistence; so he advances to himself, in the same manner, his own subsistence, which is generally suitable to the profit which he may reasonably expect from the sale of his goods. Unless they yield him this profit, therefore, they do not repay him what they may very properly be said to have really cost him.

Though the price, therefore, which leaves him this profit, is not always the lowest at which a dealer may sometimes sell his goods, it is the lowest at which he is likely to sell them for any considerable time; at least where there is perfect liberty, or where he may change his trade as often as he pleases.

The actual price at which any commodity is commonly sold is called its market price. It may either be above, or below, or exactly the same with its natural price.

The market price of every particular commodity is regulated by the proportion between the quantity which is actually brought to market, and the demand of those who are willing to pay the natural price of the commodity, or the whole value of the rent, labour, and profit, which must be paid in order to bring it thither. Such people may be called the effectual demanders, and their demand the effectual demand; since it may be sufficient to effectuate the bringing of the commodity to market. It is different from the absolute demand for a coach and six; he might like to have it; but his demand is not an effectual demand, as the commodity can never be brought to market in order to satisfy it . . .

When the quantity brought to market is just sufficient to supply the effectual demand and no more, the market price naturally comes to be either exactly, or as nearly as can be judged of, the same with the natural price. The whole quantity upon hand can be disposed of for this price, and cannot be disposed of for more. The competition of the different dealers obliges them all to accept of this price, but does not oblige them to accept of less.

The quantity of every commodity brought to market naturally suits itself to the effectual demand. It is the interest of all those who employ their land, labour, or stock, in bringing any commodity to market, that the quantity never should exceed the effectual demand; and it is the interest of all other people that it never should fall short of that demand.

If at any time it exceeds the effectual demand, some of the component parts of its price must be paid below their natural rate. If it is rent, the interest of the landlords will immediately prompt them to withdraw a part of their land, and if it is wages or profit, the interest of the labourers in the one case, and of their employers in the other, will prompt them to withdraw a part of their labour or stock from this employment. The quantity brought to market will soon be no more than sufficient to supply the effectual demand. All the different parts of its price will rise to their natural rate, and the whole price to its natural price.

If, on the contrary, the quantity brought to the market should at any time fall short of the effectual demand, some of the component parts of its price must rise above their natural rate. If it is rent, the interest of all other landlords will naturally prompt them to prepare more land for the raising of this commodity; if it is wages or profit, the interest of all other labourers and dealers will soon prompt them to employ more labour and stock in preparing and bringing it to market. The quantity brought thither will soon be sufficient to supply the effectual demand. All the different parts of its price will soon sink to their natural rate, and the whole price to its natural price.

The natural price, therefore, is, as it were, the central price, to which the prices of all commodities are continually gravitating. Different accidents may sometimes keep them suspended a good deal above it, and sometimes force them down even somewhat below it. But whatever may be the obstacles which hinder them from settling in this center of repose and continuance, they are constantly tending towards it . . .

Source: Adam Smith, *An Inquiry into the Nature and Causes of the Wealth of Nations* (London: Everyman's Library, 1910).

Summing up: Smith's key points

Does the payment of profit and rent signify that workers are exploited? Smith's answer, provided chiefly in Chapter VII, but also elsewhere, is a powerful *negative*. He argues that a commodity tends to be sold for its 'natural price,' that is, 'precisely for what it is worth' and this price is inclusive of 'the natural rates of wages, profit and rent at the time and place in which they commonly prevail.' It is thus clear that Smith's theory of value is *not* a labor theory of value and the profit of the capitalist is *not* an income derived from exploitation, even though capitalists have greater bargaining power than wage earners.

As soon as the land of a country becomes privately owned, rent appears as the third component of natural price. Smith's attitude toward the receipt of rent by the landlords is less than warm, for he tells us that landlords love to reap where they have never sowed. But they are no different from others in this respect, and Smith regards the receipt of rent as being quite as natural as the receipt of profits.

In every society or neighborhood there is an average or ordinary rate of wages, profits, and rents that is natural with respect to the time and place it prevails. Thus, when a commodity sells for a price that is just high enough to compensate the worker, the landlord, and the owner of stock at the natural rate, the commodity is being sold at its natural price. It is then being sold for precisely what it is worth. This is not to say that a commodity will always sell for its natural price. From time to time, changes in the relationship between the demand for it and the supply of it will cause the market price to rise above or fall below the natural level. But such deviations tend to be corrected, for the supply will naturally tend to suit itself to the effective demand, thus causing the market price to rise or fall, as the case may be, until it again equals the natural price. However, the long-run, or natural, price was thought to be independent of demand forces. Smith believed it is determined solely by the cost incurred on the supply side of the market. Neglect of demand in explaining value was to become typical until the advent of the marginal revolution toward the end of the nineteenth century.

What is the significance of Smith's explanation of natural price for the labor theory of value? Smith nowhere denies the right of the owner of stock to receive profit or of the landlord to receive rent. On the contrary, he regards the existence of these shares as natural once 'that early and rude state of society' (before the advent of privately owned land and accumulated stock) is past. What this implies from the standpoint of the value problem is that the cost of production tends to be the long-run determinant of value. Smith does not, of course, specifically say this. Nor does he anywhere limit the validity of the labor theory of value to a primitive society. But the door to a theory of class conflict was opened by him to those who, like Karl Marx, would later argue that the deduction of rent and profit from the total revenue of the sale of a commodity necessarily meant a discrepancy between its labor cost and its labor command.

The theory of distribution

Classical distribution theory

When Smith addressed himself to the matter of distribution, he thought the problem requiring explanation to be the division of the nation's product among the laboring class, the capitalist class, and the landlord class. All who followed him – in what became the classical tradition – explained wages, profits, and rents as the incomes of 'the three great social classes.'

This approach is very different from that of modern economists who think of labor, capital, and enterprise as factors of production that receive functional returns for their productive contribution to the economy's product. The interdependence between the problems of value and distribution that

modern writers perceive is not a matter emphasized by Smith.[33] Indeed, his original lectures at Glasgow dealt only with production. The inclusion of four chapters on distribution in Book I of *The Wealth of Nations* conceivably reflects the influence of the Physiocrats or, as suggested by Edwin Cannan, Cantillon's *Essay on the Nature of Commerce in General*. Moreover, his explanation of the distributive shares as component parts of natural price that tend toward competitive rates under his 'obvious and simple system of liberty' is not of major significance as far as the central theme of *The Wealth of Nations is* concerned. However, as England became more industrialized and the great conflict between the landed interests and the rising manufacturing class and between the latter and the growing class of wage earners became intensified, his discussion of the distributive shares assumed great social significance.

Wages

Smith's discussion of wages suggests every conceivable theory of wage rate determination. He begins by referring once again to the early and rude society, which precedes the accumulation of capital and the private ownership of land, and tells us that, under those conditions, the produce of labor constitutes the natural recompense or wages of labor.[34] In this state, it is unnecessary to share the product with either the owner of stock or the landlord, and labor's share would have increased with all the improvements in its productive powers resulting from the division of labor if this state had continued. This utopian state being no longer in existence, Smith proceeds to discuss the various factors that are operative in the determination of wage rates.

The first explanation offered is the bargaining theory. He maintains that 'what are the common wages of labour depends everywhere upon the contract usually made between these two parties, whose interests are by no means the same . . . It is not, however, difficult to foresee which of these two parties must, upon all ordinary occasions have the advantage in the dispute, and force the other into a compliance with their terms.'[35]

Although employers generally have the advantage in the wage bargain, even the poorest grade of laborers must receive at least enough to maintain themselves and their families. Subsistence, Smith believed, sets the minimum below which wages cannot fall in the long run. Wages may, of course, rise considerably above this rate if the demand for workers is great, in precisely the same way a commodity price may rise above its natural level. The demand for labor, says Smith, is governed by the size of the wage fund that employers have available to give employment. Stock comes to be accumulated 'in the hands of particular persons' who constitute a class distinct from the worker. Independent workers, who used stock they owned themselves and who received both profits and wages, had already become atypical. Instead, says Smith, 'in every part of Europe, twenty workmen serve under a master for one that is independent; and the wages of labor are everywhere understood to be, what they usually are, when the laborer is one person and the owner of the stock which employs him another.'[36]

The owners of stock have accumulated it out of revenues in excess of their own living requirements and the capital requirements of business. 'The demand for those who live by wages, therefore, necessarily increases with the increase of the revenue and stock of every country, and cannot possibly increase without it. The increase of revenue and stock is the increase of national wealth. The demand

for those who live by wages, therefore, naturally increases with the increase of national wealth, and cannot possibly increase without it.'[37]

Thus, Smith relates increasing wages to increasing national wealth. He continues with a discussion of the level of wages in different parts of the world, noting that wages are especially high in North America because of its small population and the rapidity of increase in national wealth. China, on the other hand, has a very low level of wages because it has long been stationary. Wage rates in Great Britain are not so high as in North America, but they are above subsistence for even the poorest grade of labor. This is evident, says Smith, from the fact that summer wages are always higher than winter wages, although living costs are greater in the wintertime.[38]

In his observation on wage rates in different parts of the world, Smith also notes the relationship between the rewards of labor and the growth *of* population. He notes that 'every species of animals naturally multiplies in proportion to the means of their subsistence and no species can ever multiply beyond it.'[39] Thus, when wages are high, as they are in North America, the rate of population growth tends to be high, whereas low wage rates are associated with a stationary population. If, for any reason, the wage fund fails to increase and population nevertheless continues to grow, then wage rates will fall until the wage payment per laborer just enables population to remain stationary. Constancy in the size of the population is indicative of a stationary state – a condition that Smith believed had already been experienced by China, which had long been stationary by the eighteenth century. Worse yet was the situation in Bengal, in which subsistence wages were maintained only because 'want, famine, and mortality have reduced the size of the population.'[40] Wages are thus a reliable index for identifying whether a state is advancing, stationary, or declining.

'It is in the progressive state, while the society is advancing to further acquisition, that the condition of the laboring poor seems to be the happiest and most comparable. It is hard in the stationary and miserable in the declining state. The progressive state is in reality the cheerful and hearty state for all the different orders of the society. The stationary state is dull; the declining melancholy.'[41] These relationships were later the subject of a detailed inquiry by Thomas Malthus. Smith, however, did not share the pessimism encountered in Malthus's essay with respect to the growth of population. While Malthus was concerned, in the main, with the dire consequences of population pressure and the available means of subsistence, Smith noted that high wage rates also increase the 'industry of the common people' and thus contribute to the rising standard of living associated with greater division of labor.

Smith believed that the long-run trend of wages would be upward and considered that this was not merely a symptom of an advancing economy but also a cause of great progress. For though rising wages are dependent upon increases in stock, they also enhance the productive powers of labor and thereby facilitate the accumulation of capital. Even though population tends to expand to the very limits of subsistence, Smith evidently believed that the incentive to save rather than to be prodigal is so strong that additions to the wage fund coupled with the productivity increases associated with capital accumulation would tend to make the living standard of wage workers rise. Thus, the specter of a stationary state, in which the great mass of people live in misery, did not loom upon

Smith's horizon.[42] Not until the day of Malthus and Ricardo was the optimisim of Smith to be replaced by an attitude of such general pessimisim that economics became known as the 'dismal science.'

Profits on stock and interest

The profits of stock, says Smith, are closely related to the wages of labor, falling when wages rise and increasing when wages decline. Their average level depends on the accumulation of stock. The nature, accumulation, and employment of stock are not discussed until Book II, in which it is explained that not until individuals have accumulated financial reserves (stock) in excess of their subsistence requirement, will they try to use these savings to employ additional productive hands; or for lending to other productive persons, for an interest, payment that is, for a share of their profits. Thus, it is evident that Smith thought of increases in stock as the source of additions to the wage fund. The size of this fund determines the demand for labor, and depending upon the size of the laboring population, it determines whether the average level of wages will rise or fall. Increases in stock are generally associated with falling profits as well as rising wage rates, for mutual competition in the same trade will reduce the rate of return.

The level of profits, says Smith, is so fluctuating that it cannot be ascertained precisely. The most reliable gauge of the level of profits is the level of interest. 'It may be laid down as a maxim that whenever a great deal can be made by the use of money, a great deal will commonly be given for the use of it; and that whenever little can be made by it, less will commonly be given for it . . . The progress of interest, therefore, may lead us to form some notion of the progress of profit.'[43]

Like Turgot, Smith opposed the legal prohibition of interest, maintaining that it increases rather than diminishes the evil of usury, for nobody will lend without such a consideration for the use of his money as is suitable, not only to the use that may be made of it, but to the difficulty and danger of evading the law. It is clear, therefore, that the term *interest is* used by Smith, and indeed by others before him, as a payment made for the use of borrowed funds. He tells us that there is a minimum rate of interest that must compensate for the risk of lending, and the lowest rate of profit must be enough to compensate investors after they have made interest payments to the lender. Interest is thus regarded by Smith as part of gross profit, and net profit is a rate of return on capital whose level can be inferred from the market rate of interest. It was not uncommon for business owners to provide all or most of their capital, when businesses were predominantly organized as proprietorships or partnerships and their entire income was simply regarded as profit. Today, of course, the return on equity capital would be identified as interest rather than profit. But early thinkers on the subject, not only Smith but Malthus and Ricardo as well, made no functional distinction between interest and profit. They thought of the profit of the business owner as being, essentially, a yield on capital investment. That the business owner performs other functions, such as risk bearing, management, and innovation, and is not necessarily a provider of funds, was still unrecognized or given only passing notice. Their primitive theory of profit was therefore essentially a yield-on-capital explanation of interest.

With regard to the rate of profit, Smith believed that the average would be in the neighborhood of approximately double the rate of interest on well-secured loans.[44] Reasoning that there is competition for the employment of capital, which is largely mobile enough to flow from one part of the economy to another in response to profit opportunities, Smith concluded that the same *rate* of return would tend to prevail in all industries, although the actual *amount* would vary, he believed, with the amount of capital invested. The rate of profit would tend to decline with the progress of accumulation relative to the supply of labor. While Smith did not link the decline in the rate of profit with the tendency toward diminishing returns that is experienced as additional quantities of labor and capital are applied to a fixed supply of land, as was later emphasized by Ricardo, his discussion of the trend of income shares in areas abundantly populated and capital-rich, as compared with newer and still underdeveloped economies, anticipates the Ricardian analysis of the effect of progress on income distribution.

It should also be noted that the positioning of Smith's theory of value in Chapters 4–7 shifts attention from the growth theme inherent in the practice of division of labor and the expansion of markets of Chapters 1–3, thereby skirting the possibilities, of which Smith was clearly aware in the *Lectures* and Book III of *Wealth of Nations*, for class conflict once the cessation of growth dampens the economy's progress toward riches.[45]

Rent

Although some consideration has already been given to rent as a component of natural price, along with profit and wages, Smith devotes his lengthy closing chapter of Book I to this matter. Here, he virtually abandons his earlier view of rent as a cost and makes it a differential return.

Rent, it is to be observed, therefore, enters into the composition of the price of commodities in a different way from wages and profits. High or low wages and profits are the causes of high or low prices; high or low rent is the effect of it. It is because high or low wages and profits must be paid in order to bring a particular commodity to market, that its price is high or low: but it is because its price is high or low, a great deal more, or very little more, or no more. than what is sufficient to pay those wages and profits, that it affords a high rent, or a low rent, or no rent at all.[46]

Land that is used to produce food is the only land that 'always and necessarily affords some rent to the landlord.'[47] How much this rent will be depends on the fertility and location of the land. The greater the demand for the product, the higher the price that the landlord, as a monopolist, will be able to demand for his product above the minimum necessary to pay wages and profit. This is the essence of the differential surplus theory presented later by 'Ricardo, and it is perhaps superior to it in some respect because it discusses different conditions under which rent will emerge.

Smith concludes his lengthy chapter on rent with some observations about the long-run trend of the various income shares and the role their recipients play with respect to the society as a whole. It is his expectation that every improvement in the economy as a whole will raise the real rent of land either directly or indirectly. This is not because of the efforts of the landlords, a class of men who Smith considered to be naturally indolent, but rather because of the reduction in labor requirements resulting from improvements. It was not Smith's intention, however, to single out the landed gentry as the object of his attack. Opposition to the landed interests did not become an issue until industrialization had become sufficiently advanced to make cheap labor, and therefore cheap food, a primary

requisite. But a basis for the destruction of the harmony of social interests had clearly been laid, although the eventual conflict was obscured for the time being by Smith's philosophy of a beneficent natural order. If anything, Smith's criticism was reserved for traders and manufacturers. They are 'an order of men whose interest is never exactly the same with that of the public, who have generally an interest to deceive and even to oppress the public and who accordingly have upon many occasions, both deceived and oppressed it.'

The argument for economic liberty

Economic progress among different European nations

Book III, 'Of the Different Progress of Opulence in Different Nations,' provides a historical perspective for the devastating attack on infringement against economic liberty that Smith delivers in Book IV. In it, he reviews the development of European industry and agriculture from the time of the decline of the Roman Empire. He notes that, in many nations, the progress of opulence has been impeded by the pursuit of policies that conflict with what he regards as the natural course of things. If the natural course of development is allowed to assert itself, the capital of every nation will first be directed to agriculture, then to manufacturing and domestic trade, and last of all to foreign commerce.[48] This is the order of capital development Smith believed would be most profitable and most conducive to welfare.

Having completed this comparatively brief historical survey, Smith proceeds with his examination of different systems of political economy. This is done in Book IV, which is devoted to the commercial and agricultural systems.

The attack on mercantilism

The task of exposing the fallacies of the commercial system is begun by examining the policy of seeking a favorable balance of trade to augment the nation's gold supply and wealth. Smith rejected the argument that, just as a person is judged wealthy on the basis of large gold holdings, so a nation is rich if it has a great deal of gold; this analogy erroneously identifies money with wealth. The inflow of gold is undoubtedly in the interest of merchants, but for a country that has no mines of its own, to seek to gain gold by pursuing a favorable balance of trade is as unnecessary as it is foolish. It is unnecessary because a country can always acquire all the gold it has need of in the same way it acquires any other commodity it does not produce at home, namely, by trade, which will automatically respond to the effective demand for a commodity.

> We trust with perfect security that the freedom of trade, without any attention of government, will always supply us with the wine which we have occasion for; and we may trust with equal security that it will always supply us with all the gold and silver which we can afford to purchase or to employ, either in circulating our commodities, or in other uses.[49]

The special characteristics of gold and silver are, in fact, such that they are more easily transported than most other commodities. But, if for any reason it is impossible to satisfy the effective demand for the precious metals, this shortage will cause less inconvenience than would be encountered in regard to virtually any other commodity because a well-regulated paper money could supply the need for a medium of exchange, 'not only without any inconveniency, but, in some cases, with some advantages.'[50] Nor is it necessary to accumulate treasure in order to carry on foreign wars, for 'fleets and armies are maintained, not with gold and silver, but with consumable goods.'[51]

Foreign trade is desirable, in Smith's view, when it appears spontaneously in the natural course of a country's economic development. But the acquisition of gold and silver is an insignificant benefit to be derived from it. The primary gain from trade is that it provides a market for a country's surplus products and, by extending the market, facilitates further division of labor.[52] The great gain derived from the discovery of America was not the additional gold it brought to Europe, but the advantage to all trading countries of acquiring commodities cheaper than they could be produced at home.

> Whether the advantages which one country has over another be natural or acquired is in this respect of no consequence. As long as the one country has those advantages, and the other wants them, it will always be more advantageous for the latter rather to buy of the former than to make.[53]

Thus, there is a natural distribution of products among the different countries of the world that will come into existence automatically if only restrictive measures do not prevent their development. Later on, David Ricardo and John Stuart Mill were to elaborate the basis for territorial specialization in their theory of comparative cost and to point out the advantages accruing to the consumer if there is free trade. Smith was more concerned with the disadvantages of mercantilist restrictions on traders and producers, but unlike the arguments of the early antimercantilists, his were the first such arguments to be made by a personally disinterested individual.

The Physiocrats were, of course, also free traders, but their hostility to restrictive measures was an aspect of their program for agricultural reform, and there was no attempt to demonstrate the positive advantages of international trade. Smith, however, undertook to demonstrate that protection is not only useless but may actually be disadvantageous to the economy because it will tend to bring about a different allocation of capital than would occur under conditions of free trade. 'No regulation of commerce can increase the quantity of industry in any society beyond what its capital can maintain. It can only divert a part of it into a direction into which it might not otherwise have gone; and it is by no means certain that this artificial direction is likely to be more advantageous to the society than that into which it would have gone of its own accord.[54] There are, in general, only two circumstances in which it is desirable to lay some burden on foreign industry for the encouragement of the domestic; the first is when the industry is necessary to the defense of the country, and the second is when a tax levied on a foreign commodity would merely equal the tax imposed on the domestic commodity. The later policy 'would leave the competition between foreign and domestic industry, after the tax as nearly as possible upon the same footing as before it.'[55]

The agricultural system

Having devoted eight chapters to an analysis and criticism of mercantilism, Smith turns his attention, in the concluding chapter of Book IV, to Physiocracy. During his travels to France, he had personal contact with the authors of that system. While he regarded their argument that agriculture is the sole source of revenue and wealth, and that artificers, manufacturers, and merchants are unproductive, as incorrect, he nevertheless had warm praise for them.

> Though in representing the labor which is employed upon land as the only productive labour, the notions which it inoculates are per-

haps too narrow and confined; yet in representing the wealth of nations as consisting, not in the unconsumable riches of money, but in the consumable goods annually reproduced by the labour of the society, and in representing perfect liberty as the only effective expedient for rendering this annual reproduction the greatest possible, its doctrine seems to be in every respect as just as it is generous and liberal.[56]

He commended them not only for understanding the true nature of the wealth of nations but also for realizing the essential role of economic freedom in promoting its growth.

Concluding remarks

Although *The Wealth of Nations* was, in the main, an attack on the English commercial system, it was also intended as a policy guide – a key to the wealth of nations. Smith believed that the natural trend of economic development is upward and is most likely to manifest itself within the framework of an 'obvious and simple system of liberty.' Interpreted in modern terminology, this is a system that embodies the characteristics of perfect competition. Smith conceived of a perfectly ordered social universe, which operates in accordance with wise and beneficial *natural laws*, in much the same way as Newton conceived of a perfectly ordered mechanism as governing the functioning of the physical universe. Smith's analysis of the operation of the invisible hand of nature was a major step in the direction of understanding the optimizing results of activities conducted under perfect competition.[57]

Smith's greatest insight about the economic system is that it is driven by self-interested individuals operating under the force of competition. This observation provided the analytical basis for his theory that the rate of return to a resource will tend toward equality in its various uses. This principle remains the most substantial proposition in all of economics.

If perfect competition exists, there is no area of conflict between private and social interests. Individuals, independently seeking to maximize what they consider to be their own selfish interest, will nevertheless contribute to the social welfare. This thesis, in addition to counteracting the then prevailing view that every action for private gain is necessarily antisocial, also laid the groundwork for future propositions concerning the optimal results of perfect competition.

Smith's principal concern was to maintain the system of natural liberty that would facilitate the accumulation and direction of capital into those avenues that his theory of different employments of capital identified as being most desirable from the standpoint of maximizing welfare. The premature diversion of resources away from the agricultural sector was his great concern. Capital employed in agriculture is most productive, in Smith's view, for it yields not only wages and profit but also a surplus that is paid as rent to the landlord. Manufacturing ranks second in the hierarchy of productive employments, followed by domestic trade and, finally, foreign trade. His attack on mercantilism, which is rooted in his hierarchy of productive employments of capital, laid the foundation for the classical tradition of free trade and is, thus, high on the list of Smith's successes.

Also ranking high among Smith's successes is his formulation of the wages fund theory. This analytical construct explains the short-run average level of wages as reflecting the ratio between the funds allocated for the payment of labor and the number of laborers employed. This theory of wage-rate determination dominated for the next 100 years and is marred only by Smith's failure to define explicitly the content of the wages fund.

Smith's analysis implied that the activities in which the state engages are best held to a minimum because the labor of the sovereign and other governmental servants is unproductive. The incomes they receive are transfers and do not correspond to value added. However, despite his emphasis on the desirability of economic freedom, Smith's concern with identifying legitimate areas of intervention by government should not be overlooked. He did not, for example, favor wholesale removal of protective trade duties, for this would precipitate dislocation and unemployment in the domestic economy. 'The public tranquillity' would, he believed, require control over the corn trade, and he considered import duties whose intent is to retaliate against those imposed on domestic products by foreign countries as justified.

While Smith's treatise expressed a harmony of social interests, it also showed how and why social conflict might arise. His labor theory of value and his theory of surplus laid the foundation for a dichotomy of class interests which is seldom recognized. However, a re-examination of Smith's theory of natural price in the context of the 'stages of social history' developed in Book III leads to interpreting the prospect for class conflict as a more integral and substantive aspect of *Wealth of Nations* than is generally recognized. The continuity of his argument from his *Moral Sentiments* (1759) to *Lectures on Jurisprudence* (1766) to *Wealth of Nations* is not widely recognized. This lapse obscures the fact that Smith had two views of the distribution process. One view is that wages, profit and rent are components of natural price. The other is that profits and rents are deducted from the product produced by labor. The latter implicitly augments a potential for conflict.[58]

The theme of class interests is a recurring

one in the *Wealth of Nations*. It is often over-shadowed by the equally powerful theme that natural liberty promotes harmonious outcomes. Yet, the vision of an optimal self-regulating system is subject to the caveat that it is necessary for government to correct failings which he regarded as 'subversive of the great purpose which it [i.e. the economic system] means to promote.'[59] He expressed his faith in the operation of the 'invisible hand' in securing the interests of all members of society, but also had second thoughts about the role which different classes played with respect to the society as a whole. Of landowners, he entertained a low opinion indeed; they are frequently not only incapable of understanding the significance of any proposed change in policy but are actually ignorant of their own interests. The recipients of profit are, by training and inclination, best able to understand proposed changes in policy, but they are a class of people who are 'interested to deceive and even oppress the public.' Thus, elements of disharmony were present in Smith's analysis, but social conditions were not yet ready to ripen into actual conflict. As will become evident in the next few chapters, the further development of economics by thinkers who are not identified as 'classical' explored the functioning of the economic system in terms of the paradigm that Smith developed in *The Wealth of Nations*.

Notes

1 Some notion of Smith's perception of the declining relative importance of agriculture may be gleaned from his estimate in *The Wealth of Nations* that the annual value of agricultural output amounted to 60 million pounds, whereas the *Lectures* (written about 1763) inferred that 'the whole annual produce of lands must be about 72 millions.' See Adam Smith, *Lectures on Justice, Police, Revenue and Arms* (1763), edited by E. Cannan, first published in 1896 (New York, 1964), p. 224, and Adam Smith, *An Inquiry into the Nature and Causes of the Wealth of Nations*, vol. 11, p. 775. This and following references to this work are to the edition of Ernest Rhys (London: Everyman's Library, 1910).

2 Among the several themes of Samuel Hollander's *The Economics of Adam Smith* (Toronto: University of Toronto Press, 1973) is that Smith did not fail to anticipate the Industrial Revolution as has sometimes been charged.

3 Adam Smith, *An Inquiry into the Nature and Causes of Wealth of Nations*, vol. 2, p. 255.

4 Adam Smith, *The Theory of Moral Sentiments*. p. 451. This and subsequent references to this work are to the edition published in London by George Bell & Sons, Ltd, 1911.

5 Smith, *The Wealth of Nations*, vol. 1, p. 13.

6 Smith, *The Wealth of Nations*, vol. 2, p. 208.

7 Smith, *The Wealth of Nations*, vol. 1, p. 400.

8 Smith, *The Theory of Moral Sentiments*, p. 162.

9 Smith, *The Theory of Moral Sentiments*, pp. 304–5.

10 See Glenn R. Morrow, 'Moralist and philosopher' in *Adam Smith. 1776–1920*, edited by J. M. Clark *et al.* (Chicago: University of Chicago Press, 1928), for an interesting essay on the relationship between *The Theory of Moral Sentiments* and *The Wealth of Nations*. Jacob Viner has explored the same issue, taking the point of view that there are divergences between *The Theory of Moral Sentiments* and *The Wealth of Nations* that are impossible to reconcile. His essay 'Adam Smith and laissez-faire' is included in the same volume.

11 Robert Dimand provides a detailed survey of the data with which Smith was apparently acquainted and the works of the political arithmeticians in his library in 'Adam Smith and quantitative political economy' in *Measurement Quantification and Economic Analysis*, edited by Ingrid H. Rima (London and New York: Routledge 1995). See also Laurence Klein, 'Smith's use of data' in *Adam Smith's Legacy*, edited by Michael Fry (London: Routledge, 1992).

12 Smith, *The Wealth of Nations*, vol. 1, p. 11.

13 Smith, *The Wealth of Nations*, vol. 1, p. 12.

14 Smith, *The Wealth of Nations*, vol. 1, p. 76.

15 Smith, *The Wealth of Nations*, vol. 1, p. 15.

16 Smith, *The Wealth of Nations*, vol. 1.

17 Smith, *The Wealth of Nations*, vol. 1, p. 205.

18 Smith, *The Wealth of Nations*, p. 295.

19 Smith, *The Wealth of Nations*, p. 325.

20 Smith. *The Wealth of Nations*, vol. 1, p. 302.

21 Smith, *The Wealth of Nations*, vol. 1, p. 20.

22 Smith, *The Wealth of Nations*, vol. 1, p. 25.

23 See Chapter 12.

24 See this early manuscript on interest in William Letwin, *The Origins of Scientific Economics*, Appendix 5, p. 291.

25 See H. R. Sewall, 'The theory of value before Adam Smith,' *Publications of the American Economic Association*. Series III, 2, no. 3, 1901, pp. 66–124.

26 Smith, *The Wealth of Nations*, vol. 1, p. 26.

27 Smith, *The Wealth of Nations*, vol. 1, p. 41.

28 Smith, *The Wealth of Nations*, vol. 1, p. 26.

29 Smith, *The Wealth of Nations*, vol. 1, p. 31.

30 Smith, *The Wealth of Nations*, vol. 1, p. 32.

31 Smith, *The Wealth of Nations*, vol. 1, p. 42.

32 Smith, *The Wealth of Nations*, vol. 1, p. 41.

33 Samuel Hollander's *The Economics of Adam Smith* (Toronto and Buffalo: University of Toronto Press, 1973), which interprets Smith's work from the perspective of the modern neoclassical view, argues that while the formal analysis of general equilibrium is given relatively little attention in *The Wealth of Nations*, Smith's perception of the interdependence between the problems of value and distribution are evident in the applied chapters that deal with restraints on imports and colonial trade.

34 Smith, *The Wealth of Nations*, vol. 1, p. 57.

35 Smith, *The Wealth of Nations*, vol. 1, pp. 58–59.

36 Smith, *The Wealth of Nations*, vol. 1, p. 66.

37 Smith, *The Wealth of Nations*, vol. 1, p. 61.

38 Smith, *The Wealth of Nations*, vol. 1, pp. 62–65.

39 Smith, *The Wealth of Nations*, vol. 1, p. 71.

40 Smith, *The Wealth of Nations*, vol. 1, p. 72.

41 Smith, *The Wealth of Nations*.

42 It has been suggested that the odd positioning of Smith's theory of value in Chapters 4–7, which shifts attention from the growth theme inherent in the practice of division of labor and the expansion of markets of Chapters 1–3, skirts the possibilities of which Smith was clearly aware, in the *Lectures* and Book III of *The Wealth of Nations*, for conflict among the recipients of wages, profit and rent, once the cessation of growth dampens the economy's progress toward riches. See Ingrid H. Rima, 'Class conflict and Adam Smith's "Stages of Social History",' *Journal of the History of Economic Thought*, vol. 20, 1998, pp. 103–13.

43 Smith, *The Wealth of Nations*, vol. 1, p. 79.

44 Smith, *The Wealth of Nations*, vol. 1, p. 87.

45 See Ingrid H. Rima, 'Class conflict and Adam Smith's "Stages of Social History",' *Journal of the History of Economic Thought*, vol. 20, 1998, pp. 103–13.

46 Smith, *The Wealth of Nations*, vol. 1, p. 132.

47 Smith, *The Wealth of Nations*, vol. 1, p. 147.

48 Smith, *The Wealth of Nations*, vol. 1, p. 340.

49 Smith, *The Wealth of Nations*, vol. 1, p. 381.

50 Smith, *The Wealth of Nations*, vol. 1, p. 383.

51 Smith, *The Wealth of Nations*, vol. 1, p. 386.

52 Although Smith's main argument in favor of trade is that it provides a 'vent for surplus' in that it utilizes the output of factors that would otherwise be unemployed, Ricardo subsequently noted that Smith's treatment of trade would have been more consistent with the main theme of *The Wealth of Nations* if he had emphasized the advantage of foreign trade as facilitating a more efficient utilization of resources. See David Ricardo, 'Principles of political economy,' in *The Works and Correspondence of David Ricardo*, edited by Piero Sraffa (Cambridge: Cambridge University Press, 1951) pp. 294–95.

53 Smith, *The Wealth of Nations*, vol. 1, p. 403.

54 Smith, *The Wealth of Nations*, vol. 1, p. 398.

55 Smith, *The Wealth of Nations*, vol. 1.

56 Smith, *The Wealth of Nations*, vol. 2, p. 172.

57 Samuel Hollander's *The Economics of Adam Smith* (Toronto: University of Toronto Press, 1973) undertakes a comprehensive re-examination of *The Wealth of Nations*, including several new themes, chief among which is Smith's perception of the general equilibrium tendencies of a competitive economy.

58 Ingrid H. Rima, 'Class conflict and Adam Smith's stages of social history,' *Journal of the History of Economic Thought*, vol. 20(1), 1998, pp. 103–13.

59 Smith, *Wealth of Nations*, vol. 2, pp. 550–51.

Glossary of terms and concepts

Circulating capital
That portion of the economy's stock of capital that the production process converts into finished goods in a year or less, such as raw materials and the 'wage goods' that make up the worker's subsistence. Fixed capital (i.e. tools, machinery, equipment) depreciates over a much longer period.

Division of labor
Concentration of labor effort on particular tasks in order to improve skill, save time, and promote better use of capital.

Exchange value
The ability of a good to command another good in exchange for itself. This is predicated on its having value in use (though Smith did not recognize this relationship).

Invisible hand
The harmonizing of individual profit-maximizing actions with the social good through the operation of competitive market forces.

Labor theory of value
The hypothesis that the rate at which a commodity will exchange for another is equal to the time, hardship and quality of the labor effort required to produce it.

Price
Exchange value expressed in terms of a common denominator: money.

Use value
The ability of a good to yield satisfaction.

Wages fund
Food and other items constituting the subsistence requirements of labor, or their monetary equivalent. In classical theory, the wages fund constitutes the bulk of the economy's supply of capital. The size of this fund, relative to the size of the working population, determines the average wage rate.

Questions for discussion and further research

1 Is the doctrine of sympathy that is central to Smith's *Theory of Moral Sentiments* in conflict with the self-interest doctrine of *The Wealth of Nations?*

2 What is the invisible hand concept? In what sense is it central to Smith's system of thought?

3 How did Adam Smith distinguish between value in use and value in exchange? What three fallacies did his famous illustration involve? What implication did his distinction have for the later development of value theory?

4 The following appeared in *The Wealth of Nations:*

> In that early and rude state of society which preceded the accumulation of stock and the appropriation of land, the proportion between the quantities of labor necessary for acquiring different objects seem to be the only circumstance which can afford any rule for exchanging commodities one for another. The natural price of a commodity resolves itself into wages, profit and rent.

Analyze the implication of these two sentences with respect to the determination of value. Are they consistent? In what way do they reflect Smith's social philosophy?

Notes for further reading

From *The New Palgrave*

Mark Blaug on circulating capital, vol. 1, pp. 426–27; C. A. Blyth on the wage fund doctrine, vol. 4, pp. 835–37; Peter Groenewegen on division of labor, vol. 1, pp. 901–5; Robert L. Heilbroner on wealth, vol. 4, pp. 880–82; Guido Montani on productive and unproductive labor, vol. 3, pp. 1008–10;

Andrew Skinner on Adam Smith, vol. 4, pp. 357–74; G. Vaggi on market price, vol. 3, p. 334, and on natural price, vol. 3, pp. 605–8; Karen I. Vaughn on the invisible hand, vol. 2, pp. 997–98; Fernando Vianello on labour theory of value, vol. 3, pp. 107–13.

Selected references and suggestions for further reading

Clark, John M. (ed.) *Adam Smith, 1776–1920* (Chicago: University of Chicago Press, 1928).

de Mandeville, Bernard. *The Fable of the Bees.* Edited by E B. Kaye (London: Oxford University Press, 1924).

Hollander, Samuel. *The Economics of Adam Smith* (Toronto: University of Toronto Press, 1973).

Morrow, Glenn R. 'Moralist and philosopher.' In *Adam Smith, 1776–1920*, edited by J. M. Clark (Chicago: University of Chicago Press, 1928).

Rima, Ingrid H. 'Class conflict and Adam Smith's stages of social history.' *Journal of the History of Economic Thought*, 20(1), 1998.

Robbins, Lionel. Lectures 13, 14, 'General survey of Smith's intentions – The Wealth of Nations: Analytical I, II'; Lectures 15, 16, 'The Wealth of Nations: Analytical (III) – Policy I, II.' In *A History of Economic Thought*, edited by S. Medema and W. Samuels, (Princeton, NJ: Princeton University Press, 1998), pp. 125–63.

Skinner, A. S., and Wilson, Thomas (eds), *Essays on Adam Smith* (London: Clarendon Press, 1975).

Smith, Adam. *The Wealth of Nations*. Edited by Edwin Cannan (New York: Modern Library, 1937 [1776]).

Smith, Adam. *The Theory of Moral Sentiments* (Indianapolis, Ind.: Liberty Classics, 1976 [1759]).

Stigler, G. J. 'The successes and failures of Professor Smith.' *Journal of Political Economy*, 84 (December 1976), pp. 1199–314.

Chapter 6

Thomas Malthus and J. B. Say: the political economy of population behavior and aggregate demand

....

Introduction

The economic thought of the first half of the nineteenth century was very much the product of the problems that beset England and, to a lesser degree, France, after the Napoleonic wars came to an end in 1815. While England was relatively prosperous during this lengthy and expensive struggle, the end of the war was accompanied by severe economic depression. Widespread unemployment and high food prices encouraged a re-examination of the usefulness of restoring the Corn Laws as a possible corrective policy. The Corn Laws in mercantilist time were intended to stabilize grain price through a system of import duties and bounties that were linked to changes in their domestic supply. Their object was two-fold: first, to prevent significant changes either up or down in prices of the grains which comprised the principal foods consumed by commoners and farm animals; second, to maintain a level of grain prices that were consistent with the preservation of landlord rents and lifestyles. Accordingly, if poor harvests raised grain prices to levels that attracted foreign imports, duties were imposed on them as a method for collecting revenues to pay subsidies to landowners. These would lower the price of grain (and bread) to levels consistent with worker needs

to support their families without depriving landlords of their rents. In spite of increased acreage and improved methods of cultivation, continued population growth caused English grain prices to remain high so that grain imports were virtually duty-free from 1795 to 1812.[1] Grain prices and, consequently, landlord rents were high, even without the payment of bounties, throughout the Napoleonic Wars. Thus, Parliament had no reason to continue the Corn Laws, as landlord interests were well served without them. Not until the return to peacetime conditions, and the prospect of large imports from the Continent, which threatened lower grain prices, did landlords again clamor for the bounty that had historically been provided by the Corn Laws. Manufacturers and merchants, on the other hand, were quick to realize the advantages that free trade would yield them because of the relationship between wage rates and low food prices. Malthus and his contemporary David Ricardo emerged as intellectual adversaries on the question of whether England is better served by free trade in corn and other agricultural products or by protected markets.

Also at issue was the question of whether human behavior was inherently consistent with the betterment of society as a whole, so that the necessity of intervention by a higher legal authority was precluded by people's instincts to conduct themselves in ways that are consistent with progress. The question of the possibility of human progress toward 'perfectibility' and 'happiness' was a leading topic among the intellectuals of the day, who often took William Godwin's recently published book *The Enquirer* (1797) as their starting point. His earlier *Political Justice* (1793) had already proposed a 'simple form of society without government' in which the perfectibility of the individual will ultimately be realized. His principal argument was that reason dictates that an equal division of wealth will provide for basic human requirements to live while leaving ample leisure for the intellectual and moral improvement that will ultimately establish perfection and happiness on earth.

The French philosopher Marquis de Condorcet had much the same vision, although he relied more on science than morals to produce the ideal society. Like Godwin, he believed in the perfectibility of people, but he emphasized the progress inherent in the cumulative character of knowledge in the arts and sciences, which would produce advances to offset the growth of population. The prospect of overpopulation was viewed as too distant in the future for present contemplation.

The writings of Godwin and Condorcet were primary among the influences that provoked the publication of one of the most discussed works of the times, by Thomas Malthus (1766–1834). It bore the title *An Essay on the Principle of Population, as it Affects the Future Improvement of Society with Remarks on the Speculations of Mr. Godwin, M. Condorcet and Other Writers.* Relatively few copies of the original edition were circulated by its author, for the subject of population behavior was both unpopular and controversial. But the *Essay* soon became the center of heated discussion, and six editions that appeared during the author's lifetime give it a place among the masterworks of economics.

Malthus was born to a distinguished family. His father, Daniel, a lawyer by profession, was a friend of such men as Rousseau and Hume. He sent his son to be educated in Cambridge; upon graduation, Malthus entered the ministry of the Church of England, and had a parish at the time his famous essay was written. It was subsequently revised after extensive travel in Germany, France, and the Scandinavian countries. Shortly afterward, in 1805, he was appointed professor of history and political economy at the East India College, where he remained for the rest of his life. During these years he enjoyed a close friendship with David Ricardo (1772–1823), and helped found the Political Economy Club in 1821 and the Statistical Society of London in 1834.

The span of Malthus's lifetime coincided with years that were revolutionary in the industrial as well as in the political world. The Industrial Revolution, still in its embryonic stage when Adam Smith wrote, brought with it not only improved methods of production and transportation, new forms of business organization, and better banking and credit facilities, but also the factory system with its many attendant evils. The ever-growing urban population, whose employment opportunities were reduced by technological progress, presented a troublesome problem. These difficulties were compounded by recurrent economic crises that gave rise to periodic commodity gluts. The problem of overproduction therefore became an issue, as did the whole question of the 'effect of machinery.' The possibility that French revolutionary ideas might spread into England as a result of difficulties of the working class was the great fear that haunted the wealthy. The practical aim of English politics became to forestall a similar uprising by improving the conditions of the urban working class. William Pitt's bill of 1798, calling for the extension of relief to large families, is typical of the sort of safety valve measures proposed. These included the possibility of re-passing the Corn Laws in order to restore low food prices. Malthus and wealthy stock broker, David Ricardo, deeply concerned about current economic issues, emerged as intellectual adversaries on the question of whether England is better served by free trade in corn and other agricultural products or by protected markets.

Understandably, the question of free trade and its relation to domestic prosperity and the avoidance of gluts that resulted from large quantities of unsold goods were a similarly troublesome problem in France. Like the Physiocrats, J. B. Say recognized that interruptions to the circular flow can injure the economy, but he argued against their view that prosperity requires a pattern of consumption that directs a large fraction of total expenditures toward raw produce.

J. B. Say (1767–1832), a French businessman, was appointed in 1815 to the first chair of political economy at the *Conservatoire des Arts et Metiers* and, later, the *College France*. His *Traité* (1803) offered the thesis, which later became known as the *law of markets*, that *production*, rather than consumption, underlies prosperity. The sixth edition introduced the law of markets to criticize the Physiocrats, among others, for their argument that parsimony, or excessive thrift, is the source of underconsumption and gluts. Because Say's perspective became central to the whole question of the relationship between saving, investment, and prosperity – which is among the perennial issues of

economics – his essay 'Of the demand or markets for products' stands as one of the enduring masterworks of economics. Even though he is of greater importance for moving the development of economics into the nineteenth century, his insistence on the importance of utility for explaining value challenged the central importance of labor in Smith's theory of value. His *Traité* was written with the intent of offering a presentation of economic principles that was both more systematic and concise than the *Wealth of Nations*. Indeed, the translation of *Traité*, which went through five editions between 1803 and 1826, was used as a university textbook in Europe and America.

The philosophical aspects of post-Smithian economics: utilitarianism

Post-Smithian economics, as reflected in the writings of Malthus and his contemporaries, James Mill (1773–1836) and Jeremiah Bentham (1748–1832), represented essentially the same kind of interaction between political economy and moral philosophy that characterized Smith's work. Yet, it also reflects the legalistic perspective and language that Bentham brought to codifying the English penal code. Together with his close friend James Mill, he helped found a reform movement known as *Philosophical Radicalism* or *Utilitarism*.[2] Building on ideas drawn principally from David Hume and the French philosopher Claude Adrien Helvetius, he was also an early exponent of the utility theory of value, thereby challenging the central importance of labor in Smith's theory of value. Utilitarians interpreted behavior as the product of human sense experience rather than reason. They identified the pleasant sensations that individuals experience with moral goodness, and painful sensations with evil.

Bentham was thus able to reinterpret Hume's hedonism to provide a foundation for his system of social ethics.

Practical application of this ethical system required a 'felicific calculus,' or quantitative measurement of the pleasures and pains associated with various actions or modes of behavior. Bentham thought it possible to sum up pleasures and set them against pains, conceived of as negative pleasures. 'The balance, if it be on the side of pleasure, will give the good tendency of the act upon the whole, with respect to the interests of that individual person; if on the side of pain, the bad tendency of it upon the whole.'[3] By assuming that all individuals count equally and that a given action is associated with identical experiences of pleasure or pain for everyone, he extended the felicific calculus to society as a whole. He concluded that conduct should be judged morally according to its effects on the balance of human happiness.

Utilitarianism linked the principle of utility to an economic program to address the problems of working class, poverty, which had become too pressing and widespread to be obscured by belief in a natural order in which harmony is always assured. Thus, the thinkers who followed Smith described an economic system whose laws of operation they conceived to be dictated by a supreme but not necessarily beneficent natural order, instead of the invisible hand operating for the good of all, although this is no part of human intention. The necessity to adapt to the exigencies of nature was emphasized as essential to avoiding the unpleasant consequences of inevitable human shortcomings. The measures they proposed included changes in the Poor Law and in education to encourage population growth by moral restraint, along with legal penalties to promote individual behavior consistent with public well-being.

Bentham's conception of social utility necessarily raises the question of whether the egoisms that motivate human conduct are in conflict with each other, as Smith maintained. The French philosopher Helvetius held that individuals do not spontaneously identify their personal interests with that of the general public. His influence led Bentham to the idea that education and legislation are required to promote the greatest happiness of the greatest number. Education will contribute to the more perfect attainment of the goal of maximum utility by teaching people more appropriate associations. Its influence can be strengthened by a legal system that penalizes unacceptable behavior and thus provides an incentive for individual behavior consistent with social welfare. Mankind must fulfill this purpose by selecting wisely among human impulses to carry out the design of the Creator. Thus, Bentham argued, human happiness is most likely to be attained within existing institutions, specifically the existing form of English constitutional government. His counsel was thus for the preservation of the existing legal, social, and economic status quo. Regardless of the issue – whether the Poor Laws, the Corn Laws, or the problem of maintaining effective demand – the utilitarian position was consistently in favor of preserving the then existing class structure and relying on the principle of utility to improve human society.

Diminishing returns

Although Malthus did not explicitly identify the tendency toward diminishing returns on land, it is implicitly assumed in his ratios. While human subsistence consists of lower forms of animal and vegetable life which, unchecked, also tend to increase in a geometrical ratio, the human population and its food supply are equally capable of growth only when the supply of land is large enough to accommodate the expansion. Because the earth's surface is limited, increasing the food supply necessarily means the application of added productive effort at the margin, where the returns are proportionately less, unless the existing land supply can be made more productive via technological improvements. The problem is apparent as soon as a given quantity of land has been brought under cultivation, for then only more effective use of the given supply of land can increase its food-producing potential to support the human and animal population. The power of increase of the lower plants and animals is perhaps even greater than that of humans, but their actual increase is quite slow because of the limited land supply from which all subsistence, human and otherwise, must be derived. If good land exists in abundance, the increase in food production from it would be in a geometrical ratio even greater than that of humans. But, because good lands are limited in supply and are ultimately all under cultivation, increasing the food supply can eventually proceed only at a diminishing rate. Thus, even if one could create an ideal social system such as Godwin envisioned, in which checks on population would be eliminated or greatly reduced, Malthus inferred that it would not be long before the pressure of checks would reassert itself, not from any

fault of the people, but because the earth's productive capacity does not expand with population.[4]

Godwin's view was that a 'simple form of society, without government,' is compatible with the perfectibility of the individual. Malthus's *Essay* was to shatter this utopian dream of a golden age of human equality and happiness. What Malthus foresaw was the specter of excessive population as a permanent impediment to the improvement of society. He concluded from the contradiction between the geometrical ratio of population growth and the arithmetic ratio of the growth of the food supply, that population increase must necessarily be checked in some manner. In the first edition of his *Essay*, he identified these checks as misery or vice. He concluded that William Godwin's hypothesis about the ultimate perfectibility of humans is therefore untenable. Godwin and Marquis de Condorcet were wrong, he argued, in attributing inequality to human institutions. It is human nature, with its instinct to marry and multiply, that is the most serious obstacle to improvement. The selection which follows focuses on Malthus's interpretation of the great contradiction that confronts humankind: the desire for food and the desire for marriage are equally urgent and may defy reconciliation because the tendency toward diminishing returns from land is a barrier to the provision of food.

Issues and Answers from the Masterworks 6.1

Issue

Is there a potential imbalance between the size of the human population and the available food supply? Does this make the millennium Godwin and Condorcet anticipated unattainable?

Malthus's answer

From *An Essay on the Principle of Population* (1826).

The increase of population and food

In the northern states of America, where the means of subsistence have been more ample, the manners of the people more pure, and the checks to early marriages fewer, than in any of the modern states of Europe, the population has been found to double itself, for above a century and a half successively, in less than twenty-five years. Yet, even during these periods, in some of the towns, the deaths exceeded the births, a circumstance which clearly proves that, in those parts of the country which supplied this deficiency, the increase must have been much more rapid than the general average.

In the back settlements, where the sole employment is agriculture, and vicious customs and unwholesome occupations are little known, the population has been found to double itself in fifteen years. Even this extraordinary rate of increase is probably short of the utmost power of population. Very severe labour is requisite to clear a fresh country; such situations are not in general considered as particularly healthy; and the inhabitants, probably, are occasionally subject to the incursions of the Indians, which may destroy some lives, or at any rate diminish the fruits of industry.

According to a table of Euler, calculated on a mortality of 1 in 36, if the births be to the deaths in the proportion of 3 to 1, the period of doubling will be only 12 years and 4–5ths. And this proportion is not only a possible supposition, but has actually occurred for short periods in more countries than one.

Sir William Petty supposes a doubling possible in so short a time as ten years . . . But, to be perfectly sure that we are far within the truth, we will take the slowest of these rates of increase, a rate in which all concurring testimonies agree, and which has been repeatedly ascertained to be from procreation only. It may safely be pronounced, therefore, that population, when unchecked, goes on doubling itself every twenty-five years, or increases in a geometrical ratio.

The rate, according to which the productions of the earth may be supposed to increase, will not be so easy to determine. Of this, however, we may be perfectly certain, that the ratio of their increase in a limited territory must be of a totally different nature from the ratio of the increase of population. A thousand millions are just as easily doubled every twenty-five years by the power of population as a thousand. But the food to support the increase from the greater number will by no means be obtained with the same facility. Man is necessarily confined in room. When acre has been added to acre till all the fertile land is occupied, the yearly increase of food must depend upon the melioration of the land already in possession. This is a fund, which, from the nature of all soils, instead of increasing, must be gradually diminishing. But population, could it be supplied with food, would go on with unexhausted vigour; and the increase of one period would furnish the power of a greater increase the next, and this without any limit . . .

Europe is by no means so fully peopled as it might be. In Europe there is the fairest chance that human industry may receive its best direction. The science of agriculture has been much studied in England and Scotland; and there is still a great portion of uncultivated land in these countries. Let us consider at what rate the produce of this island might be supposed to increase under circumstances the most favourable to improvement.

If it be allowed that by the best possible policy, and great encouragements to agriculture, the average produce of the island could be doubled in the first twenty-five years, it will be allowing, probably, a greater increase than could with reason be expected.

In the next twenty-five years, it is impossible to suppose that the produce could be quadrupled. It would be contrary to all our knowledge of the properties of land. The improvement of the barren parts would be a work of time and labour; and it must be evident to those who have the slightest acquaintance with agricultural subjects, that in proportion as cultivation extended, the additions that could yearly be made to the former average produce must be gradually and regularly diminishing. That we may be the better able to compare the increase of population and food, let us make a supposition, which, without pretending to accuracy, is clearly more favourable to the power of production in the earth, than any experience we have had of its qualities will warrant.

Let us suppose that the yearly additions which might be made to the former average produce, instead of decreasing, which they certainly would do, were to remain the same; and that the produce of this island might be increased every twenty-five years, by a quantity equal to what it at present produces. The most enthusiastic speculator cannot suppose a greater increase than this. In a few centuries it would make every acre of land in the island like a garden.

If this supposition be applied to the whole earth, and if it be allowed that the subsistence for man which the earth affords might be increased every twenty-five years by a quantity equal to what it at present produces, this will be supposing a rate of increase much greater than we can imagine that any possible exertions of mankind could make it.

It may be fairly pronounced, therefore, that, considering the present average state of the earth, the means of subsistence, under circumstances the most favourable to human industry, could not possibly be made to increase faster than in an arithmetical ratio.

The necessary effects of these two different rates of increase, when brought together, will be very striking. Let us call the population of this island eleven millions; and suppose the present produce equal to the easy support of such a number. In the first twenty-five years the population would be twenty-two millions, and the food being also doubled, the means of subsistence would be equal to this increase. In the next twenty-five years, the population would be forty-four millions, and the means of subsistence only equal to the support of thirty-three millions. In the next period the population would be eighty-eight millions, and the means of subsistence just equal to the support of half that number. And, at the conclusion of the first century, the population would be a hundred and seventy-six millions, and the means of subsistence only equal to the support of fifty-five millions, leaving a population of a hundred and twenty-one millions totally unprovided for.

Taking the whole earth, instead of this island, emigration would of course be excluded; and, supposing the present population equal to a thousand millions, the human species would increase as the numbers 1, 2, 4, 8, 16, 32, 64, 128, 256, and subsistence as 1, 2, 3, 4, 5, 6, 7, 8, 9. In two centuries the population would be to the means of subsistence as 256 to 9; in three centuries as 4096 to 13, and in two thousand years the difference would be almost incalculable.

In this supposition no limits whatever are placed to the produce of the earth. It may increase for ever and be greater than any assignable quantity; yet still the power of population being in every period so much superior, the increase of the human species can only be kept down to the level of the means of subsistence by the constant operation of the strong law of necessity, acting as a check upon the greater power.

Of the general checks to population, and the mode of their operation
The ultimate check to population appears then to be a want of food, arising necessarily from the different ratios according to which population and food increase. But this ultimate check is never the immediate check, except in cases of actual famine.

The immediate check may be stated to consist in all those customs, and all those diseases, which seem to be generated by a scarcity of the means of subsistence; and all those causes, independent of this scarcity, whether of a moral or physical nature, which tend prematurely to weaken and destroy the human frame.

These checks to population, which are constantly operating with more or less force in every society, and keep down the number to the level of the means of subsistence, may be classed under two general heads – the preventive and the positive checks.

The preventive check, as far as it is voluntary, is peculiar to man, and arises from that distinctive superiority in his reasoning faculties, which enables him to calculate distant consequences. The checks to the indefinite increase of plants and irrational animals are all either positive, or, if preventive, involuntary. But man cannot look around him, and see the distress which frequently presses upon those who have large families; he cannot contemplate his present possessions or earnings, which he now nearly consumes himself, and calculate the amount of each share, when with very little addition they must be divided, perhaps among seven or eight, without feeling a doubt whether, if he follow the bent of his inclinations, he may be able to support the offspring which he will probably bring into the world. In a state of equality, if such can exist, this would be the simple question. In the present state of society other considerations occur. Will he not lower his rank in life, and be obliged to give up in great measure his former habits? Does any mode of employment present itself by which he may reasonably hope to maintain a family? Will he not at any rate subject himself to greater difficulties, and more severe labour, than in his single state? Will he not be unable to transmit to his children the same advantages of education and improvement that he had himself possessed? Does he even feel secure that, should he have a large family, his utmost exertions can save them from rags and squalid poverty, and their consequent degradation in the community? And may he not be reduced to the grating necessity of forfeiting his independence, and of being obliged to the sparing hand of Charity for support?

These considerations are calculated to prevent, and certainly do prevent, a great number of persons in all civilized nations from pursuing the dictate of nature in an early attachment to one woman . . .

On examining these obstacles to the increase of population which I have classed under the heads of preventive and positive checks, it will appear that they are all resolvable into moral restraint, vice, and misery.

Of the preventive checks, the restraint from marriage which is not followed by irregular gratifications may properly be termed moral restraint.

Promiscuous intercourse, unnatural passions, violations of the marriage bed, and improper arts to conceal the consequences of irregular connexions, are preventive checks that clearly come under the head of vice.

Of the positive checks, those which appear to arise unavoidably from the laws of nature, may be called exclusively misery; and those which we obviously bring upon ourselves, such as wars, excesses, and many others which it would be in our power to avoid, are of a mixed nature. They are brought upon us by vice, and their consequences are misery.

The sum of all these preventive and positive checks, taken together, forms the immediate check to population; and it is evident that, in every country where the whole of the procreative power cannot be called into action, the preventive and the positive checks must vary inversely as each other; that is, in countries either naturally unhealthy, or subject to a great mortality, from whatever cause it may arise, the preventive check will prevail very little. In those countries, on the contrary, which are naturally healthy, and where the preventive check is found to prevail with considerable force, the positive check will prevail very little, or the mortality be very small.

In every country some of these checks are, with more or less force, in constant operation; yet, notwithstanding their general prevalence, there are few states in which there is not a constant effort in the population to increase beyond the means of subsistence, which constantly tends to subject the lower classes of society to distress, and to prevent any great permanent melioration of their condition . . .

The labourer therefore must do more work, to earn the same as he did before. During this season of distress, the discouragements to marriage and the difficulty of rearing a family are so great, that the progress of population is retarded. In the mean time, the cheapness of labour, the plenty of labourers, and the necessity of an increased industry among them, encourage cultivators to employ more labour upon their land, to turn up fresh soil, and to manure and improve more completely what is already in tillage, till ultimately the means of subsistence may become in the same proportion to the population, as at the period from which we set out. The situation of the labourer being then again tolerably comfortable, the restraints to population are in some degree loosened; and, after a short period, the same retrograde and progressive movements, with respect to happiness, are repeated.

When population has increased nearly to the utmost limits of the food, all the preventive and the positive checks will naturally operate with increased force. Vicious habits with respect to the sex will be more general, the exposing of children more frequent, and both the probability and fatality of wars and epidemics will be considerably greater; and these causes will probably continue their operation till the population is sunk below the level of the food; and then the return to comparative plenty will again produce an increase, and, after a certain period, its further progress will again be checked by the same causes.

Source: From *An Essay on the Principle of Population*, sixth edition (London, 1826).

Summing up: Malthus's key points

Malthus argued that he required only two postulates to prove the unattainability of the millennium Godwin and Condorcet foresaw: the first, 'that food is necessary to the existence of man'; the second, that 'the passion between the sexes is necessary, and will remain nearly in its present state.' The potential increase of population, when unchecked, is in a geometrical ratio, whereas subsistence can increase only in an arithmetical ratio. It is obvious therefore that the growth powers of population greatly exceed those of the food supply. This implies that there must exist a strong and constantly operating check on population because of the difficulty of obtaining subsistence. The latter is clearly attributable to diminishing returns on land.

Malthus's numeracy

Moral restraint: the preventative check

Many critics of the first edition of Malthus's essay offered the counter-argument that 'Providence never sends mouths without sending meat.'[5] Realizing that much additional work needed to be done to support the inferences he drew from his ratios, Malthus undertook a more thorough study of population behavior that became the basis for his much enlarged second edition that was published in 1803.[6] In it he undertook to illustrate the 'power and universality' of his principle of population 'from the best authenticated accounts that we have of the state of other countries.'

His investigation consisted of two parts. The first related to primitive people about whom we have learned from the writers of antiquity, among them Plato, whose *Republic* prohibited marriage for men under 30, and Aristotle, who recommended that their marriage be postponed at least until age 37. The second part contains information he collected on his visits to the continent and learned from the writings of travelers who visited the islands of the South Seas, Australia, and the Andeans. These established abundant evidence of harsh conditions tending to prevent increases in population, including infanticide, high mortality from war, unsanitary conditions, and scarcity of food.

Scandinavia and Russia were among the countries in modern Europe that were a source of actual statistical data derived from marriage, birth and death registries. He noted that Norway was substantially the only European country not experiencing war and epidemic disease, which are the two main positive checks to population growth. Yet its population increased slowly because preventative checks in the form of restrictions to early marriage were widely observed. Specifically, young men were subject to ten years of military service, and most ministers refused to marry those who were unable to demonstrate they could support a family. Malthus also visited Switzerland where he found that postponement of marriage was also part of the culture, as was also the case in England, Wales, Scotland, and Ireland. He concluded that the facts of their population growth confirmed his principle of population. More important, with respect to the Europe of his day, the positive checks were less prevalent than they were either in the past, or in the more uncivilized parts of the world. He also expressed the view that 'moral restraint' was now more prevalent, especially in modern Europe than he first believed.

Moral restraint: the preventative check

Moral restraint is interpreted to mean the postponement of marriage, coupled with sexual abstinence, until such time as a family can adequately be supported. While misery and vice were the primary checks to population growth in ancient and primitive societies, Malthus came to regard prudent restraint as the only morally acceptable check in modern civilizations. Educate the individual, he urged, to avoid instant gratification and postpone marriage until a person is capable of supporting a family.

This can best be accomplished, Malthus believed, within the framework of a social system that encourages people to be responsible in their personal behavior. The existing system of private property promises the most desirable results in this regard. Despite economic inequality, the system also assures opportunity to those who are ambitious and prudent to rise by their own efforts. Malthus was therefore critical of the Poor Laws on the grounds that they encouraged indolence and raised the level only of the weakest members of society, and this is at the expense of the others. If people knew they could not count on parish relief, the ordinary motives of self-interest would force them to help themselves. Thus, Malthus became an enthusiastic supporter of popular education to teach enlightened self-interest; at the same time, he opposed the continuation of poor relief.

The tendency toward subsistence wages

Malthus and his contemporaries theorized that the money wage rate is determined by the ratio between the labor force (i.e. the proportion of the population that is typically employed) and the size of the wage fund. It is among the main implications of Malthus's theory of population growth that, given the irrevocable tendency toward diminishing returns and the rising price of food, the level of *real* wages will tend toward subsistence unless the rate of population growth is sufficiently checked by moral restraint.

Since it was generally assumed that the wage fund is a constant proportion of the capitalists' stock, it follows that continued population growth will depress both the money and real wage rates of workers to the lowest level compatible with subsistence. This tendency could be offset if capital stock, and therefore the wage fund, increased more rapidly than the population. Thus, Malthus associated rising wage rates with a high ratio of capital to labor, whereas falling wage rates were associated with a low ratio of capital to labor. This is a conclusion with which modern economists are in accord, but for a different reason. Modern analysis maintains that a high capital-to-labor ratio affects labor's marginal productivity and consequently its claim to income.

Rent, the Corn Laws, and commodity gluts

The tendency for rents to rise

Malthus and classical thinkers associated the growth of population not only with downward pressure on wage rates (given the size of the wage fund), but also with a tendency for rents to rise. Malthus's *The Nature and Causes of Rent* primarily addressed the question of whether rent is a monopoly income, as implied by Smith and sometimes the Physiocrats.[7] Reflecting his concern about the issue of restoring the Corn Law, Malthus suggested that the subject of rent 'has perhaps a particular claim to our attention at the present moment on account of the discussions which are going on respecting the Corn Laws, and the effects of rent on the price of raw produce and the progress of agricultural improvement.' His pamphlet antedated the appearance of Ricardo's *Essay on the Influence of a Low Price of Corn on the Profits of Stock* (1815).

Malthus advanced three reasons for the appearance of rent. First, that land produces more than enough to maintain its cultivators.[8] This fact alone makes rent 'a bountiful gift from providence' rather than monopolistic scarcity. Second, he argued, the necessaries of life are uniquely capable of 'creating their own demand or of raising up the number of demanders in proportion to the quantity of necessaries produced.'[9] It is because population increases with the food supply that its price rises above its cost of production and creates rent as a surplus. Must we not therefore grant, Malthus asks, that the appearance of rent reflects a gift that God has bestowed on humans in the quality of the soil that enables them to maintain more persons than are necessary to work it?[10] Malthus clearly regards the appearance of rent as inherent in the progress of society, according to the dictates of natural law. The third cause of rent is that, except in a new country, the most fertile land is comparatively scarce, and there is not enough to supply all our wants. When population growth and diminishing returns make it necessary to resort to inferior lands, the products produced thereon will have to be priced high enough to pay their costs of production. Superior lands will then receive rent because the cost of producing on them is lower.

The comparative scarcity of fertile land was viewed in a very different light by Malthus than by his contemporary, David Ricardo. To Malthus, it seemed that the superiority of the best land is 'a bountiful gift from providence.' This view is expressed in his *Principles of Political Economy* in which he concludes his chapter 'Of the rent of land' with the statement that

> in every point of view, then, in which the subject can be considered, that quality of land which, by the laws of our being, must terminate in rent, appears to be a boon most important to the happiness of mankind; and I am persuaded that its value can only be underrated by those who still labour under some mistake as to its nature, and its effects on society.[11]

Ricardo, unlike Malthus, was persuaded that rent is due to the 'niggardliness of nature,' which not only causes rents to rise but causes them to absorb a progressively larger proportion of the national product in a closed economy. On these grounds, and in opposition to Malthus, he advocated repeal of the Corn Laws.

Rent as a differential surplus

Malthus's theory of rent (which is also that of Ricardo and the classical school), lends itself readily to modern terminology and apparatus, for it is, in essence, a marginal productivity theory, as is evident from the example that follows.[12] Unlike Turgot, whose literary example depicted capital and land as variable factors, Malthus proceeded in terms of a numerical example in which increasing inputs of labor are used to produce a product, say wheat on lands that are of equal area but successively less productive or well situated. Production proceeds by applying successive equal doses of labor and capital to fixed quantities of different grades of land. The total and marginal outputs yielded are summarized in Table 6.1. The portion of the table that relates to total output shows the tendency toward diminishing returns as additional equal doses of labor and capital are applied to progressively less productive lands A through D. The table also shows the additional, or *marginal*, output resulting from additional doses of labor and capital to each grade of land. Strictly speaking, marginal analysis involves very small increments, whereas the numbers used here are quite large, but they are convenient for illustrating the relationship between the total and the marginal product.

Table 6.1 enables us to visualize the number of doses of labor and capital that can economically be applied to each grade of land. Assume that each dose of labor and capital costs $100 to employ and that the market price of wheat is $1. It is obvious that the output potential of land grade D warrants

Table 6.1 Diminishing returns on land

Inputs of labour and capital	Total output of wheat				Marginal output of wheat			
	A	B	C	D	A	B	C	D
0	0	0	0	0	–	–	–	–
1	400	300	200	100	400	300	200	100
2	600	475	300	–	200	175	100	–
3	750	575	–	–	150	100	–	–
4	850	–	–	–	100	–	–	–

the application of one dose. This is the case because the marginal cost of these inputs is exactly equal to the *marginal* value product, which is the marginal physical product multiplied by the market price. Market price is equal to the cost of production on marginal land and is the same for all sellers under competitive conditions. On Grade D land the cost of labor and capital absorbs the entire product, whereas lands A, B, and C yield a surplus of $100, $275, and $450, respectively. These amounts go to the landlord as rent; Grade D land is the extensive margin of cultivation that yields an output whose value is just equal to the labor and capital cost of producing it. Thus, it is no-rent land.

The same principle is applicable to intra-marginal land; thus, it pays to cultivate grades A, B, and C *intensively* until the value of the marginal product produced is just equal to the marginal cost of producing it. Cultivation will therefore continue until *returns at the intensive margin of cultivation are equal to those at the extensive margin*. The variable factor, that is, the labor and capital component, receives the value of the marginal product as its return, while the fixed factor (land, in this instance) receives the difference between the total revenue and the payments going to labor and capital. This difference is the surplus called rent. Rent is not part of the cost of production in that its elimination (for example, by a tax levied on it) would not affect the size of the product that a given quantity of labor and capital could produce. Thus, rent is an *effect* rather than a cause of value; and the rent share will increase as the extensive margin of cultivation is pushed further by increasing population and the consequent need for additional food and raw materials. This is a principle which both Malthus and Ricardo understood and which

shaped their very different views on the progress of population, the Corn Laws and the problem of commodity gluts. The latter problem is examined next.

The problem of commodity gluts

The post-Napoleonic War years subjected both Great Britain and France to severe economic disruption. The economic crisis prompted the Swiss historian and economist Jean Charles Sismondi to explore its source. While his first theoretical work, *De La Richesse Commerciale* (Paris, 1803), was essentially in the tradition of Adam Smith, his later *Nouveaux Principes de l'Economie Politique* (Paris, 1819), written against the background of the crises of the early nineteenth century, questioned the self-equilibrating character of the capitalistic system. It gave particular emphasis to the ever-increasing productive powers of the modern capitalistic system and reasoned that the worker, having only the purchasing power of subsistence wages, is unable to purchase all the products the system is capable of producing. The inevitable outcome is that further technological advances will necessarily worsen matters because competition among capitalists to employ capital profitably will intensify overproduction. Thus, Sismondi emphasized the potentially adverse effect on purchasing power that may occur under capitalism because workers do not own the capital goods with which they work. Inadequacy of consumer purchasing power manifests itself in overproduction which is the most striking feature of economic crises. His argument was, however, challenged by another French economist who joined an issue that *even now* remains a centerpiece of economic controversy.

Issues and Answers from the Masterworks 6.2

Issue

Is it possible for an economy to experience a general commodity glut as a consequence of producing goods for which no market can be found? Are the resulting gluts substantially worsened when commodities are imported from abroad?

J. B. Say's answer

From *A Treatise on Political Economy,* Chapter 15.

Of the demand or market for products

It is common to hear adventurers in the different channels of industry assert that their difficulty lies not in the production, but in the disposal of commodities; that products would always be abundant, if there were but a ready demand, or market for them. When the demand for their commodities is slow, difficult, and productive of little advantage, they pronounce money to be scarce; the grand object of their desire is, a consumption brisk enough to quicken sales and keep up prices. But ask them what peculiar causes and circumstances facilitate the demand for their products, and you will soon perceive that most of them have extremely vague notions of these matters; that their observation of facts is imperfect, and their explanation still more so; that they treat doubtful points as matter of certainty, often pray for what is directly opposite to their interests, and importunately solicit from authority a protection of the most mischievous tendency.

To enable us to form clear and correct practical notions in regard to markets for the products of industry, we must carefully analyse the best established and most certain facts, and apply to them the inferences we have already deduced from a similar way of proceeding; and thus perhaps we may arrive at new and important truths, that may serve to enlighten the views of the agents of industry, and to give confidence to the measures of governments anxious to afford them encouragement.

A man who applies his labour to the investing of objects with value by the creation of utility of some sort, can not expect such a value to be appreciated and paid for, unless where other men have the means of purchasing it. Now, of what do these means consist? Of other values of other products, likewise the fruits of industry, capital, and land. Which leads us to a conclusion that may at first sight appear paradoxical, namely, that it is production which opens a demand for products.

Thus, to say that sales are dull, owing to the scarcity of money, is to mistake the means for the cause; an error that proceeds from the circumstance, that almost all produce is in the first instance exchanged for money, before it is ultimately converted into other produce: and the commodity, which recurs so repeatedly in use, appears to vulgar apprehensions the most important of commodities, and the end and object of all transactions, whereas it is only the medium. Sales cannot be said to be dull because money is scarce, but because other products are so. There is always money enough to conduct the circulation and mutual interchange of other values, when those values really exist. Should the increase of traffic require more money to facilitate it, the want is easily supplied, and is a strong indication of prosperity – a proof that a great abundance of values has been created, which it is wished to exchange for other values. In such cases, merchants know well enough how to find substitutes for the product serving as the medium of exchange or money: and money itself soon pours in, for this reason, that all produce naturally gravitates to that place where it is most in demand. It is a good sign when the business is too great for the money; just in the same way as it is a good sign when the goods are too plentiful for the warehouses.

When a superabundant article can find no vent, the scarcity of money has so little to do with the obstruction of its sale, that the sellers would gladly receive its value in goods for their own consumption at the current price of the day: they would not ask for money, or have any occasion for that product, since the only use they could make of it would be to convert it forthwith into articles of their own consumption.

This observation is applicable to all cases, where there is a supply of commodities or of services in the market. They will universally find the most extensive demand in those places, where the most of values are produced; because in no other places are the sole means of purchase created, that is, values. Money performs but a momentary function in this double exchange; and when the transaction is finally closed, it will always be found, that one kind of commodity has been exchanged for another.

It is worth while to remark, that a product is no sooner created, than it, from that instant, affords a market for other products to the full extent of its own value. When the producer has put the finishing hand to his product, he is most anxious to sell it immediately, lest its value should diminish in his hands. Nor is he less anxious to dispose of the money he may get for it; for the value of money is also perishable. But the only way of getting rid of money is in the purchase of some product or other. Thus, the mere circumstance of the creation of one product immediately opens a vent for other products . . . One kind of production would seldom outstrip every other, and its products be disproportionately cheapened, were production left entirely free.

The position of a nation, in respect of its neighbours, is analogous to the relation of one of its provinces to the others, or of the country to the town; it has an interest in their prosperity, being sure to profit by their opulence. The government of the United States, therefore, acted most wisely, in their attempt, about the year 1802, to civilize their savage neighbours, the Creek Indians. The design was to introduce habits of industry amongst them, and make them producers capable of carrying on a barter trade with the States of the Union; for there is nothing to be got by dealing with a people that have nothing to pay. It is useful and honourable to mankind, that one nation among so many should conduct itself uniformly upon liberal principles. The brilliant results of this enlightened policy will demonstrate, that the systems and theories really destructive and fallacious, are the exclusive and jealous maxims acted upon by the old European governments, and by them most impudently styled *practical truths*, for no other reason, as it would seem, than because they have the misfortune to put them in practice. The United States will have the honour of proving experimentally, that true policy goes hand-in-hand with moderation and humanity.

From this fruitful principle, we may draw this further conclusion, that it is no injury to the internal or national industry and production to buy and import commodities from abroad; for nothing can be bought from strangers, except with native products, which find a vent in this external traffic. Should it be objected, that this foreign produce may have been bought with specie, I answer, specie is not always a native product, but must have been bought itself with the products of native industry; so that, whether the foreign articles be paid for in specie or in home products, the vent for national industry is the same in both cases.

Source: Reprinted from the first American edition of Jean-Baptiste Say, *A Treatise on Political Economy, or the Production, Distribution, and Consumption of Wealth*, Chapter 15 (reprinted in 1880 by Claxton, Rensen & Haffelfinger in Philadelphia).

Summing up: Say's key points

Say's most fundamental point is that goods are intended to be exchanged for other goods; every act of production simultaneously creates a market for the product produced by making the monetary means of purchasing it available in the form of income payments to those engaged in its production. Aggregate effective demand is thus necessarily the equivalent of aggregate supply – a generalization that has become known as *Say's law*.[13] Its logic asserts that a state of general overproduction, or glut, is impossible, even though specific commodities may, at times, be produced in greater quantities than the demand for them warrants. Such maladjustments, Say argued, tend to correct themselves. If the supply of a given commodity is excessive, the losses incurred in its production will soon diminish its supply; conversely, if the supply falls short of current demand, the resulting high profits will expand output so that individual demands and supplies will tend to be balanced.

Malthus's rebuttal to Say's Law: the need for unproductive consumption

Malthus's view of gluts reflected a substantially different conception of the nature and source of aggregate demand than is implicit in Say's law of markets. Essentially, Say's view conceives of the economy as a barter society, in which goods are intended to be exchanged for other goods; every act of production simultaneously creates a market for the product produced by making available the monetary means of purchasing it. An excess supply of all goods relative to the aggregate demand for them is thus a logical impossibility. Aggregate demand and aggregate supply are necessarily equal.[14]

Malthus argued that a society composed of landowners and laborers is often likely to experience an inadequate level of effective demand for commodities. Although he did not specifically define the term *effective demand*, he meant the ability and willingness of the community to buy a commodity at a price equivalent to its labor command value; that is, at a price that will enable the producer to recover costs plus profit at the prevailing rate. Thus, Malthus regarded the market price, which results from the interaction of supply and demand, as much more important than the natural price of a commodity. He agreed with Ricardo that rising food costs will gradually eliminate profits through their impact on wages, since wages and profits vary inversely. But he also maintained that, to explain *short-run* variations in profits, it is necessary to explain the phenomenon of gluts.

When profits rise, there will be a tendency for capitalists to spend a smaller proportion of their gains and to save more. They are more interested in accumulation than in making large expenditures on consumer goods. Their savings increase the stock of capital and eventually output, which increases the problem of maintaining effective demand. It is for this reason that Malthus was concerned about the insufficiency of working class expenditures for maintaining the level of effective demand. His concern was to identify a source of purchasing power to supplement spending out of wages, and thought rent to be such a source. Whereas wage incomes are costs of production as well as sources of purchasing power, what is needed to maintain profit is a differential surplus whose expenditure adds to effective demand without adding to costs of production. Malthus therefore regarded increased rents (which could be achieved by restoring the Corn Laws) as an ideal source of 'unproductive consumption.'

There are other classes of unproductive consumers besides landowners – menial servants, statesmen, physicians, judges, lawyers, clergymen, and so forth. Their expenditures also add to the effective demand for goods and thus offset the deficiency of consumer demand that arises out of the savings process. Malthus maintained that it is absolutely essential for an economy with great powers of production to have a body of unproductive consumers. Unproductive consumption is the 'safety valve' which he viewed as potentially diminishing the undesirable effects of too rapid accumulation. Without it, the economy will experience periods of commodity glut and capital redundancy.[15]

Progress and the structure of economy

It should be apparent from Malthus's view of unproductive consumption that he was concerned about the structure of the economy. Malthus thought England's economic health would be best served by achieving a balance between the industrial and agricultural sectors that would enable the country to be independent of foreign sources of food.[16] Unlike Ricardo, he favored restricting free trade in corn on the ground that it would contribute to maintaining the effective demand for labor. His argument is presented in his *The Grounds of an Opinion on the Policy of Restricting the Importation of Foreign Corn* (1815). In it, he argues that it is desirable for England to encourage domestic production of grain on a scale that would make her independent of foreign supplies, even though it would tend to raise English crop prices. This position is, he tells us, mainly the result of French legislation to restrict the export of corn. Since England was greatly dependent

on exports from France to supplement her home supply, he argued that a system of free trade would render domestic supplies inadequate in years of scarcity abroad. In view of England's special circumstances, therefore, he argued in favor of the Corn Laws to protect crop prices and landlord rent.

Malthus's second reason for advocating restricted corn trade for England was his observation that increased industrialization tends to be accompanied by more frequent and more severe business fluctuations, which particularly burden the lower classes, and that it is therefore desirable for England, which is 'the most manufacturing [country] of any ever recorded in history, ... that its agriculture should keep pace with its manufactures, even at the expense of retarding in some degree the growth of manufactures.'[17] He thus concluded that agricultural protection was in the interest of general abundance in England, and advantageous to the working class who should be protected against adverse price movements originating abroad. It would also minimize the evil effects of unemployment where there is rapid industrialization.

Malthus also observed that while predominantly agricultural economies tend to be poorer than those which are more industrialized, the 'premature check' to the progress of the population is due to the remains of the feudal system. While he asserted the primary importance of agriculture in promoting the progress of population and wealth, subsequent editions of his *Principles* became increasingly cognizant of the fact that industrialization also contributed to maintaining and enhancing the effective demand for labor.

Concluding remarks

The impact of an individual's work manifests itself in a variety of ways. First, and perhaps foremost, it may influence subsequent work in its own discipline in terms of method or content. It may also become incorporated in some way into policy measures and so guide the solution of practical problems. Finally, it may inspire new work in other fields of knowledge. Malthus's efforts have the distinction of having borne fruit in all these directions.[18]

In Malthus's day, the principles that subsequently became known as the laws of classical economics were only beginning to be forged, and he contributed greatly to their development, in terms of both content and methodology. At a time when inquiry was at least as much on practical policy as on the discovery of principles, Malthus used the deductive method to establish formal principles. Both the principle of population and the principle of effective demand are propositions he established by means of deductive logic.

In establishing these principles, Malthus was a pioneer in applying the methods of deductive logic to the complex world of daily events. These events crystallized themselves to Malthus chiefly in the form of worker misery. The poverty suffered by the laboring classes before the Napoleonic Wars was compounded by unemployment. Anticipating the policy orientation of philosophical radicalism, Malthus concluded the best way to improve the living standards of the laboring classes was to control their number. His approach was that of the moral scientist schooled in the *a priori* method of the Cambridge tradition. To this, he added a wealth of historical and contemporary factual information that guided him in the proper selection and formulation of the premises from which he ultimately arrived, by means of deductive logic, at his conclusions. His work thus has the merit of being the first thorough application of the inductive method to study popula-

tion growth and the supply of labor. Indeed, Alfred Marshall, who is remembered by historians of economic thought as the founder of the neoclassical tradition, hailed Malthus's Essay as 'the first thorough application of the inductive method to social science.'

Malthus's principle of effective demand maintained that the aggregate demand for labor is derived from the aggregate demand for commodities and determines the ability of a population to grow. Malthus maintained, on the basis of this principle, that excessive savings are associated with gluts of commodities and capital, and therefore with an inadequate demand for labor.

Not until the worldwide depression of the 1930s was the principle of effective demand restated and extended by John Maynard Keynes. Thus, the importance of Malthus's principle of effective demand has come to be appreciated only in this century. In the interim, Say's Law led to the conclusion that an economy whose operation is guided by a freely operating price system will automatically tend fully to employ its resources, including labor. While Malthus's name and reputation have been immortalized by his principle of population behavior, Keynes's praise for his articulation of the principle of effective demand has raised his stature far beyond what it would be on the basis of the population principle only.[19]

In the Western world, the triumphs of technology and the practice of contraception have intervened to counteract the dire implications of Malthus's theory of population growth. But given the premises from which Malthus started, no other conclusion is possible than the one at which he arrived. This is all too evident in areas of the world like Asia, in which the premises on which Malthus rested his conclusions are empirically verifiable. Although the *Essay* prompted angry protests when it first appeared, its eventual impact on the English Parliament was apparent in the passage of a new Poor Law in 1834, which, in comparison with the earlier legislation, greatly limited aid to the poor, particularly those of illegitimate birth. Malthus's principle of population was also significant in causing the first census to be taken in 1801. It also inspired innumerable empirical and theoretical works on demography, besides serving as an inspiration to Charles Darwin in the development of his theory of evolution.[20]

Notes

1 Edwin Canaan, A *History of the Theories of Production and Distribution in English Political Economy* (London: Staples Press, 1953), pp. 148–52.

2 Elie Halévy, *The Growth of Philosophical Radicalism* (New York: Augustus Kelley, 1949), Chapter 1.

3 W. Stark (ed.), *Jeremy Bentham's Economic Writings*, vol. 3 (London: Allen & Unwin, 1954), pp. 436–37.

4 The tendency toward diminishing returns had, of course, already been noted by Turgot in *Observations sur le Memoire de M. de Saint-Peravy* (Paris, 1768). James Anderson, a Scottish farmer and a prolific writer, also predated Malthus in his recognition of diminishing returns in relation to rent in *An Inquiry into the Nature of the Corn Laws with a View to the New Corn Bill Proposed for Scotland* (London, 1777). Nineteenth-century English economists appear to have been influenced less by the work of their predecessors than by the actual experience of England during the Napoleonic Wars. Edward West has been credited for recognizing before Malthus or Ricardo that the high price of raw produce, which enables land to yield a high rent, is due to diminishing returns. (See the listing for Edward West, *The New Palgrave* vol. 4 p. 898.)

5 Kenneth Smith, *The Malthusian Controversy* (London: Routledge and Kegan Paul, 1951), Book 2, 'The development of controversy.'

6 In *The Malthusian Population Theory* (London:

Faber and Faber), G. F. McCleary provides a detailed account and analysis of the origins and sources of the second and subsequent editions of Malthus's *Essay on the Principle of Population*, published in 1803.

7 This was also the position of David Buchanan, whose argument that rent is the result of a monopoly of land appears to have had a good deal to do with Malthus's inquiry.

8 Thomas Malthus, *Principles of Political Economy*, 2nd (edn) (1836), Reprints of Economic Classics (New York: Augustus Kelley, 1964), p. 140.

9 Malthus, *Principles of Political Economy*, 2nd (edn) (1836), Reprints of Economic Classics (New York: Augustus Kelley, 1964)

10 Malthus, *Principles of Political Economy*, 2nd (edn) (1836), Reprints of Economic Classics (New York: Augustus Kelley, 1964), p. 147.

11 Malthus, *Principles of Political Economy*, 2nd (edn) (1836), Reprints of Economic Classics (New York: Augustus Kelley, 1964), p. 217.

12 J. B. Clark and Philip H. Wicksteed first appreciated this aspect of Ricardo's theory of rent. This is discussed in Chapter 13.

13 Jacob Hollander has maintained that the generalization known as Say's law was, in fact, conceived by James Mill before it was developed by Say. See Hollander's *Introduction to Ricardo's Notes on Malthus* (Baltimore: Johns Hopkins Press, 1928). In any event, Mill evidently taught the principle to Ricardo.

14 J. J. Spengler examines the relationship between Malthus's theory of population and his theory of aggregate demand with great insight in 'Malthus total population theory: a restatement and reappraisal,' *Canadian Journal of Economics and Political Science*, 11 (February–May 1945), reprinted in *Essays in Economic Thought: Aristotle to Marshall*, edited by J. J. Spengler and W. R. Allen (Chicago: Rand McNally, 1960). G. N. Gilbert argues that by 1817, the anti-industrial tone of Malthus's original *Essay* is displaced by the view that workers are not necessarily harmed by the reallocation of labor from farm to factory because manufactured comforts are an alternative to increased food consumption. See 'Economic growth and the poor in Malthus's essay on population,' *History of Political Economy*, 12 (1) (1980), pp. 83–96.

15 Interpretations of Malthus's analysis of aggregate demand, economic growth, and fluctuation include W. A. Eltis, 'Malthus's theory of effective demand and growth,' *Oxford Economic Papers*, 32 (March, 1980); Samuel Holland 'Malthus and the post-Napoleonic depression,' *History of Political Economy* (Fall 1969); L. A. Dow, 'Malthus on sticky wages, the upper turning point, and general glut,' *History of Political Economy*, 9 (Fall, 1977); and, S. Rashid, 'Malthus model of general gluts,' in the same volume.

16 Malthus's position on protectionism in agriculture has also become a matter of renewed discussion in response to Samuel Hollander's argument in 'Malthus's abandonment of agricultural protectionism: a discovery in the history of economic thought,' *American Economic Review*, 82 (July, 1992), pp. 650–59. Hollander's reinterpretation is challenged by J. M. Pullen in 'Malthus on agricultural protection. An alternative view,' *History of Political Economy*, 27 (Fall, 1995), pp. 517–30. Hollander replies in 'More on Malthus and agricultural protection,' *History of Political Economy*, 27 (Fall, 1995), pp. 531–38.

17 Malthus, *Observations on the Effects of the Corn Laws* (1814).

18 For general assessments of Malthus's work, see James Bonar's classic *Malthus and His Work* (London: George Allen and Unwin, 1924) and the more recent assessment of Lionel Robbins, 'Malthus as an economist,' *Economic Journal*, 77 (June, 1967). On Malthus's relation to Utilitarianism, see Elie Halévy, *The Growth of Philosophical Radicalism* (New York: Augustus Kelley, 1949).

19 J. M. Keynes; Robert Malthus, in *Essays in Biography* (London: Macmillan, 1933).

20 Francis Darwin, ed., *Life and Letters of Charles Darwin*, vol. I (New York, D. Appleton, 1897), p. 83.

Questions for discussion and further research

1 From a philosophical point of view, most post-Smithian writers were Utilitarians. What was the chief concern of Utilitarianism (or philosophical radicalism)?

Glossary of terms and concepts

Commodity gluts

An insufficiency of aggregate effective demand that results in unsold goods.

Diminishing returns

In a given state of the arts, the productive capacity of land increases at a decreasing rate beyond a certain point. Malthus inferred from this principle that the food supply could only be increased at an arithmetical rate.

Hedonism

The explanation of human behavior in terms of the objective of maximizing pleasure and minimizing pain. In economics, the counterparts of pleasure and pain are monetary gains and losses.

Principle of population

The hypothesis that, in the absence of restraints, population will tend to increase at a geometrical rate as long as there is a food supply.

Say's identity

Equality between aggregate demand and supply *in money terms*. It is predicated on the assumption that the demand for cash balances is zero. *Say's equality* assumes that money serves only as a medium of exchange and not as a store of value.

Utilitarianism

A system of ethics, primarily associated with Bentham and other philosophic radicals, that maintained that the ideal of 'the greatest good for the greatest number' could be achieved by educative and punitive measures to promote the kinds of individual choices that would maximize human happiness.

2 What was the nature of Malthus's intellectual dispute with Godwin?

3 What is Malthus's population principle? What

was the counter-argument of his critics? What sort of empirical evidence was Malthus able to provide to support his population principle in his revised *Essay*?

4 Malthus is among the first to examine the phenomenon of economic crisis. How does his position on the Corn Laws relate to his analysis of the cause of commodity gluts and his recommendations? Why was Malthus not adverse to landlords receiving increasing rents?

Notes for further reading

From *The New Palgrave*

James Griffin and Derek Parfit on hedonism, vol. 2, pp. 634–35; Ross Harrison on Jeremy Bentham, vol. 1, pp. 226–28; B. Hilton on Corn Laws, vol. 1, pp. 670–71; J. M. Pullen on Thomas Robert Malthus, vol. 3, pp. 280–85; S. Rashid on Malthus and classical economics, vol. 3, pp. 285–90; D. R. Weir on Malthus's theory of population, vol. 3, pp. 290–93; C. Welsh on Utilitarianism, vol. 4, pp. 770–75; Thomas Sowell on Jean-Baptist Say and Say's law, vol. 4, pp. 249–51 and on Simonde de Sismondi vol. 4, pp. 348–50; Mark Blaug on Edward West, vol. 4, p. 898.

Selected references and suggestions for further reading

Bentham, Jeremy. *An Introduction to the Principles of Morals and Legislation* (Oxford: The Clarendon Press, 1879 [1789]).

Blaug, Mark. *Ricardian Economics* (New Haven: Yale University Press, 1958).

Cannan, Edwin. *A History of the Theories of Production and Distribution in English Political Economy from 1776 to 1848* (London: Staples, 1917).

Cassels, John M. 'A re-interpretation of Ricardo on value.' *Quarterly Journal of Economics* 46 (May 1935).

Garegnani, P. 'The classical theory of wages and the role of demand schedules in the determination of relative prices.' *Papers and Proceedings of American Economic Association* (May 1983), pp. 309–13.

Gilbert, O. N. 'Economic growth and the poor in Malthus's essay on population.' In *History of Political Economy* 12(1) (Spring, 1980), pp. 83–96.

Grampp, W. D. 'Malthus on money, wages and welfare.' *American Economic Review*, 46 (December, 1956), pp. 924–36.

Halévy, Elie. *The Growth of Philosophical Radicalism*, chapter 1 (New York: Augustus Kelley, 1949).

Hollander, Samuel. *The Economics of David Ricardo* (Toronto and Buffalo: University of Toronto Press, 1979).

Malthus, Thomas R. *An Inquiry into the Nature and Progress of Rent, and the Principles by Which It Is Regulated.* A reprint of economic tracts edited by J. H. Hollander (Baltimore: Johns Hopkins, 1903 [1815]).

Malthus, Thomas R. *The Principles of Political Economy, Considered with a View to Their Practical Application*, 2nd edn (New York: A. M. Kelley, 1951 [1836]).

Malthus, Thomas R. *An Essay on Population.* 2 vols. (London: J. M. Dent, 1914).

O'Brien, D. P. 'Ricardian economics and the economics of David Ricardo.' *Oxford Economic Papers*, 33 (1981), pp. 1–35.

Ricardo, David. *The Works and Correspondence of David Ricardo.* 10 vols. Edited by P. Sraffa with the collaboration of M. Dobb. (London: Cambridge University Press, 1951–55).

Ricardo, David. *The Works of David Ricardo.* Edited by R. R. McCulloch (London, 1886).

Rima, Ingrid H. 'James Mill and classical economics: a reappraisal.' *Eastern Economic Journal*, 2(2) (April, 1975).

Robbins, Lionel. *Robert Torrens and the Evolution of Classical Economics* (New York: St. Martin's Press, 1958), pp. 21–24.

Robbins, Lionel. Lecture 17, 'General review – Malthus on population,' in *A History of Economic Thought*, edited by S. Medema and W. Samuels (Princeton, NJ: Princeton University Press, 1998), pp. 167–75.

Roncaglia, Allesandro. 'Hollander's Ricardo.' *Journal of Post Keynesian Economics*, 4(3) (Spring, 1982), pp. 339–75.

Say, J. B. *A Treatise on Political Economy* or *Production, Distribution and Consumption of Wealth*. American edition, chapter 15 (Philadelphia: Rensen and Hafelfinger, 1880).

Spengler, J. J. 'Malthus's total population theory; a restatement and reappraisal.' In *Essays in Economic Thought: Aristotle to Marshall*, edited by J. J. Spengler and W. R. Allen (Chicago: Rand McNally, 1960).

Stark, William. *Jeremy Bentham's Economic Writings* (London: Allen & Unwin, 1954).

Thweatt, William O. 'James Mill and the early development of comparative advantage.' *History of Political Economy*, 8(2) (Summer, 1976).

Chapter 7

David Ricardo and William Nassau Senior: income shares and their long-term tendencies

Introduction

Ricardo's life and times (1772–1823)

The classical tradition achieved its peak development with the work of David Ricardo. It is remarkable that a person of his background should have made such a distinguished contribution to economics since he was destined as a youth to a business, rather than a scholarly, career. His father, a native of Holland, of the Jewish faith, settled in England and eventually became a member of the Stock Exchange. Young David was already in his father's employ at the age of 14, and it was fully expected that this would be his lifework. Indeed, he amassed a fortune in the exchange at such an early age that he had ample time to devote himself to such studies as took his fancy. This was accomplished largely on his own resources, for his marriage to a Quaker and subsequent conversion to Christianity estranged him from his father.

His first acquaintance with the subject to which he was to contribute so importantly was through Smith's *Wealth of Nations*, which came into his hands in 1799.[1] A decade was to elapse, however, before anything bearing Ricardo's name appeared in print. His contributions clearly reflected the transformation England had undergone in the 40-odd

years since the appearance of Smith's great work. England was still able to feed its people and even exported some grain as late as 1812 and 1813. England had long since experienced diminishing returns on land, and the price of bread was a major issue. Yet land owners pressured for increased protection against imports at a time when free trade appeared to be called for. Because of the pressure of diminishing returns, Ricardo found himself unable to share Smith's optimism regarding the future well-being of an ever increasing population. Without free importation of corn, he argued, food could not be cheap. Wages, therefore, would necessarily rise, lowering profits and impeding further accumulation. Ricardo's analysis was thus oriented to the question of economic progress, which drew his attention to the 'machinery question.' Unlike Smith, he regarded progress as being closely associated with the trend of the distributive shares. This was an intensely practical issue that necessarily led him into the policy question of free trade in corn and the theory of comparative advantage that underlies it. Although his style of writing was extremely abstract, there was nothing unrealistic about the issues Ricardo addressed. Indeed, the problems were many and pressing, and hinged closely on the fact that the country was becoming ever more populous in spite of emigration. Industrial-ization did not relieve the problem, for manu-facturing processes were also dependent on a fixed supply of land subject to diminishing returns. Moreover, the introduction of machinery created new problems quite unlike those that confront a predominantly agri-cultural nation.

Senior's life and times (1790–1864)

Compared with Ricardo, Nassau Senior's contributions to economics have not secured him a leading place in history. Yet, they pres-ent an important contrast with Ricardo's in three major respects. The first relates to the nature of capital, the second to the role of utility in relation to the determination of value, and the third – and perhaps most important – relates to the methodology of economics.

Nassau Senior's life was the rather ordin-ary one of the son of an Oxford educated vicar. He was admitted to the bar in 1819, and became a member of the Political Economy Club in 1823 (the year of Ricardo's untimely death from an ear infection). In 1825 he became first Drumand Professor of Political Economy at Oxford. The first edition of his *Outline of the Science of Political Economy* was published in 1836, and incorporated his Oxford lectures on that subject. Between his first and second Oxford appointments (the latter in 1847), he was a professor of political economy at King's College in London, from which he resigned following his advocacy that some of the revenues of The Church of Ireland be confiscated for the benefit of Roman Catholics. He also was a member of the commission for administering the Poor Laws, and wrote a large number of pamphlets and letters on the Poor Laws and the Factory Acts.

Ricardo's Principles of Political Economy and Taxation *(1817)*

Controversy about interpreting Ricardo's work

Some of the best minds in the economics pro-fession have directed their attention to inter-preting Ricardo's work, in particular his *Principles of Political Economy and Taxation* (1817). Two major studies were published during the 1950s; specifically, *The Works and Correspondence of David Ricardo* (1951–55), edited by Piero Sraffa in collaboration with Maurice Dobb, and *Ricardian Economics: A Historical Study*, by Mark Blaug. The ten Sraffa–Dobb volumes, in particular, offer a comprehensive reinterpretation of the Ricard-ian contribution based on new materials and correspondence that were fortuitously dis-covered after the bombings of London and its environs during the Second World War. Samuel Hollander's mammoth volume, *The Economics of David Ricardo*, subsequently challenged not only the Sraffa–Dobb inter-pretation but also the classic interpretations of several other eminent scholars.[2]

There is agreement that Ricardo's chief problem is to explain distribution; i.e. 'the natural course of rent, profit, and wages.' However, Samuel Hollander's interpretation of the relationship between these income shares and the exchange values (prices) of commodities has become an issue that has left many historians of economic thought unconvinced.[3] Because the controversy is unlikely to be resolved soon, this chapter presents an interpretation of Ricardo's con-tribution that reflects more closely the con-ventional wisdom that this great thinker is truly consistent with the classical tradition in which the distributive shares are determined separately from exchange values.[4] It is this characteristic that sets classical economics apart from the neoclassical tradition according to which wages, profit, and rent are linked as costs of production to the theory of exchange value and price determination. The latter continues into contemporary economics.

Ricardo's principles of political economy and taxation

Introduction

The major part of Ricardo's *Principles* was written in a single year and incorporated many of the ideas that had already been presented in his tracts and pamphlets. It appears to have been undertaken at least partly at the urging of James Mill.[5] The issues to which he addressed himself raised pressing policy questions relating to the distribution of the national product between rents, wages, and profits. Because he did not allow himself a long period for revision and reflection as did Smith and, perhaps, because his style is abstract and seldom relieved by digressions into history or philosophy, his work is far less readable than is Smith's. His rigorously deductive method was to set the pattern for much of the subsequent work in the field of political economy. This is not to say that political economy became divorced from philosophy and psychology, but rather that many of the observations that were previously made concerning human behavior and social institutions could now be accepted as postulates on which subsequent analysis could be based. The high degree of abstraction we encounter in Ricardo's work should not, however, cause us to forget that he was an intensely practical man with wide experience and knowledge about his contemporary world.

Ricardo's theory of exchange value

The measurement of exchange value

Smith, it will be recalled, regarded labor as the only unvarying measure of value. This 'labor command' measure of value was adequate for Smith's problem of identifying the growth of total real income over time or between countries. However, Ricardo found it inadequate for examining changes over time in the relation between rents, wages, and profits. He maintained that the value of labor is no less variable than that of gold or silver or corn. Its value is determined in precisely the same manner as the exchangeable value of any other commodity. There is no commodity that is truly an invariable measure of value: 'Of such a measure it is impossible to be possessed, because there is no commodity which is not itself exposed to the same variations as the things the value of which is to be ascertained; that is, there is none which is not subject to require more or less labour for its production.'[6]

Ricardo, nevertheless, recognized that his analysis of price could be greatly facilitated if he could identify a measure of value that is invariable in the sense of being independent of fluctuations in wage and profit rates. He solves the problem of identifying such a measure of value by making an assumption that enables him to rely on gold as a measure. Specifically, he assumes that the amount of labor and the corresponding amount of fixed capital necessary to produce gold remains constant over time and thus can serve as a near ideal measure of value.

If this assumption is made, money made of gold can be taken as an invariable standard of value. It can then be concluded that when changes are observed in commodity prices, they are the result of changes in the past and present labor required to produce their monetary unit of account, in terms of which values are expressed, which Ricardo takes to be constant by assumption.

The theory of exchange value

The source of exchange value

Ricardo began his analysis of exchange value by recalling Smith's distinction between value in use and value in exchange. He asserts that for a commodity to have value in exchange, it is essential that it have utility, although utility is not a measure of that value. Having utility, commodities derive their exchangeable value from their scarcity and from the quantity of labor required to obtain them.

Some commodities derive value from their scarcity alone. Such objects as rare pictures, books, coins, and other art objects that no amount of labor can reproduce, are in this class. The implication is that when supply cannot be adjusted, demand will rule in the determination of exchange value. The great bulk of commodities are, however, reproducible and therefore derive their value not from scarcity but from the labor requirements of production. Ricardo thus raises the following question.

Issues and Answers from the Masterworks 7.1

Issue

Are the exchange values of commodities which are not permanently scarce determined differently from those which can be produced without limit by the application of labor?

Ricardo's answer

From *from Principles of Political Economy and Taxation*: Chapter III

Not only the labour applied immediately to commodities affect their values, but also the labour which is bestowed on the implements, tools, and buildings with which such labour is assisted.

Even in that early state to which Adam Smith refers, some capital, though possibly made and accumulated by the hunter himself, would be necessary to enable him to kill his game. Without some weapon, neither the beaver nor the deer could be destroyed, and therefore the value of these animals would be regulated, not solely by the time and labour necessary to their destruction, but also by the time and labour necessary for providing the hunter's capital, the weapon, by the aid of which their destruction was effected.

Suppose the weapon necessary to kill the beaver was constructed with much more labour than that necessary to kill the deer, on account of the greater difficulty of approaching near to the former animal, and the consequent necessity of its being more true to its mark; one beaver would naturally be of more value than two deer, and precisely for this reason, that more labour would, on the whole, be necessary to its destruction. Or suppose that the same quantity of labour was necessary to make both weapons, but that they were of very unequal durability; of the durable implement only a small portion of its value would be transferred to the commodity, a much greater portion of the value of the less durable implement would be realised in the commodity which it contributed to produce.

All the implements necessary to kill the beaver and deer might belong to one class of men, and the labour employed in their destruction might be furnished by another class; still, their comparative prices would be in proportion to the actual labour bestowed, both on the formation of the capital and on the destruction of the animals. Under different circumstances of plenty or scarcity of capital, as compared with labour, under different circumstances of plenty or scarcity of the food and necessaries essential to the support of men, those who furnished an equal value of capital for either one employment or for the other might have a half, a fourth, or an eighth of the produce obtained, the remainder being paid as wages to those who furnished the labour; yet this division could not affect the relative value of these commodities, since whether the profits of capital were greater or less, whether they were 50, 20, or 10 per cent., or whether the wages of labour were high or low, they would operate equally on both employments.

If we suppose the occupations of the society extended, that some provide canoes and tackle necessary for fishing, others the seed and rude machinery first used in agriculture, still the same principle would hold true, that the exchangeable value of the commodities produced would be in proportion to the labour bestowed on their production; not on their immediate production only, but on all those implements or machines required to give effect to the particular labour to which they were applied . . .

The aggregate sum of these various kinds of labour determines the quantity of other things for which [say] stockings will exchange, while the same consideration of the various quantities of labour which have been bestowed on those other things will equally govern the portion of them which will be given for the stockings.

Source: *The Works of David Ricardo*, edited by J. R. McCulloch
(London: John Murray, 1886), pp. 22–3.

Summing up: Ricardo's key points

Although Smith talked of that early and rude state of society that preceded the accumulation of capital, for Ricardo commodities have past labor as well as present labor embodied in them. He questions whether Smith's conception of a stage of economic development in which capital becomes accumulated only in a later stage of economic development ever existed. 'Without some weapon neither the beaver nor the deer could be destroyed; therefore their value in exchange [as commodities] is determined by the time and labour necessary to destroy them, as well as the time and labour needed to produce the weapons (capital) the hunter needs to kill both animals.'

Ricardo was, of course, conceiving of real capital rather than money capital and inclu-

ded in this category, as did Smith, not only instruments of production such as buildings, machines, tools, and equipment, but also circulating capital, which is composed primarily of the wage fund out of which productive workers are supported. The primary role of capital, for Ricardo as for Smith, is to employ labor through advances from the wage fund. The exchange values of the goods they produce is proportional to both the direct labor involved in production, and that which is completed on the implements, tools, and buildings with which direct labor is assisted.

Ricardo's assumption of money as a stable unit of account implies the constancy of the general price level (i.e. the value of money). Thus, when Ricardo refers to price, it is synonymous with exchange value; and unless he specifically refers to 'market price,' he means 'natural price,' or the price in terms of embodied labor. Thus, Ricardo accepted that the ratio of exchange between goods, e.g. stockings and hats, will reflect their costs of production including both the current rate of wages and also of profits.

However, he has often been mistakenly regarded as a proponent of the labor theory of value. Actually, his concern was not to explain the ratio of exchange between commodities. His primary interest was to explain *alterations* in exchange values because these variations affect the wage, profit and rent distributive shares going to laborers, capitalists, and landlords. Ricardo reasoned that changes in the rate at which two commodities are exchanged for one another reflect changes in their relative content of past and present labor. This implies that exchange values are *not* affected by the rents yielded by non-marginal lands or by wage rate differences between workers or by changes in the level of wages and profits. Let us proceed with each of these in turn, bearing in mind that Ricardo's theory of value is a labor theory only in a very special sense.

The influence of land rent on exchange values

Ricardo's argument is that *changes* in the relative values of pairs of commodities reflect changes in the quantities of labor required to produce them. This argument requires him to demonstrate that rent is an *effect* rather than a cause of value; that is, rent must be eliminated as a determinant of exchange value. It is also necessary to demonstrate that wage-rate differentials among different kinds of workers, and/or changes in the level (or height) of wage rates, do not affect the exchange value that prevails between pairs of commodities.

Ricardo's initial examination of the phe-nomenon of rent in the *Principles* inquires whether 'the appropriation of land, and the consequent creation of rent, will cause any variation in the relative value of commodities, independently of the quantity of labour necessary to production.'[7] He defines rent as the compensation that is paid to the owner of land for the original and indestructible powers of the soil. Rent in this sense is distinct from the return resulting from capital improvements on land. These give rise to profits rather than rent, and are regulated by different factors from those that regulate rents.

When a country is first settled and rich and fertile land is abundant, relative to the size of the population to be supported, there will be no rent on any part of the land. In effect, land is a free good under such circumstances. It is not until the growth of population and the progress of society requires land of a second degree of fertility to be brought under cultivation that rent will emerge on land of the first quality. This rent will depend on the difference in the productive powers of the two pieces of land. With each subsequent need to bring less-productive land under cultivation, rent will appear on land that previously yielded no rent and will increase on those lands that already yield rent. This principle, as has already been noted, was also known to Malthus. However, it is Ricardo who specific-ally integrated it into the theory of value.

The exchange value of outputs produced on lesser grades of land is regulated by the same principle as that with respect to the out-puts produced on the best grade of land; namely, the amount of labor and capital embodied in its production, relative to that required to produce another product. When a growing population makes it necessary to cultivate land that is inferior to the best land first cultivated, equal labor–capital inputs will yield a smaller additional wheat output. Thus, it costs more to produce the same product on land that is second-grade land, either by virtue of location and/or fertility. Since two rates of exchange between wheat and another product cannot exist in the same purely competitive market, the exchange value of the entire output of wheat is regulated by the *least favorable* production requirements, that is, by the highest labor and capital cost of producing the required output. Competition dictates that there will be a single price for all units sold in the same market.

To whom goes the difference between the cost of producing output on better grades of land and the revenue received from its sale, and why? Since only one rate of wages and one rate of profit can prevail, the differential surplus goes to the owner of superior land in the form of rent. Ricardo, like Malthus, therefore, concluded that because rent is a *differential surplus*, it is not a cause of the exchangeable value of a product but *the result* of it.

This is, similarly, the case if additional labor and capital are employed on land already under cultivation because it will produce a greater product than can be gotten from the cultivation of additional land.

> In such case, capital will be preferably employed on the old land, and will equally create a rent; for rent is always the difference between the produce obtained by the employment of two equal quantities of capital and labour . . . In this case, as well as in the other, the capital last employed pays no rent.[8]

The payment of rent does not increase the exchangeable value of raw produce. Exchange value is regulated by the quantity of labor bestowed on land that pays no rent. Thus, says Ricardo, 'corn is not high because a rent is paid, but a rent is paid because [the price of] corn is high, and it has been justly observed that no reduction would take place in the price of corn, although landlords should forego the whole of their rent.'[9]

The influence of wage and profit levels on exchange values

After explaining why rent is not a determinant of price, Ricardo undertook to explain that neither wage-rate differentials nor changes in the price level affect the exchange values of commodities. He noted that different commodities are certain to be produced with different kinds, quantities, and qualities of labor. If the labor embodied in one commodity is superior, and therefore more highly paid than that embodied in another commodity, the effect on exchange value is precisely the same *as if a greater quantity of labor* had been used.

A different problem arises if the average level of all wages change. Because labor contents of pairs of commodities remain unchanged, only the ratio between wages and profits will become altered while the exchange value of pairs of goods remains the same. Like Smith before him, Ricardo thought of wages and profits as varying inversely with each other, although, as will be noted below, their respective arguments about the cause of the falling rate of profit were different.

While there necessarily will be wage-rate differences among different kinds of workers, Ricardo maintained that capital is sufficiently mobile and its employment opportunities sufficiently competitive to ensure a uniform rate of profit in the long run. The prices of all commodities would thus include the same percentage of profit on all the capital goods used in their production, so that variations in profit levels are not a source of variations in exchange value. While this principle is later qualified to take account of different proportions of fixed and circulation capital and capitals of unequal durability, it enabled Ricardo to conclude (having already eliminated rent as a determinant of exchange values) that changes in the relative values of pairs of commodities are derived entirely from changes in the quantities of labor required to produce them.

Why Ricardo's is not a labor theory of value

Having eliminated rent as a cost of production and demonstrated that neither wage rate differentials nor price level changes affect exchange values, Ricardo next examines the effect of different capital structures in bringing about alterations of exchange values. If the labor embodied in one commodity is superior, and therefore more highly paid than that embodied in some other commodity, the effect on exchange value is precisely the same as if a greater quantity of labor had been used.

Ricardo also recognized that capital structures reflect different ratios of fixed and circulating components, as well as capitals of different durabilities. When the ratio of fixed to circulating capital is increased, or when capital of greater durability is employed, it has the effect of increasing the length of time that must elapse before the final product comes to market. It follows that goods produced with equal amounts of fixed capital or capital of durability cannot sell at the same price as those produced with more circulating capital or less durable capital, even if the same quantity of labor is involved. Thus, the effect of capital structures is to qualify the principle that the relative quantities of labor used in production determines the exchange values of pairs of commodities. More specifically, Ricardo's concern was not to explain the ratio of exchange between commodities.

His primary interest was to explain alterations (i.e. *changes*) in exchange values because such variations affect the distributive shares going to laborers, capitalists, and landlords.

Capitalists must be compensated for the greater time lapse of a production process by greater profits. Thus, the effect of different capital structures is to qualify the principle that the relative quantities of labor used in production determine the exchange value of pairs of commodities.

The significance of this qualification has been a source of controversy and discussion from the outset. Ricardo himself seemed unclear on the matter. On the one hand, he minimized the importance of the modification and maintained that commodities are valuable in proportion to the quantity of labor bestowed on them.[10] On the other, he seemed to sense that the qualification he proposed brought the role of capital in the production process to the forefront and involved the cost of the capital component. The classic case in which he and his contemporaries came to grips with this problem was their effort to explain why wine has a greater value than grape juice, although no additional labor has been applied.[11] Ricardo eventually concluded that there must be some element other than accumulated labor in capital and that this other element is *waiting*. Thus, he appeared to be on the very brink of adopting a more sophisticated concept of capital and thus of giving up a labor theory of exchange value.

To appreciate why Ricardo, in fact, did neither of these things, we need only remind ourselves that he was concerned with explaining *changes* in exchange values rather than the ratio of exchange between goods at any moment of time. Further, he was concerned with the value problem only insofar as it affected the determination of the *distributive (i.e. income) shares*. Different capital–labor ratios necessarily mean that a change in the level of money wage rates (and therefore the rate of profit) must have an impact on the price *structure*. Ricardo realized that if the level of wages is rising, it will cause the prices of goods produced with a lower capital–labor ratio to rise relative to gold and to those produced with a higher capital–labor ratio. Gold, it will be recalled, serves Ricardo as an invariable measure of value because he assumed that it is produced with an average capital–labor ratio.

The prices of agricultural outputs produced by more labor-intensive methods than either gold or manufactured goods will rise when wage levels rise. On the other hand, the prices of manufactured goods will fall because they are produced under capital-intensive rather than labor-intensive conditions. This effect (now called the *Ricardo effect*) later became the basis for the inference that a rise in real wages will lead to a substitution of machinery for labor, which is described as 'lengthening' the average period of production.[12] Since Ricardo assumed that wage goods consist of agricultural products, while manufactured products are the luxuries consumed by capitalists and landlords, he was also able to conclude that, although the long-run trend of the economy's total product is one of growth, the share going to labor in real terms will not increase.

Distribution

An overview of Ricardo's system

As already noted, Ricardo's chief theoretical concern was the determination of rent, wages, and profit, and their probable future trend. 'To determine the laws which regulate this distribution is the principal problem in Political Economy; much as the science has been improved by the writings of Turgot, Steuart, Smith, Say, Sismondi, and others, they afford very little satisfactory information respecting the natural course of rent, profit and wages.'[13]

The outline of Ricardo's theory, especially as it relates to distribution, was already evident in his *Essay on the Influence of a Low Price of Corn on the Profits of Stock* (1815). Both the theory of rent and the dominant influence of diminishing returns in agriculture were clearly stated in the *Essay*. Two further components were needed for Ricardo's complete system: the subsistence theory of wages and his measure of value, both of which were developed in the *Principles*.

While his primary emphasis is on rent, it is the trend of the rate of profit that is most significant for economic progress. For Ricardo, high rents do not cause, but rather accompany, low profits, which is a residual remaining after the wage share has been paid from the national income, *net of rent*. In the Ricardian system, wages reflect the cost of producing food at the margin of cultivation. Thus, productivity of labor is relatively unimportant in Ricardo's view in the production of non-wage goods. The doctrine of land rent is therefore the heart of his whole distribution theory.

The tendency for rent to increase in the normal course of economic development is crucial to the future of both wages and profits, and thus to the generally pessimistic conclusions that are associated with Ricardo's analysis. It is also fundamental to the possible divergence of class interests that emerges so clearly in his thinking and that forms the theoretical basis for his position on the Corn Laws and other questions of policy. For while Malthus shared the Physiocratic view that rent results from the *bounty* of nature, Ricardo viewed it as the outcome of the *niggardliness* of nature. Rent is absent in a new country, in which land is still abundant. Rent emerges only when population growth necessitates a resort to inferior lands. The interests of landlords are thus antagonistic to those of every other class in society. For, while other classes have an interest in free trade in raw produce, the interests of the landed proprietor are best served by a rapid growth of population and a continuation of the Corn Laws.

The wage share and the wage rate

The trend of the rental share determines the proportions of the income shares received by workers and capitalists. For Ricardo, the prospects are not optimistic for workers. The total available to be paid out to all who live by wages is the equivalent of the wage fund, which is that part of real capital consisting of consumer goods customarily bought with wages. At any moment the average wage per worker is determined by the ratio between the wage fund and the number of workers to be paid. The *wage rate* expresses the average payment per worker on an hourly or weekly basis. The wage fund cannot be increased except by increased savings by capitalists, and it was implicitly assumed that, in the short run at least, substantial additions are unlikely.

It is likely that there will be new savings and thus additions to the wage fund in the long run. But there will also be a continuous growth in population and consequently a persistent tendency for real-wage income to approximate the subsistence level of workers and their families. This is the essence of Ricardo's statement that 'the natural price of labour is that price which will enable the labourers one with another to subsist and perpetuate their race without increase or diminution.'[14] The real wage can rise above this level in the short run, but this would encourage larger families by encouraging earlier marriages, more births, and a greater survival rate by children to maturity.

Ricardo does not, however, hypothesize any precise functional relationship between population growth and the real wage rate. Malthus himself stressed that lower death rates and reduced rates of infant mortality affect the size of the labor force only after a lag of 16 to 18 years, which is a conclusion Ricardo apparently accepted.[15] Thus, there is a tendency that, in the long run, the increase in the supply of labor will return the wage rate to its 'natural' level. The latter reflects the subsistence requirements of the workers and their families – recognizing, of course, that the level of subsistence reflects the length of the work day and the energy it requires, as well as the influence of habits and customs on consumption.

It is because real wages constantly tend toward their natural level that even with increases in the supply of capital and the wage fund, and improvements in the state of the arts, Ricardo foresaw little, if any, long-run improvement in the workers' economic status. Agricultural production lends itself less to scientific improvement than does manufacturing, and advances in the latter do little to make the resort to inferior lands unnecessary. Simultaneously, continuous population growth tends to offset whatever real gains are made.

Profits

Ricardo, as well as Smith and Malthus, conceived of profits as consisting of the entire net income received by business owners who manage and generally provide the capital funds for their enterprises. Part of this net income, namely, the return on the capital they provided, would today be called interest.

Ricardo also believed that the rate of profit from different employments of capital will tend toward equality. But what of the trend of this uniform rate? Ricardo, again like Smith, believed that profits and wages always vary inversely with one another. However, Smith simply argued that unless the opportunities for new investment expand faster than the rate of capital accumulation, increasing competition among competing capitals will lead to a falling rate of profit. For Ricardo, however, the decline in the rate of profit in the long run is inseparably linked to the rise in the trend of wages and thus to the cost of producing food at the margin of cultivation.

As long as the rate of profit is high enough to enable capitalists to save and invest, the supply of capital, and therefore the wage fund, will increase. However, with the continued growth of population and thus a resort to inferior soils, the labor cost of producing food and other raw produce will increase. The real share going to land rent increases, as does the *nominal* wage rate.

Although this serves to reduce profit levels, the worker is no better off in terms of what money wages will purchase. The cessation of growth thus ushers in the 'stationary state,' in which neither capital nor population can experience further growth.

As a practical matter, however, Ricardo believed that with technological progress and free trade the stationary state may lie far in the future.[16] Although diminishing returns pressures food costs upward even in the short run, Ricardo expected that the introduction of machinery (i.e. the conversion of circulating capital into fixed capital) would lower the prices of manufactured commodities and benefit all classes of society. However, this was only Ricardo's initial conclusion about the effect of machinery. He reconsidered the question in the third edition of his *Principles*. Instead of concluding that machinery would invariably be beneficial to all except those who are harmed by having to shift out of agricultural employment, Ricardo's reconsideration of the issue led him to a 'most revolutionary change.'[17]

Issues and Answers from the Masterworks 7.2

Issue
How can the introduction of machinery bring about a deterioration in the conditions of the laborer?

Ricardo's answer
From *Principles of Political Economy and Taxation* (third edition).

On machinery, Chapter XXXI
In the present chapter I shall enter into some inquiry respecting the influence of machinery on the interests of the different classes of society, a subject of great importance, and one which appears never to have been investigated in a manner to lead to any certain or satisfactory results. It is more incumbent on me to declare my opinions on this question, because they have, on further reflection, undergone a considerable change; and although I am not aware that I have ever published anything respecting machinery which it is necessary for me to retract, yet I have in other ways given my support to doctrines which I now think erroneous: it therefore becomes a duty in me to submit my present views to examination, with my reasons for entertaining them.

Ever since I first turned my attention to questions of political economy, I have been of the opinion that such an application of machinery to any branch of production as should have the effect of saving labour was a general good, accompanied only with that portion of inconvenience which in most cases attends the removal of capital and labour from one employment to another. It appeared to me that, provided the landlords had the same money rents, they would be benefited by the reduction in the prices of some of the commodities on which those rents were expended, and which reduction of price could not fail to be the consequence of the employment of machinery. The capitalist, I thought, was eventually benefited precisely in the same manner. He, indeed, who made the discovery of the machine, or who first usefully applied it, would enjoy an additional advantage by making great profits for a time; but, in proportion as the machine came into general use, the price of the commodity produced would, from the effects of competition, sink to its cost of production, when the capitalist would get the same money profits as before, and he would only participate in the general advantage as a consumer, by being enabled, with the same money revenue, to command an additional quantity of comforts and enjoyments. The class of labourers also, I thought, was equally benefited by the use of machinery, as they would have the means of buying more commodities with the same money wages, and I thought that no reduction of wages would take place because the capitalist would have the power of demanding and employing the same quantity of labour as before, although he might be under the necessity of employing it in the production of a new or, at any rate, of a different commodity. If, by improved machinery, with the employment of the same quantity of labour, the quantity of stockings could be quadrupled, and the demand for stockings were only doubled, some labourers would necessarily be discharged from the stocking trade; but as the capital which employed them was still in being, and as it was the interest of those who had it to employ it productively, it appeared to me that it would be employed on the production of some other commodity useful to the society, for which there could not fail to be a demand; for I was, and am, deeply impressed with the truth of the observation of Adam Smith, that 'the desire for food is limited in every man by the narrow capacity of the human stomach, but the desire of the conveniences and ornaments of building, dress, equipage, and household furniture, seems to have no limit or certain boundary.' As, then, it appeared to me that there would be the same demand for labour as before, and that wages would be no lower, I thought that the labouring class would, equally with the other classes, participate in the advantage, from the general cheapness of commodities arising from the use of machinery.

These were my opinions, and they continue unaltered, as far as regards the landlord and the capitalist; but I am convinced that the substitution of machinery for human labour is often very injurious to the interests of the class of labourers.

My mistake arose from the supposition that whenever the net income of a society increased, its gross income would also increase; I now, however, see reason to be satisfied that the one fund, from which landlords and capitalists derive their revenue, may increase, while the other, that upon which the labouring class mainly depend, may diminish, and therefore it follows, if I am right, that the same cause which may increase the net revenue of the country may at the same time render the population redundant, and deteriorate the condition of the labourer.

A capitalist, we will suppose, employs a capital of the value of £20,000, and that he carries on the joint business of a farmer and a manufacturer of necessaries. We will further suppose that £7000 of this capital is invested in fixed capital, viz. in buildings, implements, etc., etc., and that the remaining £13,000 is employed as circulating capital in the support of labour. Let us suppose, too, that profits are 10 per cent, and consequently that the capitalist's capital is every year put into its original state of efficiency and yields a profit of £2000.

Each year the capitalist begins his operations by having food and necessaries in his possession of the value of £13,000, all of which he sells in the course of the year to his own workmen for that sum of money, and, during the same period, he pays them the like amount of money for wages: at the end of the year they replace in his possession food and necessaries of the value of £15,000, £2000 of which he consumes himself, or disposes of as may best suit his pleasure and gratification. As far as these products are concerned, the gross produce for that year is £15,000, and the net produce £2000. Suppose, now, that the following year the capitalist employs half his men in constructing a machine, and the other half in producing food and necessaries as usual. During that year he would pay the sum of £13,000 in wages as usual, and would sell food and necessaries to the same amount to his workmen; but what would be the case the following year?

While the machine was being made, only one half of the usual quantity of food and necessaries would be obtained, and they would be only one-half the value of the quantity which was produced before. The machine would be worth £7500, and the food and necessaries £7500, and, therefore, the capital of the capitalist would be as great as before; for he would have, besides these two values, his fixed capital worth £7000, making in the whole £20,000 capital, and £2000 profit. After deducting this latter sum for his own expenses, he would have a no greater circulating capital than £5500 with which to carry on his subsequent operations; and, therefore, his means of employing labour would be reduced in the proportion of £13,000 to £5500, and, consequently, all the labour which was before employed by £7500 would become redundant.

The reduced quantity of labour which the capitalist can employ, must, indeed, with the assistance of the machine, and after deductions for its repairs, produce a value equal to £7500, it must replace the circulating capital with a profit of £2000 on the whole capital; but if this be done, if the net income be not diminished, of what importance is it to the capitalist whether the gross income be of the value of £3000, of £10,000, or of £15,000?

In this case, then, although the net produce will not be diminished in value, although its power of purchasing commodities may be greatly increased, the gross produce will have fallen from a value of £15,000 to a value of £7500; and as the power of supporting a population, and employing labour, depends always on the gross produce of a nation, and not on its net produce, there will necessarily be a diminution in the demand for labour, population will become redundant, and the situation of the labouring classes will be that of distress and poverty.

As, however, the power of saving from revenue to add to capital must depend on the efficiency of the net revenue, to satisfy the wants of the capitalist, it could not fail to follow from the reduction in the price of commodities consequent on the introduction of machinery that with the same wants he would have increased means of saving – increased facility of transferring revenue into capital. But with every increase of capital he would employ more labourers; and, therefore, a portion of the people thrown out of work in the first instance would be subsequently employed; and if the increased production, in consequence of the employment of the machine, was so great as to afford, in the shape of net produce, as great a quantity of food and necessaries as existed before in the form of gross produce, there would be the same ability to employ the whole population, and, therefore, there would not necessarily be any redundancy of people.

All I wish to prove is that the discovery and use of machinery may be attended with a diminution of gross produce; and whenever that is the case, it will be injurious to the labouring class, as some of their number will be thrown out of employment, and population will become redundant compared with the funds which are to employ it.

Source: Reprinted from *The Works of David Ricardo*, edited by J. R. McCulloch (London: John Murray, 1886) Chapter XXXI, pp. 23–42.

Summing up: Ricardo's key points

Although Ricardo's numerical illustration of the effects of introducing machinery is clumsy, it is important both for the content of his argument and its introduction of the technique of *sequence analysis;* the latter technique examines the transition process from one equilibrium situation to another. The outcome of changing from production without machinery to a situation in which machinery is applied, is traced out sequentially. The transition process is initiated by the diversion of labor and resources for the construction of a machine. Subsequently, the machine is used to produce output that was previously the product of direct labor alone.[18]

Ricardo's example involves four periods $t-1$, t, $t+1$, and $t+2$. In period $t-1$, the economy is in a self-replacing equilibrium state producing without machinery. In period t, the machine is constructed; in period $t+1$, the new machine is used in production. Period $t+2$ thus poses the problem of examining the effect on laborers' well-being of shifting resources from supporting variable capital outlays (which go to workers as wage payments) to supporting outlays for constant capital. Ricardo's example may thus be examined as follows.[19]

Period $t-1$

The initial situation: a capitalist employs a capital of £20,000 in a business in which he is jointly a farmer and a manufacturer. It is supposed that £7000 of the total is allocated to fixed capital, such as buildings and implements, while the remaining £13,000 is paid as wages in the support of labor. It is further assumed that this £20,000 capital yields £2000 which is a profit of 10 percent. If the capitalist's annual gross revenue from the sale of farm output is £15,000, £13,000 is available for the maintenance of labor in the subsequent year along with £2000 for his own consumption. Thus, the economy is in a self-replacing, or stationary, equilibrium state.

Period t

Period t begins when the capital, that has been reproduced in the preceding period, is *reallocated*. The capitalist is now assumed to employ half his work force to produce farm output, as usual, and half to produce a machine. He pays out £13,000 in wages as before. However, the composition of his product is altered, for he now owns a machine worth £7500 and commodities that will provide a revenue of £7500 when they are sold. From this revenue, he will first deduct £2000 (i.e. 10 percent profit on whole capital) for his own expenses. His circulating capital is thus only £5500. The total capital remains at £20,000, but £14,500 of this total is constant capital. Ricardo's concern is thus with examining the implications of what Karl Marx later called the *organic composition of capital*.

Both Ricardo and Marx anticipated that the constant capital component of this total capital would rise.[20]

With a circulating capital of only £5,500 to carry on subsequent operations, some workers will necessarily become redundant as a result of the change in the proportions between fixed and circulating capital. Since the wage fund previously amounted to £13,000, some workers become jobless because the wage fund has decreased to £5500/£13,000, or 11/26, of its original size. At an unchanged real wage per worker, it is inevitable that there is 'substitution of machinery for human labor.' The reduced quantity of labor must now produce a product whose sale yields enough to replace the circulating capital (i.e. at £5500) plus a profit of £2000 on the whole capital of £20,000. Thus, the value that the reduced quantity of labor must produce is equal to £7500 (net of deductions for the machine's repairs).

Period $t + 2$ and beyond

Ricardo's analysis of period $t + 2$ and beyond is very sketchy, though there are tentative conclusions about some possible scenarios. In particular, he notes that as increased labor efficiency reduces costs and therefore the prices of commodities, it may increase the capitalist's possibility of saving. Ricardo anticipates that as a result of positive (net) accumulation (i.e. savings), 'a portion of the people thrown out of work in the first instance would subsequently be reemployed.' Under these conditions, 'there would not necessarily be any redundancy of people.'[21] In such a case, the condition of all classes would be improved, and the laboring classes, especially, would benefit.

The positive long-run case for machinery

While Ricardo considers the possibility that displaced workers might become reabsorbed as result of a net increase in savings, he does not give consideration to a possible fall in the real wage as an effective remedy for unemployment. Since his theory of wages does *not* imply that wage rates generally tend to be at the level of *physical* subsistence, it is not inconsistent with the rest of his analysis to explore the role of a possible decline in real wages. When Knut Wicksell, who pioneered the application of marginal analysis to the factors of production, further explored the problem of technological unemployment, he criticized Ricardo for not recognizing the role of the 'factor price–factor quantity mechanisms,' which was developed by later theorists.[22]

It is also relevant to note that, while Ricardo was most emphatic about the change in his viewpoint on the possible adverse effect of machinery on the working class, he also did not want to be interpreted as being opposed to innovation. 'The statements which I have made will not, I hope lead to the inference that machinery should not be encouraged.'[23] Three main reasons are offered in support of the continued introduction of machinery. The first is that machinery serves as a counterforce to 'the niggardliness of nature.' The law of diminishing returns in agriculture implies that money wages will have to rise (which means that the rate of profit is pressured downward) in order to maintain the level of real wages. Second, Ricardo anticipates that if the State intervened to render the introduction of machinery difficult, it would limit the possibility of reducing the cost of production of commodities. This would deteriorate the terms of trade and lead to a loss of foreign markets.[24] Third, Ricardo notes that impediments to the introduction of machinery would encourage capital exports, 'and this must be a much more serious discouragement to the demand for labor, than the most extensive employment of machinery'; the demand for labor 'will be wholly annihilated.'[25]

Concluding remarks on the wage-fund doctrine

The preceding discussion of the determination of wages and profits, and the ways in which they are likely to be affected by the conversion of circulating into fixed capital, indicates that the wage-fund theory performed a dual role in that it was used both as a theory of wages and a theory of capital. As a theory of capital, it conceived of capitalists as setting aside a predetermined portion of their revenue for making advances to workers during the course of the production process. Labor, therefore, subsists on the part of the economy's real capital that consists of the wage goods it consumes. The sale of labor's output merely replenishes the capital stock advanced, plus the capitalists' profit. As a theory of real wages, it conceived of the average real wage rate as determined by the ratio between the wage fund and the working population.[26]

The weakness of applying the wage-fund doctrine to any but a strictly agricultural economy is that production is a continuous process. Output does not typically become available for sale periodically, as is implicitly assumed in the wage-fund model, but flows continuously into inventories at more or less the same rate as inventories are depleted by consumption. The net effect, therefore, is that capital, interpreted as a supply of 'wage goods,' is maintained intact.

Another difficulty of the wage-fund doctrine is that it provides no basis for explaining the proportions in which a business employs labor and capital. These proportions depend both on the relative marginal cost of using labor and capital and on the value of their marginal products. Without the concepts of marginal cost, productivity, and factor substitution, it cannot be explained why the proportions between circulating capital and fixed capital are what they are to begin with or why these proportions change.

Nevertheless, the wage-fund doctrine enabled the classicists to reach substantially correct conclusions about the possibility of raising the average wage for a given labor force with a given level of technology. They concluded that the average wage rate can rise *only* if the capital stock rises. Today, we recognize that increasing wage rates do, indeed, require an increase in capital; however, we explain rising wages not in terms of an increasing wage fund but in terms of the increase in the marginal productivity of labor when it is combined with more capital. But, whereas the marginal productivity theory provides a basis for understanding the proportions in which the factors will be used in production, the wage-fund doctrine does not.

The wage-fund doctrine was fruitful in another direction; namely, in providing a foundation for the theory of capital. The idea that the wage fund is the source of capitalist advances to the worker ultimately led to the idea that capital bridges the time gap between production and consumption, and that there is a necessary cost inherent in shifting resources from producing goods for immediate consumption as opposed to producing goods whose final products become available only after a lapse of time. While this is essentially the logic pursued later in the Austrian theory of capital, the understanding which Nassau Senior had of the nature of capital, and its role in the production process, has been more persuasive with respect to modern thinking about the nature of capital than Ricardo's interpretation.

Senior's interpretation of capital and its return

There are two aspects to Senior's contribution to the theory of capital and its return: first, his explanation of the relationship between capital and what he termed *abstinence*; second, his explanation of the productivity of *waiting*. While he is better known for his concept of abstinence than for his explanation of the gain to be derived from *roundabout production*, the latter concept is a new idea in English economic thinking, although it is not fully developed. The desirability of waiting was, after all, inherent in Smith's concept of parsimony.

What Ricardo failed to recognize is that the use of capital, besides lengthening the waiting period until the final product matures, is also more productive. Thus, the return on capital is related to the productivity of waiting as well as on the disutility or real cost of waiting. The productivity of waiting, as Senior recognized, derives from the greater productivity of the roundabout method and thus provides a basis for explaining the demand for capital.

The supply of capital depends on abstinence; abstinence expresses 'the conduct of a person who either abstains from the unproductive use of what he can command, or designedly prefers the production of remote to that of immediate results.' While the second part of this definition implies that abstinence is waiting in the Ricardian sense, the first part implies that revenues are permanently being withdrawn from consumption in order to create intermediate products. It is on this basis that Senior regards abstinence itself, rather than the capital goods it creates, as a separate factor of production. 'By the word abstinence, we wish to express that agent, distinct from labour and the agency of nature, the concurrence of which is necessary to the existence of capital and which stands in the same relation to profit as labour does to wages.'[27] The significance of this statement is that it specifically makes capital a distinct factor of production, the cost of which must be included along with wages as part of the total cost of production. It thus contributes to undermining the view that labor cost is the only cost. Ricardo himself argued against a labor theory of value when he observed that the values of commodities produced with more fixed capital must deviate from their labor value because the producer must be compensated for the greater lapse of time before his product can come to market.

Senior conceived of costs not merely in a money sense but in a real sense, that is, as payments for the sacrifices incurred in producing goods. His appreciation of the subjective aspects of economic behavior is also apparent in Senior's inquiry into the value problem. He attempted to introduce utility as a determinant of value by insisting that value depends not only on the difficulty of acquiring goods as reflected in their labor and abstinence costs but also on their utility. He also recognized that the utility of additional units of one and the same good diminishes as additional units are acquired, but did not understand the relationship between scarcity and the utility of the *marginal unit*, which requires the application of differential calculus to economic analysis. Thus, the relationship between utility and demand was not explored by Senior in a way that sheds much light on price determination. His discussion of monopoly prices is, for example, designed to illustrate that prices will equal costs of production only under competition. But he does not show that utility limits the extent of the deviation.

His analysis of monopoly price does, however, lead in another direction. Because monopoly returns are essentially a surplus, Senior included them in his concept of rent. He also suggested that when a worker receives an 'extraordinary' remuneration because of unique natural talents, the surplus may be termed rent. He thus anticipated the generalization of the Ricardian theory of rent, which was to be fully developed subsequently by Alfred Marshall in his analysis of quasi rent.

In summary, then, Senior had a number of potentially fruitful ideas. However, his most substantive contribution is in the area of capital theory. His analysis in this area led not only to the broadening of the concept of cost of production, but also to the theory that abstinence is the source of the supply of savings. This does not of course provide an explanation of the interest rate, because this requires that the supply side be coordinated with a theory of the demand for funds if it is to explain the determination of interest rates. The interaction of demand and supply forces was not examined until Alfred Marshall integrated the 'waiting' theory of interest with the productivity theory in his *Principles of Economics* (1890).

Concluding remarks

Ricardo's primary theoretical concern was the division of the nation's product among the three main social classes in the form of wages, profit, and rent. In his view, the probable long-run tendency of these shares is governed by the cost of producing labor's subsistence. Since he implicitly assumed a given level of agricultural technology as well as a constantly growing population, the tendency toward diminishing returns forced a resort to progressively inferior lands and, consequently, rising food costs. Thus, he regarded the freedom to import food products from countries that have a comparative advantage in labor cost as the most effective way of alleviating the upward pressure on food costs that underlies the determination of the income shares in the long run.

It is because Ricardo's main concern was the problem of distribution that he addressed himself primarily to explaining alterations in exchange values over a period of time. The price of a good would, he thought, reflect its cost of production, including not only the current rate of wages but also the current rate of profits. Ricardo's value theory can therefore be interpreted as a labor theory only in a very special sense. And even this adherence to the labor theory is qualified. The relative values of commodities are not governed exclusively by embodied labor, but depend also on the proportions between fixed and circulating capital and on the durability of capital, because these affect the length of time that elapses before commodities can come to market.

While Ricardo conceived of different capital structures as influencing the time flow of labor-created values to market, as will be seen in the next chapter, Nassau Senior had a far better understanding of the nature of capital and its role in the production process, and a broader cost of production concept emerged from his analysis.

The cost of capital is not the only cost element Ricardo neglected to treat; rent is another such element. Rent in the Ricardian sense applies only to land as a whole because there is no necessary supply price that must be met in order to call forth the supply of land in the aggregate. But once it is recognized that there are competing uses for land and that land can be shifted from one alternative use to another, it follows that it will tend to be used in the alternative in which it is most productive and that it will command a scarcity payment in that alternative, which is just as much a cost factor, and hence a price determinant, as the necessary costs of labor and capital. This type of payment is now known, quite appropriately, as the 'transfer price' of an agent. From the point of view of the individual firm hiring such a factor, transfer prices are part of the production cost, even though they are a surplus from the point of view of the entire industry, or the economy as a whole, in the sense that their elimination would not affect the supply of that factor. Only if the services of a factor (say, land) are limited to a single alternative is the entire reward considered to be rent from both an individual and a social point of view because its transfer price is then equal to zero. When such rewards accrue to factors other than land, they are known as quasi rents. Such rents are unlikely, however, to exist in the long run because no factor is completely non-reproducible or incapable of alternative uses.

Modern economists have little inclination for a special theory to explain the rent of land. They recognize, in the first place, that land, far from being a free gift of nature, requires the outlay of developmental and maintenance costs, and that there are few, if any, resources available for use without such costs. In this sense, land is not very different from capital goods or even reproducible human labor, even though its supply is less elastic than that of other factors. Furthermore, it is unrealistic to think of land as being used only to produce a particular agricultural product. This is the sense in which Ricardo thought of it. He conceived of land beyond the extensive margin of agricultural use as being left idle, whereas a given area of land is likely to have several alternative uses to which it can be put. It will command a scarcity payment in any of these alternatives and will actually be

employed in that alternative in which it is most productive. The transfer price associated with this employment is necessarily a cost to the hiring firm and will therefore be price-determining rather than price-determined.

While the explanation of value generally accepted in Ricardo's day was a cost-of-production theory, there were others besides Nassau Senior who argued that utility must not be neglected. Samuel Bailey, in particular, pointed out that the relative nature of value implies that utility is a cause of value and not just a prerequisite, as Ricardo maintained.[28] It is plain from his observation that Ricardo's dictum that reproducible commodities derive their value from the quantity of labor required to make them, rather than scarcity, is untenable. Reproducible goods may be less scarce relative to the demand for them than those that exist permanently in fixed supply, but they are scarce nonetheless. Thus, demand and utility, as well as cost of production and supply, determine exchange values, whether the commodities being exchanged are reproducible or not.

Those who criticized Ricardo for neglecting the demand side of the price problem were, however, unable to show how demand affects price. Jean-Baptiste Say (1767–1835), for example, while he emphasized that exchange value is dependent on utility, failed to recognize the relationship between utility and supply. Consequently, he was no more able than Smith to explain why water, for all its utility, does not command a price. Nassau Senior, although he too emphasized utility as a cause of value, also failed to perceive the significance of the marginal unit. The net result was that criticisms of Ricardo's theory of value on the grounds of its failure to recognize the role of utility more specifically, came to naught until the marginal revolution of the 1870s. With respect to its long-term significance, Ricardo's demonstration of the construction and use of rigorous deductive analysis is no doubt his primary contribution. It was he who perfected the technique of abstraction, and this, rather than his substantive conclusions, is the basis for his long-term influence on economic analysis.

Notes

1 John R. McCulloch (ed.), *The Works of David Ricardo* (London: John Murray, 1886), pp. xvi–xxxiii, hereafter cited as *Works* (McCulloch edition).

2 Samuel Hollander, *The Economics of David Ricardo* (Toronto and Buffalo: University of Toronto Press, 1979). Hollander argues that income shares are determined by the interaction of the same demand and supply forces which modern thinkers use to explain the exchange values of commodities. In his interpretation, commodity and factor prices are linked through the economy's production processes, so that factor prices serve to allocate scarce resources among alternative uses to satisfy wants. Ricardo's work is thus interpreted by Hollander as representing the further development of a similarly integrated approach, introduced by Adam Smith which, he believes, is continued in an unbroken tradition to the later neoclassical marginalist economics of Alfred Marshall (1842–1924) and Leon Walras (1834–1910).

3 See especially Allesandro Roncaglia, 'Hollander's Ricardo,' *Journal of Post Keynesian Economics*, 4 (3) (Spring, 1982), pp. 339–75; D. P. O'Brien, 'Ricardian economics and the economics of David Ricardo,' *Oxford Economic Papers* 33 (1981), pp. 1–35; R. Garegnani, 'The classical theory of wages and the role of demand schedules in the determination of relative prices,' *Papers and Proceedings of American Economic Association*, May, 1983. pp. 309–13; and Hollander's response, 'On the interpretation of Ricardian economics.'

4 Ricardo's complete works have been edited by Piero Sraffa and M. H. Dobb in *The Work and Correspondence of David Ricardo*, 10 vols, (Cambridge: The University Press, 1951–55). Subsequent references are to this edition of Ricardo's work unless otherwise noted, abbreviated as *Works and Correspondence*. Unless specifically noted, references are to the Sraffa–Dobb editions.

5 The influence of James Mill on Ricardo has always been a matter of speculation. The general view, which reflects Sraffa's interpretation of the Ricardo–Mill correspondence, is that Mill contributed little more than friendly, though persistent, encouragement. An alternative interpretation is offered in Ingrid H. Rima, 'James Mill and classical economics: a reappraisal,' *Eastern Economics Journal*, 2(2) (April, 1975).

6 David Ricardo, *Principles of Political Economy and Taxation*, vol. 1, pp. 43–44.

7 David Ricardo, *Principles of Political Economy and Taxation*, vol. 1, p. 67. Ricardo, however, was not always consistent in his use of the term *rent*. For example, he says that the payments to the owners of mines for permission to work them are for the minerals removed and not for the original and indestructible powers of the soil. He also suggests, in a note at the end of his chapter on profit rates, that a portion of the capital used by landlords may be 'amalgamated with the land, and [so] tends to increase its productive powers, [that] the remuneration paid to the landlord for its use is strictly of the nature of rent, and is subject to all the laws of rent.'

8 David Ricardo, *Principles of Political Economy and Taxation*, vol. 1, pp. 71–72.

9 David Ricardo, *Principles of Political Economy and Taxation*, vol. 1, pp. 74–75.

10 'Letters to J. B. Say,' in *Works and Correspondence*, vol. 9, p. 169.

11 'Letter to McCulloch,' in *Works and Correspondence*, vol. 9, p. 330.

12 See E A. Hayek, 'The Ricardo effect,' *Economica* 9 (1942), reprinted in F. A. Hayek, *Individualism and the Economic Order* (Chicago: University of Chicago Press, 1948).

13 *Works* (McCulloch edition), Preface.

14 *Works* (McCulloch edition), p. 93.

15 *Work and Correspondence*, vol. 2, p. 225.

16 Hollander, *The Economics of David Ricardo*, p. 12.

17 *Works*, (McCulloch edition), p. 235.

18 Samuel Hollander, *The Economics of David Ricardo*, includes an exhaustive examination of the development of Ricardo's position on machinery. See pp. 346–73.

19 This discussion draws on Heinz Kurz's paper, 'Ricardo and Lowe on Machinery,' *Eastern Economic Journal*, 10(2) (1984).

20 It is important to note that in Ricardo's example of the business owner who is jointly a farmer and a manufacturer, the business owner does not abstain from consumption during the period in which the machine is being constructed. He simply restructures his capital stock. The additional profits received thus cannot be considered a reward for waiting. It is the workers' consumption that is reduced; i.e. their unemployment imposes *involuntary saving on* them. See Adolph Lowe, *The Path of Economic Growth* (Cambridge: Cambridge University Press, 1976), p. 75.

21 Ricardo, *Works* (McCulloch edition, 1886), p. 237.

22 Knut Wicksell, *Lectures on Political Economy* (London: Routledge & Kegan Paul, 1935), vol. 1, pp. 137–38.

23 Ricardo, *Works* (McCulloch edition), p. 240.

24 Ricardo, *Works* (McCulloch edition), p. 242.

25 Ricardo, *Works* (McCulloch edition), p. 242.

26 Money wages will, of course, tend to rise, for the increasing labor cost of producing raw produce at the margin of cultivation will raise the money price of provisions and, therefore, the nominal wage the workers must receive in order to support themselves and their families. It is even conceivable that a decrease in *real* wages will be obscured by an increase in *money* wages – that the worker may be less well-off in terms of goods even though the money wages are rising. The only hope for permanent improvement in the worker's lot is, therefore, to be found in the restriction of numbers. This is precisely in accord with Malthus' observation, but Ricardo had less faith than Malthus in the check of moral restraint of population growth.

27 *Outline of the Science of Political Economy*, 6th edn (London: Allen Unwin, 1872), pp. 58–59.

28 Samuel Bailey, A *Critical Dissertation on the Nature of Measures and Causes of Values; Chiefly in Reference to the Writings of Mr. Ricardo and His Followers* (London, 1825).

Glossary of terms and concepts

Abstinence
Postponement of consumption in order to facilitate the production of 'intermediate' (i.e. capital goods). In Senior's view, abstinence is rewarded by profit.

Economic (Ricardian) rent
A differential surplus appearing on better than marginal land because of its greater fertility or better location than 'no-rent land,' which only produces enough to pay for the labor and capital employed on it. Rent in this sense is not a cost of production and therefore not price-determining.

Ricardo effect
The lengthening of the average period of production that results when a rise in real wages favors capital-intensive, as opposed to labor-intensive, production.

Sequence analysis
Examination of the process of transition from one equilibrium to another over time. Ricardo's consideration of the machinery question used a simple arithmetical example to trace out the effects of shifting resources from the agriculture sector to the production of capital goods.

Stationary state
The ultimate state, according to classical theorists, toward which the economy is evolving. It is characterized by a stable population (i.e. the birth rate equals the death rate), a constant stock of capital (i.e. new investment merely replaces depreciated capital), and a constant income per capita.

Questions for discussion and further research

1 How did Ricardo explain the phenomenon of exchange value? To what extent can this be interpreted as adhering to a labor theory of

value? Support your answer with references to specific readings, where possible.

2 The Ricardian theory of distribution is inseparably bound up with the land factor and its margin of cultivation. Discuss Ricardo's analysis of the distributive shares received by *each* of the social classes and this probable long-run trend. How does Ricardo's position on the Corn Laws fit in with his analysis of the income shares? What is the basis for Malthus's opposite view of the Corn Laws?

3 On what basis did Ricardo reach his new position in regard to the machinery question?

4 Besides labor and land, Senior recognized a third factor of production, which he called abstinence. What is the nature of its reward and why should it go to the capitalist?

Notes for further reading

From *The New Palgrave*

Ronald Findlay on comparative advantage, vol. 1, pp. 514–17; E W. Taussig on stationary state, vol. 4, p. 484; G. de Vivo on the corn model, vol. 1, p. 671, and on David Ricardo, vol. 4, pp. 183–98; Anna J. Schwartz on banking school, currency school, free banking school, vol. 1, pp. 182–85; Roy Green on the real bills doctrine, vol. 4, pp. 101–2; Krishna Bharadwaj on wages in classical economics, vol. 4, pp. 843–45; and Ingrid H. Rima on wage goods, vol. 4, pp. 837–38.

Selected references and suggestions for further reading

Bowley, Marion. *Nassau Senior and Classical Political Economy* (New York: Augustus Kelley, 1949). Senior's *Outline of the Science of Political Economy*, 6th edn (New York: Augustus Kelley, 1951) is available as a reprint.

Cairnes, J. E. *Some Leading Principles of Political Economy Newly Expounded* (London: 1874).

Mill, J. S. *Principles of Political Economy*. Edited by W. J. Ashley (New York: A. M. Kelley, 1965 [1848]).

Mill, J. S. *Principles of Political Economy*. In *Collected Works*, edited by J. M. Robson, vols 2 and 3 (Toronto: University of Toronto Press, 1966 [1848]).

Mill, J. S. *Letters of John Stuart Mill*. 2 vols. Edited by H. S. R. Elliot (London: Longmans, 1910).

Mill, J. S. *Essays on Economics and Society*. In *Collected Works*, edited by J. M. Robson, vols 4 and 5 (Toronto: University of Toronto Press, 1967).

Mill, J. S. *The Later Letters of John Stuart Mill, 1848–1873*. In *Collected Works*, edited by F. E. Mineka and D. N. Lindley, vols 14–17 (Toronto: University of Toronto Press, 1972).

Mill, J. S. 'Thornton on labour and its claims,' *Fortnightly Review* (May, June 1869), pp. 505–18, 680–700.

Robbins, Lionel. Lectures 18, 19, 20: 'Value and distribution: historical origin I, II and III,' in *A History of Economic Thought*, edited by S. Medema and W. Samuels (Princeton NJ: Princeton University Press, 1998), pp. 176–200.

Senior, N. W. *An Outline of the Science of Political Economy* (New York: A. M. Kelley, Publishers, 1938 [1836]).

Senior, N. W. *Selected Writings on Economics* (New York: A. M. Kelley, 1966).

Stark, W. (ed.), *Jeremy Bentham's Economic Writings* (London: George Allen & Unwin, 1954), vol. 3, p. 441.

Stigler, G. L. 'Originality in scientific process.' *Economica*, 22 (November, 1955), pp. 296–99.

Thornton, W. T. *On Labour: Its Wrongful Claims and Rightful Dues, Its Actual Present and Possible Future* (London: 1869).

Chapter 8

Ricardo, Senior and John Stuart Mill: international trade, monetary theory and method in economic science

Introduction

Every nineteenth century economist, whether they were in basic agreement with David Ricardo's economic analysis or rejected it in whole or in part, was undoubtedly influenced by the tradition he shaped. His chief disciples were James Mill, his son John Stuart Mill and John Ramsey McCulloch. Of the three, John Stuart Mill (1806–73) made the greatest contribution to extending, refining, and continuing the Ricardian tradition. Indeed, he was reared in an intellectual environment precisely designed to train him to carry on the tradition of Bentham and Ricardo. Bentham's *Utilitarianism* is the chief source of agenda for reforming nineteenth century capitalism in England, while Ricardo's *Principles of Political Economy and Taxation* was the basis for the further refinement and modernization of *The Wealth of Nations* in the light of 'the more extended knowledge and improved ideas of the present age,' and also to examine economic principles with respect to 'their application to social philosophy.' The latter objective sets the tone of the book. Mill was less concerned with theoretical analysis for its own sake than with the application of the doctrines of Malthus and Ricardo, in which he had been steeped since childhood, to the solution of the problems of the age.

Chief among these, from Mill's perspective, are the 'problems of the laboring poor.' These stem from the law of diminishing returns, which inexorably raises the cost of food and raw materials and, on the other hand, the difficulties workers confront in raising their wages, and also the possibility that the funds for maintaining workers (i.e. the wages fund) might become impaired if 'the sinking or fixing of capital in machinery' proceeds too rapidly so that legislators confront the need for measures to moderate its pace.[1]

Mill's utilitarianism

Mill's *Autobiography* (1861) tells of his introduction to the study of economics at the age of 13 under his father's careful supervision of his reading of Ricardo's *Principles of Political Economy and Taxation*. This was followed by an equally intensive study of Adam Smith. Mill subsequently spent a year in France, partly at the home of Jean-Baptiste Say, and upon his return to England was assigned the task of preparing marginal notes for his father's *Elements of Political Economy* (1821). He was only 19 when he began contributing articles on economics to the *Westminster Review*. He had also studied Utilitarian philosophy and he became a member of the circle of philosophic radicals. He was not yet 20 when he edited the five volumes of Bentham's *Rationale of Evidence.*

Not long afterward, however, Mill experienced a severe mental crisis, which he described in his *Autobiography* as a 'conviction of sin,' the sin being his acceptance of Utilitarianism. Actually, although he became sharply critical of certain features of Bentham's system he never rejected Utilitarianism in its entirety. Specifically, he rejected the view that human behavior was governed by self-interest, as Bentham implied. He even ventured to suggest that Bentham attached little importance to sympathy and benevolence as influencing conduct because he himself was devoid of these characteristics.[2] He also maintained that there are qualitative differences among pleasures and that the estimation of pleasure does not depend on quantity alone. But these criticisms are a qualification of Benthamism rather than a rejection, for Mill was a hedonist who thought that the morality of behavior is to be judged in terms of its effects on happiness.

Mill's attempted revision of Utilitarianism reached out for new ideas to the writings of the English Romanticists, among them Samuel Taylor Coleridge and Thomas Carlyle, and the philosopher Auguste Comte. He was also greatly interested in the views of the utopian socialists. The ideas he derived from these sources created an intellectual dilemma for Mill, for he tried to reconcile them with the earlier and deeply ingrained influences of Benthamism and Ricardianism. Consequently, Mill's standard approach to almost every subject was to begin with a preliminary statement of received doctrine, which he subsequently qualified and revised until much of the original principle was swept away.

While these qualifications stemmed largely from his deep sense of humanitarianism and social purpose, they nevertheless created

conflicts he was unable to resolve. He was, for example, a great champion of individual liberty; the eloquence of his defense of freedom on the basis of its own moral worth made his essay *On Liberty* (1859) a classic in the English language. He was also a great social reformer. However, his political theory provided no criterion for judging the circumstances in which a society is justified in placing a limitation on personal freedom. Rather, the case that he made for social legislation is derived from his humanitarian ideals.[3]

While Mill believed that individual and social interests are generally compatible with each other within the framework of a competitive economy, there are numerous exceptions to the *laissez-faire* principles he recommended. These include taxation of the unearned increment on land, control of the rate at which technological changes are introduced, and social control of natural monopolies. He also emphasized the necessity of worker education, particularly with respect to the importance of controlling their numbers and he favorably regarded labor combinations as contributing to the improvement of the position of the working class.

Mill's economics started with Ricardian principles, but the objective of creating a complete science of society, which he learned from the French philosopher Auguste Comte, led him to the broader view of political economy as a study of people, institutions, and customs, and not just as the formulation of laws governing production, exchange, and distribution. Thus, the aim of his *Principles of Political Economy* was to provide not only an exposition of Ricardian theory but, more important, to examine the social and political milieu within which Ricardian generalizations work themselves out. Since Mill conceived of these environmental factors as exerting their main influence on the distribution of wealth, his distinction between pure economics and *applied* economics provided a foundation for a broad program of reform intended to alter the institutions that affect this distribution. This approach enabled Mill to be the last great exponent of Ricardian classicism, while also being sympathetic to the utopian socialists' aspirations for establishing cooperative communities.

Mill believed the law of diminishing returns to scale is the most important principle of political economy because of the limited supply of land. While technical progress operates to reduce the labor costs of producing wage goods, which in the main are agricultural products, the principle of diminishing returns is the critical element in establishing the well-being of the working class, which depends on the wage fund. While the modern reader would expect the subject of the distributive shares to follow that of exchange value, Mill's examination treats income shares immediately after production. Since he regards these shares as the result of human institutions, he apparently considers their determination as unrelated to the price-making forces that operate in commodity markets.[4]

Mill's Ricardianism

Mill's Ricardian classicism leads him to focus first on the laws of production which reflect the dictates of nature, before proceeding to the laws of distribution. The laws governing the production of wealth are physical truths, whereas

those of Distribution are partly of human institution . . . But though governments of nations have the power of deciding what institutions shall exist, they cannot arbitrarily determine how those institutions shall work. The conditions on which the power they possess over the distribution of wealth . . . are as much a subject for scientific inquiry as any of the physical laws of nature.[5]

Mill takes the position that the basic tenet of the institution of property is the right of each person to the 'exclusive disposal of what he or she may have produced by their own exertions.'[6] Thus, one is entitled to the product of one's labor and one's abstinence.[7] When the institution of private property prevails, the division of the produce among the various claimants is determined primarily by competition, although it may be modified by custom.

As did Ricardo before him, Mill believed that there is a fund of predetermined size destined to maintain labor in production that limits the size of the annual wage flow. He therefore reasoned that the average wage depends on the number of participants in the market and that there is nothing that can be done, either by government or by labor unions, to raise the wages of labor as a whole. The wages of any *particular group* may, of course, be raised, but only at the expense of other groups. Thus, Mill, like Ricardo, maintained that the demand for labor is enhanced by the capitalists' abstinence, for wages represent the advances that capitalists make to workers. From this, it follows that 'industry is limited by capital,' which implies that employment can only be increased by new capital.

This leads Mill to his second fundamental proposition that relates to capital, namely that 'capital is the result of saving' from which he invokes the Smith–Say principle that 'saving is spending.' According to this principle, which has come to be known as *Say's identity*, purchasing power is not destroyed or lost; income not used for consumption expenditures will be used to support investment, either as fixed or as circulating capital.

Like Ricardo before him, Mill was also

concerned with the effect that an increase in the ratio of fixed to circulating capital will have on employment. Ricardo's concern in considering the machinery question was that the conversion of circulating into fixed capital might well 'deteriorate the condition of the labourer.' However, unlike Ricardo, Mill concludes that improvements in production are seldom injurious, even temporarily, to the working class in the aggregate.[8] His argument was based on his extension of Say's law from commodity markets to labor markets. Just as the demand for consumer goods can never be insufficient to clear the market of the whole supply because their prices adjust to assure this outcome, so the demand for labor will be large enough to assure the employment of the entire workforce, even after the introduction of new machines.

This follows because cost reductions from new machinery provide capitalists with increases in fixed and circulating capital. Since circulating capital includes the wage fund, employment can be maintained at previous levels. Employment, Mill observed, had been maintained in the manufacture of cotton textiles and in printing, which were prime examples of industries that increased their stocks of fixed capital. The test, says Mill, of the relative productive efficiency of large-scale versus small-scale establishments in the same business is the ability to sell more cheaply.

However, large-scale production is accompanied by larger capitals in fewer hands. The result may be higher prices, for 'where competitors are so few, they always end up by agreeing not to compete' (Mill, *Principles*, p. 218). Mill therefore suggests that when a firm produces its output under conditions of natural monopoly, it is best to treat it as a public utility.

Although Mill appreciates the possibilities and significance of increasing returns to scale

in manufacturing, he is nevertheless a true Ricardian in pronouncing the law of diminishing returns to labor in agriculture as 'the most significant proposition in political economy. Were the law different, nearly all the phenomena of the production and distribution of wealth would be other than they are.' This law operates because a given quantity of land is cultivated in a 'given state of agricultural skill and knowledge.'[9] While Mill agreed with Henry Carey, Ricardo's American critic, that the order of cultivation does not always proceed from the best lands to the poorest, but may proceed from the poorest to the best, he maintained that diminishing returns will ultimately occur because land is fixed in quantity. Its impact may be temporarily controlled or offset as people gain control over nature. However, the limited supply of land, along with the deficiency of capital, presents fundamental impediments to continued increases in production without proportionately greater increases in the cost of production. Thus, Mill's statement of the principle of diminishing returns emphasizes that, given the state of the arts in agriculture, returns will eventually diminish regardless of the order in which lands are cultivated. Economic progress is therefore dependent on maintaining a rate of technical improvement in agriculture to offset the tendency toward diminishing returns. It is also dependent on the extension of foreign trade as Ricardo maintained in his inquiry into the link between land, rents, and the Corn Law, and the inverse relationship between the rates of wages and profits.

The Corn Laws and Ricardo's contribution to trade theory

Ricardo's interest in and contribution to international trade theory is closely related to his analysis of the inverse relationship between wages and profits, and the consequent impossibility of increasing profits except by means of reductions in wages. Any measure that operates to reduce wages, maintained Ricardo, will simultaneously operate to increase profits and contain rents.[10] The extension of foreign trade is precisely such a measure. Ricardo is therefore critical of the Corn Laws and advocates that protection be reduced, especially on agricultural commodities, which are the 'wage goods' consumed by the working class. This issue is precisely the central point of his debate with Malthus and his explanation of the gains from trade and their relationship to the long-run trend of wages and profits. It is this relationship which leads Ricardo (and, later, John Stuart Mill) to focus on the gains that are inherent in free trade in raw produce, specifically in food.

Issues and Answers from the Masterworks 8.1

Issue

How can free trade in agricultural products raise the rate of profit and raise the real wages of labor? How will a country deploy its labor and capital under a system of perfectly free commerce?

Ricardo's answer

From Chapter 7, *On Foreign Trade.*

On foreign trade

No extension of foreign trade will immediately increase the amount of value in a country, although it will very powerfully contribute to increasing the mass of commodities, and therefore the sum of enjoyments. As the value of all foreign goods is measured by the quantity of the produce of our land and labour, which is given in exchange for them, we should have no greater value, if by the discovery of new markets, we obtained double the quantity of foreign goods in exchange for a given quantity of ours. If by the purchase of English goods to the amount of 1000£., a merchant can obtain a quantity of foreign goods, which he can sell in the English market for 1200£., he will obtain 20 per cent. profit by such an employment of his capital; but neither his gains, nor the value of the commodities imported, will be increased or diminished by the greater or smaller quantity of foreign goods obtained. Whether, for example, he imports twenty-five or fifty pipes of wine, his interest can be no way affected, if at one time the twenty-five pipes, and another fifty pipes equally sell for 1200£. In either case his profit will be limited to 200£., or 20 per cent. on his capital; and in either case the same value will be imported into England. If the fifty pipes sold for more than 1200£., the profits of this individual merchant would exceed the general rate of profits, and capital would naturally double the value of wine. But if I, and others, contented ourselves with the same quantity of wine as before, fewer English commodities would be exported, and the wine-drinkers might either consume the commodities which were before exported, or any others for which they had an inclination. The capital required for their production would be supplied by the capital liberated from the foreign trade.

There are two ways in which capital may be accumulated: it may be saved either in consequence of increased revenue, or of diminished consumption. If my profits are raised from 1000£ to 1200£ while my expenditure continues the same, I accumulate annually 200£ more than I did before. If I save 200£ out of my expenditure, while my profits continue the same, the same effect will be produced; 2001£ per annum will be added to my capital. The merchant who imported wine after profits had been raised from 20 per cent to 40 per cent, instead of purchasing his English goods for 1000£ must purchase them for 857£. 2s. 10d., still selling the wine which he imports in return for those goods for 1200£, or, if he continued to purchase his English goods for 1000£. must raise the price of his wine to 1400£.; he would thus obtain 40 instead of 20 per cent. profit on his capital; but if, in consequence of the cheapness of all the commodities on which his revenue was expended, he and all other consumers could save the value of 200£. out of every 1000£ they before expended, they would more effectually add to the real wealth of the country; in one case, the savings would be made in consequence of an increase of revenue, in the other, in consequence of diminished expenditure.

If, by the introduction of machinery, the generality of the commodities on which revenue was expended fell 20 per cent. in value, I should be enabled to save as effectually as if my revenue had been raised 20 per cent.; but in one case the rate of profits is stationary, in the other it is raised 20 per cent. – If, by the introduction of cheap foreign goods, I can save 20 per cent. from my expenditure, the effect will be precisely the same as if machinery had lowered the expense of their production, but profits would not be raised.

It is not, therefore, in consequence of the extension of the market that the rate of profit is raised, although such extension may be equally efficacious in increasing the mass of commodities, and may thereby enable us to augment the funds destined for the maintenance of labour, and the materials on which labour may be employed. It is quite as important to the happiness of mankind, that our enjoyments should be increased by the better distribution of labour, by each country producing those commodities for which, by its situation, its climate, and its other natural or artificial advantages, it is adapted, and by their exchanging them for the commodities of other countries, as that they should be augmented by a rise in the rate of profits.

It has been my endeavour to shew throughout this work, that the rate of profits can never be increased but by a fall in wages, and that there can be no permanent fall of wages but in consequence of a fall of necessaries on which wages are expended. If, therefore, by the extension of foreign trade, or by improvements in machinery, the food and necessaries of the labourer can be brought to market at a reduced price, profits will rise. If, instead of growing our own corn, or manufacturing the clothing and other necessaries of the labourer, we discover a new market from which we can supply ourselves with these commodities at a cheaper price, wages will fall and profits will rise; but if the commodities obtained at a cheaper rate, by the extension of foreign commerce, or by the improvement of machinery, be exclusively the commodities consumed by the rich, no alteration will take place in the rate of profits. The rate of wages would not be affected, although wine, velvets, silks, and other expensive commodities should fall 50 per cent. and consequently profits would continue unaltered.

Foreign trade, then, though highly beneficial to a country, as it increases the amount and variety of the objects on which revenue may be expended, and affords, by the abundance and cheapness of commodities, incentives to saving, and to the accumulation of capital, has no tendency to raise the profits of stock, unless the commodities imported be of that description on which the wages of labour are expended . . .

The same rule which regulates the relative value of commodities in one country, does not regulate the relative value of the commodities exchanged between two or more countries.

Under a system of perfectly free commerce, each country naturally devotes its capital and labour to such employments as are most beneficial to each . . . It is this principle which determines that wine shall be made in France and Portugal, that corn shall be grown in America and Poland, and that hardware and other goods shall be manufactured in England . . .

If Portugal had no commercial connexion with other countries, instead of employing a great part of her capital and industry in the production of wines, with which she purchases for her own use the cloth and hardware of other countries, she would be obliged to devote a part of that capital to the manufacture of those commodities, which she would thus obtain as probably inferior in quality as well as quantity.

The quantity of wine which she shall give in exchange for the cloth of England, is not determined by the respective quantities of labour devoted to the production of each, as it would be, if both commodities were manufactured in England, or both in Portugal.

England may be so circumstanced, that to produce the cloth may require the labour of 100 men for one year; and if she attempted to make the wine, it might require the labour of 120 men for the same time. England would therefore find it in her interest to import wine, and to purchase it by the exportation of cloth.

To produce the wine in Portugal, might require only the labour of 80 men for one year, and to produce the cloth in the same country, might require the labour of 90 men for the same time. It would therefore be advantageous for her to export wine in exchange for cloth. This exchange might even take place, notwithstanding that the commodity imported by Portugal could be produced there with less labour than in England. Though she could make the cloth with the labour of 90 men, she would import it from a country where it required the labour of 100 men to produce it, because it would be advantageous to her rather to employ her capital in the production of wine, for which she would obtain more cloth from England, than she could produce by diverting a portion of her capital from the cultivation of vines to the manufacture of cloth . . .

It would undoubtedly be advantageous to the capitalists of England, and to the consumers in both countries, that under such circumstances, the wine and the cloth should both be made in Portugal, and therefore that the capital and labour of England employed in making cloth, should be removed to Portugal for that purpose . . . Experience, however, shews, that the fancied or real insecurity of capital, when not under the immediate control of its owner, together with the natural disinclination which every man has to quit the country of his birth and connexions, and intrust himself with all his habits fixed, to a strange government and new laws, [will] check the emigration of capital . . . Gold and silver having been chosen for the general medium of circulation, they are, by the competition of commerce, distributed in such proportions amongst the different countries of the world, as to accommodate themselves to the natural traffic which would take place if no such metals existed, and the trade between countries were purely a trade of barter.

Thus, cloth cannot be imported into Portugal, unless it sell there for more gold than it cost in the country from which it was imported; and wine cannot be imported to England, unless it will sell for more there than it cost in Portugal. If the trade were purely a trade of barter, it could only continue whilst England could make cloth so cheap as to obtain a greater quantity of wine with a given quantity of labour, by manufacturing cloth than by growing vines; and also whilst the industry of Portugal were attended by the reverse effects . . .

England exported cloth in exchange for wine, because, by so doing, her industry was rendered more productive to her; she had more cloth and wine than if she had manufactured both for herself; and Portugal imported cloth and exported wine, because the industry of Portugal could be more beneficially employed for both countries in producing wine. Let there be more difficulty in England in producing cloth, or in Portugal in producing wine, or let there be more facility in England in producing wine, or in Portugal in producing cloth, and the trade must immediately cease.

Thus then it appears, that the improvement of a manufacture in any country tends to alter the distribution of the precious metals amongst the nations of the world: it tends to increase the quantity of commodities, at the same time that it raises general prices in the country where the improvement takes place.

To simplify the question, I have been supposing the trade between two countries to be confined to two commodities – to wine and cloth; but it is well known that many and various articles enter into the list of exports and imports. By the abstraction of money from one country, and the accumulation of it in another, all commodities are affected in price, and consequently encouragement is given to the exportation of many more commodities besides money, which will therefore prevent so great an effect from taking place on the value of money in the two countries as might otherwise be expected . . .

In the former part of this work, we have assumed, for the purpose of argument, that money always continued at the same value; we are now endeavouring to shew that besides the ordinary variations in the value of money, and those which are common to the whole commercial world, there are also partial variations to which money is subject in particular countries; and in fact, that the value of money is never the same in any two countries, depending as it does on relative taxation, on manufacturing skill, on the advantages of climate, natural productions, and many other causes . . . Wages may therefore be precisely the same in two countries; they may bear too the same proportion to rent, and to the whole produce obtained for the land, although in one of those countries the labourer should receive ten shillings per week, and in the other twelve.

In the early stages of society, when manufactures have made little progress, and the produce of all countries is nearly similar, consisting of the bulky and most useful commodities, the value of money in different countries will be chiefly regulated by their distance from the mines which supply the precious metals; but as the arts and improvements of society advance, and different nations excel in particular manufactures, although distance will still enter into the calculation, the value of the precious metals will be chiefly regulated by the superiority of those manufactures.

Source: *The Works of David Ricardo*, edited by J. R. McCulloch
(London: John Murray, 1886), Chapter 7, pp. 72–86.

Summing up: Ricardo's key points

Ricardo's inquiry into foreign trade proceeded in the context of his argument that the rate of profit depends on the labor cost of producing the food supply of the working population. His now classic illustration hypothesizes a situation in which a work force of 120 laborers in England can produce a quantity of wine that can be produced in Portugal by the labor of 80, while the same quantity of cloth can be produced in England with the labor of 100 workers, and in Portugal, with the labor of 90. That is, the wine-to-cloth ratio in England is 6:5 whereas it is 8:9 in Portugal. Portugal thus produces both wine and cloth at a lower labor cost than does England, but she produces wine at a comparatively cheaper cost than cloth. England has a comparative *disadvantage* in both, but produces cloth at a comparatively lower labor cost than wine. Thus Ricardo concludes, under free-trade conditions, England will specialize in producing cloth and will import wine from Portugal in exchange for cloth. By the same principle, Portugal imports cloth because it requires relatively less labor to produce wine in Portugal than to produce cloth.

The crucial element in this conclusion is that there is a mechanism which makes international trade attractive to profit seeking capitalists. This mechanism derives from the relationship between international gold flows and domestic prices. In Ricardo's famous example, given Portugal's absolute advantage in terms of labor cost, she would initially export both wine and cloth to England which would be paid for in gold. This gold outflow raises money prices in Portugal, while lowering money prices in England, which makes British cloth and wine progressively cheaper. As long as a trade imbalance persists, the outflow of gold from England would make British cloth and wine progressively cheaper until, at some point, England becomes able to undersell Portugal in some products. Since England is assumed to have a lesser disadvantage in producing cloth than wine, it is cloth production to which capitalists will direct resources, while Portuguese capitalists will find it profitable to specialize in wine.

Because the critical part of Ricardo's argument was to demonstrate the basis for free trade as part of his polemic against the Corn Laws, the precise terms of trade between wine and cloth were not critical either to Ricardo's example or his argument. Thus, he did not find it necessary to explain how the ratio at which wine and cloth would be exchanged for each other are determined, but assumed that they would exchange for one another at a ratio of one unit of cloth to one unit of wine. This is close to being midway between their comparative cost ratios, and the gains of trade are almost equally divided at this ratio.[11] This gain reflects the saving of labor made possible by importation.

England is saving the equivalent of 20 labor-hours by importing wine, because it would have cost 120 labor-hours if she chose to acquire wine by producing it at home. Similarly, if one unit of wine is exchanged for one unit of cloth, Portugal will save 10 labor-hours by importing cloth instead of relying on domestic production. Both countries will therefore gain from specialization and exchange. England can obtain more wine per labor-hour by importing it than by producing it; conversely, Portugal can obtain more cloth per labor-hour by importing it than by producing it herself. Trade is therefore advantageous to both countries.

Mill's alternative statement of comparative advantage

Ricardo's illustration of the prospective gains from trade supposed that the given hypothetical outputs of wine and cloth in Portugal and England can be produced at labor costs that differ as represented in Table 8.1. If trade commences between them, the terms of trade will lie between 6:5 and 8:9, which is an approximate ratio of 1:1, and *implies* that the gains from trade will be equally divided. His contemporaries, James Mill and J. R. McCulloch, specifically stated that the benefits from trade would be equally divided.

It was subsequently pointed out that the terms of trade are determined by reciprocal demand of the two countries for one another's products. Robert Torrens has been credited as the earliest exponent of this idea, but it was John Stuart Mill's extension of Ricardo's statement of the principle of comparative advantage which stated the concept in a way which gained it general acceptance among economists.[12]

Mill assumed the 'equivalent inputs' of comparative labor are able to produce two commodities, say cloth and linen, in Germany and England. As shown in Table 8.1, both countries produce ten yards of broadcloth per unit of labor and are thus equally efficient in that product. But their comparative efficiencies in the production of linen are different. With an equivalent input of labor, Germany is assumed to produce 20 yards of linen, whereas England produces only 15 yards. Germany thus has a comparative advantage in the production of linen. Ricardo's example hypothesized a given quantity of wine and cloth produced in Portugal and England, and expressed their respective costs of production in terms of the labor inputs required in each country. Mill, however, assumes given labor inputs and expressed comparative advantage in terms of each country's output.

Without trade, both countries produce linen and broadcloth. In England, the domestic ratio of exchange without trade is 10 yards of broadcloth for 15 of linen; in Germany, it will be 10 yards of broadcloth for 20 of linen.

From these domestic exchange ratios, it follows that trade will be profitable to England if more than 15 yards of linen can be exchanged for 10 of broadcloth, while Germany will gain if 10 yards of broadcloth can be traded for fewer than 20 yards of linen. Comparative output with equivalent labor inputs limits the international ratios of exchange that are possible; within these limits any ratio might come about. The question Mill undertook to answer is posed in Issues and Answers from the Masterworks 8.2.

Table 8.1 Comparative advantage in international trade

	Ricardo's example Labor cost for production			Mill's example Output in yards	
	Wine	*Cloth*		*Broadcloth*	*Linen*
Portugal	80 hours	90 hours	England	10	15
England	120 hours	100 hours	Germany	10	20

Domestic terms of exchange without trade:
  England: W = 6/5C
  Portugal: W = 8/9C

International terms of trade:
  Not less than W = 8/9C
  Not more than W = 6/5C

Domestic terms of exchange without trade:
  England: 10B = 15L
  Germany: 10B = 20L

International terms of trade:
  Not less than 10B = 15L
  Not more than 10B = 20L

Issues and Answers from the Masterworks 8.2

Issue
How are the values of internationally traded commodities established and how are the gains from trade shared between trading partners?

Mill's answer
From *Principles of Political Economy, with Some of Their Applications to Social Philosophy*, Book 3, Chapter 18.

Of international values

1. The values of imported commodities depend on the terms of international interchange

The values of commodities produced at the same place, or in places sufficiently adjacent for capital to move freely between them – let us say, for simplicity, of commodities produced in the same country – depend (temporary fluctuations apart) upon their cost of production. But the value of commodity brought from a distant place, especially from a foreign country, does not depend on its cost of production in the place from whence it comes. On what, then, does it depend? The value of a thing in any place, depends on the cost of its acquisition in that place; which in the case of an imported article, means the cost of production of the thing which is exported to pay for it.

Since all trade is in reality barter, money being a mere instrument for exchanging things against one another, we will, for simplicity, begin by supposing the international trade to be in form, what it always is in reality, an actual trucking of one commodity against another. As far as we have hitherto proceeded, we have found all the laws of interchange to be essentially the same, whether money is used or not; money never governing, but always obeying, those general laws.

If, then, England imports wine from Spain, giving for every pipe of wine a bale of cloth, the exchange value of a pipe of wine in England will not depend upon what the production of the wine may have cost in Spain, but upon what the production of the cloth has cost in England. Though the wine may have cost in Spain the equivalent of only ten days' labour, yet, if the cloth costs in England twenty days' labour, the wine, when brought to England, will exchange for the produce of twenty days' English labour, *plus* the cost of carriage; including the usual profit on the importer's capital, during the time it is locked up, and withheld from other employment.

The value, then, in any country, of a foreign commodity, depends on the quantity of home produce which must be given to the foreign country in exchange for it. In other words, the values of foreign commodities depend on the terms of international exchange. What, then, do these depend upon? What is it, which, in the case supposed, causes a pipe of wine from Spain to be exchanged with England for exactly that quantity of cloth? We have seen that it is not their cost of production . . .

2. The terms of international interchange depend on the Equation of International Demand

When the trade is established between the two countries, the two commodities will exchange for each other at the same rate of interchange in both countries. Supposing, therefore, for the sake of argument, that the carriage of the commodities from one country to the other could be effected without labour and without cost, no sooner would the trade be opened than the value of the two commodities, estimated in each other, would come to a level in both countries.

Suppose that 10 yards of broadcloth cost in England as much labour as 15 yards of linen, and in Germany as much as 20. In common with most of my predecessors, I find it advisable, in these intricate investigations, to give distinctness and fixity to the conception by numerical examples. These examples must sometimes, as in the present case, be purely suppositions. I should have preferred real ones; but all that is essential is, that the numbers should be such as admit of being easily followed through the subsequent combinations into which they enter.

This supposition then being made, it would be the interest of England to import linen from Germany, and of Germany to import cloth from England. When each country produced both commodities for itself, 10 yards of cloth exchanged for 15 yards of linen in England, and for 20 in

Germany. They will now exchange for the same number of yards of linen in both. For what number? If for 15 yards, England will be just as she was, and Germany will gain all. If for 20 yards, Germany will be as before, and England will derive the whole of the benefit. If for any number intermediate between 15 and 20, the advantage will be shared between the two countries. If, for example, 10 yards of cloth exchange for 18 of linen, England will gain an advantage of 3 yards on every 15, Germany will save 2 out of every 20. The problem is, what are the causes that determine the proportion in which the cloth of England and the linen of Germany will exchange for each other?

As exchange value, in this case as in every other, is proverbially fluctuating, it does not matter what we suppose it to be when we begin: we shall soon see whether there be any fixed point about which it oscillates, which it has a tendency always to approach to, and to remain at. Let us suppose, then, that by the effect of what Adam Smith calls the 'higgling' of the market, 10 yards of cloth in both countries, exchange for 17 yards of linen.

The demand for a commodity, that is, the quantity of it which can find a purchaser, varies as we have before remarked, according to the price. In Germany the price of 10 yards of cloth is now 17 yards of linen, or whatever quantity of money is equivalent in Germany to 17 yards of linen. Now, that being the price, there is some particular number of yards of cloth, which will be in demand, or will find purchasers, at that price. There is some given quantity of cloth, more than which could not be disposed of at that price; less than which, at that price, would not fully satisfy the demand. Let us suppose this quantity to be 1000 times 10 yards.

Let us now turn our attention to England. There, the price of 17 yards of linen is 10 yards of cloth, or whatever quantity of money is equivalent in England to 10 yards of cloth. There is some particular number of yards of linen which, at that price, will exactly satisfy the demand, and no more. Let us suppose that this number is 1000 times 17 yards.

As 17 yards of linen are to 10 yards of cloth, so are 1000 times 17 yards to 1000 times 10 yards. At the existing exchange value, the linen which England requires will exactly pay for the quantity of cloth which, on the same terms of interchange, Germany requires. The demand on each side is precisely sufficient to carry off the supply on the other. The conditions required by the principle of demand and supply are fulfilled, and the two commodities will continue to be interchanged, as we supposed them to be, in the ratio of 17 yards of linen for 10 yards of cloth.

But our suppositions might have been different. Suppose that, at the assumed rate of interchange, England has been disposed to consume no greater quantity of linen than 800 times 17 yards: it is evident that, at the rate supposed, this would not have sufficed to pay for the 1000 times 10 yards of cloth which we have supposed Germany to require at the assumed value. Germany would be able to procure no more than 800 times 10 yards at that price. To procure the remaining 200, which she would have no means of doing but by bidding higher for them, she would offer more than 17 yards of linen in exchange for 10 yards of cloth: let us suppose her to offer 18. At this price, perhaps, England would be inclined to purchase a greater quantity of linen. She would consume, possibly, at that price, 900 times 18 yards. On the other hand, cloth having risen in price, the demand of Germany for it would probably have diminished. If, instead of 1000 times 10 yards, she is now contented with 900 times 10 yards, these will exactly pay for the 900 times 18 yards of linen which England is willing to take at the altered price: the demand on each side will again exactly suffice to take off the corresponding supply; and 10 yards for 18 will be the rate at which, in both countries, cloth will exchange for linen.

The converse of all this would have happened, if, instead of 800 times 17 yards, we had supposed that England, at the rate of 10 for 17, would have taken 1200 times 17 yards of linen. In this case, it is England whose demand is not fully supplied; it is England who, by bidding for more linen, will alter the rate of interchange to her own disadvantage; and 10 yards of cloth will fall, in both countries, below the value of 17 yards of linen. By this fall of cloth, or what is the same thing, this rise of linen, the demand of Germany for cloth will increase, and the demand of England for linen will diminish, till the rate of interchange has so adjusted itself that the cloth and the linen will exactly pay for one another; and when once this point is attained, values will remain without further alteration.

It may be considered, therefore, as established, that when two countries trade together in two commodities, the exchange value of these commodities relatively to each other will adjust itself to the inclinations and circumstances of the consumers on both sides, in such manner that the quantities required by each country, of the articles which it imports from its neighbour, shall be exactly sufficient to pay for one another . . . The ratios, therefore, in which the advantage of the trade may be divided between the two nations, are various. The circumstances on which the proportionate share of each country more remotely depends, admit only of a very general indication.

Source: Reprinted from the revised edition of John Stuart Mill, *Principles of Political Economy, with Some of Their Applications to Social Philosophy*, Book 3, Chapter 18 (New York: The Colonial Press, 1900), pp. 100–11.

Summing up: Mill's key point on reciprocal demand

Mill's examination of the principle of comparative advantage proceeded in terms of the comparative effectiveness of labor rather than comparative labor cost. Ricardo, it will be recalled, took the output of each commodity in two countries as given and assumed their respective labor costs to be different. Mill, however, assumed a given input of labor in each of the two countries, so the comparative efficiency of labor in production becomes reflected in differing outputs. The product in which a country has the greatest comparative advantage, or the least comparative disadvantage, can then be determined in terms of the comparative efficiency of labor in producing the outputs in question. The real cost of a commodity, then, is the sacrifice its production imposes in terms of the alternative output forgone. In modern terminology, this real cost is termed *opportunity cost*. The rate at which the product of one country will be exchanged for that of a second country depends on the state of *reciprocal demand*, and it is the latter principle that Mill maintained explains how gains from trade will be divided. He concluded that, within the limits set by comparative cost conditions (i.e. 10 yards of cloth cannot exchange for more than 20 yards of linen or for less than 15), the *actual* ratio at which goods are traded internationally depends on the strength and elasticity of each country's demand for the other country's product. In Mill's own words:

It may be considered, therefore, as established, that when two countries trade together in two commodities, the exchange value of these commodities relatively to each other will adjust itself to the inclinations and circumstances of the consumers on both sides, in such manner that the quantities required by each country, of the articles which it imports from its neighbor, shall be exactly sufficient to pay for one another.[13]

It does not follow, however, that the gains from trade will necessarily be equally divided, although both gain from trade. If, for example, country X has a relatively greater demand for commodity A than country Y has for commodity B, the actual rate of barter exchange would favor country Y. That is, Y would be acquiring commodity B by exchanging it for A at a relatively greater saving in terms of labor than that which is enjoyed by country X in importing A from country Y. This idea is expanded by recognizing that the benefit of cost-reducing improvements in the production of a good that is exported may be enjoyed entirely by the importing country if its demand for the product increases proportionately with the reduction in price. Mill thus demonstrates his appreciation of what is today called the *price elasticity of demand*. Mill also recognized that the benefits from trade are reduced by increases in transportation costs and that transportation costs may make it uneconomical to trade certain goods regardless of their production costs.

Classical monetary theory

Mercantilist origins

David Hume, who wrote during the latter part of the mercantilist period, although he was not a mercantilist himself, conceived nominal or money prices as reflecting levels of economic activity that are determined by non-monetary (or 'real') factors. He hypothesized that the quantity of money (which in his day consisted chiefly of gold and silver) had no permanent effect on the level of economic activity. What it affects is the *price level*, i.e. money prices are proportional to a country's quantity of money. The physical quantity of money (e.g. gold) in a country is

unimportant, for any physical quantity can 'do the work of money,' which is to serve as a medium for exchanging goods for one another. The exchange values of these goods are determined by their costs of production and, depending on the (nominal) price level, may be high or low. A country with a relatively small stock of gold will have relatively low prices and, in an open economy, will tend to have a balance of trade surplus. Since the money equivalent of trade surpluses must be paid in gold by those countries which, because of their high prices develop import surpluses, the world's stock of gold becomes redistributed among trading partners so that their respective price levels reflect their relative real costs of production. In the long run, the quantity of the money commodity in a country adjusts so that commodity prices in individual countries are at levels which require no further gold movements, i.e. the balance of payments is in equilibrium.

The validity of Hume's argument depends on the stage of development of the banking system. Like the rest of the economy, the English monetary system underwent a substantial change between the periods of mercantilism and classicism. In Smith's day, money consisted largely of coin and paper notes, redeemable in gold, issued by the Bank of England and relatively few rural banks. Smith was concerned to establish the rule that banks be required to hold sufficient gold against the bank notes they issued to prevent a depreciation in their value. According to the 'real bills' doctrine, banknotes were to be issued only in conjunction with loans to creditors who would repay their debts when their products were sold, thereby taking the bills out of circulation. In the meantime, anyone receiving a paper note during the course of trade had the legal right to exchange it for gold. In principle, therefore, banks would be restrained in their note issue by the obligation to redeem them in gold. Thus Smith and Hume maintained that the quantity of money – whether convertible paper or bullion – has a determining influence on interest rates which they interpret as being determined by the level of profits. The latter, in turn, reflect the level of wages and the costs of worker subsistence, chiefly food. Hume and Smith thus focused chiefly on the 'long run' in which commodity prices came to reflect their 'real' (i.e. labor) costs of production, and it is unnecessary for gold stocks to be redistributed further.

The rather different situation that can arise in the intermediate period during which a country's nominal quantity of money may be inappropriate because banks have improperly controlled their volume of their note issues is one that did not arise until the Napoleonic Wars, when the Bank of England suspended the convertibility of its banknotes into gold. The market price of gold had by then risen to a substantial premium over its official (i.e. mint) price. The experience prompted a famous debate about the reasons for the premium on gold, and to articulate a policy appropriate for dealing with it. David Ricardo became an important contributor to the issues of the so-called Bullion Controversy.

Ricardo and the bullion controversy

For Ricardo, the rise in the market price of gold bullion and its relation to the depreciation of the sterling rate of exchange and the associated rise in commodity prices required careful inquiry. His analysis, intended chiefly for his own clarification, was shown to the editor of the *Morning Chronicle*, who urged its publication in letter form. His letter eventually led to an essay entitled 'The High Price of Bullion: A Proof of the Depreciation of Bank Notes.'[14] Ricardo thus became an active participant in the famous bullion controversy, one of the major issues of the day about which the Bullion Committee issued a report in 1810. Ricardo argued that the cause of both high prices in England and the fall of the rate of exchange of the English pound internationally was the overissue of paper notes. Thus, the issue of 'redundancy' was central to the bullion controversy.

The events leading up to this controversy may be reviewed briefly.[15] The Bank of England had issued paper currency (notes) in excess of the gold available to redeem the supply. With the outbreak of the war with France in 1793, and the demands for advances by the government, the Bank of England found it necessary to suspend specie payments of its notes early in 1797. Suspension initially induced an inward flow of bullion, which eased the strain on the bank and produced a general resurgence of confidence. Subsequently, however, toward the end of 1799, and more particularly from 1809 to the end of the war, the sterling exchange rate fell, and gold rose to a substantial premium over paper. This would not have occurred over such a prolonged period of time on a fully convertible international gold or bimetallic standard, because the convertibility of paper into either gold or silver would have prevented more than temporary divergence from par.

The situation in England, however, was that the sterling exchange rate was at a marked and prolonged discount, while bullion commanded a premium over paper. At the same time, English prices rose substantially relative to those prevailing abroad. The bullionists, with whom Ricardo aligned himself, took the position that currency was depreciated.

Ricardo's essay set forth the view that the premium of bullion over paper currency, the relative rise in English prices over those abroad, and the fall of the sterling exchange below par, are prima facie evidence of depreciation. He attributed this depreciation to the fact that the quantity of currency was greater than it would have been possible to maintain if there had been adherence to the principle of currency convertibility into gold or silver.[16]

The Report of the Bullion Committee proposed reducing the excess supply of currency within two years by restoring the convertibility of bank notes into gold or silver. Ricardo found himself in complete accord with this proposal. He urged that the Bank of England gradually diminish the volume of notes in circulation until the price of gold and silver returned to their mint par. He maintained that, without such a measure, foreign exchange rates would remain unfavorable to England, domestic prices would continue to be high, and gold would continue to be exported. His argument in The High Price of Bullion argued as follows:

> If the Bank directors had kept the amount of their notes within reasonable bounds; if they had acted up to the principle which they have avowed to have been that which regulated their issues when they were obliged to pay their notes in specie, namely, to limit their notes to that amount which should prevent the excess of the market above the Mint price of gold, we should not have been now exposed to all the evils of a depreciated, and perpetually varying currency.[17]

He concluded that if the price of bullion rises above its mint price by more than the cost of shipping it abroad, this is conclusive proof of overissue, or *redundancy*. Redundancy is the 'invariable cause' of disequilibrium in the balance of trade, whether it is produced by 'a diminution of goods or by an actual increased quantity of money (or, which is the same thing, by an increased economy in the use of it) in one country; or by an increased quantity of goods or by a diminished amount of money in another.'[18] In other words, redundancy can be caused either by forces operating on the supply of goods or by the supply of money.

Ricardo made another important contribution to the literature of money and banking in his *Proposals for an Economical and Secure Currency with Observations on the Profits of Stock* (1816). The latter essay concerned itself with the value of money. Ricardo took the position that it is unnecessary for a currency to have intrinsic worth. Rather, what is essential is that the supply of a paper currency be sufficiently limited to maintain its value on a par with the value of gold. He offered a plan for accomplishing this without the expense of making paper convertible into coin to save the expense associated with metallic currency. This plan, which was subsequently adopted by the Bank of England, proposed that bank notes be made convertible into bars of gold bullion of a standard weight and purity instead of making them convertible into gold coin. Although the plan was effective in checking the overissue of notes, it was later decided to continue a mixed currency, even though it was more expensive to maintain than one that consisted exclusively of paper, because the pound notes that replaced sovereigns became subject to forgery.[19]

Concluding thoughts: theory versus policy in economics

Unlike Ricardo, J. S. Mill and Bentham, William Nassau Senior had extensive opportunity to address policy questions in economics. But he was concerned with keeping these inquiries strictly separated from those of a theoretical nature. He believed that as long as the science of political economy is associated with controversial issues of public policy, it cannot develop the body of universal truths which are the hallmarks of science. He was a member of the commission for administering the Poor Laws, and wrote numerous pamphlets relating to the Poor Laws and Factory Acts but, unlike Ricardo and J. S. Mill, his discussions of social problems were always undertaken as a moralist or statesman and not as an economist. His efforts to present economics as a body of generalizations deduced from a small number of postulates give him the distinction of being, methodologically speaking, the first of the pure theorists in England.

Senior's contribution to the methodology of economics

The four postulates

While the technique of establishing economic laws by the process of deduction was already well established when Senior published his *Outline of the Science of Political Economy* (1836), he was the first to explicitly state the postulates or axioms on which economic theory is constructed.[20] His list is extremely limited in that it includes only four postulates from which economic reasoning is properly to proceed. It is preceded by a definition of wealth as all goods and services that possess utility and are scarce.

Senior's first postulate is as follows: '*That every person is desirous to obtain, with as little sacrifice as possible, as much as is possible of the articles of wealth.*' This proposition was, of course, an integral part of economics long before Senior's explicit formulation. The only difference derives from his definition of wealth as including services as well as

material goods. While this conception of wealth obscures the difference between the stock of tangible goods and the flow of money income, it has the advantage of facilitating inquiry into the pricing of services as well as goods. It also facilitates more specific attention to the role of demand in the pricing process than was given by Ricardo. Senior was extremely critical of Ricardo's failure to deal more specifically with utility and demand in the pricing process and considered his first postulate a basis for constructing a theory of value that would take cognizance of utility.

Senior's three remaining postulates are significant for the theory of production and distribution as well as value. His second postulate states '*That the Population of the World, or, in other words the number of persons inhabiting it, is limited only by moral or physical evil, or by a fear of a deficiency of those articles of wealth which the habits of the individuals of each class of its inhabitants lead them to require.*' Although this proposition is reminiscent of Malthus, Senior did not accept the popular doctrine that population tended to expand more rapidly than the food producing potential of land. He maintained, instead, that with the advance of civilization, there is a natural tendency for subsistence to increase in a greater ratio than population.

The difference between Senior's and Malthus's positions on the relationship between the growth of population and the food supply derives from the third postulate, which is stated as follows: '*That the powers of labour, and of the other instruments of production which produce wealth, may be indefinitely increased by using their products as the means of further production.*' This is fundamental to Senior's conception of increasing returns in manufacturing as the result of the application of additional labor.

In contrast with the experience of manu-facturers, the application of additional labor in agriculture results in diminishing returns. Thus, the fourth proposition: '*That agri-cultural skill remaining the same, additional labor employed on the land within a given dis-trict produces in general a less proportionate return, in other words, that though, with every increase of the labor bestowed, the aggregate return is increased, the increase of the return is not in proportion to the increase of the labor.*'

Although these four propositions had already been stated by Senior in his lectures, they assumed a new importance in his *Outline of the Science of Political Economy*, published in 1836, because Senior recognized the use-fulness of separating economic principles (i.e. science) from questions of policy. Senior con-ceived of economics as 'the science which treats the nature, the production and the dis-tribution of Wealth.'[21] The significance of this definition is that it limited economics exclusively to pure theory in order to make it an exact science based on the four postulates and the definition of wealth noted above. Within this conception of the scope of eco-nomics, all questions of policy are part of the science of legislation and are not the concern of the economist.

Mill's objective on the other hand was to modernize *The Wealth of Nations* in the light of 'the more extended knowledge and improved ideas of the present age,' and to examine economic principles with respect to 'their application to social philosophy.'[22] The latter objective sets the tone of the book. Mill is less concerned with theoretical analysis for its own sake than with the application of the doctrines of Malthus and Ricardo, in which he had been steeped since childhood, to the solution of the problems of the age. Thus, he is led at the very outset of his work to dis-tinguish between the laws of production and

those of distribution. The laws governing the production of wealth are physical truths, whereas

> those of Distribution are partly of human insti-tution . . . But though governments of nations have the power of deciding what institutions shall exist, they cannot arbitrarily determine how those institutions shall work. The condi-tions on which the power they possess over the distribution of wealth are as much a subject for scientific inquiry as distribution of wealth . . . are as much a subject for scientific inquiry as any of the physical laws of nature.[23]

His distinction between the laws of produc-tion and the laws of distribution became the vehicle by which Mill reconciled his concern for reform with Malthusian and Ricardian economic principles. The distinction later became unacceptable to neoclassical writers because it implies that the income shares of the factors are independent of the process of production and the determination of exchange values. However, from the stand-point of Mill's reform objectives, the distinc-tion enabled him to tackle questions of social justice on a basis different from that used for questions of productive efficiency.

These reforms, clearly premised on the Utilitarian principle of the 'greatest good for the greatest number,' were conceived of as necessary improvements in the system of individual property, which functions within the framework of human, and therefore alter-able, institutions. Thus, Mill's distinction between the laws of production and exchange and the laws of distribution enabled him to go beyond pure theory, while at the same time adhering to the 'immortal principles' of Ricardo. From the standpoint of doctrine, therefore, the work of Ricardo virtually com-pleted the architecture of classical political economy, although Mill gave the doctrine its most refined statement. This system remained substantially intact, commanding respect and attention throughout most of the nineteenth century, although it encountered criticisms and reactions on several fronts. Except for the efforts of Karl Marx to construct an alternative system on classical foundations, however, no new system of economic analysis was to emerge until that of the marginal utility economists in the latter part of the nineteenth century.

Notes

1 John Stuart Mill, *Principles of Political Economy*, edited by W. J. Ashley (London: Longmans, Green 1885), p. 99.

2 'Bentham,' reprinted in John Stuart Mill, *Dissertations and Discussions*, 3rd edn, vol. 1, (London: Longmans, Green, 1875), p. 353.

3 George Sabine, *A History of Political Theory*, revised edition (New York: Holt, Rinehart & Winston, 1950), pp. 705–15.

4 Departing from this conventional view, Samuel Hollander's *Economics of John Stuart Mill* (Toronto: University of Toronto Press, 1985, vols, 1 and 2) once again advances his earlier theme, this time with specific reference to Mill, that there is an unbroken tradition of thought from Smith to Alfred Marshall; that is, from classical to non-classical thought.

5 John Stuart Mill, Preface, *Principles of Political Economy*, edited by W. J. Ashley (London: Longmans, Green, 1885), p. 2.

6 John Stuart Mill, Preface, *Principles of Political Economy*, edited by W. J. Ashley (London: Longmans, Green, 1885), p. 218.

7 While Mill admits that those who have inherited the savings of others have an advantage, which he believes should be curtailed as much as is consistent with justice to those who left their savings to their descendants, he also points out that laborers share in this advantage (John Stuart Mill, Preface, *Principles of Political Economy*, edited by W. J. Ashley (London: Longmans, Green, 1885), p. 219).

8 The causes and advantages of large-scale production in achieving increasing returns to scale are also examined by Mill with considerable insight. The test, says Mill, of the relative productive efficiency of large-scale versus small-scale establishments in the same business is the ability to sell more cheaply (John Stuart Mill, Preface, *Principles of Political Economy*, edited by W. J. Ashley (London: Longmans, Green, 1885), p. 143).

9 John Stuart Mill, Preface, *Principles of Political Economy*, edited by W. J. Ashley (London: Longmans, Green, 1885), p. 177

10 The argument to contain land rent had decidedly antisocial implications, not so much to Ricardo as to some of his contemporaries. James Mill, for example, argued in favor of the confiscation of rent. Ricardo admits the possibility of doing this by means or taxation, for tax on rent would affect rent only; it would fall wholly on landlords and could not be shifted to any class of consumers. Nevertheless, he appears reluctant to burden the owners of property, *Works* (McCulloch edition) p. 235.

11 The ratio exactly midway between the comparative cost ratio is one cloth to 47/48 wine.

12 Lionel Robbins, *Robert Torrens and the Evolution of Classical Economics* (New York: St. Martins Press, 1955), pp. 21–24.

13 John Stuart Mill, *Principles of Political Economy*, vol. II (1902), p. 142.

14 A rebuttal to Ricardo's views was written by a Mr. Bonsanquet, a merchant who presented his opinions in his *Practical Observations*. Ricardo subsequently published his *Reply to Mr. Bonsanquet's Practical Observations on the Report of the Bullion Committee*, which is generally regarded as one of the most brilliant essays ever written on a controversial issue in the field of economics.

15 These events are the subject of Ricardo's letter to Malthus, 18 June, 1815, reprinted in *Works and Correspondence*, vol. 6, pp. 25–28.

16 Before the suspension of specie payments, England was legally on a bimetallic standard, although the undervaluation of silver at the mint kept it in fact, on a gold standard. Gold coin, however, could not legally be melted down, nor could gold bullion be exported. Metallic money was supplemented by Bank of England notes, which circulated largely in the London area; by bills of exchange drawn on local banks; and, to a limited extent, bank

deposits that could be drawn upon by check. See Jacob Viner, *Studies in the Theory of International Trade* (New York: Harper & Row, 1937), p. 137.

17 David Ricardo, 'The high price of bullion' in *Works* (McCulloch edition), p. 287.

18 Letter to Malthus, *Works and Correspondence*, vol. 6, pp. 25–26.

19 In opposition to the bullionists, adherents of the currency school, however, contended that convertibility alone is an inadequate safeguard and that what is required is the regulation of note issue in such a manner as to correspond to the fluctuations that would have taken place if the currency were purely metallic.

20 Nassau Senior, *Outline of the Science of Political Economy*, 6th edn (London: Allen & Unwin, 1872), p. 22.

21 Nassau Senior, *Outline of the Science of Political Economy*, 6th edn (London: Allen & Unwin, 1872), p. 1.

22 John Stuart Mill, Preface, *Principles of Political Economy*, edited by W. J. Ashley (London: Longmans, Green, 1885), p. 2.

23 John Stuart Mill, Preface, *Principles of Political Economy*, edited by W. J. Ashley (London: Longmans, Green, 1885), p. 21.

Questions for discussion and further research

1 William Nassau Senior maintained that for economics to be a science, it must concern itself with establishing general laws about the behavior of the economy. Explain the proper methodology for establishing these laws.

2 What are the four postulates, or axioms, that Senior argued the economist should use as the basis for discovering economic laws? Be specific.

3 Besides labor and land, Senior recognized a third factor of production, which he called abstinence. What is the nature of its reward and why should it go to the capitalist?

4 Mill recognized that the gains from trade are not always shared equally. What is

Glossary of terms and concepts

Abstinence

Postponement of consumption in order to facilitate the production of 'intermediate' (i.e. capital) goods. In Senior's view, this act is rewarded by profit.

Barter terms of trade

The ratio (in physical terms) at which two goods exchange in international exchange.

Principle of comparative advantage

Under conditions of free trade, a region will tend to specialize in the production of those goods in which it has the greatest comparative advantage in terms of cost, or the least comparative disadvantage.

The real bills doctrine

The principle maintains that banks should restrict their loans to businessmen whose collateral consists of commodities that can be sold if necessary to redeem a promise to pay. The loans are made in paper currency in amounts no larger than each bank can redeem in gold.

Reciprocal demand

The relative urgency of demand that trading partners have for one another's goods. This concept was introduced by J. S. Mill to explain how the benefits of trade would be shared. Unlike Ricardo, Mill did not assume they would be shared equally.

Senior's four postulates

Senior was the first to stipulate specifically the premises on which he considered it appropriate as a basis for constructing a deductive argument in economics. The first relates to the basic human propensity to acquire as much wealth as possible with minimum effort; the second relates to the principle of human population to increase in accordance with the food supply; the third relates to diminishing returns; the fourth is that the powers of labor and other instruments of wealth (i.e. capital) are able to yield an increasing product when their products are used in further production. Senior's postulate is thus an early statement of the gains inherent in roundabout production.

the principle according to which they are shared?

5 What is the concept of the wage fund? On what basis did Mill recant his earlier view as regards its role in establishing the compensation of labor?

Notes for further reading

From *The New Palgrave*

Peter Groenewegen on political economy and economics, vol. 3, pp. 904–6; K. H. Hennings on waiting, vol. 4, pp. 846–48; Samuel Hollander on John Stuart Mill as economic theorist, vol. 3, pp. 471–75; N. de Marchi on abstinence, vol. 1, p. 8, and on William Nassau Senior, vol. 4, pp. 303–5; D. H. Monro on self-interest, vol. 4, pp. 297–99; Alan Ryan on John Stuart Mill, vol. 3, pp. 466–71; and Donald Winch on James Mill, vol. 3, pp. 465–66.

Selected references and suggestions for further reading

Baumol, W. J. *Economic Dynamics*. 3rd edn (New York: Macmillan, 1970).

Coats, A. W. (ed.) *The Classical Economists and Economic Policy* (London: Methuen, 1971).

Eagley, Robert V. *The Structure of Classical Economic Theory* (New York: Oxford University Press, 1974).

Fetter, Frank W. 'The influence of economists in parliament on British legislation from Ricardo to John Stuart Mill.' *Journal of Political Economy*, 83 (October, 1975), pp. 1051–67. See especially p. 1054.

Grampp, William. 'Economic opinion when Britain turned to free trade.' *History of Political Economy*, 14(4) (Winter, 1982) pp. 496–520.

Halévy, Elie. *The Growth of Philosophical Radicalism* (New York: Augustus Kelley, 1949).

Henderson, James P. 'The oral tradition' in British economics: influential economists in the 'Political Economy Club of London.' *History of Political Economy*, 15(2) (Summer, 1983) pp. 149–79.

Hicks, J. R. *Capital and Growth* (London: Oxford University Press, 1965), chapter 4.

Marvel, H. P. 'Factory regulation: a reinterpretation of early English experience.' *Journal of Law and Economics*, 20 (October, 1977), pp. 379–402.

Robbins, Lionel. *The Theory of Policy in Classical Political Economy* (New York: Macmillan, 1952).

Robbins, Lionel. Lecture 22 'International Trade,' Lecture 23 'John Stuart Mill', in *A History of Economic Thought*, edited by S. Medema and W. Samuels (Princeton NJ: Princeton University Press, 1998), pp. 210–28.

Viner, Jacob. 'Bentham and J. S. Mill: the utilitarian background.' Reprinted in *The Long View and the Short* (New York: Free Press, 1958).

Viner, Jacob. *Studies in the Theory of International Trade* (London: G. Allen, 1937).

Chapter 9

Classical theory in review: from Quesnay to McCulloch

Scope and method

In the first half of the eighteenth century, it was France, rather than England, that had a school of theoretical economists; Quesnay and the Physiocrats conceived of political economy as the science that seeks the laws governing the distribution of wealth. While Adam Smith did not distinguish between economics as a science and economics as a branch of politics, his French disciple, Jean-Baptiste Say, used the deductive method to derive the laws that govern the production, distribution, and consumption of wealth. His method and logical arrangement of the subject matter of economics were probably introduced into England through James Mill, who studied the work of the Physiocrats and was also well acquainted with Say.[1] Mill taught the deductive method to David Ricardo, whose work became the prototype for a school of thinkers who reasoned from premises that were accepted *a priori* or that had been previously arrived at by deduction to discover universal laws of production, exchange, and distribution.

It was Karl Marx (1818–83) who coined the term 'classical' political economy to characterize the writings of economists from William Petty to David Ricardo. Their tradition was continued by William Nassau Senior, John Stuart Mill, John Elliott Cairnes, and J. R. McCulloch. All elaborated and refined in some way the economic principles and methodological tools introduced by the Physiocrats, Smith, and Say. Their predominantly deductive methodology and the economic laws which they discovered were almost universally accepted until about 1870. Characterizing their work as classical also serves to distinguish it from that of the various dissenting schools that appeared coincidentally, or shortly afterward, in England and to an even greater extent on the Continent. It is, however, an over-simplification to suggest that the contributions made before 1870 came from writers who were exponents of classical economics, while those who came afterwards dissented in some major way from the basic themes that characterized the classical tradition. Classical economics is not so pure a tradition that one cannot discern elements of difference, even though the characteristic of heterogeneity and continuity dominates.

The writings of the later classicists were more rigorous, but also had less popular appeal than Adam Smith's in *The Wealth of Nations*. The scope of their inquiry was more narrowly restricted than Smith's because of their conception of economics as a science for discovering the laws governing the production, exchange, and distribution of wealth.

Smith was concerned with policy almost as much as he was with analysis. But later members of the classical school generally took the position that, if economics is to be a science, it must restrict itself to analyzing the functioning of the economy and not intrude into policy-making, where value judgments necessarily come into play and inject bias.

At least in principle, economists have since attempted to preserve the distinction between pure economics and *applied* economics. The former seeks only to establish laws, while the latter is normative and seeks to alter the results that emanate from economic laws. This distinction became particularly important in the writings of later classicists. John Stuart Mill went so far as to consider communism as an alternative to capitalism. His chapter 'On property' examines the origin of private property and proceeds to an extremely sympathetic discussion of socialism and communism. He observes that if

the choice were to be made between Communism with all it choices, and the present [1852] state of society with all its suffering and injustices; if the institution of private property necessarily carried with it as a consequence, that the produce of labour should be apportioned as we now see it, almost in an inverse ratio to the labour ... if this or communism were the alternative, all the difficulties, great or small of Communism would be but as dust in the balance.[2]

Mill is not, however, prepared to take an unequivocal stand in favor of communism, feeling that we must first consider 'the regime of individual property, not as it is, but as it might be made.'[3] Mill takes the position that the basic tenet of the institution of property is the right of each person to the 'exclusive disposal of what he or she may have produced by their own exertions.'[4] Thus, one is entitled to the product of one's labor and one's

abstinence.[5] Accordingly, Mill's *Principles of Political Economy* which enjoyed a position of unchallenged leadership from the time of its publication in 1848 until the publication of Marshall's *Principles of Economics* published in 1890, began by distinguishing between (a) the immutable laws of production and exchange, rooted in nature, and (b) the laws of distribution, or income sharing, which are primarily the result of human institutions. To discover the first set of laws, classical writers examined the theme of *production*, in contrast with the mercantilist focus on the potential for increasing wealth via exchange. Examination of the laws of distribution, on the other hand, led Mill to the mature classical view that they are alterable by intervention and, therefore, different from the laws of production, which are rooted in nature and cannot be changed.

Bearing in mind the limitation of lists, the laws of classical economics may conveniently be collected in summary form as follows: (1) the law of value, (2) the law of wages, (3) the law of capital accumulation, (4) the law of population growth, (5) the law of diminishing returns, (6) the law of rent, (7) the law of comparative advantage, (8) the quantity theory of money, and (9) the law of markets.

Most of these generalizations or 'laws' relate to the central classical theme of economic growth and the economy's tendency toward an ultimate stationary state. They were thought to be irrevocable and universally applicable regardless of time, place, or existing institutions. That is, economic laws were seen as operating in the same impersonal way as physical laws, so that they are neither good nor bad, moral or immoral, in and of themselves.

Unlike earlier classicists who believed in the inherent benevolence of nature, later classical writers did not view the laws of economics as inherently beneficent, i.e. able to promote the welfare of the majority of the persons comprising society. Naturally, not all who are collectively referred to as classical economists dealt exhaustively with each of these laws or accepted them without modification.

Classical value theory

The distinction which Adam Smith makes at the end of Chapter 4 between a commodity's value in use and its value in exchange sets the classicist's inquiry into the question of exchange value into motion. He tells us at the outset that 'the things which have the greatest value in use (e.g. water) frequently have little or no value in exchange, while some other commodities (a diamond for example) commands a high price, even though it has little or no value in use.' This juxtaposition of value in use and value in exchange has come to be called 'the Adam Smith problem.' This is because subsequent thinkers were confounded by the Smithian notion that a commodity could command a price without having value in use. Thus, he sets classical thinking on the road to being essentially a cost of production theory.

Once the 'early and rude state of society' which precedes private ownership of land and the accumulation of capital is over, a commodity's 'natural price' resolves itself into the wages of labor, the profits of capital, and the rents of land, each of which tends toward its own natural level. In the absence of a clear theory of profit and confusion as to whether rent is a cause of price (i.e. a cost of production), or an effect of it (i.e. a differential surplus), at least some of Smith's followers were understandably led to interpret it as a labor theory of value. Clearly, Smith set classical value theory onto a rocky road in requiring

those who came after him not only to rethink the demand side of price determination, but also to rethink what is the nature of capital, how it relates to the understanding of profit and interest, and whether rent is a differential surplus or a cost of production.

Ricardo struggled mightily with all of these questions, particularly as they relate to capital. Less progress was achieved with respect to the importance of use value, which he thought of as a 'prerequisite' to exchange value, especially for those commodities which are not reproducible without limit through the application of additional labor. Thus, it is not until John Stuart Mill's treatment of exchange value, which he placed after his examination of production and distribution, that a substantially correct statement of the law of demand and supply and the idea of price as representing an equilibrium between demand and supply in a schedule sense was developed. However, like Ricardo, Mill apparently thought of supply and demand as determining short-run prices, while costs determine long-run prices. Thus, the role of demand never achieves the importance in classical analysis that it would be given in the analyses of subsequent writers on the value problem, such as Léon Walras, Carl Menger, William Stanley Jevons and Alfred Marshall. The notable exception is the classical analysis of the barter terms of trade which J. S. Mill explained with the aid of a distinctly new concept – reciprocal demand.[6]

Wages and capital accumulation

It is a basic premise of classical economics that laborers are maintained out of the wage fund, whose size depends on the decision of capitalists to expend their earnings in advance to productive labor rather than in unproductive consumption. Thus, the demand for labor is enhanced by the capitalists' abstinence, because wages represent the advances that capitalists make to workers during the production process. It thus led classicists to the law of wages, which conceives of the average wage rate as being dependent on the relationship between the number of workers seeking employment and the size of the wages fund available.[7]

This leads Mill to his second fundamental proposition with respect to capital, namely that 'capital is the result of saving.' It is at this point that the Smith–Say principle that 'saving is spending' is invoked. According to this principle, which has come to be known as *Say's identity*, purchasing power is not destroyed or lost; income not used for consumption expenditures will be used to support investment, either as fixed or as circulating capital. Mill identifies the capitalists' reward for abstinence as representing net profit and interest, for gross profit also includes a return for the risks and superintendence of the 'undertaker.'[8] It is thus Mill, rather than Senior, who deserves credit that the classical school eventually recognized that interest and profit are returns associated with the performance of *different* functions. Nevertheless, the classical explanation of the level of the interest rate leaves much to be desired, for it proceeds only in terms of abstinence and the supply price of savings. The demand for savings based on the productive services of capital was not part of classical thinking. This is evident in Mill's observation that, strictly speaking, capital has no productive power, but only sets productive labor into motion. The classicists seem not to have understood the significance of the concept of roundabout production in connection with explaining the phenomenon of interest.

The law of rent emerges because the tendency toward diminishing returns forces a resort to the inferior margin of cultivation, and competition causes price to equal the cost of producing a product on the least productive land in cultivation. A differential surplus in the form of rent will therefore make its appearance on superior grades of land. This principle is primarily associated with Thomas Malthus and David Ricardo, who relied on it to explain the basis for the distribution income share received by landowners as a social class separate and distinct from that of the wage earning and capital owning classes. The classical approach to explaining distribution as the sharing of income among the three great social classes – workers, capitalists and landlords – which was also the treatment it was given by Nassau Senior and John Stuart Mill as latter day classicists, was quite different from the so-called 'functional distribution' perspective which conceived of incomes as factor rewards that reflect the contributions of labor, capital, land and enterprise to the value of the product. This is the perspective of both the great French thinker J. B. Say (of law of markets fame) and the marginalist thinkers whose ideas dominated after 1870 as part of the dissent from classicism.

It is also worth noting at this juncture that Say, unlike the classicists, accorded a unique role to the entrepreneur who arranges and manages production for which, if he is successful, he earns profit. Classical economists were invariably confused by the distinction between interest and profit as separate income in the sense that they reward different functions.

Say's law

Both Malthus and Ricardo considered the possibility that demand insufficiency might arise. For Malthus the possibility of insufficient aggregate demand was linked to the different spending habits of wage and profit receivers. Wage earners direct all their wages to the purchase of 'wage goods' (in a 'corn into corn' fashion), whereas capitalist's savings support not only the wages fund, but also 'machinery' which worsens the prospect that there will be sufficient purchasing power to pay for the entire output at high enough prices to sustain the process. It is for this reason that he emphasized the potential power of landlord rents to offset any difference that might arise, and supported the Corn Law as a vehicle for maintaining high corn prices and consequently landlord rents.

The link between classical growth and distribution theory

The laws of diminishing returns, population growth, wage determination, rent, and capital accumulation jointly provide the basis for linking the classical models of economic growth and income distribution. Classical economists conceived of growth in much the same way we do today; that is, in terms of an increase in per capita income. Economic development is thus the result of both population growth and net capital accumulation. The former depends on, and is limited by, the availability of subsistence, while the latter depends on the savings propensities of capitalists, because workers are assumed to spend all of their wages. Smith's dictum that 'parsimony and not industry is the immediate cause of the increase of capital' is thus fundamental to the classical conception of the growth process. It is perhaps intuitively obvious that the growth phenomenon is a dynamic process in which one or more of the magnitudes that relate to the determination of income in the present 'carry over' and determine the income level achieved in the next period. In the classical model this surplus provided the basis for

savings and the accumulation of the capital stock. Growth requires a sufficiently large product to leave a residual for profit, after the wage requirements of the laboring population and the rental payments of the landlord class have been met.

The relationships among the key variables lend themselves readily to graphic representation. In terms of Figure 9.1, output is shown on the vertical axis and population and the labor force are on the horizontal. When population is relatively small, say at N_1, and only the best soils are required to produce output Y_1; food costs and, therefore, wage rates are relatively low. Economic rent, which is the surplus that appears on the superior land, is zero when only the simple best grade is cultivated. It has a positive, but nevertheless low, value as 'second best' lands are brought under cultivation in the early stages of development. Profit levels are relatively high because they are inversely related to wage rates. This encourages accumulation and supports an increased wage fund, which, at least in the short run, facilitates wage rate increases and improved levels of living for workers.

As population grows to N_2, cultivation of poorer grades of land is required. Output grows, say, to Y_2 as additional labor is applied at the margin, although the increase proceeds at a decreasing rate, as is reflected in the shape of the output curve. The size of the wage bill required to support the working class then absorbs an increasing share of the economy's output. This *depresses* the level of profits remaining to capitalists as a residual, which necessarily *discourages* accumulation and further growth. Only the proportion of output accruing to the landowning class as rent continues to rise. Thus, the impetus to growth winds down and the economy eventually approaches the classical stationary state. The

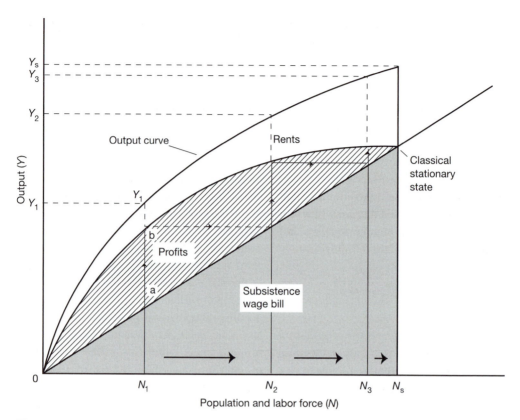

Figure 9.1 Population and labor force (N)

Source: Based on William J. Baumol, *Economic Dynamics*, 2nd edn (New York: Macmillan, 1969)

inexorable law of diminishing returns, coupled with the requirements of a growing population for food and necessaries at some culturally set level, will then have pressured the level of profits to such a low level (though not necessarily to zero) that net capital accumulation can no longer be supported. The stationary state in which both population growth and net capital accumulation cease will then come into existence. Concern about international trade follows directly from the ultimate threat of the stationary state, for access to cheap food offers a means for postponing, as far as possible into the future, its inevitable onset. It is for this reason that

Ricardo supported free trade in corn to keep food prices low. On the other hand, Malthus, reasoning from the same set of circumstances, supported the Corn Laws not only to protect pushing additional workers into the unhealthy environment of factory life, but to maintain landlord rents as a source of aggregate demand.

Classical writers conceived of international trade as governed by the same laws that govern individual exchange. Like individual exchange, international exchange yields a gain to both participants. If there is freedom to buy in the cheapest market, those commodities that would impose the greatest costs if produced domestically will be purchased abroad. The value of a commodity that is imported from abroad depends on the cost of producing the commodity exported in exchange for it. This is the essence of Ricardo's famous law of comparative cost, which was further elaborated by John Stuart Mill.

Classicism and utilitarianism

Most post-Smithian economists denied that there is a *natural* harmony of egoisms, which was such an important idea to Smith. They were thus persuaded by the Utilitarian view that education, religious sanctions, the criminal justice system, and legislative policy must be directed at shaping human conduct to make it compatible with the common good. For J. S. Mill and Bentham, the goal of public policy ought to be the 'greatest good for the greatest number'; Mill was thus persuaded of the necessity for distinguishing between an individual's 'happiness' and what is 'good' for him and ultimately for society.

This policy objective raises the question of whether 'the rules of arithmetic are applicable in the valuation of happiness, as of all other measurable quantities.'[9] Mill's belief that individuals differ in their capacities for feeling and that pleasures differ in kind as well as in magnitude, implies that they cannot be sufficiently uniform to be measurable. 'Competent judges' may be able to evaluate the quality of different pleasures and pains. Yet Mill objected to this possible way around the measurement problem, because in emphasizing the central importance of individual liberty as integral to human happiness, he rejected the idea that progress can be achieved by social reforms that rely on a central rather than local authority and on individual self-reliance, especially on the part of the worker.

The ultimate problem of translating Utilitarianism into social policy is that individual utilities are neither measurable or additive. Thus, as a practical matter, the economic analysis of mid-nineteenth century English writers was essentially based on Smith's psychology of individual behavior, which emphasizes the natural inclination of people to maximize their personal gains, if they are free to do so. This does not imply that people's interests are only pecuniary, but rather that pecuniary interests have been singled out for special consideration.

Classicists thus envisaged business owners as seeking to decrease costs to maximize profits and minimize losses, while workers seek to increase wages and work fewer hours, and landlords and moneylenders seek to maximize rent and interest. This view of human behavior owes nothing to the hedonistic psychology of Utilitarianism, although it is compatible with it.

The independence of classical economics from Utilitarianism and its hedonistic psychology is particularly evident in the emphasis on cost of production in the determination of natural price. Even though Smith and his followers explained the oscillations of market price around natural price in terms of demand and supply, they had little understanding of the relationship between utility and demand. Otherwise Bentham's felicific calculus might have added a new dimension to post-Smithian economics by leading to a theory of value that accorded a greater role to the demand side of price determination. This, in turn, could have led to an understanding of the conditions of maximum consumer satisfaction and optimum resource allocation. Bentham did, after all, understand the principle of diminishing marginal utility, which was later to figure so importantly in the thinking of the marginal utility theorists; he observed that while happiness is associated with the possession of wealth, each addition to an individual's wealth will not produce a corresponding, increase in happiness. On the contrary, 'the quantity of happiness produced by a particle of wealth, each particle being of the same magnitude, will be less and less at every particle. The second will produce less than the first, the third less than the second and so on.'[10] This observation did not, however, lead Bentham to a utility theory of value. The fact that his felicific calculus was nothing more than a table or list of the various sources of human pleasure is probably a major reason why it did not serve as a fruitful beginning for a utility-oriented theory of value. This sort of theory developed only after it was understood that a mathematical calculus is required to define the conditions under which consumer satisfactions are maximized by balancing infinitely small increments of utility and disutility.

Neglect of the role of utility in explaining decision making may also be the result of the classicist's orientation to business rather than consumer behavior. While it was shown that the competitive market leads to an optimum allocation of resources among different industries, the effectiveness of this process was interpreted in terms of monetary gains for the business owner, rather than the maximization of consumer satisfaction, or utility, as it was later called. Thus, classical writers chose to refine Smith's labor cost theory of value instead of developing a value theory premised on a theory of consumer behavior. Only Say and Senior gave utility a significant role by maintaining that prices are proportional to utilities. But their failure to recognize that it is the utility of *marginal* unit that is important prevented them from developing a utility-oriented theory of value.

The quantity theory of money: dichotomizing the pricing process

The chief architects of mature classicism did not break new ground in the area of monetary theory. Like Ricardo, their analytical approach was to dichotomize the pricing process in the sense that they explained the determination of individual commodity prices and the general price level (which is the average of all commodity and factor prices) as *unrelated* to one another. Individual commodity prices reflect the exchange values of pairs of commodities, based on their relative labor and capital costs. The general price level, on the other hand, was thought to reflect the relationship between the quantity of money (i.e. gold and paper notes) and the supply of commodities that the money stock was to circulate.

In the language of Smith, money serves as a 'wheel of circulation,' but it is neutral in the sense that it has no effect on output or other real magnitudes. The preceding perspective underlies Ricardo's argument that such monetary abuses as the issue of bank notes with insufficient gold backing to assure their redemption in specie if the public presented them for collection, lead to domestic inflation and depresses the country's rate of exchange in the international market. It will be recalled that this was precisely the reason why he advocated convertibility for the paper notes issued by the Bank of England.

Ricardo's *Plan of a National Bank* (1823), published posthumously, thus proposed to give the *state* (as opposed to the Bank of England) a monopoly over issuing paper currency, but only against new gold holdings. This plan, in essence, reflected the old Smithian principle that paper money is an efficient substitute for gold and silver. Ricardo's refinement was to suggest that currency *elasticity* could be achieved by giving the central bank power to engage in open-market purchases and sales of government securities, based on alterations in the exchange rate between sterling and other currencies.

Classical writers as parliamentarians

While one would, perhaps, not expect men whose intellectual interests made them great economic thinkers also to be political leaders, the fact is that their parliamentary representation was most impressive. The 49 years that elapsed between February 1819, when David Ricardo took his seat in Parliament, to November, 1868, which marks the end of John Stuart Mill's brief three-year parliamentary career, was a period of high representation by economists in the national legislature, unparalleled in Britain or any other country. Between the founding date of the Political Economy Club of London, in 1821, and 1868, 52 of its 108 members were also members of Parliament.[11] Even though half this number might be termed passive economists, their recorded voting record suggests their influence was substantially higher than that of the entire House of Commons.

Ricardo and Mill sought Parliamentary seats because they and their supporters believed they could be persuasive in bringing about social and political reforms on the basis of sound economic principles. Although their influence, and that of less well known economists – among them Robert Torrens, Sir Henry Parnell, and Richard Whately – was often that of opposing legislation they considered hostile to the reforms they wanted, their backbench influence was enhanced by the extraordinary political talent of men like Sir Robert Peel. Though Peel made no contribution to economic analysis, he played a leading role in the passage of the Specie Resumption Act of 1817, The Bank Act of 1844, and the repeal of the Corn Laws in 1846.

Most economists who were members of Parliament aligned themselves with the Whigs, whose political persuasion was liberal and, at times, even radical, in comparison with the conservative Tories. Their thinking on political and social issues was an expression of Utilitarian principles as a basis for bringing about economic reforms. Their aim was to guarantee the public interest by means of legislation, for they doubted that Smith's doctrine of the natural harmony of interests could be relied on to promote the general welfare in England's burgeoning textile industry; in which children under 14 worked in excess of 60 hours a week. This gave rise to the so-called Ten Hour Movement, which led to the Factory Acts of 1802, 1819, and 1833, and regulated the hours and working conditions of children. The Act of 1833 introduced a unique policing technique that provided for a system of factory inspectors to identify infringements and report them to the Home Office for correction.[12]

Nevertheless, the English economy retained a high degree of freedom from governmental intervention during the nineteenth century. This is attributable, in part, to the efforts of William Gladstone to induce Parliament to limit the tax funds available to government. Specifically, sales and excise taxes were prohibited, and income taxes were reduced, as were revenues from tariffs when the Corn Laws were repealed in 1846. Intervention was thus necessarily limited by the funds available to government for spending. In addition, England adhered to a metallic gold standard, which was suspended only during extraordinary periods of financial strain, like that produced by the Napoleonic Wars. The requirement for convertibility of notes, restored in 1821, strictly limited the ability of government to finance itself by issuing paper money. In spite of pressure by economists for positive steps by government to help the poor and aid productive business (often at the expense of landowners), they were also opposed, in principle, to a large role by government in making expenditures that also provided employment for the sons of the aristocracy and supported the Establishment.

Appraisal of classicism

Classical economic theory attempted to provide, first, a simplified model of the operation of the actual economic system. Second, it attempted to offer a hypothesis concerning its probable future long-run development. Finally, its philosophical and psychological foundations were thought to offer a basis for a policy of economic liberalism which would leave businesses substantially free from governmental regulations. How well were these objectives satisfied?

The conception of the operation of the economic system – which is fundamental to classical analysis – is that its functioning is comparable to a self-correcting physical mechanism capable of automatic adjustment to external forces disturbing its equilibrium. This assumption proved to be most valid while the economy was in its preindustrial stage of development. Later, as industrialization altered the system, the assumption of automatic adjustment became less valid and rendered analysis conducted on that assumption less tenable. Malthus's theory of gluts was in the nature of an internal attack on the classical system in this regard. The impact of this theory was, however, undermined by the prominence that Say's law of markets assumed in Ricardo's thinking. Ricardo's views about the ability of markets to become

cleared of output were so persuasive that subsequent analyses of the nature and cause of economic crisis came largely from such heretics as Jean Charles Sismondi and Karl Marx. Even though his chapter on machinery suggested that workers might become 'redundant' as a result of technological change, the overall perception of an economy capable of self-regulation for the common good persisted into the twentieth century. Indeed, its influence both on analytical economics and practical policy was so persuasive that it led John Maynard Keynes to lament the limited influence of Malthus's thinking about aggregate demand, 'If only Malthus [whom Keynes referred as 'the first of the Cambridge economists'] instead of Ricardo had been the parent stem from which nineteenth century economics proceeded, what a much wiser and richer place the world would be today.'[13]

The classical system was conspicuously successful in providing a basis for political theory. Philosophically, the roots of its political system stem from John Locke's conception of the natural order. Thus, political *laissez-faire* became the logical counterpart of classical economic theory. Not everyone agreed, however, that the property relations that came into existence in the course of time coincided with the requirements of the natural order. This was much in evidence in the policy reforms that economists pressed for as members of Parliament.

Bentham's system of Utilitarianism, which is a later expression of the philosophy of natural law compared with Locke's, can be used to lend support to a radical movement as well as to a conservative one.[14] The principle of utility provides an unequivocal basis for *laissez-faire* only if egotistic behavior can be relied on to produce socially altruistic behavior, as would be the case if the same basic desires can be attributed to all people, so that they engage in essentially the same behavior to maximize pleasure and avoid pain. But this presupposes, not only that individuals are, in fact, the best judges of their own interests and that the pleasures and pains of different persons are homogeneous and comparable, but also that individuals commonly and regularly make rational calculations with respect to the pleasures and pains associated with the various modes of behavior open to them. If these conditions are not realized, it is a simple matter to make out a case for state intervention. If, for example, competition cannot be relied upon to assure everyone a just share of society's product, or if general overproduction is possible, or if the urge for procreation is so powerful that population tends to multiply without reference to the supply and fertility of land, there is a basis for arguing that the state should properly intervene to improve and correct these conditions.

Bentham himself prescribed that governmental intervention in economic matters be limited, but the limits he suggested were not so narrow as to support the doctrine that a natural harmony of interests always exists in a society unregulated by government. More to the point was that the problem of measuring the 'greatest good' to provide a basis for reforms intended to increase the 'sum of happiness' was imperiled for lack of data and a technique for establishing the hedonic balance sheet needed to provide guidance to policy makers. In principle the classical economists who followed him advocated *laissez-faire* as a general rule, they also recognized that legislation is sometimes required when interests are naturally divergent; they thus recommended numerous exceptions to *laissez-faire* on the basis of the principle of utility. This was, indeed, the position of Ricardo and Mill as members of Parliament.

The frequently expressed notion that the classicists regarded the functions of government as being wholly negative is quite erroneous in spite of its persistence.[15]

Indeed, the concern which Parliament was beginning to have about the hardships that the industrial revolution had imposed on the working class is reflected in the support given to data collection to provide a factual basis for policy. While Adam Smith, as has already been noted, 'had no great faith in political arithmetick,' his disenchantment stemmed chiefly from his disagreement with the political objectives of mercantilism and Colbertism. Thus, in keeping with his commitment to the natural order philosophy of the enlightenment, he and those who followed him in the classical tradition relied on deductive logic to infer the functioning of the natural order. But those who came later, among them Malthus and J. S. Mill, appreciated the necessity for factual information. This need also coincided with the methodological attack, which was about to emerge against Ricardian deductive economics for the 'second stage' in the development of numeracy in economics.

Notes

1 Elie Halévy, *The Growth of Philosophical Radicalism* (New York: Augustus Kelley, 1949), pp. 266–82.
2 John Stuart Mill, *Principles of Political Economy*, edited by W. J. Ashley (London: Longmans Green, 1885), p. 208.
3 John Stuart Mill, *Principles of Political Economy*, edited by W. J. Ashley (London: Longmans Green, 1885), p. 208.
4 John Stuart Mill, *Principles of Political Economy*, edited by W. J. Ashley (London: Longmans Green, 1885), p. 218.
5 While Mill admits that those who have inherited the savings of others have an advantage, which he believes should be curtailed as

much as is consistent with justice to those who left their savings to their descendants, he also points out that laborers share in this advantage (John Stuart Mill, *Principles of Political Economy*, edited by W. J. Ashley (London: Longmans Green, 1885), p. 219).

6 The role of demand is also recognized in Mill's explanation of the prices of commodities produced under conditions of true joint supply. Neither of these problems had been dealt with by Ricardo, and Mill's treatment is both original and correct.

7 Nothing can therefore be done, either by workers' labor unions or government, to raise the wages of workers as a whole. Only the wages of *particular groups* can be raised, which would necessarily be achieved only at the expense of others. The fallacy of this explanation of the average wage rate, as Mill later recognized, is that the wage flow may be altered by employers of other non-wage recipients. If these groups reduce their own consumption expenditure and divert it to giving more employment, neither the wage fund nor the flow of wages is predetermined. It was this line of reasoning that led Mill to recant the wage-fund doctrine in an 1869 article in the *Fortnightly Review* and to take the position that it is possible for wages to rise so that they absorb, not only the funds initially intended for the maintenance of labor, but also funds intended by the capitalist for other businesses. *Some Unsettled Questions of Political Economy* (London: London School of Economics, 1924), he concluded that, even under competition, there are numerous possible wage rates at which the supply of labor can be absorbed. Since employers generally have greater bargaining power than individual employees, the wage bargain will usually be to the employer's advantage. However, labor unions can, within limits, raise the wage rate by reducing the disparity between the relative strength of the parties to the wage bargain. The practical significance of Mill's recognition of the fallacy of the wage-fund doctrine was that it provided him with a theoretical basis for supporting labor unions.

8 John Stuart Mill, *Principles of Political Economy*, edited by W. J. Ashley (London: Longmans Green, 1885), p. 405

Glossary of terms and concepts

Dichotomization of the pricing process
The examination of individual commodity prices as though the process were unrelated to the determination of the general price level.

Economic liberalism
The economic policy of allowing the market process to reconcile divergent individual interests on the assumption that all people have the same basic desires and are equally capable of asserting themselves in the economic decision-making process.

9 Mill, *Principles*, p. 258n.

10 W. Stark, (ed.), *Jeremy Bentham's Economic Writings* (London: George Allen & Unwin, 1954), vol. 3, p. 441.

11 Frank W. Fetter, 'The influence of Economists in parliament on British legislation from Ricardo to John Stuart Mill,' *Journal of Political Economy*, 83 (October, 1975), pp. 1051–67. See especially p. 1054.

12 However, H. P. Marvel has interpreted this legislation as 'an early example of a regulated industry controlling its regulators to further its own interests.' See his 'Factory regulation: a reinterpretation of early English experience,' *Journal of Law and Economics*, 20 (October, 1977), pp. 379–402.

13 J. M. Keynes, *Essays in Biography* (London: Rupert Hart Davis, 1951) p. 120.

14 Halévy, *Philosophical Radicalism*, Part III, Chapter 1.

15 This question is examined at length by Lionel Robbins in *The Theory of Economic Policy in Classical Political Economy* (New York: Macmillan, 1952).

Questions for discussion and further research

1 Classical economic theory attempted to identify the laws governing the operation of the economic system. It also offered a hypothesis concerning its probable future

long-run development. Identify and explain the laws classical writers identified. Explain the nature of the long-run trend they expected the economy to exhibit.

2 Later classical writers were philosophically committed to utilitarianism. What effect, if any, did this have on their economics? Who among the classical writers served in England's parliament? How did this role tend to reflect their utilitarian sympathies?

3 What aspects of classical economics appear most vulnerable in the sense of inviting criticisms that might lead to alternative systems of thought?

4 What is the nature of the methodological attack against Ricardian deductive economics? How do these foreshadow the revival of economists' interests in 'numeracy' in which Smith had 'little faith'?

Notes for further reading

From *The New Palgrave*

Mark Blaug on classical economics, vol. 1, pp. 434–44; Krishna Bharadwaj on wages in classical economics, vol. 4, pp. 843–45; Lawrence A. Boland on methodology, vol. 3, pp. 455–58; John Eatwell on competition: classical conceptions, vol, 1, pp. 537–40; Giorgio Gilibert on production; classical theories, vol. 3, pp. 990–92; Roy Green on the classical theory of money, vol. 1, p. 451; Donald Harris on classical growth models, vol. 1, pp. 445–48; Massimo Piretti on distribution theories: classical, vol. 1, pp. 872–75; and C. Welch on Utilitarianism vol. 4, pp. 770–75.

Selected references and suggestions for further reading

The German historical school

H. K. Betz. 'How does the German historical school fit?' *History of Political Economy*, 20 (Fall, 1988), pp. 409–30.
Dorfman, Joseph. 'The role of the German historical school in American Economic thought.' *American Economic Review*, 45 (May, 1955).
List, Friedrich. *The National System of Political Economy*. Translated by S. S. Lloyd (New York: Longmans, 1928 [1841]).
Roscher, Wilhelm. *Principles of Political Economy* (New York: 1878 [1854]).

The socialist critique

Condorcet, Marquis de Marie-Jean. *Esquisses d'un tableau historique des progres de l'esprit humain* (Paris: 1795). Gerd and Dicter Herdack Karras with Ben Fine, translated by James Weckham, *A Short History of Socialist Economic Thought* (New York: St. Martin's Press, 1978).
Manuel, F. E. and E. P. Manuel (eds) *French Utopias: An Anthology of Ideal Societies* (New York: Free Press, 1966).
Morton, A. L. *The Life and Ideas of Robert Owen* (New York: Monthly Review Press, 1963).
Ritter, Allan. *The Political Thought of Pierre-Joseph Proudhon* (Princeton, NJ: Princeton University Press, 1969).
Robbins, Lionel. Lecture 24, 'Mill – Saint-Simon and Marx,' in *A History of Economic Thought*, edited by S. Medema and W. Samuels (Princeton NJ: Princeton University Press, 1998), pp. 231–37.
Saint-Simon, Henri. *Oeuvres de Saint-Simon et d'Enfantin*, 47 vols (Aalen: Otto Zeller, 1963).
Sismondi, J. C. L. Simonde de. *De la richesse commerciale, ou principes d'économie politiques appliquées a' la legislation du commerce*, 2 vols (Geneva: 1803).
Sismondi, J. C. L. Simonde de. *Nouveaux principes d'économie politique*, 2nd edn, 2 vols (Paris: Delaunay, 1827).

Part III

The Critics of Classicism

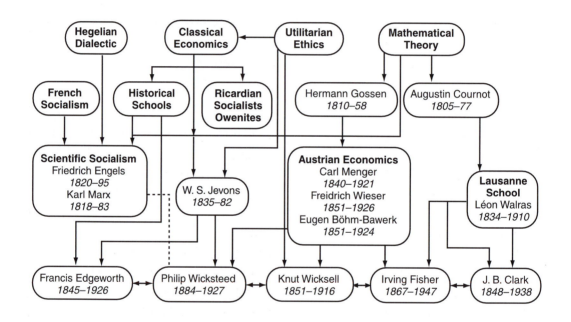

Legend:
Direct influence ——
Indirect influence ----

Key dates

1826	Johann von Thünen	The Isolated State
1838	Augustin Cournot	Researches into the Mathematical Principles of Wealth
1844	Jules Dupuit	On the Measurement of the Utility of Public Works
1844	Friedrich Engels	The Condition of the Working Class in England
1848	Friedrich Engels and Karl Marx	Communist Manifesto
1854	Hermann Gossen	The Development of Laws of Human Commerce
1867	Karl Marx	Capital
1871	William Stanley Jevons	The Theory of Political Economy
1871	Carl Menger	Grundsätze der Volkswirtschaftslehre
1874	Léon Walras	Elements d'economie politique pure
1885	John Bates Clark	The Philosophy of Wealth
1888	Eugen Böhm-Bawerk	Positive Theory of Capital
1889	John Bates Clark	The Distribution of Wealth
1889	Friederich V. Wieser	Natural Value
1893	Knut Wicksell	Value, Capital, and Rent
1898	Knut Wicksell	Interest and Prices
1901–6	Knut Wicksell	Lectures on Political Economy
1907	Irving Fisher	The Rate of Interest
1911	Irving Fisher	The Purchasing Power of Money
1924	Eugen Böhm-Bawerk	Karl Marx and the Close of His System

An overview of dissent

The two decades following the publication of John Stuart Mill's work were comparatively sterile as far as the development of economic analysis is concerned. The 1850s and 1860s were relatively prosperous decades for the British economy, but continued industrialization and the spread of the factory system imposed hardships on the working classes. Yet, orthodox economic thinking, with its ideological bias in favor of the free market system dominated throughout the nineteenth century. Nevertheless, there were also important voices of dissent that flourished alongside the classical tradition. The English historical school (like its German counterpart) challenged the economic laws that the classical school claimed to have established using the deductive method; at the same time, members of the English socialist movement were mounting programs to reform the capitalist system to alleviate the adverse effects that the system imposed on wage-workers.

A very different kind of critique emanated from other English thinkers who returned to the earlier Bentham–Mill effort to conceptualize and measure utility. The emphasis that both Samuel Bailey (1791–1870) and Nassau Senior (1790–1864) gave to utility to explain the phenomenon of value in the 1840s was an early sign of the weakening of the doctrinal facade of English classicism. Their work, in fact, signaled a prospective shift away from the cost of production theory of value in England. By the last third of the nineteenth century the time had become ripe for a new paradigm – which became known as marginalism – to explain commodity values in terms of subjectively perceived changes in the utility of additional increases in a consumer's stock of a good. Marginalist thinkers, in particular William Stanley Jevons, established diminishing marginal utility as the basis for value in exchange, while also relying on the mathematics of calculus as an expository and analytical tool. Together with Léon Walras in Switzerland, and Carl Menger in Austria, these three first-generation marginalists made almost simultaneous, independent efforts to reconstruct the theory of value in the 1870s. The common thread in their work is their emphasis on marginal utility rather than cost of production as the determinant of value in exchange, which effectively challenged the classical theory of value.

Little work was, however, done with respect to reformulating the theory of *distribution*; i.e. the determination of wage, profit, interest and rent incomes. Indeed, there was no separate and distinct theory of distribution in the 1870s in the sense of a body of principles that explained the division of the economy's product among those who perform different functions in the production process. The problem of distribution was still being approached in the classical manner, which viewed wages, profits, and rents as the income shares of the three main social classes, rather than as *functional returns* to productive factors that are, at one and the same time, costs of production and factor incomes. It was 'second-generation' marginalists who undertook to bridge this hiatus by formulating a theory of distribution that was integrated with the theory of value.

Chief among them were the Austrians, Friedrich von Wieser and Eugen Böhm-Bawerk, who followed in the tradition established by Carl Menger. The Swedish economist Knut Wicksell and the Americans, John Bates Clark and Irving Fisher, were also among the thinkers who made their most substantive contributions in the area of distribution theory and the related fields of production theory and the theory of capital and interest. Thus, second generation marginalists, with the exception of Francis Edgeworth, Philip Wicksteed and Alfred Marshall, were not English.

The methodology of the marginalists was deductive (as was that of the classicists), and emerged as a doctrine more or less simultaneously in Austria, France, Italy and America. In addition to its emphasis on utility as the foundation for value, marginalism shifted the focus of analysis to short-term relationships expressed in mathematical terms instead of the classicists' concern with tendencies toward natural prices in the long run, and with wage, profit, and rent shares whose trends reflect the economy's tendency toward the stationary state.

Many nineteenth-century thinkers were also inclined to make use of empirical observation, such as had long been relied on in physics, astronomy and other physical sciences, and to collect and classify data that might potentially be useful in induction. The apparent failure of Ricardian deduction to develop hypotheses (besides that relating to the machinery question) that were useful in explaining the problems imposed by the industrial revolution, led scholars to strike out methodologically in a new direction: specifically, toward, *induction* as a tool for advancing knowledge.

German and English historical economists practiced the only kind of induction that was possible before the beginning of large scale data collection and the development of statistics as a new science. They focused on the study of bygone economic events and institutions, with a view to inferring economic laws from past experience. While the science of statistics differs from political economy in that it is concerned with collecting and arranging numerical information, including

information that relates to economic events and outcomes, it is not concerned with formulating hypotheses to explain them. Yet, over time, the science of statistics has become the foundation for econometrics, which is today the sister science of economics. Thus, the practice of data collection, which Malthus had tried to pioneer with respect to population behavior, and the development of statistics as a science, marks the beginning of 'stage two' of numeracy as a tool for advancing economic knowledge.

In addition to the willingness of nineteenth-century thinkers to rely on quantitative observations, there was also a growing recognition that prevailing business practices could become a basis for identifying empirical relationships and laws. Business journals, such as *The Economist* and *The Commercial and Financial Chronicle*, which were published weekly in London and New York, had the objective of providing accurate trustworthy permanent records of commercial and financial events. Graphic representation also became an essential adjunct of economic analysis and pedagogy in the late nineteenth century. As long ago as René Descartes's *Geometria*, published in 1637, it has been recognized that every equation can be represented by a curve (and conversely, that every curve is an equation). In the generations that followed, the diagrams in use in mathematics, meteorology, and engineering became models for those drawn by political economists.

Political economists schooled in Germany, France and Italy came from an intellectual tradition that led them to focus on group behaviors studied in the context of historical changes. Theirs was an intellectual and political environment which nurtured the German historical school and the socialist movement, which were sources of inspiration for Karl Marx. Intellectually speaking, Marx is a descendant of David Ricardo, so that his work reflects a continuation of the classical tradition, albeit with a different philosophical foundation, and a different political message. Philosophically, Marx's political economics is grounded in the dialectic of the German philosopher Georg Hegel rather than on the philosophical radicalism of English Utilitarians. Marx forged a system of economic analysis on the basis of Hegel's dialectic that rivaled the classical one, although, as an economist, he built on the classical tradition. His analysis of the origin, functioning, and inevitable destruction of the capitalistic system is a completely articulated rival to the classical analysis. It was, and even today continues to be, intellectually influential, even though it did not become the basis for an intellectual revolution in economics. Marginalism ultimately provided such a model; but it required the unique talent of Alfred Marshall to use its insights to reinterpret the classical legacy to establish neoclassicism as the next paradigm in economics. Nevertheless, Marx's model and those offered by Jevons, Walras, and the Austrians, are alternative models of economic puzzle-solving to which the proponents of historicism and induction also provided valuable insights. Our concern in this part is thus to examine these challenges to classicism and how they contributed to the subsequent development of economics.

Chapter 10

Socialism, induction, and the forerunners of marginalism

The concern of this chapter is to enlarge on contributions made in the nineteenth century by the extremely diverse group of individuals who divorced themselves from the deductive methodology and the generalizations (or laws) of the classical tradition, and often from its conservative *laissez-faire* political tradition. Our particular interest is in those who wrote up to 1870, the latter date coinciding with the work of the 'first generation' marginalists. Although the contributions that appeared in the first half of the century are important in their own right, they are of greater significance for the development of *political* thought rather than *economic* theory. Accordingly, the contributions of the so-called 'utopian' socialists, Claude-Henry de Rouvroy de Saint-Simon (1760–1825) and Charles Fourier (1772–1837), lie beyond our concern. While their proposals for reforming capitalism differ from one another, the common thread of their thinking (as well as that of later socialists), is their agreement with the criticisms which the French philosopher Rousseau directed at the natural law philosophers. They challenged the concepts of the state and private property as 'natural' because, in practice, instead of promoting the utilitarian ideal of the greatest good for the greatest number, they were the source of an inequitable distribution of wealth and income. Thus, we begin with the work of those socialists who, in England, were associated with the cooperative movement known as Owenism, and the arguments by Jean-Charles-Leonard Simonde de Sismondi (1773–1842) in France. Robert Owen (1771–1858) attracted large numbers of followers who championed the English reform movement known as 'Chartism.' Sismondi dissented from J. B. Say's law of markets, which claims that the process of production simultaneously generates an equivalent of purchasing power so that a general glut of commodities is an impossibility.

The socialist critique

'Ricardian' and other socialists

The socialist movement, and the critiques its proponents directed against the classical tradition, were inspired chiefly by the exploitation and genuine misery that the Industrial Revolution imposed on the working class. However, both also had a philosophical root in the doctrine of the natural order. As has already been noted, the thesis that society is governed by natural laws can as readily be used to support radical as conservative political views. Thus, English socialists started with the Ricardian theory of value and joined it to

Bentham's Utilitarianism in a revolutionary way. Instead of supporting the existing social order, their interpretation of the utilitarian principle of the 'greatest good' proposed a more egalitarian system of income distribution, in which individuals would receive the whole product of their labor.

In the 1820s, the philosopher and social revolutionary, Robert Owen, promoted a strong cooperative and subsequently a militant trade union movement in England which eventually merged with the Chartist party. Political economists who supported the Owenist movement are often referred to as 'Ricardian' socialists, because they began from a labor theory of value, and invoked their version of the natural law doctrine of property to arrive at the conclusion that each person has a natural right to the product of his own labor. Thus, they interpreted the capitalistic system as an instrument for worker exploitation in the sense that they saw the private property rights of the capitalist class as effectively depriving workers of the fruits of their labor, because the subsistence wages they were paid transferred the surplus they produced to their employers.

Richard Jones (1790–1855) should also be remembered as among those who criticized Ricardo and the classical tradition of constructing general laws and purporting them to be 'natural' and immutable. Although he was politically conservative, and thus not a socialist, his most important works (*An Essay on the Distribution of Wealth and the Sources of Taxation*, 1831, and *An Introductory Lecture on Political Economy*, 1833) make the argument that political economists should study institutions and the class structure of society. In effect, he anticipated Karl Marx's later hypothesis that capitalism is merely the present phase of the system's economic development, which will evolve into a subsequent phase sometime in the future. Marx was so appreciative of Jones's work that he gave over Chapter 10 of his *Theories of Surplus Value* (1905–10) to offering a favorable review.

The French socialists

Sismondi's two most important works, *New Principles of Political Economy* (1819) and *Studies in Political Economy* (1837–38,) in common with those of the Owenists, interpreted the policy of *laissez-faire* as operating as an instrument which enabled capitalists to exploit workers. It produced an 'anarchy of capitalist production,' which forced workers to accept subsistence wages because their lack of ownership of the tools and machines forced them to work as employees. The value of the output they produced exceeded their wages, so that a deficiency of purchasing power was seen by Sismondi as inherent in the structure of production. This is an important conclusion because it is completely inconsistent with the Say's Law conclusion that a general lack of purchasing power is an impossibility.

Sismondi's argument thus puts us in mind of Malthus's theory of gluts. Malthus, it will be recalled, favored re-establishing the Corn Laws to ensure higher farm prices and landlord rents in order to maintain the level of aggregate demand. Sismondi's very different proposal was to alleviate the insufficiency of purchasing power by redistributing income from capitalists to workers instead of shifting it from capitalists to landowners.

Induction as dissent

The German historical school

While British thinkers were concerned chiefly with discovering immutable and universal laws of the natural order, Continental thinkers more typically focused on historical change to produce human progress in the direction of truth and reason. The essentially ahistorical perspective of the classical school thus provided a basis for the *methodological* criticism that was launched by the German historical school.

The historical school took the position that the laws of the classical school are neither absolute nor perpetually valid. Economic laws, if they can be discovered at all, necessarily exist only relative to time and place. Because economic laws operate within the framework of constantly changing environments, historicists argued that it is necessary to replace the classical method of deduction by *induction*, in order to discover the specific characteristics of national economies and the nature of their changing environments. Induction was also expected to shed new light on the motives of human conduct, which historicists believed to be far more complex than can be explained by the self-interest premise which underlies classical thinking. German scholars, among them Wilhelm Roscher and Karl Knies of the 'older' school, and Gustav von Schmoller, who was among the younger thinkers who carried on the tradition of *historismus*, took the position that the historical method ought to be the principal way of studying political economy, and that little can be learned by relying exclusively on deduction.

Roscher (1817–94) favored what he termed the 'historical–physiological' method as an inductive basis for identifying and describing the course of real economic life. His emphasis was on comparing the histories of different people and nations to establish the stages of their development based on their particular historic and national conditions. More specifically, a national economy is more the sum of its individual members. His most important contribution is thus in his classification of economic development into stages, and he is best known for his history of Cameralism, which is the German counterpart of English Mercantilism and French Colbertism. He also developed a theory of the location of towns but, like his fellow practitioners of *historismus*, he contributed chiefly to developing the *method* of studying political economy rather than the formulation of explanatory theories.

Karl Knies (1821–98,) who is remembered as among the most important members of the 'older' German historical school, took the lead not only in criticizing Ricardo's deductive logic but also in arguing that political economy cannot be 'absolutist' in the sense of maintaining that it is possible to establish economic laws that are valid for all time. His emphasis was thus on historical relevance, which requires a study and comparison of different countries and different periods of time. While a comparative approach may yield analogous generalizations, laws of causality such as those claimed by the classical school are an impossibility in a world of changing institutions and human habits and behaviors. Thus, Knies's chief work *Political Economy and Method* (1853), focuses on the relevance of the history and geography of an economy and the characteristics of its people. Disputing the classical self-interest perspective of behavior, Knies maintains that behavior is equally dependent on the cultural and political life of a population and their sense of identity as members of a community. His perspective is that different nations and races have distinctively different characteristics, which led him to emphasize the interdependence of economics and other social sciences.

Schmoller is remembered as the leading member of the 'younger' German historical school, as well as the most influential political economist of Imperial Germany, in the sense that his views directly affected the outcomes of most academic appointments in the German Reich. Echoing the teachings of Knies, he challenged the usefulness of deductive analysis in classical economics with a vigor that provoked a bitter and prolonged debate with Carl Menger, the leader of the Austrian marginal utility school, about the relative usefulness of *deduction* versus *induction* as the preferred method for studying economic outcomes.

Schmoller had a special interest in detailed historical studies of German artisan guilds, including the seventeenth- and eighteenth-century guilds of Brandenburg, Prussia's Strasbourg weavers' guild (1879,) and the eighteenth-century Prussian silk industry. He also studied the history of German towns, Strasbourg in particular, and the historical development of the class struggle in Germany. His interests extended to examining the absence of a centralized German national state and Prussian dominance of the German monarchy, for which he had a particular reverence.

These studies clearly reflect the perspective of *historismus* that the study of political economy should proceed by collecting a mass of historical data from which generalizations eventually will be drawn. It cannot be determined in advance precisely what the nature of these generalizations will be, for the necessary data must first be assembled. Accordingly, the historical school embarked on an ambitious program of study that produced a remarkable volume of historical detail. On this basis, their contribution is primarily descriptive rather than analytical, although they urged that the facts established by induction are also a prolegomenon to better deductive arguments. Undoubtedly, the criticisms of the

historical school caused deductive economists to be more selective about their premises and more cautious about putting forward their generalizations. However, the historical school contributed little to the body of economic analysis, and this English counterpart of the German movement attracted few adherents. The disagreement over methodology (the *Methodenstreit*), eventually resolved itself, as the participants to the dispute came to recognize that both deduction and induction have their place in economic analysis and mutually fructify one another.

Data collection and statistics: the second stage of numeracy

Section 'F' and the Royal Statistical Association

While the use of induction as a basis for advancing knowledge in modern times dates from David Hume's *Treatise on Human Nature* (1739) and J. S. Mill's *A System of Logic* (1843), it is the establishment of the Statistical Section of the British Association for the Advancement of Science (later known as Section F) and the Statistical Society of London (later the Royal Statistical Society) that provided the foundation for the modern empirical tradition. Indeed, it marks the beginning of the 'second stage' of the development of numeracy as it relates to political economics.

The Society identified its mission as follows: 'to collect, arrange, and compare facts' relating to economic activities, events, and outcomes, and present them in numerical form. By 1840 the Society had developed a classification system that consisted of 'fifteen well defined sub-divisions of statistics, universally available for purposes of comparison, and susceptible of the minutest sub-division, according to the multifarious detail of the affairs of life.'[1] The collection and classification of data became the foundation for a systematic inductive discipline. It would serve as an adjunct to political economy, but also have status as a separate science of statistics. As stated in the first issue of the new journal,

> The Science of Statistics differs from Political Economy because, although it has the same end in view, it does not discuss causes, nor reason upon probable facts; it seeks only to collect, arrange and compare that class of facts which alone can form the basis of correct conclusions with respect to social and political government. (*Journal of the Statistical Society*, May, 1838:1)

The investigations undertaken by Section F and the Statistical Society were to be devoted to 'collecting fresh statistical information and of arranging, condensing, and publishing much of what already exists.'[2]

The specific types of data to be collected were identified as 'Economical statistics,' 'Political statistics,' 'Medical statistics,' and 'Moral and intellectual statistics' and, in so far as possible, the Society's attention was to be addressed to facts that can be expressed numerically and presented in tabular form. It was emphasized that, in order to meet the test of science, the scope of investigation conforms to the Society's classification format.

While the research of Section F was initially intended to be limited to data collection and classification, it was not very long before it moved beyond science into fact-gathering as a basis for inferring economic laws and (reminiscent of the political arithmeticians) mounting social policy by returning to the Bentham–Mill idea that a 'felicific calculus' is possible. The question that Mill was confronted with was whether 'the rules of arithmetic are applicable to the valuation of happiness, as of all other measurable quantities.'[3]

William S. Jevons reconsidered the Bentham–Mill question of measuring utility and arrived at the conclusion that 'the numerical expression of quantities of feeling seems to be out of the question.'[4] Nevertheless, another Cambridge colleague, the mathematical economist Francis Edgeworth, believed that Jevons's mathematical logic might become the basis for a cardinal ranking of units of utility, and pioneered the development of indifference curves as a graphical technique for representing equally preferred combinations of two commodities. He was also concerned with the possibility of developing a 'psycho–physical machine' which could register the height of pleasure experienced by an individual according to a law of errors.'[5]

The contribution of business practices

In addition to the willingness of nineteenth century thinkers to rely on quantitative observations, there was also a growing recognition that prevailing business practices could become a basis for identifying empirical relationships and laws. Business journals, such as *The Economist* and *The Commercial and Financial Chronicle*, which were published weekly in London and New York, had the objective of providing accurate trustworthy permanent records of commercial and financial events.

Jevons, in particular, concerned himself with arranging commodity prices and discount rates into tabular form and calculating and plotting their mean values and identifying seasonal variations. It is he who developed the technique now known as *moving averages*, which transformed the traditional 'rule of thumb knowledge' of the merchant into a tool of scientific investigation.

Graphic representation also became an

essential adjunct of economic analysis and pedagogy in the late nineteenth century. As long ago as René Decartes' *Geometria*, published in 1637, it was recognized that every equation can be represented by a curve (and conversely, every curve is an equation). In the generations that followed, the diagrams in use in mathematics, meteorology, and engineering became models for those drawn by political economists. Public utility engineers were, for example, concerned with developing principles on the basis of which they could establish rates for selling the services of a bridge or toll road, which required them to understand how the quantity of services demanded varies with the rate charged. [6] These price–quantity relationships are translated into a graph that depicts a continuous convex function (or law curve) in logical time. Thus, the drawing up of rate tables requires a decision as to whether the objective is to set a rate that will maximize the value of service made available, or maximize the profit that is earned from the sale.

The utility concept before the marginal revolution

The classical and early continental conception

The concern of classical economists with the problem of exchange value and their failure to appreciate any relationship between value in use and value in exchange caused them to give little emphasis to the role of utility and demand in the determination of prices. They conceived of utility as a general characteristic of a commodity rather than as a relationship between a consumer and a unit of a commodity. This was true even of Senior, who was more aware of the subjective aspects of value than most other English thinkers. Thus, the 'paradox of value' posed by Smith's example of the diamond and the water went

unresolved for lack of the marginal increment concept.

Continental, rather than English, thinkers were the first to use the concept of the marginal increment. It is interesting to speculate why Continental thinkers were appreciative of the role of utility in the determination of value so much earlier than their English counterparts. One suggested hypothesis is that Protestant theology, with its greater emphasis on the virtue of work, was more compatible with a labor-oriented theory of value than the more subjective doctrine of Catholicism.[7] The dominance of Protestant theology in England may conceivably be a reason for the general lack of interest of the classical economists in consumer wants, while thinkers in Catholic countries like France and Italy placed greater emphasis on utility.

Daniel Bernoulli, who was Swiss, was among the earliest anticipators of the concept of utility, which he examined in connection with the significance of the margin as it relates to increments of income. His hypothesis, presented in the 1730s, was that the importance of an additional dollar to an individual is inversely proportional to the number of dollars already in possession. From this relationship, he deduced that, in a situation of risk, an individual will not be guided exclusively by the mathematical probability of gain or loss of future receipts, but will also be influenced by their significance relative to means.[8] Bernoulli did not, however, explore the concept of the margin as it relates to utility, consumer behavior, or the determination of exchange value.

The concept of marginal utility expresses the subjective value or want-satisfying power of an additional unit of a given good to a particular user. The importance an individual attaches to an additional unit of a particular good depends in part on its relative scarcity.

The larger the supply of a given commodity, the smaller will be its relative significance at the margin. Thus, the reason why water usually commands no price is because its supply is so large relative to the demand for it that the utility of the marginal unit is zero. Joseph A. Schumpeter noted that there were a number of eighteenth-century Italian and French thinkers who understood this paradox of value and that its existence did not, as Smith thought, bar the way to a theory of exchange value based upon value in use.[9]

Dupuit's conception of utility

Inquiry into the monopoly problem – especially as it is associated with large fixed and low variable costs, and therefore increasing returns to scale – made a pioneering contribution to the development of marginal utility analysis. Those who dealt with the pricing problems of railroads and other public utilities addressed the kinds of issues that contributed to the rise of the marginal utility analysis.

Jules Dupuit, a French railway engineer, made a particularly noteworthy contribution. The essence of his thinking is contained in an article published in 1844, 'On the measurement of the utility of public works.'[10] His inquiry into the monopoly problem – especially as it relates to the increasing returns to scale associated with large fixed and low variable costs – made a pioneering contribution to our understanding of the distinction between utility and exchange value and how they relate to one another. The utility of everything consumed, observed Dupuit, varies according to the person consuming it. This may be illustrated by observing how consumers react if the government imposes a tax on a commodity they enjoy. For example, a tax of five *sous* per bottle of wine will raise its

price by the amount of the tax, but adds nothing to the utility of the product. Thus, if a bottle of wine is bought for 15 *sous* instead of 10, it is because the buyer finds at least an equivalent degree of utility in it. If a buyer were willing to pay more than 15 *sous* in order to enjoy its utility, but only had to pay the price of 15 *sous*, the difference would be what Dupuit called *utilité relative*, or *consumer surplus*. He subsequently used this concept as a basis for a tax theorem and a theory of discriminatory pricing among consumers with different demand elasticities in order to increase the profitability of selling public utility services.

Dupuit's tax theorem concerned the relationship between the revenue a tax yields and the loss its collection imposes on society. To illustrate the principle he had in mind, he depicted a downward sloping curve for water supplied by a public system, such as that represented in Figure 10.1, in which DD' represents total utility. Users are assumed, initially, to be required to pay a price of P at which they demand quantity OM.[11] The segment Da of the utility curve represents the willingness of some users to pay prices in excess of P for some units of water. Because the actual price is only P, they enjoy a consumers' surplus that can be represented by the triangle, PDa. This surplus would be reduced if the price of water were raised to P' as a consequence of a tax, T, that reduces the quantity demanded to OM_1.[12] As shown in Figure 10.1, this results in a tax yield represented by the shaded rectangle, but since consumer surplus is reduced, there is also a net loss of utility to society represented by the adjacent triangle.

This relationship is a basis for two principles for establishing tolls for publicly used goods, such as canals and bridges, in accordance with alternative social objectives. Different social objectives require that different

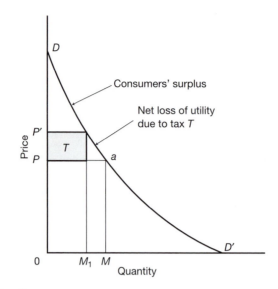

Figure 10.1 Dupuit's tax theorem

rates be charged. If, for example, the demand curve for the services of a bridge can be expressed as $y = f(x)$, and the objective is to set a toll rate sufficient to raise the cost of capital to build it, Dupuit reasoned that the appropriate toll rate can be established by solving the equation

$$R = xy$$

where R is the required amount of revenue.

If, on the other hand, the objective is to raise the maximum revenue possible then, given the demand curve for the service, it is appropriate to set a rate at which the marginal revenue will be zero. This requires solving the equation

$$\frac{\mathrm{d}(yx)}{\mathrm{d}x} = 0.$$

Figure 10.2 is useful for understanding the difference in outcome when the first equation, rather than the second, is used for establishing a toll rate. If the toll for the service is set at T, the total revenue the public utility will earn is $T_0 Tnr$. If Dupuit's interpretation of the demand curve as a utility curve is accepted, the consumer surplus enjoyed by those who use the service can be represented as the triangle TnT'. Analogously, the utility lost by the public because the service is not free (i.e. the rate is *not zero*) is represented by the triangle nrN. From this, Dupuit concluded that the rate imposed for the services of publicly used goods like bridges, canals, and roads should ideally be set at the lowest rate consistent with providing a revenue to cover costs. He also reasoned that it is possible to increase the revenue collected and diminish the loss of utility to consumers by choosing an appropriate combination of tolls, if consumers can be grouped according to the utility each category of user derives from the same service. Dupuit's analysis is thus an early example of the relevance of what is today called *price discrimination* in the setting of public utility rates. However, what Dupuit's analysis failed to do was to distinguish between the utility curve and a demand curve. The clarification of this distinction is attributable to another Frenchman, Augustin Cournot.

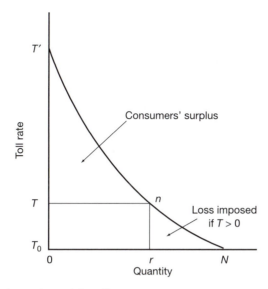

Figure 10.2 Dupuit on alternative public utility rates

Issues and Answers from the Masterworks 10.1

Issue
On what basis can a law of demand be formulated and represented?

Cournot's answer
From *Researches into the Mathematical Principles of the Theory of Wealth* (1838, translated 1897 by Nathanial Bacon), Chapter 4.

Of the law of demand

To lay the foundations of the theory of exchangeable values, we shall not accompany most speculative writers back to the cradle of the human race; we shall undertake to explain neither the origin of property nor that of exchange or division of labour. All this doubtless belongs to the history of mankind, but it has no influence on a theory that could only become applicable at a very advanced state of civilization, at a period when (to use the language of mathematicians) the influence of the *initial* conditions is entirely gone.

We shall invoke but a single axiom, or, if you prefer, make but a single hypothesis, i.e. that each one seeks to derive the greatest possible value from his goods or his labour. But to deduce the rational consequences of this principle, we shall endeavour to establish better than has been the case the elements of the data which observation alone can furnish. Unfortunately, this fundamental point is one which theorists, almost with one accord, have presented to us, we will not say falsely, but in a manner which is really meaningless.

It has been said almost unanimously that 'the price of goods is in the inverse ratio of the quantity offered, and in the direct ratio of the quantity demanded.' It has never been considered that the statistics necessary for accurate numerical estimation might be lacking, whether of the quantity offered or of the quantity demanded, and that this might prevent deducing from this principle general consequences capable of useful application. But wherein does the principle itself consist? Does it mean that in case a double quantity of any article is offered for sale, the price will fall to one-half? Then it should be more simply expressed, and it should only be said that the price is in the inverse ratio of the quantity offered. But the principle thus made intelligible would be false; for, in general, that 100 units of an article have been sold at 20 francs is no reason that 200 units would sell at 10 francs in the same lapse of time and under the same circumstances. Sometimes less would be marketed; often much more.

Furthermore, what is meant by the quantity demanded? Undoubtedly it is not that which is actually marketed at the demand of buyers, for then the generally absurd consequence would result from the pretended principle, that the more of an article is marketed the dearer it is. If by demand only a vague desire of possession of the article is understood, without reference to the *limited price* which every buyer supposes in his demand, there is scarcely an article for which the demand cannot be considered indefinite; but if the price is to be considered at which each buyer is willing to buy, and the price at which each seller is willing to sell, what becomes of the pretended principle? It is not, we repeat, an erroneous proposition – it is a proposition devoid of meaning. Consequently all those who have united to proclaim it have likewise united to make no use of it. Let us try to adhere to less sterile principles.

The cheaper an article is, the greater ordinarily is the demand for it. The sales or the demand (for to us these two words are synonymous, and we do not see for what reason theory need take account of any demand which does not result in a sale) – the sales or the demand generally, we say, increases when the price decreases.

We add the word *generally* as a corrective; there are, in fact, some objects of whim and luxury which are only desirable on account of their rarity and of the high price which is the consequence thereof. If any one should succeed in carrying out cheaply the crystallization of carbon, and in producing for one franc the diamond which today is worth a thousand, it would not be astonishing if diamonds should cease to be used in sets of jewelry, and should disappear as articles of commerce. In this case a great fall in price would almost annihilate the demand. But objects of this nature play so unimportant a part in social economy that it is not necessary to bear in mind the restriction of which we speak.

The demand might be in the inverse ratio of the price; ordinarily it increases or decreases in much more rapid proportion – an observation especially applicable to most manufactured products.

The demand might be in the inverse ratio of the price; ordinarily it increases or decreases in much more rapid proportion – an observation especially applicable to most manufactured products. On the contrary, at other times the variation of the demand is less rapid; which appears (a very singular thing) to be equally applicable both to the most necessary things and to the most superfluous. The price of violins or of astronomical telescopes might fall one-half and yet probably the demand would not double; for this demand is fixed by the number of those who cultivate the art or science to which these instruments belong; who have the disposition requisite and the leisure to cultivate them and the means to pay teachers and to meet the other necessary expenses, in consequence of which the price of the instruments is only a secondary question. On the contrary, firewood, which is one of the most useful articles, could probably double in price, from the progress of clearing land or increase in population, long before the annual consumption of fuel would be halved; as a large number of consumers are disposed to cut down other expenses rather than get along without firewood.

Let us admit therefore that the sales or the annual demand D is, for each article, a particular function $F(p)$ of the price p of such article. To know the form of this function would be to know what we call *the law of demand or of sales*. It depends evidently on the kind of utility of the article, on the nature of the services it can render or the enjoyments it can procure, on the habits and customs of the people, on the average wealth, and on the scale on which wealth is distributed.

Since so many moral causes capable of neither enumeration nor measurement affect the law of demand, it is plain that we should no more expect this law to be expressible by an algebraic formula than the law of mortality, and all the laws whose determination enters into the field of statistics, or what is called social arithmetic. Observation must therefore be depended on for furnishing the means of drawing up between proper limits a table of the corresponding values *of D* and *p*; after which, by the well-known methods of interpolation or by graphic processes, an empiric formula or a curve can be made to represent the function in question; and the solution of problems can be pushed as far as numerical applications.

But even if this object were unattainable (on account of the difficulty of obtaining observations of sufficient number and accuracy, and also on account of the progressive variations which the law of demand must undergo in a country which has not yet reached a practically stationary condition), it would be nevertheless not improper to introduce the unknown law of demand into analytical combinations, by means of an indeterminate symbol; for it is well known that one of the most important functions of analysis consists precisely in assigning determinate relations between quantities to which numerical values and even algebraic forms are absolutely unassignable.

We will assume that the function $F(p)$, which expresses the law of demand or of the market, is *a continuous function*, i.e. a function which does not pass suddenly from one value to another, but which takes in passing all intermediate values. It might be otherwise if the number of consumers were very limited: thus in a certain household the same quantity of firewood will possibly be used whether wood costs 10 francs or 15 francs the stere, and the consumption may suddenly be diminished if the price of the stere rises above the latter figure. But the wider the market extends, and the more the combinations of needs, of fortunes, or even of caprices, are varied among consumers, the closer the function $F(p)$ will come to varying with p in a continuous manner. However little may be the variation of p, there will be some consumers so placed that the slight rise or fall of the article will affect their consumptions, and will lead them to deprive themselves in some way or to reduce their manufacturing output, or to substitute something else for the article that has grown dearer, as, for instance, coal for wood or anthracite for soft coal. Thus the 'exchange' is a thermometer which shows by very slight variations of rates the fleeting variations in the estimate of the chances which affect government bonds, variations which are not a sufficient motive for buying or selling to most of those who have their fortunes invested in such bonds.

If the function $F(p)$ is continuous, it will have the property common to all functions of this nature, and on which so many important applications of mathematical analysis are based: *the variations of the demand will be sensibly proportional to the variations in price so long as these last are small fractions of the original price*. Moreover, these variations will be of opposite signs, i.e. an increase in price will correspond with a diminution of the demand.

Suppose that in a country like France the consumption of sugar is 100 million kilograms when the price is 2 francs a kilogram, and that it has been observed to drop to 99 millions when the price reached 2 francs 10 centimes. Without considerable error, the consumption which would correspond to a price of 2 francs 20 centimes can be valued at 98 millions, and the consumption corresponding to a price of 1 franc 90 centimes at 101 millions. It is plain how much this principle, which is only the mathematical consequence of the continuity of functions, can facilitate applications of theory, either by simplifying analytical expressions of the laws which govern the movement of values, or in reducing the number of data to be borrowed from experience, if the theory becomes sufficiently developed to lend itself to numerical determinations.

But even if it were impossible to obtain from statistics the value of p which should render the product $pF(p)$ a maximum, it would be easy to learn, at least for all articles to which the attempt has been made to extend commercial statistics, whether current prices are above or below this value. Suppose that when the price becomes $p + \Delta p$, the annual consumption as shown by statistics, such as customhouse records, becomes $D - AD$. According as

$$\frac{\Delta D}{\Delta P} \text{ or } \frac{D}{P}$$

the increase in price, Δp, will increase or diminish the product $pF(p)$; and, consequently, it will be known whether the two values p and $p + \Delta p$ (assuming Δp to be a small fraction of p) fall above or below the value which makes the product under consideration a maximum.

Commercial statistics should therefore be required to separate articles of high economic importance into two categories, according as their current prices are above or below the value which makes a maximum of $pF(p)$. We shall see that many economic problems have different solutions, according as the article in question belongs to one or the other of these two categories.

Any demonstration ought to proceed from the simple to the complex: the simplest hypothesis for the purpose of investigating by what laws prices are fixed, is that of monopoly, taking this word in its most absolute meaning, which supposes that the production of an article is in one man's hands. This hypothesis is not purely fictitious: it is realized in certain cases; and, moreover, when we have studied it, we can analyze more accurately the effects of competition of producers.

Source: Reprinted from the American edition (Macmillan Company, 1897), translated by Nathaniel Bacon from the 1838 French edition. Originally appeared as Chapters 4, 5, and 7, with footnotes deleted and equations renumbered.

Summing up: Cournot's key points

Cournot's examination of demand is a major step forward from an analytical point of view. While not concerned with linking demand to utility, as was Dupuit, Cournot conceived of demand *in a schedule sense*, that is, as a physical quantity of a good that an individual or group of buyers might purchase at alternative market prices. The basic assumption is that the quantity demanded is a continuous function that can be represented as $D = F(p)$, in which quantity demanded varies inversely with price.

The relationship can also be represented in the form of a table that shows corresponding values of D and p. Cournot also considered the possibility of empirical studies that would make it possible to complete the tables with actual values that would be useful for solving actual problems. Among the problems that particularly interested him are those that relate to 'investigating by what laws prices are fixed' in order to analyze 'the effects of competition of producers.' It was this insight which led Cournot to the concept of marginal revenue and its significance for the behavior of the individual firm.

Cournot and marginal revenue

Building on his recognition that increments of revenue are related to increments of demand, Cournot developed the marginal revenue concept in connection with his analysis of monopoly.[13] In the case of pure monopoly, which Cournot thought of as the polar opposite of 'illimited competition' (our pure competition), the firm is the entire industry, so the monopolist is confronted with the same demand curve as the industry.

While a pure competitor confronts a given market price and maximizes profits by adjusting output, monopolists can maximize profits with respect to variations in either price or output. Given their respective demand curves, they can select the output they wish to sell and let consumers determine the price, or they can set the price and let consumers determine the quantity they will take. The demand curve $q = f(p)$, therefore, has a unique inverse, $p = f(q)$. Thus, if the monopolists' selling price is p and the demand curve is $p = f(q)$, total revenue may be written either as $R = p(q)$ or as $R = R(p)$. Total cost may also be expressed as a function of output. Thus, $C = C(q)$. The difference between total revenue and total cost is profit. This difference is maximized when the additional revenue associated with an extra increment of output is equal to the additional cost of that incre-

ment. It follows that monopolists will maximize profit when they set a price that equates the first derivative of total revenue to the first derivative of total cost or, what amounts to the same thing, when marginal revenue equals marginal cost.[14]

Although Cournot did not identify the first derivative of total revenue as marginal revenue, his proof that profits are maximized when $MR = MC$ is a fundamental concept, which is now contained in every textbook on economic principles. It was, however, neglected after Cournot initially introduced it in his *Researches* in 1838. This is due partly to Alfred Marshall's subsequent analysis of monopoly profit maximization in terms of the monopolist's total net revenue rather than in marginal terms. Marshall's procedure, coupled with the fact that neoclassical price analysis, until the 1930s, was typically conducted under the assumption that the structure of the market is purely competitive, accounts for the neglect of the concept of marginal revenue after Cournot described it.

Although Cournot recognized that monopolists can set the price for their products in such a way as to maximize total revenue by offering to sell that volume of output at which marginal revenue will equal marginal cost, he apparently failed to appreciate the additional opportunities for adding to total profits that are inherent in discriminatory pricing. This is the policy of offering a product or service to different groups of demanders at different prices, rather than at the same price, depending upon the strength of their demands. Total profits will then be maximized when the marginal revenue *in each separate market* is equated to marginal cost. The success of this type of policy depends on the ability of monopolists to segregate their buyers according to the urgency (elasticity) of their demands and the ability to keep those who are able to buy at low prices from reselling to those to whom the product is made available only at higher prices. Dupuit and others in the applied fields – transportation in particular – appreciated this aspect of the theory of price discrimination.

Cournot on duopoly

Cournot sketched out the kinds of market conditions that lie between pure monopoly and what he termed *illimited competition* (our pure competition). His most famous case was that of duopoly – two competing monopolists whom he assumed to be selling a costless homogeneous commodity (water from a mineral spring). Assuming, to begin with, that one seller is in possession of the entire market, he proceeded to examine what would happen if a second seller enters to compete with the first. Cournot's explanation of the nature of the ultimate equilibrium position derived from the assumption he made about the behavior of the two rivals.

Cournot assumed that neither seller has the power to name a price. However, each has the power to adjust the quantity offered for sale and, as a result, influences buyers bidding for this product. Thus, a rival who enters the market to compete with a former monopolist is conceived to offer that particular quantity that will maximize total revenue, on the assumption that the former monopolist will not alter the quantity offered for sale. But, says Cournot, this assumption on the part of the newcomer will prove to be invalid, for these sales cut into the former monopolist's market and force adjustments in price and output. These adjustments are similarly assumed by Cournot to be made on the invalid premise that the rival seller will not alter the output. Each seller, in turn, will always have to adjust to the new situation created by the change the

rival makes in the quantity offered for sale. This will necessitate corresponding adjustments by the rival until a stable equilibrium is reached. Cournot reasoned that, in an equilibrium situation, the amount offered in any market that is not purely competitive can be determined according to the formula

$$\frac{n}{(n+1)}$$

multiplied by the competitive output. Thus, the amount offered in a duopoly equilibrium is equal to two thirds of the competitive output, with half the amount being offered by each of the sellers.[15] The equilibrium price will be below the monopoly price and above the competitive price, and any departure from this level will cause its re-establishment as a result of 'a series of reactions, constantly declining in amplitude.'

The Cournot solution of the duopoly problem is only one among several that are possible, for there are numerous behavior assumptions that might be made. Cournot assumed that a duopolist maximizes profit on the basis of a conjectural variation of zero with respect to the rival's output. His solution was subsequently criticized by Joseph Bertrand, who offered an alternative solution based on the assumption that each seller tries to maximize profits, on the assumption that rivals will not alter their prices.

Actually, neither Cournot's solution nor Bertrand's is based on realistic assumptions, for duopolists, as well as oligopolists, are likely to realize that their decisions are interdependent with respect to both price and output. Various behavior patterns may result from this interdependence. For example, the monopolists may agree to cooperate so that both set a monopoly price, or they may engage in a price war designed to drive the competitor out of business. This is why it has often been said that the problem posed by Cournot is *indeterminate*. That is, there is no general solution possible without introducing further assumptions about the behavior of the two competitors.

Gossen's conception of utility

The German writer Wilhelm Gossen (1810–58) introduced the concept of marginal utility in *Development of the Laws of Human Commerce and of the Consequent Rules of Human Action* (1854). Using the term *Werth* to express utility, Gossen noted that there is no such thing as absolute utility, but rather that *Werth* is a relationship between an object and a person. He observed that as an individual acquires additional units of the same kind of good, each successive act of consumption

yields continuously diminishing pleasure up to the point of satiety. This principle later became known as the law of satiable wants, or Gossen's First Law.

If we are willing to assume that pleasure or utility can be measured in cardinal numbers, the relationship between increases in consumption and the behavior of total and marginal utility inherent in Gossen's first law may be demonstrated graphically by means of a hypothetical curve of total utility. This is done in the upper portion of Figure 10.3, in which the maximum utility derived from the consumption of a given commodity is reached when quantity *OX* is consumed per unit of time. The relationship between total utility and marginal utility may be easily perceived from this graph. If an individual is assumed to be taking quantity X_0 per unit of

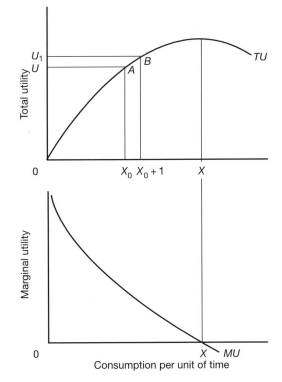

Figure 10.3 Gossen's First Law: The behavior of total and marginal utility

time, and consumption is increased to $X_0 + 1$, total utility increases from U_0 to U_1. The marginal utility of the unit $(U_0 + 1) - X_0$ is therefore $U_1 - U_0$ and is approximately equal to the average slope of the total utility curve between points A and B. If the change in quantity and the utility associated with it are both infinitely small, marginal utility at any given level of consumption is equal to the slope of the total utility curve at that point. Symbolically, the slope of the curve is equal to

$$\frac{\mathrm{d}(TU)}{\mathrm{d}X}$$

It is evident from the total utility curve that marginal utility decreases as consumption per unit of time increases between 0 and X. Thus, the slope of the total utility curve becomes progressively less until it is zero when quantity OX is consumed, and it is negative beyond that point.

In the lower section of Figure 10.3 a marginal utility curve is plotted on the ordinate axis. Since the slope of the total utility curve is decreasing as consumption level OX is approached and reaches zero at that level, the marginal utility curve slopes downward and passes through the horizontal axis when OX units are consumed. The curve MU represents the marginal utility for all levels of consumption per unit of time; including those that yield diminishing total satisfaction. This function is significant because it subsequently became the basis for drawing consumer demand curves.

In addition to the law of satiable wants, Gossen is also given credit for formulating a second law that expresses the optimum allocation of income among alternative uses. Since separate units of the same good yield different degrees of satisfaction, each individual will, in general, derive utility only from a limited number of such units. Continued consumption beyond this point does not, therefore, continue to add to total satisfaction. From this, Gossen inferred that each person should distribute money income among the various goods consumed so that the last unit of income spent on each commodity yields an equal degree of satisfaction. His statement of the equimarginal principle as it applies to consumption has become known as Gossen's Second Law.

Gossen must thus be credited with the statement of the basic principles on which the marginal utility theory of value is grounded. Yet, the fact is that he did not utilize them in connection with the problem of value and price, perhaps because his mathematical training was compromised by his education in law and government. His work attracted virtually no attention until it was rediscovered by William Jevons of England in the 1870s. Nevertheless, Gossen's 1854 book introduced the principle of diminishing utility as the basis for value and succeeded in presenting a mathematical formulation of what is today known as the *maximization principle*, that is, the balancing of marginal increments. Thus, Gossen's work actually introduced a new point of view and a potentially powerful new analytical tool. The new point of view concerned the role of utility in the determination of value; the new tool was the concept of the additional, or *marginal*, increment.

Marginal revolution

The classical theory

It has already been noted that the observation of the tendency toward diminishing returns on land marked the beginning of marginal productivity theory, but failed to develop the concept of marginal cost. Ricardo, as well as Malthus, understood that if additional doses of labor and capital are applied to a given land area, output will increase at a decreasing rate beyond a certain point. These observations were made in connection with the emergence of rent and the apparent tendency of this share of income to increase. The unique social and political implications of the rent problem undoubtedly helped to obscure the fact that the principle of diminishing returns, or productivity, is equally applicable to labor and capital. Thus, the classicists treated the problem of distribution as the sharing of the social income among the three main economic classes of society. No attempt was made to explain income shares from a *functional* point of view, that is, as a problem of valuing the services of factors in the production process under conditions of competition or monopoly.

Von Thünen and the marginal product

A brilliant pioneering effort was made by a little-known German thinker, Johann Heinrich von Thünen (1783–1850), to explain factor rewards in terms of the contributions that marginal increments make to the total product. He made a fundamental contribution to economics with his method of deriving economic propositions from explicit optimizing models, and may have been the first to apply differential calculus to economic problems. His explanation was developed in conjunction with his effort to explain the location of different kinds of agricultural production in relation to the market. His analysis, as set forth in his leading work, *Der Isolierte Staat* (The Isolated State) in 1826, supposes a city surrounded by uniformly fertile agricultural land, isolated by an impenetrable wilderness from the rest of the world. The problem von Thünen postulates is that of explaining to what use land will be put as the distance from the city increases. He reasoned that the further a piece of land is removed from the city, the less intensive production on it will become. More distant areas will concentrate on products that are relatively non-perishable and yet valuable enough to bear the cost of transportation to market. He represented the different types of production, which were located with varying degrees of proximity to a city, by a series of concentric circles. The lands immediately surrounding the city, represented by the first circle, are devoted to garden and dairy products that are highly perishable and/or difficult to transport. The next circle represents forest lands that provide fuel and building materials. Various kinds of extensive farming activities, such as the raising of animal stocks for meat and hides, are located in areas still farther from the city.

The principle involved in this example is that production must be guided by the additional, or marginal, cost incurred by moving further away from the market. Von Thünen concluded that the added application of a factor should stop when the additional cost exactly equals the value of the added product and that the return to a factor is determined by the productivity of the last unit employed. Thus, von Thünen anticipated the marginal productivity theory of factor rewards – although he never used the term – in the process of developing his location theory. His contributions were, however, largely unnoticed, and it was not until the 1890s, as will be seen in Chapter 14, that the marginal productivity principle was rediscovered and the theory of distribution revolutionized.

Concluding remarks

Two observations are in order concerning early efforts to develop the marginal concept as an analytical tool. The first is that while the concept of the margin is obviously applicable to any magnitude of economic significance, such as utility, cost, revenue, and productivity, not one of the individuals who pioneered its use understood the possibility of its general application. Bernoulli understood the concept of the margin and applied it to increments of income. Gossen and Dupuit appreciated the concept of marginal utility and its relationship to consumer behavior. Cournot developed the concept of marginal revenue and its relationship to marginal cost in a profit-maximizing situation. Von Thünen understood the relationship between additional applications of a factor of production and its marginal output, and used these concepts as a basis for developing a theory of location and an explanation of factor rewards. All, however, understood the concept of the margin and its significance only in relation to a particular problem. They therefore failed to develop the marginal concept as a general analytical tool.

A second, and perhaps related, observation is that their embryonic efforts failed to bear fruit; indeed, as is often the case, essential truths had to be rediscovered or developed anew by others before they could become incorporated into the body of economic analysis. Thus, the reconstruction of the theory of value and distribution was delayed until the 1870s, when the marginal concept was reintroduced through the virtually simultaneous and independent efforts of William Jevons in England, Léon Walras in Switzerland, and Carl Menger in Austria. The contributions of this trio will be examined in the next chapter.

Notes

1 Cited by E. Gide and C. Rist, *A History of Economic Doctrine*, 2nd English edn (London: George G. Harrap, 1948), p. 214. *A Short History of Socialist Economic Thought*, by Gerd Hardach and Dieter Karras with Ben Fine, translated by James Weckham (New York: St. Martin's Press, 1978), includes a most useful first chapter, 'The critique of capitalism and perspectives of socialist society before Marx.'

2 *Annuals of the Royal Statistical Society*, 1834–1934, pp. 31–2.

3 *Collected Works of John S. Mill*, edited by J. M. Robson (Toronto: University of Toronto Press, 1962), vol. IX, p. 258n.

4 *Theory of Political Economy*, 1871 (reprinted London: Macmillan 1911).

5 F. Y. Edgeworth, *Mathematical Psychics*, 1881, (reprinted New York: Augustus Kelly), p. 101.

6 It has become conventional to refer to this 'moment in time' as logical, as opposed to 'historical time.'

7 See R. S. Howey, *The Rise of the Marginal Utility School,* 1870–1889 (Lawrence Kans: University of Kansas Press, 1960), p. 2.

8 Some of the more sophisticated aspects of economic behavior under conditions of risk have only recently been explored. See, for example, John von Neumann and Oskar Morgenstern, *The Theory of Games and Economic Behavior* (Princeton, NJ: Princeton University Press, 1944).

9 Joseph A. Schumpeter, who is remembered as being among the great modern historians of economic thought, noted that there were a number of eighteenth-century Italian and French thinkers who understood this paradox of value and that its existence did not, as Smith thought, bar the way to a theory of exchange value based upon value in use. While these thinkers realized that utility is more than the prerequisite of value David Ricardo thought it to be, none of them understood the significance of scarcity. They thus continued to be confounded by the paradox of value. Although they appreciated the importance of utility, they lacked the concept of rate of change at the margin. Neither a utility theory of value nor a concept of demand that related quantities to

prices was therefore able to germinate from their efforts. In his *History of Economic Analysis*, Joseph Schumpeter specifically mentions the Neapolitan Abbé Ferdinando Galiani (1728–87) and the Frenchman Abbé Étienne de Condillac (1714–80) in this connection. J. B. Say, the early-nineteenth-century French thinker who is best known for popularizing *The Wealth of Nations*, also appreciated the significance of utility as a value determinant, although he lacked the concept of the margin.

10 *Annales des Ponts et Chaussées* (1844). This article was not available in English until it appeared in *International Economic Papers*, No. 2 (London and New York: Macmillan, 1952), pp. 83–110.

11 'On the measurement of the utility of public works,' *International Economic Papers*, No. 2 (London and New York: Macmillan, 1952), pp. 83–110 (translated from the 1844 original in *Annales des Fonts et Chaussées*).

12 Dupuit showed price on the horizontal and quantity on the vertical axis. These have been reversed to conform to standard practice in economics today.

13 Augustin Cournot, *Researches into the Mathematical Principles of the Theory of Wealth* (1838), translated by Nathaniel Bacon (New York: Macmillan, 1897).

14 Where P is profit, $P = R(q)$, $\dfrac{dp}{dq} = R'(q) - c'(q) = 0$, $R'(q) = C'(q)$.

15 Cournot's formula $n/(n + 1)$ times the competitive output is applicable to any number of sellers. Competitive output is approached as the number of sellers (n) increases, whereas when the number of sellers decreases, the monopolistic situation is approached. Monopoly output is half the competitive output.

Questions for discussion and further research

1 Cournot, Dupuit, Gossen, and von Thünen each anticipated modern marginal concepts and analyses. Identify the specific concerns and interest of each and summarize their main legacy to marginal utility and demand theory and marginal productivity theory.

Glossary of terms and concepts

Bernoulli's law
In a case of uncertainty about future receipts, behavior is guided, not only by the mathematical probability of gain or loss, but also by the significance of the gains and losses in relation to the individual's financial capability.

Cardinal utility
Measurement of satisfaction in terms of cardinal numbers, for example, 1, 2, 3, and so on.

Consumer surplus
If consumers would have been willing to pay more for a particular good than the price actually paid, they may be said to be enjoying a consumer surplus.

Demand curve
A curve that depicts the relationship between the possible prices at which consumers might purchase corresponding quantities in a given market at a point in time. It is a graphic representation of a demand schedule such as Marshall was to use in his *Principles* (1890).

Diminishing marginal utility
The satisfaction an individual derives from additional quantities of a particular good diminishes as more units are consumed in a given finite period

Discriminatory pricing
The practice of identifying different groups of consumers according to differences in the urgency (elasticity) of their respective demands in order to charge them different rates for service. Dupuit recognized the potential inherent in this pricing technique for maximizing monopoly profit.

Dupuit's tax theorem
Evaluates the relationship between the revenue a tax yields and the loss its collection imposes on society. In raising the price of a commodity, a tax generates a revenue. It also deprives the consumer of the utility he gives

up at the higher price. The optional tax is one which best meets the objective of either maximizing tax collected vs. achieving a given level of consumer surplus for users.

Gossen's First Law

From the principle of diminishing utility, Gossen inferred that if individuals distribute their income among the various goods they consume in such a way that the last unit of each good consumed will satisfy equally, they will have maximized satisfaction; that is, a reallocation of expenditures cannot increase satisfaction.

Induction

The process of inferring information from historical observation or data to establish possible future scenarios.

Marginal analysis

An analysis that focuses on infinitely small increments of such economic magnitudes as utility, cost, output, revenue, and so forth.

Marginal productivity

The additional output Q attributable to an added input of a factor F, when the input of other factors with which it is combined are held constant. Expressed mathematically it is the first order partial derivative of the production function with respect to the input in question: $\partial Q/F$. The rate of change of that productivity, with respect to the associated input, is the second-order partial derivative, $\partial[\partial Q/\partial F]/\partial F = \partial^2 Q/\partial F^2$.

Methodenstreit

A disagreement about the relative merits of using the method of deducing conclusions from an underlying set of premises as opposed to induction, either on the basis of descriptive historical observations or from factual data that can be analyzed statistically. The early participants of the dispute were the German historical school *vis-à-vis* members of the Austrian school.

Ordinal utility

The ranking of preferences. The statement that A is preferred to B means that a particular individual prefers A to B. It does not imply that the extent of the preference is measurable.

Ricardian socialism

Nineteenth-century champions of utilitarian principles predicated on Ricardian value theory. The expectation was that the political reforms of the Fabians could achieve socially better outcomes by means of changes in income distribution.

Von Thünen's law

The principle that each factor will tend to receive a return equivalent to the value added by the last unit employed.

Von Thünen's location principle

This variant of the equimarginal principle establishes the least-cost location for each productive activity that serves a central market. Assuming labor and capital are equally effective in producing all outputs at all locations, resources become allocated among alternative locations to maximize profits. Production of low valued and/or bulky outputs is near the point of consumption, while products of greater value and/or lesser bulk can profitably be located in more remote locations.

Notes for further reading

From *The New Palgrave*

M. T. Beckmenn on location of economic theory, vol. 3, pp. 223–28; Robert Dorfman on marginal productivity theory, vol. 3, pp. 323–25; Robert B. Ekelund on Arsene-Jules-Emile Juvenal Dupuit, vol. 1, pp. 943–44; Jurgen Niehans on Hermann Heinrich Gossen, vol. 2, pp. 550–54, and on Johann Heinrich von Thünen, vol. 3, pp. 636–39; Martin Shubik on Antoine-Augustin Cournot, vol. 1, pp. 708–12; Akira Takayama on consumer surplus, vol. 1, pp. 607–12; S. C. Zabell on Daniel Bernoulli, vol. 1, pp. 231–32.

Selected references and suggestions for further reading

Acton, H. B. *The Illusion of the Epoch*, Part I (Boston: Beacon Press, 1957).

Hilferding, Rudolph in *Das Finanz-kapital* (Berlin: Dietz, 1955 [1923]).

Marx, Karl. *A Contribution to the Critique of Political Economy*. Translated by N. W. Stone (Chicago: Charles H. Kerr, 1904).

Marx, Karl. *Capital*. Translated by Ernest Untermann, and edited by E. Engels, 3 vols (Chicago: Charles Kerr, 1906–9).

Marx, Karl. *Grundrisse der Kritik der Politischen Ökonomie*, 2 vols (Berlin: Dietz-Verlag, 1953).

Marx, Karl and E. Engels. *The Communist Manifesto*. Translated by Samuel Moore (Chicago: Regnery, 1954).

Marx, Karl. *Economic and Philosophic Manuscripts of 1844*. Translated by Martin Milligen, and edited by D. J. Struik (New York: International Publishers, 1964).

Marx, Karl. *Precapitalist Economic Formations*. Translated by J. Cohen and edited by E. J. Hobsbawm (New York: International Publishers, 1965).

Meek, Ronald L. *Studies in the Labour Theory of Value* (London: Lawrence and Wishart, 1956).

Robbins, Lionel. Lecture 25, 'Marx (cont.) – List and the Historical School'. In *A History of Economic Thought* edited by S. Medema and W. Samuels (Princeton, NJ: Princeton University Press, 1998), pp. 238–45.

Robinson, Joan. *An Essay on Marxian Economics* (New York: St. Martin's, 1967).

Sabine, George. *A History of Political Theory*. Revised edition (New York: Holt, Rinehart & Winston, 1950).

Sherman, Howard J. 'Marxist models of cyclical growth.' *History of Political Economy*, 3 (Spring, 1971).

Sweezy, Paul M. *The Theory of Capitalist Development* (New York: Oxford University Press, 1942).

Wolfson, Murray. *A Reappraisal of Marxian Economics* (New York: Columbia University Press, 1966).

Chapter 11

Karl Marx: an inquiry into the 'Law of Motion' of the capitalist system

••

Introduction

Life and times (1818–83)

Not only is the name Karl Marx intimately associated with the socialist movement, but his ideas have had greater influence than those of any other socialist advocate. 'Scientific' socialism – that distinctively Marxian fusion of philosophy, socialism, and economics, put forward as a revelation of the ultimate collapse of capitalism and the inevitable triumph of socialism – is largely attributable to the influence of his thinking.

Marx was born in the German Rhineland, the son of a moderately well-to-do Jewish lawyer who became a convert to Lutheranism and raised his children in that faith. At 17, Marx entered the University of Bonn to study law, but transferred after a year to the more stimulating atmosphere of the University of Berlin, where his interests turned to philosophy and history. His religious views now abandoned like many others of his generation, he became profoundly affected by the ideas of the philosopher Georg Hegel (1770–1831). Hegel's views of the individual, the state, and the mode of historical change contrasted sharply with the tenets of rationalism that characterized the Age of Enlightenment. Initially, Hegelian ideas led Marx in the direction of the 'higher criticism,' which kept him from securing a university post. He turned his attention to journalism and became editor of the *Rheinische Zeitung* in Cologne, a moderately liberal paper sponsored by business interests.

The suspension of the newspaper a year later caused Marx and his wife to move to Paris, where he felt people would be more sympathetic to his liberal views in social and economic matters. His contacts with revolutionary socialist and communist thinkers encouraged him to study history, politics, and economics. The French social philosopher, Pierre Proudhon, appears to have suggested to him the possibility of interpreting economic phenomena in terms of ideas drawn from the philosopher Georg Hegel. This approach appears to have become the foundation for the Marxian system, although Marx later denounced Proudhon as an incompetent proponent of Hegel's ideas.

His 'Paris period' also brought Marx into close personal contact with Friedrich Engels, whose friendship with Marx spanned a lifetime. Engels's family was in the textile business in Barmen (now Wuppertal), Germany, and he later became the prosperous part-owner of a cotton business in England. His intimate knowledge of economic and social conditions in that country, the basis for his work on *The Condition of the Working Class in England* (1844), was invaluable to Marx. It was also through Engels that Marx made contact with the English socialists of the day.

Marx's sojourn in Paris was brief, lasting little more than a year. He was expelled from France at the request of the Prussian government, and moved to Belgium. His intellectual system had by then already taken shape, and he turned his attention to political activity. He helped found a German Workers' Union that joined with other such groups into an international Communist League. Marx and Engels together drafted a statement of principles they called the *Communist Manifesto* (1848), which became the best-known of all Marxist writings. A powerful and brilliant document, now available in virtually all languages, the *Manifesto* was intended to present a theoretical basis for communism, a critique of utopian socialist movements, and a program of socialist aims with methods for achieving them.

The year 1848 brought many revolutionary uprisings in Europe. The outbreak of revolutionary feelings in France forced the abdication of Louis Philippe and the proclamation of the Second French Republic. Although there were efforts to direct the new government in accordance with socialist principles, the coup of 1852 established Louis Napoleon as Emperor Napoleon III. However, in all likelihood, Marx's *Manifesto* had little to do with the revolution. Nevertheless, he was deported from Belgium for revolutionary activity, returning first to Paris, then briefly to Germany, before taking refuge in London. He lived there for the remainder of his life, supported largely by gifts and loans from friends, relatives, and sympathizers (Engels, in particular), and stipends from his intermittent journalistic activity. The most note-worthy of the latter was his work as foreign correspondent for the *New York Tribune*, an association that lasted from 1851 to the 1860s. This was also the period during which he utilized the facilities of the British Museum to gather material for the first volume of *Capital*, which appeared in print in 1867. The remaining two volumes were put together by Engels from partial drafts and notes. This was the trilogy that Marx, had he lived, intended to comprise the reconstruction of the science of political economy.

The background for Marxian economic theory

Socialist thought

Marx's *Capital* sets forth his theory of the development of the capitalistic system. The book has remarkably little to say about socialism, the system Marx expected ultimately to succeed capitalism. His analysis derives partly from the social reform movements of the Enlightenment, which nurtured the idea that human society can be rationally reconstructed to promote the best interests of its members.

There were two broad views as to how this reconstruction might take place. One continued the tradition of classical liberalism and maintained that society's best interests are served by assuring individual freedom. In seeking their own best interests, individuals would automatically also assure the ideal functioning of society as a whole. *Philosophical radicalism* was this sort of reform movement. It stressed the preservation of private property rights and individual enterprise with minimal government restriction.

The *socialist–anarchist* movement was similar to philosophical radicalism in its aims but fundamentally different in the *modus operandi* it visualized would achieve them. It was socialistic in its view that the only rational society is one that substitutes collective for private ownership of the means of production as a foundation for an egalitarian distribution of income. It was anarchistic in its conception of government as the outgrowth of the property rights of the wealthy who needed the coercive influence of the state to survive and retain economic and political power.

Like classical liberalism, the socialist–anarchist movement was initially an idealistic one that attracted intellectual, rather than working-class, support. Its primary early development was in France during the early nineteenth century, before it experienced the Industrial Revolution and associated labor discontent. The Revolution destroyed the absolute monarchy of the *ancien regime*, and raised the bourgeoisie to such a high level of economic and political power that calls for further reform emerged. Comte Henri de Saint-Simon (1760–1825) called for the reorganization of society on the model of the factory. The new industrial state was urged to supplant the church as the supreme authority for achieving harmony. He maintained that all would enjoy the advantages of an industrial system built on the basis of capital and science, and also benefit from the spirit of cooperation that characterizes factory life.[1] Saint-Simon favored drastic reforms in the ownership of land but did not advocate the abolition of private property. On the contrary, he maintained that capital as well as labor are legitimately entitled to some form of remuneration.

Charles Fourier (1772–1837), another Frenchman who developed a theory of socialism at about the same time as Saint-Simon, maintained that a principle akin to Newton's physical principles underlies social relations.

He argued that the industrial world ought to be organized on the principle of mutual attraction and proposed the group as the basic social unit composed of at least seven persons of similar tastes who pursue a common art, science, or industry. Five or more groups would constitute a series, and a union of series would make up a phalanx. Each phalanx, consisting of approximately 1600 persons, would, in his scheme, occupy about 500 acres of land, and its members would live together in a *phalanstere* or garden city. Since the organization of the phalanx is essentially like that of a joint-stock corporation, Fourier does not, however, recommend that land be distributed solely among those who own stock: 5/12 would go to labor, 4/12 to capital, and 3/12 to talent. Thus, the wage system would be abolished in Fourier's scheme because labor would be rewarded by a share in profits.

Not all of the early French socialists shared the view of Saint-Simon and Fourier that it is unnecessary to abolish private property in order to achieve major reforms. Proudhon's contrary view is typical. 'Property,' he said, 'is theft'; when there is private property, the state becomes the agency required to perpetuate it. He reasoned that after private property has been abolished and the people have renounced acquisition in favor of cooperation for the common good, government can be abolished because it will have no further function to perform.

While Saint-Simon and Fourier approached reform on an intellectual level, Robert Owen (1771–1858) attempted to put some of the principles of a socialist society into practice. He bought an impoverished textile village at New Lanark, Scotland, and approximately 2500 people were encouraged to participate in a model community he sought to establish there. He also purchased a tract of land in the state of Indiana in the United States, where he established a settlement known as New Harmony. The success of these communities was, however, short-lived. The experiment is, however, an interesting chapter in the history of what Karl Marx dubbed *utopian socialism.*

Marx was in substantial agreement with these early socialists about the aims of socialism and shared many of their visions of the future society. But he felt they were unrealistic in believing that a major transformation of existing society could be brought about simply by an appeal to reason. The prosperous upper classes, in particular, could never be led by reason alone to accept the reforms proposed by the socialists. Even workers were not yet ready, in his view, for a radically different society. Not until the effects of the Industrial Revolution became widespread did socialism become a mass movement of the working class. It is perhaps worth noting, in this regard, that the German Workers' Union, which Marx helped found while he was in Belgium, had no workers in it, but existed primarily to study socialist thought. Marx maintained that workers would not be ready for socialism until the evils of the present system greatly worsened their positions. It became his aim to demonstrate how the deterioration of the working class would inevitably come about and necessarily call forth socialism. This is the difference between Marx's scientific socialism and earlier utopian movements. He argued that socialism will be the inevitable result of an evolutionary process that might be hastened by proper strategy and tactics, and that the approach of the utopians would, in fact, serve to hinder rather than serve that ultimate aim. Precisely why socialism was inevitable, according to Marxian thinking, turns upon the use he made of Hegel's philosophy of history.

Hegel's philosophy of history

Marx's analytical system appears to have begun with its general philosophy. He was still a student at the University of Berlin when he came under the influence of Hegel's philosophy of history and its dialectic. The origin of the dialectic is ancient Greek philosophy, which refers to the method by which two persons engaged in argument or debate, can modify, and eventually correct, one another's views until they arrive at a third view incorporating elements of both. Thus, there is a thesis that is confronted with a conflicting antithesis. The controversy between them leads to corrective argument and modification until a synthesis emerges in which thesis and antithesis are reconciled. This is the method used by Plato in his *Dialogues* and, later, this became an important intellectual tool of the Scholastics.

Hegel's adaptation of the dialectic was little concerned with the opposing ideas of individual human beings.[2] He conceived of the dialectic as the process by which change takes place in the universe. There is, he thought, an inherent pattern according to which this development takes place and about which we can learn from the study of history. Under his influence, European scholars came to believe that knowledge of the past is necessary to foresee and influence the future. Conservative and radical thinkers alike embraced anew the study of history; and there followed an age, particularly in Germany but also elsewhere in Europe, in which the historical method became regarded as the only truly scientific one and was applied to virtually all fields of inquiry.

Hegel himself undertook to utilize the dialectic to predict the next stage of German history. The next and inevitable step, he maintained, would be the amalgamation of the several German states under a single monarchy. The new German state would thus be the apex of history. Hegel's political philosophy not only rejected individualism on the grounds that it failed to recognize the intimate relationship between the individual and society, but also endowed the state with a spirit all its own. This is the conception of the state that characterized German political theory even into the twentieth century.

Ricardian economics

Ricardian economics or, more specifically, Ricardo's labor theory of value, was the third source of inspiration for Marx's analysis of the functioning of the capitalistic system. Ricardo, it will be recalled, wrote as follows: 'Possessing utility [which he discarded both as a cause and as a measure of value], commodities derive their exchangeable value from two sources: from their scarcity and from the quantity of labour required to obtain them.'[3] Scarcity is of primary significance for a commodity that is not reproducible, like a rare work of art. Most commodities, however, are products of labor and can be supplied 'almost without any assignable limit, if we are disposed to bestow the labour necessary to obtain them.'[4] Since Ricardo reasoned that rent, as a differential surplus, is not a determinant of exchange value, and that variations in wages or profits do not affect value in exchange, commodities are exchanged in proportion to the labor used in their production.

Marx's serious study of economics dates from his early Paris days, when he became impressed with the treatment that Smith, and more particularly Ricardo, gave to labor as the cause of value. Both were, however, favorably disposed toward competitive capitalism and *laissez-faire* policy, whereas Marx was hostile to that system in every form on the grounds that the laboring class is exploited by capitalist employers. However, he regarded Smith and Ricardo's labor theory of value as providing an essential foundation for his labor exploitation hypothesis and the eventual destruction of the capitalist system. Indeed, Marx considered himself to be, intellectually speaking, a lineal descendant of the great classical tradition.

The origin, nature, and functioning of capitalism

The economic interpretation of history

Marx's objective was 'to lay bare the economic law of motion of modern society.'[5] He maintained the prime mover of social change is to be found in changes in the mode of production. This premise was a firm part of his thinking for some considerable time before he published volume I of *Capital*. In the preface to *A Contribution to the Critique of Political Economy*, he wrote as follows:

> The mode of production in material life determines the general character of the social, political and spiritual processes of life. It is not the consciousness of men that determines their existence, but on the contrary, their social existence determines their consciousness. At a certain stage of their development, the material forces of production in society come in conflict with the existing relations of production, or what is but a legal expression for the same thing, with the property relations within which they had been at work before. From forms of development of the forces of production these relations turn into their fetters. Then comes the period of social revolution. With the change of the economic foundation the entire immense superstructure is more or less rapidly transformed.[6]

The impetus to social change is thus to be found in the 'mode of production.' The mode of production of a particular period reflects the social relationships inherent in the ownership and use of the material means of production. As the mode of production becomes appropriate to the altered production process, contradictions develop between existing social relationships and the altered mode of production that generates social change. This is the Hegelian aspect of Marx's thinking. However, unlike Hegel, Marx saw the arena of conflict to be the material world, with its existing social system, rather than locating it in the realm of ideas. Human minds do not originate conflicting theses and antitheses according to Marx, but only perceive the material world of reality. This is the essence of Marx's materialism as opposed to Hegel's idealism. For Marx, the conflicts to be resolved are between social classes – the ruling class of the era versus the exploited class. Thus, Marx began the *Communist Manifesto* with the observation that 'the history of all hitherto existing society is the history of class struggles.'

The economic source of class conflict was also of special interest to the classicists. Class conflict was the basis for Ricardo's concern about 'the distribution of the produce of the earth.' For Ricardo, the basic antagonism between social classes was that which existed between the landlords and the industrial capitalists. This is the reason why the doctrine of rent loomed so large in the Ricardian analysis. Marx, however, regarded the emphasis on land and rent as inappropriate in a capitalist economy, in which the antagonistic classes are *the bourgeoisie and the proletariat*. It is the relationship between those two that determines the nature of the mode of production and hence the character of the whole society.

In analyzing the relationship between the bourgeoisie and the proletariat, Marx relies heavily on the deductive methodology so strongly associated with Ricardo and his followers. Marx's application is, of course, different, in that it is oriented towards demonstrating the transitory nature of capitalism. To do this, Marx finds it necessary to isolate the capital–labor relationship from all other social relationships in order to examine its basic character. Reduced to its simplest form, the capital–labor relationship is one of *exchange*. Marx identifies the commodity that is being bought and sold as *labor power*. Labor power is merely one commodity among many, but it is the only commodity labor has available for sale. The exchange relationship that results from the sale of labor power is also one among many. Thus, Part I of the first volume of *Capital*, entitled 'Commodities,' analyzes the phenomenon of exchange. Exchange begins with simple commodity production, such as that which takes place when individuals own the means of production and uses them to satisfy wants that cannot be fulfilled directly by exchanging their surpluses with others. This is not what happens under capitalism, in which the ownership of all means of production is in the hands of the bourgeoisie, while the work is performed by the members of the proletariat. The means of production and labor power are thus given commodity form, and exchange relationships are involved in their purchase and sale. This is the mode of production that is typical of capitalism.

It should now be clear that the concept of the mode of production does not refer to the technical aspects of production alone. The mode of production includes, not only the technology surrounding the physical means of production, but also the social relationships deriving from the whole complex of the socioeconomic, political, and cultural institutions that accompany a given stage of development. This superstructure is a major aspect of the mode of production and historical process. Thus, what is so often referred to as the *economic interpretation of history* is at least as much in the realm of sociology as of economics.

Use value and exchange value

The manner in which the conflict between the mode of production and the superstructure of social organization will make itself felt, and the reason the capitalistic system will eventually become untenable, are questions that Marx's economic analysis is intended to answer. His focus is on the value problem and his analysis begins by noting that every commodity has a use value and an exchange value. Although these terms are given their usual meaning, Marx regards the analysis of use value as outside the sphere of political economy. Political economy, in Marx's view, properly involves only social relations. The study of use values does not come within the province of the political economist because these values involve a relationship between a person and an object. Exchange values between goods, although they seemingly do not involve social relationships, are the concern of the political economist because every *exchange of commodities is also an exchange of labor*. Marx thus conceives of the value problem as having a qualitative aspect as well as a quantitative one. It has been suggested that the great originality of Marx's value theory lies in its attempt to deal simultaneously with both.[7]

Marx's insistence that an object can have exchange value only if it represents embodied labor, led him to distinguish between value and price. An object like uncultivated land may command a price but has no exchange value because there is no labor congealed in it.[8] While Marx thought all value derives from labor, he was aware that labor is sometimes more proficient because of natural ability or superior training. When a more effective worker is employed side-by-side with one who is less productive, their comparative efficiency is measurable in physical terms. Once the ratio of their output has been established, the two kinds of labor can be reduced to a common denominator, namely, 'human labor pure and simple.' 'Skilled labor counts only as simple labor intensified, or rather, as multiplied simple labor, a given quantity of skilled labor being considered equal to a greater quantity of simple labor.'[9] The labor embodied in a commodity is thus measurable in time units that express the proportion of the community's labor force that a commodity absorbs. From this, Marx deduces that there is a correspondence between the labor–time ratios involved in the production of two commodities and their exchange ratios.

There is an obvious qualification to this principle: the fact that more labor time is lavished on a commodity does not necessarily give it greater value. Unnecessary or inefficient expenditures of labor time do not enhance value. Only 'socially necessary' labor time contributes to value. 'The labor time socially necessary is that required to produce an article under the normal conditions of production and with the average degree of skill and intensity prevalent at this time.'[10] Thus, commodities are exchanged for one another at a rate that is determined by the quantity of socially necessary labor each embodies. When this ratio of exchange prevails in the market between any pair of commodities, there is no incentive for the producers of either commodity to shift from the production of one to the production of the other, and the price of each will be proportional to the labor time required to produce it. In other words, if the forces of supply and demand have free play, an equilibrium price that is proportional to labor time will be established. Competitive market forces, then, are the mechanism through which deviations between market prices and real (labor) values are eliminated. Thus, the supply and demand explanation of price determination is really an essential part of the labor theory, although Marx did not always express this point clearly.

Marx did not completely overlook the role of demand in determining exchange values; he specifically emphasized that use value is a prerequisite for exchange value and that, therefore, the social need for a commodity is the determining factor of the amount of social labor to be allocated to a particular type of production. Thus, if too much of a commodity has been produced or if more labor has been expended than is socially necessary, it will be reflected in a reduced exchange value. Nevertheless, it is true that Marx did not approach the value problem from the standpoint of consumer choice, any more than did Smith or Ricardo. It has been suggested that to have done so would have been inconsistent with his objective of investigating the causes of social change, for consumer wants, except insofar as they originate in physical requirements, are a reflection of the mode of production and are therefore passive as regards the process of change.[11]

Simple reproduction and extended reproduction

In common with the Physiocrats and the classicists, Marx recognized that the process of production must be continuous, in the sense that it constantly converts a part of its products into means of production; that is, it *reproduces* itself. The Physiocrats and the classicists envisioned a system of production in which producers owning means of production typically exchange their surplus products for those of others, either by barter or by using money, to enjoy consumption. But they were not describing the system of 'extended reproduction' that characterizes an advanced capitalistic system. Under advanced capitalism, the means of production are owned by a property-owning, or capitalist class (the bourgeoisie), which employs working class persons (the proletariat) to produce goods for sale. By employing them, the capitalist class, in fact, purchases the use of *labor power* as a commodity and directs its efforts into the production of commodities whose sale yields the capitalists' revenue. The difference between the exchange values of the commodities the capitalists buy and those they sell, when the production process is completed, is *surplus value,* which supports *accumulation* rather than consumption. Surplus value raises an issue that goes to the heart of capitalism as a system. In fact, it is an issue that Smith left unresolved when he argued that profit is not just another name for the wages of management.

Issues and Answers from the Masterworks 11.1

Issue

How does the capitalist manage to create surplus value? Given that he hires his workers in a competitive market at a wage rate that equals the labor cost of their families' requirement for 'food and necessaries' and sells their product at a competitive price equal to their labor cost of production, surplus value seems an impossibility.

Marx's answer

From *Capital*, Vol. I, Part 3, Chapter 6.

The general formula for capital

The circulation of commodities is the starting point of capital. The production of commodities, their circulation, and that more developed form of their circulation called commerce, these form the historical ground-work from which it rises. The modern history of capital dates from the creation in the sixteenth century of a world-embracing commerce and a world-embracing market. If we abstract from the material substance of the circulation of commodities, that is, from the exchange of the various use-values, and consider only the economic forms produced by this process of circulation, we find its final result to be money: this final product of the circulation of commodities is the first form in which capital appears.

As a matter of history, capital, as opposed to landed property, invariably takes the form at first of money; it appears as moneyed wealth, as the capital of the merchant and of the usurer. But we have no need to refer to the origin of capital in order to discover that the first form of appearance of capital is money. We can see it daily under our very eyes. All new capital, to commence with, comes on the stage, that is, on the market, whether of commodities, labour, or money, even in our days, in the shape of money that by a definite process has to be transformed into capital.

The first distinction we notice between money that is money only, and money that is capital, is nothing more than a difference in their form of circulation. The simplest form of the circulation of commodities is C-M-C, the transformation of commodities into money, and the change of the money back again into commodities; or selling in order to buy. But alongside of this form we find another specifically different form: M-C-M, the transformation of money into commodities, and the change of commodities back again into money; or buying in order to sell. Money that circulates in the latter manner is thereby transformed into, becomes capital, and is already potentially capital.

Now let us examine the circuit M-C-M a little closer. It consists, like the other, of two antithetical phases. In the first phase, M-C, or the purchase, the money is changed into a commodity. In the second phase, C-M, or the sale, the commodity is changed back again into money. The combination of these two phases constitutes the single movement whereby money is exchanged for a commodity, and the same commodity is again exchanged for money; whereby a commodity is bought in order to be sold, or, neglecting the distinction in form between buying and selling, whereby a commodity is bought with money, and then money is bought with a commodity. The result, in which the phases of the process vanish, is the exchange of money for money, M-M. If I purchase 2,000 lbs. of cotton for £100, and resell the 2,000 lbs. of cotton for £110, I have, in fact, exchanged £100 for £110, money for money.

Now it is evident that the circuit M-C-M would be absurd and without meaning if the intention were to exchange by this means two equal sums of money, £100 for £100. The miser's plan would be far simpler and surer; he sticks to his £100 instead of exposing it to the dangers of circulation. And yet, whether the merchant who has paid £100 for his cotton sells it for £110, or lets it go for £100, or even £50, his money has, at all events, gone through a characteristic and original movement, quite different in kind from that which it goes through in the hands of the peasant who sells corn, and with the money thus set free buys clothes. We have therefore to examine first the distinguishing characteristics of the forms of the circuits M-C-M and C-M-C, and in doing this the real difference that underlies the mere difference of form will reveal itself.

Let us see, in the first place, what the two forms have in common. Both circuits are resolvable into the same two antithetical phases, C-M, a sale, and M-C, a purchase. In each of these phases the same material elements – a commodity, and money, and the same economic dramatis personae, a buyer and a seller – confront one another. Each circuit is the unity of the same two antithetical phases, and in each case this unity is brought about by the intervention of three contracting parties, of whom one only sells, another only buys, while the third both buys and sells.

What, however, first and foremost distinguishes the circuit C-M-C from the circuit M-C-M, is the inverted order of succession of the two phases. The simple circulation of commodities begins with a sale and ends with a purchase, while the circulation of money as capital begins with a purchase and ends with a sale. In the one case both the starting-point and the goal are commodities, in the other they are money. In the first form the movement is brought about by the intervention of money, in the second by that of a commodity.

In the circulation C-M-C, the money is, in the end, converted into a commodity, that serves as a use-value; it is spent once and for all. In the inverted form, M-C-M, on the contrary, the buyer lays out money in order that, as a seller, he may recover money. By the purchase of his commodity he throws money into circulation, in order to withdraw it again by the sale of the same commodity. He lets the money go, but only with the sly intention of getting it back again. The money, therefore, is not spent, it is merely advanced.

In the circuit C-M-C, the same piece of money changes its place twice. The seller gets it from the buyer and pays it away to another seller. The complete circulation, which begins with the receipt, concludes with the payment, of money for commodities. It is the very contrary in the circuit M-C-M. Here it is not the piece of money that changes its place twice, but the commodity. The buyer takes it from the hands of the seller and passes it into the hands of another buyer. Just as in the simple circulation of commodities the double change of place of the same piece of money effects its passage from one hand into another, so here the double change of place of the same commodity brings about the reflux of the money to its point of departure.

Such reflux is not dependent on the commodity being sold for more than was paid for it. This circumstance influences only the amount of the money that comes back. The reflux itself takes place, as soon as the purchased commodity is resold, in other words, as soon as the circuit M-C-M is completed. We have here, therefore, a palpable difference between the circulation of money as capital, and its circulation as mere money.

The circuit C-M-C comes completely to an end, as soon as the money brought in by the sale of one commodity is abstracted again by the purchase of another . . . It is otherwise in the circulation M-C-M, which at first sign appears purposeless, because it is tautological. Both extremes have the same economic form. They are both money, and therefore are not qualitatively different use-values; for money is but the converted form of commodities, in which their particular use-values vanish. To exchange £100 for cotton, and then this same cotton again for £100, is merely a roundabout way of exchanging money for money, the same for the same, and appears to be an operation just as purposeless as it is absurd. One sum of money is distinguishable from another only by its amount. The character and tendency of the process M-C-M, is therefore not due to any qualitative difference between its extremes, both being money, but solely to their quantitative difference. More money is withdrawn from circulation at the finish than was thrown into it at the start. The cotton that was bought for £100 is perhaps resold for £100 + £10, or £110. The exact form of this process is therefore M-C-M, where $M' = M + \Delta M$ = the original sum advanced, plus an increment. This increment or excess over the original value I call 'surplus-value.' The value originally advanced, therefore, not only remains intact while in circulation, but adds to itself a surplus-value or expands itself. It is this movement that converts it into capital . . . The simple circulation of commodities – selling in order to buy – is a means of carrying out a purpose unconnected with circulation, namely, the appropriation of use-values, the satisfaction of wants. The circulation of money as capital is, on the contrary, an end in itself, for the expansion of value takes place only within this constantly renewed movement. The circulation of capital has therefore no limits.

As the conscious representative of this movement, the possessor of money becomes a capitalist. His person, or rather his pocket, is the point from which the money starts and to which it returns. The expansion of value, which is the objective basis or main-spring of the circulation M-C-M, becomes his subjective aim, and it is only in so far as the appropriation of ever more and more wealth in the abstract becomes the sole motive of his operations, that he functions as a capitalist, that is, as capital personified and endowed with consciousness and a will. Use-values must therefore never be looked upon as the real aim of the capitalist; neither must the profit on any single transaction. The restless never-ending process of profit-making alone is what he aims at. This boundless greed after riches, this passionate chase after exchange-value, is common to the capitalist and the miser; but while the miser is merely a capitalist gone mad, the capitalist is a rational miser. The never-ending augmentation of exchange value, which the miser strives after, by seeking to save his money from circulation, is attained by the more acute capitalist, by constantly throwing it afresh into circulation . . .

Buying in order to sell, or, more accurately, buying in order to sell dearer, M-C-M', appears certainly to be a form peculiar to one kind of capital alone, namely, merchants' capital. But industrial capital too is money, that is changed into commodities, and by the sale of these commodities, is reconverted into more money. The events that take place outside the sphere of circulation, in the interval between the buying and selling, do not affect the form of this movement. Lastly, in the case of interest-bearing capital, the circulation M-C-M' appears abridged. We have its result without the intermediate stage, in the form M-M', '*en style lapidaire*' so to say, money that is worth more money, value that is greater than itself. M-C-M' is therefore in reality the general formula of capital as it appears prima facie within the sphere of circulation . . .

The buying and selling of labour-power

The change of value that occurs in the case of money intended to be converted into capital, cannot take place in the money itself, since in its function of means of purchase and of payment, it does no more than realise the price of the commodity it buys or pays for; and, as hard cash, it is value petrified, never varying. Just as little can it originate in the second act of circulation, the re-sale of the commodity, which does no more than transform the article from its bodily form back again into its money-form. The change must, therefore, take place in the commodity bought by the first act, M-C, but not in its value, for equivalents are exchanged, and the commodity is paid for at its full value.

The labour-process and the process of producing surplus-value

Section 1. The labour-process or the production of use-values

The capitalist buys labour-power in order to use it; and labour-power in use is labour itself. The purchaser of labour-power consumes it by setting the seller of it to work. By working, the latter becomes actually, what before he only was potentially, labour-power in action, a labourer. In order that his labour may re-appear in a commodity, he must, before all things, expend it on something useful, on something capable of satisfying a want of some sort. Hence, what the capitalist sets the labourer to produce, is a particular use-value, a specified article . . .

The labour-process, turned into the process by which the capitalist consumes labour-power, exhibits two characteristic phenomena. First, the labourer works under the control of the capitalist to whom his labour belongs; the capitalist taking good care that the work is done in a proper manner, and that the means of production are used with intelligence, so that there is no unnecessary waste of raw material, and no wear and tear of the implements beyond what is necessarily caused by the work.

Secondly, the product is the property of the capitalist and not that of the labourer, its immediate producer. Suppose that a capitalist pays for a day's labour-power at its value; then the right to use that power for a day belongs to him, just as much as the right to use any other commodity, such as a horse that he has hired for the day. To the purchaser of a commodity belongs its use, and the seller of labour-power, by giving his labour, does no more, in reality, than part with the use-value that he has sold. From the instant he steps into the workshop, the use-value of his labour-power, and therefore also its use, which is labour, belongs to the capitalist. By the purchase of labour-power, the capitalist incorporates labour, as a living ferment, with the lifeless constituents of the product. From his point of view, the labour-process is nothing more than the consumption of the commodity purchased, i.e. of labour-power; but this consumption cannot be effected except by supplying the labour-power with the means of production. The labour-process is a process between things that the capitalist has purchased, things that have become his property. The product of this process belongs, therefore, to him, just as much as does the wine which is the product of a process of fermentation completed in his cellar.

Section 2. The production of surplus-value

The product appropriated by the capitalist is a use-value, as yarn, for example, or boots. But, although boots are, in one sense, the basis of all social progress, and our capitalist is a decided 'progressist,' yet he does not manufacture boots for their own sake . . . Our capitalist has two objects in view: in the first place, he wants to produce a use-value that has a value in exchange, that is to say, an article destined to be sold, a commodity; and secondly, he desires to produce a commodity whose value shall be greater than the sum of the values of the commodities used in its production, that is, of the means of production and the labour-power, that he purchased with his good money in the open market. His aim is to produce not only a use-value, but a commodity also; not only use-value, but value; not only value, but at the same time surplus value . . .

The fact that half a day's labour is necessary to keep the labourer alive during 24 hours, does not in any way prevent him from working a whole day. The owner of the money has paid the value of a day's labour-power; his, therefore, is the use of it for a day, a day's labour belongs to him. The circumstance, that on the one hand the daily sustenance of labour-power costs only half a day's labour, while on the other hand the very same labour-power can work during a whole day, that consequently the value which its use during one day creates, is double what he pays for that use, this circumstance is, without doubt, a piece of good luck for the buyer, but by no means an injury to the seller . . .

By turning his money into commodities that serve as the material elements of a new product, and as factors in the labour-process, by incorporating living labour with their dead substance, the capitalist at the same time converts value, i.e. past, materialised, and dead labour, into capital, into value big with value, a live monster that is fruitful and multiplies.

Source: Reprinted from the English edition (London: Swan Sonnenschein, Lowry & Company, 1887), translated from the third German edition. The selection reprinted here originally appeared as Part 2, Chapters 4, 6, and 7. Footnotes deleted.

Summing up: Marx's key points

Marx's basic concern is to undermine the perception that abstinence by capitalists is the source of capital accumulation and that the profits they earn are their just return. To refute this classical view, he begins by noting that, under conditions of simple reproduction, money served only as a medium to circulate commodities. In this stage the process of production and exchange involved the exchange (sale) of individuals' commodity surpluses for money which, in turn, became used to buy other commodities. The process whose purpose is to satisfy wants can be represented by C-M-C.

A different process is at work when the possessor of money becomes a capitalist, for his objective is to make profit by appropriating surplus value. The capitalist uses money to buy labor power as a commodity whose use value is at his disposal for the entire working day. The selling price of workers' products (in which their labor power is congealed) returns an amount of revenue to the capitalist that exceeds the wage cost of the labor power he purchased. The differential is surplus value and the process, which Marx calls *extended reproduction*, can be represented as M-C-M′ or 'buying in order to sell dearer.' If the average working day is, let us say, 12 hours, and

the worker can produce the equivalent of his family's subsistence in 6 hours, then 6 hours remain during which the worker continues to create new exchange values. The working day is, therefore, divisible into two parts, necessary labor and surplus labor. The value of the output resulting from necessary work in the form of wages, but the product of labor power for which workers are not paid goes to the capitalist in the form of surplus value. According to Marx, this is the basis of ongoing accumulation under capitalism.

Since Marx is concerned with the degree of labor exploitation, he also focuses on the *rate of surplus value*, which he designates as s'. This is the ratio between surplus value (s) and the variable capital outlays (v) the capitalist makes. Thus,

Rate of surplus value $= s' = s/v$

The rate at which surplus value can be created depends on three factors: (1) the length of the working day; (2) the productivity of labor; and (3) the quantity of commodities making up the worker's real wage. Individually, or in combination, these factors can be altered by the capitalist to increase surplus value. It is thus obvious that Marx associated the creation of surplus value strictly with labor. That part of the machinery and tools that is actually used up, and the materials utilized in the production process, are incapable of creating a surplus, but only transfer an equal value to the final good. Marx assumes that the rate of surplus value (i.e. the degree of labor exploitation) will be 100 percent.

The equalization of rates of profit

In Volume I of *Capital*, Marx maintains that the rate of surplus value tends to become equalized among sectors of the economy because of labor's tendency to move from low-wage areas to high-wage areas while producers utilize productive techniques as efficient as those used by their competitors. He maintains that the rate of surplus value will tend to be the same for all firms within an industry and also among all the industries in the economy.

In Volume III of *Capital*, which was edited by Engels and published after Marx's death, it is, however, argued that *rates of profit*, rather than rates of surplus value, tend toward equality. Under competitive conditions, surplus values are redistributed among different industries so that rates of profit are equal among industries. The rate of profit is the ratio of surplus value to total capital outlay. Thus,

Rate of profit $= \pi' = s/c + v$

The argument that *rates of profit* (rather than rates of surplus value) tend to become equalized is a more realistic perspective: business owners are not interested in profit per unit of labor cost, but in profit per unit of total invested capital. Only if the rate at which capital depreciates annually and the turnover rate of inventory are the same in every industry, which they clearly are not, could rates of surplus value and rates of profit both be equalized.

But Marx's argument that it is rates of *profit* rather than surplus value that tend toward equality raises another important intellectual puzzle: it implies that a commodity will sell at its cost of production rather than at its labor value. Marx's critics have thus argued that the problem of transforming values into prices necessarily determines the entire labor theory of value.[12]

Marx himself recognized the problem: 'It would seem therefore, that here the theory of value is incompatible with the actual process, incompatible with the real phenomena of production, and that for this reason any attempt to understand these phenomena should be given up.'[13] He did, however, offer a solution to the problem. The essence of Marx's solution is that the market 'transforms' values into prices that differ individually from labor-determined values of commodities. Some capitalists will therefore *sell above value* and enjoy more surplus value, and others will sell below value and enjoy less surplus value. Capitalists will thus share in the aggregate of surplus value in accordance with the *organic composition of capital* in their industry. The latter term is Marx's way of expressing what is today called the *capital intensity* of an industry. The higher the ratio of (c), constant capital, to ($c + v$), or total capital, the greater is the industry's capital intensity: Thus,

Organic composition of capital $K = c/c + v$

Marx assumed five industries with organic compositions of capital like those represented in Table 11.1. By assumption, the capital for the economy as a whole is $390c + 110v = 500$; each industry is assumed to have a capital of 100. Industries 5 and 4 are the most capital-intensive since they make the smallest variable capital outlays; analogously, industries 3 and 2 are the least capital-intensive.

The numerical example reproduced in Table 11.1 became the basis for Marx's

Table 11.1 The transformation of values into prices

Capital composition by industry*	Surplus value (s)	Rate of surplus value* (s′ = s/v)	Used up* (c′)	Commodity's labour cost (c′ + v)	Commodity's value (c′ + v + s)	Industry rate of profit π ($\frac{s}{c+v}$)
1. 80c + 20v	20	100%	50	70	90	20%
2. 70c + 30v	30	100	51	81	111	30
3. 60c + 40v	40	100	51	91	131	40
4. 85c + 15v	15	100	40	55	70	15
5. 95c + 5v	5	100	10	15	20	5
390c + 110v	110	100%				22%

*By assumption

Table 11.2 Deviation of prices from values based on 22 percent profit

Capital composition by industry	Commodity's labour cost (c′ + v)	Surplus value (s)	Commodity's value (c′ + v + s)	Price of production (c′ + v + s ± d)	Average profit (π)	Deviation of price from value (d)
1. 80c + 20v	70	20	90	92	22%	+ 2
2. 70c + 30v	81	30	111	103	22	− 8
3. 60c + 40v	91	40	131	113	22	−18
4. 85c + 15v	55	15	70	77	22	+ 7
5. 95c + 5v	15	5	20	37	22	+17

explanation of the transformation of values into prices. Each industry is assumed to enjoy a rate of surplus value equal to 100 percent of the variable capital outlay made in the industry. Thus, the *amount* of surplus value is highest in industries 3 and 2, whose organic composition of capital is *least* intensive with respect to constant capital.

A portion of the constant capital will be used up and thus become congealed in the commodity in the process of production. Marx computes the value of the commodities produced by each industry on the basis of socially necessary labor time as c′ + v + s, recorded in column 4 of Table 11.2. If each industry sold its commodities at a price equal to their values, each would experience a different rate of profit, as shown in the last column of Table 11.1.

Different profit rates, however, are incompatible with the operation of competitive forces. These forces, Marx maintains, will tend to redistribute the total amount (110) of surplus value in such a fashion that each industry will receive a share of the aggregate surplus value that will yield a 22 percent rate of profit to each, as shown in Table 11.2. Arithmetically, the rate of profit π = s/c + v or 110/500 = 0.22.

Economy-wide equalization is brought about by inter-industry capital movements. If the rate of profit is above average, as is the

234

case in industries 1, 2, and 3 in Table 11.1, capital will tend to be attracted from industries 4 and 5, where the rate of profit is lower than average, until the average rate of profit is 22 percent for all.

The implications of profit equalization are twofold. It implies, first of all, that products will be sold at what Marx calls their *Price of Production* or by $c' + v + s + d$. *Individual commodity prices will therefore deviate from value*. As is shown in Table 11.2, which demonstrates the effects of equal rates of profit of 22 percent on each individual capital of 100, individual prices will deviate from values by the amounts shown in the last column. It will be noted, however, that these deviations of prices from values *cancel one another out*. These deviations imply that, while individual commodity prices differ from their labor costs, commodity values in the aggregate are nevertheless, consistent with explaining values in terms of labor cost. This is the manner in which Marx rescues the labor theory of value from the abyss into which it appears to fall as a result of transforming values into prices.

Capital accumulation and the tendency toward a failing rate of profit

It has already been noted that the rate of profit is the critical inducement to investment and is thus more important to the capitalist than the rate of surplus value. The tendency for the rate of profit to become equal throughout the economy implies that commodity prices will deviate from their values in the manner discussed above, and also that individual capitalists, in order to increase their shares of the aggregate surplus value, will make additions to constant capital. One of the ironies of capitalism is that the pricing system redistributes surplus values among industries in accordance with their stocks of constant capital, rather than with their allocation to variable capital, which is the source of surplus value. The question of how capital funds accumulate is therefore relevant.

Marx's economic interpretation of history explains the original source of capital funds. Primitive accumulation, which occurred in England during the late fifteenth and early sixteenth centuries, created, for the first time, the free proletarian (in the sense of being emancipated from the soil and therefore free to sell his labor) and the money-owning capitalist. Describing the demise of the feudal system and the related destruction of the agricultural economy, Marx observes:

> The spoliation of the church's property, the fraudulent alienation of the state domains, the robbery of the common lands, the usurpation of feudal and clan property, and its transformation into modern private property under circumstances of reckless terrorism, were just so many idyllic methods of primitive accumulation. They conquered the field for capitalistic agriculture, made the soil part and parcel of capital, and created for the town industries the necessary supply of a 'free' and outlawed proletariat.[14]

After the era of primitive accumulation ended, the source of further accumulation is surplus value. Accumulation is accompanied by increased mechanization in the production process. A given amount of labor, now combined with a greater supply of more efficient equipment, will be able to process a greater volume of raw materials into finished goods. Although labor productivity is enhanced, the organic composition of capital is altered as increasing amounts of constant capital relative to variable capital are now acquired by the capitalist. Because only variable capital yields a surplus, the rate of surplus value, that is,

$$s/v$$

will fall. From this, Marx deduced his 'law of

the falling tendency of the rate of profit.' The latter naturally tends to dampen the enthusiasm for new investment and encourages the capitalist to seek ways of counteracting it.

Since the rate of profit depends on both the rate of surplus value and the organic composition of capital, it follows that measures that tend to raise the rate of surplus value, or reduce the constant capital component of total capital, will tend to keep the rate of profit from falling. Marx notes six possibilities, the most obvious being the lengthening of the working day, which operates to increase the amount of surplus labor. The speed-up has essentially the same effect. The increase in surplus value tends to keep the rate of profit from falling. The technique of cutting wages is not one which Marx seriously entertains, for he assumes that wages, like prices, are determined in a purely competitive market that is beyond the power of an individual employer.

Marx saw a tendency for wages to be depressed as a result of the growing constant capital component rather than an aggressive employer wage policy. This growth creates a situation of technological unemployment that Marx regards as the primary factor operating to push wages toward the subsistence level. He regarded as a 'libel on the human race,' the population theory by which Malthus and Ricardo explained the tendency of the market wage to equal the natural wage. He emphasized, instead, the development of a surplus population. The workers who are set free by machine power constitute an industrial reserve army that depresses the rate of wages and thereby tends to raise the level of surplus value. Unlike the classicists, Marx did not regard technological changes as fortuitous occurrences but as labor-saving devices necessary for the continued existence of capitalist production. The existence of a reserve army

is necessary for the maintenance of surplus value. Thus, Marx observed in the *Communist Manifesto*: 'The bourgeoisie cannot exist without constantly revolutionizing the instruments of production, and thereby, the relations of production, and with them the whole relations of society.' It is in this manner that Marx lays bare an area of inherent conflict within the framework of capitalism, from which he deduces one of the laws of motion of the capitalistic system.

The human aspect of these observations is 'the increasing misery of the proletariat.' On the one hand, the degree of worker exploitation is enhanced through the speed-up and the lengthening of the working day; and on the other, the value of the worker's labor power is depressed through the reduced labor requirements of producing labor's subsistence. It is another of capitalism's internal contradictions that the increasing productivity of labor is associated with increasing exploitation and diminished ability to consume goods.

Capitalist crisis

The classical economists, as has already been noted, largely assumed away the problem of economic crisis by their acceptance of Say's law. Marx rejected Say's law because he regarded it as applicable only to a barter economy. In a capitalistic economy, commodities are exchanged first for money and then for one another. In the process, qualitatively different use values represent quantitatively equal exchange values. The exchange value of commodities is transformed into money form and then back again to commodity form. The transformation of commodities into money and back into commodities is not necessarily synchronized with regard to time and place. Marx maintains that endogenously created crises are inherent in capitalism for this reason: 'If the interval in time between two complementary phases of the complete metamorphosis of a commodity becomes too great, if the split between the sale and the purchase becomes too pronounced, the intimate connection between them, their oneness, asserts itself by producing a crisis.'[15] Thus, Marx regarded a crisis as being indicative of, and taking the form of, a state of general overproduction. Crisis is the process by which equilibrium between the production and circulation of goods is forcibly restored. The actual cause of periods of general overproduction is among the problems to which Marx returned again and again, although he nowhere presents a systematic and thorough treatment. He seems more concerned to show, contrary to the fundamental theorem of Say's law, that partial gluts are always possible in a capitalistic system and that they tend to culminate in general overproduction instead of being corrected.

Marx offered several hypotheses about the possible causal mechanisms of crises that manifest themselves in overproduction (or underconsumption) and declining rates of profit. Marxist interpreters and revisionists have, however, considerably more to say on the specific causes of crisis than Marx himself. His followers extended and embellished hypotheses that Marx does not develop completely, although he did introduce them in his works.[16]

Among the hypotheses suggested by Marx on the matter of crisis, that which undertakes to link this phenomenon with the declining rate of profit is of particular interest. One interpretation stresses the fact that the growth of accumulation stimulates the demand for labor power, thus raising the level of wages and diminishing profits. Diminished profits, in turn, discourage further accumulation and

precipitate a crisis, the immediate cause of which, in more modern terminology, is underinvestment. In other words, an interruption to the circular flow takes place as a result of a decline in the rate of profit below normal. This hypothesis finds its modern counterpart in the Keynes hypothesis of the declining marginal efficiency of capital, although the Marxian formulation is far less well developed, especially regarding its failure to take into account the significance of the interest rate, the money market, institutional credit arrangements, and the role of expectations. Some writers, such as Maurice H. Dobb, argue that Marx regarded the tendency of the rate of profit to fall as the primary explanation of a crisis.[17]

Another hypothesis about economic crises that may be derived from Marx's fragmentary observations is that a crisis is traceable to the atomistic character of capitalist production. The essence of this view is that crises originate because individual business owners have, at best, only partial knowledge of the market and tend to produce either too much or too little. These errors call forth adjustments, but only small errors can be corrected without general disturbance. Michael Tugan-Baranowsky, in particular, is associated with this view.

A third hypothesis about crises, and the one most clearly stated by Marx himself, stresses the role of underconsumption. The capitalist, he maintains, creates surplus value in the process of production in the form of commodities. However, in order that capitalists may realize their surplus value, they must *sell* their products. The consumption of the great mass of the people, however, is restricted by low wage rates and unemployment, with the result that the capitalist has to sell products at prices below the cost of production. Labor is not less exploited, but the capitalist benefits little from this exploitation. Consumption is further restricted by the tendency to accumulate and expand capital in order to introduce labor-saving technological improvements. These are undertaken in order to improve the level of profits but the reduction in variable capital, relative to constant capital, defeats this goal through its impact on the labor component, which is the source of surplus value. The quest for profit is thus the reason for its falling rate. Although this tendency is counteracted from time to time (the problem of timing was not specifically dealt with), it is nevertheless an inexorable tendency that will grow more pronounced as the counteracting forces become attenuated. Thus, crises will become increasingly severe, and each successive occurrence will increase their threat to capitalism's future.

Monopoly capitalism

Marx's entire economic analysis is intended to demonstrate the impossibility of an indefinite expansion of the capitalistic system and the consequent inevitability of a revolution, during which the proletariat will overthrow the existing structure of production and its associated social relations, and establish a socialistic organization of production in its place. The prelude, in Marx's thinking, to the ultimate overthrow of capitalist production is the change in the organic composition of capital. The proportion between constant and variable capital will grow, and the fixed component of constant capital – that is, the proportion in buildings, machinery, and equipment, as opposed to raw materials – will increase. As a result, there is an increase in the optimum size of the production unit. This implies not only a concentration of capital, but what Marx called *centralization of capital*.[18]

The causes of the centralization of capital are only briefly sketched by Marx. The major factor is, of course, the economies inherent in large-scale production. As the optimum-size production unit grows larger, 'the larger capitals beat the smaller.'[19] In other words, interfirm competition for profits is, in itself, a force of centralization. In addition, the credit system, which Marx conceives to include not only banks but all financial institutions, facilitates the development of the large corporation, which alters the production structure from one in which there is competition among a large number of producers to competition among a few. In the process of this phase of capitalist development, there is a divorce between the ownership of capital and the entrepreneurial function.[20] The owner of capital becomes a shareholder, and the actual function of the entrepreneur is assumed by professional managers. The ultimate stage in the development of the capitalistic system gets underway when corporations unify in the form of cartels, trusts, and mergers in order to control production and prices. At the same time, there is also the tendency, because of the close relations between the banks and industry, for capital to be concentrated in the stage of *monopoly capitalism*, in which social production is under the virtual control of a single bank or a small group of banks.

During this phase of capitalist development, the contradictions of capitalism become even more acute. Monopoly tends to increase the rate of accumulation out of surplus value, since centralization of capital, in decreasing the number of competitors, tends to increase the portion accruing to each one. Monopolists, however, tend to invest in the remaining competitive areas of the economy rather than in their own industry in which the marginal rate of profit is low, although the average rate may still be high. This tends to strengthen the tendency in those sectors toward a declining rate of profit. Also, to the extent that additional monopoly profits are a deduction from labor's share, the tendency toward underconsumption is further strengthened. The declining rate of profit further encourages the adoption of labor-saving technology, with a resultant expansion in the size of the industrial reserve army. Monopoly, therefore, intensifies the contradictions inherent in capitalism and strengthens the forces leading to social revolution. 'Centralization of the means of production and socialization of labor at last reach a point where they become incompatible with their capitalist integument. The integument is burst asunder. The knell of capitalist private property sounds. The expropriators are expropriated.'[21]

Thus, the internal contradictions created by capitalist production ultimately make its continuation untenable. Conditions are then ripe for the proletariat to seize the instruments of production and establish socialism, which is the first stage of full communism. This, in Marx's view, could not come about without violent revolution. The questions of precisely what the pattern and tactics of revolution should be or the nature of the proletariat state, while interesting, are not only outside the scope of economic analysis, but are also a matter to which Marx, himself, gave little expression.

Concluding remarks

While Marx's technical apparatus was built on Ricardian foundations, the political implications he derived from the Hegelian interpretation he gave to the labor theory of value made his analysis unacceptable in modern orthodox circles, whose inquiries were directed by the classical paradigm. Then, too, Marx adhered to the tradition of the labor theory of value at a time when Austrian thinkers were stressing the importance of utility and the subjective cost elements inherent in interest and profit. His theory, therefore, met with an attitude of almost complete rejection, except among those who sympathized politically. His analysis of capitalism was indicative of an intellectual crisis, but his rejection of the classical paradigm failed to generate a scientific revolution that would establish an alternative paradigm in economics. However, Marx's observations about the functioning of capitalism were later taken more seriously, when such problems as monopoly, mass unemployment, excess production, recurrent crises, and other phenomena that he had described, became so prevalent that they could no longer be glossed over.

Marx's theory of socially necessary labor as the determinant of value has been widely criticized. However, the ultimate use to which he put his theory of value – namely, as the basis for a model in which economic breakdown is ascribed to internal insufficiencies – was a ground-breaking conception. Marx's precapitalist model of simple commodity production envisages an economy in which there is no technical progress and no change in the capital–labor ratio. Thus, there is no net accumulation of capital. However, his model of a capitalist economy is one in which there is capital accumulation and, consequently, a continuous reduction in the labor requirements of production. This is associated with a declining rate of profit that affects not only the process and composition of capital accumulation but the entire structure of the system. He envisaged constant capital as increasing more rapidly than the output of consumer goods, so that the economic structure becomes increasingly imbalanced.

This principle is very suggestive of the Keynesian conception, in which a declining marginal efficiency of capital causes a lack of effective demand. Marx, however, went even further, for his model implies that stable economic growth requires a proportionate expansion of both the consumer and the capital goods industries. Thus, the law of capitalist motion that Marx discovered is also surprisingly anticipatory of the principle, recently established by modern growth theorists, that a growing equilibrium requires that the rate of increase in capacity must equal the rate of increase in income and that both must be expanding at a compound interest rate in order to avoid deflationary tendencies. The change that is required to update Marx's model is, of course, quite substantive, especially insofar as it hinges on the labor theory of value; but once the philosophical and sociological overtones are removed, the remaining differences are in no small measure terminological. The richness of his legacy can best be appreciated by abstracting the Hegelian elements and the sociology of revolution that obscure the contribution of Marx as an economist.

Notes

1 Cited by E. Gide and C. Rist, *A History of Economic Doctrine*, 2nd English edn (London: George G. Harrap, 1948), p. 214. *A Short History of Socialist Economic Thought*, by Gerd Hardach and Dicter Karras with Ben Fine, translated by James Weckham (New York: St. Martin's Press, 1978), includes a most useful first chapter, 'The critique of capitalism and perspectives of socialist society before Marx.'

2 Excellent treatments of Hegelian philosophy are available in George Sabine, *A History of Political Theory*, revised edn (New York: Holt, Rinehart & Winston, 1950); and in H. B. Acton, *The Illusion of the Epoch*, Part I (Boston: Beacon Press, 1957).

3 David Ricardo, 'Principles of political economy and taxation,' in *The Works and Correspondence of David Ricardo*, 10 vols, edited by Piero Sraffa and Maurice Dobb (Cambridge, UK: The University Press, 1951–55), vol. 1, p. 11.

4 *The Works and Correspondence of David Ricardo*, 10 vols, edited by Piero Sraffa and Maurice Dobb (Cambridge, UK: The University Press, 1951–55), vol. 1, p. 12.

5 Karl Marx, *Capital*, Ms. from the 3rd German edn (1883) by Samuel More and Edward Aveling, edited by Friedrich Engels (Moscow: Foreign Languages Publishing House, 1959), vol. 1, Preface to 1st edn, p. 10.

6 Karl Marx, *A Contribution to the Critique of Political Economy*, translated by N. I. Stone (Chicago: Charles H. Kerr, 1904), p. 11.

7 See Paul M. Sweezy, *The Theory of Capitalist Development* (New York: Oxford University Press, 1942).

8 Marx, *Capital*, vol. 1, p. 102.

9 Marx, *Capital*, vol. 1, p. 44.

10 Marx, *Capital*, vol. 1, p. 39.

11 Sweezy, *Capitalist Development*, p. 51.

12 See, in particular, Eugen Bohm-Bawerk, *Karl Marx and the Close of His System* (New York: Augustus Kelley, 1949).

13 Marx, *Capital*, vol. 2, p. 151.

14 Marx, *Capital*, vol. 1, p. 732.

15 Marx, *Capital*, vol. 1, pp. 113–14.

16 The subsequent discussion is greatly indebted to the analysis presented by Sweezy, *Capitalist Development*, p. 3. Albert O. Hirshman's essay 'Rival interpretations of market society: civilizing, destructive, or feeble,' *Journal of Economic Literature* 20 (December, 1982), pp. 1463–84, is particularly recommended for the perspective it provides about changing views of the relationship between the expansion of commerce, human behavior, and ideology. Marx's self-destruction thesis is contrasted with Schumpeter's version and also with the 'feudal shackles' thesis.

17 See Maurice H. Dobb, *Political Economy and Capitalism* (New York: International Publishers, 1944), especially Chapter 4.

18 Marx, *Capital*, vol. 1, pp. 625–26.

19 Marx, *Capital*, vol. 1, p. 626.

20 This aspect of Marx's work was greatly extended by Rudolph Hilferding in *Das Finanzkapital* (Berlin: Dietz, 1955), first published 1923.

21 Marx, *Capital*, vol. 1, p. 763.

Glossary of terms and concepts

Capitalistic 'law of motion'
A Marxist expression referring to the dynamic tendencies of the capitalistic system that drive it inevitably toward a zero rate of return and toward economic crises that threaten the continued existence of the entire bourgeois society.

Constant capital (c)
That portion of total capital that is unable to create surplus values, but only transfers an equal value to the final good. Specifically, it consists of machinery, tools, equipment, and materials used in production.

Dialectic
A process through which the phenomenon of change has been explained. The conflict between a thesis (in the real world or in the world of ideas) and an antithesis results in a synthesis that provides the basis for subsequent conflicts and further change.

Economic interpretation of history
The hypothesis (principally associated with Marx) that human history is basically the product of economic forces that determine the character of the other aspects of human experience.

Extended (versus simple) reproduction
A Marxian concept that relates the process of reproduction and surplus creation to the accumulation of capital (rather than to consumption) and thus to the growth of the capitalistic system.

Industrial reserve army
A Marxian term referring to labor that becomes unemployed as variable capital is converted into constant capital.

Mode of production
A distinctively Marxian term referring to the social relationship inherent in ownership and use of the material means of production.

Monopoly capitalism
The last phase through which the capitalistic system will pass, according to Marxian theory. It is characterized by an increase in the optimum size of the production unit, the concentration of capital in the hands of a few large financial institutions, and a separation between the ownership of capital and the function of entrepreneurship.

Organic composition of capital (k)
The ratio of constant capital to variable capital. A higher proportion of variable capital in an industry yields a larger surplus value. However, a higher proportion of constant capital enables an industry to enjoy a disproportionate share of the economy's total surplus value, for this is redistributed as profit rates become equalized.

Proletariat
A class that is propertyless in the sense that it owns only its labor power.

Surplus value
A distinctively Marxian term referring to the difference between the value of the commodities workers produce in a given period, and the value of the labor power they sell to the capitalists hiring them. The surplus value realized by the capitalist is indicative of the degree of labor exploitation. The rate of surplus value is the ratio s/v.

Transformation problem
Critics of the Marxian theory of value have argued that the proposition, found in Volume III of *Capital*, that rates of profit, $s/(c + v)$, are equalized as opposed to the equalization of rates of surplus value, s/v, as is argued in Volume I, undermines the labor theory of value. Marx's own solution to the transformation problem was that individual commodity prices might well deviate from their labor costs of production and that capitalists would not share equally in surplus value. But these deviations would cancel one another out, so

commodity prices would, on average, reflect their labor content.

Variable capital (*v*)
That portion of total capital that is used in the support of labor. It tends to be equal to labor's subsistence and creates a surplus, *s*, because *v* is transformed into labor power.

Questions for discussion and further research

1 What is the chief concern of Marx's *Capital*? How does it relate to Marx's view that class conflict is inevitable in all the societies of history? Who are the antagonists under capitalism?

2 Marx's economic interpretation of history identified the prime mover of social change to *be changes in the mode of production*. What does this phrase refer to?

3 Hegel's dialectic is an important fundamental of Marx's theory. How does Hegel's dialectic explain the phenomenon of change in the universe?

4 The theory of surplus value, and its related prediction of increasing misery, is an integral part of Marx's analysis of capitalism. Explain the source of surplus value and its relation to Marx's theoretical model.

5 What is the industrial reserve army? How does it relate to the concerns of *Capital*?

Notes for further reading

The New Palgrave offers a veritable treasure trove of entries that relate to Marx and Marxian economics: Andrew Arato on Marxism, vol. 3, pp. 387–90; R. P. Bellamy on Hegelianism, vol. 2, pp. 635–36; Meghnad Desai on simple and extended reproduction, vol. 4, pp. 335–37, and on value and price, vol. 4, pp. 789–91; Roy Edgley on dialectical materialism, vol. 1, pp. 830–32; S. Foster on class, vol. 1, pp. 432–34; Ernest Gellner on economic interpretation of history, vol. 2, pp. 47–51; Andrew Glyn on Marxist economics, vol. 3, pp. 390–94; R. Jessop on mode of production, vol. 3, pp. 489–91; Ernest Mandel on Karl Heinrich Marx, vol. 3, pp. 367–83; N. Okishio on constant and variable capital, vol. 1, pp. 580–84; Fabio Petri on rate of exploitation, vol. 4, pp. 249–51; J. E. Roemer on Marxian value analysis, vol. 3, pp. 383–86; Willi Semmler on competition: Marxian conceptions, vol. 1, pp. 540–42; Anwar Shaikh on capital as a social relation, vol. 1, pp. 333–36, on exploitation, vol. 2, pp. 249–51, on market value and market price, vol. 3, pp. 347–48, on organic composition of capital, vol. 3, pp. 755–57, and on surplus value, vol. 4, pp. 574–76; and Paul M. Sweezy on monopoly capitalism, vol. 3, pp. 341–44.

Selected references and suggestions for further reading

Cournot, A. A. *Principes de la théorie des richesses* (Paris: Librarie Hachette, 1863).

Cournot, A. A. *Researches into the Mathematical Principles of the Theory of Wealth*. Translated by N. T. Bacon (New York: A. M. Kelley, Publishers, 1960 [1838]).

Dupuit, Jules. 'On the measurement of the utility of public works.' In *International Economic Papers*, no. 2, translated by R. H. Barback (London: Macmillan, 1952 [1844]) pp. 83–110.

Dupuit, Jules. 'On tolls and transport charges.' In *International Economic Papers*, no. 11, translated by E. Henderson (London: Macmillan, 1962 [1849]) pp. 7–31.

Dupuit, Jules. 'Tolls.' In *Dictionnaire de l'économie politique*, vol. 11, translated by Charles Coquelin (Paris: Guillaumin, 1852–53).

Dupuit, Jules. 'On utility and its measure.' *Journal des Économistes*, 1st series, vol. 35 (July–September 1853), pp. 1–27.

Gossen, Herman Heinrich. *The Laws of Human Relations and the Rules of Human Action Derived Therefrom* (1854). Translated by Rudolph C. Blitz with an introductory essay by Nicholas Georgescu-Roegen (Cambridge, Mass: MIT Press, 1983).

Leigh, Arthur H. 'von Thünen's theory of distribution and the advent of marginal analysis.' *Journal of Political Economy*, 54 (December, 1946). Reprinted in *Essays in Economic Thought: Aristotle to Marshal.*, edited by J. J. Spengler and W. Allen (Chicago: Rand McNally, 1960).

Robbins, Lionel. Lecture 26, 'The historical school (cont.) – Precursors of change: Cournot, von Thünen, and Rae,' in *A History of Economic Thought*, edited by S. Medema and W. Samuels (Princeton NJ: Princeton University Press, 1998) pp. 249–257.

von Thünen, Johann H. *Isolated State*. Translated by Carla Wartenberg and edited by Peter Hall (Oxford: Pergamon Press, 1966).

Chapter 12

'First-generation' marginalists: Jevons, Walras, and Menger

The first area of economic theory to be revolutionized through the rediscovery of the marginal principle was the theory of value. Three brilliant men, William Stanley Jevons (1835–82), Carl Menger (1840–1925), and Léon Walras (1834–1910), working, respectively, in England, Austria, and Switzerland, independently formulated a theory of exchange value based on the principle of diminishing utility. Jevons's work, *The Theory of Political Economy* (1871), was preceded by *Notice of a General Mathematical Theory of Political Economy*. Menger's *Grundsätze der Volkswirtschaftslehre* was also published in 1871, and Walras's *Elements d'économie politique pure ou theorie de la richesse sociale*, was published in two parts in 1874 and 1877.

The principle that unites the efforts of Jevons, Walras, and Menger is their emphasis on the role of marginal utility as opposed to cost of production as the determinant of exchange value. They established the nexus between value in use and value in exchange that Smith's paradox of value obscured and that Ricardo and Marx failed to recognize. Their analyses thus mark a clear departure from the cost-of-production and labor theories of value of the classical paradigm and Marxian theory.

Jevons was only 24 years old and a graduate student at the University of London when he incorporated the concept of marginal utility into his thinking. His private correspondence indicates that he arrived at the marginal utility principle as early as 1860, which is an earlier date than the initial efforts of either Menger or Walras. Although his theory of production and distribution is essentially classical, his subjective theory of value and its exposition in mathematical terms set it apart from the classical tradition. However, the classical school of thought was so dominant in England that Jevons attracted few followers to build on the ideas he introduced. Jevons, in particular, concerned himself with arranging commodity prices and discount rates into tabular form, and calculating and plotting their mean values, and identifying seasonal variations. It is he who developed the technique now known as moving averages, which transformed the traditional 'rule of thumb knowledge' of the merchant into a tool of scientific investigation.[1]

Léon Walras was the most mathematically inclined of the first generation of marginal utility economists and lavished his greatest concern on the formulation of his general equilibrium equations. This is his great contribution to economic theory; in the opinion of Schumpeter, it has earned him the distinction of being rated as the greatest of the pure theorists. He built on the work of Quesnay,

Condillac, Say, Cournot, and his father Augustin Walras, who was professor of philosophy and an economist in his own right. From his father, he drew the notion of the general interdependence of all social phenomena; from Quesnay, the idea of the general equilibrium of the economic system; and from Say, the notion that value derives from utility and scarcity rather than cost of production. He hoped to produce separate volumes on price theory, applied theory, and social economy, but, unfortunately, his work in the latter two fields did not develop into treatises.

Walras invited a young Italian nobleman, Vilfredo Pareto, who left his country because of political disturbances, to succeed him at Lausanne. Pareto adopted Walras's concept of the general equilibrium of the static state and developed a technique, already introduced by Francis Edgeworth and known as an *indifference curve*, as an analytical tool for the purpose of defining the nature of the economic optimum. Since the indifference curve technique has come into general use only since the 1930s, particularly in connection with the theory of rational consumer behavior and welfare theory, Pareto's contribution will be examined in a later chapter, along with recent developments in microeconomic theory.

The Austrian Carl Menger is the first-generation marginalist whose work had the greatest immediate impact. A whole group of able economists, who collectively became known as *the Austrians*, followed in his footsteps. Friedrich von Wieser (1851–1926) and Eugen Böhm-Bawerk (1851–1914) directed their considerable talents toward advancing the cause of theoretical analysis, as opposed to the historical method, and extended Menger's opportunity cost principle to the problem of valuing goods of a higher order

(productive resources) or what they termed 'goods' of a higher order. In addition, both forged ahead in new directions, Wieser in the area of utility theory and Böhm-Bawerk in the area of capital theory. Their joint efforts were persuasive in diminishing the intellectual influence of Karl Marx as well as that of the German historical school.

Their preference for a literary approach to economics sets the work of the Austrians apart from that of Jevons, who utilized calculus to express his notion of the final degree of utility (which is equivalent to marginal utility), and Walras, who invented general equilibrium equations. But, in spite of this methodological difference, their emphasis on individual utility maximization as the key to the problem of valuation provides a rationale for grouping the work of Jevons, Walras, and Menger together in a single chapter.

It is, however, Walras who exerted the chief intellectual influence on economic theory as it developed on the European continent at the turn of the century. His general equilibrium analysis, which focuses on interdependencies between markets and maintains that the valuation process occurs simultaneously in all of them, today provides the framework for much of contemporary mainstream theory. His present-day influence has come to rival that of Alfred Marshall, who founded the great neoclassical tradition and became the dominant English economist after Mill. His work will be examined in detail in Part IV.

The economics of William Stanley Jevons (1835–82)

The subjective aspects of exchange value

Jevons maintained that investigation of the 'nature and conditions of utility . . . doubtless furnishes the true key to the problem of

Economics.'[2] Since 'the whole theory of Economics depends upon a correct theory of consumption,'[3] 'we must necessarily examine the character of the wants and desires of men.'[4] The influence of Bentham's felicific calculus is apparent in Jevons's definition of a commodity as 'any object or, it may be, any action or service which can afford pleasure or ward off pain,' while utility is 'the abstract quality whereby an object serves our purposes, and becomes entitled to rank as a commodity.' Its negative counterpart is disutility. In the process of gaining utility, an individual necessarily makes sacrifices, or incurs disutility.[5]

While Jevons had considerable insight into the subjective side of the value problem, the issue that was of particular concern to him was the matter of exchange value. For Jevons, the preoccupation of the classical school with cost of production to explain value, and their neglect of value in use, was one reason for their inability to untangle Smith's water–diamond puzzle. The other is the failure of economists to recognize that their science must be mathematical.

Issues and Answers from the Masterworks 12.1

Issue

Why does the solution of the water–diamond paradox require the application of differential calculus to the notions of utility and supply?

Jevons's answer

From *The Theory of Political Economy*, Introduction and Chapter 3.

Theory of political economy

Introduction

The science of Political Economy rests upon a few notions of an apparently simple character – utility, wealth, value, commodity, capital, are the elements of the subject; and whoever has a thorough comprehension of their nature must possess or be soon able to acquire a knowledge of the whole science . . . Accordingly, I have devoted the following pages to an investigation of the conditions and relations of the above-named notions.

Repeated reflection and inquiry have led me to the somewhat novel opinion, that *value depends entirely upon utility*. Prevailing opinions make labour rather than utility the origin of value; and there are even those who distinctly assert that labour is the *cause* of value. I show, on the contrary, that we have only to trace out carefully the natural laws of the variation of utility, as depending upon the quantity of commodity in our possession, in order to arrive at a satisfactory theory of exchange, of which the ordinary laws of supply and demand are a necessary consequence. This theory is in harmony with facts; and, whenever there is any apparent reason for the belief that labour is the cause of value, we obtain an explanation of the reason. Labour is found often to determine value, but only in an indirect manner, by varying the degree of utility of the commodity through an increase or limitation of the supply . . .

It is clear that Economics, if it is to be a science at all, must be a mathematical science. There exists much prejudice against attempts to introduce the methods and language of mathematics into any branch of the moral sciences. Many persons seem to think that the physical sciences form the proper sphere of mathematical method, and that the moral sciences demand some other method – I know not what. My theory of Economics, however, is purely mathematical in character. Nay, believing that the quantities with which we deal must be subject to continuous variation, I do not hesitate to use the appropriate branch of mathematical science, involving though it does the fearless consideration of infinitely small quantities. The theory consists in applying the differential calculus to the familiar notions of wealth, utility, value, demand, supply, capital, interest, labour, and all the other quantitative notions belonging to the daily operations of industry. As the complete theory of almost every other science involves the use of that calculus, so we cannot have a true theory of Economics without its aid.

To me it seems that *our science must be mathematical, simply because it deals with quantities*. Wherever the things treated are capable of being *greater* or *less*, there the laws and relations must be mathematical in nature. The ordinary laws of supply and demand treat entirely of quantities of commodity demanded or supplied, and express the manner in which the quantities vary in connection with the price. In consequence of this fact, the laws *are* mathematical. Economists cannot alter their nature by denying them the name; they might as well try to alter red light by calling it blue. Whether the mathematical laws of Economics are stated in words, or in the usual symbols, *x, y, z, p, q*, etc., is an accident, or a matter of mere convenience. If we had no regard to trouble and prolixity, the most complicated mathematical problems might be stated in ordinary language, and their solution might be traced out by words. In fact, some distinguished mathematicians have shown a liking for getting rid of their symbols, and expressing their arguments and results in language as nearly as possible approximating to that in common use.

The theory of utility

Utility is not an intrinsic quality

To return, however, to work, the theory here given may be described as *the mechanics of utility and self-interest*. Oversights may have been committed in tracing out its details, but in its main features this theory must be the true one. Its method is as sure and demonstrative as that of kinematics or statics, nay, almost as self-evident as are the elements of Euclid, when the real meaning of the formulae is fully seized . . .

Law of variation of utility

Let us imagine the whole quantity of food which a person consumes on an average during twenty-four hours to be divided into ten equal parts. If his food be reduced by the last part, he will suffer but little; if a second tenth part be deficient, he will feel the want distinctly; the subtraction of the third tenth part will be decidedly injurious; with every subsequent subtraction of a tenth part his sufferings will be more and more serious, until at length he will be upon the verge of starvation. Now, if we call each of the tenth parts *an increment*, the meaning of these facts is, that each increment of food is less necessary, or possesses less utility, than the previous one. To explain this variation of utility we may make use of space representations, which I have found convenient in illustrating the laws of economics in my college lectures during fifteen years past [see Figure 12.1].

Let the line *ox* be used as a measure of the quantity of food, and let it be divided into ten equal parts to correspond to the ten portions of food mentioned above. Upon these equal lines are constructed rectangles and the area of each rectangle may be assumed to represent the utility

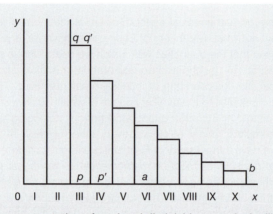
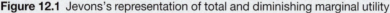

Figure 12.1 Jevons's representation of total and diminishing marginal utility

of the increment of food corresponding to its base. Thus, the utility of the last increment is small, being proportional to the small rectangle on *x*. As we approach towards *o*, each increment bears a larger rectangle, that standing upon III being the largest complete rectangle. The utility of the next increment, II, is undefined, as also is that of I, since these portions of food would be indispensable to life, and their utility, therefore, infinitely great.

We can now form a clear notion of the utility of the whole food, or of any part of it, for we have only to add together the proper rectangles. The utility of the first half of the food will be the sum of the rectangles standing on the line *oa*; that of the second half will be represented by the sum of the smaller rectangles between *a* and *b*. The total utility of the food will be the whole sum of the rectangles, and will be infinitely great.

The comparative utility of the several portions is, however, the most important. Utility may be treated as *a quantity of two dimensions*, one dimension consisting in the quantity of the commodity, and another in the intensity of the effect produced upon the consumer. Now the quantity of the commodity is measured on the horizontal line *ox*, and the intensity of utility will be measured by the length of the upright lines, or *ordinates*. The intensity of utility of the third increment is measured either by *pq*, or *p'q'*, and its utility is the product of the units in *pp'* multiplied by those in *pq*.

But the division of the food into ten equal parts is an arbitrary supposition. If we had taken twenty or a hundred or more equal parts, the same general principle would hold true, namely, that each small portion would be less useful and necessary than the last. The law may be considered to hold true theoretically, however small the increments are made; and in this way we shall at last reach a figure which is indistinguishable from a continuous curve. The notion of infinitely small quantities of food may seem absurd as regards the consumption of one individual; but when we consider the consumption of a nation as a whole, the consumption may well be conceived to increase or diminish by quantities which are, practically speaking, infinitely small compared with the whole consumption. The laws which we are about to trace out are to be conceived as theoretically true of the individual; they can only be practically verified as regards the aggregate transactions, productions, and consumptions of a large body of people. But the laws of the aggregate depend, of course, upon the laws applying to individual cases.

The law of the variation of the degree of utility of food may thus be represented by a continuous curve *pbq*, and the perpendicular height of each point at the curve above the line *ox*

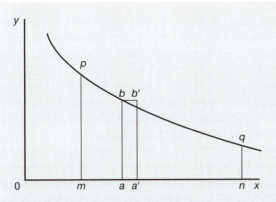

Figure 12.2 Jevons's representation of diminishing utility as a continuous function

represents the degree of utility of the commodity when a certain amount has been consumed [see Figure 12.2].

Thus, when the quantity *oa* has been consumed, the degree of utility corresponds to the length of the line *ab*; for if we take a very little more food, *aa'*, its utility will be the product of *aa'* and *ab* very nearly, and more nearly the less is the magnitude of *aa'*. The degree of utility is thus properly measured by the height of a very narrow rectangle corresponding to a very small quantity of food, which theoretically ought to be infinitely small.

Total utility and degree of utility

We are now in a position to appreciate perfectly the difference between the *total utility* of any commodity and the *degree of utility* of the commodity at any point. These are, in fact, quantities of altogether different kinds, the first being represented by an area and the second by a line. We must consider how we may express these notions in appropriate mathematical language.

Let *x* signify, as is usual in mathematical books, the quantity which varies independently – in this case the quantity of commodity. Let *u* denote the *whole utility* proceeding from the consumption of *x*. Then *u* will be, as mathematicians say, *a function of x*; that is, it will vary in some continuous and regular, but probably unknown, manner, when *x* is made to vary. Our great object at present, however, is to express the *degree of utility*.

Mathematicians employ the sign prefixed to a sign of quantity, such as *x*, to signify that a quantity of the same nature as *x*, but small in proportion to *x*, is taken into consideration. Thus, Δx means a small portion of *x*, and $x + \Delta x$ is therefore a quantity a little greater than *x*. Now when *x* is a quantity of commodity, the utility of $x + \Delta x$ will be more than that of *x* as a general rule. Let the whole utility of $x + \Delta x$ be denoted by $u + \Delta u$; then it is obvious that the increment of utility Δu belongs to the increment of commodity Δx; and if, for the sake of argument, we suppose the degree of utility uniform over the whole of Δx, which is nearly true, owing to its smallness, we shall find the corresponding degree of utility by dividing Δu by *x*.

We find these considerations fully illustrated by the last figure, in which *oa* represents *x*, and *ab* is the degree of utility at the point *a*. Now, if we increase *x* by the small quantity *aa'*, or Δx, the utility is increased by the small rectangle *abb'a'*, or Δu; and since a rectangle is the product of its sides, we find that the length of the line *ab*, the degree of utility, is represented by the fraction $\Delta u/\Delta x$.

As already explained, however, the utility of a commodity may be considered to vary with perfect continuity, so that we commit a small error in assuming it to be uniform over the whole increment Δx. To avoid this, we must imagine Δx to be reduced to an infinitely small size, Δu decreasing with it. The smaller the quantities are the more nearly we shall have a correct expression for ab, the degree of utility at the point a. Thus, the *limit* of this fraction $\Delta u / \Delta x$, or, as it is commonly expressed, du/dx, is the degree of utility corresponding to the quantity of commodity x. The degree of utility is, in mathematical language, *the differential coefficient of u considered as a function of x*, and will itself be another function of x.

We shall seldom need to consider the degree of utility except as regards the last increment which has been consumed, or, which comes to the same thing, the next increment which is about to be consumed. I shall therefore commonly use the expression *final degree of utility*, as meaning the degree of utility of the last addition, or the next possible addition of a very small, or infinitely small, quantity to the existing stock. In ordinary circumstances, too, the final degree of utility will not be great compared with what it might be. Only in famine or other extreme circumstances do we approach the higher degrees of utility. Accordingly, we can often treat the lower portions of the curves of variation (*pbq*) which concern ordinary commercial transactions, while we leave out of sight the portions beyond p or q. It is also evident that we may know the degree of utility at any point while ignorant of the total utility, that is, the area of the whole curve. To be able to estimate the total enjoyment of a person would be an interesting thing, but it would not be really so important as to be able to estimate the additions and subtractions to his enjoyment which circumstances occasion. In the same way a very wealthy person may be quite unable to form any accurate statement of his aggregate wealth, but he may nevertheless have exact accounts of income and expenditure, that is, of additions and subtractions.

Variation of the final degree of utility

The final degree of utility is that function upon which the theory of economics will be found to turn. Economists, generally speaking, have failed to discriminate between this function and the total utility, and from this confusion has arisen much perplexity. Many commodities which are most useful to us are esteemed and desired but little. We cannot live without water, and yet in ordinary circumstances we set no value on it. Why is this? Simply because we usually have so much of it that its final degree of utility is reduced nearly to zero. We enjoy every day the almost infinite utility of water, but then we do not need to consume more than we have. Let the supply run short by drought, and we begin to feel the higher degrees of utility, of which we think but little at other times.

The variation of the function expressing the final degree of utility is the all-important point in economic problems. We may state, as a general law, that *the degree of utility varies with the quantity of commodity, and ultimately decreases as that quantity increases*. No commodity can be named which we continue to desire with the same force, whatever be the quantity already in use or possession. All our appetites are capable of *satisfaction* or *satiety* sooner or later, in fact, both these words mean, etymologically, that we have had *enough*, so that more is of no use to us. It does not follow, indeed, that the degree of utility will always sink to zero. This may be the case with some things, especially the simple animal requirements, such as food, water, air, etc. But the more refined and intellectual our needs become, the less are they capable of satiety. To the desire for articles of taste, science, or curiosity, when once excited, there is hardly a limit.

Disutility and discommodity

A few words will suffice to suggest that as utility corresponds to the production of pleasure, or, at least, a favorable alteration in the balance of pleasure and pain, so negative utility will consist in the production of pain, or the unfavorable alteration of the balance. In reality we must be almost as often concerned with the one as with the other, nevertheless, economists have not employed any distinct technical terms to express that production of pain which accompanies so many actions of life. They have fixed their attention on the more agreeable aspect of the matter. It will be allowable, however, to appropriate the good English word *discommodity*, to signify any substance or action which is the opposite of *commodity*, that is to say, *anything which we desire to get rid of*, like ashes or sewage. Discommodity is, indeed, properly an abstract form signifying inconvenience, or disadvantage; but as the noun *commodities* has been used in the English language for four hundred years at least as a concrete term, so we may now convert discommodity into a concrete term, and speak of *discommodities* as substances or things which possess the quality of causing inconvenience or harm. For the abstract notion, the opposite or negative of utility, we may invent the term *disutility*, which will mean something different from inutility, or the absence of utility. It is obvious that utility passes through inutility before changing into disutility, these notions being related as +, 0, and −.

Source: *Theory of Political Economy*, W. S. Jevons (London: Macmillan and Co. Ltd, 1888).

Summing up: Jevons's key points

Once it is recognized that it is necessary to view utilities and quantities from a marginal perspective – that is, from the perspective of differential calculus – Smith's error is resolved. Jevons conceives of the marginal utility of a commodity as a diminishing function of the quantity in a consumer's possession, for example, $U_w = f(W)$, $U_d = f(D)$, and so forth. If W, the quantity of water at a particular location, exists in large supply relative to the need for it, then indeed 'scarce anything can be had in exchange for it,' precisely as Smith observed to be the case. In the case of a diamond, on the other hand, because it is part of a small supply relative to the demand for it, 'a very great quantity of other goods may frequently be had in exchange for it.'

Having recognized that the marginal, or 'final degree,' of utility acquired by an individual decreases with each increase in total supply, Jevons explains that given a stock of a particular commodity, individuals will exchange additional units for units of someone else's stock of some other commodity if he believes they will also have utility to him. Exchange will take place until both individuals maximize their positions by bartering units from their given supply in exchange for the commodity they do not have; exchanges continue until there is no additional utility for either trader. His concern therefore is to deduce the *limits of exchange* and define the nature of the *equilibrium position*. Equilibrium is achieved when the ratio of exchange of any two commodities is the reciprocal of the ratio of the final degrees of utility of the quantities of the commodity available for consumption after the exchange is completed.[6]

The limits of exchange

Jevons's argument continues with an example intended to illustrate when trade between two individuals will end. Each individual is assumed to have an initial stock of goods, for example corn and beef. Following Jevons's notations, let a denote a quantity of corn held by one person, while b denotes a quantity of beef held by a second. Each person exchanges successive small increments of the commodity he owns for successive small increments of the commodity he does not have. If the market is purely competitive and has an established exchange value of quantity x of corn for y of beef, the ratio of exchange will be:

$$dy/dx = y/x$$

After exchange has taken place, one person will have $(a - x)$ of corn and y of beef, and the second will have x of corn and $(b - y)$ of beef. Now, if the expressions $\Phi_1(a - x)$ and $\psi_1(Y)$ represent the marginal utilities of beef and corn to the first person, while $\Phi_2(x)$ and $\psi_2(b - y)$ express the marginal utilities of corn and beef to the second person, the conditions of maximum satisfaction for each of the two parties in a barter exchange are expressed by the following equation:

$$\Phi_1(a - x)/\psi_1(y) = y/x = \Phi_2 x/\psi_2(b - y)$$

This equation expresses the principle that neither party to an exchange of two goods will be satisfied unless the ratio of the marginal utilities between them is inversely proportional to their ratio of exchange.[7]

While Jevons's example was intended to demonstrate the limits of barter exchange, the equimarginal principle also easily explains how consumers will allocate their incomes to maximize their total satisfaction. The rational consumer will allocate a given income to two or more goods in such a way that the marginal utility of the last cent spent on good A is equal to that of the last cent spent on good B. If this were not the case, the consumer could add to total satisfaction by buying more of the commodity that offers greater marginal utility per additional expenditure because the loss of utility associated with giving up a unit of the second good would be less than the gain gotten from buying more of the first. This principle is, of course, applicable to any number of goods a consumer might buy.

Rational allocation of money income does not imply that a consumer will spend *the same dollar amount* on every commodity. Rather, it means that *differences in expenditures must be balanced by differences in utility*, so if the expenditure on good A is twice as high as on good B, the marginal utility associated with good A will be twice as high as that associated with good B. Thus, a consumer who makes a rational allocation of expenditures on any pair of goods acquires them in proportions to make

$$\frac{\text{Marginal utility of good } A}{\text{Price of good } A} = \frac{\text{Marginal utility of good } B}{\text{Price of good } B}$$

which is the same as making

$$\frac{\text{Marginal utility of good } A}{\text{Marginal utility of good } B} = \frac{\text{Price of good } A}{\text{Price of good } B}$$

This is a conclusion that is not dependent on the *cardinal measurement* of utility. That is, even if utility cannot be measured directly in real numbers, the expression of quantities in terms of a ratio has the effect of eliminating the unit of measurement. Thus, the principle laid down by the marginal utility theorists concerning the maximization of satisfaction is not contradicted by later work in demand

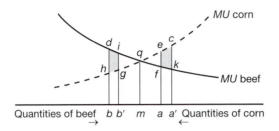

Figure 12.3 Jevons's consumer equilibrium with fixed stocks

theory, which introduced a system of *ordinal ranking* of consumer preferences (i.e. good, better, best), instead of assuming that utility is cardinally measurable (i.e. one *util*, two *utils*, etc), as it is implicitly assumed to be in the older analysis.

The concept of the trading body

Jevons's equation of barter exchange is repeated below to facilitate examination of his concept of the trading body.

$$\Phi_1(a-x)/\psi_1(y) = y/x = \Phi_2 x/\psi_2(b-y)$$

While the equation was designed to illustrate equilibrium in the case of an isolated exchange taking place at fixed prices, Jevons attempted to make a transition from the *subjective* valuations of two trading partners to exchanges among many traders and, ultimately, to multiple exchange and the formation of market price.

To do this, he employed the concepts of the *trading body* and the *law of indifference*. The trading body is composed of the aggregate of buyers and sellers of a commodity in a purely competitive market. The law of indifference implies that only one price can prevail between a pair of commodities at any point in time in a competitive market. Jevons used these concepts to extend his conclusion that

the equilibrium achieved by two traders also relates to the case of a large number of traders engaged in multiple exchange.

Jevons's logic was supplemented by a graph that is reproduced, with minor changes, as Figure 12.3. Trading body (*A*) with its stock of beef (*a*) is presumed to exchange increments from its stock with trading body (*B*), which has a stock of corn (*b*). Quantities of corn and beef are measured along the horizontal axis of the graph. The marginal utilities associated with increases and decreases in the quantities held by each trading body are represented by curves *MU* of corn and *MU* of beef, which express increasing or decreasing functions of the changes in the quantities held. Thus, an increase in the quantity of corn held by *A*, as represented by the line segment *a'a*, implies a decrease in the stock of beef and loss of the utility represented by area *afka'*. The marginal utility associated with increased quantities of corn is represented by *aeca'*, which implies a *net* gain from trade of *kfec*.

Trading party *B* acquires a comparable gain equivalent to area *hdig* when s/he decreases the stock of corn in order to acquire additional beef. Both parties will continue their trading activities until equilibrium is reached at *m*, which represents the optimum division of both stocks between the trading bodies, in the sense that further trade would reduce the net gain of each of the parties.

Jevons's approach involves some rather obvious difficulties, the first of which is the possibility that the relative utilities of the two commodities to either or both traders *may* preclude any exchange. The latter limitation is recognized in his discussion of the Failure of the Equations of Exchange.[8] He is also aware that utility functions may not be continuous. However, for simplicity, his analysis proceeds on the premise that marginal utilities vary continuously with variations in the quantities held. His logic is that, while a single individual may not vary the quantity bought with every small variation in price, this will not be true of a large number of individuals.

The concept of the trading body, which may represent any combination from a pair of individuals to the sum total of a country's inhabitants, poses other difficulties. It implicitly assumes that the utilities of different individuals are additive, which Jevons himself recognized is not possible.[9] Even more important is that the equilibrium rate of exchange is *assumed* as given at the outset, and is thus not explained, so the analysis begs the question of price determination. What Jevons's analysis really amounts to, therefore, is a definition of consumer equilibrium with given supplies. It is only in the exceptional case of given commodity stocks that utility functions do determine exchange ratios or relative prices.

Jevons himself seemed to sense these limitations. While he stated categorically 'that value depends solely on the final degree of utility,' he amended this principle by asserting: 'Cost of production determines supply; supply determines the final degree of utility.'[10] Thus, it would seem that, while Jevons emphasized the role of utility in determining

exchange value, he was groping toward an analysis of price that would also take the role of supply into account.

The marginal utility explanation of market price is only valid when supplies are given. It demonstrates only that each consumer with given tastes and income maximizes his or her utility at given prices when the marginal utility per dollar expended is obtained from every product bought. It omits the whole problem of variations over time in supply and cost of production, and their effects on exchange value. Just as each consumer maximizes utility, so each producer maximizes the profit position within the framework of factor prices by employing factors in proportions that will yield an equal marginal value product per dollar of factor outlays. This is the sort of analysis suggested by Fleeming Jenkin, and actually undertaken by Alfred Marshall, who solved the problem of the determination of particular prices, without resorting to the fiction of the trading body, by explaining that the price of a commodity is determined by the interaction of the schedule of demand for it and its schedule of supply.[11]

Jevons on the supply of labor effort

Jevons's extension of his theory of utility to explain the relationship between the supply of labor effort and the disutility of work is a particularly perceptive aspect of his work. He conceived of labor as the 'painful exertion of mind or body undergone partly or wholly with a view to future income.' The worker is envisioned as trading the disutility of work against the utility of the real wages labor can command. Work, in Jevons's view, entails disutility as well as utility.

Initially, the pleasure work yields offsets the disutility, or pain, inherent in work. As illustrated in Figure 12.4, which assumes the

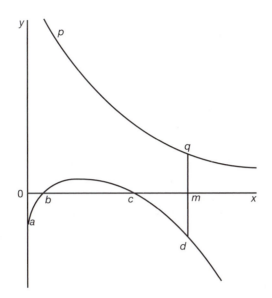

Figure 12.4 Jevons's illustration of the net pain of work

Source: William S. Jevons, *The Theory of Political Economy*, 5th (edn) (New York: Kelley and Millman, 1957), p. 173.

measurability of utility and disutility along the vertical axis, the 'degree,' or marginal utility, of real wages (i.e. future consumption) declines continually along a curve such as *pq*. The utility inherent in work, measured on the horizontal axis, initially offsets the *disutility* of added exertion. However, the painfulness of labor in proportion to output, which is represented by a curve such as *abcd*, overcomes the utility of work so that 'net pain' increases over the range *cd* of the pain curve. That is, the net pain of labor is first a decreasing function of the rate of production before it becomes an increasing function. Thus, the worker will not produce in excess of *om*, at which the marginal utility of the real wage is equal to the net pain of labor. The logic of Jevons's analysis is thus essentially the same as that which underlies the representation of a labor supply curve, as sloping upward until at some point it bends backward to represent the greater utility derived from leisure, in comparison with the net gain of utility from work.

Jevons as an inductive economist

Jevons believed that the science of Political Economy 'might gradually be erected into an exact science, if only commercial statistics were far more complete and accurate than they are at present, so that the formulae could be endowed with exact meaning by the aid of numerical data.'[12] His argument was predicated on his understanding of the laws of probability, trusting that the principle of mathematical odds would, 'out of a great multitude of cases lead us most often to the truth.'[13] More specifically, what he meant was that the cause that produces an event is its most probable cause. For example, his 1863 pamphlet on the value of gold undertook to measure the extent of its depreciation during the 1850s. He attributed depreciation to the

discoveries of gold in California and Australia and not to such other circumstances as
a variation in the production of commodities.
To establish this hypothesis, Jevons explained
that he offered an 'inverse or inductive application of the theory of probability.' Such an
investigation requires a careful marshaling of
the facts of trade and industry in order to
compute arithmetical and geometric means
and deviations from them, which he represented by plotting them graphically as in Figure 12.5. In searching for the laws governing
seasonal and cyclical laws, he pioneered the
use of semi-log graphs, cycle-time framework,
index numbers, geometric means and moving
averages in time series analysis.[14]

Jevons went far beyond the tabulations of
weekly, monthly and quarterly information
that had long been part of business record
keeping. Among the hypotheses he developed
on the basis of his study of commercial fluctuations is that the demand for manufactured
products is high only when the price of food
is low. The latter observation was based partly

on his 1878 study of the link between solar
activity (i.e. 'sunspots') and agricultural harvests in India, which Jevons inferred was the
determinant of the Indian demand for British
exports. In *The Solar Period and the Price of
Corn* (1875) Jevons traced commercial crises
to periodic appearances of sunspots, which
generated cycles in harvests and, thus, agricultural prices, and later to manufactured
goods prices.

While Jevons was at the forefront of exploring the links between meteorological and
agricultural and manufacturing outputs and
prices as starting points for quantitative
observations about economic phenomena, his
view that empirical observation is the way of
the future in economics was not universally
shared by other political economists. There
were other quite prominent political economists, among them John Elliott Cairnes
(1823–75), who rejected Jevons's enthusiasm
for empirical observation as the way of the
future in economics.

Following Senior and J. S. Mill, Cairnes

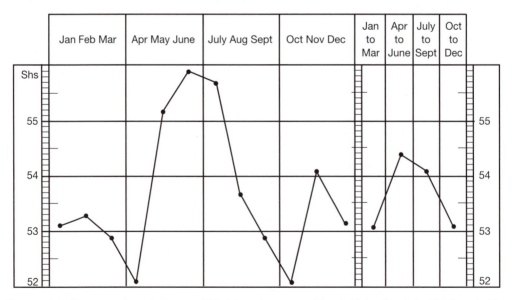

Figure 12.5 Average price of wheat, 1846–61, as interpreted by J. Klein, *Statistical Visions in Time*
(Cambridge, Cambridge University Press, 1997).

emphasized the appropriateness of using the deductive method in economics on the grounds that the subject is a hypothetical science whose concern is 'not what *will* take place, but what would or what tends to take place.'[15] In his *Essays Towards a Solution of the Gold Question*, Cairnes undertook to determine the likely course of trade and prices if an increase in the supply of gold were to take place on the basis of classical principles of deduction. While his and Jevons's studies produced remarkably similar findings, Cairnes's deductive approach (i.e. reasoning from certain premises or postulates to conclusions in the classical tradition of Senior and Mill) was, methodologically speaking, totally different from Jevons's inductive approach.[16] The methodological controversy that arose between them remains relevant because the history of economics as a science reflects ongoing methodological controversy. It became increasingly heated as political economists became more sophisticated in their knowledge of statistical tools and mathematics.

The economics of Léon Walras (1834–1910)

The subjective aspects of value

Léon Walras's great achievement with respect to clarifying the subjective aspects of exchange was to integrate explicitly the process of individual optimization into the analysis and representation of the circular flow. However, unlike Jevons, who insisted that inquiry into the subjective value of goods is the necessary foundation for the theory of exchange value, Walras introduced his analysis of marginal utility (*rareté*) after his inquiry into the theory of exchange value. He was also, like Jevons, fully aware that utility is

subjective and that it has no measurable relationship to time or space. Nevertheless, he proceeded boldly and suggested:

> We need only assume that such a direct and measurable relationship does exist, and we shall find ourselves in a position to give an exact mathematical account of the respective influences on prices of extensive utility, intensive utility and the initial stock possessed.... I shall, therefore, assume the existence of a standard measure of intensity of wants or intensive utility, which is applicable not only to similar units of the same kind of wealth, but also to different units of wealth.[17]

This is the basis on which Walras proceeded to the solution of the two-commodity exchange problem and the derivation of individual demand curves. He begins his theory of exchange in essentially the same way as Jevons, by analyzing the nature of an equilibrium between two goods. Initially, exchange is, as already noted above, explained without referring to utility, which is introduced only in the second stage as the analytical foundation for exchange, eventually arriving at the proposition that, in equilibrium, there must be equilibrium between the marginal utilities of the quantities. This proposition is the equivalent of Gossen's 'Second Law.' From this principle, he subsequently deduced that in equilibrium the marginal utilities derived from pairs of commodities must be proportional to the ratio of their prices.

The derivation of individual demand curves

Walras's primary objective was to demonstrate the establishment of *general equilibrium*. Going from two goods he proceeds to three and ultimately to *m* commodities, and *n* factors (land, labor, and capital) are mutually determined.

The first portion of his analysis, however, is devoted to the problem of individual demand curves. Whereas Augustin Cournot had neglected the relationship between utility and demand and Jevons had interpreted demand curves as representing individual utility curves, Walras was fully aware of the relationship between utility and demand, Thus, he introduces the theorem of maximum utility, which, in substance, holds that an individual maximizes satisfaction by equating the ratios of marginal utilities to the ratio of their prices for all the *m* commodities acquired by exchange.

If one among the *m* commodities is selected as a *numéraire* (common denominator) in terms of which all other prices are expressed, $P_1 = 1$, an individual maximizes satisfaction when

$$MU_1 = MU_2/P_2 = MU_3/P_3 = \ldots Mu_n/P_n .$$

It follows directly from this rule that a reduction in price will increase the quantity demanded, while a price increase will decrease the quantity demanded. Postulating a market in which there are only two goods, and in which the price of one is expressed in terms of units of the other, Walras showed how to establish a consumer demand curve for either good.

He followed the standard mathematical procedure of placing the *independent* variable on the abscissa, and the quantities demanded on the ordinate as the *dependent* variable. The derivation of a consumer's demand curve for a commodity, say *A*, begins with the initial equilibrium position. The coordinate of the initial price, P_{a1}, and the quantity, Q_{a1}, taken at that price constitutes point D_a on the demand curve shown in Figure 12.6, which follows the economist's practice of placing price on the ordinate axis.[18] The problem is then to establish other price–quantity relationships with respect to commodity A.

If the price of *A* is assumed to increase to P_{a2}, a consumer would be left with less income to spend on commodity *B* if he or she buys the same quantity at the higher price. It would also mean that the marginal utility per dollar expended on *A* would have decreased, whereas the marginal utility of a dollar's worth of the now smaller quantity of *B* at an unchanged price would have increased. That is:

$$MU_{Qa2}/P_{a2} < MU_{Qb1}/P_{b1}$$

marginal utility of expenditure on both commodities – in other words, when

$$MU_{Qa2}/P_{a2} = MU_{Qb2}/P_{b1}$$

The relationship between the quantity Q_{a2} and the price P_{a2} yields a point upward to the

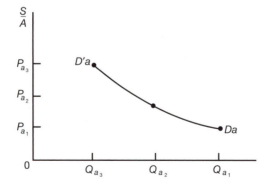

Figure 12.6 Walras's derivation of a demand curve

left of *Da* on the consumer's demand curve. This procedure may then be repeated until a whole series of price–quantity relationships for commodity *A* is obtained. These price–quantity combinations constitute a demand schedule and may be presented graphically as *D'aDa*, as in Figure 12.6. It should not be inferred, however, that Walras conceived of an individual's demand for a given commodity as a function of its price alone. Cournot (and, later, Alfred Marshall) defined the demand curve as $D = f(p)$, a form that continues to be used in present-day partial equilibrium analysis. Walras's demand function is the relationship between the quantity of a commodity and all prices.[19] Only money income and tastes are assumed constant, whereas the Marshallian demand curve assumes also that all prices other than that of the commodity in question are held constant.

General equilibrium analysis

Cournot expressed the rationale for a general equilibrium approach to the problem of price determination when he wrote that 'for a complete and rigorous solution of the problems relative to some parts of the economic system, it is indispensable to take the entire system into consideration.'[20] It was, however, Léon Walras who constructed a *mathematical system* to demonstrate general equilibrium. Instead of embracing only two commodities to establish the equilibrium rate of exchange between them, his analysis is broadened to include simultaneous equilibria in *all* commodity and factor markets.

Like a partial analysis, a general equilibrium analysis is constructed on the basis of certain assumptions. In Walras's system, these givens are (1) the quantities of *m* finished goods to be consumed in a given period of time; (2) the supplies of *n* factors of production that may be offered for hire in the factor market or employed directly by their owners; (3) the technical coefficients of production, that is, specific combinations of land, labor, and capital required by technical considerations to produce finished goods; and (4) the marginal utility, or *rareté*, functions of individuals for goods and self-employed factor services. These are the data of Walras's system.

The system seeks to determine four sets of unknowns: the quantities of *n* productive services offered for sale, the quantities of *m* finished goods demanded, the prices of *n* productive services, and the prices of *m* finished goods. In practice, of course, quantities and prices are determined in the marketplace through the interaction of demand and supply forces. However, Walras demonstrated that, given the necessary data, it is possible to achieve a solution mathematically. If one of the commodities whose prices we seek to establish is chosen as a common denominator in terms of which all prices are expressed, so that $P_a = 1$, there is one less price to be established, so there are $(2m + 2n - 1)$ unknowns to be determined. Therefore, $(2m + 2n - 1)$ independent equations must be written; thus, the solution of Walras's general equilibrium equations is thus precisely like the solution of a system of simultaneous equations.

The achievement of general equilibrium in all markets is premised on the achievement of simultaneous individual equilibria. Assuming that the quantities of productive resources available to be supplied by each household are known, once commodity and factor prices are established, two conditions must be satisfied before each individual consumer of finished goods or supplier of resources can be in a state of general equilibrium. Both of these conditions can be expressed in terms of equations. The first is that the marginal utilities of the finished goods bought and the productive services of self-owned factors retained by individuals for their own use must be proportional to their prices. If this condition is not satisfied, maximum satisfaction from expenditures is not achieved.

The second condition derives from the fact that every individual is subject to a *budget constraint* imposed by the requirement that individual expenditures must equal individual receipts. Individual budget equations, together with marginal utility equations, determine the quantity of each good bought or factor retained by the household for its own use. These consumer equations express the optimum allocation of income for each individual among alternative goods and services when their prices and the marginal utilities consumers derive from them are given. By contrast, Jevons's equation of the ratio of exchange expressed the conditions of maximum satisfaction for two parties to a barter exchange.

Consumer utility and budget equations provide part of the information needed to define the conditions of general equilibrium for the economy as a whole. Individual demands for each good, expressed as a function of all commodity and factor prices, are aggregated into a group of market demand equations. There are m such equations, each of which is a summation of individual consumer demand equations for each good. Unlike a particular equilibrium analysis in which the demand for each good is expressed as a function of its price alone, each of the m equations of demand in the Walrasian general equilibrium analysis is expressed as a function of all commodity and factor prices. Similarly, individual supply equations for productive resources, expressed as a function of individual commodity and factor prices, are aggregated to provide a group of equa-

tions of factor supplies. There are n such equations.

The technical coefficients of production (which are one part of the data of Walras's system) and the demands for finished goods establish the quantity of each resource required to produce each good. Since Walras assumed full employment, it is axiomatic that the sum of these requirements is equal to the total supply of each resource. This, too, may be expressed in terms of a group of equations that are n in number. A final group of equations expresses equality between the prices of consumer goods and their average costs of production. Since one of these goods is the *numéraire*, or common denominator, there are $m - 1$ such equations. Summing up, then, there are $2m + 2n - 1$ independent equations to solve for the same number of unknowns, so the system is determinate.

The preceding verbal description of the Walrasian system may be supplemented by a symbolic presentation. Let the quantity of finished goods to be consumed be designated as

$$a, b, \ldots m.$$

Let the supply of factors used to produce these goods be designated as

$$S_{f1}, S_{f2}, \ldots S_{fn}$$

Let the technical coefficients, that is, the quantities of the various factors $f_1, f_2, \ldots f_n$ that enter into the production of finished goods $a, b, \ldots m$, be represented as

$$a_{f1}, a_{f2}, \ldots a_{fn}$$
$$b_{f1}, b_{f2}, \ldots b_{fn}$$
$$\vdots$$
$$m_{f1}, m_{f2}, \ldots m_{fn}$$

Let the quantities of finished goods demanded be represented as

$$d_a, d_b, \ldots d_m$$

and let the demands for the services of owner-employed factors be represented as

$$d_{f1}, d_{f2}, \ldots d_{fn}.$$

The marginal utility, or *rareté*, functions of each of the m consumer goods are:

$$u_a = F_a(d_a)$$
$$u_b = F_b(d_b)$$
$$\vdots$$
$$u_m = F_m(d_m)$$

The *rareté*, functions for n productive services retained by owners are:

$$u_{f1} = F_{f1}(s_{f1} - d_{f1})$$

$$u_{f2} = F_{f2}(s_{f2} - d_{f2})$$
$$\vdots$$
$$u_{fn} = F_{fn}(s_{fn} - d_{fn})$$

There are m unknown demand functions for finished goods as follows:

$$d_b = f_b(p_{f1}, p_{f2}, \ldots p_{fn}, p_b, p_c \cdots p_m)$$
$$d_c = f_c(p_{f1}, p_{f2}, \ldots p_{fn}, p_b, p_c \cdots p_m)$$
$$\vdots$$
$$d_m = f_m(p_{f1}, p_{f2}, \ldots p_{fn}, p_b, p_c \cdots p_m)$$

No equation is required for good a, which is the *numéraire*, or common denominator, in terms of which values are expressed. There are also n equations representing the supplies of resources r, labor (l) and capital (k) whose productive services and offered at prices (also expressed in terms of the numéraire as follows:

$$s_{f1} = f_1(p_{f1}, p_{f2}, \ldots p_{fn}, p_b, p_c \cdots p_m)$$
$$s_{f2} = f_2(p_{f1}, p_{f2}, \ldots p_{fn}, p_b, p_c \cdots p_m)$$
$$\vdots$$
$$s_{fn} = f_n(p_{f1}, p_{f2}, \ldots p_{fn}, p_b, p_c \cdots p_m)$$

The summation of $m - 1$ individual demand equations for finished goods and n factor supply functions results in two of the four sets of equations Walras required to define the conditions of general equilibrium.

The third group of n equations expresses equality between the quantity of productive services employed to produce each good, given the technical coefficients of production, and the quantity offered:

$$a_{f1}d_a + b_{f1}d_b + \ldots m_{f1}d_m = s_{f1}$$
$$a_{f2}d_a + b_{f2}d_b + \ldots m_{f2}d_m = s_{f2}$$
$$\vdots$$
$$a_{fn}d_a + b_{fn}d_b + \ldots m_{fn}d_m = s_{fn}$$

Finally, the fourth group of equations expresses equality between the prices of n consumer goods and their average costs of production. Thus, there are m equations as follows:

$$a_{f1}p_{f1} + a_{f2}p_{f2} + \ldots a_{fn}p_{fn} = 1$$
$$b_{f1}p_{f1} + b_{f2}p_{f2} + \ldots b_{fn}p_{fn} = p_b$$
$$\vdots$$
$$m_{f1}p_{f1} + m_{f2}p_{f2} + \ldots m_{fn}p_{fn} = p_m$$

Summing up, there are $2m + 2n - 1$ independent equations to solve for the same number of unknowns. The determinacy of the system follows from the equality of the number of independent equations with the number of unknowns. This demonstration has become the inspiration for all subsequent work on general equilibrium.

The process of *tâtonnement*

When the price of the first commodity (or numéraire) is arbitrarily established as p_1 and all other prices are expressed as though the *numéraire* served as money, the equilibrium (or optimum) condition of exchange for each commodity requires their marginal utilities are equal to the ratio of their prices to the price of the numéraire. It is possible that sellers find no buyers at an initial price and, vice versa, that buyers will not find anyone to sell (i.e. the price might be 'false'). It would then become necessary for a new set of prices to become established until there is some set of mutually agreeable prices to all trading partners.

Walras described what he called the *tâtonnement* process as a sort of 'groping' towards equilibrium. He envisions an auctioneer as 'calling out' an initial price. If there is either excess supply or excess demand at this price (at which no actual trades take place if the price is revealed as being 'false' in the sense that it is inconsistent with market clearing), a higher or lower price is 'announced.' The process continues until there is a simultaneous equilibrium in all markets. Until such a price is identified, no actual trades take place.

It is not difficult to appreciate some of the problems inherent in the general equilibrium approach. To establish and solve such a system of equations is certainly to perform Herculean labor. Furthermore, equality between the number of equations and the number of unknowns does not necessarily mean that there will be a single positive solution. Sets of simultaneous equations may have multiple solutions or may be satisfied by zero or negative prices, which imply that the good is either a free good or a nuisance good. Negative prices for goods are more easily accommodated in the equations than negative factor prices, for the latter imply that factors are paying firms to employ them. Yet, it is obvious that if factor supplies and technical coefficients of production are fixed, as Walras assumed them to be, it may not always be possible to satisfy the market-clearing equations at positive factor prices.

Walras took his analysis a step beyond demonstrating the determinacy of a general market equilibrium. He tried to show that the problem for which he gave a theoretical explanation is, in practice, solved in the market by the mechanism of free competition through a process of recontracting. People are assumed to come to the market with cer-

tain stocks of commodities and certain dispositions to trade, from which a set of prices will emerge. If demand and supply are equal at these prices, there is an immediate equilibrium. If, on the other hand, demand and supply are not equal, people will recontract until none of the parties sees any advantage in further recontracting. The price ultimately established by this process is the equilibrium price.

The two cardinal points in Walras's description of exchange equilibrium are (1) that the amounts demanded and supplied by particular individuals depend on the system of market prices and (2) that there must be an equilibrium between demand and supply in particular markets. What Walras does not make clear in his analysis of exchange equilibrium is whether exchanges do or do not take place at the prices originally proposed if these prices are not equilibrium prices. If there is no actual exchange (i.e. 'false trading') until the equilibrium prices are reached by bidding, then it follows that the equilibrium state is *postulated*; that is, the system is in equilibrium before the analysis begins and can, in fact, never be out of equilibrium. The classicists' distinction between market and natural prices is therefore meaningless in the Walrasian general equilibrium framework. The Walrasian equilibrium is an instantaneous equilibrium that is *timeless* in the sense that it does not envision the passing of clock-time in the process of achieving equilibrium.

There is a further important aspect of Walras's general equilibrium to be noted. General equilibrium is, conceptually, very different from the classical idea of the stationary state in which all prices converge to their natural levels and net savings and population growth are zero. Classical thinkers, like Quesnay and Marx, were concerned chiefly with identifying the conditions under which the economic system will be able to *reproduce itself* next year. Walrasian general equilibrium, on the other hand, poses a different problem, that of identifying the system of prices that is compatible with *market clearing*. This notion of equilibrium is fundamentally different from that inherent in the classical notion of the stationary state.

The economics of Carl Menger

Menger on the subjectivity of value and negative imputation

Carl Menger gave even more detailed attention than Jevons to the subjective aspects of value. His most enduring work is *Grundsätze der Volkswertshafts lehre* (1871) (*Principles of Social Economics*), whose pioneering inquiry established the foundation for the so-called Austrian or Vienna School.[21] He notes that there must be a human want for an object and that it must have characteristics that will satisfy this want.[22] Further, consumers must be aware of its want-satisfying power and have the object at their disposal. *Güterqualität* is thus seen as deriving from human wants in relation to objects that have the potential for satisfying them. Because objects having *Güterqualität* are generally in smaller supply than the needs (*Bedarf*) for them, people will economize in their use. Individuals will therefore classify wants in accordance with their importance, given the circumstances that govern the particular situation. Menger illustrates this hypothesis with an arithmetical example that presents a hierarchy of wants from the point of view of an individual consumer designated by Roman numerals from I to X as in Table 12.1.

Arabic numbers listed in each column represent the satisfaction associated with a unit increase in the stock of goods acquired to satisfy that want. Declining numerical values were selected to represent the diminishing want-satisfying power of additional units of the same good. No additions are made to any stock when the utility of the marginal increment becomes zero. This observation was the basis for Menger's incisive solution to the water–diamond puzzle, to which classical value theory was unable to provide an answer. He recognized that the critical consideration is the relationship between the quantity needed and the available supply of both

Table 12.1

I	*II*	*III*	*IV*	*V*	*VI*	*VII*	*VIII*	*IX*	*X*
10	9	8	7	6	5	4	3	2	1
9	8	7	6	5	4	3	2	1	0
8	7	6	5	4	3	2	1	0	
7	6	5	4	3	2	1	0		
6	5	4	3	2	1	0			
5	4	3	2	1	0				
4	3	2	1	0					
3	2	1	0						
2	1	0							
1	0								
0									

diamonds and water. Drinking water is available in such copious quantities that humans are unable to use all that is available under ordinary cirumstances.[23]

Menger's alternative approach to explaining the value of goods that satisfy consumer needs directly (i.e. goods of a lower order) led to an alternative way of viewing the problem of explaining the valuation of factors of production. Menger thought of modern-day factors of production as *goods of a higher order* whose value is determined by negative *imput-*ation from the anticipated value of the goods of a lower order in whose production they serve. He was the first economist to consider the problem as one of imputing the value of higher order goods from their contributions to the value of their products. This alternative approach would correct the classicists' error of failing to understand that the values of factors of production are related to the values of the goods in whose production they assist. How to correct this error is the basis of Menger's theory of negative imputation.

Issues and Answers from the Masterworks 12.2

Issue

What is the relationship between goods employed in production (i.e. factors) and the values of the goods themselves? How does this principle alter the conventional view that the payment of interest reimburses the owner of capital for abstinence?

Menger's answer

From *Principles of Economics* (1871), Chapter 3.

The laws governing the value of goods of higher order

The principle determining the value of goods of higher order

Among the most egregious of the fundamental errors that have had the most far-reaching consequences in the previous development of our science is the argument that goods attain value for us because goods were employed in their production that had value to us. Later, when I come to the discussion of the prices of goods of higher order, I shall show the specific causes that were responsible for this error and for its becoming the foundation of the accepted theory of prices (in a form hedged about with all sorts of special provisions, of course). Here I want to state, above all, that this argument is so strictly opposed to all experience that it would have to be rejected even if it provided a *formally* correct solution to the problem of establishing a principle explaining the value of goods.

Hence the principle that the value of goods of higher order is governed, not by the value of corresponding goods of lower order of the present, but rather by the prospective value of the product, is the universally valid principle of the determination of the value of goods of higher order . . . The value of goods of *higher order is* therefore, in the final analysis, nothing but a special form of the importance we attribute to our lives and well-being. Thus, as with goods of first order, the factor that is ultimately responsible for the value of goods of higher order is merely the importance that we attribute to those satisfactions with respect to which we are aware of being dependent on the availability of the goods of higher order whose value is under consideration. But due to the casual connections between goods, the value of goods of higher order is not measured directly by the expected importance of the final satisfaction, but rather by the expected value of the corresponding goods of lower order.

The productivity of capital

The transformation of goods of higher order into goods of lower order takes place, as does every other process of change, in time. The times at which men will obtain command of goods of first order from the goods of higher order in their present possession will be the order of these goods. While it is true, as we saw earlier, that the more extensive employment of goods of higher order for the satisfaction of human needs brings about a continuous expansion in the quantities of available consumption goods, this extension is only possible if the provident activities of men are extended to ever more distant time periods . . . but only on condition that they lengthen the periods of time over which their provident activity is to extend in the same degree that they progress to goods of higher order.

There is, in this circumstance, an important restraint upon economic progress. The most anxious care of men is always directed to assuring themselves the consumption goods necessary for the maintenance of their lives and well-being in the present or in the immediate future, but their anxiety diminishes as the time period over which it is extended becomes longer. This phenomenon is not accidental but deeply imbedded in human nature. To the extent that the maintenance of our lives depends on the satisfaction of our needs, guaranteeing the satisfaction of earlier needs must necessarily precede attention to later ones. And even where not our lives but merely our continuing well-being (above all our health) is dependent on command of a quantity of goods, the attainment of well-being in a nearer period is, as a rule, a prerequisite of well-being in a later period. Command of the means for the maintenance of our well-being at some distant time avails us little if poverty and distress have already undermined our health or stunted our development in an earlier period. Similar considerations are involved even with satisfactions having merely the importance of enjoyments. All experience teaches that a present enjoyment or one in the near future usually appears more important to men than one of equal intensity at a more remote time in the future . . .

The circumstance that places a restraint upon the efforts of economizing men to progress in the employment of goods of higher orders is thus the necessity of first making provision, with the goods at present available to them, for the satisfaction of their needs in the immediate future; for only when this has been done can they make provision for more distant time periods. In other words, the economic gain men can obtain from more extensive employment of goods of higher orders for the satisfaction of their needs is dependent on the condition that they *still have further quantities of goods available for more distant time periods* after they have met their requirements for the immediate future.

In the early stages and at the beginning of every new phase of cultural development, when a few individuals (the first discoverers, inventors, and enterprisers) are first making the transition to the use of goods of the next higher order, the portion of these goods that had existed previously but which until then had had no application of any sort in human economy, and for which there were therefore no requirements, naturally have a non-economic character. When a hunting people is passing over to sedentary agriculture, land and materials that were not previously used and are now employed for the first time for the satisfaction of human needs (lime, sand, timber, and stones for building, for example) usually maintain their non-economic character for some time after the transition has begun. It is therefore not the limited quantities of these goods that prevents economizing men in the first stages of civilization from making progress in the employment of goods of higher orders for the satisfaction of their needs.

But there is, as a rule, another portion of the complementary goods of higher order, which has already been serving for the satisfaction of human needs in some branch or other of production before the transition to the employment of a new order of goods, and which therefore previously exhibited economic character. The seed grain and labor services needed by an individual passing from the stage of collecting economy to agriculture are examples of this kind.

These goods, which the individual making the transition previously used as goods of lower order, and which he might continue to use as goods of lower order, must now be employed as goods of higher order if he wishes to take advantage of the economic gain mentioned earlier. In other words, he can procure this gain only by employing goods, which are available to him, if he so chooses, for the *present* or for the *near future*, for the satisfaction of the needs of a *more distant time period*.

Meanwhile, with the continuous development of civilization and with progress in the employment of further quantities of goods of higher order by economizing men, a large part of the other, previously non-economic, goods of higher order (land, limestone, sand, timber, etc, for example) attains economic character. When this occurs, each individual can participate in the economic gains connected with employment of goods of higher order in contrast to purely collecting activity (and, at higher levels of civilization, with the employment of goods of higher order in contrast to the limitations of means of production of lower order) only if he already has command of quantities of economic goods of higher order (or quantities of economic goods of any kind, when a brisk commerce has already developed and goods of all kinds may be exchanged for one another) in the present for future periods of time – in other words, only if he possesses *capital*.

With this proposition, however, we have reached one of the most important truths of our science, the 'productivity of capital.' The proposition must not be understood to mean that command of quantities of economic goods in an earlier period for a later time can contribute anything by itself *during* this period to the increase of the consumption goods available to men. It merely means that command of quantities of economic goods for a certain period of time is *for economizing individuals* a means to the better and more complete satisfaction of their needs, and therefore a *good* – or rather, an *economic good*, whenever the available quantities of capital services are smaller than the requirements for them.

The more or less complete satisfaction of our needs is therefore no less dependent on command of quantities of economic goods for certain periods of time (on capital services) than it is on command of other economic goods. For this reason, capital services are objects to which men attribute value, and as we shall see later, they are also objects of commerce.

Some economists represent the payment of interest as a reimbursement for the abstinence of the owner of capital. Against this doctrine, I must point out that the abstinence of a person cannot, by itself, attain goods-character and thus value. Moreover, capital by no means always originates from abstinence, but in many cases as a result of mere seizure (whenever formerly non-economic goods of higher order attain economic character because of society's increasing requirements, for example). Thus the payment of interest must not be regarded as a compensation of the owner of capital for his abstinence, but as the exchange of one economic good (the use of capital) for another (money, for instance).

Source: Carl Menger, *Principles of Economics*, volume 1, reprint no. 17 (London: London School of Economics, 1870), Chapter 3.

Summing up: Menger's key points

Menger's theory of imputation is a radical departure from the classical approach not only with respect to explaining the value of consumer goods (i.e. goods of a lower order) but also with respect to explaining the values of goods of a higher order, or factors of production. The change in perspective is especially critical, for it challenges the classical explanation of income shares, especially of interest, which goes to the capitalist as a reward for abstinence. Böhm-Bawerk was later to build, in an important way, on Menger's rejection of the idea that capital is the product of abstinence, but it is to Menger that we owe the foundation for this 'Austrian' perspective. Menger thought of capital as a good of a higher order and that the correct procedure for imputing the value of goods of a higher order is to withdraw one unit of a good of a higher order from production and observe the effect on utility resulting from the loss of output. The loss in the total product is the marginal product of the variable factor in question, and the *utility* of the product forgone establishes the value of the unit of the good of a higher order in the production process. This value may also be conceived as the alternative *opportunity cost*, of using the factor in the production of some other good. This alternative cost is equal to the difference in utility that is attributable to the withdrawal of a unit of the resource in question.

Within the framework of Menger's reasoning, it is immaterial whether the factors are used in fixed proportions or variable proportions. In the case of fixed proportions, the withdrawal of a unit of one resource necessitates the employment of some portion of cooperating resources elsewhere. The total loss of product minus the product produced by the complementary factors in their new employment establishes the loss of utility, and thus the value, of the variable factor.

Concluding remarks

The threads of the preceding examination may now be drawn together to see what positive contribution to economic analysis was made by the marginal utility theorists and how they differed from their classical predecessors. While classical thinkers were chiefly concerned with explaining how the self-serving behaviors of individuals and businesses propel the economy forward toward economic growth, marginalists focused on individual optimizing behaviors. In particular, they introduced the marginal utility apparatus to deduce the exchange ratios that will be established between commodities in competitive markets. This approach enabled them to establish the link between value in use and value in exchange that Smith, Ricardo, and Marx failed to recognize. Their analyses thus mark a clear departure from labor and cost of production theories of value.

While they did not emphasize the weaknesses of the labor theory of value as a basis for advancing their views on marginal utility, they pointed out that a labor theory of value is deficient in several respects. They noted, first, that a large expenditure for labor will not necessarily result in a high commodity value because future demands may be inaccurately forecast. They also noted that a labor theory of value lacks generality, for it does not explain the value of land or objects like works of art, that exist in permanently fixed supply.

While their concern with marginal utility and its significance for the determination of value in exchange is conventionally regarded as the chief feature of the marginal revolution, some less obvious (and consequently often neglected) aspects of their analysis are also important. First, it is relevant that, in spite of the common element of marginal utility, if one contrasts what happened to economic theory in England with what happened on the Continent, the *specifics* are really quite different. In England, the rejection of the classical theory of value and wages by Jevons and a new generation of thinkers who followed *might* be described as a revolution. But the authority of classical theory did not extend to the Continent; Menger did not launch an extensive attack, as Jevons did, on the cost of production theories of value, which gave little scope to utility and the wants of consumers. Nor did Menger confront a long-entrenched tradition of wages-funds and natural-wage theories. Thus, the unified approach to the value of consumer goods and the values of the factors of production (i.e. higher order goods), which Menger's theory of imputation pioneered and which Wieser and Böhm-Bawerk further developed, did not encounter the kind of resistance that prevailed in England. Although Menger was most disappointed that his ideas were not received with greater enthusiasm, this was not the result of the strong entrenchment of an alternative theory. Rather, it reflects the entrenchment of the German historical school, which had little use for theory of any kind. The dominance of *historismus* later became the basis of the famous *Methodenstreit* (conflict over methodologies) that erupted between Menger and Gustav Schmoller.

Nor were English theories influential in France during the middle of the nineteenth century. Going back to Condillac and Say, French economic theory had long emphasized the significance of utility and scarcity

in the determination of value. Walras began his own work from this tradition, reinforced by the work of Cournot and his father, A. A. Walras. Unlike Jevons, Walras did not confront the cost of production theory of value or the wage-fund and natural-wage theories that prevailed in England, and which Jevons repeatedly described as 'Ricardo–Mill Economics.'[24] The precipitous collapse in England of 'credibility and confidence' in the Ricardo–Mill theoretical system in the space of relatively few years, in the late 1860s and the early 1870s, may reasonably be described as a revolution, although in a negative, rather than in a positive, sense.[25]

A second point that is important to emphasize is that two separate traditions emerged on the Continent; specifically, the Laussane tradition that grew out of Walras's general equilibrium analysis and the Austrian tradition that built on the work of Menger. These brought with them essentially different notions of equilibrium from the classical concept of long-run equilibrium toward which the system tends as it moves through historical time.

The Austrian analysis stands apart from the classical analysis, not only in terms of its emphasis on utility, and the unity that its theory of imputation achieves between commodity values and factor values, but also because it utilizes an essentially different concept of capital. In pioneering this new approach, Carl Menger laid the foundation for the work of Friedrich von Wieser and Eugen Böhm-Bawerk. These second-generation Austrians extended Menger's interpretation of the determination of 'remote,' or 'higher order,' goods as a reflection of the valuation consumers placed on near goods. In Menger's formulation, the imputation procedure was *negative* in the sense of envisioning the loss of utility that would follow if one unit of a remote good is released from the production process.

This procedure, in Wieser's view, would lead to incorrect results, for the withdrawal of a unit of any one agent reduces the productivity of those that remain. The reduction in the total product is due not just to the withdrawal of an individual unit of the factor in question but also to a change in proportions. Hence, he proposed the alternative method of *positive imputation*, which measures the product gained by adding a unit of the factor in question.

Wieser assumed that factors are combined in fixed proportions in each industry, though these proportions vary from one industry to another. By assuming that the values of the factors are simply reflections of the marginal utility of consumer goods, and therefore equal to the value of the product, he was able to demonstrate that factor payments just exhaust the final product. However, this procedure does not prove that a factor's reward is determined by the value of its marginal product because the separate productivity of a factor cannot be imputed at all when factors are combined in fixed proportions. A factor's marginal product can be isolated *only* if proportions are variable and substitution is possible. Otherwise, the concept of marginal product is without meaning.

In the more usual case of variable factor proportions, Menger's analysis implies that the withdrawal of one unit of a factor necessitates a rearrangement of complementary factors. The loss of utility associated with the reduction of the product determines the value of the withdrawn factor unit. What is not made clear in Menger's analysis is the effect that the tendency toward diminishing returns exerts on output when the input of one variable resource is altered. Nor does he examine the problem of whether his method of valuing the factors will result in payments that will exactly exhaust the total product. This question was to become a major issue of the marginal productivity theory of distribution. Menger does not have a theory of capital that distinguishes between capital goods themselves and the services they render. However, his work provides the analytical basis for a whole school of eminent thinkers, beginning with Wieser and Eugen Böhm-Bawerk, who are known as *the Austrians*.

Notes

1 Judy Klein, 'Institutional origins of econometrics' in Ingrid H. Rima (editor) *Measurement, Quantification and Economic Analysis* (London: Routledge, 1994), p. 92.
2 William Jevons, *The Theory of Political*, Economy, 5th edn (New York: Kelly and Millman, 1957), p. 46.
3 William Jevons, *The Theory of Political*, Economy, 5th edn (New York: Kelly and Millman, 1957), p. 47
4 William Jevons, *The Theory of Political*, Economy, 5th edn (New York: Kelly and Millman, 1957), p. 46.
5 William Jevons, *The Theory of Political*, Economy, 5th edn (New York: Kelly and Millman, 1957), p. 37.
6 Jevons's single variable utility functions ignore the possibility that the utilities of at least some commodities are interrelated rather than independent of the quantities and prices of other goods, changes in income (and therefore the marginal utility of money), and other people's utility functions.
7 Jevons, *Theory*, p. 100.
8 Jevons, *Theory*, pp. 11–27.
9 Jevons, *Theory*, p. 21
10 Jevons, *Theory*.
11 Fleeming Jenkin, *The Graphic Representation of the Laws of Supply and Demand and Other Essays on Political Economy 1868–84* (London:

London School of Economics and Political Science, 1870, reprinted 1931).

12 The principle of inverse probability expounded by Thomas Bayes (1702–61) and refined by Pierre Simon de Laplace (1749–1827).

13 Jevons, W. S. *The Theory of Political Economy*, p. 21.

14 Jevons, W. S. *Principles of Science: A Treatise on Logic and the Scientific Method*, London: Macmillan, 1877.

15 Jevons, W. S. *Principles of Science: A Treatise on Logic and the Scientific Method* (London: Macmillan, 1877).

16 Klein, Judy, *Statistical Visions in Time* (Cambridge: Cambridge University Press, 1997).

17 Léon Walras, *Elements of Pure Economics*, translated by William Jaffé (London: George Allen & Unwin, 1954), p. 11.

18 The convention of placing price on the ordinate axis, even though it is the independent variable, and quantity on the abscissa was introduced by Alfred Marshall.

19 See his general equilibrium analysis.

20 Augustin Cournot, *Researches into the Mathematical Principles of the Theory of Wealth* (1838), translated by Nathaniel Bacon (New York: Macmillan, 1897), p. 127.

21 The perspective which derives from Menger's *Principles* continues to command a sufficiently large number of adherents to the present day to warrant their recognition as a separate school of contemporary thinkers. Their work will be further examined in Chapter 22.

22 Carl Menger, *Principles of Economics*, vol. 1, reprint no. 17 (London: London School of Economics, 1870), p. 3.

23 Carl Menger, *Principles of Economics*, vol. 1, reprint no. 17 (London: London School of Economics, 1870), p. 140.

24 W. S. Jevons, *Theory of Political Economy*, 4th edn (1931), p. Ii.

25 Terrence W. Hutchison, 'The marginal revolution' and 'Decline and fall of English political economy,' *History of Political Economy*, vol. 4 (Fall, 1972), pp. 442–68.

Glossary of terms and concepts

Imputation

The process of valuing factors of production (goods of a 'higher order' in Austrian terminology) on the basis of their contributions to the value of production.

Methodenstreit

The conflict over method between the Austrian approach, which was abstract and theoretical, and the approach of the historical school, which looked to comparative historical studies to lead eventually to generalizations that are relevant to particular economies at particular times in their history. One important feature of their intellectual disagreement related to the rejection by the historical school of the premise that it is possible to arrive at economic laws that are relevant at all times and places.

Numéraire

A commodity arbitrarily chosen to serve as a common denominator of unchanging value, that is, as constant value money, in terms of which all other prices are expressed. Thus, all prices vary relative to P_a where $P_a = 1$.

Opportunity cost

The price a factor of production can command in its best paying alternative use.

Recontracting

Walras's notion of hypothetical resales of commodities as a process for establishing a true equilibrium. The process is known as *tâtonnement*.

Walras's law of general equilibrium

Demonstration of simultaneous individual equilibriums in all commodity and factor markets. A mathematical solution can be found if it is possible to write as many equations on the basis of known data as there are unknown prices to be established.

Questions for discussion and further research

1 What is Jevons's equation for identifying the conditions of maximum satisfaction for two parties in a barter exchange? Explain in words what this equation means.

2 Rational allocation of money income does not mean that a consumer will spend equal amounts of money on every commodity. Using Jevons's logic, why is this the case?

3 What is the nature of Walras's general equilibrium model? What is the chief thing it purports to show?

4 What is Walras's notion of *rareté*? May it be compared with Jevons's final degree of utility?

Notes for further reading

From *The New Palgrave*

R. D. Collison Black on William Stanley Jevons, vol. 2, pp. 1008–13; James M. Buchanan on opportunity cost, vol. 3, pp. 718–21; Antonietta Campus on marginalist economics, vol. 3, pp. 320–22; Gerard Debreu on existence of general equilibrium, vol. 2, pp. 216–18; Meghnad Dtsai on value and price, vol. 4, pp. 789–91; John Eatwell on Walras's theory of capital, vol. 4, pp. 868–72; K. H. Hennings on Eugen von Böhm-Bawerk, vol. 1, pp. 254–58, and on roundabout methods of production, vol. 4, pp. 224–25; Israel M. Kirzner on Austrian School of Economics, vol. 1, pp. 145–50; Lionel W. McKenzie on general equilibrium, vol. 2, pp. 498–511; Paul J. McNalty on competition: Austrian conceptions, vol. 1, pp. 536–37; Takashi Negishi on *tâtonnement* and recontracting, vol. 4. pp. 589–95; G. O. Orosel on period of production, vol. 3, pp. 843–46; Don Patinkin on Walras's law, vol. 4, p. 863; Terry Peach on Jevons as economic theorist, vol. 2, pp. 1014–19; Murray N. Rothbard on imputation, vol. 2, pp. 738–39; Karen I. Vaughn on Carl Menger, vol. 3, pp. 438–44; Donald A. Walker on Léon Walras, vol. 4, pp. 852–63.

Selected references and suggestions for further reading

Bowman, R. S. 'Policy implications of W. S. Jevons's economic theory.' *Journal of the History of Economic Thought* 19(2), (Fall, 1997), pp. 196–221.

History of Political Economy 4 (Fall, 1972) This complete issue is devoted to papers on the marginal revolution in economics.

Howey, R. S. *The Rise of the Marginal Utility School, 1870–1899* (Lawrence: University of Kansas Press, 1960).

Hutchison, Terrence W. 'The marginal revolution' and 'Decline and fall of English political economy.' *History of Political Economy* (Fall, 1972) pp. 442–68.

Jenkin, Fleeming. *The Graphic Representation of the Laws of Supply and Demand and Other Essays on Political Economy 1868–84* (London: London School of Economics and Political Science, 1870, reprinted 1931).

Jaffé, William. 'The birth of Leon Walras' *Elements.' History of Political Economy*, 1 (Spring 1969).

Jaffé, William. 'Leon Walras' role in the marginal revolution of the 1870s.' *History of Political Economy*, 4 (Fall, 1972).

Jevons, W. S. *The Theory of Political Economy* (New York: Kelley and Millman, 1957).

Jevons, W. S. 'On the study of periodic commercial fluctuations.' In *Investigations in Currency and Finance*, edited by H. S. Foxwell (London: Macmillan, 1862), pp. 1–12.

Klein, Judy. *Statistical Visions in Time* (Cambridge: Cambridge University Press, 1998).

Robbins, Lionel. Lecture 27, 'The Marginal Revolution (I): Jevons'; Lecture 28, 'The Marginal Revolution (II): Jevons and Menger.' In *A History of Economic Thought*, edited by S. Medema and W. Samuels (Princeton, NJ: Princeton University Press, 1998), pp. 258–276.

Robertson, R. M. 'Jevons and his precursors.' *Econometrica*, 19 (July, 1951), pp. 229–49.

Stigler, George J. *Production and Distribution Theories: The Formative Period* (New York: Macmillan, 1941).

Van Daal, J. 'From utilitarianism to Hedonism: Gossen, Jevons and Walras.' *Journal of the History of Economic Thought* 18(2) (Fall, 1996), pp. 271–86.

Viner, Jacob. 'The utility concept in value theory and its critics.' In *The Long View and the Short* (New York: Free Press, 1958).

Walker, Donald A. 'Leon Walras in the light of his correspondence and related papers.' *Journal of Political Economy*, 78 (July/August, 1970).

Walras, Léon. *Elements of Pure Economics*, (Homewood, Ill.: Richard D. Irwin, 1954).

Chapter 13

'Second-generation' marginalists and the Austrian school

It is something of an enigma that the marginal productivity theory was not clearly developed alongside the theory of subjective value. It seems that, once the revolutionary concept of explaining the value of consumer goods in terms of marginal utility theory was developed, the next logical step would have been to explain how the values of the productive services themselves are determined. Yet, it was approximately 20 years later that second-generation marginalists developed the marginal productivity theory.

Among the English pioneers of marginal productivity theory, pride of place surely must be accorded to Francis Ysidro Edgeworth (1845–1926), who was elected to the Drummond Professorship in Political Economy at Oxford University in 1890. During his lifetime, he was, perhaps, second only to Alfred Marshall – his contemporary at Cambridge – as one of the leading figures of English political economy. At the present time, the almost universal use of mathematics and statistical inference in economics and econometrics weighs at least somewhat against Marshall and in favor of Edgeworth, but in their day it was quite the reverse. Nevertheless, Edgeworth is to be remembered as one among the great toolmakers of our discipline; both the indifference curve and the box diagram are among his intellectual legacies.

Philip Wicksteed (1884–1927) is best remembered for his understanding of what is known in contemporary theory as *the returns to scale*. However, he should perhaps also be remembered for his 1884 critique of Marx's *Capital*, volume I. By that date he had become steeped in Jevonsian theory, although he was also interested in British socialism and social movements, and he was a friend of G. B. Shaw, whom he is said to have led from Marxian thinking to Jevons. His most important books in economics are *The Alphabet of Economic Science* (1888), *An Essay on the Coordination of the Laws of Distribution* (1894), and *The Common Sense of Political Economy* (1910).

As in the case of marginal utility theory, marginal productivity theory also appeared more or less simultaneously in several countries besides England. The Swedish economist Knut Wicksell (1851–1926), whose principal works are *Value, Capital and Rent* (1893), *Interest and Prices* (1898), and *Lectures on Political Economy* in two volumes (1901 and 1906), was a thoroughgoing marginalist who integrated the utility theory of value with the marginal productivity theory of distribution.[1] His special contribution to the theory of distribution, for which he shares the honor of discovery with Philip Wicksteed, is the theorem concerning the exhaustion of the product.

Eugen Böhm-Bawerk (1851–1914) and Friedrich von Wieser (1851–1926) were the chief followers of Carl Menger, who directed their considerable talents toward advancing the cause of theoretical analyses, as opposed to the historical method, and to extending Menger's opportunity cost principle to the problem of valuing goods of a higher order. Their joint efforts were persuasive in diminishing the intellectual influence of Karl Marx and the German historical school and, at the same time, reaffirmed the intellectual basis for the Austrian school. Their great contribution is to the theory of capital and interest, which laid the foundation for contemporary work in the theory of entrepreneurship.

The second generation of marginalists also includes the first major American economist, John Bates Clark (1847–1938), who is remembered as the most distinguished American marginalist who contributed to the development of distribution theory during the period under consideration. He brought to economics a lifelong interest in philosophy and ethics acquired in his undergraduate days at Brown University and Amherst College. This philosophic bent led him to the view that the economic aspects of life cannot be divorced from questions of morality. This perspective is evident in each of his three books: *The Philosophy of Wealth* (1885), *The Distribution of Wealth* (1899), and *Essentials of Economic Theory* (1907). His reputation rests chiefly on *The Distribution of Wealth*, in which he developed the hypothesis that the functional distribution of income in the long run is determined in the long run under static and perfectly competitive conditions, according to the principle of factor productivity at the margin.

From 1895 well into the 1920s, Clark was a professor of economics at Columbia University. Most of his work aligns him with the orthodox tradition of English economists and makes him an intellectual cousin of his English contemporary, Alfred Marshall. There is little, especially as regards his mature work, to mark his contribution as distinctively American. The early Clark, as reflected in his first work, *The Philosophy of Wealth*, gave promise of a departure from English tradition in its criticism of the assumptions on which classical economics rested. In it, Clark undertook to question the premise that human economic behavior is motivated by material self-interest and urged the necessity of a more valid psychological basis for economic inquiry. He also questioned the inherent desirability of competition as the regulator of economic life and introduced into economics the Spencerian conception that society is an organic whole. While many of these ideas were novel when Clark introduced them into economics, the body of economic analysis that he ultimately perfected and which is given expression in *The Distribution of Wealth* places him, in terms of viewpoint, among the ranks of the orthodox thinkers who believed that competitive forces could be relied upon to work economic justice and social harmony. Thus, while Clark gave promise of leading the revolt against the body of orthodox economics, it was in fact his student, Thorstein Veblen, who became the most prominent critic of received doctrine.

Irving Fisher (1867–1947) was another noted American theorist, who was a statistician and mathematician as well as an economist. From the standpoint of the development of distribution theory, Fisher's special contribution is in the theory of the interest rate. His ideas are given their most fully developed exposition in *The Theory of Interest* (1930), a revision of his earlier volume *The Rate of Interest* (1907). The central idea of this book, which is dedicated to both Eugen Böhm-Bawerk and his fore-runner, John Rae, is that interest is not a separate form of income but is an element common to all income shares that accrue over a period of time.

Fisher's other work is aimed at advancing economic theory in relation to mathematics and statistics. This objective was already evident in his first work, *Mathematical Investigation in the Theory of Value and Prices* (1892), which was his Ph.D. thesis. He is perhaps best known for *The Purchasing Power of Money* (1911), in which he attempted to measure the elements in the equation of exchange in order to test the relationship between changes in the quantity of money and changes in the general price level.

The theory of production

Edgeworth on the laws of return in the short run

The chief problem 'second-generation' marginalists addressed was that of income sharing; i.e. to explain how the earnings of landowners, workers and capitalists are related to their productive contributions at the margin. Their theory of distribution is therefore necessarily related to their theory of production; i.e. to the relationship between factor inputs and production outputs.

Although the concept of a *production function* is implicit in von Thünen's analysis and in the classical theory of diminishing returns, Léon Walras was the first to express these relationships in mathematical form. His initial assumption with respect to the production function was that the coefficients of production are fixed: i.e. there is only one possible combination of inputs that will yield any product. The significance of this assumption from the standpoint of the theory of

distribution is that it makes it impossible to isolate the productive contribution of any individual factor. Even though Walras eventually introduced the concept of variable proportions into his theory of production, it is interesting to note that he never arrived at a theory that related the distributive shares to the marginal productivities of their factors.

It is only in the very short run that the extreme situation, in which factor substitution is a complete impossibility, is likely to be encountered. It is more than likely that at least one input will be variable. Ricardo's theory of rent was premised on a production function of this sort. The presence of a fixed factor (land) was recognized as imposing a constraint on the production process that causes the returns to the variable factor (labor) to increase at a decreasing rate beyond a certain number of inputs. The operation of this law accounted for Ricardo's explanation of rent as a differential surplus on better-than-marginal land.

Ricardo's analysis had its shortcomings, both as a theory of production and as a theory of distribution. Not only did it fail to distinguish between diminishing average and marginal products, but it also implied that the law of diminishing returns applied only to land and agricultural output. Classical theorists therefore failed to recognize that it is impossible to generalize Ricardo's theory of rent. That is, the return to any factor may be conceived either as a differential surplus or as the equivalent of its marginal product, depending upon whether the factor is a fixed constant or a variable in the production function.

While the classical theorists stated the law of diminishing returns, Francis Edgeworth is credited with making a clear-cut distinction between the average and marginal changes in the output that an increase in a variable factor can yield. He also made it plain that if, for any reason, it is not possible to vary all factor inputs simultaneously, diminishing returns are due to the change in *the ratio* in which the factors are used.

To demonstrate the distinction between diminishing average and marginal returns, Edgeworth assumed that successive small doses of labor and capital are applied to a given plot of land and that the total output, marginal output, and average output behave as recorded in Table 13.1.[2] This table provides a clear demonstration that there is a differ-

ence between diminishing marginal returns and diminishing average returns, although the two were usually confused.[3]

The behavior of marginal product and average product when the land-to-labor ratio is varied may also be shown graphically. Figure 13.1 plots the labor-to-land ratios from Table 13.1 on the horizontal axis, and the average and marginal product associated with varying the labor-to-land ratio on the vertical axis. It is evident that as long as additional increments of a variable factor can cause total output to increase at an increasing rate,

Table 13.1 Returns from varying amounts of labor and equipment applied (in small doses) to a given plot of land

Day's labor with team and tools	Total crop in bushels	Increments due to successive doses	Bushels per day's labor
–	–	–	–
13	220	–	16.92
14	244	24	17.43
15	270	26	18.00
16	294	24	18.38
17	317	23	18.65
18	339	22	18.83
19	360	21	18.95
20	380	20	19.00
21	396	16	18.86

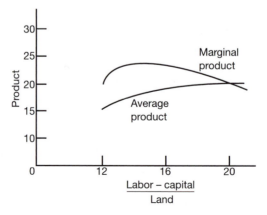

Figure 13.1 Average and marginal product of a variable factor

both marginal and average output will increase, and the marginal physical product of the variable factor will be greater than its average product. The marginal product curve will then lie above the average product curve.

When additional units of the variable factor can no longer raise the total product at an increasing rate, as in the case in Edgeworth's example after the application of the fifteenth dose of labor and equipment, the marginal product will diminish, and the marginal product curve will slope downward. When additional inputs of the variable factor can no longer raise the average product beyond the maximum already reached, the average product of the variable factor will equal the marginal product. Beyond that point, additional applications of the variable factor will cause the average product to diminish. This takes place, in Edgeworth's example, with the application of the twenty-first dose of labor and equipment to a given plot of land. The marginal physical product is then smaller than the average product. While Table 13.1 and Figure 13.1 do not show it, additional applications of the variable factor to a given amount of a fixed factor will, at some point, be associated with an absolute decrease in total product; the marginal product would then become negative.

Edgeworth's distinction between diminishing average productivity and diminishing marginal productivity is fundamental to understanding the behavior of production costs in the short run, which later became fundamental to the neoclassical understanding of business firms' demands for factors of production. Just as a consumer is conceived to maximize gain by allocating income among alternative uses until the ratios of the marginal utilities of the goods consumed are equal to the ratios of their prices, so a producer maximizes gains from factor inputs when the ratios of the marginal revenue products of the factors hired are equated to the ratios of their prices.

Wicksteed on returns to scale: Euler's theorem

Philip Wicksteed is credited with being the first to appreciate that the laws of return are different when factor inputs are fixed than when inputs are variable.[4] The output possibilities when all factors are variable are now commonly described by the term *returns to scale*. There are three possibilities: constant returns, increasing returns, and decreasing returns.

If an increase in all factor inputs increases output proportionately, the returns to scale are constant. In this special case, the production function also satisfies the requirement that the eighteenth-century mathematician, Leonhard Euler, laid down in his theorem concerning *linear homogeneity*. A function is linearly homogeneous if the multiplication of every variable it contains by a given real number increases the value of the total function by the same multiple. Applying this principle to the relationship between factor inputs and the resulting product, a production function is homogeneously linear if a given increase in all factor inputs increases the total product in precisely the same proportion. If, however, a proportionate increase in all factor inputs increases output more than proportionately, the returns to scale are increasing. Conversely, if a proportionate increase in all factor inputs increases output less than proportionately, the returns to scale are decreasing.

Wicksteed was especially concerned with the relevance of returns to scale with respect to the problem of coordinating the laws of distribution.[5] He conceived the latter problem to involve the demonstration that each of the distributive shares is governed by the principle of marginal productivity, and that the total product available for distribution is the exact sum of the shares that that principle assigns to each of the several factors. He understood that it is possible to pay each factor the equivalent of its marginal product and *exactly exhaust the total product* only if returns are constant. In this case, the marginal product of the factors is independent of the absolute amount of the factors employed, and a proportionate change in the quantity of all factors does not affect their marginal product. The increase in total product resulting from additional quantities of all factors is precisely equal to the sum of the marginal products of each of the separate factors. The problem Wicksteed posed concerning the exhaustion of the total product thus revealed what neoclassical thinkers perceived as the *essential link* between the theory of production and the theory of distribution; i.e. that the production of a factor at the margin establishes the basis for its wage, rent or interest payment, and that under competition the sum of their payments exhausts the value of the total product. Profit (loss) is a residual which tends toward zero in the long run.

The marginal productivity theory of distribution

Clark's generalization of Ricardo's theory on rent

The marginal productivity theory is an alternative hypothesis to the Austrian theory of imputation for explaining the functional distribution of income. The individual most closely associated with marginal productivity theory is John Bates Clark, who gave this hypothesis its fullest exposition in *The Distribution of Wealth* (1899). Independently of

Jevons, Menger, and Walras, Clark had already formulated the hypothesis that the value of a commodity expresses the utility of the marginal unit to society as a whole. The problem of distribution was therefore the logical sequel to his inquiry into the problem of value.

The notion that persons should be rewarded in accordance with the productivity of their labor and/or other factors that they own has gained wide currency. Its association with the widely misunderstood *marginal productivity theory of distribution* suggests the importance of gaining a clear understanding of what precisely the theory means and what its limitations are. The starting point of the marginal productivity theory of distribution is the demand for, and the supply of, the factors to individual hiring firms. Firms are assumed to have production functions in which factor proportions are *variable* so that it is a technical possibility to change factor inputs independently of one another. If the input of one factor remains fixed, the contribution of the variable factor to the total product increases at a decreasing rate beyond a certain point. The result is that added inputs then cause the marginal physical product curve to be downward sloping. If the market price for a firm's product is competitive so that $P = AR = MR$, the marginal physical revenue product curve is $MPP(P) = MRP$. This curve is also the firm's demand curve for the factor in question because it identifies the revenue attributable to an additional unit of that factor.

If firms are also assumed to be hiring factors in a purely competitive market, their factor supply curves are perfectly elastic at the ruling market price. If each firm hires its factors in profit-maximizing proportions, each variable factor will be employed until the marginal revenue product it produces is equal to its price of hire. Since all factor inputs are variable in the long run, all factors will be employed in proportions that will make the ratio of their marginal revenue products equal to the ratio of their prices. Thus, if the variable inputs are labor and capital, each is employed until $MRP_l/MRP_k = w/r$, where w/r is the ratio between the rate of wages and the rate of interest. From the point of view of an individual firm, the marginal productivity theory is, therefore, a theory of *employment*; that is, it explains the demand for a factor, say labor, at a given wage rate. It is *not* a theory of wage-rate determination.

Is a transition possible, conceptually speaking, from the demand curve of a firm for a factor to the demand curve of a group of firms? If the factor is homogeneous, its market demand curve represents the summation of the demand curves of individual firms with the necessary adjustment in the market price of the commodity being sold. The commodity price is, of course, no longer a parameter when the analysis is extended from the individual firm to the industry as a whole. Since the market price of a competitively produced product will fall as output is increased, the industry demand curve for a factor will fall more rapidly than the marginal revenue product curve of a factor to a firm. Given the supply of the factor available for employment, the market price per unit that would tend to prevail for a homogeneous factor in a static state would follow from the logic of productivity theory. According to Clark's conception, a static state would exist 'if labor and capital were to remain fixed in quantity, if improvements in the mode of production were to stop, if the consolidation of capital were to cease and if the wants of consumers were never to vary.'[6] The essential departure from reality of these static state requirements makes it abundantly clear that,

at best, marginal productivity theory is useful for understanding employment decisions at the level of the individual firm. However, it *cannot* explain the prevailing rate of payment, that is, the wage rate in a market; and nor can it explain the share of any factor in the economy's total product.

Yet, Clark and Wicksteed were correct in recognizing that the marginal productivity theory of distribution is a generalization of Ricardo's theory of rent.[7] Ricardo's theory viewed rent as the differential surplus that appears on land as a result of the difference between the value of the total product and the value of the marginal product of labor and capital in their intramarginal applications. There is no rent at the margin of cultivation because the marginal product of capital and labor is exhausted by wages and interest. In Ricardo's case, land is assumed to be the fixed factor to which variable labor-capital inputs are applied. The surplus he called *rent* arises because the payment to the variable factor is determined by the productivity of labor and capital at the margin.

Wicksteed and Clark demonstrated that if the input of labor (including that congealed as capital) is assumed to be fixed while land is the variable factor, rent is the marginal product of land, and wages are the residual surplus. Figure 13.2 represents the gist of their reasoning graphically. The right-hand portion of the diagram shows the classical case, in which a fixed quantity of land is combined with increasing quantities of a given grade of labor. The curve DC represents the diminishing marginal product of labor. Since it is being assumed that all units of labor are homogeneous, and therefore perfect substitutes, the marginal productivity curve of labor establishes BC as the demand price per unit. Thus, the rectangle labeled 'Wages'

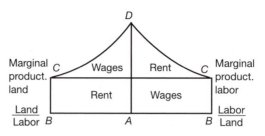

Figure 13.2 The generalization of Ricardo's rent theorem

represents labor's share of the total product on the basis of its productive contribution when the total product is *ABCD*. The area under the marginal productivity curve is, therefore, the return to land as the fixed factor. Rent is thus a differential surplus remaining after the payment of wages at a rate established by the marginal productivity of labor. This is simply a graphic representation of Ricardo's rent theory.

The left-hand portion of Figure 13.2 utilizes the same vertical axis (in the middle of the diagram) to facilitate comparison when *labor* is assumed to be the fixed factor and land is the variable factor. Assuming also the same total product, *ABCD*, the productivity curve is now that of land. In this case, rent is determined by the marginal productivity of land, while wages are a residual surplus. From this, Wicksteed and Clark deduced that *all* factors can be rewarded according to their marginal productivities, and that the total product will be exhausted if each factor is paid the equivalent of its marginal product. Proof of this proposition was, however, not provided by either Clark or Wicksteed, but by A. W. Flux in his review of Wicksteed's book.[8] Flux recognized that the distribution of factor rewards whose sum will equal the sum of the marginal products of the factors is consistent with production functions that are linearly homogeneous.

Without intending to deny the technical validity of the Clark–Wicksteed–Flux contributions, the point must again be made that, because they are based on the extremely limiting assumption of perfectly competitive factors and product markets, production functions in which factors are continuously substitutable for one another and technical change is absent, they offer only a starting point for understanding the operation of present-day factor markets. But it is also relevant that without these formulations our understanding would be far less than it is.

Clark's ethical interpretation of marginal productivity theory

The laws of income distribution that Clark undertook to formulate in *The Distribution of Wealth* are those that would operate in a static state from which all changes have been abstracted. If they were able to work without friction, these laws 'would (naturally) give to every agent of production the amount of wealth that agent creates.'[9] Thus, Clark's conception of the problem of functional distribution was, at the very outset, placed squarely in the realm of ethics. The position taken was that if all receive precisely the value of what they or the resources they own create, there is no basis for grievance. If, on the other hand, a factor does not receive its full product, there is 'institutional robbery' and therefore a potentially disruptive condition in the society.

Hence, in Clark's view, an understanding of the laws of distribution is basic to providing insight into the 'right of society to exist in its present form, and the probability that it will continue so to exist.'[10]

While Clark's earlier work, *The Philosophy of Wealth*, questioned the efficiency and justice of competition in the economic sphere, a fundamental change of attitude is evident in *The Distribution of Wealth* with respect to the role of competitive forces as a beneficial influence. In the earlier volume, competition was thought to be self-destructive, and the immorality of the marketplace was viewed as incompatible with economic justice and social harmony. In the later volume, competition is viewed in a different light, namely, as the force that 'insures to the public the utmost that the existing power of man can give in the way of efficient service.'[11]

The logic by which Clark came ultimately to have faith in competition as a perfect regulatory mechanism is not difficult to perceive. Competition forces product prices to equal costs of production. Pure profits are therefore absent because all the changes associated with entrepreneurial risk are absent and the entrepreneurial function is reduced to that of a special kind of labor. Incomes that accrue in excess of contractual costs and imputed wages and interest to the owner, exist only because they are imperfectly eliminated by competitive forces or because new frictions develop. These frictions are the source of what Frank Knight, writing during the 1920s, called 'uncertainty.'[12] In Knight's view, it is the entrepreneurs' uncertainty about the demand for their products, and therefore the price at which they can be sold, that causes them to hire productive factors, not on the basis of the actual value of their marginal products, but on the basis of expected value. Profits or losses thus materialize if actual product values diverge from those that are anticipated.

Competition also forces all factor rewards to be equal to the value of the factor's marginal product. The fact that entrepreneurial demands for factors are based on their marginal revenue product rather than on their marginal value product creates no difficulty within Clark's framework of perfect competition for, in this case, the two are equal. Thus, Clark argued that, in the static state, competition among workers would keep the wage rate from rising above the point at which the value of the marginal product of labor equals its marginal revenue product, while competition among employers would prevent it from being less. Competition among the suppliers of capital funds and those who demand them would likewise ensure that the interest rate is neither more nor less than that at which the value of the marginal product of capital is equal to its marginal revenue product.

A further reason for Clark's laudatory attitude toward competition stems from the relationship he perceived to exist between the natural laws of distribution and the natural laws of value. Although Clark does not systematically develop a theory of value, he accepts as correct the Ricardo–Mill view that the natural price of a commodity is its cost price.[13] But whereas the classicists conceived of prices as being determined by the cost of production in the long run, Clark conceived of price as reflecting the social cost of commodities, i.e. the pain and sacrifice incurred by factors in production. These costs are *subjectively* identified by individuals, as are the utilities of goods. The market, however, transforms individual costs into social costs and individual utilities into social utilities.

The universal law of economics is that costs and benefits are everywhere equalized. The social organism as a whole is visualized as capable of rationally weighing the social marginal utility of goods against the social marginal cost of acquiring them and maximizing the social welfare by balancing one against the other. Thus, for Clark, the static state constitutes the ideal in much the same way that the natural order was ideal for the thinkers of the eighteenth century. The major impediment, in his view, to the attainment of this static state is the growth of monopoly power and the consequent necessity for government regulation to hold its spread in check.

The marginal productivity theory of distribution

The marginal productivity theory of distribution, associated most particularly with John Bates Clark, is a hypothesis that relates the per unit price of a homogeneous factor of production to the value of the product it produces in its marginal application. This theory is premised on the assumption that factor proportions are variable and that the return to the variable factor will increase at a decreasing rate beyond a certain point. It is, therefore, a generalization of Ricardo's theory of rent, in that any factor, not just land, may be the fixed factor whose return appears as a differential surplus remaining after the variable factor, is paid at a rate established by its marginal productivity.

The marginal productivity theory of income distribution maintained that, in the long run, under perfect competition, all factors of production, including entrepreneurs, tend to receive a real rate of return equal to the *social value* of their marginal physical product. Since the profits of entrepreneurs tend to be no higher than normal (i.e. they tend to equal the marginal productivity of that kind of labor), the total product of soci-

ety is exactly exhausted by the payments made to the factors. In Clark's interpretation, the payment of factor rewards, which are determined according to the marginal productivity principle, is consistent with the natural law of income distribution. In his view, every agent is justly compensated when it receives the equivalent of its own product; and the payment of each factor according to the value of its marginal product will, in the competitive long-run static state, exactly exhaust the total product.

Wicksell and the adding-up problem

Some of the most penetrating observations on the *adding-up problem* – as the question of whether the total product is exactly exhausted by factor rewards equal to their marginal products has become known – were made by the Swedish economist Knut Wicksell. He recognized that the sum of the marginal products will equal the total product (a) if the production function is homogeneous and linear or (b) if the presence of pure competition causes firms to achieve an optimum size in the long run.[14] The entry and exodus of firms in response to short-run profits or losses will result in a tendency for firms to operate at an output level that is consistent with the lowest point of their long-run average-cost curve. When output is at this level, it will coincide with that point on the production function that is linear and homogeneous. Thus, even if the production function as a whole is not linearly homogeneous, Euler's theorem applies at the long-run, least-cost point, for at this point returns are constant.

If either increasing or decreasing returns to scale prevail, the payment of the factors in accordance with the value of their marginal products cannot exactly exhaust the value of the total product. In the case of increasing returns, the marginal return to outlay is greater than the average return; while in the case of decreasing returns, it is smaller. Thus, in the case of increasing returns, the value of the total product is too small to reward all factors according to the value of their marginal products; and in the case of decreasing returns, a surplus will remain after the factors have received rewards equal to the value of their marginal products.

Wicksell maintained that neither increasing nor decreasing returns to scale are likely to prevail in the long run under competition because of the tendency for firms to achieve optimum size and, therefore, to operate under conditions of long-run constant cost. Instead of conceiving of increasing returns, decreasing returns, and constant returns as being mutually exclusive situations, Wicksell regarded these conditions as governing different phases of a firm's long-run cost curve. Increasing returns are likely to prevail in the initial phases of a firm's expansion and decreasing returns will assert themselves beyond some point. The transitional phase, in which these forces are balanced, is the stage of constant returns and costs, which is the optimum long-run condition for a firm under pure competition. The output at which long-run marginal cost equals long-run marginal revenue is also the one at which total cost equals total revenue. Therefore, the payment of the factors according to the value of their marginal product would exactly exhaust the value of the total product.

Limitations of the marginal productivity theory: a recapitulation

The notion that there is a universal tendency toward a system of payment based on some measure of individual productivity has a strong overtone of both efficiency and fairness and has, on this basis, appealed not only to the proverbial man on the street, but also to many economists. It is therefore important to understand precisely the assumption on which the theory is based and what the limitations are to the validity of the marginal productivity principle as a *theory of distribution*.

The marginal productivity theory is premised on the behavior of an individual firm under perfect competition with respect to the purchase of a single variable factor when all other factor inputs and their prices and the states of the arts are fixed. In this case, a firm is always confronted with a given sales price for its output, so its total revenue is a function of its output. Its marginal revenue, therefore, expresses the share of the sales proceeds of a firm that will be available to pay any given factor of production.

The marginal productivity theory was not, however, intended simply as a theory of the behavior of the individual firm with respect to the employment of a homogeneous factor at the going market price. It was also intended as a theory of per-unit price determination, especially in versions of Clarkian inspiration. There are limitations inherent in its use for this purpose. Specifically, the marginal productivity theory neglects completely the influence of factor supplies in determining the factor process. The marginal productivity of a factor explains the demand for a factor, but a complete theory of factor price determination must also consider the economic and social factors that determine factor supplies. This is precisely why Alfred Marshall, the foremost English contributor of the period, shied away from a marginal productivity theory of distribution in favor of a theory that recognized the interaction of demand and supply forces.

A much more formidable difficulty is

encountered in making the transition from the demand for a variable factor by a firm to the demand by an industry, and from there, to the demand by the economy. The marginal revenue product of a factor to a given firm is calculated on the basis of an assumed product price. This price is itself premised on a given product demand curve, which is drawn up on the assumption that consumer preferences, the prices of other goods, and the level of income are given. The latter assumption poses a special difficulty for the theory of income determination because every change in the marginal revenue product of a factor, and therefore in its compensation, must necessarily affect the product demand curves of the firms in the economy. This must, in turn, affect the marginal revenue product on which the demand for the factor depends. Nevertheless, marginal productivity theory implicitly ignores the interdependence of factor demand curves and product demand curves.

This interdependence is the reason why John Maynard Keynes, writing during the 1930s, objected to wage cuts as a suitable method for dealing with the problem of mass unemployment. A wage cut will cause an *individual firm* to employ additional workers until the marginal revenue product of labor equals the new wage rate, because the demand for its product is not likely to be affected. However, if wage rates everywhere are reduced, product demand curves – and therefore the demand for labor itself – become altered, so the derivation of industry and market demand curves for a factor cannot be accomplished by the simple process of summing up individual firms' factor demand curves. Marginal productivity theory has a microeconomic bias that limits the validity of the conclusions it can yield when its application is extended. What the marginal productivity principle provides

is not an explanation of factor prices but rather a basis for understanding an employer's demand for a particular factor of production at a given market price.

The normative implications inherent in the marginal productivity theory have been another source of criticism. The theory implies that if a factor is compensated according to the value of its marginal product, it is receiving a just payment. Yet, when a firm hires a factor in a market that is not purely competitive or sells its product in a market that is not purely competitive, the value of its marginal product (i.e. the marginal physical product multiplied by the sale price of the good) is not equal to its marginal revenue product (i.e. the marginal physical product multiplied by the marginal revenue the sale of a product yields). It follows that the absence of pure competition, either in the product market or in the factor market, is associated with exploitation in the sense that the marginal increment of the factor cannot then receive a compensation equivalent to the value of its marginal product.[15]

The Austrian school

The works of Wieser and Böhm-Bawerk overlap in time with those of Edgeworth, Wicksteed, Clark, and Wicksell in much the same way as Menger's overlapped with those of Jevons and Walras. Their analyses stand apart, not only from that of the classicists, but from that of their contemporaries in other countries. For this reason alone, it is important to give them their due as constituting a separate school of thinkers who are not simply second-generation marginalists. A useful starting point for making the Austrian perspective concrete is to articulate what may be termed their *linear view of production*. Their model of production is linear in the sense that it proceeds from 'goods of a higher order' to consumption goods. In this linear view of the production process, capital simply consists of goods not consumed during the production process. Thus, the distinction that the classicists and Marx made between circulating and fixed capital is not relevant. Capital is, as Menger made clear in his *Principles*, quite simply, intermediate goods moving steadily towards the final goal of consumption. What Menger lacked was a theory that distinguished between capital goods themselves and the services they provide. It is this aspect of Menger's imputation theory that Böhm-Bawerk was chiefly interested in extending. His objective was partly to undermine the abstinence theory of interest, but also to articulate a positive rationale for the receipt of profits.

Böhm-Bawerk's point of departure was Menger's marginal utility theory of value, to which he added his own solution, different from Wieser's, of the imputation problem. His theory of capital and interest was developed within this typically Austrian conception of the problem of valuation. It was presented in a three-volume magnum opus entitled *Capital and Interest*, whose first volume. *History and Criticism of Interest Theories* (1884), set the groundwork for the two subsequent volumes. This volume presents a detailed review and criticism of all the theories on the subject of interest previously formulated. It thus provides the background for Böhm-Bawerk's definitive statement of his own views on capital and interest in his *Positive Theory of Capital* (1889), the second of his three volumes.

The key to the problem of capital as a means of production and as a source of a net return is, in Böhm-Bawerk's view, an understanding of the nature of the production process in which the original factors, labor and resources, transform matter into want-satisfying goods. These may be either consumer goods or 'produced means of production.' When production proceeds with the aid of produced means of production, the same input of original factors results in a larger total product than when direct methods of production are employed. This observation, which was not completely original to Böhm-Bawerk, but which had never been given detailed formulation before, became one of the pillars of his theory of capital and interest.

Capital goods are, in Böhm-Bawerk's view, not original and independent factors of production, but intermediate products that yield final goods after a period of waiting. The more capitalistic, or roundabout, a process of production is, the longer will be the interval of waiting time to elapse before the final goods emerge from the production process. Any good available in the present has a greater value than an equal quantity of the same kind available at some time in the future. Present goods, therefore, command an *agio*, or premium, over future goods.

There are three separate reasons for the higher value placed on present goods. The first two are of a psychological nature and are relevant to the demand for consumer loans, namely, the hope that most people entertain of being better able to provide for future wants and the human tendency to underestimate future wants. These factors reinforce one another and enhance the value of present goods. The third reason for the greater value of present goods is technical rather than psychological. Böhm-Bawerk illustrates this principle with an example intended to demonstrate that the want-satisfying power of any presently available productive resource, say 30 days of labor now available, is greater than that of 30 days of labor to be used in the same production process that will become available in a year's time. By the same reasoning, 30 days of labor available last month are technically superior to the same quantity that becomes available only this month. Precisely the same principle applies to the utilities produced by capital goods. Capital goods already on hand are technically superior to those not yet available. Hence, their use in time-consuming, roundabout methods of production yields a product that contains some surplus value.

If only the third reason for interest were operative, the greater productivity of the roundabout method would result in an infinitely long period of production. The operation of the first and second reasons, however, which cause the value of future goods to be discounted in the present, implies that the period of production cannot be infinitely long. It is therefore the interaction between the first two and the third of Böhm-Bawerk's 'three grounds' that determine the optimum length of the production period in terms of its yield of present value. Thus, the agio in the exchange of present goods for future goods derives, on the one hand, from the fact that future values are discounted in the present for psychological reasons and, on the other, from the fact that the roundabout method of production yields a greater value product.[16] It is precisely because the three grounds for the value, agio, of present goods

over future goods are not equally operative for all individuals that there is a market for exchanging present against future goods.

The simplest form of interest is that arising in connection with consumer loans. The preference at the margin for present, versus future, goods is objectively expressed in the rate of interest. This rate is the price phenomenon that reflects the difference in value between present and future goods. A borrower must pay interest to a lender who makes funds available to acquire present goods. Profit to entrepreneurs is, however, the principal form in which interest is received. Capitalists buy *remote goods* such as raw materials, tools, machines, and the use of land and labor and transform them into finished goods ready for consumption. They receive a gain proportional to the amount of capital invested in their business. This gain, which has variously been called 'profit,' 'surplus value,' and 'natural interest on capital,' is in addition to the compensation received for managerial services. It is, Böhm-Bawerk argues, for this reason that profit gives the appearance of being simply a tool for worker exploitation. Marx's theory of surplus value, in particular, has had the effect of compromising the receipt of profit and interest as a just return from the standpoint of both ethics and the performance of an identifiable function. The critical issue for Böhm-Bawerk is thus the nature of capital.

Issues and Answers from the Masterworks 13.1

Issue

What is the true nature of capital? Why can our understanding of interest and profit not be separated from our understanding of capital?

Böhm-Bawerk's answer

From *The Positive Theory of Capital* (1889), Chapter 3, pp. 24–39, and Chapter 9, pp. 358–64.

Chapter III

Historical development of the conception

It will be most convenient to open the discussion by a historical survey of the deve
the conception.

Originally the word Capital (*Capitale* from *Caput*) was used to signify the Principal of
loan (*Capitalis pars debiti*) in opposition to Interest. This usage, already foreshadowe
Greek formation ΚΦραλαιον, became firmly established in medival Latin, and appears
remained the prevailing one for a very long time, even pretty far down in the new era.
therefore, Capital meant the same thing as 'an interest-bearing sum of money.'

In the meantime, the disputes which had arisen over the legitimacy or illegitimacy of
interest brought about an essential deepening and widening of the conception. It had beco
apparent that the interest-bearing power of 'barren' money was at bottom a borrowed one
borrowed from the productive power of things that the money could buy. Money only gave th
exchange form – to a certain extent the outward garb – in which the interest-bearing things
passed from hand to hand. The true 'stock' or parent stem which bore interest was not money
but the goods that were acquired for it. In these circumstances the obvious course was to
change the conception that, besides embracing the representative thing, money, it would
embrace the represented thing, goods.

Thus, Turgot gave the second reading in historical succession to the conception of capital.

It was very soon superseded by a third. For when Turgot designated all saved goods indiscriminately as Capital, he seemed to have gone too far in broadening the conception. To replace
the word 'money' in the definition by the word 'goods' only reflected, indeed, the more thorough
grasp, which was now taken of the subject. But to give the name of Capital, without any further
discrimination, to stocks of goods, was to give up, without sufficient reason, the second feature
in the old conception . . . It was no less a man than Adam Smith who changed and rectified
Turgot's definition. The 'saved' stocks, he said, must be distinguished as containing two parts.
One portion is destined for immediate consumption, and gives off no kind of income; the other
portion is destined to bring in an income to its owner, and this part alone rightly bears the name
of Capital.

With this distinction, however, Adam Smith connected another consideration, that was destined to have very serious consequences on the development of the conception. He remarked
that his use of the term was applicable as well to the case of individuals as to that of a whole
community; only, with this shifting of the standpoint, the group of things embraced by the
conception was also somewhat changed. Individuals, that is to say, can make a gain, not only
by the production of goods, but also by lending to other individuals for a consideration goods
which are destined in themselves to immediate consumption, such as houses, masquerade
dresses, furniture, etc. But the community, as a whole, cannot enrich itself otherwise than by the
production of new goods.

But all the time, in virtue of the old parent conception – that known later as Private Capital –
the term capital remained connected with the phenomenon of interest, which belonged to
the theory of distribution or income. Thus, from that time onward appeared the peculiar
phenomenon, which was to be the source of so many errors and complications, that two
series of fundamentally different phenomena and fundamentally different problems were
treated under the same name. Capital, as National Capital, became the central figure of the

; as Private Capital, of the fundamentally distinct problem

lowers of Adam Smith not only failed to get rid of the confu-
ption of capital, but, on the contrary, positively put their seal
did not notice that, in what Adam Smith and they themselves
damentally distinct conceptions; they considered the capital
of production as identical with the capital which bears interest.
already noticed that there was a certain difference in the mean-
d capital, and that, for instance, rented houses, hired furniture, or
capital in one sense and not in another, and his followers had not
he remark. But obviously they attached no importance to it, – what was
ss about a distinction which referred only to a few hired fancy dresses and
d fast by their conception of capital, the factor of production being capital,
est. And now one confusion resulted in another. Before, it was the concep-
mixed; now, it was the phenomena and the problems. Capital produces, and it
. What is more natural than to say shortly; – it bears interest *because* it produces.
itroduced and made possible by the confusion in the conception of capital, origin-
naive and one-sided theory of the Productivity of capital which, from Say's days to our
s held, and still, in some measure, holds economic science under its baneful influences.
every one knows he [Marx] sees in interest a profit got by the capitalist at the expense of
wage-earner. This element of exploitation seems to him so important that he brings it in to
he conception of capital as a constitutive feature of it: he conceives of capital as only those
productive instruments which, in the hand of the capitalists, serve as 'instruments for the
exploitation and enslaving of the labourer.' The same things in the possession of the labourer,
on the other hand, are not capital.

Chapter IX

Results

We have traced all kinds and methods of acquiring interest to one identical source – the increasing value of future goods as they ripen into present goods. Thus it is with the profit of the
undertakers, who transform labour – the future good which they purchase – into products for
consumption. Thus it is with landlords, property-owners, and owners of durable goods generally, who allow the later services of the goods they possess to gradually mature, and pluck them
when they have ripened into full value. Thus, finally, it is with the loan. Even here it is not the
case, as one might easily think at first sight, that the enrichment of the capitalist comes from the
creditor receiving more articles than he gives – for at first, indeed, the articles concerned are less
in value – but from the fact that the loaned objects, at first lower in value, gradually increase in
value, and on the moment of fruition enter into their complete higher present value.

What, then, are the capitalists as regards the community? – In a word, they are merchants
who have present goods to sell. They are the fortunate possessors of a stock of goods which
they do not require for the personal needs of the moment. They exchange this stock, therefore,
into future goods of some form or another, and allow these to ripen in their hands again into
present goods possessing full value. Many capitalists make this exchange once for all. One who
builds a house with his capital, or buys a piece of land, or acquires a bond, or gives a loan at
interest for fifty years, exchanges his present goods, wholly or in part, for goods or services

weightiest problems of Production; as Private Capital, of the fundamentally distinct problem of Interest . . .

The principal point is that the followers of Adam Smith not only failed to get rid of the confusion in which he had left the conception of capital, but, on the contrary, positively put their seal to one of its worst mistakes. They did not notice that, in what Adam Smith and they themselves called 'capital,' there were two fundamentally distinct conceptions; they considered the capital of which they spoke in the theory of production as identical with the capital which bears interest. As we know, Adam Smith had already noticed that there was a certain difference in the meanings usually given to the word capital, and that, for instance, rented houses, hired furniture, or masquerade dresses were capital in one sense and not in another, and his followers had not failed to loyally transmit the remark. But obviously they attached no importance to it, – what was the use of making a fuss about a distinction which referred only to a few hired fancy dresses and such like? – and held fast by their conception of capital, the factor of production being capital, the source of interest. And now one confusion resulted in another. Before, it was the conceptions that were mixed; now, it was the phenomena and the problems. Capital produces, and it bears interest. What is more natural than to say shortly; – it bears interest *because* it produces. And thus, introduced and made possible by the confusion in the conception of capital, originated that naive and one-sided theory of the Productivity of capital which, from Say's days to our own, has held, and still, in some measure, holds economic science under its baneful influences.

As every one knows he [Marx] sees in interest a profit got by the capitalist at the expense of the wage-earner. This element of exploitation seems to him so important that he brings it in to the conception of capital as a constitutive feature of it: he conceives of capital as only those productive instruments which, in the hand of the capitalists, serve as 'instruments for the exploitation and enslaving of the labourer.' The same things in the possession of the labourer, on the other hand, are not capital.

Chapter IX

Results

We have traced all kinds and methods of acquiring interest to one identical source – the increasing value of future goods as they ripen into present goods. Thus it is with the profit of the undertakers, who transform labour – the future good which they purchase – into products for consumption. Thus it is with landlords, property-owners, and owners of durable goods generally, who allow the later services of the goods they possess to gradually mature, and pluck them when they have ripened into full value. Thus, finally, it is with the loan. Even here it is not the case, as one might easily think at first sight, that the enrichment of the capitalist comes from the creditor receiving more articles than he gives – for at first, indeed, the articles concerned are less in value – but from the fact that the loaned objects, at first lower in value, gradually increase in value, and on the moment of fruition enter into their complete higher present value.

What, then, are the capitalists as regards the community? – In a word, they are merchants who have present goods to sell. They are the fortunate possessors of a stock of goods which they do not require for the personal needs of the moment. They exchange this stock, therefore, into future goods of some form or another, and allow these to ripen in their hands again into present goods possessing full value. Many capitalists make this exchange once for all. One who builds a house with his capital, or buys a piece of land, or acquires a bond, or gives a loan at interest for fifty years, exchanges his present goods, wholly or in part, for goods or services which belong to a remote period of time, and consequently creates, as it were at a blow, the opportunity or condition of a permanent increment of value, and an income called interest which will last over this long period. One, again, who discounts a three months' bill, or enters on a one year's production, must frequently repeat the exchange. In three months or in one year, the future goods thus acquired become full-valued present goods. With these present goods the business begins over again; new bills are bought, new raw material, new labour, these in their turn ripen into present goods, and so on again and again.

In the circumstances, then, it is very easily explained why capital bears an 'everlasting' interest. We may dismiss any idea of an inexhaustible 'productive power' in capital, assuring it eternal fruitfulness, – any idea of an eternal 'Use' given off, year out year in, to the end of time by a good perhaps long perished. It is because the stock of present goods is always too low that the conjuncture for their exchange against future goods is always favourable. And it is because time always stretches forward that the prudently purchased future commodity steadily becomes a present commodity, grows accordingly into the full value of the present, and permits its owner again and again to utilise the always favourable conjuncture.

I do not see that there is anything objectionable in this. For natural reasons, present goods are certainly more valuable commodities than future goods. If the owner of the more valuable commodity exchanges it for a greater quantity of the less valuable, there is nothing more objectionable in this than that the owner of wheat should exchange a peck of wheat for more than a peck of oats or barley, or that a holder of gold should exchange a pound of gold for more than a pound of iron or copper. For the owner not to realise the higher value of his commodity would be an act of unselfishness and charity which could not possibly be translated into a general duty, and as a fact would not be so translated in regard to any other commodity.

It is undeniable that, in this exchange of present commodities against future, the circumstances are of such a nature as to threaten the poor with exploitation of monopolists . . . The capitalists who have present goods for sale are relatively few; the proletarians who must buy them are innumerable.

But what is the conclusion from all this? Surely that, owing to accessory circumstances, interest may be associated with a usurious exploitation and with bad social conditions; not that, in its innermost essence, it is rotten . . . [But] before we abolish interest as such, we must first draw out a balance-sheet to show whether human wellbeing is better promoted in a society which permits gain from capital and recognises it, or in one which permits only income from labour.

In making this calculation it will not be overlooked that the institution of interest has its manifold uses; particularly as the prospect of interest induces saving and accumulation of capital, and thus, by making possible the adoption of more fruitful methods of production, becomes the cause of a more abundant provision for the whole people. In this connection the much-used and much-abused expression, 'Reward of Abstinence,' is in its proper place. The existence of interest cannot be theoretically *explained* by it: one cannot hope in using it to say anything about the essential nature of interest: everyone knows how much interest is simply pocketed without any 'abstinence' that deserves reward. But, just as interest sometimes has its injurious accompaniments, so in its train it bangs others, fortunately, that are beneficent and useful; and to these it is due that interest, which has its origin in quite different causes, acts, among other things, as a wage and as an inducement to save. I know very well that private saving is not the only possible way to the accumulation of capital, and that, even in the Socialist state, capital may be accumulated and added to. But the fact remains that private accumulation of capital is a proved fact, while socialist accumulation is not, – and there are, besides, some very serious *a priori* doubts whether it can be.

Source: Böhm-Bawerk, *Positive Theory of Capital* (1889, translated by William Smart, London).

Summing up: Böhm-Bawerk's key points

The propriety of profit and interest and their relationship to capital has been a matter of frequent controversy in the history of economic thought. Turgot brought some clarification to the matter by distinguishing between capital as money and capital as goods. Further clarification was provided by Smith, although even he failed to distinguish the notion of productive instruments from their ownership as private capital. This failure obscured the true nature of interest and profit as deriving from the difference in value between present and future commodities.

A borrower must pay interest to the lender who makes the funds available to acquire present goods. However, the principal form in which interest is received is entrepreneurial profit. Capitalists buy *remote goods* – such as raw materials, tools, machines, and the use of land and labor – and transform them into finished products ready for consumption. They receive a gain proportional to the amount of capital invested in their business. This gain, which has variously been called *profits, surplus value*, and *natural interest on capital*, is an addition to the compensation received for managerial services. It arises, according to Böhm-Bawerk, from the fact that the goods of remote rank that the business owner transforms are, from an economic point of view, future commodities. Profit is therefore a price agio appearing in exchange transactions between capitalists, on the one hand, and

workers and landlords who own the original means of production, on the other.

Differently expressed, profit is a discount from the money value of the future marginal product of the original means of production. It follows that, even in a socialist society, the value of labor effort is only equivalent to the discounted value of their product rather than the whole product, and the same is true of land. That is, both rent and wages are the monetary expression of the marginal products of a given quantity of labor and land discounted to the present. This would, in Böhm-Bawerk's view, be equally true in a socialist society, for labor and land can in any case receive only the present or discounted value of their future product.[17]

Wicksell's theory of capital and interest

Capital accumulation and the distributive shares

Wicksell's concern with the theory of capital and interest grew out of his study of Böhm-Bawerk's works. His critical examination and restatement of Böhm-Bawerk's theory is itself a contribution, particularly as it relates to his introduction of the concept of the *capital structure*. The capital structure reflects the 'height' and the 'width' of the land and labor inputs invested in real capital goods. The width of the capital structure is the number of land and labor input units invested, while its height reflects the length of time over which such inputs must remain invested before the maturation of their services in production. The economic value of this structure can be determined by multiplying the input units by the relevant rate of wages and rent, and then applying the rate of interest, properly compounded, over the average length of the investment period. Or, expressed in terms of Böhm-Bawerk's agio principle, the value of a capital structure is equal to the discounted value of the products that the invested inputs yield until they mature.

Wicksell's capital structure concept was intended to provide new insight into the effect of capital accumulation and invention on national income and the relationship between the distributive shares. He reasoned that, given a constant supply of labor and land, net investment initially expands the capital structure by extending its width. Subsequent expansion extends its height; that is, in more modern terminology, it is 'capital deepening' as opposed to 'capital widening.' Expansion of the capital structure always increases the national income by the marginal product of new investment. But it will affect the share going to capitalists differently from that going to workers and landowners. Capital widening (i.e. net investment that proportionately increases capitals regardless of their maturity) decreases the marginal productivity of capital so that the interest rate tends to fall while wages and rents tend to rise. This was essentially also the conclusion of the classical economists. Eventually, however, accumulation increases the height or intensity of capital as well as the width because the profitability of investments of longer maturity becomes relatively greater as wages and rents rise. This effect, Wicksell maintained, serves to retard their further increase and slows down the reduction of the relative share going to capital. It cannot, however, stop the increase in the

share going to land and labor or prevent the decline in the relative share going to capital.

Wicksell also examined the effect of technological change on the distributive shares. He reasoned that, even in the absence of net investment, technological improvements always increase national income if there is perfect competition, because they increase the average and marginal productivity of all factors, although not all are affected equally. Even though labor may experience hardship because of displacement by capital and a consequent fall in wages, it will find employment elsewhere. Thus, Wicksell was critical because Ricardo failed to recognize the possibility that, at the lower wage rates associated with unemployment, labor would tend to be substituted for capital.[18] It was on this basis that Wicksell concluded that invention does not, in and of itself, reduce labor's share of the national income because of its productivity-enhancing nature. Wicksell's conclusion about the potentially adverse effect of capital accumulation on labor is thus consistent with Ricardo's conclusion. But it is important to recognize that the *basis* for this conclusion is essentially different. Ricardo recognized that 'machinery and labor are in constant competition but that the former can frequently not be employed until labor rises.'[19] In other words, machinery usually cannot be employed until the wage share in the national product rises. Capital is thus perceived by Ricardo as being *complementary* to labor rather than as a potential substitute for it. It follows that, in Ricardo's analysis, the growth rates of labor and capital would tend to increase in tandem.

Wicksell, on the other hand, perceived of the possibility of substitution between labor and capital, although he concluded that invention does not in itself seriously reduce labor's share of the national income because of its productivity-enhancing nature.

Invention injures labor only if it serves to make long-term capital absolutely more profitable than before. Net investment will then result in the relative deepening of capital. When this occurs, a smaller quantity of capital will be used in current production, so that its marginal productivity will rise both relatively and absolutely. If the supply of land and labor is constant, this has the effect of reversing both the downward trend of the interest rate and the increase in rent and wages that normally results when there is net capital accumulation. Wicksell thus concluded that 'the capitalist saver is fundamentally the friend of labor, though the technical inventor is not infrequently its enemy.'[20]

The Wicksell effect

Wicksell's analysis of the effect of net accumulation led him to the conclusion that, in addition to technical invention, there is still another factor that tends to halt the downward trend of the interest rate. The classicists, it will be recalled, anticipated that the trend toward a zero rate of interest would accompany the tendency toward a stationary state. Wicksell argued that a zero rate of interest would not come about in an economy in which there is capital growth. Because Wicksell thought of capital in the Austrian sense, that is, as 'goods of a higher order,' these goods eventually 'mature out.' Their product is continually being absorbed, Wicksell argued, by rising wages and rents, so the supply of capital (i.e. goods of a higher order) never becomes large enough to reduce its marginal productivity to zero. This principle, which has come to be called the *Wicksell effect*, in effect challenged the classical notion of the stationary state.

The relationship between Böhm-Bawerk's conception of capital as an intermediate good and Wicksell's analysis of the tendency of a uniform rate of return as a condition of long-period equilibrium, is clear. Goods of a higher order eventually emerge as goods of a lower order, some are in a 'free form' and can thus be reincorporated as other higher-order goods or enjoyed as lower-order (i.e. consumer) goods. The nature and the direction of their flow are dependent on profit levels among different industries. There is a flow of capital (i.e. goods of higher order) from low-profit to high-profit industries, until the distribution of capital goods (i.e. the height and width in each industry) is compatible with long-period prices. In long-run equilibrium, these values are made consistent with a uniform rate of profit or return among industries.

Wicksell utilized the principle of the partial absorption of the product of capital by labor and land, in the form of rising wages and rents, as the basis for his argument that the marginal productivity principle applies in a different way to real capital than it does to labor and land. According to the marginal productivity principle, or *von Thünen's law*, as Wicksell called it, every factor will tend to receive the equivalent of its marginal social product.

The social marginal productivity rate of real capital is determined by dividing the increment of output by the increase in real capital. According to von Thünen's law, the rate of interest should tend to be equal to the social marginal productivity rate of return of real capital. But this is not the case, according to Wicksell, because part of the social marginal productivity of capital is absorbed by rising wages and rents. The quantity of capital actually created is smaller than it would have been if part of the net saving had not been absorbed in this manner. The rate of interest therefore tends to be equal, not to the marginal social product of capital, but to the somewhat smaller marginal product of the real capital actually created. Thus, Wicksell concluded, von Thünen's law cannot apply to real capital for the economy as a whole, but can only apply on a microeconomic level.

The reason why the application of von Thünen's law is qualified only in the case of capital and not in the case of labor and land is not hard to find. It is the result of the valuation process. Wicksell conceives of an index valuation of capital stock that is determined by its physical size multiplied by the rate of wages and rent relevant to the labor and land inputs that constitute it, discounted to the present. Thus, given a constant supply of labor and land, an increase in the index number expressing the stock of capital alters the rates of wages and rents and, thus, its own value.

The indirect mechanism of price change

Wicksell's greatest contribution was his pioneering effort to integrate monetary analysis with real analysis. Monetary analysis, in Wicksell's day, was largely concerned with the behavior of the general price level. It proceeded on the implicit assumption that changes in the purchasing power of money are unrelated to real phenomena such as the level of output and employment. Changes in the price level and the value of money were attributed only to changes in the *quantity of money* and its *velocity*. The level of output was thought to depend on the supply of resources and the state of the arts that determined the efficiency of their use at full employment. Acceptance of Say's Law led to the conclusion that resources, including labor, would always tend to be fully employed.

Wicksell contended that monetary phenomena and real phenomena are interrelated in that changes in the general price level take place not directly, as implied by the quantity theories of money, but *indirectly* as a result of changes in the interest rate. He argued that any theory of money worthy of the name must show the interrelationship between changes in the quantity of money, the interest rate, and the price level.[21] To demonstrate these interrelationships, he conceived of a natural rate of interest and a market rate of interest. The natural rate of interest is the rate at which the demand for loan capital, which reflects the demand for capital for investment purposes, is equal to the supply of savings. It is also the rate that corresponds to the yield on newly created capital. The market rate of interest is the money rate charged by banks. Unlike the natural rate, its level can be observed. Whether its level coincides with the natural rate or diverges from it can, Wicksell believed, be inferred from the behavior of the price level.

If, for example, there is an increase in the demand schedule for funds, reflecting perhaps innovation and an improvement in the marginal productivity of capital, it will cause the natural rate of interest to rise. The market rate of interest will not, however, rise as long as banks have excess reserves. The rise in the natural or real rate above the money rate 'will provide a stimulus to trade and production and alter the relation between supply and demand for goods and productive services.'[22] The total demand for goods increases as a result of an increase in investment demand. Its source is the expansion of bank credit, which enables business owners receiving credits to bid factors away from the consumer goods industries. The consequent rise in factor prices increases factor income at a time when fewer consumer goods are available because factors have been diverted to the capital goods industries. In turn, rising consumer goods prices deprive consumers of increased real consumption out of higher incomes; they create a situation of 'forced saving,' which may moderate the price rise. In a pure credit system, the expansion made possible by the divergence of the natural rate and the money rate of interest becomes cumulative and is self-perpetuating. The rise in prices will continue indefinitely unless a shortage of reserves forces the bank rate up to the market rate. This will eventually happen under gold standard conditions because the loss of specie by external drain as well as internal drain into currency circulation will ultimately bring about a shortage of reserves. Such shortages will cause banks to raise the market rate. Their action will bring the expansion to a halt.[23] Needless to say, such an expansion could never have started in a banking system requiring 100 percent reserves.

Wicksell's analysis also demonstrated how a reduction of the natural rate below the market rate would produce a cumulative contraction. The demand for investment funds is diminished in this situation. Falling factor prices and incomes are accompanied by reduced employment and production. The contraction is cumulative because the deficiency of demand associated with falling factor incomes offsets the stimulus arising from falling money costs. Demand will remain insufficient until either investment demand or consumption increases, and this cannot take place as long as the banks absorb funds. This requires either that the market rate of interest is reduced to the natural rate or that the natural rate rises until it is above the market rate. The implication of Wicksell's analysis is, therefore, that if the monetary authority will act to *prevent divergences* between the natural rate of interest and the market rate, it can prevent cumulative expansion and contraction and achieve a stable price level. The existence of a stable price level is indicative of, and consistent with, a monetary equilibrium in which money is 'neutral.'

Concluding remarks

Second-generation marginalists – Edgeworth, Wicksteed, Clark, Wicksell, and the Austrians – focused their chief attention on explaining the phenomenon of income distribution. For Edgeworth and Wicksteed, an inquiry into the nature of the production process was an important first step toward distribution theory. For Wicksell, as for Böhm-Bawerk – who, along with Wieser, carried forward Menger's tradition – the nature of capital and its return was of particular interest.

The era of the second generation – the late nineteenth and early twentieth centuries – was characterized by increasing reliance on mathematics. Edgeworth's work, in particular, anticipated the mathematical style that has come to characterize the discipline in the present century.

The theory of capital and interest also came into its own as a result of second-generation thinkers – Böhm-Bawerk in particular. As has already been noted, there was little written about production and its relation to capital before the middle of the eighteenth century. The Physiocrats developed a view of production that recognized the role of capital as advances, although without using the term *capital*. Physiocratic usage thus began to distinguish between capital as goods and capital as money. Their view, and that of Smith – that production requires advances for the maintenance of labor (i.e. the wage fund) – focused on circulating, rather than durable, capital. This view later paved the way for Ricardo's machinery question and its notion of capital goods as stored up labor, which was a prelude to Marx's perception that increases in the proportion of fixed to variable capital are the chief modality under capitalism for increasing surplus value and, thus, for the exploitation of labor. Senior's view, that capitalists earned profit to reward them for their 'abstinence,' was thus a chief target of Marx's contempt. Therefore, Böhm-Bawerk's explicit attempt to link profit and interest to the process of production in a new way was an important departure. Unlike the classical view that capital goods have value because they represent past land and labor services, the Austrians emphasized the role of capital in the production of future goods, commanded by present as compared with future goods. Accordingly, the length of the production process is chosen to achieve maximum profit, and both profit and interest are thus viewed as an agio; that is, the money equivalent of the premium commanded over future goods.

Although Böhm-Bawerk's theory of capital is consistent with the classical view of production as requiring time and advances in the form of goods of a higher order, the Austrian emphasis on the technical superiority of presently available goods as providing a separate reason for a positive rate became an issue of controversy. Irving Fisher, in particular, argued that a positive rate of interest could not arise from this reason alone. Fisher's argument was that the greater productivity of roundabout methods of production explains only the *willingness* of borrowers to pay a premium. However, the *necessity of paying* a premium derives from Böhm-Bawerk's first two reasons, which explain why people discount the future. Thus, Fisher's conception of interest is that it is an index of the community's preference for a dollar of present over a dollar of future income.

Fisher's theory of interest was first advanced in *The Rate of Interest* (1907)

which, when revised in 1930 as *The Theory of Interest*, was received as 'the peak achievement, so far as perfection within its own frame is concerned, of the literature of interest.'[24] Fisher suggested that the nature of interest and its determination can best be understood if interest is conceived in relation to *income* rather than capital because 'capital wealth is merely the means to the end called income, while capital value is merely the capitalization of expected income.'[25] He therefore objected to that part of Böhm-Bawerk's explanation of interest that relates to the technical superiority of present goods. He objected to the concept of the production period and also to the thesis that the longer the period of production, the larger the final product will be. But he considered Böhm-Bawerk's fatal error to be the notion that the greater productivity of lengthier processes over shorter ones, which makes present goods technically superior to future goods, is an independent cause of interest.[26]

Fisher did not deny the technical superiority of present goods in Böhm-Bawerk's sense of the term, but maintained that this is not an independent cause of interest but one that operates through its effect on wants and the provision for them in the present and in the future. The fact that capital is productive will not, in and of itself, cause people to prefer income today in preference to income tomorrow. However, the productivity of capital will affect the relative abundance of present and future goods, and therefore the willingness of people to pay a premium for income available today instead of in the future. Thus, Fisher sees the interest rate as being determined by the actions of people to alter the time flow of their income receipts. There is any number of possible combinations of real present and future income with which the individual might be equally well satisfied. Whether an individual will alter the time flow of his other income depends on his or her degree of impatience, investment opportunities, and the interest rate to which he or she must adjust. Individuals will optimize the stream of present and future income by (1) saving and lending an amount of present income to acquire a claim on additional income and/or (2) investing an amount of present income that will yield an expected rate of return equal to the rate of interest. These activities adjust this year's income until its present value is equal to the interest rate. Fisher's approach thus shifted thinking away from the 'advances' view of capital. Thus, capital has come to be viewed as a homogeneous mass of wealth, created by savings decisions and measured in money that can be invested in any industry. This is essentially the concept of capital that has found its way into the contemporary textbook tradition.[27]

Notes

1 Interest and Prices (1898) was translated into English in 1936. *Lectures on Political Economy* (1901 and 1906) were translated in 1934–35.

2 Francis Edgeworth, *Collected Papers Relating to Political Economy*, vol. 1 (London: Macmillan, 1925), p. 68.

3 Even Alfred Marshall was among those who confused the two concepts. See Chapter 14.

4 Philip Wicksteed, *The Commonsense of Political Economy*, edited by Lionel Robbins (London: George Routledge, 1935), p. 529.

5 Philip Wicksteed, *An Essay on the Co-ordination of the Laws of Distribution* (London: Macmillan, 1894).

6 John Bates Clark, *The Distribution of Wealth* (London and New York: Macmillan, 1899), Preface.

7 Wicksteed's generalization of Ricardo's theorem appears in *An Essay on the Co-ordination of the Laws of Distribution*. Clark's first exposition is in 'Possibility of a scientific law of wages,' in *Publications of the American Economic Association*, 4, no. 1 (1889); also 'Distri-

bution as determined by the law of rent,' *Quarterly Journal of Economics*, 5 (October 1890–July 1891), pp. 289–318.

8 *Economic Journal*, 4 (June, 1894), p. 305.

9 Clark, *The Distribution of Wealth*, Preface, p. v.

10 Clark, *The Distribution of Wealth*, p. 3.

11 Clark, *The Distribution of Wealth*, p. 77.

12 Frank Knight, *Risk, Uncertainty and Profit* (Boston: Houghton Mifflin, 1921).

13 Clark, *The Distribution of Wealth*, p. 230.

14 Knut Wicksell, *Lectures on Political Economy* (New York: Macmillan, 1934), vol. 1, pp. 126–31.

15 See Chapter 16 on monopolistic exploitation.

16 The issue of whether the third reason, which Böhm-Bawerk advanced as a basis for a positive rate of interest, is really independent of the other two has given rise to a considerable body of literature. Böhm-Bawerk himself regarded the technical superiority of presently available goods as a separate reason; see Eugen Böhm-Bawerk, *Positive Theory of Capital* (1889; translated by William Smart, London), pp. 960–75. Others, Fisher in particular, argued that a positive rate of interest could not arise from this reason alone. Fisher's argument was that the greater productivity of roundabout methods of production explains only the *willingness* of borrowers to pay a premium. But the *necessity of paying* a premium derives from the first two reasons, which explain why people discount the future; see Irving Fisher, *The Theory of Interest* (New York: Macmillan, 1930), pp. 476–85.

17 The American theorist Frank Taussig combined the marginal productivity theory of factor rewards with Böhm-Bawerk's theory of time preference to develop the hypothesis that competitive wages tend to be equal to the discounted value of labor's marginal product because wages represent an advance made by employers against the finished product. See his *Wages and Capital* (New York: Appleton-Century-Crofts, 1898).

18 Knut Wicksell, *Lectures on Political Economy* (1901; reprint New York: Macmillan, 1934).

19 Sraffa (ed.), *Works and Correspondence of David Ricardo*, vol. 1, p. 388.

20 Wicksell, *Lectures on Political Economy*, vol. 1, p. 164.

21 Wicksell, *Lectures on Political Economy*, (1935), vol. 2, p. 160.

22 Knut Wicksell, *Interest and Prices* (1899), translated by Richard F. Kahn (London, 1936; reprinted New York: A. M. Kelley, 1965), p. 89.

23 Wicksell, *Lectures*, vol. 2, pp. 200–01.

24 Joseph A. Schumpeter, *Ten Great Economists*, (London: Oxford University Press, 1965), p. 230.

25 Irving Fisher, *The Nature of Capital and Income* (New York: Macmillan, 1906), p. 61.

26 Irving Fisher, *The Rate of Interest* (New York: Macmillan, 1907), p. 55.

27 Paul A. Samuelson, *Economics: An Introductory Analysis* (New York: McGraw Hill, 1948 and subsequent editions).

Questions for discussion and further research

1 How did Clark generalize Ricardo's theory of rent?

2 What is the adding-up problem? What is its significance for distribution theory?

3 What is the marginal productivity theory of distribution? Does J. B. Clark come close to committing to it? What limitations need to be recognized before this theory can be given real-world application?

4 What is Wicksell's hypothesis for explaining changes in the general price level? How does it compare with Fisher's quantity theory hypothesis?

5 How did Böhm-Bawerk use Menger's imputation theory to explain the capitalist's receipt of profit and interest?

6 In the view of Joseph Schumpeter, the essential rebuttal to Marx was delivered by Böhm-Bawerk. How, in the context of the Austrian theory of imputation, did Böhm-Bawerk develop his theory of the agio to negate Marx's interpretation of the relationship between surplus value and exploitation?

Glossary of terms and concepts

Adding-up problem

The question of whether the total product is equal to the sum of the marginal products. If it is, then each factor can be paid the equivalent of its marginal product and the sum of their shares will exactly exhaust the total product.

Agio

The premium commanded by present goods over future goods.

Deepening of capital

The process in which the structure of capital is altered in such a manner that investment in capital of longer maturity is increased.

Euler's theorem

A mathematical theorem concerning the properties of linearly homogeneous equations. An equation is linearly homogeneous if a change in any of the variables on one side of the equation proportionately changes the other side. Applied to a production function, this means that a given increase in all factor outputs will increase the total product in precisely the same proportion.

Fisher's concept of capital

Any asset that yields a stream of income over time. Thus, assets that yield rent (i.e. land), as opposed to interest, are merely different forms of capital. Contemporary theorists (e.g. Gary Becker and T. W. Schultz) have extended Fisher's concept also to include human capital.

Generalization of Ricardian rent

The principle that the returns of any factor that exists in fixed supply (not just labor) may be viewed as rent.

Imputation

The process of valuing factors of production (goods of a higher order, in Austrian terminology) on the basis of their contributions to the value of production.

Indirect mechanism of price change

Wicksell's hypothesis that the general price level does not change directly, as implied by the quantity theories of money, but indirectly as a result of changes brought about by divergences between the natural and money rates of interest.

Inferior goods

Goods of a kind purchased less often as income increases.

Marginal productivity theory of distribution

The theory that, in the long run, under competition, all factors would tend to receive a real rate of return equal to the value of their marginal physical products.

Opportunity cost

The price a factor of production can command in its best paying alternative use.

Production function

A mathematical expression concerning the relationship between the output. O, of good a and the factors required to produce it. For example $O_a = f(x,y,z)$.

Returns to scale

An expression describing the behavior of the production function in the long run when all inputs are variable. If an increase in inputs, say, x,y,z increases the output of a proportionately, the returns to scale are said to be *constant*. This means the production function has the property of linear homogeneity. If returns increase proportionately more than inputs, returns to scale are *increasing*. Conversely, if output increases proportionately less, returns are *decreasing*.

Notes for further reading

The New Palgrave Dictionary offers the most accessible contemporary survey and evaluation of the topics and contributors included in this chapter. The most readable among these are the following: K. H. Henning on capital as a factor of production, vol. 1, pp. 327–33; on Eugen von Böhm-Bawerk, vol. 1, pp. 254–59; Donald Dewey on John Bates Clark, vol. 1, pp. 428–31; Peter Newman on Francis Ysidro Edgeworth. vol. 2, pp. 84–98; and Carl G. Uhr on Johan Gustav Knut Wicksell, vol. 4, pp. 901–8; Massimo Pivetti on Wicksell's theory of capital, vol. 4, pp. 912–15; Ian Steedman on Philip Henry Wicksteed, vol. 4, pp. 915–19; E. Streissler on Friedrich Freiherr von Wieser, vol. 4, pp. 921–22; and Israel M. Kirzner on the Austrian School of Economics, vol. 1, pp. 145–51.

Selected references and suggestions for further reading

Böhm-Bawerk, Eugen. 'The Positive Theory of Capital.' In *Capital and Interest*, vol. 11. Translated by George D. Huncke (South Holland, Ill.: Libertarian Press, 1959 [1889]).

John Bates Clark. *The Distribution of Wealth* (London and New York: Macmillan, 1899), Preface. 'Distribution as determined by the law of rent.' *Quarterly Journal of Economics* (October 1890–July 1891), pp. 289–318.

Douglas, Paul. *Theory of Wages* (New York: Macmillan, 1934), chapters 1 and 2.

Edgeworth, E. Y. *Mathematical Psychics: An Essay on the Application of Mathematics to the Moral Sciences* (London: Kegan Paul, 1881). *Collected Papers Relating to Political Economy*, Vol. 1. (London: Macmillan, 1925).

Fisher, Irving. *The Nature of Capital and Income* (New York: Macmillan, 1906).

Fisher, Irving. *The Rate of Interest* (New York: Macmillan, 1930).

Fisher, Irving. *The Theory of Interest* (New York: Macmillan, 1930).

Knight, Frank. *Risk, Uncertainty and Profit* (Boston: Houghton Mifflin, 1921).

Pareto, Vilfredo. *Manual of Political Economy*. Translated by Ann S. Schwier, and edited by Ann S. Schwier and Alfred Page (New York: A. M. Kelley, 1971 [1906]).

Robbins, Lionel. Lecture 29, 'The Marginal Revolution (III): Costs (Wieser) – The Pricing of Factor Services (Wieser, Clark, Wicksteed)'; Lecture 30, 'Capital Theory: Böhm-Bawerk and Fisher'. In *A History of Economic Thought* edited by S. Medema and W. Samuels (Princeton, NJ: Princeton University Press, 1998), pp. 277–294.

Robinson, Joan. 'Euler's theorem and the problem of distribution.' Reprinted in *Collected Economic Papers*, vol. 1 (London: Basil Blackwell & Mott, 1951).

Stigler, Stephen, M. 'Francis Ysidro Edgeworth, statistician.' *Journal of the Royal Statistical Society*, series A. vol. 141 (1978) pp. 287–322.

Stigler, Stephen, M. *Production and Distribution Theories* (New York: Macmillan, 1941), chapters 1–7, 12.

Taussig, Frank. *Wages and Capital* (New York: Appleton-Century-Crofts, 1898).

Wicksell, Knut. *Lectures on Political Economy*. 2 vols. Edited by L. Robbins (London: Routledge & Kegan Paul, 1935).

Wicksell, Knut. *Interest and Prices*. Translated by R. E. Kahn (London: Macmillan, 1936).

Wicksteed, Philip. *The Commonsense of Political Economy*. Edited by Lionel Robbins. (London: George Routledge, 1935).

Wicksell, Knut. *An Essay on the Co-ordination of the Laws of Distribution* (London: Macmillan, 1894).

Wieser, Friedrich. *Natural Value*. Translated by A. Malloch and edited by William Smart (New York: Kelley and Millman, 1956 [1889]).

Wieser, Friedrich. *Social Economics*. Translated by A. Ford Hinrichs (New York: A. M. Kelley, 1967 [1914]).

Uhr, Carl G. *Economic Doctrines of Knut Wicksell* (Berkeley: University of California Press, 1962).

Part IV

The Neoclassical Tradition, 1890–1945

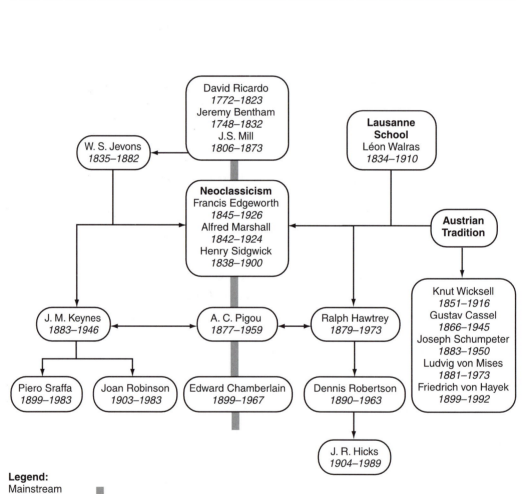

David Ricardo
1772–1823
Jeremy Bentham
1748–1832
J.S. Mill
1806–1873

W. S. Jevons
1835–1882

Lausanne School
Léon Walras
1834–1910

Neoclassicism
Francis Edgeworth
1845–1926
Alfred Marshall
1842–1924
Henry Sidgwick
1838–1900

Austrian Tradition

J. M. Keynes
1883–1946

A. C. Pigou
1877–1959

Ralph Hawtrey
1879–1973

Knut Wicksell
1851–1916
Gustav Cassel
1866–1945
Joseph Schumpeter
1883–1950
Ludvig von Mises
1881–1973
Friedrich von Hayek
1899–1992

Piero Sraffa
1899–1983

Joan Robinson
1903–1983

Edward Chamberlain
1899–1967

Dennis Robertson
1890–1963

J. R. Hicks
1904–1989

Legend:
Mainstream
Direct influence

Key dates

1890	Alfred Marshall	Principles of Economics
1891	John Neville Keynes	The Scope and Method of Political Economy
1913	Ralph Hawtrey	Good Trade and Band Trade
1919	Alfred Marshall	Industry and Trade
1920	Arthur C. Pigou	Wealth and Welfare
1921	Frank Knight	Risk, Uncertainty, and Profit
1923	Alfred Marshall	Money, Credit, and Commerce
1926	Piero Sraffa	The Laws of Return under Competitive Conditions
1932	Gustav Cassel	Theory of Social Economy
1933	Edward Chamberlin	The Theory of Monopolistic Competition
1933	Joan Robinson	The Economics of Imperfect Competition
1934	Joseph Schumpeter	The Theory of Economic Development
1939	John R. Hicks	Value and Capital
1939	F. A. Hayek	Profits, Interest, and Investment
1939	Bertil Ohlin	Studies in the Theory of Money and Capital
1939	Gunner Myrdal	Monetary Equilibrium

An overview of neoclassicism

When Alfred Marshall published his *Principles of Economics* in 1890, with the intention of completing and generalizing Mill's exposition of Ricardo's theory of value and distribution, he, in fact, provided a fully integrated theory of commodity and factor pricing. This body of principles is thought of as *neoclassical* in the sense that it incorporates the new insights of the marginal utility theorists, while also retaining the classical emphasis on the relevance of cost of production in the determination of value in exchange. Economics is still conceived as a moral science with a concern for deriving economic laws as a basis for mounting social policy, but hedonic calculation and interpersonal comparisons of utility became recognized as impractical. As a result, nineteenth-century British economists disassociated themselves from the notion that utility is measurable, and that Edgeworth's 'hedonometer' could become a means to evaluate social utility. Marshall preferred deductive logic (as did Ricardo, Senior, J. S. Mill and Cairnes) to statistical methods for discerning cause–effect relationships and, except for his development of the technique of a chain index to calculate changes in the general price level, relied on deductive representation rather than logic as a basis for inductive methods of statistics and the graphic plots generated from time series data.

The analytical tradition of neoclassicism after Alfred Marshall's *Principles*, and the *laissez-faire* policy conclusions that most interpreters inferred from it, dominated economic thought for at least the first three decades of the twentieth century. It was continued by several able theorists who undertook to extend the oral and written tradition inherited from Marshall. Marshall's work was continued by Arthur Cecil Pigou (1877–1959), who was among Marshall's most brilliant students and his successor at Cambridge. Much of Pigou's work places him firmly in the mainstream of neoclassicism. His inquiry into the conditions required for maximizing welfare and his argument concerning the need for special concern about social costs and benefits generated a heated controversy with Frank H. Knight (1885–1972), of the University of Chicago, who founded a more conservative tradition than Marshall's.

An important extension of Marshall's work was accomplished by Professor John R. Hicks (1904–89). Hicks's objective was to identify the conditions under which the divergent interests of consumers seeking to maximize their satisfaction can be reconciled with those of profit-maximizing producers by the operation of the competitive price mechanism. His work is a major contribution to the theory of consumer choice and is the basis for a theoretical development known as the *new welfare theory*.

The development of the new welfare economics a decade after Marshall's death in 1924 reflects Hicks's concern with social objectives within the framework of a value free analytical model. William Nassau Senior had already urged that the proper scope of economics is to concern itself with what is, not what ought to be.

This view was echoed by Marshall's contemporary, John Neville Keynes (John Maynard's father) in *The Scope and Method of Political Economy* (1891). It also became the uncompromising position of Lionel Robbins in his *Essay on the Nature and Significance of Economic Science* (1932). Robbins maintained that propositions with ethical content are not appropriate to positive economics. The designation of economics as a science requires that it limit itself to two types of generalizations: tautologies, or generalizations derived by logical deduction from one or more premises, and therefore acceptable *a priori* (i.e. without proof), and generalizations that are empirically verifiable. This was consistent with the objective of a philosophical movement known as *logical positivism*, which maintains that the ideal of all science is to be neutral among alternative ends.

Neville Keynes's description of political economy as 'standing neutral between competing social sciences'[1] is assuredly implicit in Marshall's effort to construct what he called his *engine of analysis*. This body of *positive* economics is a system of abstract analysis based on logical inference from simple postulates. Unlike Léon Walras's, his general equilibrium analysis, Marshall's partial equilibrium analysis undertook to explain price determination under the convenient assumption of perfect competition. This assumption implies that the individual firm can sell as much as it chooses without having an impact on market price. It also implies that there is freedom for new firms to enter if they are attracted by the profits that can be earned, with the result that long-run competitive prices tend to be equal to long-run average costs of production, and profits are no higher than what is normal. There is also a tendency for all resources to become optimally allocated (i.e. each resource will tend to earn an equal rate of return in all its uses) and yield the maximum possible output. Thus, Marshall's assumption of perfect competition, in fact, had considerable *normative bias*, even though its analysis was intended to be value free. But it was possible for Hicks and other proponents of the new welfare analysis to maintain that their approach (which introduced indifference curves as an analytical tool to avoid Marshall's notion of consumer surplus) also avoided the possibility of reading normative implications into the analyses.

While Marshall's analysis assumed purely competitive markets as the norm (and their opposite, pure monopoly, as an exception), he was not unaware of the possibility that the prices and outputs of individual firms that produced similar commodities might be *interdependent* rather than independent, as is required by the assumption of pure competition. But he did not examine the case of markets exhibiting a *mixture* of competitive and monopolistic characteristics. Thus, when the theories of imperfect and monopolistic competition were developed during the 1930s, they were, essentially, refinements of Marshall's work. Marshall lavished almost all of his concern on firms that produced their products under conditions of free competition, even though he noted, in his *Industry and Trade*, that competition and monopoly are 'interlaced.' Nowhere, however, did he examine the nature of this interlacing or its significance for price determination. Not until the 1920s and early 1930s did there emerge a growing concern with the gaps in Marshall's work, particularly with respect to pricing situations that were intermediate between competition and monopoly.

While the initial breakthrough for this work was made by Piero Sraffa (1899–1983), the two definitive works of this period are *The Theory of Imperfect Competition* (1933), by Joan Robinson, and *The Theory of Monopolistic Competition*, by Edward H. Chamberlin (1933). Both writers examined the optimizing problem from the standpoint of the individual firm, with special reference to markets that are neither purely competitive nor purely monopolistic. Although their analyses differed in important ways from Marshall's theory of price determination, their price theories are essentially Marshallian. Their emphasis on the imperfectly competitive character of typical market situations is a departure from orthodox theory that was readily accommodated by neoclassical theorists simply by extending their conception of market types to include the gray area of markets that are neither purely competitive nor purely monopolistic.

Late in his career, Marshall established the oral tradition of monetary theory, which had the long-term effect of changing the focus of the quantity theory of money, which dated back to the pre-Ricardian era in which attention had always been on 'quantity doctrines.' Marshall was to go beyond the naive quantity theory, focusing not only on the rapidity with which money circulates but, more important, on the importance of money as a 'store of value' that generates a demand for cash balances.

Traditional monetary theory conceived of money as neutral in the sense that changes in monetary variables were thought to affect only the value of money itself (i.e. the price level) but not the level of output or employment. However, a different perspective was adopted by those who studied the work of Knut Wicksell. As has already been noted, Wicksell's analysis is a major innovation in several respects. First, it demonstrates that the price level changes, not directly, as is implied by the quantity theory of money, but indirectly as a result of changes in the rate of interest. Second, by relating changes in investment to changes in the interest rate, and therefore factor and commodity prices, it provides an explanation of the process of income determination. Wicksell's analysis became the foundation for various monetary theories of the business cycle.

The implication of Wicksell's analysis is, therefore, that if the monetary authority will act to prevent divergences between the nat-ural rate of interest and the market rate, it can prevent cumulative expansion and contraction and achieve a stable price level. This type of theorizing and its associated policy view became associated with several of Marshall's followers, among them Arthur Pigou and Ralph Hawtrey. Their analyses reflected a belief that the economy has an internal self-adjusting mechanism that is capable, after a period of depression, of restoring a full-employment equilibrium.

The influence of Wicksell's monetary theory is also evident in the work of Joseph A. Schumpeter (1883–1950); who also went beyond the problem of economic fluctuation to the larger question of economic growth and development. Schumpeter's hypothesis, which linked economic development in a capitalistic economy to entrepreneurship and innovation, reflects a concern with the kinds of secular changes that so greatly interested the classical school. Since World War II, there has been a resurgence of interest in growth theory. But modern growth theory (i.e. growth theory in the post-World War II period) assumes that population growth and the state of the art, which were the concerns of the classicists and Schumpeter, are exogenously determined data outside the mechanism of the model. With respect to theorizing about economic fluctuation and growth, the close of World War II (1945) thus marks the end of an intellectual era.

Refinement of the microeconomic aspects of Marshall's work were also substantially complete by that time. The second edition of John R. Hicks's persuasive *Value and Capital* was published in 1946. Chamberlin's *The Theory of Monopolistic Competition*, which first appeared in 1933, the same year as Robinson's *Theory of Imperfect Competition*, added only one new feature in the 1948 revision, specifically, the application of the theory of monopolistic competition to the determination of factor shares. Thus, the neoclassical paradigm (that is, the body of thought the profession uses as the basis for its own research and that it passes on to the next generation in the textbooks it writes) was full-blown by the end of World War II, which is thus an appropriate closing date for the inquiry of this Part.

Note

1 J. N. Keynes, *Scope and Method of Political Economy* (London: Macmillan, 1891), p. 95.

Chapter 14

Alfred Marshall and the neoclassical tradition

•••

Introduction

Life and times (1842–1924)

Alfred Marshall described his *Principles of Economics* (1890) as 'an attempt to present a modern version of old doctrines with the aid of new work, and with reference to the new problems of our age.' This description was, in many ways, an unfortunate introduction to that great work, which became the fountainhead for the tradition of *Neoclassicism*. It was unfortunate because it obscured the time sequence of his own intellectual development. His work on the theory of value and distribution was practically completed in the years 1867–70, when he translated Mill's version of Ricardo's doctrines into mathematics. In a letter written to J. B. Clark in 1908 Marshall noted: 'Between 1870 and 1874 I developed the details of my theoretical position and I am not conscious of any perceptible change since the time Böhm-Bawerk and Wieser were still lads at school.'[1] But the long delay before the publication of the *Principles* virtually denied Marshall's claim to priority in the discovery of many economic truths associated with him.[2] It was also unfortunate for a second reason: it reflected Marshall's dissatisfaction with a book that was already the product of 20 years' labor. He spent much of the next

30 years making relatively minor changes and refinements in a work that went through eight editions during his lifetime, but which was essentially the same work he had laid out mentally no later than the 1870s and, certainly, no later than the publication of Jevons's work.

Marshall had originally planned to become a minister in the Church of England. But his wide range of intellectual interests, which included mathematics, history, Utilitarian and Hegelian philosophy, and social Darwinism, led him to the study of John Stuart Mill's work on political economy. He was particularly concerned about the problem of poverty and was attracted into economics by the prospect of addressing problems of human improvement. These he approached with a Utilitarian spirit inherited from Mill and an analytical approach firmly anchored in Ricardianism.

Marshall came into economics at a time when the influence of the classical tradition was on the wane. The twist that Marx gave to Ricardian doctrines, coupled with the attack of the German historical school and the challenge of Jevons's marginal utility economics, contributed to its eclipse. While Marshall believed in the essential validity of Ricardo's principles, he maintained that utility must be accorded a greater role in the determination of value and that the evolutionary approach derived from Darwin's thesis could be utilized to revitalize Ricardian economics. He thus founded a new tradition, later known as *Neo-classicism*, which became the source from which much of modern economic thought and analysis springs. Even those who later reacted against the tradition he founded, employ concepts and analytical tools that are Marshallian in origin.

His greatest theoretical work, and the source of most of this chapter, is his *Principles of Economics*, published in 1890. The success of this treatise was so great that it almost totally eclipsed works of lesser stature for many decades after. In England, as well as the United States, the study of economics became, perforce, the study of Marshall's *Principles*. It is generally agreed that it was unfortunate that he devoted so much time to its original formulation that publication was delayed until 1890, and that he labored over seven revisions, none of them substantive, instead of turning his attention to other work. His other publications are *Industry and Trade* (1919), which is a historical study of the development of industry, and has little analysis; *Money, Credit and Commerce* (1923); and a brief book he co-authored before the *Principles* with his wife, Mary Paley Marshall, in addition to numerous occasional papers and lectures.[3]

Principles of economics

Objectives

Marshall begins the *Principles of Economics* with the observation that 'political economy or economics is the study of mankind in the ordinary business of life; it examines that part of individual and social action which is most closely connected with the attainment and use of the material requisites of well-being.'[4] Unlike Nassau Senior, therefore, he intends to study economics as a science of human behavior rather than as a science of wealth.

He is concerned, above all, that his analysis be scientific; that is, that it bring to light such regularities or patterns of orderliness as are inherent in economic phenomena. These regularities can then be expressed as generalizations or laws that describe the economic forces that have been examined. The primary aim of the *Principles* is, therefore, to study the economic aspects of human behavior in order to derive the laws governing the functioning of the economic system.

Although the primary aim of the *Principles* is the analysis of the functioning of the economic system, Marshall believed that the system he was analyzing reflected the progress of Western civilization, not only in terms of material achievement, but also in the improvement of human character. In his eyes, the present system is the product of a gradual but progressive extension of individual independence, freedom, and competitiveness. Although fully aware that competition can have negative results both from a social and from an individual standpoint, Marshall regarded the rivalry of men against one another as having a wholesome effect on individual character and behavior, in addition to providing economic gain. He believed that individuals become more rational in their goals and decision making, more sportsman-like and socially conscious of their behavior as they gain freedom, so that in seeking their own success, they also promote the common good. The study of economics can contribute to this progress because the laws it discovers reveal more than knowledge for its own sake; they also contribute to the solution of social problems. Humanitarian motives thus pervade all Marshall's inquiries. He is interested not only in what is, but equally in what ought to be. His pure analysis of the economy's functioning is therefore frequently interspersed with what Schumpeter has called Marshall's *Victorian moralizing.*

Methodology

Marshall recognizes that the complexity of the economic system he is studying is so great and the motives of human behavior so diverse that it is necessary to devise techniques for their systematic study. This requires reducing the number of variables to manageable proportions and finding a method to measure them. In common with the Utilitarians and Jevons, he was concerned with the problem of measuring the motives for human behaviour, especially those that relate to 'man's conduct in the business part of his life.' He inferred that the effects of these (though not the motives themselves) 'can be approximately measured by a sum of money which we will just give up to secure a desired satisfaction . . .'[5].

Marshall introduces the method of abstraction to single out one variable or sector of the economy at a time, on the assumption that its behavior is incapable of exerting any appreciable influence on the rest of the economy. This does not necessarily imply that the rest of the economy remains unchanged, but rather that if the small sector being analyzed is subjected to an external change, it adjusts itself without producing more than a negligible effect on the rest of the economy. This is Marshall's principle of the *negligibility of indirect effects.* By invoking this principle, all of the effects and counter-effects taking place in the real world between a sector and the rest of the economy are impounded by the assumption *ceteris paribus*; that is, 'other things remaining equal.'

Marshall's famous Book 5 of the *Principles* has become the classic example of the use of the technique of abstraction to investigate the interaction of demand and supply forces to explain the emergence of an equilibrium price. His premise is that the individual industry is so small relative to the rest of the economy that he can draw up industry demand and supply curves that are completely *independent* of one another. It is assumed that indirect effects are so negligible that changes in the quantity of output produced by the industry do not have a sufficient impact on the incomes earned in that industry to shift even the demand curve for its product, much less the aggregate demand for output as a whole.

The assumption of an industry that is a minuscule part of the whole implies that the market is 'perfect'; the industry supply curve is composed of the *outputs* of a large number of small firms. These outputs are perfectly homogeneous, or identical, from the point of view of the buyers, so the industry faces a definite market demand curve that, when set against the supply curve, will result in a single, competitive market price for all buyers. The use of the term *competition* in connection with Marshall's *Principles* can be confusing to modern students of economics who are already familiar with the more precise terms of *pure competition* and *perfect competition.* He himself thought that the term *competition* is not well suited to describe the special characteristics of industrial life in the modern age.[6] He suggested *freedom of industry and enterprise* or, more briefly, *economic freedom,* because these terms have no moral implication. It would be convenient if Marshall had been precise about the assumptions on which he constructed his analytical model of the industry. But his assumptions are nowhere precisely set forth; on the contrary, he avoided their specification, believing that each real problem investigated would require modifications in the model. Marshall's followers, rather than Marshall himself, have supplied us with such rigorous concepts as pure and perfect competition.

The concept of pure competition, as it is used in modern economics, is rather precise with respect to both the demand side and the supply side of the market. It requires, on the demand side, that the commodity be one that absorbs only a small portion of the consumer's income and on which total expenditures constitute only a small part of the nation's income. It requires, on the supply side, a sufficiently large number of small selling units offering a homogeneous product, so that only one selling price can emerge as a result of the interaction of demand and supply forces. The concept of perfect competition is even more rigorous, requiring, in addition, perfect knowledge on the part of market participants and perfect mobility of buyers and resources. It represents an ideal set of circumstances that, if they existed, would facilitate the perfect functioning of the economy. The precise results that would be obtained under these conditions were subsequently to be detailed by the modern welfare school.[7]

Marshall's concept of economic freedom was considerably less refined than these more modern concepts. However, he conceived of an economy functioning within the framework of enough of the elements of what is conceived as pure competition to make the typical firm an insignificant part of the whole industry. Each individual firm produces such a small portion of the total market output that output variations cannot affect either the total supply of the product or the price that emerges.

The passage of time complicates the explanation of prices because the strength and the relative importance of the forces operating both on the side of demand and on the side of supply may change. Marshall's appreciation of the impact of change was too keen to ignore these possibilities by reasoning from unchanging static assumptions. On the other hand, his commitment was to uncover *regularities*, that is, to explain the *normal* behavior of prices. The method he chooses is therefore a compromise that does not eliminate change but reduces it to manageable proportions by introducing the assumptions of a *stationary state*.

In Marshall's stationary state, consumer tastes and production techniques remain unchanged. However, unlike the classical stationary state, population and capital are allowed to increase slowly and at the same rate. Business enterprises therefore grow and decline; change is not entirely absent. But always there will be certain firms regarded as being *representative* of the others in an industry. Change has been abstracted sufficiently to show how prices would be adjusted in the long run if the conditions under which they are determined are stable enough to allow these forces the opportunity to work themselves out.

There are times when Marshall seems to imply that the long-run results he describes actually occur in the real world. However, except for occasional lapses, he reminds his reader that his concept of the stationary state is an *analytical construct* designed to cope with the many variables operating in the real world. For while Marshall aimed at realism, his method was to start with simplifying assumptions. He singled out variables, specifically consumer tastes, incomes, the prices of other goods, and the value of money, which he treated as data to arrive at conclusions that represented *tendencies* or first approximations. Marshall's sense of history kept him from inferring that the generalizations economists arrive at are universal and permanent. 'That part of economic doctrine which alone can claim universality has no dogmas. It is not a body of concrete truth, but an engine for the discovery of concrete truth.'[8] He never lost sight of the complexity and changeability of the universe within which economic forces operate and of the consequent difficulty of arriving at valid generalizations. His reluctance to claim universality for economic propositions is evident in his paper 'The old generation of economists and the new,' in which he maintains that qualitative analysis, by which he meant deductive analyses, 'will not show the resultant drift of forces . . . The achievement of quantitative analysis stands over for the 20th century.'[9]

These observations appear to suggest that, in Marshall's view, pure theory has been carried as far as it fruitfully can be for the present, besides being unable to yield universal or permanent laws. In fact, he frequently depreciated even the present significance of pure analysis; for example, he hesitated to publish his diagrammatic analyses, fearing that 'if separated from all concrete study of actual conditions they might seem to claim a more direct bearing on real problems than they in fact had.'[10] He regarded theory as essential, but he warned against regarding it as economics proper. Nevertheless, much of modern microeconomic analysis has developed out of Marshall's theory of value and distribution.

The theory of demand

Utility and demand

While Marshall's theory of value is fully developed in Book 5, which treats the 'General relations of demand, supply and value,' the analysis presented there builds on the two books that precede it. Book 3, 'On wants and their satisfaction,' begins with the observation that insufficient attention has been paid to demand and consumption until just recently. He was alluding here, in particular, to Jevons, who 'did excellent service by calling attention to it [the demand side of the theory of value] and developing it.'[11]

While Marshall regarded consumer wants and their satisfaction as an important part of the theory of value, and was an important contributor to the development of demand theory himself, he believed that marginal utility is not the dominant factor in the determination of value. Ricardo, he agreed, tended to slight the role of demand; but he did not, as Jevons maintained, think of value as being governed by cost of production without reference to demand. Thus, for Marshall, the Ricardian emphasis on cost of production remained the fundamental basis for explaining long run normal values, and the theory of utility and demand merely supplemented and rounded out the classical analysis. Marshall's analysis was therefore designed to demonstrate the *interaction* of demand and supply forces. As a result, he has frequently been thought of as a synthesizer of the Ricardian cost-oriented type of analysis with the newer approach of the marginal utility theorists. Marshall himself was, however, irritated at being cast in the role of an eclectic, although his failure to publish earlier his own work on utility and demand makes such an interpretation understandable, even though incorrect.[12]

Demand schedules and curves

Marshall's analysis of demand begins by translating the law of diminishing utility into terms of price. He reasons that the larger the quantity of a commodity a person has, the smaller (other things being equal) will be the price that person will pay for a little more of it. Impounded in the phrase 'other things being equal' is the assumption that the amount of money the individual has available, and its purchasing power, remain constant. Marshall assumes a constant marginal utility of money, and thereby rules out any income effects resulting from price changes. On this basis, the curve representing the marginal utility of a commodity to a consumer is converted into a demand schedule and then into a demand curve.

Any individual demand for certain commodities may be discontinuous; that is, it may not vary continuously for every small change in price. The aggregate demands of many persons will, however, vary in response to price changes; thus, the quantity to be taken at alternative possible prices causes the demand curve to take on a characteristic downward slope to the right.[13] It is also the basis for the generalization known as the law of demand: 'The amount demanded increases with a fall in price and diminishes with a rise in price.'[14] Thus, there will be a movement along a *given* demand curve as a result of a change in the price of the commodity itself if none of the other factors which can influence the demand for it – for example, taste or the prices of other goods – have changed.

Only if the factors which have been held constant in defining a given demand situation become altered does the position, and perhaps shape, of the demand curve itself change. In a schedule sense, this means that buyers will be willing to buy either more or less of the commodity per unit of time at every possible price. This will shift the entire demand schedule from its original position, either upward to the right or downward to the left.

Price elasticity of demand

While the law of demand expresses the inverse relationship between the demand for a commodity and its price, it does not indicate how sensitive the demand for a commodity is to a change in price. The concept of the *price elasticity* of demand is needed to supply this sort of information. The simplest way to determine whether the demand for a particular commodity is elastic or not is to observe the behavior of total expenditures when the price of the good in question is changed. If total expenditures are greater at a lower price than at a higher price, the demand is elastic. Conversely, if total expenditure is smaller at a lower price, the demand for the good is inelastic. The limitation of this method is that it cannot indicate the degree of demand elasticity or inelasticity.[15]

Because the measurement of elasticity by the slope of the curve is crude, Marshall defined price elasticity as the percentage change in quantity demanded divided by the percentage change in the price when both changes are infinitely small.[16] In symbols, then:

$$e_d = \frac{\left(\dfrac{dq}{q}\right)}{\left(\dfrac{dp}{p}\right)} = \frac{dq \times p}{dp \times q}$$

The resulting number (coefficient) is independent of the units in terms of which prices and quantities are measured because it is derived by dividing one percentage by another. The coefficient denoting elasticity will always be negative since price change and quantity change take place in opposite directions and therefore have different signs. In speaking of demand elasticity, however, it is customary to ignore signs and refer to the numerical values of elasticity magnitudes simply as equal to 1, greater than 1, or smaller than 1. When elasticity equals 1, it is referred to as *unitary elasticity*. When elasticity is greater than 1, demand is said to be *elastic*, and when it is less than 1, it is said to be *inelastic*.

The Marshallian formula is now a standard analytical tool for calculating the degree of sensitivity of the demand for a commodity to a change in its price. It lends itself to measuring elasticity either at any point on a given demand curve or between two points on a demand curve. The latter measurement involves the computation of what is known as *arc elasticity*. The formula for computing elasticity between two points on a demand curve will result in two *different* elasticity coefficients, depending on the direction in which the change is measured.[17] The farther apart these points are, the greater will be the discrepancy between the resulting elasticity coefficients.[18] If price-quantity data are sufficiently continuous to result in any two points, A and B, that are very close together on the curve, greater precision can be achieved in measurement. This is precisely why Marshall's elasticity formula is intended to measure infinitely small changes in price and quantity.

A change in the price measurement unit thus distorts the ratio that purports to measure the slope of the demand curve. A similar distortion would result from altering the unit in terms of which quantities are measured; for example, a shift from pounds to bushels.

The theory of production

The theory of production, the central topic of Marshall's Book 4, is the foundation for his analysis of costs and supplies of goods. It is also fundamental to explaining the pricing of the factors, their allocation among alternative uses in the economy, and the distribution of the economy's product among the various claimants. Thus, Marshall's discussions of the agents of production, and the laws of return under which they operate, precede the analysis of price determination, which is the subject matter in Book 5. His analysis of income distribution is in Book 6.

The laws of return are significant in the short run and in the long run, but not in the market period. Since the time of Marshall, the market period is conceived as a situation in which the available output has already been produced. Physical supply is on hand in this period and cannot be increased, while a decrease results only from sale or destruction, not changes in output.

Output changes can be accomplished during the short run by altering some, though not all, of the factor inputs required to produce output. The long run is a period during which the supply of a product can be varied by altering *all* of the factor inputs. Only those changes in output associated with economic growth or decline are absent.

The laws of return in the short run

Since a production unit is always confronted with one or more fixed factors and a given state of technology in the short run, its production function is governed by the law of diminishing returns. Marshall, like his classical predecessors, examined this tendency with respect to agricultural production and concluded that, when land is a fixed constant in the production function, 'the application of increased capital and labor to land will add a less than proportionate amount to the produce raised, unless there be meanwhile an increase in the skill of the individual cultivator.'[19] His treatment restricted the operation of diminishing returns to agriculture. However, he undoubtedly understood that *any* variable factor of production will yield diminishing marginal returns when it is combined in production with a given quantity of a fixed factor.[20] This is implied by his *principle of substitution*, according to which the desire to maximize profits causes the business owner to substitute less expensive factors for more expensive ones. It is precisely because one factor is not a perfect substitute for another that diminishing returns occur. If the ratio of a variable factor, A, to a fixed factor, B, is progressively increased, A becomes a less effective substitute for B, and returns to the variable factor increase at a decreasing rate.

According to the principle of substitution, a firm will alter the proportions in which it uses its variable inputs to achieve the least-cost combination. It will experiment with different combinations of its variable factors until it achieves the greatest revenue product for a given expenditure. This principle is analogous to that previously examined with respect to the maximization of consumer satisfaction. The consumer maximizes satisfaction by distributing income among different goods so as to equate the marginal utility of each dollar's worth of goods purchased. A firm achieves its objective of maximizing its product (minimizing its cost) by distributing its expenditures so as to equate the marginal revenue product of each dollar's worth of variable resources it purchases.

The value of a factor's marginal product underlies the demand for it (i.e. the extent to which it will be given employment) at the prevailing factor price. A firm's demand curve for a factor is therefore related to its marginal productivity in much the same way as a consumer demand curve is related to marginal utility. The best combination of variable resources depends on the respective marginal physical products of these resources, the cost at which they can be employed, and the price at which the product they produce can be sold. *The marginal productivity principle therefore serves to integrate Marshall's theory of value with his theory of income distribution.* It enters into the neoclassical theory of value through its effect on the cost and supply of commodity outputs, and it enters into its theory of distribution through the effect on factor demands. It is, however, important to emphasize that Marshall's use of the marginal productivity principle for examining the demand for factors did *not* lead him to a marginal productivity theory for explaining the distributive shares.

The laws of return in the long run

Marshall's concern with the laws of return in the long run was to establish a basis for depicting the long-run supply curve of an industry. He identified three possible output behavior patterns that might result when an industry expands in the long run. In the case of constant return, output will increase proportionately with an increase in factor input; in the case of increasing return, the increase in output will be proportionally greater than the increase in factor input; in the case of diminishing return, it will be proportionately smaller. Marshall thought of increasing and diminishing returns as forces that 'press constantly against one another.'[21] He observed that 'the part which nature plays in production shows a tendency to diminishing return, the part which man plays shows a tendency to increasing return.'[22] When the two forces are balanced, there is a tendency toward constant returns.[23]

The concepts of external and internal

economies are central to Marshall's analyses of the laws of return. Their role is that they facilitate the production of a proportionately larger output with a given increase in expenditures. External economies are those that result from 'the general progress of the industrial environment' and enable the firms of an expanding industry to experience decreasing costs; the development of better transportation and marketing facilities, and improvements in resource-furnishing industries, are possible sources of such economies which Marshall specifically mentions.[24] Internal economies are those that a firm gains as it enlarges its size to achieve greater advantages of large-scale production and organization.[25] Marshall observed that 'an increase of labor and capital leads generally to improved organization, which increases the efficiency of the work of labor and capital.'

It is not clear from the preceding statements whether Marshall conceived of the laws of return in the long run as relating strictly to the results accomplished by changing *all* factor inputs (i.e. to changes in scale). Only in the case of increasing returns resulting from internal economies is it clear that a change in the scale of production is involved. Increasing returns resulting from external economies, that is, 'the general progress of the industrial environment,' does not necessarily involve a change in scale in Marshall's analysis. This part of his analysis is thus the source of considerable confusion and has been criticized for its inconsistency. Diminishing returns is a short-run phenomenon. In the short run, as has already been noted, a change in scale is not possible. The impossibility of varying all factor inputs results in a production function that is governed by the law of diminishing returns beyond some point. It is therefore not possible for the tendency toward diminishing returns and

increasing returns to 'press against one another' in the manner conceived by Marshall, as these tendencies are operative in different time periods.[26]

Marshall's distinction between internal and external economies as the source of long-run increasing returns has important implications for the competitive tendencies of the economy. He recognized that a condition of increasing returns is incompatible with competition. 'Insofar as the economies of production on a large scale are 'internal,' i.e. belonging to the internal organization of individual firms, the weaker firms must speedily be driven out of existence by the stronger.' However, he did not think it possible for such economies to continue indefinitely. 'The continued existence of weaker firms is evidence that a strong firm cannot indefinitely increase its output. This is partly because of the difficulty of extending its market and partly because the strength of a firm is not permanent.'[27] The reason, Marshall suggested, is that the growth of individual enterprises is likely to be limited by the probably inferior business talents of the descendants of present business leaders.[28] He also anticipated increased difficulties of marketing as limiting the possibilities for securing advantages of large-scale production.[29] Increasing long-run returns were therefore attributed by Marshall to the presence of *external* rather than internal economies. The basis for subsequent disagreement with this conclusion is discussed in Chapter 16.

Costs of production and supply

Real costs and money costs

Examination of Marshall's inquiry into production costs is a logical extension of his theory of production. Except in the very short run (market period), when the supply of a good has already been produced, costs of production underlie the supply schedules of firms and industries. While these costs are necessarily monetary, Marshall is also concerned with the real costs imposed by the disutilities of labor and the 'abstinences or rather the waitings required for saving the capital' required to produce capital goods.[30] All factors of production except land, which is a free gift of nature requiring neither abstinence nor labor effort, impose a real cost when they are used in production. In Marshall's view, the money costs of production are the prices that must be paid 'in order to call forth an adequate supply of the efforts and waitings that are required for making it; or, in other words, they are its [a commodity's] supply price.'[31]

Marshall's emphasis on the subjective or psychological aspects of cost reflects a continuation of the Utilitarian philosophy of the British classicists. Insofar as they explained money costs, they referred them back to the discomforts of work and saving. Marshall followed this tradition, to which he added the subjective costs inherent in effort and waiting on the part of enterprise.[32] Some normal rate of profit is therefore included by Marshall as part of the cost of producing a commodity.

The money costs of production consist of prime costs and supplementary costs. In the terminology of the present day these are identified as fixed and variable costs. Prime costs, or operating expenses, vary directly with output, whereas supplementary costs are standing charges that do not vary with output. In the short run, the inputs represented by supplementary costs are fixed. Only variable inputs, and therefore prime costs, are subject to change. In the long run, all inputs, and therefore all costs, are variable.

Diminishing returns and short-run cost behavior

Although Marshall's discussion of diminishing returns implies that it is a land law, he is aware that when increasing quantities of any variable input are employed, together with a fixed factor, there will be diminishing returns beyond some level of output. Production of the profit-maximizing (loss-minimizing) output (i.e. $MC = MR$) will therefore cause the firm to be producing on the rising portion of its marginal cost curve. The segment of the marginal cost curve lying above average variable (or prime) costs is its short-run supply curve which will be rising from the point which corresponds to diminishing marginal product.

While Marshall did not make cost calculations of the sort that have now become standard in most texts on economic principles, or draw the cost curves these calculations describe, such calculations are implicit in his distinction between prime and supplementary costs. They are also useful in understanding why Marshall drew upward-sloping industry supply curves for the short run. Since the industry supply curve is a summation of individual firms' supply curves, it must be upward-sloping in the short run. This is not necessarily the case in the long run. However, in the short run, the fixed factors in the firm's production function cause rising marginal costs because of the tendency toward diminishing marginal returns to the variable factors. Individual firms and the industry as a whole will therefore offer larger quantities only at higher prices. The typical upward slope of the supply schedule of a purely competitive industry in the short run reflects this relationship.

Long-run cost and supply curves

There is no reason to assume that the cost curves of individual firms are identical in the short run, even if all firms purchase factors in the same purely competitive market. Some firms may enjoy lower costs because of superior capital equipment, more favorable location, or better management. These advantages yield what Marshall terms *quasi-rents* in the short run. These incomes accrue in the short run from using factors that are fixed in supply and are akin to the economic rent of land.

In the long run, quasi-rents tend to be eliminated, either through an increase in the supply of a reproducible factor or, in the case of one that is not reproducible, through a price rise that results from competitive bidding for its use. In the long run under competition, therefore, each firm will tend to produce along identical cost curves that include the quasi-rents of the short run. These costs may be explicit or imputed, depending on whether the firm hires the factor in the market or owns it.

Marshall himself did not examine the long-run cost curves of the individual firm, but dealt only with the long-run supply curve of the entire industry.[33] He conceived of the shape of the industry supply curve in the long run as depending on whether it is one of constant returns (constant cost), decreasing returns (increasing cost), or increasing returns (decreasing cost). The predominant tendency in each industry will manifest itself in the experience of what Marshall terms the *representative firm*. The representative firm 'has had a fairly long life, and fair success, which is managed with normal ability and which has normal access to the economies, external and internal, which belong to that aggregate volume of production; account

being taken of the class of goods produced, the conditions of marketing them and the economic environment.'[34] This firm is not an actual firm, but rather an analytical tool that Marshall conceived of for the purpose of identifying the cost of production, and therefore the supply schedule of a commodity, in the long run. '[The] normal supply price of any amount of that commodity may be taken to be its normal expenses of production (including gross earnings of management) by that firm.'[35] Thus, Marshall examines the long-run supply curve of the industry with reference to the costs of the representative firm.

Marshall presents his concept of the representative firm within the framework of a biological analogy. The life cycles of business firms are compared to those of trees in a forest, which first grow to maturity and then decay. During its growth phase, a firm will enjoy internal economies of scale; in its declining phase, these economies will be offset by diseconomies that limit its growth potential and its ability to experience decreasing costs as a result of internal economies. A firm therefore cannot, in Marshall's view, expand its size to an extent that will enable it to dominate an industry. Competition remains pure, and an increase in the output of the industry in the long run results from an increase in the *number* of firms rather than from an increase in the *size* of firms.

Given pure competition, the long-run supply curve of an industry may be constant, upward sloping, or downward sloping as the industry expands in size to accommodate an increase in demand. The case of constant cost implies that the internal and external economies of production are canceled out by internal and external *diseconomies*. Increasing quantities of the product can therefore be supplied at a constant long-run average cost.

The long-run supply curve may also be upward sloping. This will be the case, for example, if the expansion of the industry raises the average cost curve of each firm, because the increasing scarcity of a non-reproducible factor increases the cost of using it. The quasi-rents that accrued as a producer's surplus in the short run are capitalized in the long run and become embodied in the long-run cost curves and supply curves when the supply of factors that gave rise to them is less than infinitely elastic. Increasing quantities of the product can then be supplied only at increasing long-run average costs, and the industry supply curve will be upward sloping.

Marshall believed that the long-run supply curve in a competitive industry could also be downward sloping. Perceiving that this kind of supply curve might be incompatible with pure competition, he attributed its existence to the possibility that firms might enjoy *external* economies that enable them to experience falling average costs as the industry expands in size. External economies derive from having input or output advantages that are available to all the firms in the industry. The implication is that they are attributable to changes in the state of the arts so that they cannot be charged for by any factor. They thus have the effect of *reducing costs* rather than creating rents. Their presence makes it possible to supply at decreasing long-run costs.

Decreasing costs, which are the result of external economies, must not be confused with decreasing costs that result from *internal* economies. Internal economies are under the control of the firm and can be achieved by enlarging the scale of its plant. External economies, as Marshall defined them, are those that firms sometimes enjoy if there are improvements, *outside* of the control of individual firms, which all firms can share, but for which no factor of production can charge a price. Writers who came after Marshall questioned that the kind of external economies he had in mind could be identified. As will be examined in Chapter 16, this was part of their reason for eventually rejecting Marshall's explanation of decreasing long-run cost.

The theory of price determination

The analyses of Books 3 and 4, with their detailed examinations of utility and of demand and cost of production and supply, provide the basis for Marshall's theory of price determination, which is the subject matter of his Book 5. This lengthy prelude to price determination was Marshall's approach to resolving the critical issue that Jevons's insistence on the role of utility brought to the fore.

Issues and Answers from the Masterworks 14.1

Issue
Is it cost of production or utility that governs value?

Marshall's answer
From *Principles of Economics* (1890), 8th edn (1920), Book 5, Chapter 3.

Equilibrium of normal demand and supply
§5. To give definiteness to our ideas let us take an illustration from the woollen trade. Let us suppose that a person well acquainted with the woollen trade sets himself to inquire what would

be the normal supply price of a certain number of millions of yards annually of a particular kind of cloth. He would have to reckon (i) the price of the wool, coal, and other materials which would he used up in making it, (ii) wear-and-tear and depreciation of the buildings, machinery and other fixed capital, (iii) interest and insurance on all the capital, (iv) the wages of those who work in the factories, and (v) the gross earnings of management (including insurance against loss), of those who undertake the risks, who engineer and superintend the working. He would of course estimate the supply prices of all these different factors of production of the cloth with reference to the amounts of each of them that would be wanted, and on the supposition that the conditions of supply would be normal; and he would add them all together to find the supply price of the cloth.

Let us suppose a list of supply prices (or a supply schedule) made on a similar plan to that of our list of demand prices: the supply price of each amount of the commodity in a year, or any other unit of time, being written against that amount. As the flow, or (annual) amount of the commodity increases, the supply price may either increase or diminish; or it may even alternately increase and diminish. For if nature is offering a sturdy resistance to man's efforts to wring from her a larger supply of raw material, while at that particular stage there is no great room for introducing important new economies into the manufacture, the supply price will rise; but if the volume of production were greater, it would perhaps be profitable to substitute largely machine work for hand work and steam power for muscular force; and the increase in the volume of production would have diminished the expenses of production of the commodity of our representative firm. But those cases in which the supply price falls as the amount increases involve special difficulties of their own; and they are postponed to chapter XII of this Book.

§6. When therefore the amount produced (in a unit of time) is such that the demand price is greater than the supply price, then sellers receive more than is sufficient to make it worth their while to bring goods to market to that amount; and there is at work an active force tending to increase the amount brought forward for sale. On the other hand, when the amount produced is such that the demand price is less than the supply price, sellers receive less than is sufficient to make it worth their while to bring goods to market on that scale; so that those who were just on the margin of doubt as to whether to go on producing are decided not to do so, and there is an active force at work tending to diminish the amount brought forward for sale. When the demand price is equal to the supply price, the amount produced has no tendency either to be increased or to be diminished; it is in equilibrium.

When demand and supply are in equilibrium, the amount of the commodity which is being produced in a unit of time may be called the *equilibrium-amount*, and the price at which it is being sold may be called the *equilibrium-price*.

Such an equilibrium is *stable*; that is, the price, if displaced a little from it, will tend to return, as a pendulum oscillates about its lowest point; and it will be found to be a characteristic of stable equilibria that in them the demand price is greater than the supply price for amounts just less than the equilibrium amount, and *vice versa*. For when the demand price is greater than the supply price, the amount produced tends to increase. Therefore, if the demand price is greater than the supply price for amounts just less than an equilibrium amount; then, if the scale of production is temporarily diminished somewhat below that equilibrium amount, it will tend to return; thus the equilibrium is stable for displacements in that direction. If the demand price is greater than the supply price for amounts just less than the equilibrium amount, it is sure to be less than the supply price for amounts just greater: and therefore, if the scale of production is somewhat increased beyond the equilibrium position, it will tend to return; and the equilibrium will be stable for displacements in that direction also.

When demand and supply are in stable equilibrium, if any accident should move the scale of production from its equilibrium position, there will be instantly brought into play forces tending to push it back to that position; just as, if a stone hanging by a string is displaced from its equilibrium position, the force of gravity will at once tend to bring it back to its equilibrium position. The movements of the scale of production about its position of equilibrium will be of a somewhat similar kind.

To represent the equilibrium of demand and supply geometrically we may draw the demand and supply curves together as in the accompanying figure. If then *OR* represents the rate at which production is being actually carried on, and *Rd* the demand price is greater than *Rs* the supply price, the production is exceptionally profitable, and will be increased. *R*, the *amount-index*, as we may call it, will move to the right. On the other hand, if *Rd* is less than *Rs*, *R* will move to the left. If *Rd* is equal to *Rs*, that is, if *R* is vertically under a point of intersection of the curves, demand and supply are in equilibrium.

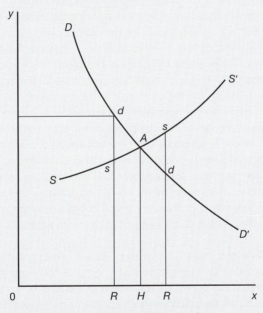

Figure 14.1 Marshall's representation of demand and supply

This may be taken as the typical diagram for stable equilibrium for a commodity that obeys the law of diminishing return. But if we had made SS′ a horizontal straight line, we should have represented the case of 'constant return,' in which the supply price is the same for all amounts of the commodity. And if we had made SS′ inclined negatively, but less steeply than DO′ (the necessity for this condition will appear more fully later on), we should have got a case of stable equilibrium for a commodity which obeys the law of increasing return. In either case the above reasoning remains unchanged without the alteration of a word or a letter; but the last case introduces difficulties which we have arranged to postpone.

But in real life such oscillations are seldom as rhythmical as those of a stone hanging freely from a string; the comparison would be more exact if the string were supposed to hang in the troubled waters of a mill-race, whose stream was at one time allowed to flow freely, and at another partially cut off. Nor are these complexities sufficient to illustrate all the disturbances with which the economist and the merchant alike are forced to concern themselves. If the person holding the string swings his hand with movements partly rhythmical and partly arbitrary, the illustration will not outrun the difficulties of some very real and practical problems of value.

For, indeed, the demand and supply schedules do not in practice remain unchanged for a long time together, but are constantly being changed; and every change in them alters the equilibrium amount and the equilibrium price, and thus gives new positions to the centres about which the amount and the price tend to oscillate.

These considerations point to the great importance of the element of time in relation to demand and supply, to the study of which we now proceed. We shall gradually discover a great many different limitations of the doctrine that the price at which a thing can be produced represents its real cost of production, that is, the efforts and sacrifices which have been directly and indirectly devoted to its production. For, in an age of rapid change such as this, the equilibrium of normal demand and supply does not thus correspond to any distinct relation of a certain aggregate of pleasures got from the consumption of the commodity and an aggregate of efforts and sacrifices involved in producing it: the correspondence would not be exact, even if normal earnings and interest were exact measures of the efforts and sacrifices for which they are the money payments. This is the real drift of that much quoted, and much-misunderstood doctrine of Adam Smith and other economists that the normal, or 'natural,' value of a commodity is that which economic forces tend to bring about *in the long run*. It is the average value which economic forces would bring about if the general conditions of life were stationary for a run of time long enough to enable them all to work out their full effect.

But we cannot foresee the future perfectly. The unexpected may happen; and the existing tendencies may be modified before they have had time to accomplish what appears now to be their full and complete work. The fact that the general conditions of life are not stationary is the source of many of the difficulties that are met with in applying economic doctrines to practical problems.

Of course Normal does not mean Competitive. Market prices and Normal prices alike are brought about by a multitude of influences, of which some rest on a moral basis and some on a physical; of which some are competitive and some are not. It is to the persistence of the influences considered, and the time allowed for them to work out their effects that we refer when contrasting Market and Normal price, and again when contrasting the narrower and the broader use of the term Normal price.

§7. The remainder of the present volume will be chiefly occupied with interpreting and limiting this doctrine that the value of a thing tends in the long run to correspond to its cost of production. In particular, the notion of equilibrium, which has been treated rather slightly in this chapter, will be studied more carefully in chapters V and XII of this Book: and some account of the controversy whether 'cost of production' or 'utility' governs value will be given in Appendix I. But it may be well to say a word or two here on this last point.

We might as reasonably dispute whether it is the upper or the under blade of a pair of scissors that cuts a piece of paper, as whether value is governed by utility or cost of production. It is true that when one blade is held still, and the cutting is effected by moving the other, we may say with careless brevity that the cutting is done by the second; but the statement is not strictly accurate, and is to be excused only so long as it claims to be merely a popular and not a strictly scientific account of what happens.

In the same way, when a thing already made has to be sold, the price which people will be willing to pay for it will be governed by their desire to have it, together with the amount they can afford to spend on it. Their desire to have it depends partly on the chance that, if they do not buy it, they will be able to get another thing like it at as low a price: this depends on the causes that govern the supply of it, and this again upon cost of production. But it may so happen that the stock to be sold is practically fixed. This, for instance, is the case with a fish market, in which the value of fish for the day is governed almost exclusively by the stock on the slabs in relation to cost of production, then he may be excused for the demand: and if a person chooses to take the stock for granted, and say that the price is governed by demand, his brevity may perhaps be excused so long as he does not claim strict accuracy. So again it may be pardonable, but it is not strictly accurate to say that the varying prices which the same rare book fetches, when sold and resold at Christie's auction room, are governed exclusively by demand.

Taking a case at the opposite extreme, we find some commodities which conform pretty closely to the law of constant return; that is to say, their average cost of production will be very nearly the same whether they are produced in small quantities or in large. In such a case the normal level about which the market price fluctuates will be this definite and fixed (money) cost of production. If the demand happens to be great, the market price will rise for a time above the level; but, as a result, production will increase and the market price will fall: and conversely if the demand falls for a time below its ordinary level.

In such a case, if a person chooses to neglect market fluctuations, and to take it for granted that there will anyhow be enough demand for the commodity to insure that some of it, more or less, will find purchasers at a price equal to this cost of production, then he may be excused for ignoring the influence of demand, and speaking of (normal) price as governed by cost of production – provided only he does not claim scientific accuracy for the wording of his doctrine, and explains the influence of demand in its right place.

Thus we may conclude that, *as a general rule*, the shorter the period which we are considering, the greater must be the share of our attention which is given to the influence of demand on value; and the longer the period, the more important will be the influence of cost of production on value. For the influence of changes in cost of production takes as a rule a longer time to work itself out than does the influence of changes in demand. The actual value at any time, the market value as it is often called, is often more influenced by passing events and by causes whose action is fitful and short lived, than by those which work persistently. But in long periods these fitful and irregular causes in large measure efface one another's influence; so that in the long run persistent causes dominate value completely. Even the most persistent causes are however liable to change. For the whole structure of production is modified, and the relative costs of production of different things are permanently altered, from one generation to another.

Source: *Principles of Economics*, 8th edition, Alfred Marshall (London: Macmillan, 1920) Chapter 3 (some footnotes deleted).

Summing up: Marshall's key points

In Marshall's view, price is governed neither by cost of production alone nor by marginal utility alone, but by the interaction of these forces as they express themselves in the demand for, and the supply of, a good. Normally, the price of a commodity will tend to be equal to its long-run cost of production. The longer the relevant period of time, the more accurately it is possible to adjust supply to changes in demand. The mechanism for this adjustment is the exodus of unprofitable firms or the entry of new firms when short supply causes higher than normal profit.

Marshall himself illustrates this principle in the figure reproduced on page 326 of *Principles*. The industry demand curve *DD* is the summation of consumer demand curves, and the cost-experience of the representative firm underlies the supply curve *SS'*. (Contemporary practice is to identify an industry demand curve as the sum of the segments of the firms' marginal cost curves that lie above their average variable costs.) The interaction of industry demand and supply forces establishes the equilibrium amount of industry output and its corresponding equilibrium price. The longer the period over which output can become adapted to changes in demand, the greater will be the influence of cost of production on price. The precise behavior of cost of production depends on whether the commodity obeys the law of diminishing returns, constant returns, or increasing returns. Although Marshall often used biological analogies to describe the forces of change he believed to be operative (recall, for example, his analogy to the life cycle of a forest in his concept of the representative firm), the analysis of Book 5, Chapter 3, is an example of Marshall's reliance on a *mechanical* analogy drawn from physics to explain the pricing

process and the tendency toward an industry competitive equilibrium in which price equals long-run average cost of production.

While this part of Marshall's inquiry emphasizes the dominant role of cost of production in the determination of commodity prices, there are three cases in which the price of a product will reflect its *demand* rather than its cost of production. One of these, namely, the case of competitive price determination in the market period, requires little elaboration. When the supply of a commodity has already been produced, the force of demand will necessarily be relatively more important than supply in determining price, so there is no necessary tendency for price to approximate the cost of production. However, Marshall's explanation of the reason why long-run price bears no necessary relationship to cost of production in the cases of *true joint supply* or *monopoly* warrants separate examination.

Prices that deviate from cost of production

Joint production and cost

Marshall reformulated Mill's principle that the prices of joint products produced in fixed proportions cannot be governed by the cost of producing them because their individual costs *cannot be determined*. If two or more products are produced in fixed proportions (e.g. cotton and cotton silk, beef and hides, wheat and straw), the marginal cost of one product cannot be identified. We can speak only of the marginal cost of a combined unit of production (i.e. the marginal cost of a bushel of wheat and so many pounds of straw), but we cannot separate the cost of the wheat from the cost of the straw. Thus, Marshall concluded that the price of a particular joint product will be governed, even in the long run, by the relative intensity of the market demand, rather than by its cost of production. Further, whenever a change in the demand for one joint product induces a change in the joint supply, their prices will vary inversely with each other.

For example, Marshall showed that if there is an increase in the demand for wool, the supply of both wool and mutton will increase as the high price of wool stimulates the production of sheep. The increased cost of output is as attributable to the extra output of mutton as it is to the extra output of wool, but since there is no change in the demand for mutton, its price must fall. Uniform prices for two jointly produced products would result only in those accidental cases in which the demand schedules for both jointly produced products are exactly alike. Only the case of joint cost with variable proportions presents no unusual value problem because it is possible to assign a separate supply price to each of the products.[36]

Monopoly prices

Marshall likewise noted that cost of production is no guide to the price that will be charged in a monopoly situation. 'The prima facie interest of the owner of a monopoly is clearly to adjust the supply to the demand not in such a way that the price at which he can sell his commodity shall just cover its expenses of production, but in such a way as to afford him the greatest possible total net revenue.'[37] The price a monopolist will charge, given the demand schedule for his product, may be determined, Marshall tells us, by calculating the monopoly revenue associated with the production and sale of various quantities of output.

To calculate what portion of the total revenue will be the *monopoly net revenue* at every level of output, it is necessary to draw up a supply schedule that represents the normal expenses of production of each of the several amounts supplied, including interest on capital and managerial salaries. For small outputs, the supply price, or average cost, will be high, so the supply curve will be above the demand curve; for larger outputs, average cost of production will diminish, and the supply curve will therefore lie below the demand curve before it ultimately rises again. If the supply price of each quantity of output is subtracted from the corresponding demand price, the differential remaining is monopoly net revenue. The object of a monopolist is to select the volume of output that, given the demand for the product, will make the aggregate net revenue the greatest.

Marshall's method of finding the price–quantity combination at which monopoly net revenue is at a maximum, yields the same results as Cournot's method of equating the first derivative of total cost with the first derivative of total revenue.[38] Net revenue is at a maximum when marginal revenue and marginal cost are equal. That is, we can measure monopoly profit as the difference between average cost and average revenue multiplied by output. Or, alternatively, we can measure monopoly profit as the difference between the area lying under the marginal revenue curve (aggregate revenue) and the area lying under the marginal cost curve (aggregate cost). Thus, in Figure 14.2, monopoly profit is equal to the area *YXZ* and to the area *P'PCC'* when output *OA* is produced at an average cost of *AC*.

Long-run competitive price determination

In the absence of monopoly and production under joint supply, the long-run price (or *normal* price as Marshall calls it), will be

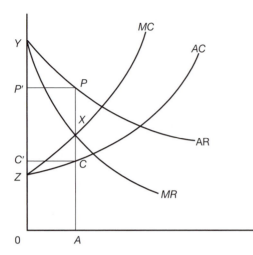

Figure 14.2 Maximizing monopoly net revenue (profit)

equal to the cost of production, including the normal earnings of management, of the representative firm. This is the competitive equilibrium towards which the industries in the economy are always moving. His emphasis on the predominant influence of cost of production in the determination of value in the long run led him to conclude 'that the foundations of the theory as they were left by Ricardo remain intact; that much has been added to them, and that very much has been built upon them, but that little has been taken from them.'[39] This is as much of a concession as he was willing to make to the marginal utility theory of value. He accorded utility a role, but by no means the dominant one, in the determination of competitive price. The longer the period of time under consideration, the greater the influence of cost of production on price. In the long run, when all the forces of adjustment have had time to work themselves out, price will be equal to the cost of producing the supply needed to satisfy the demand for the product.

The long-run cost tendencies that prevail, coupled with the demand for an industry's products, determine whether the long-run price will be higher, lower, or the same as an industry expands or contracts in response to changes in demand. A change in demand will cause output to expand or contract in the long run in a constant cost industry, but the long-run equilibrium price will be neither higher nor lower than that which prevailed in the short run.

If, on the other hand, the firms in an industry experience diseconomies as they expand their factor inputs, the industry's long-run supply curve will slope upward, and it will produce a larger output at a higher cost than previously if increases in demand cause it to expand. Conversely, if external economies cause the cost curves of an industry to decrease as its scale is increased, an increase in demand will enable the industry to produce a larger output than previously at a lower price. Marshall regarded these cases as constituting a possible basis for interfering with the free operation of the price mechanism through a system of taxes and subsidies.

Marshall's analysis of the effect of imposing a tax or granting a subsidy in different industries clearly demonstrates that he did not share the position of the classical and utility schools that welfare is always maximized under free competition. When production takes place under long-run increasing cost or long-run decreasing cost, there will be a loss in economic welfare under *laissez-faire* conditions. These cases lend themselves best, Marshall believed, to the partial type of analysis in which it is possible to concentrate on net changes in economic welfare as a result of given changes in particular sectors of the economy, the rest of the system being assumed constant. Marshall measures these changes in terms of the effect that altered opportunities to buy or sell a particular commodity have on the surpluses consumers are able to reap.

Consumer surplus

While the concept of consumer's surplus originated with Dupuit, it was Marshall who named the idea and used it in a context that led to its subsequent importance in what later became known as *welfare economics*. Marshall used the concept in more than one sense. He first defined it as the monetary value of the utility a consumer gains when the price at which a good can be purchased is lower than the price an individual would pay rather than go without it. If, as in Figure 14.3, the market price of the commodity is p, those buyers who would be willing to pay more than this price enjoy a consumer surplus. Adding individual surpluses together, Marshall represents consumers' surplus as the shaded area $DA'p_1$ under the demand curve. At a lower price, say p_0, consumers' surplus is the area $DB'p_0$. The change in consumer surplus is measured in terms of a sum of money that will offset the gain or loss resulting from price changes brought about by the imposition of a tax or the granting of a subsidy in industries operating with different laws of return.

The chief difficulties that arise when the consumers' surplus is conceived as above are, first, that it assumes individual utilities are additive and, second, that it assumes the marginal utility of money is constant. An obvious way around the additivity problem is to relate the concept to a single consumer; that is, to conceive of a particular consumer's surplus, rather than consumers' surplus as a whole. However, the problem of a change in the marginal utility of the monetary unit in which prices are expressed (say, shillings, dollars, francs, and so forth) remains. A fall in price from p_1 to p_0 is equivalent to an increase in real income, and, assuming that money is valued like other normal goods, the utility of

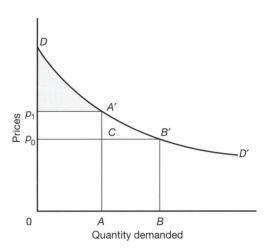

Figure 14.3 Consumers' surplus

an additional increment of income falls as income rises. Thus, unless the utility of money remains constant, there is no common denominator in terms of which to measure the utility that consumer's surplus is intended to represent.

Marshall was aware of this problem and attempted to circumvent it by assuming that the marginal utility of money income remains approximately constant, if there is a change in the price of an unimportant commodity. A commodity such as tea (Marshall's own example) represents such a small proportion of a household's expenditure that a small change in its price would not produce a significant real income effect (i.e. it would not change the utility of money income). Later, many modern economists avoided both the concept of marginal utility and consumer surplus by utilizing the indifference curve technique of Francis Edgeworth and Vilfredo Pareto.[40]

Marshall developed the concept of consumer's surplus to examine the larger question of increasing consumer welfare by taxing or subsidizing certain industries. In this application, he preferred to focus on the *change* in consumer surplus when price changes from one level to another. If, for example, it is possible to introduce a subsidy that reduces the price of a commodity from p_1 to p_0 as in Figure 14.3 then (again assuming a constant marginal utility of money) the change in consumer surplus is represented by the triangle $A'B'C$. This application of the concept of consumer surplus is examined somewhat further in connection with the price and output results of increasing and decreasing cost industries.

Welfare effects of taxes or subsidies

The effects a tax or subsidy will have are most easily demonstrated in a constant-cost industry. Assume the imposition of a tax raises the long-run supply curve from SS' to ss' as in Figure 14.4. The demand curve DD will then cut the new supply curve at W and output will be contracted from OB to OA. Consumer surplus will be reduced from DYS before the tax to DWs after the tax. The loss in consumer surplus due to the tax is therefore $sWYS$, while tax receipts are $sWXS$. Thus, the loss of consumer surplus is greater than the tax receipts by the amount WXY. This triangle on the graph represents the net loss to the community.

The effect of a subsidy given to the same commodity can be demonstrated by similar logic. Assume ss' is the original supply curve and SS' is the new supply curve that results when a subsidy of $sZYS$ facilitates an expansion of output from OA to OB. In this case, the gain in consumer surplus is smaller than the subsidy spent to acquire it, and the triangle WYZ represents the net loss to the community. Marshall concludes, therefore, that the imposition of a tax or the granting of a subsidy to a constant-cost industry can make no positive contribution to the economic well-being of consumers.

It may be desirable, however, to tax an industry operating under diminishing returns and subsidize one operating under increasing returns. A tax will be beneficial in an industry subject to sharply diminishing returns because, in this case, a small reduction in output is associated with a substantial reduction in cost, so the receipts from the tax will be greater than the loss in consumer surplus. Conversely, a subsidy will increase welfare in an industry operating under increasing returns if a small increase in output is associated with a considerable reduction in cost, for here the gain in consumer surplus will be greater than the amount spent on the subsidy. Thus, Marshall concludes that it might be 'for the advantage of the community that the government should levy taxes on commodities which obey the laws of diminishing returns, and devote part of the proceeds to bounties on commodities which obey the law of increasing returns.'[41] He warns, however, that his analysis does not, in and of itself, 'afford a valid ground for government interference.'

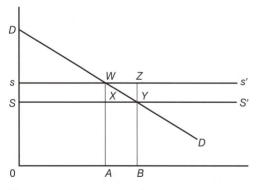

Figure 14.4 No net gain from a tax or subsidy under constant returns

The pricing of productive factors

Distribution theory in relation to value theory

Marshall's theory of distribution, as already observed, is an application of his theory of value to the pricing of the factors of production. Factor prices are explained as being determined through the interaction of demand and supply forces precisely as are commodity prices. The prices that rule in the factor markets are, at one and the same time, costs of production to the business owners who employ and pay out incomes to the factors. Since, under free competition, long-run commodity prices are equal to production costs, they are also equal, in the aggregate, to long run factor incomes. Thus, Marshall established an interdependence or complementarity between value theory and distribution theory that was absent in the thinking of his classical predecessors. He also included organization, or enterprise, in his classification of the factors of production along with land, labor, and capital. The incomes of these factors, which, in the aggregate, constitute the national dividend, are rent, wages, interest, and profit. Each of these shares, with the exception of the profit residuum, is a market-determined price that needs to be explained in terms of the demand and supply conditions operative in the long run as well as in shorter periods.

Marginal productivity and factor demand

Marshall emphasized that the demand for a factor of production by a firm or industry is a *derived demand*, which depends on the value of its services in the production of output. Since the employment of increasing quantities of a variable resource combined with one or more fixed resources will result in diminishing marginal returns to that resource beyond some point, it follows that the marginal revenue, which the sale of its output yields, will also diminish beyond some point. A firm's demand curve for a variable resource like labor will therefore be downward sloping.

All firms using a given variable factor will experience diminishing returns beyond some point as they employ greater quantities of it. In addition, the increased product of a variable factor employed by all the firms in an industry is likely to depress the sale price of the product and, hence, the marginal revenue product of the variable factor. A market-demand curve for a factor cannot, therefore, be drawn on the basis of an assumed product price, as is done for a single firm.

While the marginal revenue product of a factor governs the demand for it, it does not, in Marshall's view, explain the price it will command any more than utility governs the price of a commodity. To explain distributive shares therefore requires an examination of the influences on the supplies of all productive agents, because factor prices are governed by the interaction of demand and supply forces, for the latter govern factor prices as well as commodity prices. 'The nominal value of everything, whether it be a particular kind of labor or capital or anything else, rests, like the keystone of an arch, balanced in equilibrium between the contending pressures of its two opposing sides; the forces of demand press on the one side, and those of supply on the other.'[42]

The supply of productive factors

Time is relevant to the examination of the supply of productive factors, just as it is for the supply of commodities. Marshall maintained that while the short-run supply of the factors is, for all practical purposes, fixed, the long-run supply of reproducible factors exhibits the reflex influence of remuneration.[43] Thus, the supply of labor in the aggregate and of each grade, including that of enterprise and organization, is viewed as a positive function of the wage rate, and the supply of savings and capital are seen as responding positively to the interest rate.

Turning specifically to the supply of labor, Marshall recognizes that there are complex sociological influences at work, which he examines with great insight. But he maintains that, in the long run, the supply of various kinds of labor responds to economic factors. Unusually high wages in the short run in specific occupations increase the supply of that type of labor in the long run. His emphasis on the functional relationship between the remuneration of labor and its supply is somewhat reminiscent of Malthus's position. Unlike Malthus, however, he conceived of the growth of the labor supply as including, not merely increased numbers, but also the greater quality of labor that accompanies a rising standard of life when there is increased efficiency.

Marshall's explanation of the motives for saving and the supply of capital also emphasizes the reflex influence of remuneration on supply. Thus, he states that 'a rise in the rate of interest offered for capital . . . tends to increase the volume of savings . . . It is a nearly universal rule that a rise in the rate increases the desire to save; and it often increases the power to save.'[44] Although it is recognized that the motives for saving are very complex and that the rate of interest frequently has little effect on individual savings, the long-run aggregate supply of savings is seen as being responsive to a rise in the demand price for it. Only land and other gifts of nature are unique in that their supply in a settled country is fixed, even in the long run, so that earnings have no influence on their supply.

The pricing of productive factors

Because the rewards of reproducible factors are similar to those of land (whose supplies are relatively fixed in the short run), it is convenient to examine land rent first and then proceed to the incomes of the other factors. Because the supply of land is fixed in a settled country, Marshall hypothesizes that the parcels comprising the total supply are transferred from one use to another as changes in the demands, supplies, and prices of various crops alter profit opportunities. The active factor that determines the uses to which land is put is the relative demand for the various crops it can produce. 'Each crop strives against others for the possession of the land; and if any one crop shows signs of being more remunerative than before relatively to others, the cultivators will devote more of their land and resources to it.'[45] Thus, the rent secured from any one use must equal that possible from any other use in an equilibrium situation. Therefore, from the point of view of the individual landowner, land is not notably different from capital, for free capital can be invested either in land or in industrial equipment. In either case, the income is a rate of return on an investment whose value is established by capitalizing the income it yields.

When land is leased to a tenant, the payment made for its use is obviously related to the return the owner could earn by cultivating it himself. The rent paid is therefore one of the costs that must be covered by the market price of the product. This conclusion differs from the Ricardian view that rent is *price-determined* rather than *price-determining*. Marshall makes it clear that it *is only* within the framework of the implicit Ricardian hypothesis – that land has no use alternative to producing the raw products of labor's subsistence – that rent is *not* a cost of production. Since the long-run price of any agricultural commodity must cover the cost of the marginal application of the labor and capital required to produce it, all units of land on which labor and capital are not marginal yield a surplus that is rent in the Ricardian sense. Conceived in this way, Marshall agreed, rent is not a cost of production and exerts no influence on price. But when rent is looked at from a private point of view, it is not a surplus but a competitive price that must be paid in order to bid land away from an alternative use.

The difference between Ricardo's treatment of rent and Marshall's stems largely from the problems with which they dealt. Ricardo, it will be recalled, was primarily concerned with explaining the incomes of various social classes, particularly as they were affected by the Corn Laws. He conceived of rent as making its appearance when population growth required less fertile or less well-situated land to be taken out of idleness and used in the production of raw produce. Ricardo's concern was not with the rent paid by particular agricultural producers for particular fields, but with the rent yields to agricultural landowners as a whole. Competing uses of land for different kinds of raw products, or for non-agricultural uses, were not considered because Ricardo's concern was chiefly to determine the laws that regulate the distribution of the produce of the earth among the three social classes under the names of rent, profit, and wages.

Thus, it is the difference in the hypotheses from which Marshall and Ricardo started that is at the root of the issue of whether rent is a cause or an effect of price. Marshall's own conclusion was that 'it is wisest not to say that 'Rent does not enter into the cost of production because that will confuse many people.' But it is wicked to say that 'Rent *does* enter into the cost of production,' because that is sure to be applied in such a way as to lead to the denial of subtle truths.'[46]

In the short run, the rewards of labor and capital are governed by essentially the same principles as the rent of land. Since their supply is relatively fixed, the demand for them is the primary factor governing their remuneration. Their marginal productivity rules the demand for them, and the application of each factor up to its profitable margin of use causes the marginal increment of each factor to earn a reward equivalent to its addition to the value of the total product. Competition among homogeneous units of the same factor will operate to secure the same reward for each increment of a factor as the marginal one, since all units are interchangeable. Short-run factor rewards are therefore adjusted by the current market situation without reference to the cost of producing the factor. They may thus exceed the cost of bringing the factors to market, and thus, a surplus in the form of quasi-rent is contained in their prices.

The tendency of short-run factor rewards to equal the contribution of the factor at its margin of employment is not, however, in Marshall's view, a theory of distribution. It merely serves to 'throw into a clear light the action of one of the causes' that govern factor rewards. This cause operates on the demand side. However, supply forces must also be taken into account. Thus, *Marshall's theory of distribution is not a marginal productivity theory of distribution*, but one that holds that we must look to the margin to discover the forces governing the determination of factor rewards. Supply forces as well as those of demand are operative.

Unlike land, labor and capital are reproducible. While the reflex action will be slow, their supply will tend to increase with their remuneration. With respect to labor, the marginal productivity of each grade will govern the demand for it, so wages will tend to equal the marginal revenue product of labor. At the same time, however, wages also bear an indirect and complex relationship to the cost of rearing and training labor, and therefore to its supply and quality. Thus, unlike the classicists, Marshall does not see the real wage of labor as a constant determined in the long run by the cost of producing raw produce at the margin. Resorting once more to static assumptions, he concludes that if the economic conditions of a country remain stable for a sufficiently long period of time, the adjustment of the supply of labor to the demand for it will cause human beings to earn an amount that corresponds fairly well to their cost of rearing and training.[47] It follows that there is a separate rate of wages for each grade of labor that depends, in the long run, on the amount of that grade demanded and supplied.

Demand and supply forces are similarly at work in the determination of the income of capital. Such capital may be free capital available for new investment, or capital already invested in concrete appliances. The present rate of interest reflects the temporary equilibration of the current demand for, and supply of, funds. Because the supply of capital is relatively fixed, its short-run earnings are not necessarily equal to the present rate of interest. Its earnings reflect the market values of its products and are comparable to the earning of land. Such earnings are properly conceived as *quasi-rents* rather than interest, although they can be expressed as a percent by capitalizing them at the current rate of interest.

The long-run earnings of capital reflect the influence of altered supplies of industrial equipment over time. Types of capital yielding high returns will tend to be augmented in the long run, while those that yield relatively lower earnings will be decreased in supply. As a result, all types of capital will tend to yield a normal rate of return in the long run that corresponds to the additional amount of value product created by the capital applied at the margin.

Marshall's theory of profits involves much the same reasoning as his inquiry into wages and interest. Each industry will tend to develop the type of organization that provides the greatest opportunity for profit at the margin of advantage. That portion of profit representing the 'wages of management' is governed by the same principle that governs the determination of wages. These are the normal profits that are part of the normal costs of production and that, therefore, enter into the long-run supply prices of goods. Pure profits exist under competitive conditions only as a short-run phenomenon. Like other quasi-rents, they tend to be eliminated, so in the long run there remains only the normal rate of profit required to attract the appropriate type of entrepreneurial ability into each industry. Thus, we see that Marshall's theory of distribution is an integral part of 'a continuous thread running through and connecting the applications of the general theory of the equilibrium of demand and supply to different periods of time.'[48]

Concluding remarks

While Marshall intended to complete and generalize Mill's exposition of Ricardo's theory of value and distribution with the aid of mathematical techniques, he actually produced, as our presentation has shown, a more comprehensive transformation than he himself originally anticipated. The main features of this transformation consist of (1) the assumption that the effects of human motives as they relate to behavior in the marketplace are uniquely measurable in terms of sums of money that would be given up to gain particular satisfactions; this is in contrast with human motives in a social environment, such as neighborly and charitable acts; (2) the explicit introduction of demand equations in the explanation of commodity values; (3) recognition that the technical coefficients of production are not fixed but vary with the costs of factor substitution at the margin and that this will affect the marginal cost of producing a commodity in the short run; (4) an inquiry into the laws of return that govern the cost of production in the long run: (5) recognition that the real wage of labor is not a constant that depends on the cost of producing raw produce at the margin, and that there is a separate wage rate for each grade of labor that depends in the long run on the amount of that grade demanded and the amount supplied; (6) recognition that the return to capital is distinct from that of organization; and (6) recognition that factor prices and commodity prices are interrelated, and that the theories of value and distribution are therefore different aspects of a single problem.

While Marshall chose to conduct his analysis with the aid of the partial equilibrium technique, he also developed concepts that led outside its confines. The concept of demand elasticity, particularly in such modern developments as cross-elasticity and income elasticity, and the principle of substitution and consumer surplus all lead toward the exploration of interrelationships. So do his concepts of joint demand, joint supply, composite demand, and composite supply. His treatment of these cases in his Note 21 leads him to the

formulation of equations of the Walrasian type and the conclusion that 'however complex the problem may become, we can see that it is theoretically determinate, because the number of unknowns is always exactly equal to the number of equations which we obtain.' Marshall himself saw the general equilibrium analysis of the Walrasian type as the logical complement of his partial analysis. But even within the framework of his partial analysis, the principle of substitution at the margin – involving as it does the balancing of small increments of payments and satisfaction, costs and receipts, effort and income, by consumers, producers, and factors – provides the connecting link among all sectors of the economy. Thus, the principle of interdependence and mutual determination pervades every aspect of Marshall's analysis, even though the technique of abstraction is employed to reduce the number of variables to manageable proportions.

Marshall also went beyond Ricardo and Mill in emphasizing the efforts and sacrifices that constitute the real costs of production and the satisfactions of consumption. Ricardo and Mill consistently thought of costs in objective, rather than subjective, terms. But Marshall emphasized the psychological factors underlying behavior in the marketplace and considered them measurable in terms of money. Although the first edition of the *Principles* equated optimizing behavior with the hedonistic pleasure-maximizing, pain-minimizing choices of Utilitarian ethics, subsequent editions tried to avoid Bentham's terminology, as well as its reformist spirit.

While Marshall examined the nature and sources of monopoly power, most of his analysis was conducted on the assumption of 'freedom of industry and enterprise' – not perfect competition but pure competition of the atomistic variety in which there are a sufficiently large number of small economic units to prevent any one of them from exerting a dominant force in the market. He believed in the power of competitive forces to overcome the forces leading to monopoly. He also valued competition as a stimulus to individual initiative and achievement, and believed it would lead to social progress more surely than any form of socialism. He was not, however, opposed to reform measures so long as they did not tend to stultify individual opportunities for growth.

The main departure modern theory has made from the *Principles* has been in the realm of macroeconomics. Whereas Marshall regarded money as a passive factor with respect to the level of economic activity and accepted the conclusions inherent in Say's law, modern macroeconomic theorists explain the determination of output on non-Sayian assumptions. Their concern is, therefore, to explain the level of resource use (i.e. employment and income levels) rather than the allocation of resources. Even though many Marshallian concepts and tools are indispensable to their analysis, much of the inspiration for modern macroeconomic analysis derives from contributions to the theory of economic crisis and business fluctuation made by persons not associated with the neoclassical tradition. Neoclassical theorists literally assumed away the whole problem of explaining economic fluctuations as a result of their acceptance of Say's law, and in their preoccupation with real phenomena, they also failed to appreciate the role of monetary phenomena in the determination of real magnitudes. It is not until the Keynesian revolution that the role of money and interest rates with respect to the level of employment and income began to be understood. But once this understanding was gained, its practical significance became so great that microeconomic analysis

was almost shunted aside as macroeconomic analysis came to dominate contemporary economic theory.

The earliest criticisms leveled against the neoclassical tradition, however, were directed at its *microeconomic* aspects. The notion of consumer sovereignty and the reliability of the price mechanism with respect to maximizing welfare were primary issues in the revolt against neoclassicism that began to gather momentum during the 1920s. The chapter that follows examines this aspect of the challenge against the Marshallian tradition and how it became amended in consequence of competitive analysis.

Notes

1   Arthur C. Pigou (ed.), *Memorials of Alfred Marshall* (London: Macmillan, 1925), p. 417.
2   Mrs. Marshall is said to have commented that Marshall hit upon the concept of demand elasticity in Salerno in 1881, while spending an hour of contemplation on a rooftop. He introduced it 'without any suggestion that the idea was novel' (J. M. Keynes on Alfred Marshall, in Pigou, *Memorials*, p. 45).
3   Consult Pigou, *Memorials*, pp. 500–8, for a list of Marshall's writings.
4   Alfred Marshall, *Principles of Economics*, 8th edn (London: Macmillan, 1920), p. 1.
5   Marshall, *Principles*, p. 15.
6   Marshall, *Principles*, p. 9.
7   See Chapter 15.
8   Pigou, *Memorials*, p. 159.
9   Pigou, *Memorials*, p. 30.
10 Pigou, *Memorials*, p. 21.
11 *Principles*, Appendix 1, pp. 813–21.
12 See, for example, Joseph A. Schumpeter's discussion of Marshall's originality in *History of Economic Analysis* (London: Oxford University Press, 1954), pp. 835–40.
13 Marshall introduced the now-standard practice of putting pace on the ordinate axis.
14 *Principles*, p. 99.
15 For example, if a 10-cent price reduction results in a 500-pound increase in the quantity

demanded, the slope of that portion of the demand curve is

$$\frac{-10}{500} \text{ or } \frac{-1}{50}$$

This measure is crude in the sense that a change in the unit in terms of which prices are measured, say from cents to dollars, yields the following measure:

$$\frac{\frac{-1}{10}}{500} \text{ or } \frac{-1}{5000}$$

16 *Principles*, mathematical appendix, note III.
17 This can be easily verified by measuring elasticity from point A to B and then from B to A using the data in the accompanying table:

	Price	Quantity
A	$2.00	100,000
B	1.00	200,000

Using the formula to measure elasticity from point A to B, the demand is elastic:

$$e_d = \frac{\frac{100,000}{100,000}}{\frac{1}{2}} = \frac{\frac{1}{1}}{-2} = -2$$

But measuring from B to A, it is inelastic:

$$e_d = \frac{\frac{-100,000}{200,000}}{\frac{1}{1}} = \frac{\frac{-1}{2}}{1} = \frac{-1}{2}$$

18 This discrepancy may be reduced by modifying the formula for calculating elasticity as follows: calculate the change in pace from the lower of the two prices and the change in quantity from the smaller of the two quantities. This results in an average of the two results obtained in the original formula. For the problem given in Note 17, elasticity would be −1.

19 Marshall, *Principles*, p. 153.
20 George Stigler, *Production and Distribution Theories* (New York: Macmillan, 1941), pp. 66–67.
21 Marshall, *Principles*, p. 319.
22 Marshall, *Principles*, p. 318.
23 Marshall, *Principles*, p. 310.
24 Marshall, *Principles*, p. 317
25 Marshall, *Principles*, p. 318
26 See Stigler, *Production and Distribution*, p. 68.
27 Marshall, *Principles*, pp. 808–9 n.
28 Marshall, *Principles*, p. 316.
29 Marshall, *Principles*, pp. 286–87.
30 Marshall, *Principles*, p. 339.
31 Marshall, *Principles*.
32 Marshall, *Principles*, p. 362.
33 This problem was later dealt with by Jacob Viner in his article 'Cost curves and supply curves,' *Zeitschrift fur Nationalökonomie*, 3 (1931), pp. 23–46; reprinted in Kenneth E. Boulding and George Stigler (eds), *Readings in Price Theory*, vol. 6 (Homewood, Ill.: Richard D. Irwin, 1952), and in R. V. Clemence (ed.), *Readings in Economic Analysis* (Reading, Mass.: Addison-Wesley, 1950), vol. 2.
34 Marshall, *Principles*, p. 317.
35 Marshall, *Principles*, p. 343.
36 Marshall, *Principles*, p. 388.
37 Marshall, *Principles*, pp. 477–88.
38 This was demonstrated by Joan Robinson, *Economics of Imperfect Competition* (London: Macmillan, 1933), D. 56.
39 Marshall, *Principles*, p. 503.
40 See Chapter 15.
41 Marshall, *Principles*, p. 475.
42 Marshall, *Principles*, p. 526.
43 Marshall, *Principles*, Book 6, Chapter 2.
44 Marshall, *Principles*, p. 236.
45 Marshall, *Principles*, p. 435.
46 Pigou, *Memorials*, p. 436 (from letter to Francis Edgeworth).
47 Marshall, *Principles*, p. 577.
48 The links between Books V and VI of *Principles* and their relation to Marshall's appreciation of the methodological problems inherent in examining problems of income distribution are examined in greater detail in Ingrid H. Rima 'Marshall's concern about poverty: a hundredth anniversary retrospective,' *Review of Social Economy*, 48, no. 4 (Winter, 1990).

Glossary of terms and concepts

Ceteris paribus

A Latin phrase meaning 'other things remaining equal.' In microeconomic analysis, it is customary to assume that tastes, incomes, the price level, and the level of technology remain unchanged.

Demand (supply) schedule

A list of the quantities of a given good buyers (sellers) would be willing to purchase (offer) at a corresponding schedule of prices.

External economies

Economies associated by Marshall with 'the general progress of the industrial environment.' Because they are equally available to all firms, they do not tend to reduce competition. (Both Marshall's conception of external economies and his estimate of their impact on competition were later challenged.)

Internal economies

Economies achieved by *individual firms* as they expand their scale of production and organization. Because they are not equally available, their effect is to reduce competition.

Joint supply

An output situation in which two or more products are simultaneously produced (e.g. cottonseed and fiber) and, thus, individual costs are not separable. Individual costs can be identified only if proportions are variable.

Law of demand and supply

The price of a commodity varies directly with the quantity demanded and inversely with the quantity supplied.

Neoclassical economics

The integration, principally associated with Marshall, of the utility theory of values with the cost of production theory of the classicists. Its main concern is to explain commodity and factor prices and the allocation of resources with the aid of marginal analysis.

Partial equilibrium analysis

An analysis that focuses on the determination of individual commodity or factor prices, unlike a general equilibrium analysis in which all prices are determined simultaneously.

Perfect competition

A market characterized by perfect information on the part of participants and perfect resource mobility, in addition to the requirements associated with pure competition.

Price elasticity of demand

The percentage change in the quantity of a good demanded divided by the percentage change in price when both changes are infinitely small.

Pure competition

A market characterized by a large number of suppliers of a homogeneous commodity on which a large number of buyers spend only a small part of their income with the result that only one selling price emerges from the interaction of supply and demand forces.

Quasi-rents

Returns to factors that are temporarily in excess of the value of their marginal products.

Representative firm

A hypothetical firm with average access to resources, information, and markets, which is, in this sense, typical of the experience of the industry as a whole.

Questions for discussion and further research

1 How did Marshall's Book V reconcile the classical cost of production theory of value with that of the utility theorists, in particular, of Jevons? How does *time* relate to the relative importance of demand and supply?

2 Marshall was at great pains to maintain that the marginal productivity principle is not a theory of distribution. Why is this the case? How does it apply in particular markets, say the labor market?

3 Explain (a) the conditions under which rent is a price-determined form of income, not a cost of production, and the conditions under which rent is a cost of production and, as such, a factor in determining prices, and (b) the nature of *quasi-rents* and how, in the long run, they are either eliminated or absorbed in long run costs of production.

4 On the basis of Marshall's discussion, explain the following. (a) The nature of and distinction between internal and external economies or returns, and whether such economies or returns are phenomena of the short run or the long run. (b) Explain the meaning of changes in scale as used in the phrase 'returns to scale,' and which of the foregoing economies require changes of scale to occur. (c) Explain why marginal cost in excess of minimum prime cost (or, which comes to the same, marginal cost in excess of minimum variable average cost) is the firm's supply schedule or supply curve of output.

Notes for further reading

From *The New Palgrave*

M. Ali Kahn on perfect competition, vol. 3, pp. 831–33; Giacomo Becattini on internal economics, vol. 2, pp. 889–91; Peter Bohm on external economies, vol. 2, pp. 261–63; W. E. Diewert on cost functions, vol. 1, pp. 690–96; F. H. Hahn on neoclassical growth theory, vol. 3, pp. 625–33; James C. Moore on cost and supply curves, vol. 1, pp. 681–87; Milshaq Nadiri on production: neoclassical theories, vol. 3, pp. 992–95; Akira Takayama on consumer surplus, vol. 1, pp. 607–12; J. K. Whitaker on *ceteris paribus*, vol. 1, pp. 396–97, and on Alfred Marshall, vol. 3, pp. 350–62.

Selected references and suggestions for further reading

Review of Social Economy, 48, no. 4 (Winter, 1990). Complete issue on Alfred Marshall.

The Eastern Economic Journal, 8, no. 1 (January/ March, 1982). Complete issue on Alfred Marshall.

Frisch, Ragnar. 'Alfred Marshall's theory of value.' *Quarterly Journal of Economics*, 64 (November, 1950).

Guillebaud, Claude, W. 'Some personal reminiscences of Alfred Marshall.' *History of Political Economy*, 3 (Spring, 1971).

Keynes, J. M. 'Alfred Marshall.' In *Essays and Sketches in Biography* (New York: Meridian, 1957).

Marshall, Alfred. *Principles of Economics*, 9th edn (London: Macmillan, 1961).

Pigou, A. C. (ed.) Memorials of Alfred Marshall (New York: Kelley and Millman, 1956).

Rima, Ingrid H. 'Marshall's concern about poverty: a hundredth anniversary retrospective.' *Review of Social Economy*, 48, no. 4 (Winter, 1990).

Rima, Ingrid H. 'Neoclassicism and dissent: 1890–1930.' In Sidney Weintraub (ed.), *Modern Economic Thought* (Philadelphia University of Pennsylvania Press, 1977), pp. 7–21.

Robbins, Lionel. Lecture 32, 'Marshall', in *A History of Economic Thought* edited by S. Medema and W. Samuels (Princeton NJ: Princeton University Press, 1998), pp. 303–11.

Robertson, H. M. 'Alfred Marshall's aims and methods illustrated from his treatment of distribution.' *History of Political Economy*, 2 (Spring, 1970).

Shove, O. E. 'The place of Marshall's "Principles" in the development of economic thought.' *Economic Journal*, 52 (December, 1942).

Viner, Jacob. 'Marshall's economics, in relation to the man and to his times.' *American Economic Review*, 31 (June, 1941).

Whitaker, John K. 'Alfred Marshall: the years 1877 to 1885.' *History of Political Economy*, 4 (Spring, 1972).

Whitaker, John K. *The Early Economic Writings of Alfred Marshall, 1867–1900* (New York: Free Press, 1975).

Whitaker, John K. 'Some neglected aspects of Marshall's economic and social thought.' *History of Political Economy*, 9 (Summer, 1977).

Chapter 15

Chamberlin, Robinson, and other price theorists

Introduction

Marshall focused chiefly on the determination of commodity and factor prices in markets characterized by freedom of industry and enterprise because large numbers of buyers and sellers of homogeneous commodities and services were trading in them. He had a well-developed model of monopoly, although he accorded the problem of pricing in this type of market much less attention than he lavished on the behavior of competitive markets. Furthermore, he hardly perceived the possibility that some markets might have characteristics that enabled sellers to exert individual control over their prices even though they were not monopolists. Yet, it is precisely this gray area of pricing in markets, which are *neither* purely competitive nor purely monopolistic, that became a major area of investigation during the 1930s.

Marshall himself pointed in this direction when he noted that 'when we are considering the individual producer, we must couple his supply curve – not with the general demand curve for his commodity in the wide market – but with the particular demand curve of his own special market.'[1] Though he did not pursue this kind of analysis himself, there were writers in the 1930s who did, specifically, Piero Sraffa (1898–1983), an Italian scholar

working at Cambridge University in England, Joan Robinson (1903–83), also at Cambridge, and Edward H. Chamberlin (1899–1967), an American doctoral candidate and later a professor at Harvard University.

Development of economic analysis

Although Marshall provides hints about the possible direction future work might take, one cannot help but speculate whether the more rigorous treatment of imperfectly competitive market structures by contemporary theorists was triggered by concern with the problem of big business. It is certainly true that, in the United States at least, there was renewed public concern over the concentration of economic power during the 1920s and 1930s and many institutional studies of the problem appeared at that time.[2] Still, no one could have been more concerned with the problem of monopoly than Marshall or John Bates Clark, although both conducted their theoretical analyses on the premise that most markets approximate free competition. While the problem of big business and its regulation may indeed have been more pressing in the 1930s than it had been 50 or so years earlier, there is no evidence that the new theoretical developments in the area of price theory were in any way a response to the challenge created by this aspect of the institutional environment.

If any environmental influences were at work in stimulating the development of price theory, they derived from the intellectual, rather than the institutional, environment. In particular, greater interest in mathematical economics focused attention on the work of Cournot, whose *Researches into the Mathematical Principles of the Theory of Wealth* (1838) was then nearing its 100th anniversary. Cournot's theory of monopoly and his conclusion that monopolists will maximize profit when they equate the first derivative of total revenue (i.e. marginal revenue) to the first derivative of total cost (i.e. marginal cost) were the first major achievements of mathematical economics. Unfortunately, Cournot's work was not widely studied until the late 1870s. Thus, the more rigorous classification of market structures along the lines he suggested, along with greater terminological precision and development of new analytical concepts, is a twentieth century development. Currently, it is the problem of oligopoly, or competition among a few sellers, that has been of greatest interest in the area of price theory. The paragraphs that follow will provide acquaintance with the names of, and brief biographical information about, the main contributors to price theory since Marshall.

Contributors to modern price theory

With respect to the theory of monopoly, the improvement since Cournot has been mainly in terms of exposition. The main substantive contributions have been the theory of monopoly price discrimination and the development of the case of monopsony, or buyer monopoly, to parallel the traditional case of seller monopoly. With respect to the theory of monopoly price discrimination, the most substantial contributions have come from Arthur C. Pigou (1877–1959) and Joan Robinson (1903–83). Pigou's examination of the nature and results of monopoly pricing was conducted within the framework of the welfare analysis of his *Economics of Welfare*, which has already been discussed.

Other than Pigou's, the most substantive contribution to the theory of monopoly pricing is to be found in Robinson's *Economics of Imperfect Competition* (1933), which is also concerned with the analysis of pricing situations that lie in the gray area between pure monopoly and pure competition. Robinson, of Cambridge University, is the most famous among the women who have achieved recognition as economic theorists. She rediscovered Cournot's first derivative of total revenue and christened it *marginal revenue*, and her simple yet elegant geometry popularized the use of marginal cost and marginal revenue curves in price analysis. She also made the most substantial contribution of any contemporary writer since Pigou to the theory of monopoly price discrimination, as well as developing the case of monopsony, or buyer monopoly, to parallel the traditional case of seller monopoly. Her contributions are not, however, limited to the field of price theory. She was equally accomplished in the area of macroeconomic theory and had a particular interest in the theory of capital and secular growth. She was professionally active virtually to the end of her life and left behind a major legacy of contributions, some of which will be noted elsewhere.

Pierro Sraffa (1898–1983) pointed out the vulnerability of Marshall's 'external economies' as a device for reconciling increasing returns with the assumption of pure competition in his now classic 1926 article on the laws of return.[3] Sraffa, who came from Italy to study, and later teach, at Cambridge, is also remembered for his edition of Ricardo's *Collected Works* and for his monograph *The Production of Commodities by means of Commodities* (1960). But he is equally well known for his provocative 1926 article on the laws of return, which focused analytical attention on the main dark spots in the Marshallian theory of value and urged its reconstruction. Even though he did not participate further in bringing about this reconstruction, the keenness of his observations on the technical shortcoming of Marshall's long-run supply curve alone are sufficient to secure him a place among contemporary contributors to value theory.

Sraffa's 1926 article on the laws of return had already appeared when Edward Chamberlin (1899–1967), still a graduate student at Harvard in 1927, submitted a doctoral dissertation in which he undertook to examine the determination of prices in markets in which monopolistic and competitive elements are blended. This dissertation, *The Theory of Monopolistic Competition* (1933), appeared so nearly at the same time as Joan Robinson's *Economics of Imperfect Competition* in England, that both writers are equally recognized as pioneers in the theory of pricing situations that are intermediate between pure competition and pure monopoly. Unlike Robinson, Chamberlin, who was a professor of economics at Harvard, devoted his professional efforts almost exclusively to exploring the various ramifications of his original thesis, including the implications of the theory of monopolistic competition for the theory of distribution.

While the leading contributions to contemporary literature on price theory are those of Chamberlin and Robinson, Henrich von Stackelberg (1905–46) published his *Marktform und Gleichgewicht* (Market structures and equilibrium), which is especially concerned with duopoly and oligopoly, in 1934.[4] This work appeared in the period during which the National Socialist party was achieving full power in the Third Reich. It is interesting to note that von Stackelberg's conclusions with respect to the proper role of the state in oligopolistic markets is compatible with the policies of the Nazi party, although von Stackelberg supported his conclusions by economic analysis.

Original contributions to the literature of price theory have been scant since the leading works of the 1930s. A notable contribution was made at the close of the decade by Robert Triffin (1911–), in *Monopolistic Competition and General Equilibrium Theory* (1940), which provides an analytical comparison of the works of Chamberlin, Robinson, von Stackelberg, and others, and suggests that the theory of monopolistic competition may provide the bridge needed to reconcile the particular equilibrium approach of Marshall with the general equilibrium approach of Walras.

J. R. Hicks (1904–89), who closed his professional career at Oxford University, was affiliated with the London School of Economics during the time when he wrote his first theoretical article, 'Edgeworth, Marshall and the indeterminateness of wages' (1930). It was followed by his book *The Theory of Wages* (1932), and indicated his strong interest in the pricing aspects of the labor market, and reflected the then predominant dichotomy between real and monetary economics. His interest in monetary theory came only later as he came to be influenced by the Austrians – in particular Friedrich Hayek's 1928 work translated in 1931 as *Prices and Production* and Gunnar Myrdal's *Monetary Equilibrium* (1933) – and his ideas on money began to develop. These ideas attracted the attention of Cambridge economists Dennis

Robertson and J. M. Keynes, with whom he eventually affiliated himself between the years of 1935 and 1938, before taking up the post of Stanley Jevons Professor of Political Economy where he remained until 1946.[5]

Thus, his contributions to value theory, including 'A revision of demand theory' (1934) and *The Theory of Wages* (1932), reflect the first part of his contributions to economics. These are the contributions which will be reviewed in this chapter and the next, leaving his contributions to macroeconomics to a subsequent chapter. They belong to that part of his professional life during which his work was in the neoclassical tradition, earning him a knighthood from Queen Elizabeth in 1964 and the Nobel Prize in Economics for 1972.[6]

Some dark spots in neoclassical value theory

Assumptions concerning the firm's demand curve

While Marshall's theory of value is unquestionably superior to its predecessors, it nevertheless has certain shortcomings that made themselves increasingly apparent as time went on. One of these is the implicit assumption that most firms produce and sell their products under conditions of free competition, that is, in markets in which they must accept a price determined by the interaction of forces outside their individual control. The individual firm was conceived to have an infinitely elastic demand for its product at the going market price. Unless a firm was a monopolist, there was therefore no need to single it out for separate examination because its experience was essentially that of every other firm in its industry. Thus, Marshall solved the problem of determining the

equilibrium price of a commodity in terms of the industry as a whole by setting an industry supply curve, which was conceived of as a simple summation of the supply curves of a large number of firms producing an essentially homogeneous commodity, against an industry demand curve, constructed by the summation of individual demand curves for a given product.

The shortcoming of Marshall's procedure is its lack of analytical concern about the pricing effects that occur if buyers are not indifferent about the particular commodity of individual sellers of similar goods. The causes for their preferences are very diverse, and may range from long custom, personal acquaintance, confidence in the quality of the product, proximity, knowledge of particular requirements, and the possibility of obtaining credit, to the reputation of a trademark or sign, or a name with high traditions, or to such special features of modeling or design in the product. This is without constituting it as a distinct commodity intended for the satisfaction of particular needs, having as the principal purpose that of distinguishing it from the products of other firms.[7]

Joan Robinson, in *The Economics of Imperfect Competition*, made essentially the same observations about the causes of buyer preferences and viewed their existence as the source of 'imperfect' competition.[8] Edward Chamberlin likewise cites essentially the same factors as creating what he terms *product differentiation*, which significantly distinguishes the goods of one seller from those of his or her rivals and creates a market in which there is 'monopolistic competition.'[9]

Regardless of the particular method a seller uses to attract and hold customers, the effect of such techniques is always to make the demand (or sales) curve for the product less than perfectly elastic. This effect was succinctly expressed by Sraffa in his observation that

> the peculiarity of the case of the firm which does not possess an actual monopoly but merely has a particular market is that, in the demand schedule for the goods produced by it, the possible buyers are entered in descending order according to the price which each of them is prepared to pay, not rather than go entirely without, but rather than not buy it from that particular producer instead of elsewhere.[10]

That product differentiation will cause the demand (or sales) curves of an individual seller to diverge from the horizontal position they would have if no seller had any individual control over price, was similarly pointed out by Chamberlin and Robinson.[11]

Product differentiation also has the effect of making a firm's demand curve and its cost curves interdependent, for the firm's demand curve then depends partly on the expenditure it makes to attract customers. Chamberlin, in particular, has distinguished between selling costs and production costs, and has pointed out that the existence of selling expenditures is *prima facie* evidence that the market is not one in which there is pure competition.[12] If a seller conducts a successful selling effort, 'this means a shift of the demand curve for his product upward and to the right.'[13] The position and slope of an individual seller's demand curve depends not only on the product but also on the extent to which firms can, by their selling expenses, build up preferences for their particular output as opposed to that of rivals. It follows that when there is product differentiation, the sales and cost curves, and therefore the profits of rival firms, are interdependent in various degrees. Thus, there arises what Chamberlin has chosen to call the *group problem*. His *Theory of Monopolistic Competition* lavishes great attention on defining the nature of group equilibrium and

examining the mode of its establishment. Robinson's *Economics of Imperfect Competition*, though it parallels in many ways Chamberlin's work, is not concerned directly with the group problem at all, although it describes the phenomenon of product differentiation in almost the same language as Chamberlin.

Assumptions regarding the laws of return

An equally troublesome feature of the Marshallian analysis, along with his assumptions regarding the demand curve confronting the typical *firm*, is his treatment of the long-run laws of return and their effect on the industry supply curve. Marshall, it will be recalled, conceived of the possibility of long-run constant, decreasing, and increasing returns. He recognized that if it were possible for an individual firm, as distinct from an industry as a whole, to experience economies that would give it increasing returns to scale in the long run, free competition would be destroyed. But he rejected as unlikely the premise that economies that are sources of increasing returns are exclusively available to any one firm. He thought increasing returns are, in fact, likely to be the result of external economies equally available to all firms and therefore compatible with the continuation of competition. This conclusion was, in Sraffa's view, such a vulnerable part of Marshall's analysis of the long-run supply curve that he was led to make the following observation in his 1926 article:

> In the tranquil view which the modern theory of value presents us there is one dark spot which disturbs the harmony of the whole. This is represented by the supply curve, based upon the laws of increasing and diminishing returns. That its foundations are less solid than those of the other portions of the structure is generally recognized. That they are so weak as to be unable to support the weight imposed on them is a doubt which slumbers beneath the

consciousness of many, but which most succeed in silently suppressing. [14]

The crucial question with respect to the long-run supply curve of a particular industry was, as Sraffa viewed the matter, the compatibility of Marshall's explanation of the tendency toward long-run increasing returns and decreasing supply price with his insistence on a particular equilibrium analysis. A particular equilibrium methodology requires that variations in output or demand in one industry have neither a direct nor an indirect effect on any other industry. Such long-run independence is unlikely, Sraffa contended, in industries subject to either diminishing or increasing returns because, in these cases, changes in the output of the commodity in question have an effect on the cost of using factors that also enter into the production of other commodities. The requirements of a particular equilibrium methodology are thus violated.

He objected, for the same reason, to Marshall's reliance on external economies resulting from the general progress of the industrial environment as a means of explaining why some industries are able to enjoy long-run increasing returns. Such economies are compatible with the continuation of competitive conditions because they are equally available to all the firms in an industry. This was precisely the source of their appeal to Marshall, but, maintained Sraffa, a particular equilibrium analysis requires that the economies from which long-run decreasing costs derive be *internal* to the industry, even though they are external to the individual firms.

The only economies which could be taken into consideration would be such as occupy an intermediate position between these two extremes; but it is just in the middle that nothing, or almost nothing, is to be found. Those economies which are external from the point of view of the individual firm but internal as regards the industry in its aggregate, constitute precisely the class which is most seldom met with. [15]

Sraffa therefore advised that we abandon the path of free competition and turn in the opposite direction, namely towards monopoly. [16]

While few undertakings fit the case of pure monopoly, Sraffa believed that the theory of monopoly could provide a guide to the relationship between price and the quantity that can be sold when competition is absent for other reasons. The theory of monopoly is, therefore, useful to us in studying those cases in the real world (and they are in majority) that do not fit either the case of pure competition or pure monopoly but are 'scattered along the intermediate zone.' [17] He also suggested that the task of reconstructing the theory of value could be immediately begun, for an analytical tool equal to the task was already at hand in Marshall's concept of monopoly net revenue. Joan Robinson was among those who responded to Sraffa's urging that the time had come to reconstruct the theory of value to recognize that real-world markets do not fit the black/white model of monopoly or pure competition. But, she maintained, in order to do so, it is necessary first to identify a proper analytical tool.

Issues and Answers from the Masterworks 15.1

Issue

What is the most appropriate analytical tool for explaining the pricing and output decisions of a seller who is not offering its product to a perfectly competitive market?

Robinson's answer

From *The Economics of Imperfect Competition*, Introduction, pp. 3–6.

In the older text-books it was customary to set out upon the analysis of value from the point of view of perfect competition. The whole scheme appeared almost homogeneous and it had some aesthetic charm. But somewhere, in an isolated chapter, the analysis of monopoly had to be introduced. This presented a hard, indigestible lump which the competitive analysis could never swallow. To quote Mr. Sraffa's comment:[18] 'Of course, when we are supplied with theories in respect to the two extreme cases of monopoly and competition as part of the equipment required in order to undertake the study of the actual conditions in the different industries, we are warned that these generally do not fit exactly one or other of the categories, but will be found scattered along the intermediate zone, and that the nature of an industry will approximate more closely to the monopolist or the competitive system according to its particular circumstances.' But the books never contained any very clear guidance as to how these intermediate cases should be treated; as a picture of the real world the theory was unconvincing, and as a pure analytical construction it had a somewhat uncomfortable air.

Moreover, the relations between the real world and the competitive analysis of value were marred by frequent misunderstandings. The economists, misled by the logical priority of perfect competition in their scheme, were somehow trapped into assumptions of perfect competition, they were inclined to look for some complicated explanation of it, before the simple explanation occurred to them that the real world did not fulfil the assumptions of perfect competition. Or they were tempted to introduce into the theoretical scheme elements which, at a superficial glance, appeared to account for the phenomena of the real world, but which completely destroyed the logical self-consistency of the theoretical scheme.

It was at such a moment of confusion that Mr. Sraffa declared: 'It is necessary, therefore, to abandon the path of free competition and turn in the opposite direction, namely, towards monopoly.'[19] No sooner had Mr. Sraffa released the analysis of monopoly from its uncomfortable pen in a chapter in the middle of the book than it immediately swallowed up the competitive analysis without the smallest effort. The whole scheme of analysis, composed of just the same elements as before, could now be arranged in a perfectly uniform manner, with no awkward cleavage in the middle of the book. Two simple examples will show this process at work.

First consider the problem of defining a monopoly. It was tempting, under the old scheme, to arrange actual cases in a series of which pure monopoly would be the limit at one end and pure competition at the other, but a definition of pure monopoly which would correspond to the definition of pure competition was extremely hard to find. At first sight it seems easy enough to say that competition exists when the demand for a commodity in a certain market is met by a number of producers, and that monopoly exists when it is met by only one. But what is a commodity? Must we group together as a single commodity all articles which compete against each other to satisfy a single demand? In that case, since every article must have some rivals, and since in the last resort every article represents a use of money which is rival to every other, we should be compelled to say that no such thing as complete monopoly exists at all. Or must we define as a single commodity only a group of articles which is perfectly homogeneous? Then the slightest degree of difference, from the point of view of their customers, between rival producers even of one sufficiently homogeneous commodity, must be taken as a sign that we are dealing not with one commodity but with several. For if the individual buyer has any reason to prefer one producer to another, the articles which they sell are not perfectly interchangeable from the point of view of the buyer, and we are reduced to regarding the output of each producer as a separate commodity. Thus any attempt at a logical definition of a monopolist drives either monopoly or competition quite out of the field. It is easy enough to find the limiting case at the competitive end of the scale. The limiting case occurs when the demand for the product of an individual producer is perfectly elastic. But what is the limiting case at the other end? The case in which the demand for the product of the individual is the same as the total demand for the commodity? Then we are back at the original problem of how to define a commodity. We know what we mean by 'selling in a perfect market', but what is a perfectly imperfect market?

Now as soon as we abandon the attempt to confine monopoly in a pen by itself the whole of this difficulty disappears. Every individual producer has the monopoly of his own output – that is sufficiently obvious – and if a large number of them are selling in a perfect market the state of affairs exists which we are accustomed to describe as perfect competition. We have only to take the word monopoly in its literal sense, a single seller, and the analysis of monopoly immediately swallows up the analysis of competition.

The reader may object that there is clearly some sense in which Messrs. Coats have got a monopoly of sewing cotton, and in which a Bedfordshire market gardener has not got a monopoly of brussels-sprouts. But this objection is easily answered. All that 'monopoly' means, in this old-fashioned sense, is that the output of the individual producer happens to be bounded on all sides by a marked gap in the chain of substitutes. Such a gap in nature provides us with a rough-and-ready definition of a single commodity – sewing cotton or brussels-sprouts – which is congenial to common sense and causes no trouble. When a single producer controls the whole output of such a commodity the plain man's notion of a monopolist and the logical definition of a monopolist as a single seller coincide, and the difficulty disappears.

A second example of the manner in which monopoly analysis engulfs competitive analysis can be illustrated from the technique of analysis itself. When Mr. Sraffa declared that the time had come to re-write the theory of value, starting from the conception of the firm as a monopolist, he suggested that the familiar tool, 'maximum monopoly net revenue', was ready to hand and that the job could begin at once. But that tool is at best a clumsy one and is inappropriate to many of the operations which are required of it. In its place the 'marginal' technique must be borrowed from the competitive chapters of the old textbooks, and adapted to new purposes.

Whilst many pieces of technical apparatus have no intrinsic merit, and are used merely for convenience, the use of marginal curves for the analysis of monopoly output contains within itself the heart of the whole matter. The single assumption which it is necessary to make in order to set that piece of apparatus at work is the assumption that the individual firm will always arrange its affairs in such a way as to make the largest profits that can be made in the particular situation in which it finds itself. Now it is this assumption that makes the analysis of value possible. If individuals act in an erratic way only statistical methods will serve to discover the laws of economics, and if individuals act in a predictable way, but from a large number of complicated motives, the economist must resign his task to the psychologist. It is the assumption that any individual, in his economic life, will never undertake an action that adds more to his losses than to his gains, and will always undertake an action which adds more to his gains than to his losses, which makes the analysis of value possible. And it is this assumption that underlies the device of drawing marginal curves. With bricks of this one simple pattern the whole structure of analysis is built up.

Source: Reprinted from *The Economics of Imperfect Competition* by Joan Robinson (London: Macmillan, 1933) Introduction, pp. 3–6.

Summing up: Robinson's chief points

Robinson addressed the problem of decision making about price and output determination by introducing the concept of marginal revenue. Under free competition, a firm maximizes profits or minimizes losses by equating its marginal cost to price. But since price (average revenue) is equal to marginal revenue, in this case, the firm also equates marginal cost and marginal revenue. A monopolist will do precisely the same thing, although this behavior is not apparent when expressed in terms of monopoly net revenue. It matters not in the least whether we say, as did Marshall, that a monopolist maximizes profit by maximizing net revenue or whether we say, as did Cournot, that a monopolist will maximize profit when a price is set that will equate the first derivative of total revenue (marginal revenue) with the first derivative of total cost (marginal cost). The latter expression, however, has the advantage of being a principle equally applicable to competition and monopoly or to any market structure combining elements of both. Marshall's tool of monopoly net revenue is unsatisfactory because 'it introduces an artificial cleavage between monopoly and competition.[20]

Robinson's discovery of the marginal revenue curve has greatly facilitated both the verbal and the graphical exposition of the behavior of a firm to maximize profits or minimize losses. It is much simpler to say that a firm equates marginal revenue and marginal cost than that it equates the first derivative of total revenue with the first derivative of total cost. In addition, the intersection of the marginal cost and marginal revenue curves as the determinant of a firm's output facilitates a much clearer graphic representation of the behavior of a firm than one that proceeds by means of average revenue and average cost. Chamberlin's diagrams in *The Theory of Monopolistic Competition* depict the behavior of firms with the help of average curves only. His diagrammatic technique is cumbersome in comparison with Robinson's, which employs marginal curves. Her terminology and her geometry have become standard for the profession.

Robinson herself demonstrated the versatility of her tool in her examination of the relationship between the average and marginal revenue curves of a monopoly firm as opposed to a purely competitive firm. Their difference derives, she explained, from the fact that *under conditions of pure competition*, the individual firm does not depress market price by offering additional units for sale, with the result that its demand curve is *infinitely elastic*. Since there is no change in average revenue regardless of the volume of sales, marginal revenue does not change either. It is, therefore, graphically a horizontal line, identical with average revenue.

A monopolist, on the other hand, is supplying the total market, and this demand curve has the same characteristics as the industry demand curve for a purely competitive market. It is the summation of the demand curves of individual consumers and is therefore downward sloping. The price a monopolist can get for an additional unit of output is always less than can be got for a smaller volume. Average revenue declines as output increases, so marginal revenue will be less than average revenue. Graphically, therefore, the marginal revenue curve will lie below the average revenue curve.[21]

The equilibrium of the firm, as distinct from the equilibrium of the group, is Robinson's main concern and her main contribution to the extension of the neoclassical theory of value. It is therefore relevant to examine further what contemporary theorists have accomplished with respect to eliminating the so-called dark spots in neoclassical value theory under two headings: the first is 'Equilibrium of the firm,' which focuses on the individual seller of commodities in isolation from any rivals it may have. The second is 'Equilibrium of the group,' which examines the impact rival sellers and buyers have on one another's behavior.

Equilibrium of the firm

The conditions of stable equilibrium

Chamberlin and Robinson reflect the Marshallian origins of their studies on price in theory, in their concern with the establishment of equilibrium. Marshall's analysis was conducted almost entirely in terms of the *industry*, the notable exception being the case of monopoly, in which the firm *is* the industry. Contemporary theorists, on the other hand, having discarded the notion that the

firms of an industry have infinitely elastic demand curves, are concerned with the individual firm as a separate entity. Robinson, following Sraffa's suggestion, proceeds by allowing the theory of monopoly to swallow up the analysis of competition. It is, however, not the behavior of the pure monopolist that Robinson is concerned with, but rather the behavior of a firm that is a monopolist of its own particular product. The equilibrium position of such a firm is necessarily affected by the nature of the reaction that its price–output decisions have on its competitors. Some method must therefore be devised to deal with the problem of interdependence.

In the latter respect, there is a striking difference between Robinson's approach and Chamberlin's. Whereas Chamberlin is concerned with analyzing the nature of interdependence and the effect that the price–output decisions of one firm will have on those of its rivals, and therefore on the equilibrium of the group, Robinson makes the implicit assumption that every firm in the group, but one, is in equilibrium. It is thus possible for her to study in isolation the movement of that firm toward an equilibrium position, guided by the objective of maximizing its monetary profits. For this reason, her analysis leaves the impression of being concerned with simple monopoly.

Since the individual firm is thought to move toward its equilibrium position guided by the objective of maximizing its monetary profits, *the first condition* which must be satisfied is that its *marginal revenue must equal marginal cost*. Satisfaction of this condition will not, however, assure a stable equilibrium. Obviously, if the production of a larger output than the one at which $MC = MR$ adds more to total revenue than to total cost, it will pay a firm to expand. Robinson has therefore shown that equality between marginal cost and marginal revenue is only a first-order condition. The stability of monopoly equilibrium depends also on the relationship between the marginal revenue and marginal cost curves of a firm. A stable monopoly equilibrium requires, as its *second condition*, that the production of a larger output than that at which $MC = MR$ adds more to total cost than to total revenue, so that a further expansion of output is unprofitable. This is illustrated in Part A of Figure 15.1, in which MC cuts MR from below.

Since the marginal revenue curve of a firm is downward sloping, unless it is a pure competitor, the second-order condition specified by Robinson for a stable equilibrium of a firm is satisfied if marginal cost is increasing or, at least, decreasing less rapidly than marginal revenue. In either case, the MC curve cuts the MR curve from below, as in Part A and Part B of Figure 15.1. If MC cuts MR from above, as in Part C of Figure 15.1, so that MC lies below MR for outputs larger than that at which $MC = MR$, the second-order condition is not satisfied; that is, the maximum profit is indeterminate, and there is no stable equilibrium price or output.

Equilibrium when monopoly price discrimination is possible

Monopoly price discrimination, or the practice of charging different prices to different buyers of a product or service, is the ultimate technique for profit maximization. It is possible only if a seller who is in a position to control the selling price has the additional power of distinguishing among customers on the basis of differences in their demand elasticities. Customers having different demand elasticities for a particular product or service, as, for example, is the case with respect to most users of a public utility service, enable a seller to group buyers according to their demand elasticities and to charge a different price to each. The essential requirement for discrimination is the effective segregation of the various parts of the total market. Pigou has shown that this depends on the non-transferability of various units of output and demand from one market to another.[22]

During the 1920s, Pigou was greatly interested in the special price problems of railroads and showed that the factor of non-transferability is significant in explaining why a discriminatory price structure prevails in this field. A shipper who buys a transportation

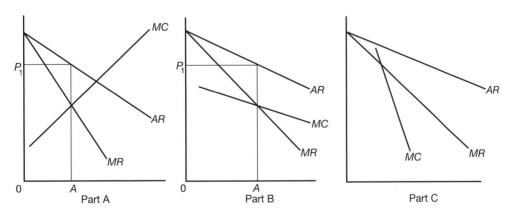

Figure 15.1 Robinson's 'second order' condition for firm equilibrium

service generally cannot resell a part of the service to some other shipper to whom the railroad has quoted a higher rate.[23] The same factor explains discriminatory rate patterns in the sale of public utility services generally. For example, gas or electric power is sold to industrial users at a lower rate than to residential users, but they cannot redistribute it, at least not without considerable expense, to residential users. Thus, the ability of a utility to maintain a policy of price discrimination derives from the fact that ready transference of service from customer to customer is impossible. If units of a product or service were transferable from one market to another, a monopolist would, for all practical purposes, be forced to adhere to a single-price system.

A monopolist who can effectively segregate markets and who is not subject to public regulation can maximize returns by charging high prices to those customers whose demands are relatively inelastic, while at the same time cultivating sales to other buyers, whose demands are more elastic, through the offer of low prices.[24] Robinson demonstrated that profits will be at a maximum when marginal revenue in each submarket is equal to the marginal cost of the whole product. That is, the total output of a discriminating monopolist is determined by the intersection of the marginal cost curve and the aggregate marginal revenue curve.

Profit maximization by a discriminating monopolist is represented in Figure 15.2, in which MR_1 is the marginal revenue curve in the market having a less elastic demand and MR_2 is the marginal revenue curve in the market having a more elastic demand. They are derived from their respective demand curves, D_1 and D_2, and their lateral summation results in the aggregate demand curve, AD. The aggregate marginal revenue curve, AMR, is obtained by summing MR_1 and

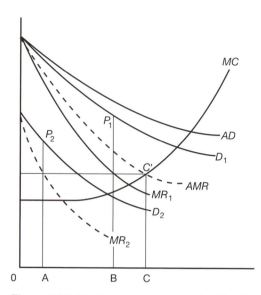

Figure 15.2 Robinson: monopoly price discrimination

MR_2. The total output is therefore OC, which is determined by the intersection of the aggregate marginal revenue curve with the marginal cost curve. It is composed of output OA, sold at price P_2 to those whose demands are relatively more elastic, and OB, sold at P_1 to those whose demands are relatively less elastic. This is the output that maximizes profit for the discriminating monopolist since marginal revenue in each market is equal to the marginal cost of the whole output. Monopoly net revenue for output OC is the area under the aggregate marginal revenue curve (total revenue) minus the area under the marginal cost curve (total costs).[25]

The chief argument against monopoly is that it affects welfare adversely because it restricts output. Robinson, however, demonstrates that if production takes place under conditions of decreasing average cost, it contributes to the welfare of consumers instead of being detrimental to their interests because it may result in the offer of a larger output. If a monopolist is able to segregate consumers into distinct market groups to which he or she charges different prices, the output may be either equal to, greater than, or smaller than, it would be if a single monopoly price were charged.

Output will be larger as a result of price discrimination if the more elastic demand curve is concave while the less elastic curve is convex or linear. In this case, the expansion in output sold in the first market at a price lower than the single monopoly price will be greater than the reduction in output sold in the second market at a price higher than the single monopoly price. This is so because discrimination results in an aggregate marginal revenue curve that is above the simple monopoly marginal revenue curve.[26] If demand curves in both markets are linear, however, the aggregate marginal revenue curve will equal the simple monopoly marginal revenue curve, and output will be no larger than it would be under a single monopoly price. The only difference will be in the way in which output is allocated between the two markets and the price that is charged in each.

Equilibrium of the group

Chamberlin's concept of small and large groups

The duopoly models of Augustin Cournot and Joseph Bertrand, which were discussed in Chapter 11, are a convenient beginning to further inquiry into the so-called *group problem*. Their models are based on the highly artificial assumption of a conjectural variation of zero with respect to the behavior of competing duopolists. This assumption means that a duopolist is depicted as behaving as though his behavior is independent of that of his rivals. Cournot hypothesized two sellers of a costless homogeneous commodity, each of

whom tries to maximize net revenue on the assumption that competitors will not alter the quantity they offer for sale. Bertrand created a different model as part of his criticism of Cournot's solution to the duopoly problem, in which the competitors behaved on the assumption that, regardless of the rival's action, the other would keep the *price* unchanged.

The oligopoly case is an extension of the duopoly problem in which there are more than two sellers, but the number is sufficiently small so that each seller realizes that his or her own behavior will influence not only the price at which he or she can sell but also rival price policies. The solution to the small group or oligopoly problem depends on the assumptions the particular model makes with respect to the behavior of the various participants. Edward Chamberlin's is the first among the several models we shall examine.

Chamberlin simplified the problem of analyzing the behavior of the group by assuming that all the firms have identical cost and demand functions. The group can then be described in terms of a single firm that is representative of all firms. The essential difference between the small group and the large group is to be found in the reaction pattern that any individual firm will stimulate among its competitors when it alters either its price, its product, or its selling expenses.[27]

Chamberlin pictures this reaction pattern in terms of the elasticity and movement of the sales or demand curve confronting the individual firm. The demand curve confronting the representative firm depends on whether its sales are a function solely of its own price, or also the prices charged by its competitors. The curve *dd* in Figure 15.3 shows how much the representative firm thinks it can sell at all possible prices, provided other firms keep their prices fixed instead of responding to price changes it

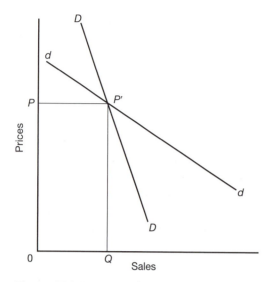

Figure 15.3 Interdependence between firms: the 'kinked' demand curve

might initiate. This kind of curve is associated only with a large group because, in a case like this, the impact of price change by one firm on its competitors is likely to be negligible. The large group is, in this sense, akin to pure competition. However, it is also akin to monopoly, in that each seller has a negatively sloped demand curve for particular products. There are many sellers in the market, but their products are heterogeneous rather than homogeneous because of advertising and other techniques of product differentiation. The absence of homogeneous commodities enables each seller to determine the profit-maximizing price, which may be quite different from that of other competitive sellers.[28] Chamberlin therefore introduced the term *monopolistic competition* to describe it. He reasoned that if there is monopolistic competition, a price cut will significantly increase the sales of the firm that introduces it because the cut draws away customers from rivals. But the effect of the price cut is spread over so many competitors that the volume of sales it

draws away from any one firm is too small to cause any such firm to alter its policy.

The *DD* curve in Figure 15.3, on the other hand, shows how much the representative firm thinks it can sell at all possible prices if its competitors always charge the same price it charges. This curve is drawn on the assumption that if a particular firm alters its price, say from *OP*, an identical change is made by every other firm in the group. The result, Chamberlin suggests, is a sales curve that is less elastic than the *dd* curve the firm would face if it were able to alter its price and not call forth a similar price change by its competitors. If the market had only one firm, *DD* and *dd* would be the same curve. However, if there is more than one firm, the *DD* curve represents the actual market share the representative firm will enjoy at every possible price it might charge if competing firms charge exactly the same price.[29] This will be the case only if the group is small.

Figure 15.3 also sheds some light on the tendency for oligopoly prices to remain rigid once they have been determined. Paul M. Sweezy suggested that, in an oligopoly situation, a seller is not confronted with the entire length of *DD* but with a 'kinked' demand curve like *dP'D*.[30] If an oligopolist can raise the price above *OP* without rivals following suit, but finds that the sales curve confronting him at prices above this level is a highly elastic curve like *dP'*, a price increase cannot provide a larger share of the market. If, on the other hand, the price is reduced below *OP'* and rivals do the same, a price cut will not increase the oligopolist's share of the market.

Thus, a firm that confronts a demand curve that is relatively inelastic at prices below *OP* and relatively elastic at prices above *OP* has little incentive either to raise or to lower price from *OP*. Sweezy therefore reasoned that once an oligopolistic seller has fixed his or her price, it will tend to stay rigid, as will the prices of rival sellers.

The tendency for oligopoly prices to be 'sticky' may thus reflect the presence of a kinked demand curve for the product.

Chamberlin's equilibrium analysis

While Chamberlin's diagrams demonstrate the profit-maximizing behavior of the representative firm of the group with the aid of average revenue and average cost curves, the same thing can be illustrated more conveniently with diagrams that also show the now standard marginal cost and marginal revenue curves. Thus, in Figure 15.4, if $DD = AR$ is the sales curve of the representative firm in a small group, and SMC and SAC are its short-run cost curves, output OQ will be offered for sale at a price of OP per unit, assuming that rivals sell at an identical price.

At a price of $OP = OP'$, there is a pure profit equivalent to the area $CC'P'P$. Whether pure profit will continue to be enjoyed depends on the entry of new firms into the market in response to higher-than-normal

profits. If entry into the group is free, new-comers will encroach on the sales of existing sellers until pure profit has been eliminated. Thus, a long-run equilibrium with only normal profit is possible when the group is small. The very existence of a small group, however, usually implies that entry is restricted in some way. Chamberlin therefore conceives of small-group equilibrium as being compatible with any level of pure profit, even in the long run.

If, on the other hand, a group is large, new firms tend to be attracted by the presence of pure profits, precisely as is the case when competition is pure. Thus, if there are pure profits, the group will move to a position of equilibrium in which pure profit is eliminated. Chamberlin pictured this move via the demand curve of the representative firm. Equilibrium is achieved when a sufficient number of new firms have entered to shift $DD = AR$ to a level at which it is tangent to the average cost curve, as in Figure 15.5, such that price equals long-run average cost. Total cost will then equal revenue; thus, only a normal profit is made and net revenue is zero.

For the firm and the group both to be in equilibrium in the long run, it is necessary that it be unprofitable to alter output from

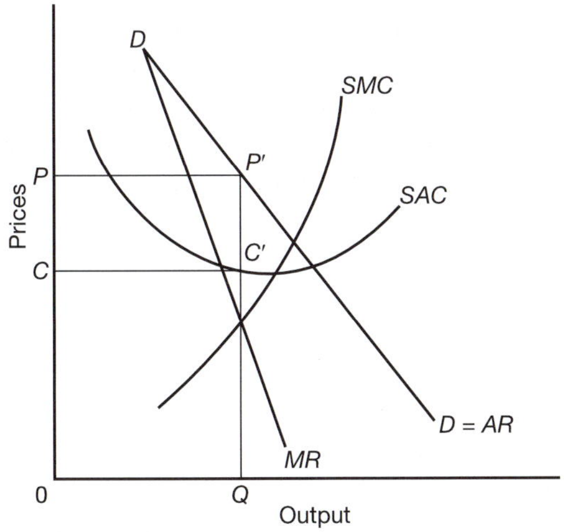

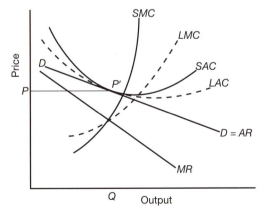

Figure 15.4 Short-run pure profit: the monopoly or oligopoly case

Figure 15.5 Long-run equilibrium in the 'large group.' The case of monopolistic competition

existing capacity (i.e. neither exit from nor entry into the group can occur). This condition requires that price equals short-run and long-run average cost, and that short-run and long-run marginal costs are increasing and equal to marginal revenue. This is shown in Figure 15.5, in which the curve $DD = AR$ is tangent to both the long-run and the short-run average cost curves. Short-run and long-run marginal costs are equal to marginal revenue at output OQ, and the price is equal to both long-run and short-run average cost at OP'. Thus, total revenue and total cost both are equal to $OQP'P$, and net revenue is zero. Chamberlin conceives of this result as being possible only if the group is large. If the group is small, which implies that entry is restricted, any level of positive profits can persist even in the long run.

In addition to the insight it provides into the difference between the behavior of oligopolistic firms and those that are monopolistically competitive, the preceding analysis also shows that the equilibrium output of firms producing under monopolistic competition *cannot* be optimal. This is because the demand curve will always be tangent to the average cost curve somewhere to the left of its lowest point, as in Figure 15.5. Price equals average cost but not marginal cost, as is the case under pure competition. Thus, in comparison with pure competition, the firm under monopolistic competition necessarily produces a smaller output at a higher average cost.[31] Does this mean that there is a waste of resources in monopolistically competitive markets? No definite answer can be given to this question. Product differentiation provides consumers with a variety of similar commodities among which to choose, and the information advertising provides facilitates choice among them. Scarce resources that could be used in other alternatives are neces-

sarily employed for these purposes, but the question as to whether consumers are, on balance, better off is a value judgment.

Robinson's full equilibrium

Robinson, unlike Chamberlin, draws no distinction between the large group and the small group. Yet, her concept of *full equilibrium*, as expressed in the following quotation, coincides with Chamberlin's tangency solution for large-group equilibrium:

> Full equilibrium . . . requires the double condition that marginal revenue is equal to marginal cost and that average revenue is equal to average cost. The double condition of full equilibrium can only be fulfilled when the individual demand curve of the firm is tangent to its average cost curve.[32]

While she does not specifically limit the applicability of the tangency solution by distinguishing between the large group and the small one, she indirectly recognizes the effect that the absence of free entry has on profits. She observes that 'in trades into which there is no possibility of entry . . . there is no upper limit to profit, though there must be a lower limit at the level of profits which is just sufficient to maintain the existing number of firms in business.'[33]

Robinson's definition of costs provides another possible way of reconciling her generalized tangency solution with pure profits. Her treatment of costs includes not only normal profits but also entrepreneurial and factor rents.[34] Chamberlin also includes factor rents and the wages of management as costs, but he has a less-inclusive definition of normal profit than she does. Thus, the differences between Robinson's exposition and Chamberlin's of the requirements of equilibrium in the firm and industry appear to be mainly terminological, despite the differences between them in the presentation of the oligopoly case.[35]

Imperfect competition and factor rewards

Factor rewards under competition

In general, a factor of production is said to be exploited if the payment it receives is less than its marginal physical product valued at its selling price.[36] In light of this definition, Robinson has investigated the relationship between factor rewards and their marginal productivities under conditions of buyer monopoly, or monopsony, in the factor market.[37] The impact of monopsony is most easily understood by first examining the relationships that result in a competitive factor market.

In a purely competitive labor market, such as is represented in Figure 15.6, the labor supply curve is perfectly elastic and is represented as $W = AC_1 = MC_1$. In a long-run equilibrium situation, $W = AC_1 = MC_1$ will be a tangent to the average revenue product curve at its maximum level. This tangency is represented by the point W' on the average revenue product curve in Figure 15.6. The firm maximizes profit from employing labor as a variable factor when it equates the marginal cost

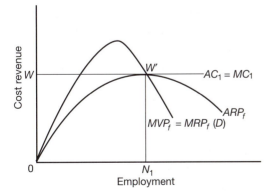

Figure 15.6 Competitive factor pricing: $W = MVP = MRP$

of its hire with the marginal revenue product, which can be got from the sale of its product. It will therefore hire quantity ON_1, for which it will pay $OW = N_1W'$ per unit. This payment is equivalent to both the average revenue product and the marginal revenue product of the factor. Thus, the factor receives the *full value* of its output.

Monopsony and factor exploitation

Robinson's analysis of the effect of monopsony begins with the observation that the factor supply curves confronting a monopsonistic buyer cannot be infinitely elastic, any more than the product demand curve confronting a seller who is not a pure competitor can be infinitely elastic. A firm that is a monopsonist in the purchase of a factor is confronted with *upward sloping average and marginal cost curves*.[38] The upward slope of these curves is significant because it alters both the amount of factor employment in an equilibrium situation and the size of its reward. When the marginal cost of hiring a factor lies above its average cost, as in the case when there is not pure competition in the factor market, the firm will employ a smaller quantity of the factor than it would under pure competition, and the price it pays for its hire will be less than the value of its marginal product.[39]

These relationships are illustrated in Figure 15.7. In this diagram, which represents the factor demand and supply curves of the monopsonistic buyer, the firm faces an upward-sloping average and marginal cost curves like AC_2 and MC_2. Their shape reflects the inability of a monopsonist to purchase additional units of the same factor at an unchanged price as is the case in a purely competitive factor market. For the purposes of comparison, the perfectly elastic factor

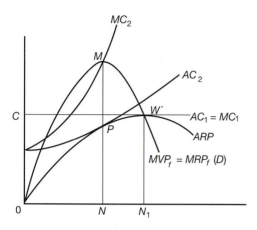

Figure 15.7 Monopsony exploitation: less employment and lower than competitive wages

supply curve that characterizes a purely competitive factor market is reproduced from Figure 15.6.

Both a purely competitive buyer of a factor of production and a monopsonist will seek the most profitable level of a factor employment. This is the level at which its marginal cost of employment is equal to the factor's marginal revenue product. A monopsonistic employer following this principle would, as is illustrated in Figure 15.7, employ only quantity ON of the factor, as opposed to the larger quantity ON_1 that would be bought by a competitive buyer. It would pay the factor a reward equal to NP, its average product. The average revenue product of the factor, however, is less than NM, its marginal revenue product. Thus, there will be *monopsonistic exploitation* to the extent of MP, which is the amount by which the value of the marginal revenue product of ON units of the factor exceeds NP', its price of employment. Thus, these observations bear, in an important way, on the problem of factor exploitation.

If the factor in question is labor, Robinson has shown that exploitation can be reduced

or eliminated and employment increased by introducing a minimum wage at which the supply of labor will be perfectly elastic.[40] In a situation such as that depicted in Figure 15.7 an enforced minimum wage rate of OC will eliminate exploitation and result in the employment of ON_1 labor units, which is the equivalent of the competitive amount of employment. A competitive firm, guided by the equimarginal rule, will employ workers until the weighted marginal physical product of labor is the reciprocal of its marginal cost or the price of its product. Alternatively it hires labor up to the point at which the marginal value product of labor is equal to the money wage rate. In symbols, $MP_n/w = 1/p = 1/MC$ and $MP_n \, p = w$.

J. R. Hicks and *The Theory of Wages*

Just as Sraffa's 1926 article challenged Marshall's argument regarding external economies as the source of falling supply prices on the part of business firms, so in 1929 Maurice Dobb's short article 'A skeptical view of *The Theory of Wages*' attacked the relevance of the marginal theory of value to the labor market.[41] It attracted the attention of J. R. Hicks of the London School of Economics, leading him to write 'Edgeworth, Marshall and the indeterminateness of wages' (1930) which was followed by his book *The Theory of Wages* (1932). Among his critical arguments is his argument that, in practice, wages are at times higher than the equilibrium wage either as a result of government actions or of trade unions. Also, at times, there is unemployment precisely because actual wages are higher than the equilibrium wage. This outcome, Hicks observed, reflected the changes that had come into existence in the post-1930s world. In particular he noted the monetary system had become relatively elastic so that it had become able to accommodate to wage changes. This flexibility has become even greater since the end of World War II in the sense that, in an economy that is no longer on the gold standard (England and the US departed the gold standard in 1932 and 1933 respectively), monetary conditions are no longer dictated from the outside.[42] He suggested that, indeed, it is no exaggeration to say that 'instead of being on a Gold Standard we are on a Labor Standard.'[43] It follows that wages need to be thought of as determined by an interplay between social and economic factors, instead of being based on economic factors – and crude economic factors at that – alone.[44]

A further important aspect of Hicks's *Theory of Wages* is his argument that there is an inverse relationship between real wages and the real rate of profit. A rise in real wages, he argued, is likely to penalize savings, which would lead to reductions in investment and output and thus still lower profits, which encourages the substitution of more capital-intensive methods for labor-intensive methods.[45] Firms react to falling rates of profits by seeking out new techniques which have, at least, the *potential* for raising profit rates and eventually savings and capital accumulation so that a new equilibrium level of output is achieved. Hicks began with an examination of the workings of the labor market that ultimately led him in the direction of examining the process via which the economy shifts to a higher level of investment and income. This is the *problem of the traverse*, which Ricardo addressed when he considered the machinery question. That is, Hicks became interested in examining how an economy shifts from one equilibrium level to another.[46]

Concluding remarks

Modern price theory is, analytically speaking, largely a refinement of the work of Cournot and Marshall. These sources are plainly evident in the static particular equilibrium framework within which optimal behavior is investigated in terms of the relationship between marginal cost and marginal revenue. This implies that, whenever possible, a firm will continue to engage in a particular activity until the net gain at the margin is zero. If there are several activities, then ideally they should all be pursued until they yield the same marginal return.

The application of this analytical tool for predicting the price–output behavior of business firms has centered primarily on market situations that lie intermediate between pure competition and pure monopoly (i.e. monopolistic competition and oligopoly). Most modern theorists conceive of a monopolistically competitive market as one in which each firm is in competition with so many rival producers of close substitutes that its long-run equilibrium position approximates that of the pure competitor, in the sense that none is able to earn 'pure' profit, even though each firm is a monopolist of its own product.

Chamberlin's term *monopolistic competition*, rather than Robinson's *imperfect competition*, has become the preferred terminology, but it is Robinson's marginal revenue concept, and its coupling with marginal cost, that has become the standard analytical tool of modern microanalysis. However, the conclusions both reached were precisely the same when they dealt with the same questions. Indeed, Robinson commented that she never regarded the distinction between her imperfect, and Chamberlin's monopolistic, competition as being the relevant distinction between them.[47]

It does, however, seem relevant to note that Mrs. Robinson has had occasion to reassess her earlier contribution. Twenty years after the publication of *The Theory of Imperfect Competition*, she remarked, 'The assumptions which were adequate are by no means now a suitable basis for an analysis of the problems of prices, production and distribution which present themselves in reality.'[48] In particular, she notes that the treatment of the entrepreneur and profits in *Economics of Imperfect Competition* is 'extremely primitive.' It is not only hard to generalize about profit rates and the 'normal level of profits' but, also, the notion of 'equilibrium size' with respect to a firm has little application to reality. Methodologically speaking, therefore, by the 1950s, Robinson was distancing herself from the neoclassical tradition, which her 1934 work helped to refine. Based on her work of the last 25 years of her life, she became recognized as a post-Keynesian anxious to move beyond her neoclassical forbears.[49]

Notes

1 Alfred Marshall, *Principles of Economics*, 8th edn (London: Macmillan, 1920), pp. 376–79.

2 Claire Wilcox, *Competition and Monopoly in American Industry*, Temporary National Economic Committee Monograph No. 21 (Washington, DC: US Government Printing Office, 1941), A. A. Berle and G. C. Means, The Corporation and Private Property (New York: Commerce Clearing House, 1932); and Frank Fetter, *Masquerade of Monopoly* (New York: Harcourt Brace & Jovanovich, 1931).

3 Piero Sraffa, 'The laws of return under competitive conditions,' *Economic Journal* 36 (December, 1926), pp. 535–50.

4 Translated as *Theory of the Market Economy* by Allen T. Peacock (New York: Oxford University Press, 1952).

5 Omar Hamouda, *John R. Hicks*, Oxford: Blackwell, 1993) chapter 1.

6 His later work represents something of an intellectual 'turnabout,' for his thinking evolved in the direction of what has become known as 'non-neoclassical.' Indeed, in his pivotal article 'Review of political economy: the old and the new' (a reply to Harcourt) *Economic Record*, September (1975), pp. 365–7, he wrote 'Clearly I needed to change my pen name. Let it be understood that Value and Capital (1939) was the work of J. R. Hicks, a "neoclassical" economist now deceased; while *Capital and Time* (1973) and "A Theory of Economic History" (1969) are the work of John Hicks, a non-neoclassic who is quite disrespectful towards his "uncle".'

7 Sraffa, 'The Laws of Return,' pp. 535–37.

8 Joan Robinson, *The Economics of Imperfect Competition* (London: Macmillan, 1933), pp. 89–90 (subsequently cited as *Imperfect Competition*).

9 Edward Chamberlin, *The Theory of Monopolistic Competition* (Cambridge, Mass.: Harvard University Press, 1933, revised 1948), p. 8.

10 Sraffa, 'The laws of return,' p. 546.

11 Chamberlin, *Monopolistic Competition*, p. 71; J. Robinson, *Imperfect Competition*, p. 21.

12 Chamberlin, *Monopolistic Competition*, Chapter 6.

13 Chamberlin, *Monopolistic Competition*, Chapter 7, p. 130.

14 Sraffa, 'The laws of return,' p. 536.

15 Sraffa, 'The laws of return,' p. 540.

16 Allyn Young was a little known, but nonetheless important, participant in the cost controversy of the 1930s. This role is carefully assessed by Charles R. Blitch in 'Allyn A. Young: a curious case of professional neglect,' in *History of Political Economy*, 15, no. 1 (Spring, 1983), pp. 1–24; see also his companion paper 'Allyn Young on increasing returns,' *Journal of Post-Keynesian Economics*, Spring, 1983, pp. 359–72.

17 Sraffa, 'The laws of return.'

18 The Laws of Returns under Competitive Conditions,' *Economic Journal*, December 1926, p. 542.

19 Ibid.

20 Robinson, *Imperfect Competition*, p. 54.

21 Robinson, *Imperfect Competition*, pp. 52–54.

22 Arthur C. Pigou, *Wealth and Welfare* (London: Macmillan, 1912), chapter 27. This work rejects the explanation of multiple railway rates

offered by Frank W. Taussig. As early as 1891, Taussig argued that services being supplied by railroads are produced under conditions of joint cost. Following Marshall (see above), he reasoned that the services are not one homogeneous commodity but several commodities characterized by different elasticities of demand and consequently differing abilities to bear the joint cost of producing them. He thus concluded that multiple railway rates are compatible with pure competition and do not provide a basis for government ownership of railways.

23 The freight forwarder does perform this function to a limited extent.

24 J. Robinson, *Imperfect Competition*, Chapter 15.

25 J. Robinson, *Imperfect Competition*, pp. 182–83, Figure 61.

26 J. Robinson, *Imperfect Competition*, pp. 190–93.

27 E. Chamberlin, *Monopolistic Competition*, pp. 81–104.

28 In 'The origin and early development of monopolistic competition,' *Quarterly Journal of Economics*, 75 (November, 1961), pp. 515–43, Chamberlin relates that his investigation was influenced by Taussig's argument with Pigou about the effect of product heterogeneity on pricing. Taussig maintained multiple rates for a railway service can be explained in terms of Marshall's joint supply thesis. Because the services bought by different groups of railroad customers are not homogeneous commodities, they will not sell at uniform prices even under competition.

29 Chamberlin, *Monopolistic Competition*, pp. 83–85.

30 Paul M. Sweezy, 'Demand under Conditions of Oligopoly,' *Journal of Political Economy*, 47 (August, 1939); also reprinted in *Readings in Price Theory* 6, (edn) Kenneth F. Boulding and George Stigler (Homewood, Ill.: Richard D. Irwin, 1952). See also the empirical study by George Stigler on the basis of which the latter denies the existence of the kinked oligopoly demand curve, 'The kinky oligopoly demand curve and rigid prices,' *Journal of Political Economy,* 55 (October, 1947).

31 E. Chamberlin, *Monopolistic Competition*, pp. 113–16.

32 J. Robinson, *Imperfect Competition*, p. 94.

33 J. Robinson, *Imperfect Competition*.

34 J. Robinson, *Imperfect Competition*, p. 125.

35 The German economist Heinrich von Stackelberg was also concerned with the problem of few sellers. His *Marktform und Gleichgewicht* (Vienna: Julius Springer, 1934) which followed within a year the Robinson–Chamberlin inquiries, began with the simple case of two sellers. In this case each seller is conceived to be confronted with the alternative of leadership or following the lead of a rival. The profit of each is a function of the output levels of both. Unlike Cournot and Bertrand, who assumed conjectural variations of zero with respect to quantity and price, von Stackelberg assumes that both sellers are aware of their mutual interdependence. A follower will adjust output to maximize profit, given the decision of the rival, who is assumed to be a leader with respect to output. The leader, on the other hand, maximizes profit on the assumption that the rival acts the part of follower. Stackelberg believed that the usual market result under duopoly is one of *disequalibrium*.

One of the two must change its behavior pattern and act as a follower before equilibrium can be reached. The implication is that there is inherent conflict that can be resolved only by collusion or a fight to the finish, in which one of the sellers is forced to yield to the leadership of the other. Disequilibrium and destructive competition are even more likely in the case of oligopoly. This inference is the basis for von Stackelberg's view that direct action by the state, or organizations such as cartels, is necessary to achieve equilibrium. This argument is consistent with the legalization in many European countries of cartels in oligopolistic industries, such as steel and chemicals, to assign output quotas to individual firms for the purpose of price control. In the United States, antitrust legislation prohibits cartels and other forms of price-fixing behavior.

36 Arthur C. Pigou, Economics of Welfare, 4th edn (London: Macmillan, 1952), p. 549.

37 Robinson, *Imperfect Competition*, chapter 18.

38 J. Robinson, *Imperfect Competition*, p. 220.

39 J. Robinson, *Imperfect Competition*, p. 250.

40 J. Robinson, *Imperfect Competition*, pp. 294–95.

41 Dobb, M., 'A skeptical view of *The Theory of*

Wages,' *Economic Journal*, 39(4), (1929), pp. 506–19.

42 Hicks, J. R., 'Economic foundations of wage policy,' *Economic Journal* (September, 1955), p. 196.

43 Hicks, J. R., 'Economic foundations of wage policy,' *Economic Journal* (September, 1955).

44 Hicks, J. R., 'Economic foundations of wage policy,' *Economic Journal* (September, 1955), pp. 199–200.

45 'The mainspring of economic growth,' *Swedish Journal of Economics* (December, 1973), especially pp. 9–12.

46 Omar Hamouda examines this and other aspects of Hicks's work in *John R. Hicks: The Economist's Economist* (Oxford: Blackwell, 1993).

47 Joan Robinson, 'Imperfect competition revisited,' *Economic Journal*, 63 (September, 1953), pp. 579–93, p. 579n.

48 Joan Robinson, 'Imperfect competition revisited.'

49 *The Joan Robinson Legacy*, edited by Ingrid H. Rima (Armonk, NY: M. E. Sharpe, 1991).

Questions for discussion and further research

1 What are decreasing long-run costs? What criticism did Piero Sraffa make of Marshall's reconciliation between the tendency toward decreasing long-run costs and pure competition? What has been the significance of Sraffa's criticism for modern price theory as developed by Joan Robinson and Edward Chamberlin?

2 Describe Chamberlin's concept of 'the group.' What is the distinction between 'the small group' and 'the large group'? Demonstrate graphically. How does the 'tangency solution' (equilibrium solution) for a large group differ from that of a small group?

3 The tendency towards price rigidity in an oligopoly situation has been observed many times. How does Professor Sweezy think this phenomenon can be explained?

Glossary of terms and concepts

Kinked demand curve

A demand curve associated with oligopolistic markets that is relatively elastic in the upper ranges and relatively inelastic in the lower ranges. It therefore displays a 'kink' at which the selling price will tend to be rigid. This follows because it is not profitable to reduce price within that segment of the demand curve that is inelastic, and it is not possible to sell at higher prices within the segments in which demand is elastic.

Marginal revenue curve

A curve showing the revenue that will be added from the sale of an additional unit of output. Under imperfect competition, it will always be downward sloping (and will be below the average revenue curve) because additional output can only be sold at a reduced price. Mathematically, it is the first derivative of the total revenue curve.

Monopolistic competition

A market situation characterized by product differentiation.

Monopoly price discrimination

A technique for maximizing profits that can be utilized by a monopolist who sells to different groups of buyers who can be identified on the basis of their demand elasticities. Buyers whose demands are relatively elastic will be offered a lower price than those whose demands are less elastic, provided it is impossible for the first group to resell to the second. The monopolist will divide output among various markets in such a manner as to equate marginal revenue in each market to the marginal cost of producing the output.

Monopsony

Buyer's monopoly. If a firm is a monopsonist in its labor market it has the power to exploit workers by paying wages less than the value of the workers' marginal revenue product.

Oligopoly

A market situation characterized by relatively few sellers, each of whom produces a large enough share of the total output to be in a position to influence market price. Chamberlin called this the *small group* case, as opposed to the large group, in which individual firms can influence price. An oligopoly situation may also be characterized by product differentiation.

Product differentiation

Various techniques – among them packaging, trademarks, brand names, advertising – for the purpose of creating buyer preference for a particular seller's product. If successful, it gives the seller some degree of freedom with respect to pricing.

4 How did the German writer Heinrich von Stackelberg amend the Cournot–Bertrand example of duopoly to arrive at the conclusion that the usual outcome of duopoly is disequilibrium rather than equilibrium.

5 Describe the contributions to economic theory that you particularly associate with Joan Robinson.

6 What is the basis for the challenge Hicks offers to the traditional view that labor markets establish equilibrium wage rates?

Notes for further reading

From *The New Palgrave*

G. C. Archibald on theory of the firm, vol. 2, pp. 357–62, and on monopolistic competition, vol. 3, pp. 531–34; Wilhelm Krelle on Heinrich von Stackelberg, vol. 4, pp. 469–70; Robert Kuenne on Edward Hastings Chamberlin, vol. 1, pp. 398–401; K. J. Lancaster on product differentiation, vol. 3, pp. 988–89;

Edward J. Nell on accumulation of capital, vol. 1, pp. 14–18; Luigi L. Pasinetti on Joan Violet Robinson, vol. 4, pp. 212–17; M. Sawyer on kinked demand curve, vol. 3, pp. 52–53; Stanley Wong on positive economics, vol. 3, pp. 920–21.

Selected references and suggestions for further reading

Blitch, Charles P. 'Allyn A. Young: a curious case of professional neglect.' *History of Political Economy*, 15, no. 1 (Spring, 1983), pp. 1–24.

Blitch, Charles P. 'Allyn Young on increasing returns.' *Journal of Post-Keynesian Economics* (Spring, 1983) pp. 359–72.

Chamberlin, Edward H. *The Theory of Monopolistic Competition* (Cambridge: Harvard University Press, 1962).

Clapham, J. H. 'Of empty economic boxes.' *Economic Journal*, 32 (1922), pp. 305–14.

Cournot, Antoine Augustin. *Researches into the Mathematical Principles of the Theory of Wealth* (1838), translated by Irving Fisher (New York and London: Macmillan, 1927).

Leontief, Wassily. 'Stackelberg on monopolistic competition.' *Journal of Political Economy*, 44 (August, 1936), pp. 554–59.

Robinson, Joan. 'Imperfect competition revisited.' *Economic Journal*, 63 (September 1953), pp. 579–93.

Robinson, Joan. *The Economics of Imperfect Competition* (London: Macmillan, 1933).

Samuelson, Paul A. *Foundations of Economic Analysis* (Cambridge: Harvard University Press, 1955).

Sraffa, Piero. 'The laws of returns under competitive conditions.' *Economic Journal*, 36 (December, 1926), pp. 535–50.

Sweezy, Paul M. 'Demand under conditions of oligopoly.' *Journal of Political Economy*, 47 (August, 1939); also reprinted in *Readings in Price Theory* 6, edited by Kenneth E. Boulding and George Stigler (Homewood, Ill.: Richard D. Irwin, 1952).

Wilcox, Claire. *Competition and Monopoly in American Industry.* Temporary National Economic Committee Monograph no. 21 (Washington, DC: US Government Printing Office, 1941).

Chapter 16

The 'new' theory of welfare and consumer behavior

Introduction

Certain areas of Marshall's theory were vulnerable, because of their reliance on questionable assumptions, as is the case with the long-run supply curve, or because they gave rise to controversial policy questions. One such question is whether a system of taxes and subsidies is the best way to deal with 'externalities' that impose costs on society. Marshall's successor, Arthur C. Pigou, became embroiled in a controversy about that matter with the American economist Frank Knight, who is remembered as the founder of the Chicago tradition of economics. Pigou's approach to the problem, articulated in his Economics of Welfare, built on Marshall's theory of consumer's surplus, which depended on the twin assumptions that the marginal utility of money is constant to consumers and that utility, which is *subjective*, *is* measurable in cardinal units (e.g. 1, 2, 3 . . .).

Marshall himself recognized that the first assumption, in effect, made a consumer's demand for a good independent of income. However, resolution of this difficulty was not apparent until it was suggested by J. R. Hicks and R. G. D. Allen that economists do not require the concept of measurable utility if they proceed from the alternative notion that consumers have preferences that can be ranked (i.e. alternatives are 'more preferred' or 'less preferred'). This approach to the theory of consumer behavior will avoid the problem of measurability, and also the problem of making value judgments. This would satisfy the aim of making economics a value-free science, which is the goal of logical positivism.

The leading participants

Arthur Cecil Pigou (1877–1959) was a man of broad intellectual concern. Indeed, he won prizes for his essays 'The causes and effects of changes in the relative values of agricultural produce in the United Kingdom during the last fifty years' and 'Robert Browning as a religious teacher' (published as Pigou's first book in 1901). He was also known for his somewhat eccentric behavior and dress.[1] More to the point, however, Pigou represents one of the most paradoxical figures in the history of economics. He was, on the one hand, a pioneer in questioning the social efficacy of unregulated private capitalism and, on the other hand, the very epitome of the neoclassical tradition. He studied under Marshall and succeeded to his chair of political economy. It was his work that J. M. Keynes took, during the 1930s, as representative of 'the classics,' whose conclusions about the tendencies of the economy fully to employ its resources he refuted in *The General Theory of Employment, Interest, and Money*. Pigou's counterattack was to demonstrate that full employment is theoretically possible under the neoclassical assumptions of wage–price flexibility. But in his earlier works, particularly *The Economics of Welfare* (1920), he is among the critics of *laissez-faire* capitalism.

Pigou was, however, not a critic who maintained that the answer to society's problems is the replacement of the capitalistic system. Where others argued in favor of abolishing capitalism, whether by revolutionary or evolutionary means. Pigou explored the possibility of improving the existing system. The thrust of his theoretical arguments and policy recommendations commanded only limited interest at the time. However, it has recently been observed that 'now that the Keynesian Revolution has been digested, and the political divisions of the thirties and forties have been reconciled in a system of welfare capitalism, economists are becoming increasingly occupied with policy problems of the kind with which Pigou was concerned, and in whose analysis he was a pioneer.'[2]

Frank Knight (1885–1972) was skeptical of positive action as a means of combating social and economic ills. Harking back to the classical liberalism of Smith and Hume, he helped mold the economic views now associated with the economics faculty of the University of Chicago, which he joined in 1927. His mistrust of reformers never altered and was never more cogently expressed than in his 1950 presidential address to the American Economic Association in which he remarked, 'when a man or group asks for power to do good, my impulse is to say, "Oh, yeah, who ever wanted power for any other reason?" And what have they done when they got it?

So, I instinctively want to cancel the last three words, leaving simply "I want power,"– that is easy to believe.'[3]

Sir John R. Hicks (1904–89) of Oxford University, became an especially important British participant in the reaffirmation of the neoclassical tradition. The refinement of modern utility, demand, and equilibrium analysis is, in large measure, attributable to the foundation he laid in *Value and Capital* (1939) published while he was Stanley Jevons Professor of Political Economy at the University of Manchester. It is largely due to Hicks that the Paretian technique of the indifference curve has become a standard tool of modern microeconomic analysis. He used this tool to demonstrate that it is possible to examine consumer behavior without resorting to the assumption that utility is a cardinally measurable magnitude. He was eventually able to join Pareto's utility analysis to welfare, general equilibrium and capital theory, with the unified theoretical apparatus set forward in *Value and Capital*, for which he was recognized with the Nobel Prize (jointly with Kenneth Arrow) in 1972.

Hicks's rationale for eliminating utility as a measurable magnitude (and the value judgments associated with such measurements) is that it makes it possible to eliminate latent elements of Utilitarianism in economics. As he put it, 'If one is a Utilitarian in philosophy, one has a perfect right to be Utilitarian in one's economics. But if one is not (and few people are Utilitarians nowadays), one also has the right to an economics free from Utilitarian assumptions.'[4] The objective of theoretical neutrality thus underlies Hicks's reconstruction of neoclassical demand theory and the new welfare economics quite as much as it underlies the thinking of Frank Knight and the Chicago tradition.

Controversy about the price mechanism and resource allocation

Sidgwick and Pigou on 'externalities'

From the time of Adam Smith, it was recognized that there are certain undertakings so necessary to the commonwealth but so unprofitable for the private business owner to undertake that their performance by government is essential. Certain other activities were also identified as requiring governmental regulation because they are of a unique public nature or are performed under conditions of 'natural monopoly.' Common defense, industries regulated under common law as public institutions, and those few activities that individuals are unable to perform for themselves, were viewed as appropriate activities for government. Apart from recognizing these exceptional activities as appropriate for government to perform, the corollary of neoclassical analysis was that society's welfare is best served by a government that allows the market mechanism to function without restraint.

Although this sharply circumscribed role for government was generally accepted, the English economist Henry Sidgwick (1838–1900) expressed his reservations even before Marshall. Unlike his contemporaries, Sidgwick recognized the possibility of a divergence between the private product and the social product.[5] He reasoned that an individual's claim to wealth is not, under all circumstances, the precise equivalent of his net contribution to society. There may be 'externalities' associated with activities that either impose costs on others for which the individual is not charged or yield benefits to others for which the person is not paid. Sidgwick's now classic illustrative example hypothesized a lighthouse erected by an individual at his own expense for his own

benefit, which simultaneously yields benefits to others who are free riders in the sense that they bear no part of its cost. In other cases, individuals have unreimbursed monetary or psychological costs imposed on them as a result of another's activities. In either case, the private net product of an activity is not the equivalent of the social net product. Thus, Sidgwick inferred there is a prima facie basis for government intervention on grounds other than those traditionally accepted.

Sidgwick's pioneering inquiry into the problem of the possibility and significance of divergences between the private and social product was raised anew by Marshall and still later by A. C. Pigou in his *Wealth and Welfare* (1920). Pigou considered it to be a major responsibility of the economist to identify the presence of externalities that caused divergences between marginal private and social products, and to work out means to eliminate them.[6] For example, he argued that a railroad ought to be made to compensate farmers and other property owners whose crops and woodlands are damaged by the emission of sparks and smoke. Society's output is overestimated if this type of uncompensated damage is understated in the absence of a compensatory liability charge. The addition of such a charge to private costs makes it possible to identify the whole cost of an operation and thus provide a basis for eliminating the divergence between the private and social product. Regulation is therefore necessary in industries that do not operate under conditions of constant cost in order to prevent the misallocation of resources.

Pigou on increasing- and decreasing-cost industries

Pigou was also concerned to explore further Marshall's inquiry into the social significance of increasing- and decreasing-cost industries and the possibility of using taxes and subsidies to regulate their outputs. Following Marshall, he argued that increasing-cost industries tend to attract excessive investment, whereas constant- and decreasing-cost industries are predisposed toward underinvestment. His most provocative example of the limitations inherent in the market mechanism concerned the hypothetical case of highway traffic on alternative roads between two cities. One of the two roads is poorly surfaced and graded but, being sufficiently wide to accommodate whatever volume of traffic is likely to use it, it provides service under conditions of decreasing cost as the number of cars using it increases. The second road is significantly better with respect to surfacing and grading, but its narrowness limits its capacity. Service is, therefore, provided under increasing-cost conditions. The object of Pigou's example was to demonstrate that, under pure competition, traffic will tend to distribute itself so that the average cost of travel is the same on both roads. This balance occurs because the cost advantage of using the better road is offset as a result of the *externalities* associated with increasing congestion. There tends to be excessive traffic on the well-surfaced road and too little on the other because the route each user chooses is based on the marginal private cost of his or her choice.

The costs that users of the better road impose on others by the additional congestion their traffic causes do not concern them; they have no reason to include the *social costs* they generate in their private-cost calculations. Under competition, the volume of traffic on each road will tend to become distributed so that, in equilibrium, marginal and average private costs are equal for both alternatives. The marginal private cost any

particular car must pay as traffic increases on the better road is, however, less than the total *social* cost. The total social cost is the marginal private cost multiplied by the number of cars using this alternative. The larger the volume of traffic on the better road, the larger the discrepancy between marginal private cost and total social cost as a result of externalities. Given the volume of traffic, a user who is charged the amount at which the private average cost equals marginal cost, is paying a price that is necessarily lower than the true marginal cost of adding an additional vehicle. Because of its failure to assess social costs, the market mechanism produces a tendency towards the misallocation of resources between increasing-cost and decreasing-cost industries.

The difference in the marginal social costs of using the better road versus the poorer road suggests that a pure gain could be achieved for all traffic by altering the use pattern that the market mechanism tends to establish. The transfer of one unit of traffic to the poorer road would not impose a loss on the user who is shifted, because the marginal private costs of service are the *same* on both routes in an equilibrium situation. The transfer would, however, *decrease* the marginal social cost of using the better road. Thus, rerouting traffic can produce a net gain to society. The question, therefore, arises, how can a socially optimal distribution of traffic best be brought about?

Pigou argued that an optimal distribution of traffic can be accomplished by imposing a tax equal to the difference between the marginal private and the marginal social cost on each vehicle using the better road. The route a user chooses to travel will then, as always, be guided by an estimate of the cost of traveling over alternative routes. If a tax is levied to use the better road, the individual necessarily includes it in his private estimate of the cost of travel. The effect is to reduce traffic on the better road until the true (i.e. inclusive of social costs) marginal cost of using it is equal to the marginal cost of using the inferior road. Since the tax for the use of the better road is equal to the cost associated with excessive crowding, its imposition does not add to total travel costs. However, by increasing the money cost of using the better road, it encourages a redistribution of the total volume of traffic and thus contributes to the total welfare.

Knight's response to Pigou

Pigou's argument in favor of using the device of taxes and subsidies to correct divergences between private and social marginal products was subjected to critical examination by Knight in 'Fallacies in the interpretation of social cost.'[7] In this essay and subsequent writings, he reasserted the traditional neoclassical view that competition would tend to produce an efficient allocation of resources. Pigou's demonstration of the failure of the market mechanism is, in fact, urged Knight, indicative of the failure of government to establish and protect private property rights.[8] The results Pigou anticipates with respect to highway use follow only if it is assumed that the owner of the better road fails to set a toll equivalent to the difference in value to the user between it and the wider, but otherwise inferior, road. As a profit maximizing entrepreneur, the owner of the better road will charge a toll equivalent to the differential surplus, or rent associated with the service of the good road. A toll that recaptures this differential surplus, which is rent in the Ricardian sense of the term, will be exactly equal to the tax prescribed by Pigou. Furthermore, it will cause traffic to adjust itself in such a way

that social interests are not abused by private decisions to use alternative transportation routes. Thus, Knight maintains, Pigou's conclusion is not evidence of market failure calling for government interference, but rather evidence of the failure of government to identify and protect property rights.[9]

The Menger heritage of Frank Knight

The microeconomic propositions of modern Chicagoans build chiefly on the work of Carl Menger, as interpreted and transmitted by Frank Knight. Their analyses proceed from the premise that choice is governed by individual perceptions of the utility associated with alternative courses of action. Following Menger, Knight maintained that the relevant cost of any economic decision is the utility of the alternatives sacrificed. No resource has any value other than that imputed to it by the consumer, whose objective it is to maximize the returns yielded by a given supply of resources. Knight credits Menger for establishing the validity of this principle.[10]

Modern writers in the Chicago tradition have built on the Menger–Knight perspective of the relationship between utility and cost (i.e. the cost of any choice is the utility lost in choosing one alternative rather than another) to explore the behavior of the household in managing its time and income resources. An impressive range of topics traditionally examined by sociologists or psychologists has come within their scope of analysis. Using the framework provided by economic theory, the new microeconomics has examined such topics as the allocation of time to education and training as investment in human capital, the rearing of children, criminal behavior as an alternative to market behavior, and choice among sex partners.[11] These inquiries represent contemporary efforts to explore Knight's classic observation: 'To live, in the human plane, is to choose.'[12] It should be noted that the modern microeconomic interpretation of time as a scarce allocatable input reflects a conception different from the Marshallian one that relates time to on-going processes.

Knight on the methodology of economics and consumer sovereignty

Frank Knight's effort to clarify the nature and role of economic man is fundamental to his defense of neoclassicism. Knight recognized that the determinants of human behavior are multifaceted; all of these aspects cannot be incorporated and reflected in the behavioral assumptions made by economists. Knight maintains that it is necessary to abstract from reality and focus on only those aspects that are relevant to explaining economic behavior. Thus, the reasoning of the economist is predicated on the assumption that when it comes to the material aspects of life, individuals make choices which will maximize their gains, both as consumers of goods and services and as producers. In making this abstraction, the economist is following precisely the same procedure as the natural scientist who also excludes the influence of those variables whose operation is either irrelevant or prejudicial to the conclusion the researcher is seeking to establish.

An 'economic person' does not and, indeed, cannot approximate the individual of the real world. But the abstraction is useful, in Knight's view, for helping us understand the purely economic dimension of human behavior. His premise is that economic activity is directed toward maximizing producer and consumer gains and that it is pecuniary behavior the economist is trying to explain. The consumer is sovereign and, in an uncertain world, it is the producer who correctly anticipates what consumers want who will be rewarded with profit. To Knight profit is thus the return for bearing *uncertainty*. It comes as a residual, after all contractual obligations have been met, and only because there is no guarantee that sovereign consumers will actually purchase what has been produced. Thus, Knight's contribution to the theory of profit is directly related to his argument about consumer sovereignty.[13]

Hicks on demand theory

Indifference curves and optimum allocation of income

The marginal utility theorists established the principle that a consumer maximizes satisfaction from a given income when it is spent in such manner as to make

$$\frac{MU_x}{Px} = \frac{MUv}{PY}$$

The chief difficulty with this formulation is its implicit assumption that economic behavior is explainable in terms of pleasure–pain principles and that rational consumers can actually quantify those subjective satisfactions economists refer to as utility. Both ideas became an embarrassment to thinkers who, like J. R. Hicks, were concerned with making economics more scientific.

Issues and Answers from the Masterworks 16.1

Issue

Is utility theory, and the assumption that utility is measurable in cardinal terms, the essential foundation for a theory of demand? Can a demand curve be derived, or the allocation of income among alternative uses explained, without *a theory of utility?*

Hicks's answer

From *Value and Capital* (1939), Chapter 1.

Utility and preference

1. The pure theory of consumer's demand, which occupied a good deal of the attention of Marshall and his contemporaries, has received far less notice in the present century. The third book of Marshall's *Principles* still remains the last word on the subject so far as books written in English are concerned. Now Marshall's theory of demand is no doubt admirable, but it is remarkable that it has remained so long upon such an unquestioned eminence. This would be explicable if there were really no more to say on the subject, and if every step in Marshall's analysis were beyond dispute. But this is clearly not the case; several writers have felt very uncomfortable about Marshall's treatment, and that it is actually the first step, on which everything else depends, which is the most dubious.

Let us first remind ourselves of the bare outline of Marshall's main argument. A consumer with a given money income is confronted with a market for consumption goods, on which the prices of those goods are already determined; the question is, How will he divide his expenditure among the different goods? It is supposed, for convenience, that the goods are available in very small units.

Marshall's argument therefore proceeds from the notion of, maximizing total utility, by way of the law of diminishing marginal utility, to the conclusion that the marginal utilities of commodities bought must be proportional to their prices.

But now what is this 'utility' which the consumer maximizes? And what is the exact basis for the law of diminishing marginal utility? Marshall leaves one uncomfortable on these subjects. However, Pareto threw further light on them.

2. Pareto's *Manuel d'economie politique* (1909) has to be reckoned as the other classical treatment of the theory of consumer's demand, from which any modern investigation must begin ... For the purpose of studying related goods, Pareto took over from Edgeworth[14] a geometrical device – the Indifference Curve. When we are concerned, like Marshall, with one commodity only, we can draw a total utility curve, measuring amounts of that commodity along one axis, and total amounts of utility derived from those various amounts of commodity along the other axis. Just in the same way, when we are interested in two commodities, we can draw a utility surface. Measuring quantities of the two commodities *X* and *Y* along two horizontal axes, we get a diagram in which any point *P* represents a collection of given quantities (*PM* and *PN*) of the two commodities. From every such point, we can erect an ordinate in a third dimension whose length represents the amount of utility derived from that particular collection of quantities. Joining the tops of these ordinates, we get a 'utility surface'. (Exhibit 1)

In principle, this is simple enough; but three dimensional diagrams are awkward things to handle. Fortunately, having once visited the third dimension, we need not stay there. The third dimension can be eliminated, and we can return to two.

Instead of using a three-dimensional model, we can use a map (Exhibit 2). Keeping quantities

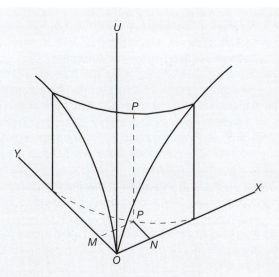

Exhibit 1. Hicks's three-dimensional representation of utility

of the two commodities *X* and *Y* along the two axes, we can mark off on the horizontal diagram the contour lines of the utility surface (the broken line in Exhibit 1). These are the indifference curves. They join all those points which correspond to the same height in the third dimension, that is, to the same total utility . . .

What will be the shape of these indifference curves? So long as each commodity has a positive marginal utility, the indifference curves must slope downwards to the right. For if *X* has a positive marginal utility, an increase in the quantity of *X*, unaccompanied by any change in the quantity of *Y* (that is to say, a simple movement to the right on the diagram), must increase total utility and so bring us on to a higher indifference curve. Similarly, a simple movement upwards must lead on to a higher indifference curve. It is only possible to stay on the same indifference curve if these movements are compensated – *X* increased and *Y* diminished, or *X* diminished and *Y* increased. The curves must therefore slope downwards to the right.

The slope of the curve passing through any point *P* has indeed a very definite and important meaning. It is the amount of *Y* which is needed by the individual in order to compensate him for the loss of a small unit of *X*. Now the gain in utility got by gaining such an amount of *Y* equals amount of *Y* gained x marginal utility of *Y*; the loss in utility got from losing the corresponding amount of *X* equals amount of *X* lost x marginal utility of *X* (so long as the quantities are small). Therefore, since the gain equals the loss, the slope of the curve

$$\frac{\text{amount of } Y \text{ gained}}{\text{amount of } X \text{ lost}} = \frac{\text{marginal utility of } X}{\text{marginal utility of } Y}$$

The slope of the curve passing through *P* measures the ratio of the marginal utility of *X* to the marginal utility of *Y*, when the individual has quantities *PM* and *PN* of *X* and *Y* respectively.

Have we any further information about the shapes of the curves? There ought, it would seem, to be some way of translating into terms of this diagram the principle of diminishing marginal utility. At first sight, it looks as if such a translation were possible. As one moves along an indifference curve one gets more *X* and less *Y*. The increase in *X* diminishes the marginal utility of *X*, the dimunition in *Y* increases the marginal utility of *Y*. On both grounds, therefore, the slope of the curve must diminish. Falling curves, whose slope diminishes as we move to the right, will be convex to the origin, as they have been drawn in the diagram.

But does this quite necessarily follow? As far as the direct effects just taken into account are concerned, it must; but there are other indirect effects to take into account too. The increase in *X* may affect not only the marginal utility of *X*, it may also affect the marginal utility of *Y*. With such related goods the above argument does not necessarily follow. Suppose that the increase in *X* lowers the marginal utility of *Y*, and the diminution in *Y* raises the marginal utility of *X*; and that these cross-effects are considerable. Then the cross-effects may actually offset the direct effects, and a movement along the indifference curve to the right may actually increase the slope of the curve. This is no doubt a very queer case, but it is consistent with diminishing marginal utility. Diminishing marginal utility and convexity of the indifference curves are not the same thing.

3. We come now to the really remarkable thing about indifference curves – the discovery which shunted Pareto's theory on to a different line from Marshall's, and opened a way to new results of wide economic significance.

Suppose that we have a consumer with a given money income, who is spending the whole of that income upon the two commodities *X* and *Y*, no others entering into the picture. Suppose that the prices of those commodities are given on the market. Then we can read off the amounts that he will buy directly from his indifference map, without any information about the amounts of utility he derives from the goods.

Mark off a length *OL* along the *X*-axis (Exhibit 3), representing the amount of *X* which he could buy if he spent all of his income upon *X*; and an amount *OM* on the *Y*-axis, representing the amount of *Y* he could buy if he spent all his income upon *Y*; and join *LM*. Then any point on the line *LM* represents a pair of quantities of the two commodities that he could buy out of his income. Starting from *L*, in order to acquire some *Y*, he will have to give up *X* in the proportion indicated by the ratio of their prices; and the price-ratio is indicated by the slope of the line *LM*.

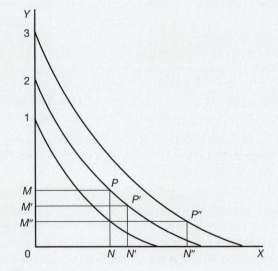

Exhibit 2. Hicks's indifference curves

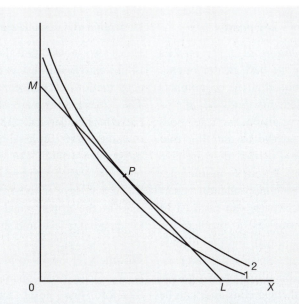

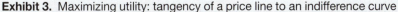

Exhibit 3. Maximizing utility: tangency of a price line to an indifference curve

It is only when the line *LM* touches an indifference curve that utility will be maximized. For at a point of tangency, the consumer will get on to a lower indifference curve if he moves in either direction.

Tangency between the price-line and an indifference curve is the expression, in terms of indifference curves, of the proportionality between marginal utilities and prices.

4. Thus we can translate the marginal utility theory into terms of indifference curves; but, having done that, we have accomplished something more remarkable than a mere translation, we have left behind some of the original data; and yet we have arrived at the desired result all the same.

In order to determine the quantities of goods which an individual will buy at given prices, Marshall's theory implies that we must know his utility surface; Pareto's theory only assumes that we must know his indifference map. And that conveys less information than the utility surface. It only tells us that the individual prefers one particular collection of goods to another particular collection; it does not tell us, as the utility surface purports to do, *by how much* the first collection is preferred to the second . . .

From this point of view, Pareto's discovery only opens a door, which we can enter or not as we feel inclined. But from the technical economic point of view there are strong reasons for supposing that we ought to enter it. The quantitative concept of utility is not necessary in order to explain market phenomena. Therefore, on the principle of Occam's razor, it is better to do without it. For it is not, in practice, a matter of indifference if a theory contains unnecessary entities. Such entities are irrelevant to the problem in hand, and their presence is likely to obscure the vision. How important this is can only be shown by experience; I shall hope to convince the reader that it is of some considerable importance in this case.

Source: Reprinted from *Value and Capital* by J. R. Hicks (2nd edn, 1946), Part 1, chapter 1, pp. 1–6.

Summing up: Hicks's key points

Among the contributions of J. R. Hicks's *Value and Capital*, none had greater impact than his demonstration that the economist's understanding of demand (and the allocation of income among alternative uses) does not depend either on the assumption that consumers are rational or that they are able to measure utility. Pareto's indifference curve, which was also independently generated by Francis Edgeworth, can be used to study market behavior as a problem of choice that is constrained by the income available to be spent. Specifically, increasingly preferable combinations of two goods, *X* and *Y*, to a hypothetical consumer can be represented by a family of indifference curves. Hicks determined that, given the prices of the two goods in question and the consumer's income, all indifference curves must slope downward and be convex to the origin of an indifference map. The reason for convexity is that the marginal rate of substitution of *X* for *Y*, which is the amount of *Y* the consumer is willing to give up for an extra unit of *X*, decreases as more of *X* is acquired, the ratio between income and the highest indifference curve.[15] Thus, given the prices of the two goods and given income, a consumer with an indifference map, such as shown in Exhibit 3 of Hicks's *Value and Capital*, maximizes his satisfaction when the quantities of goods *X* and *Y* consumed are consistent with Point *P* because this combination places the consumer on the highest possible indifference curve. However, unlike the older marginal utility analysis, satisfaction is not equated with specific measurable quantities of utility.

Derivation of a demand curve

Hicks also showed that the concept of diminishing marginal utility is not essential to the construction of consumer demand curves. The typical downward slope of a demand curve may be derived with the aid of a family of indifference curves and various assumed budget constraints. For example, one point on an individual demand curve for commodity *X* may be derived from the indifference map in the upper panel of Figure 16.1(a). Given income level and the prices of goods *X* and *Y*, the quantity of commodity *X* that a hypothetical consumer would buy at price p_1 is X_1. This price–quantity relationship is therefore one point on the individual's demand curve for *X*, as shown in Figure 16.1(b).

To demonstrate that more *X* will be taken at a lower price, assume that its price has fallen to p_{x2}. More of a good *X* can then be purchased. There will be a new line of attainable combinations drawn from point I/p_y, (which represents the ratio between the consumer's income and the price of good *Y*) to point I/p_{x2} (see Figure 16.1) which represents the ratio between income and the *new price* of good *X*. The new price line is a tangent to the higher indifference curve *III* at *D*, at which quantities OY_2 and OX_2 represent the optimum allocation of the consumer's income between goods *X* and *Y*. The relationship between the lower price, Px_2, and the larger quantity x_2, is now a second point on the demand curve in Figure 16.1(b). If this operation is repeated using other assumed prices of *X*, other points such as X_3 can be identified from which the demand curve is generated. This demonstration, which follows Hicks, shows that downward-sloping demand curves can be drawn *independently of the assumption of diminishing marginal utility*

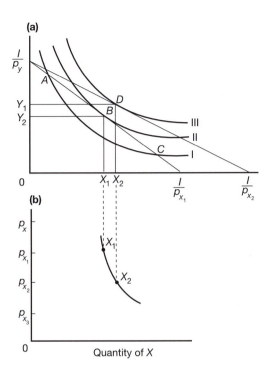

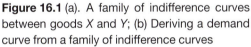

Figure 16.1 (a). A family of indifference curves between goods *X* and *Y*; (b) Deriving a demand curve from a family of indifference curves

and the notion that utility is *measurable in cardinal terms.*[16]

Although Hicks maintains that the indifference curve approach avoids the notion of measurable utility by using the concepts of the marginal rate of substitution, his critics argue that the assumption of measurable utility and diminishing marginal utility is no less implicit in the new formulation than it is in the older one.[17] They point out that a consumer cannot know which of several combinations are a matter of indifference unless the person is able to evaluate the amount of utility they represent, and that there is a set of marginal utility curves underlying every set of indifference curves. Further, if the analysis is generalized so that the marginal rate of substitution expresses the relationship between one good and the

best combination of other goods, this is the same as establishing the marginal rate of substitution between that good and money. The marginal rate of substitution then expresses the utility of that good in terms of the best combination of other goods or in dollars.

Separation of income effects and substitution effects

Even if the indifference-curve approach does not really avoid the assumption of measurable utility, it has the advantage of making it possible to separate the income effect of a price change from the substitution effect. A conventional demand curve is only able to show that a good will be purchased at a lower price, but there is no way of knowing to what extent the increase is the result of substituting the lower priced good for other higher priced goods and to what extent it is due to the increase in *real* income resulting from a fall in the price of a good in the consumer's market basket.

Hicks demonstrated that it is possible to separate the income effect of a price change from the substitution effect, by introducing a *hypothetical* compensating variation in income that is sufficient to enable a consumer to reach the same indifference curve that is made possible by an assumed change in the price of the good. Figure 16.2 identifies indifference curves I and II which represent more preferred and less preferred combinations of (say) goods *A* and *B*. At given prices p_a and p_b and an income of *Y*, the consumer's optimum consumption of both commodities is identifiable as *H* on indifference curve I. This is established by drawing a budget line from Y/p_a on the vertical axis to Y/p_b on the horizontal. Y/p_a represents the quantity of *A* which could be purchased at p_a

371

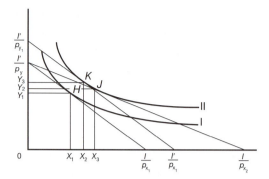

Figure 16.2 Separating income and substitution effects

effect of a price change from the substitution effect.

The new welfare economics

Logical positivism and the new welfare economics

As was seen in the preceding section, the persuasiveness of logical positivism was instrumental in recasting the problem of maximizing utility into a problem of *constrained choice*, in which the rational agent selects the best outcome from among many possible outcomes. A further objective of Hicks's *Value and Capital* (1939) was to show that this logic can also extend to explaining producer behavior, and can also be envisioned as optimizing decisions that choose between alternative factor input combinations or product output combinations, subject to a budget constraint. Thus, the new welfare economics (as distinct from the welfare economics of Marshall and Pigou) concerned itself only with the requirements for achieving an ethically neutral optimum with respect to production and consumption. It brought the era of welfare economics that began with Pigou's *Economic of Welfare* to a definitive close. The new welfare theorists searched for value-free propositions in the sense that they inquired only into the conditions under which the resources of a private ownership economy are best used to satisfy given wants within the framework of a given distribution of income.[18]

The choices made by each participant are guided by the *equimarginal principle*, which operates to ensure that the following optimum conditions of consumption and production will be satisfied, despite the fact that each participant acts in his or her own

if the whole income were allocated to that good while Y/p_b represents the quantity of B that could be purchased with income Y at price p_b.

If the price of good B is now assumed to fall to p_b, the increase in *real* income enables our hypothetical consumer to purchase a larger quantity of A. This enables a move to the higher indifference curve *II*. The tangency of the new budget line drawn from point Y/p_a to $Y/p_{b'}$ is tangent at J to the higher curve.

The question then, is, what portion of the increased consumption of both goods is attributable to the income effect of the price fall and what portion is due to the substitution effect? To determine this, a *compensating variation* in *money* income is drawn parallel and above the original budget line that will enable the individual to reach indifference curve *II* without the reduction in the price of good B. Its tangency at K means that the increase in the consumption of B from OA_1 to OB_2 reflects the *substitution* effect, while the difference between OB_2 and OB_3 is the result of the substitution effect. The older marginal utility approach obscures this difference between these two effects because it does not lend itself to separating the income self-interest. This is maximum welfare in the Paretian sense.[19] Their approach is *value free* and in this sense is compatible with the conception of *maximum welfare* as a state in which there is no alternative distribution of commodities that can improve the position of anyone without making someone else worse off. Nor is there an alternative allocation of factors that can yield a larger output *given the distribution of income and the supply of resources.*

1. *Optimum conditions of exchange.* Every household will purchase each pair of consumer goods it consumes until the marginal rate of substitution between them is equal for all households consuming both. Satisfaction of this condition implies that households cannot add to their satisfaction by further exchanges.

2. *Optimum conditions of production.* Given the technical conditions of production, each output will be produced with the optimal combination of factors. The marginal rate of substitution between each pair of productive factors being used to produce a particular product must be such that total output cannot be increased by factor substitution. Alternatively expressed, this condition means that factor substitution cannot reduce the factor cost of the product.

3. *Optimum composition of output.* The production of any product *A* implies *the loss of an alternative product B.* Thus, the marginal rate of transformation between *A* and *B* must be such that it is not possible to increase the output of either without reducing that of the other. Together with the second condition, the satisfaction of this condition implies that the least cost has been achieved for every pair of outputs. That is,

the marginal rate of transformation between *pairs of products* is equal to the marginal rate of substitution between the *pairs of factors* producing them. If the first condition is also satisfied, the marginal rate of substitution between pairs of products by each household will be equal to the marginal rate of substitution between them in production. The optimum in the producing sector will then be reached simultaneously with the optimum in the consuming sector.[20] The more important details of neoclassical optimization theory follow.

Optimum conditions in the consumer sector

J. R. Hicks shows that Francis Edgeworth's box diagram readily demonstrates the simultaneous optima required for general equilibrium. Figure 16.3 is drawn on the assumption that the quantity of two goods available for exchange between two consumers is Q_0 of good *A* and Q_1 of good *B*. Curves *I, II, III,* and *IV* represent successively

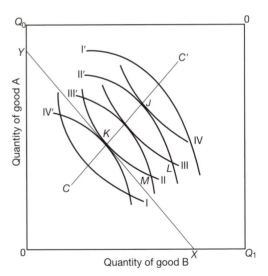

Figure 16.3 Box diagram illustrating optimum conditions of consumer exchange

better combinations of the two goods from the vantage point of one consumer, while curves *I'*, *II'*, *III'*, and *IV'* show the same thing for a second consumer. The second set of indifference curves has simply been rotated to be convex to the origin *O'* (concave to *O*) and superimposed on the first set in order to visualize the trading opportunities between them. There are, of course, numerous other indifference curves not shown in the diagram.[21]

Given their incomes and their indifference curves, a pair of consumers have various possible quantities of both goods that each could acquire by trade. Any point of intersection or tangency between two indifference curves represents a possible distribution of goods *A* and *B* between trading partners by moving toward some point on the line *CC'*, which is known as the contract curve. It is drawn through the point of tangency between the two sets of indifference curves. For example, if point *L* represents the distribution of goods *A* and *B* between the two first consumers, one of them is on indifference curve *III*, and the other is on the indifference curve *II'*. If point *J* is established by trade, the second consumer remains on indifference curve *II'*, but the first enjoys an improvement represented by a move up to curve *IV*. Every point on the line *CC'* represents a more preferred position for each of the two individuals than any point not on the curve. Any exchange that results in a movement toward the contract curve may be construed as an increase in welfare.

In order to demonstrate which point on the contract curve becomes relevant as a result of trade, it is necessary to make some assumptions concerning the rate of exchange between commodities *A* and *B*. If the rate of exchange is assumed to be *OY* of *A* or *OX* of *B*, a price line or line of attain-able combinations can be drawn, shown by *YX*. As we have seen previously, each consumer will do best by seeking the point at which the price line is tangent to the highest indifference curve reachable. In this case, the preferred point for both will be *K*, at which the price line is a tangent, simultaneously, to indifference curve *II* for the first consumer, and to curve *IV'* for the second. *K* represents an optimum for the consuming sector in the sense that neither individual could move to a higher indifference surface by trading without pushing the other party to a lower one. Figure 16.3 thus demonstrates that consumers will maximize their gains from exchange by moving to a point on the contract curve that equates the marginal rate of substitution between goods *A* and *B* for consumer 1 to that for consumer 2, and that equates both to the prevailing price ratio.[22]

Vilfredo Pareto, who followed Walras in the general equilibrium tradition, generalized this conclusion by defining the optimum as a situation in which it is impossible to improve anyone's position by either exchange or production without diminishing that of someone else. The necessity for achieving the optimum in the producing sector as well as the consuming sector is therefore implicit in Pareto's formulation, although complete exposition of the requirements of the general optimum did not appear until the 1930s, when they were spelled out by Lerner, Lange, Bergson, and Hicks.[23]

Optimum conditions in the producing sector

The indifference curve technique for analyzing consumer behavior also led Hicks to develop substitution curves and transformation curves to study the behavior of firms in the rational utilization of factor inputs and the production of outputs. Just as an indifference curve indicates the various combinations of two commodities that yield equal satisfaction to a consumer, so a *substitution curve*, or *isoquant*, shows various combinations of two factor inputs yielding the same total quantity of a given product to a firm.

Like an indifference curve, an isoquant is convex to the origin. Because different resources are not perfect substitutes for one another, it will take increasing quantities of resource *B* to substitute for resource *A* in order to produce the same quantity of a product. This is the same thing as saying that the marginal rate of technical substitution of factor *A* for factor *B* is diminishing. The slope of an isoquant at any point measures the marginal rate of substitution of *A* for *B*. The marginal rate of substitution of *A* for *B* to produce some output, *Z*, may be either positive or negative. But rational producer behavior rules out a positive substitution ratio because it implies that the use of more of *A and B* results in the *same* output. Clearly, it would be unprofitable for a firm to apply more than the minimum factor input required to produce a particular volume of output.

This is represented in Figure 16.4, in which ridge lines *X* and *Y* are drawn to mark off the limits of rational factor employment. Those segments of the isoquants that lie outside the ridge lines *X* and *Y*, as shown by the broken lines in Figure 16.4, are uneconomic factor combinations and are therefore not relevant to production decisions.

To determine the optimum output that can be produced with a given factor expenditure, it is necessary to know the prices at which the factors can be purchased. Given that the elasticity of substitution between labor and capital is expressed as:

$$\sigma = \frac{\delta(a/b)(b/a)}{\delta(p_b/p_a)(p_a/p_b)}$$

where *a* and *b* represent the quantities of labor and capital, p_a and p_b are their prices, and measures the effect of a change in relative factor prices on the factor proportion *a/b* along the same isoquant. Thus, in Figure 16.4 a firm can purchase any combination of factors *A* and *B* that lies on $p_a p_b$, which is the outlay, or *isocost* line. This line connects the point on the vertical axis, which represents the use of a given budget to purchase only factor *A*, to that point on the horizontal axis that represents the purchase of only factor *B*. The isocost line is therefore analogous to the price line in indifference curve analysis. A firm could purchase any factor combination lying on it, such as *H*, *I*, and *J*. But the best combination is *I*, for this combination enables the firm to achieve a bigger output (i.e. to produce on a higher isoquant) with a given factor input. This is the combination at which the ratio of the marginal rates of substitution between *A* and *B* is equal to the ratio of their prices. It is therefore the optimum factor combination. Generalizing this conclusion for all firms using *A* and *B* implies that the marginal rate of technical substitution must

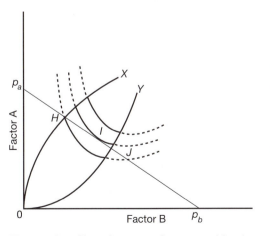

Figure 16.4 Choosing an optimum combination of inputs

be the same for both factors. If this condition is not satisfied, it is possible to increase the total product by substituting one factor for another until a further shift will no longer add anything to the total product.

Maximum efficiency of resource use also requires that each firm produce an optimum amount of each product it turns out. The various combinations of two products, say X and Y, that can be produced with a given input of factor A, can be represented by a *transformation curve*. Unless the two products are jointly produced in fixed proportions (e.g. hides and meat), outputs of X must be sacrificed to obtain outputs of Y, given the input of A. Thus, a product transformation curve will be *concave* to the origin.[24] Its slope at any point measures the marginal rate of transformation between the two products or, what amounts to the same thing, the ratio of the marginal costs of the two products. The individual firm produces the optimum combination of two products, say X and Y, with a given factor input when the marginal rate of transformation between them is equal to the ratio of their prices. If this condition is not satisfied, the firm could produce more of X and less of Y (or vice versa) and add to its profits. Generalizing this conclusion to all firms producing X and Y, and paying the same price for their factor inputs, implies that the ratio of their marginal rates of transformation to the marginal cost of producing the two goods must be equal. If this condition is not satisfied, a reallocation of inputs could increase the outputs of either or both products without any change in factor input or the output of other commodities. This general equilibrium approach of the new welfare theorists thus demonstrates that a competitive equilibrium can exist.

This is essentially the problem posed by Adam Smith in 1776. The divergent interests of consumers seeking to maximize their satisfactions and producers seeking to maximize their profits can, in principle, be reconciled by the operation of the competitive price mechanism.[25] Modern welfare theory has thus shown that there exists a set of non-negative prices for each competitive market that would emerge and be compatible with consumer and producer optimization behavior.[26]

Technical change and changes in factor shares

A central problem that Hicks addressed in *The Theory of Wages* related to the likely response of the demand for labor to a change in wages. He recognized that the degree of substitutability between labor and capital is the critical determinant. Remembering that the elasticity of substitution between labor and capital has been expressed as:

$$\sigma = \frac{\delta(a/b)(b/a)}{\delta(p_b/p_a)(p_a/p_b)}$$

it follows that the size of the wage share relative to the capital share in aggregate income is the product of their respective prices and their level of employment. That is, the distribution of income between labor and capital is established by the ratio of their earnings.

Hicks's representation of the substitutability of factors along a given isoquant subsequently led to the classification of inventions as 'neutral,' 'labor saving,' or 'capital saving,' and to understanding the effects of technical progress on income shares. Technical progress implies that a technical change makes it possible for an economy, with given endowments $0a$ of labor and $0b$ of capital, to produce output Q with lesser inputs. This can be represented by shifting the isoquant in Figure 16.5 downward to the left.

Hicks describes as 'neutral' the type of technical progress which improves the prod-

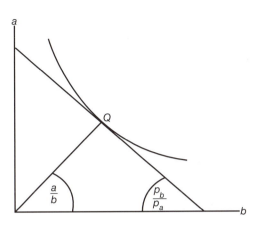

Figure 16.5 'Neutral' technical progress

uctivity of labor and capital equally. Their relative incomes increase equally so that income distribution remains unchanged. This would be the case if the isoquant in Figure 16.5 had originally been somewhere upward and to the right of Q before taking on the same shape as the isoquant passing through Q as a result of technical progress.

If, on the other hand, technical progress is 'labor saving,' it means that the marginal product of labor rises proportionately less than that of capital, so that the new isoquant is steeper than previously. At constant factor prices, firms will be inclined to employ less labor and more capital. Labor saving technical change will thus alter the distribution of income in favor of capital. Conversely, if technical progress is 'capital saving' and factor prices remain constant, producers are induced to employ more labor but less capital because the marginal product of labor rises relative to that of capital. The distribution of income then changes in favor of labor.

Concluding remarks

This chapter has focused on the theory of resource allocation and consumer choice as post-Marshallian developments of neoclassical economics. Its starting point is Arthur C. Pigou's analysis of social welfare. Using Marshall's concept of consumer surplus, he demonstrated that a system of taxes and bounties could be developed to increase welfare. He showed that the problem of externalities (i.e. social costs that individuals generate but do not include in their decision making) could be addressed by levying a tax on a socially harmful activity to limit its extent.

Frank Knight, who is remembered as the founder of the present-day Chicago tradition, disagreed with Pigou's proposed solution. All that is necessary, Knight argued, is for the state to guarantee the right of private property; the owner of a resource will then charge a toll or fee for its use which, under pure competition, will be precisely equal to the tax Pigou recommends. Although Knight is surely correct that externalities can be addressed via a property rights approach, Pigou nevertheless emerges as a scholar who was considerably ahead of his contemporaries in his concern about the discrepancies between the neoclassical theoretical model and the real world.

Before the publication of his *Wealth and Welfare* (1920), no one who commanded the respect of the academic community, other than Henry Sidgwick, undertook to inquire about the social consequences that private actions for profit might have. Pigou's distinction between private costs and social costs constituted an analytical breakthrough that he himself extended by recommending that problems of uncompensated damage, such as air and water pollution, might be dealt with through a system of fines and subsidies.

The legacy of Frank Knight's work is also much in evidence today. Specifically, his counter argument – that the misallocation of resources that Pigou attributed to *market failure* is, in fact, related to the failure of government clearly to identify *property rights* – laid the groundwork for important contemporary work in that area. Knight's influence is also apparent in both the analysis and policy recommendations of the Chicago school, whose most prominent member, Milton Friedman, was honored with the Nobel Prize in Economics in 1976.

The influence of Hicks's work is also much in evidence in contemporary theory. The foundations he laid, together with Wald and von Neumann, clarified the conditions under which a decentralized economic system, governed by the independent choices of consumers and business firms in the marketplace, can achieve efficient resource allocations. Contemporary theory is indebted to Hicks for the reintroduction of Edgeworth's indifference curve and box diagram for showing that the production isoquant is the analytical counterpart of the indifference curve as regards producer behavior.

Hicks's *Theory of Wages* also offered a format for classifying inventions and technical progress, and for examining their relationship to the relative size of factor shares. While Hicks's model of technical change related to the economy as a whole, individual agents are assumed to base their decisions on an optimizing calculus. This is implicitly the idea on which Smith premised the *Wealth of Nations*, but in that the calculus remains implicit, whereas Hicks makes it explicit. The result is a linkage between Marshallian and marginalist optimization analysis and the focus of classical thinkers on the macroeconomic question of the sharing of income among the three great social classes.

Before turning (in Chapter 17) to business cycle theory as a forerunner of the macroeconomic theorizing that began with J. M.

Keynes's *General Theory of Employment, Money, and Interest* (1936), it is interesting to note that modern theorists generally accept the proposition that the relative wage and capital shares in aggregate income have remained fairly constant. Just prior to the outbreak of World War II, the great English economist, J. M. Keynes, observed the 'the stability of the proportion of the national dividend accruing to labor is one of the most surprising yet best established facts in the whole range of economic statistics.'[27] Some two decades later the constancy of the wage share relative to the profit share was identified by American economists Lawrence Klein and Richard Kosabud as one of the 'great ratios of econometrics.'[28] These observations suggest that technical progress may have been consistent with what Hicks described as 'neutral.'[29]

Notes

1 D. G. Champernowne, 'Arthur Cecil Pigou, 1877–1959,' *Royal Statistical Society Journal*, 122 (1959), p. 11.
2 Harry Johnson, 'Arthur Cecil Pigou, 1877–1959,' *Canadian Journal of Economics and Political Science*, 26, no. 1 (February, 1960), p. 155.
3 'The role of principles in economics and policies,' *American Economic Review*, 41 (March, 1951), p. 29.
4 J. R. Hicks, *Value and Capital*, 2nd edn (Oxford: Clarendon Press, 1946), p. 18.
5 Henry Sidgwick, *The Principles of Political Economy* (1833), Book 3, especially chapter 4.
6 A. C. Pigou, *Economics of Welfare*, 4th edn (London: Macmillan, 1932), pp. 129–30.
7 *Quarterly Journal of Economics*, 38 (May, 1924), pp. 582–606; reprinted in *Readings in Welfare Economics*, edited by Kenneth B. Arrow and Tibor Scitovsky (Homewood, Ill: Richard D. Irwin, 1969), pp. 213–27.
8 The best contemporary statement of this position is in Ronald Coase's 'The problem of social costs,' *The Journal of Law and Economics*, 3 (October, 1960).
9 Pigou eliminated this particular example from

subsequent editions of *The Economics of Welfare* as a result of Knight's refutation.

10 Frank Knight, *Introduction to Carl Menger's Principles of Economics*, translated and edited by James Dingwell and Bert Hoselitz (New York: The Free Press, 1950), p. 15.

11 A further extension of these principles by Gary Becker into the realm of social interactions is to be found in 'A theory of social interactions,' *Journal of Political Economy*, 82 (November–December, 1974). Special attention is directed to the effects of different kinds of income change on charitable contributions and expenditure to allocate envy. For a popular exposition of application of the theory of choice to problems generally not treated by economists, see Richard B. McKenzie and Gordon Tullock, *The New World of Economics* (Homewood, Ill: Richard D. Irwin, 1975).

12 Frank Knight, 'Economic psychology and the value problem' (1925), reprinted in *The Ethics of Competition and Other Essays* (New York: Augustus Kelley, 1951), p. 88.

13 Frank Knight, *Risk, Uncertainty and Profit* (Boston: Houghton Mifflin, 1921).

14 *Mathematical Psychics*, pp. 21–22.

15 If an indifference curve were concave to the origin, the satisfaction of the marginal conditions would define a position of minimum satisfaction for a consumer rather than maximum satisfaction, for in such cases a consumer could improve his position by moving from the point of tangency between the price line and an indifference curve to either axis. The convexity of indifference curves is associated with the diminishing marginal rate of substitution between commodities. This condition is a second-order requirement, whereas the marginal conditions are of the first order. See Hicks, *Value and Capital*, chapter 2.

16 Frank Knight objected to Hicks's technique of generating a demand curve by keeping the price of all other goods and money income constant, while changing the price of the good in question, which implies a change in real income. This procedure, according to Knight, separates consumption from production. The correct way of viewing their relation, according to Knight, is to follow Menger and recognize that production reflects the choices made by the consumer. See Frank Knight, 'Realism and relevance,' *Journal of Political Economy*, 52 (December, 1944), pp. 289–318.

17 See, for example, Dennis Robertson, 'Utility and all what,' *Economic Journal*, 64 (December 1954).

18 It is relevant to note that while Hicks and Knight were both concerned with the extension of neoclassical economics, there was, by no means, agreement between them. Specifically, Knight was negative about Hicks's formalization of demand theory, precisely because it weakened the importance of analytical propositions regarding human behavior. See Frank H. Knight, 'Realism and relevance,' *Journal of Political Economy*, 52 (December, 1944).

19 Papers published by Abraham Wald in 1936 and John von Neumann in 1938 provided mathematical proof that a competitive equilibrium is compatible with this conception of welfare. Modern welfare theorists were thus returning to the central thesis of *The Wealth of Nations*, namely, that a competitive market reconciled the divergent interests of consumers and producers (as well as those who supply and those who hire factors of production). Wald's paper is translated as 'On some systems of equations in mathematical economics,' *Econometrica*, 19 (October, 1951), pp. 368–403. John von Neumann's paper is translated by Oskar Morgenstern as 'A model of general equilibrium,' *Review of Economic Studies*, 13 (1945–46), pp. 1–9.

20 Additional marginal conditions require optimal work–leisure combinations and optimal combinations between hours of work and the product produced and optimal allocations of factor inputs and product outputs through time.

21 John R. Hicks, 'Foundations of welfare economics,' *Economic Journal*, 49 (December, 1939), pp. 696–712.

22 The reader should realize that in the case of bilateral trade (trade between two monopolists), individual maximizing behavior does not result in determinate equilibrium prices. Depending on their relative bargaining power, any point along the contract curve is a possible equilibrium point. In the case of competitive exchange, such as that assumed in Figure 16.3, indeterminacy does not arise because relative prices are the same for all.

23 The concept of the social optimum is introduced in Chapter 6 of Vilfredo Pareto's *Manual of Political Economy*, (1906), translated by Ann S. Schwier, edited by Ann S. Schwier and Alfred Page (New York: Augustus Kelley, 1971). The marginal conditions are developed in the mathematical appendix, where they are used to demonstrate that perfect competition maximizes welfare.

24 If transformation curves were convex to their origins, satisfaction of the marginal conditions would define an economic minimum. Similarly, if isoquants were concave, satisfaction of the marginal conditions would define an economic minimum.

25 Proof that rational pricing of the factors of production is even possible in a socialist economy was first offered by Oscar Lange and Fred M. Taylor in *On the Theory of Socialism* (Minneapolis: University of Minnesota Press, 1938). Their argument was a rebuttal to Ludwig von Mises that a socialist economy is necessarily chaotic because of the absence of a free price market. Von Mises's view is published in *Collectivist Economic Planning*, edited by E. A. Hayek (London: Routledge, 1935). See also the view of Enrico Barone, 'The ministry of production in a collectivist state,' republished in the same volume.

26 Paul Samuelson's *Foundation of Economic Analysis* (Cambridge: Harvard University Press, 1947) examines the relationship between stable states and equilibrium states. A parameter change in an unstable system will not necessarily produce a new equilibrium. See also his 'The stability of equilibrium, comparative statistics and dynamics,' *Econometrica*, 9 (April, 1941), pp. 97–120.

27 J. M. Keynes, 'Relative movements of real wages and output,' *Economic Journal*, 49 (March, 1939), p. 48.

28 'Some econometrics of growth: great ratios of econometrics,' *Quarterly Journal of Economics*, 75 (May, 1961), pp. 173–98.

29 For a readable and comprehensive summary of the empirical aspects of wage share and capital ratio estimates up to the mid-1960s consult Sidney Weintraub's *Some Aspects of Wage Theory and Policy* (Philadelphia: Chilton Books, 1963), Chapters 3 and 4.

Glossary of terms and concepts

Box diagram (sometimes called an Edgeworth box)
A closed diagram that encloses the total quantities of two goods available to be exchanged and the indifference curve families of a pair of potential trading partners.

Collective goods
Goods consumed by the population as a whole, for example, police protection, military hardware, and so forth.

Constrained choice
The process of consumer or producer maximizing behavior subject to given budgets and consumer goods or factor prices that limit (or constrain) choices. The optimal choice is the commodity (or factor) bundle represented by the tangency of the budget line to the highest possible indifference curve.

Consumer sovereignty
A term describing individual ability and freedom to make rational choices among all alternative goods so that the marginal gain will tend to equal the marginal expenditure for each good.

Contract curve
The curve formed by the locus of all the points of tangency between the indifference curves of potential trading partners.

Elasticity of factor substitution
The elasticity of (factor) substitution is the percentage change in a factor input ratio to a given percentage change in the price ratios of the factors to produce a given output. Given a and b as factor quantities and p_a and p_b their prices, the elasticity of substitution can be written as

$$\sigma = \frac{\delta(a/b)(b/a)}{\delta(p_b/p_a)(p_a/p_b)}$$

Externalities
Social costs (or benefits) that unintentionally

accompany private production (or consumption) activities. Because these are not incorporated into market prices, it has been proposed that they be corrected via a system of taxes and bounties. Present concern focuses particularly on externalities that pollute the environment. The recipient of an unpaid benefit is sometimes referred to as *a free rider*.

Income effect
The change in the quantity of a good demanded as real income changes. The latter may be the result of a price change or a change in money income.

Indifference map
A three-dimensional representation of various combinations of a pair of goods, among which a consumer is indifferent. Indifference may equally well be represented by an indifference curve that will be convex to the origin and downward sloping because the rate at which one of the commodities will have to be substituted for the other will have to be increased in order for the individual to continue to be indifferent among the combinations.

Isoquant
A curve illustrating the various combinations of two factors that can be traded off against one another to produce a specific quantity of a good. Each point on an isoquant curve represents the marginal rate of substitution between the two factors. Because the rate at which one factor will have to be substituted for another in order to keep output constant must increase, an isoquant, like an indifference curve, is convex to the origin.

Neutral technical progress
A reduction in input requirements which are consistent with proportion improvements in the productivity of both labor and capital, and which preserves the relative proportions of their factor shares.

Questions for discussion and further research

1 Explain the difference or distinction between Pigouian welfare economics and the new welfare economics.

2 Explain how Hicks improved on demand theory with the application of indifference curve analysis.

3 Explain the difference between cardinal and ordinal measurements of such matters as utility.

4 In terms of the new welfare economics (which draws heavily on Hicks), explain the optimum conditions in the consumer sector and the corresponding optimum conditions in the producing sector.

Notes for further reading

From *The New Palgrave*

Christopher Bliss on John Robert Hicks, vol. 2, pp. 641–45; Phyllis Deane on Henry Sidgwick, vol. 4, pp. 328–29; Allan M. Feldman on welfare economics, vol. 4, pp. 889–94; Jide V. Graef on Arthur Cecil Pigou, vol. 3, pp. 876–78; J. J. Laffont on externalities, vol. 2, pp. 263–65; R. A. Musgrave on public finance, vol. 3, pp. 1055–60; Peter Newman on Francis Ysidro Edgeworth, vol. 2, pp. 84–97; Don Patinkin on real balances, vol. 4, pp. 98–101; Agno Sandmar on public goods, vol. 3, pp. 1061–65; George J. Stigler on Frank Hyneman Knight, vol. 3, pp. 55–59; M. W. Reder on Chicago School, vol. 1, pp. 413–17.

Selected references and suggestions for further reading

Coase, Ronald. 'The problem of social costs.' *The Journal of Law and Economics*, 3 (October, 1960).

Hicks, John R. *Value and Capital* (Oxford: Clarendon Press, 1946).

Knight, Frank. *Introduction to Carl Menger's Principles of Economics*. Translated and edited by James Dingwell and Bert Hoselitz (New York: The Free Press, 1950, p. 15).

Knight, Frank. 'Economic psychology and the value problem' (1925). Reprinted in *The Ethics of Competition and Other Essays* (New York: Augustus Kelley, 1951), p. 88.

Lancaster, Kevin, J. 'A new approach to consumer theory.' *Journal of Political Economy*, 74 (April, 1966), pp. 132–57.

Little, I. M. D. *A Critique of Welfare Economics* (London: Oxford University Press, 1957).

Pareto, Vilfredo. *Manual of Political Economy* (1906). Translated by Ann S. Schwier and edited by Ann S. Schwier and Alfred Page (New York: Augustus Kelley, 1971).

Pigou, A. C. *Economics of Welfare*. 4th edn (London: Macmillan, 1932).

Robertson, Dennis. 'Utility and all what?' *Economic Journal*, 64 (December, 1954).

Samuelson, Paul. *Foundation of Economic Analysis* (Cambridge: Harvard University Press, 1947).

Chapter 17

Neoclassical monetary and business-cycle theorists

••

Introduction

Marshall's *Money, Credit and Commerce* (1923) was published virtually at the end of his long professional career. There had, however, developed an oral tradition of monetary theory based on Marshall's teaching that was to be continued chiefly by Arthur C. Pigou, Ralph Hawtrey, Dennis Robertson, and John Maynard Keynes. Keynes, especially, has pointed out that it was a theoretical breakthrough, as far as the treatment of money is concerned, for Marshall to 'explain how each individual decides how much money to keep in a ready form as the result of a balance of advantage between this (i.e. cash) and alternative forms of wealth.'[1] This emphasis was, analytically, an important shift from Irving Fisher's equation of exchange formulation of the quantity theory. Under Marshall's influence, it led to the Cambridge concern with cash balances (k) in place of V, the velocity with which money circulates. Marshall's k is conceptually equal to $1/v$, which is the reciprocal of V.

Marshall's analysis did not, however, extend to inquiring about the possible impact of changes in monetary variables on changing the level of economic activity. That is, Marshall assumed that money is neutral. Changes in its quantity or rate of turnover affect the price level (i.e. the value of money) but have no impact on the *level of economic activity*.

A quite different type of analytical approach came from the followers of Knut Wicksell. Wicksell contended that monetary and real phenomena are interrelated and, as developed in Chapter 13, he offered the hypothesis that cumulative expansions and contractions in business are generated by a divergence between market rates of interest and real rates.

Wicksell's thesis was the starting point for all who identified monetary forces as playing a central role in generating, or at least facilitating, cyclical disturbances. Ralph G. Hawtrey of England was among the first to put money at the center of his scheme of causation, with *Good Trade and Bad Trade* (1913) which also anticipated his own later work. The issue of the nature and operation of monetary forces as the critical source of cyclical disturbance emerged as a matter of special concern for many in the economics profession. Besides Hawtrey, Friedrich von Hayek, Ludwig von Mises, and Fritz Machlup were among the Austrians who identified monetary forces, as they operated within the framework of modern banking systems, as essential to the disequilibrium between 'lower and higher stages of production' that they identified as the chief feature of cyclical disturbance. Members of another group, among them Gustav Cassel, Arthur Spietoff, and Joseph Schumpeter, stress factors that operate in the sphere of production, such as inventions and discoveries that provide new investment opportunities, besides identifying monetary forces as indispensable accompanying factors in cyclical disturbance.

Wicksell's conception of a possible divergence between the market and natural rates of interest may also be thought of in terms of saving and investment magnitudes as they come into being *ex ante*, as plans or expectations, and as they are realized *ex post*. Some of Wicksell's Swedish followers, who are sometimes identified as members of the Stockholm school, emphasized the effect of divergences between saving (S) and investment (I) *ex ante* and *ex post* in bringing about cumulative expansions or contractions. Bertil Ohlin, Erick Lundberg, and Erick Lindahl are chief among those who adopted the *ex ante–ex post* construct. Their analyses are based on definitions of saving and investment compatible with the possibility that $S > I$ or $S < I$ at the planning stage. Divergences between saving and investment are conceived to generate a process through which, ultimately, $S = 1$. This construct also had appeal for several English writers, among them Dennis Robertson and J. M. Keynes, who used it in his *Treatise on Money*. The work of all of these writers is neo-Wicksellian. Their common thread is the emphasis on money as the active factor in producing changes in real magnitudes, and the concern with analyzing the process of economic change in response to differences between expected and realized phenomena.

Neoclassical monetary theory

The theory of the general price level

The oral tradition of monetary theory that developed at Cambridge associated price level changes with fluctuations in the supply of gold and bank credit in the form of notes that were supported by gold reserves. In addition, in the United States, the Gold Standard Act of 1900 established a link between gold stocks and the supply of money in the form of bank notes. Since the process of note issue was linked to the needs of trade, and since high prices appeared generally to be associated with prosperous business conditions (and, conversely, falling prices with contracting money supplies and business contractions), the issue of changes in the price level became the early focus of thinkers seeking to explain economic fluctuation. The best known hypothesis about the behavior of the general price level is Irving Fisher's transactions version of the quantity theory of money, which emphasized changes in M, the quantity of money, as the causal factor in bringing about changes in the general price level.[2] His explanation related the price level (P) to the quantity of money in circulation (M), its velocity of circulation (V), and the volume of trade (T). The statistical measurement of these components led him to introduce checking deposits (M') and their velocity (V'); thus, his equation of exchange reads $MV + M'V' = PT$. His statistical studies concluded that, in virtually all cases of substantial price change, the active variable in the equation of exchange was M, the quantity of money in circulation. One basis for this conclusion is that P is 'normally the one absolutely passive element in the equation of exchange.'[3] In addition, V and V', which reflect the spending habits of the community, are short-run constants. Moreover, autonomous variations in M' cannot take place because there is a stable relationship between primary money, bank reserves, and the volume of checking deposits. Thus, Fisher concluded that changes in the quantity of money are the source of changes in the general price level.

What bearing does a change in the general price level have on money rates of interest? Fisher's inquiry into the interaction of what he termed 'the impatience principle' and 'the investment opportunity principle' only explained the phenomenon of the real rate of interest. If, however, the price level is changing, this will be reflected in the behavior of the *money rate of interest*. More specifically, the money rate of interest on a risk-free loan will be equal, says Fisher, to the real rate as determined by the opportunity to invest, plus or minus the change in the general price level.[4]

Marshall's formulation, unlike Fisher's, emphasized changes in the *use* of money. The public holds some portion of the annual money value of goods and services in its cash balances at any moment of time. Marshall thought the essential reason why people demand cash, or – in modern terminology – have a *preference for liquidity*, is to bridge the time gap between the receipt of money income and its disbursement. If the demand for money for transaction purposes is such that the money stock turns over, say, at a rate of four times a year, the equivalent of one quarter of the annual money value of output will be in cash balances at any moment of time. Thus, the demand for cash, which Marshall represented by the letter k, is equivalent to the velocity of circulation which is the reciprocal of V or $1/V$. By substituting k for velocity in the equation $MV = PT$ and rearranging, Marshall's equation of exchange reads $M = PTk$, where M is the quantity of money at any instant of time and $PT \cdot k$ is the average level of prices, given the volume of trade and the demand for cash to satisfy transaction needs.

Marshall's introduction of cash balances into the equation of exchange has the advantage of facilitating the examination of changes in the price level initiated by changes in the liquidity preferences of the public as well as changes initiated by alterations in the quantity of money itself. Marshall's introduction of the k factor did not, however, lead to different conclusions from those associated with Fisher's quantity theory. This is because k in the Marshallian formulation, like V in the Fisher formulation, is a stable factor. The demand for money for transaction purposes is a function of the level of income and institutional factors such as the frequency of the pay period. It is therefore not subject to autonomous variations that will affect the general price level independently of the quantity of money.

While Marshall recognized the possibility that people might have a demand for money as an asset, he viewed holding cash as somewhat irrational. He reasoned that if people find themselves with excess cash balances, say because of wage and price reductions associated with unemployment somewhere in the economy, that they would simply increase their expenditures on other goods (perhaps indirectly through investments in capital goods). This mechanism would maintain the general price level in the face of reduced rates of money wages, thereby facilitating the *real wage* reductions essential to promoting re-employment of labor if there were layoffs anywhere in the economy. Thus, for Marshall, the problem of *levels of resource use* was considerably less challenging than the need to explain individual commodity and factor prices. It was consequently left to the proponents of the underconsumption doctrine, such as John A. Hobson and Thorstein Veblen, and the proponents of the disproportionate investment doctrine, such as Michael Tugan-Baranowsky, Arthur Spietoff, and Joseph A. Schumpeter, to challenge Say's law and give the problem of crisis its place in the economic theory of the period between 1870 and 1914.

Marshall also left to others the examination of the relationship between changes in the general price level and the demand for money as an asset. His approach was to dichotomize the pricing process; that is, the forces operating in the money market were seen as operating *separately* from those operating in the commodity markets, as though there were no relationship between them. This is, of course, the case if there is no demand for money as an asset. In effect, this assumption has it that a money economy functions like a barter economy. The demand for cash balances is then zero, and the money market is always in a state of equilibrium. This implies that the money received from the sale of commodities is always used to purchase other commodities, which is to say, the requirements for Say's identity are fulfilled in Marshall's analysis as they were in the classical analysis that preceded his.

While Marshall regarded the holding of cash in excess of transactions needs as irrational, his introduction of the concept of a demand for cash balances was subsequently to become an important part of the thinking of John Maynard Keynes, who emphasized the speculative motive for holding cash.[5] He viewed the demand for cash as a function of interest rates (bond prices) and, by showing the relationship between interest rates and the investment demand schedule, integrated monetary theory with the theory of income and output. But until this was done, monet-ary theory dwelt largely in a compartment separate from the theory of income, output, and employment, and its content was virtually limited to the quantity theory of money.

Acceptance of Say's law

Since Marshall's analysis is almost wholly microeconomic in character and is little concerned with the behavior of the economy as a whole, it seems appropriate to reflect briefly on the reasons for his apparent lack of interest in what is today called macroeconomic analysis. Macroeconomic analysis, it will be recalled, began with the Physiocrats. The *Tableau Économique* was concerned, not only with the allocation of resources, but also with the size of the net product and the requirements for its reproduction. While the Physiocratic emphasis on the unique productivity of land and the prime importance of consumption in maintaining the circular flow was subsequently found to be unacceptable, it is nevertheless to the Physiocrats that we are indebted for a fundamental concept of macroeconomic analysis. This is the concept that production creates incomes that constitute the source from which the circular flow is maintained. Say's law is derived from this basic relationship, although it was directed against those aspects of the Physiocratic analysis that Say regarded as untenable.

The conclusions that Ricardo and Mill drew from Say's law effectively limited further macroeconomic analysis on the part of their classical contemporaries and followers because they used the law as the basis for their conclusion that overproduction for the economy as a whole is an impossibility, and that there cannot be an overaccumulation of capital.

Marshall, like his classical forebears, was much more interested in the normal equilibrium tendencies of the economy than in its tendency to generate crises and cycles. He paid limited attention to the problem of oscillations in trade in his *Principles*. Say's law, with respect to the impossibility of over-production for the economy as a whole, was implicitly accepted. He also concluded that the labor resources of the economy would tend to be fully employed and receive a real wage equivalent to the value of its marginal product. Full employment is assured because the tendency for money wages to fall if there are unemployed workers is associated with corresponding reductions in *real* wages. Since the latter govern the profitability of hiring, wage-rate reductions were regarded as a reliable mechanism for assuring full employ-ment. A fully operating price mechanism, Marshall believed, could be relied on to achieve what is today called *full employment*. Unfortunately, the substantial prosperity that England's industrial development had brought her became threatened in the last quarter of the nineteenth century. Germany and the United States emerged as trade rivals in the production of manufactured goods, and agricultural raw materials and food stuffs were being exported into England from other Commonwealth countries and Argentina.[6] The worsening in the terms of trade, accom-panied by lower money incomes and domestic prices, thus precipitated a theoretical issue that was substantially outside of Marshall's con-cerns. The nature of this issue is examined next.

Issues and Answers from the Masterworks 17.1

Issue

What is the source of alternating periods of good and bad trade?

Hawtrey's answer

From 'The monetary theory of the trade cycle and its statistical test,' *Quarterly Journal of Economics*, 41 (1926–1927).

The trade cycle is an empirical discovery. That is to say, experience first showed periodical fluctuations to occur in the state of trade, and then economists set themselves the task of finding a deductive explanation of the phenomenon.

The experience was not in the first instance statistical. In 1837, when Jones Loyd (afterwards Lord Overstone) wrote his often-quoted description of the cycle, very little statistical material was available. 'The history,' Jones Loyd said, 'of what we are in the habit of calling 'the state of trade' is an instructive lesson. We find it subject to various conditions that are periodically returning; it revolves apparently in an established cycle. First we find it in a state of quiescence– next, improvement–growing confidence–prosperity–excitement–overtrading–convulsion– pressure–stagnation–distress–ending again in quiescence.'

Jones Loyd was generalizing from the experience since the Napoleonic wars. The climax had been reached by three successive cycles, in 1818, in 1825, and in 1836. Since his day an ever-increasing wealth of statistical evidence has enabled us to describe the characteristics of the cycle with growing fullness and precision.

Theories of the trade cycle have, one and all, been invented *to fit the statistical evidence*. That in itself makes a statistical test to discriminate among them difficult. All those theories which palpably conflict with the known statistics have already been rejected or ought to have been. If a crucial test as between any two of those which survive is to be found, either it must be some fact not taken into account by the holders of the theory which it disproves, or there must be a flaw in the deductive argument by which they reconciled their theory with the fact. In fact, the application of a statistical test is not a purely inductive process; there is nearly always room for doubt as to the validity of some part of the deductive argument by which it is shown what statistical results ought or ought not to follow from the doctrine to be tested.

The monetary theory of the trade cycle includes two principal theses: (1) that certain monetary or credit movements are *necessary* and *sufficient* conditions of the observed phenomena of the trade cycle, and (2) that the periodicity of these phenomena can be explained by purely monetary tendencies, which cause the movements to take place in succession and to be spread over a considerable period of years . . .

The essential characteristic of the trade cycle is that maximum productive activity synchronizes with the maximum price level, and minimum productive activity with the minimum price level. That is itself a monetary phenomenon. If the consumers' income and the consumers' outlay (the aggregate income and expenditure of the community reckoned in monetary units) remained unchanged, the price level would rise when production falls and fall when production rises. The changes in the consumers' income and the consumers' outlay are nonetheless a monetary phenomenon, even if they are accompanied with no corresponding changes either in the unspent margin (the total stock of means of payment, whether money or credit), or in credit conditions.

These monetary movements are a necessary condition of the trade cycle as we know it. That is a mere matter of arithmetic. But according to the monetary theory of the trade cycle they are not merely a necessary but a sufficient condition.

This proposition depends upon monetary theory. It cannot be regarded as universally true without qualification. All that we can show is that, in general, the train of causes which bring about a contraction of the consumers' outlay will be accompanied by reduced production, and the train of causes which bring about an expansion of the consumers' outlay will be accompanied by a stimulus to production. The stimulus to production will evoke an actual increase in productive activity if industry is not already employed up to capacity . . .

The statistical records of the trade cycle are themselves a striking verification of the relation between consumers' outlay and production. They are amply confirmed by the experience of monetary changes occurring outside the trade cycle. Countries with unstable paper currencies have repeatedly found, both before the World War and since, that every fresh rise in prices is accompanied by active production, every reaction to lower prices, unless it be very fleeting, by depression. In fact, if the 'catastrophe boom' and the 'deflation crisis' have become familiar to men of affairs at the present day, that is on empirical rather than theoretical grounds. Experience has of itself afforded the materials for a generalization which is hardly disputed. Theory has arrived at the same generalization deductively and independently . . .

If there is to be a statistical test of the monetary theory of the trade cycle, the main function of the test will be to distinguish between that theory and any other which claims to account for the periodicity of the fluctuation in productive activity.

Our first step must be to state the deductive basis of the monetary theory itself. What ground have we for expecting a periodical movement in the amount of the consumers' income and the consumers' outlay extending over intervals of from 7 to 11 years?

It may be admitted at once that there is no way of arriving at the number of years in the period by *a priori* reasoning. All we can hope to do is to show that processes are at work at a rate of progress not inconsistent with attaining their turning point after an interval approximating to that ascertained.

The period for the observation of the trade cycle is the century that separated the Great War from Waterloo. It was a period of international metallic standards (bimetallic till 1872, and there-after gold). The regulation of credit was in the hands of a limited circle of Central Banks and discount markets, the leadership coming more and more into the hands of the Bank of England. Specie was largely used in active circulation, and in the latter part of the period, when it was replaced in many countries by convertible paper money, the note issue required – by law or practice – a proportional gold backing.

The reserves of the Central Banks were therefore always being drawn upon to meet the needs of active circulation. Gold passed from one country to another and back, and credit policy was directed in large measure to checking such international movements. But the reserve position of all gold standard countries together depended upon the demands for active circulation. So long as some countries had redundant gold, they could supply the needs of those which ran short. If all were approaching the limits of safety, there was no resource left (consistently with the main-tenance of the gold standard and the reserve law in which it was embodied) but to check the passage of currency into circulation.

The periodical development of this position is the foundation of the monetary theory of the trade cycle. Under the conditions described, the absorption of currency into active circulation was a very gradual process. If at any time there was a surplus of gold in reserve, the banks would be induced, for the sake of profit, to increase their lending. But any country that expanded credit faster than its neighbours, would lose gold and have to slow down again. The countries that received the gold would then have the opportunity of expansion till they in turn went a little too fast. Thus those countries that were slowest in expanding credit retarded the others, and had to be driven by heavy imports of redundant gold to join in the general movement . . .

A bare statistical compilation would be of little value in a subject of such complexity. It should be combined at every step with a record of the principal economic and political factors affecting credit, such as international movements of capital, crop conditions, wars and diplomatic crises, etc.

The general result to which, according to the monetary theory, it ought to lead would be on the following lines. Each period of depression should be found to start with high discount rates, accompanied by an increase in gold reserves and a contraction (or relative contraction) of active circulation. As gold reserves increase and rise above requirements, there should supervene a regime of low discount rates. This regime of cheap credit should persist for a considerable time (probably several years) while the gold reserves remain adequate.

Meanwhile an improvement in employment and a rise in commodity prices should be accom-panied by a decline in the surplus gold reserves, which ought to be traceable to increased circulation of coin or notes in some (or even in all) gold-using countries . . .

The statistics ought to show a culmination of the price level, followed after an interval by a decline in employment and the reductions of wages. After the decline in employment and the reductions of wages have set in, currency ought to begin to come back from circulation and relieve the reserve situation. Thereupon a new period of cheap money should set in, while gold reserves for a time increase and become excessive. In due course the gold reserves should begin to decline, and then should reach a level at which they are no longer redundant, and so a new cycle takes its course.

An investigation of pre-war statistics may go far to verify the monetary theory of the trade cycle (and also both to elucidate and to modify it), but we still have to consider how far a statistical test can discriminate between it and rival theories. It is commonly supposed that the theories of the trade cycle are very numerous. Nevertheless it is not easy to find more than two or three theories which put forward a plausible claim to account for the entire phenomenon. And here it will suffice to examine two: one which traces the cycle to variations in the demand for instrumental or capital goods; the other which finds the explanation in the psychology of the trader . . .

The psychological theory of the trade cycle is especially identified with Professor Pigou. Professor Pigou attributes the cycle to the mutual generation of errors of optimism and errors of pessimism. If people are led to increase output by excessive expectations of a favorable market, they will eventually be disappointed, and will have to reduce output as much below normal as they previously increased it. If output is curtailed through excessive expectations of an adverse market, there will be a shortage, and output must be increased to meet it.

It must be admitted that it is not easy to find a statistical test of this theory. We cannot measure people's states of mind. Moreover there is much ground common to it and the monetary theory. Credit expansions and credit contractions are worked through the mental states of borrowers, who have to be induced to increase or decrease their borrowings. It is 'optimism' that stimulates them to borrow, 'pessimism' that deters them. Nor does the psychological theory exclude the cumulative intensification of optimism and pessimism through the consequent creation or curtailment of credit . . .

The difference between the two theories lies mainly in the explanations they respectively give to the periodicity of the cycle. The transition from activity to depression is caused, according to the monetary theory, by the credit expansion being brought to an end through a shortage of gold reserves and giving place to a credit contraction which curtails demand. According to the psychological theory, the transition is caused by the disappointment of expectations.

Professor Pigou[7] argues that a wave of optimism will lead people to embark on a variety of enterprises, some of which will consist of no more than supplying current demands, while others will take several years to complete. The optimism, he implies, will not be completely dispelled till the more distant results have materialized and those who undertook them have been confronted with disappointment. It is not very clear why the optimism is not dispelled or at any rate sensibly diminished by those disappointments which come earliest. The explanation might be found in the monetary accompaniments of the optimism. Credit is created and demand stimulated. But if disappointment is to be staved off by the inflation of demand in the early stages, will it not be equally avoided in the later stages, so long as credit expands? To make optimism and pessimism *dependent* upon credit expansion and credit contraction is to concede the whole case of the monetary theory.

Statistical investigations do not seem likely to throw much light on this part of the subject. To support the psychological theory, it would be necessary to show that optimism or pessimism can not only be originated but sustained independently of the position in regard to gold reserves and credit; that productive activity can be brought to an end by the disappointment of expectations while reserves are still adequate and banks willing to expand credit: that pessimism and depression can come to an end in the face of inadequate gold reserves and a restrictive credit policy.

Source: Adapted from *Quarterly Journal of Economics*, 41 (1926–1927), pp. 471–86.

Summing Up: Hawtrey's key points

Ralph Hawtrey built on Marshall's oral tradition and Wicksell's analysis of credit expansion and contraction. According to his analysis, changes in bank credit disturb equilibrium by altering the effective demand for commodities, which is supported by the money outlay of consumers. In equilibrium, consumption equals production and consumers' outlay equals consumers' income. Consumers and traders are neither increasing nor decreasing their cash balances; banks are not changing the volume of bank credit; and there is no net export or import of gold. This equilibrium – an extremely delicate balance, which is readily disturbed – will give way to cumulative disequilibrium.

The least likely source of disturbance in Hawtrey's view, anticipating Keynes's emphasis on the stability of the consumption function, is increased spending by consumers out of their balances. Improvements in expectations cause traders to release cash and seek increases in bank credit to increase their working capital. Hawtrey conceived of traders to be extremely sensitive to changes in interest rates, which he thought to be a principal expense associated with working capital. But he rejected Pigou's psychological theory of the cycle because it requires a monetary mechanism to bring about expansions and contractions. Gold inflows are essential to increase reserves and cause banks to lower their discount rates in order to stimulate loans.

If banks release cash as a result of increasing loans, the aggregate money income of the community is increased. Given conventional attitudes toward cash balances, Hawtrey assumes the increased income will largely be spent, thus stimulating excess demand. This result sets up a cumulative process of expansion in which additional cash is released by traders and banks, which adds to consumer income and outlay. Traders' stocks are subsequently reduced, which encourages them to use idle balances and seek additional bank loans, which will be available as long as there are excess bank reserves; this process further increases consumer income and outlay. Profits increase because of the relative short-run rigidity of wages and interest rates. Further borrowing is stimulated because consumers will want more cash. The cash drain, which may be exacerbated by an increase in imports and a flow of gold abroad, inevitably depletes bank reserves, which forces interest rates higher, which halts the expansion. This discourages traders from investing in commodity stocks or inventory and leads, via layoffs, to a contraction in consumer income. Eventually, consumer outlay and effective demand also contract; subsequently, output and the volume of credit required for financing it decline. This sequence culminates in crisis and depression.

Hawtrey continues with identifying the forces that will eventually halt the decline; these get underway during the contraction phase of the cycle. One such force is the easing of the reserve position of banks as depression continues to reduce cash needs and improve reserve ratios. Banks then assume more liberal attitudes about lending. Revival is facilitated by low interest coupled with falling stocks of goods. In short, *variations in bank credit* that result from changes in the state of reserves is, in Hawtrey's view, the sole cause of cyclical variations. Most writers of the period would agree with Hawtrey that bank credit plays a critical role in the cycle; but, as is elaborated in the next several sections, they generally do not hypothesize a purely monetary theory of the cycle. Most other early twentieth-century business-cycle theorists did not join Hawtrey in hypothesizing a purely monetary theory of the cycle.

Yet, monetary disturbances are so widely viewed as central to explaining economic conditions in the aggregate economy that Hawtrey's issue of credit fluctuations as the source of good trade and bad was surely seminal for subsequent inquiries into what is now known as macroeconomics. Equally important, Hawtrey's early use of statistical analysis anticipates the empirical revolution made possible by the modern computer.

Hayek's monetary overinvestment theory

Friedrich von Hayek is among those theorists who argued that monetary forces alone are not sufficient to explain the phenomenon of the business cycle. The instability of bank credit is the ultimate cause of cycles, but its impact is on the *structure of production* rather than on variations in the consumer's outlay.[8]

In Hayek's view, the chief problem of business-cycle theory is to explain the extraordinary variation in the production of capital goods, as compared with consumer goods. The allocation of resources between the consumer and capital goods industries of the economy corresponds to the savings habits of the community and determines what the Austrians termed the *structure of production*. Increased savings reduce the interest rate and encourage increased 'roundaboutness,' or 'lengthening,' of the production process. Conversely, a decrease in saving raises interest rates and tends to shorten the process of production. Given the stability of spending habits, however, violent changes in the structure of production are unlikely, in Hayek's view, in the absence of an elastic money supply.

If the market rate of interest falls below the natural rate, the volume of bank credit demanded by borrowers increases. Their loans are used to expand the commitment of resources to the capital goods industries. The shortages of consumer goods then raise prices and bring about so-called forced savings. The real capital required for more roundabout processes of production is thus extorted via rising prices from consumers, who have not intentionally changed their consumption patterns.

Consumers can be kept from reverting to their original spending patterns as long as the market rate of interest is below the natural rate, namely, as long as banks have excess reserves. Thus, the process of transferring resources out of relatively shorter production processes (i.e. the consumer goods industries) into the capital goods industries continues until banks are forced to halt the lending process by raising interest rates.

The structure of production cannot be restored to compatibility with the level of voluntary savings, in Hayek's view, without economic crisis and depression. The crisis that precedes depression reflects a shortage of real voluntary savings relative to the volume of investment that has taken place. There is overinvestment in the capital goods industries, which, in effect, wipes out or, at a minimum, severely reduces the value of investments in capital-intensive industries. Thus, workers and other resources are released from longer processes more rapidly than they can be reabsorbed into shorter processes. The result is large-scale unemployment and general deflation. Hayek thus agrees with Hawtrey that repeated episodes of prosperity and depression can be avoided only by exercising proper control over the size of the money supply. However, whereas Hawtrey interprets cyclical disturbance as a strictly monetary phenomenon, Hayek interprets cyclical variations as reflecting changes in the structure of production that are incompatible with the voluntary savings choices of the community.

Both hypotheses are in the tradition of Wicksell in the sense that they represent a definitive break with the simplistic quantity theory view of the relationship between the quantity of money and the price level. Both maintain, on the contrary, that changes in the money supply affect the *real* magnitudes of the system. Money plays a decisive role in bringing about the cycle and periodically causing real maladjustments; but in Hayek's theory, unlike Hawtrey's, the business cycle is not interpreted as a purely monetary phenomenon.

Other considerations

While there are fundamental differences between Hawtrey's view that monetary movements are sufficient to explain cyclical phenomena and Hayek's theory that stresses the role of forced saving brought about by monetary forces, a common feature of both theories is their presumption that business owners are uniquely sensitive to small changes in the bank rate of interest. Their responsiveness to these changes is central to the mechanism purported to trigger cumulative upswings and downswings.

This hypothesis about the mechanism of change is at odds with contrary evidence that business is not much influenced by changes in the rate of interest, which are generally too small or too delayed to be very consequential. Long-term changes in capital production may be related to changes in interest rates, but short-term variations of the cyclical variety are more likely to be induced by spurts of invention and innovation and changes in the potential for making a profit.[9] There are a

number of writers whose theories identify the unique role of *real* factors in producing cyclical disturbance, although they do not negate the contributory role of fluctuations in credit in exacerbating the influence of more fundamental real causes. Joseph Schumpeter's theory of innovation is among the more highly regarded real theories of the cycle. Although it is Austrian, rather than Marshallian in inspiration, Schumpeter's view is neoclassical in its premise that the economy has strong tendencies toward recovery from a depression phase of the cycle that will return it to a full-employment equilibrium.

Theories of innovation

Schumpeter's theory of innovation

Invention, innovation, and technological changes are among the most characteristic aspects of a competitive capitalistic economy. Joseph Schumpeter viewed their impact as being so pervasive that he interpreted the cyclical fluctuations and development experience of dynamic economies as having their origin in the changes they initiate.[10] According to his view of the process, innovational changes are spearheaded by the unique few entrepreneurs who, by virtue of their vision and daring, assume a position of economic leadership. As their entrepreneurial expectations are enhanced, they generate a demand for new productive equipment to take advantage of the innovated opportunities. If these arise at a time when the economic system is in a state of equilibrium, with all factors fully employed and entrepreneurs making zero profits (i.e. there is a static state), the equilibrium is disturbed. Innovation interrupts the circular flow because it is facilitated by bank credit, which enables innovators to bid resources away from other sectors of the economy.

As long as the banking system is able to provide credit, the system expands on a wave of innovation to a new level of prosperity because the profits of successful innovators are great and attract imitators whose investments carry the expansion into a full-blown prosperity. Innovation does more than alter the technical aspects of production and promote a prosperous business environment. Because of their inconsistency with existing economic relationships, innovations induce reorganizations in the sociological superstructure. The logic of Schumpeter's analysis of the far-reaching effects of innovation on the structure of society is analytically reminiscent of Marx's examination of the impact of changes in the mode of production.[11] The imitators who follow on the heels of the captains of industry are less able than the original innovators, and they arrive at a less propitious time. Their miscalculations, coupled with the tightening of credit which accompanies the expansion of bank loans, tend to force marginal firms into bankruptcy. These failures are the harbingers of depression, for they reflect the need to correct the errors made in the process of expansion. Error correction is the painful process of weeding out inefficiencies. This process is, to Schumpeter, the essence of depression.

However, for all its destructiveness, depression is also creative in Schumpeter's view, for the gains of innovation are truly assimilated by the economy only during depression. Depression also stimulates and encourages the next surge of innovation which will propel the economy to a new level of economic achievement. Thus, Schumpeter views the process of capitalist development as being inherently unstable because it is always accompanied by the turbulence of cyclical expansion and contraction. Depression is part of the growth process because it is during this phase of the cycle that the fruits of earlier innovation are assimilated. Depression also causes a more active search for methods to reduce costs, which is the chief impulse to innovation. The reduction of interest rates, which is characteristic of depression, makes it profitable to exploit new inventions which are able to initiate a new phase of expansion.

Innovation and capitalist development

There is still another aspect of Schumpeter's theory of capitalist development which is relevant, especially in relation to the views of Karl Marx and J. M. Keynes, with whom he subsequently found himself locked in fundamental disagreement. In *Capitalism, Socialism, and Democracy*, Schumpeter expressed the view that the process of capitalist development will not continue indefinitely. The system maintained its vitality as long as the rugged individualism of early capitalism predominated. But with the emerging dominant role of the corporation, control of industry passed into the hands of hired managers. As a result, the position of the bourgeoisie has degenerated relative to that of a stockholder; thus, instead of leading the capitalist process, capitalists merely participate indirectly. As a result, Schumpeter, like Marx, believed capitalism will eventually destroy itself, but for fundamentally different reasons.

Schumpeter thought capitalism was destined to lose its vitality not as a result of the increasing misery of the exploited proletariat, but rather because the bourgeoisie loses control of the entrepreneurial process. The productive system becomes, not less efficient as capitalist development advances, but rather more so; however, in spite of its technical superiority, the system will cease to command popular support because so few persons have the opportunity for individual action in a bureaucratic society. Capitalism, Schumpeter believed, will tend to become *sociologically* untenable. This is one reason why he rejected so violently Keynes's political economy with its prescriptions for reforming the capitalistic system. Quite apart from his belief that pre-scription has no place in scientific economics, Schumpeter was of the opinion that the measures proposed by Keynes would hasten capitalism's decline because they are inher-ently anti-capitalistic.

Cassel's theory of innovation and crisis due to undersaving

The Swedish economist Gustav Cassel was among those who, like Schumpeter, identified the force of progress as the chief cause of the cycle. But whereas Schumpeter traces the cri-sis that always follows expansion to price dis-locations that occur when the gestation period is completed and the results of innov-ation are ready for the market, Cassel attrib-utes the end of the expansion to investment that is excessive relative to the supply of sav-ing. According to Cassel, cycles, or *con-junctures*, as he preferred to call them, are essentially the result of progress.[12] These forces include not only technical progress, which is the chief force, but also population growth and the opening of new countries and new resources. All innovations and discover-ies generate opportunities to use fixed capital profitably on a large scale. A new, high con-juncture develops when progress has lowered the cost of exploiting these opportunities relative to the existing rate of interest.

At the beginning of a period of high con-juncture interest rates are relatively low, which encourages investment plans. When profits are high, as they are in the beginning of a boom, saving and capital formation are at their highest. Much of this saving comes

from profit makers, who tend to have high rates of savings.

Expansions commonly end abruptly; that is, crises occur. These crises, in Cassel's view, are indicative of miscalculation about the community's capacity to save. But the mis-calculation does not relate either to the needs of the community for fixed capital or to con-sumer demands. What has been miscalculated is the community's capacity to save. A period of 'high conjuncture' is dependent on the community's willingness to supply the savings to facilitate the flow of resources into invest-ment.[13] The process of expansion sharply limits the growth of savings; the scarcity of labor that characterizes the prosperity phase raises wages at the expense of profits; and, as this occurs, the level of saving becomes inadequate relative to the needs of investors.

The capital shortage evidences itself in ris-ing interest rates that make it difficult for businesses to complete previously planned undertakings. The ability of the banking system to expand credit can offset these dif-ficulties only temporarily, for, as the prices of capital goods fall and enterprises are aban-doned, the real scarcity of capital will become apparent. Cassel therefore viewed the essen-tial cause to be an undersupply of savings relative to the volume of fixed-capital produc-tion undertaken to exploit the opportunities generated by innovation. Like Hayek, Cassel associates crises with an insufficiency of sav-ing. However, whereas Hayek blames the banking system for facilitating more round-about production processes that force add-itional saving via higher consumer prices, Cassel associates cyclical instability with the forces of progress and innovation that char-acterize the capitalistic system. Whereas a monetary theorist like Hawtrey would control fluctuations by proper control of the money supply, Cassel (like Schumpeter) sees no way of overcoming cyclical instability except at the expense of curbing the progress and innovational activities of the capitalistic system.

The savings–investment controversy

Another possible approach to explaining expansions and contractions in economic activity is to examine more specifically the savings–investment process. While the concepts of saving and investment, and the differences between them, have arisen numerous times in the preceding discussion, neither of these terms has been given a precise definition. This is because the writers who used them thought that they could rely on their everyday meaning. Subsequent inquiry by the Swedish or 'Stockholm School,' which built on Wicksell's work, and by Dennis Robertson and J. M. Keynes, made it apparent that it was important to define 'saving' and 'investment' when using them as part of an analytical inquiry.

In the overinvestment theories reviewed above, the equality of S and I is associated with an equilibrium state. If I exceeds S (i.e. $I > S$) within this framework, the result is inflation; an excess of S over I (i.e. $S > I$) produces deflation. These concepts lent themselves well to expressing what was generally inferred to be happening during periods of prosperity and depression. There remains, however, the matter of how saving and investment should be defined if one is to be consistent in speaking about the differences between them.

Keynes's treatise on money

Keynes's *Treatise on Money* popularized the concepts of an 'excess of saving over investment' and an 'excess of investment over saving' in English economic literature. Its novelty in the mid-1930s is attested to by the reference made to it as 'the new-fangled view, sponsored by Mr. Keynes in his *Treatise*, that the volume of saving may be unequal to the volume of investment.'[14]

In the *Treatise*, Keynes defined investment as the 'value of unconsumed output'; savings was defined as 'income minus consumption.' The implication is that an excess of saving over investment is a state in which the economy experiences losses; analogously, by definition, an excess of investment over savings implies that the economy is experiencing profit. Profits and losses are defined in the *Treatise* as the amount by which actual entrepreneurial income exceeds or falls short of the level that induces entrepreneurs to alter aggregate output and employment.

The main theme of the *Treatise* is the problem of price level stability, whereas the short-run problem of changes in output, employment, and income is the chief focus of *The General Theory of Employment Interest and Money* (1936). According to the schematic of the *Treatise*, output is divided into what Keynes called *available* and *non-available* output. These categories correspond to consumption and capital goods output. Wage costs are the primary costs of production *for both types of output*. In order for the price level to be stable over time, wage earners, together with profit receivers, must save enough of their income to equal the value of the non-available output (i.e. investment) produced. In other words, if the price level is to be stable, saving (S) must equal investment (I). If this condition is not met (i.e. if $S < I$ or $S > I$), the price level will change. This will create windfall gains or losses that will cause the balance between saving and investment to be restored. For example, if there are windfalls, more resources will be utilized in the investment sector. The accompanying increase in the price level increases profits while at the same time reducing real wages (i.e. there is a transfer of income to capitalists). Their higher savings propensities generate an increase in total savings until their level is equal to the new level of investment.

The definitions of saving and investment that Keynes found useful in the *Treatise* for explaining price-level changes were discarded in his subsequent, and more famous, *General Theory of Employment, Money and Interest* (1936). What is important here is to recognize that he fashioned definitions of saving and investment in the *Treatise* that were compatible with his emphasis on the critical role of entrepreneurial decisions about investment as the chief determinant of the system. Furthermore, he emphasized that investment decisions do not automatically match decisions to save out of income. This point was to become as central to Keynes's later intellectual dispute with Classicism as his repudiation of the quantity theory of money.[15] Thus, there is a common thread running between the *Treatise* and *The General Theory*, in which his focus shifts from the problem of explaining *price-level stability* to the problem of explaining the phenomenon of *less-than-full employment*.

The *ex ante–ex post* construct of the Stockholm School

A group of Swedish writers, among them Erick Lundberg,[16] Bertil Ohlin,[17] and Gunnar Myrdal,[18] developed an alternative set of definitions to those Keynes proposed in *The Treatise on Money*. Their scheme distinguished between 'plans' or 'expectations' and the income, savings, and investment amounts that are actually 'realized.' Magnitudes that are associated with plans are *ex*

ante manifestations. Thus, households and businesses formulate plans to save based on the incomes they expect. Entrepreneurs expect certain demands, interest rates, costs of production, and prices, and they formulate their investment plans on the basis of these expectations. *Ex ante* magnitudes for the economy as a whole represent the summing up of these expectations.

There is no reason, according to this school, for planned saving and planned investment to be equal *ex ante*. But they will be equal *ex post*. How does this equality come about? An inequality between saving and investment *ex ante* sets into motion a process that causes realized income to be different from expected income, realized saving to be different from planned saving, and actual new investment to differ from what was planned.[19] *Unexpected* income, *unexpected* new investment, and *unintentional* new savings materialize. An excess of investment *ex ante* over savings has a stimulating effect and is characteristic of the prosperity phase of the cycle. Conversely, if savings exceed investment *ex ante*, retailers find themselves with greater stocks than they expected (unintentional investment) or lower receipts (unintentional dissavings). This generates a contraction (or, alternatively, expansion if *ex ante I > S*), which brings about equality between saving and investment *ex post*. No more can be saved than is compatible with realized income; the latter depends on entrepreneurial decisions about investment.

In general, then, and in spite of different definitions of saving and investment, Keynes and the Stockholm School are in agreement that (1) saving and investment reflect decisions made by two different groups who are motivated by different criteria; and (2) entrepreneurial decisions about investment are the dominant factor in generating change.

Both would agree that *forced saving* is not an appropriate term to apply to the increase in savings that accompanies an increase in income. Even though the increase is unexpected and unplanned, it is *unintentional* rather than *forced* in the Hayekian sense of the term. The terms *ex ante* and *ex post* seem more descriptive of the process by which income changes are generated than is Keynes's own terminology. They are now quite standard terminology for referring to plans and the results that actually materialize.[20]

Concluding remarks

Business-cycle theory progressed very rapidly during the 1920s and 1930s; indeed, it became a major concern of writers who, unlike Marx and other socialist crisis theorists, were respectably orthodox politically and in their theories of value and distribution. Much of the inspiration came from the work of Knut Wicksell, whose theory of the relationship between interest rates, the allocation of resources, the process of price change, and changes in the quantity of money was a fundamental departure from the simplistic quantity theory of money.

Hawtrey, in particular, identified the link between credit supply changes, interest rates, and periods of good and bad trade. Hayek, Cassel, Schumpeter, and a host of others also focused on the central role of elastic credit systems in generating the phases of the trade cycle. Although there are important differences among them, in common with Hawtrey they implicate money, as generated by the credit system, as the active factor in determining the real magnitudes of the economy.

Hayek, Schumpeter, and Cassel conceive of the prosperity phase as being associated with the lengthening of the production process. They thus also follow in the tradition of the

Austrians – such as Menger, Wieser, and Böhm-Bawerk. Hayek blames the phenomenon of the cycle on the elasticity of credit, while Schumpeter and Cassel, emphasizing the positive effect of innovations and their effect on entrepreneurial expectations, see the role of the banking system as being accommodating rather than initiating.

The notion of saving and investment as *unrelated phenomena* is evident in the writings of the overinvestment and innovation theorists. However, an analytical construct, designed to focus more precisely on differences between savings and investment magnitudes and on the impact of such differences, awaited the writing of J. M. Keynes, Robertson, and the Stockholm School. The critical feature of their analyses is their focus on the key role of entrepreneurial investment decisions in bringing about the changes in income levels at which savings and investment are equal *ex post*. These analyses pointed in the direction of future thinking, especially as it became crystallized in J. M. Keynes's *General Theory of Employment, Money and Interest.*

Although it includes 'Notes on the trade cycle,' Keynes's *General Theory is* not a theory of the business cycle. As such, it signals an important shift of emphasis that distinguishes it from the analyses examined in this chapter. The hypothesis formulated by cycle theorists conceived of full employment as an *equilibrium condition* towards which the economy tended to return via the adjustment mechanism the theory purported to explain. The forces that generated revival from a depression were conceived to carry along the seeds of their own destruction. Ultimately, crisis would cut short the prosperity phase and produce the cumulative decline from which it would eventually recover as forces of revival operated to restore a new equilibrium.

This representation of alternating phases of prosperity and depression brought about by the economy's internal mechanism of self-adjustment reflects an essentially different conception of its functioning from that presented by Keynes in *The General Theory*. His preconception, in this work, is not that of an economy possessing strong tendencies toward restoring the full employment of its labor resources, but one that exhibits tendencies toward equilibrium at less-than-full employment. Keynes's criticism of the neoclassical theory maintaining the economy's tendency toward full employment on the basis of Say's law and Marshall's law of factor substitution became the basis for what is sometimes called the *Keynesian Revolution*. Despite his Marshallian background, Keynes was to launch the single most powerful attack on the neoclassical tradition.

Notes

1 J. M. Keynes, 'Essays in biography,' vol. 10, *Collected Works* (London: Macmillan, 1971–72) p. 191.

2 Irving Fisher, *The Purchasing Power of Money* (New York: Macmillan, 1911, revised 1922). See Chapter 13 of this text for a discussion of Fisher's quantity theory.

3 Fisher, *The Purchasing Power of Money*, p. 172.

4 Irving Fisher, *The Theory of Interest* (New York: Macmillan, 1930), Chapter 19.

5 See Chapter 20.

6 F. G. H. Clapham, *An Economic History of Modern Britain* (Cambridge, UK: Cambridge University Press, 1926) vol. 1, Chapter 12.

7 *Industrial Fluctuations* (1927), Chapter 7.

8 Frederich A. von Hayek, *Prices and Production*, 2nd edn (London: Macmillan, 1934).

9 In an alternative statement of his hypothesis, Hayek argued that variations in the structure of production will occur in response to changes in the level of profits; thus, cyclical disturbances will occur even if interest rates are unchanged. See F. A. Hayek, Profits, *Interest and Investment* (London: Routledge, 1939), essay 1.

10 Joseph A. Schumpeter, *The Theory of Economic Development*, translated by Redvers Opie (Cambridge, Mass.: Harvard University Press, 1954).

11 It should not, of course, be inferred from this similarity that Schumpeter was intellectually sympathetic to Marx's analysis, for, on the contrary, he was opposed to Marx's thinking as he was, for quite different reasons, to Keynes's.

12 Gustav Cassel, *Theory of Social Economy*, vol. 2, revised edn translated by S. L. Barron (London: Ernest Benn, 1932).

13 Cassel, *Theory of Social Economy*, vol. 2, p. 649.

14 Roy Harrod, 'Mr. Keynes and traditional theory,' *Econometrica*, 5 (1937), p. 75.

15 It is worth noting that the *Treatise* also shows Keynes's concern with the problem of income distribution, i.e. which of the two groups – wage earners or profit recipients – do the necessary saving and how does the change in the price level distribute the burden of non-consumption (real saving) between them? There is implicit in the *Treatise*, an alternative conception of income distribution that reflects institutional forces rather than factor productivities. These alternative explanations of income distribution are critical matters of current controversy.

16 *Studies in the Theory of Economic Expansion*, translated by Nils G. Sahlin and Florianne Dahlberg (London: R S. King & Staples, 1937).

17 *Studies in the Theory of Money and Capital* (London: G. Allen, 1939).

18 *Monetary Equilibrium* (London: Hodge, 1939).

19 Bertril Ohlin, 'Some notes on the Stockholm theory of saving and investment,' *Economic Journal*, 47 (1937), Part 1, pp. 53–69; Part 11, pp. 221–40.

20 Dennis Robertson introduced an alternative construct. He thought in terms of periods he called 'days.' Income received during a given day is available for disposal only on the following day. In his terminology, saving is the difference between yesterday's income and today's expenditure. If income is increasing or decreasing, the income earned in any day is greater or less than the disposable income of that day. Thus, there is a disequilibrium of saving and investment that generates expansion or contraction. See D. H. Robertson, 'Saving and hoarding,' *Economic Journal*, 43 (September, 1933).

Glossary of terms and concepts

Business cycles

Recurrent but non-periodic fluctuations in general economic conditions. Each phase is believed to carry the seeds that bring about the succeeding phase. Thus, *prosperity* – which is characterized by high employment, income, and prices, including interest rates – is interrupted by a crisis that generates *recession* that degenerates into *depression*, which continues until expansionary forces promote *revival*, which eventually culminates in a new prosperity.

Cambridge equation

$M = PTk$, where M is the quantity of money and PTk is the average level of prices given the volume of trade and the transactions for cash. The latter is written as $1/V$, which is reciprocal of V, the velocity of circulation in the Fisherine equation $PT = MV$.

Ex ante and *ex post* phenomena

The plans and expectations of households and business firms with respect to consumption, saving, income, and investment are *ex ante* phenomena. If the plans households and business firms make with respect to saving and investment diverge from each other, it sets a process in motion that causes them to be equal as realized, or *ex post*, magnitudes.

Innovation

Schumpeter's term for changes in production and/or marketing processes introduced by uniquely talented entrepreneurs. They anticipate opportunities for making profits that are so fundamental that they induce reorganizations in the sociological superstructure while promoting the revival of the economy during the depression phase of the cycle.

Overinvestment theories and the cycle

Theories that identify the cause of cyclical disturbance with excessive investment. Monetary theorists typically associate excessive investment with excessive credit expansion.

Underconsumption theories and the cycle

Theories that identify the cause of cyclical disturbance with purchasing power insufficiencies. Some, like the *A* plus *B* theorem, attribute the deficiency to the presence of interbusiness payments which, unlike payments to individuals, do not finance the purchase of consumer goods. Others attribute purchasing power insufficiency to excessive saving by capitalists and high-income groups. Depending on their special emphasis, underconsumption theories are akin to oversaving theories

Questions for discussion and further research

1   A critical feature of business-cycle analysis is the necessity for providing an explanation of the turning points of a cycle. Explain why the matter of turning points is so central to business-cycle theorizing. What are the phases of the business cycle and what are the characteristics of each phase?

2   Ralph Hawtrey's theory of the business cycle is among the important monetary theories of the cycle that were offered during the 1920s. Explain the key features of Hawtrey's theory, especially as regards its monetary character. How is his theoretical hypothesis related to empirical findings about cyclical phenomena?

3   Joseph Schumpeter has argued that *innovation* is among the most characteristic features of competitive capitalistic economies. What is the nature of an innovation and how is the process related to the role of the entrepreneur as the personification of economic leadership. How does innovation set into motion the forces that

are necessary to generate an economic revival whose cumulative effect is the prosperity phase of the cycle?

4 Why does a prosperity period typically come to an end? In what sense does Schumpeter argue that the depression phase of the cycle is the one during which the economy consolidates the gains from the preceding prosperity?

5 Schumpeter's theory of economic development considered the possibility that the capitalistic system will eventually become socially untenable. Why? How does his analysis of the possible end of capitalism differ from that of Karl Marx?

6 How has the Stockholm school used the concept of savings and investment *ex ante* and *ex post* to distinguish between economic plans and outcomes as an analytical tool to explain what happens over the course of a business cycle?

7 How is the Cambridge equation useful for explaining changes in the price level? How is it different (or similar) from Irving Fisher's equation $PT = MV$?

Notes for further reading

From *The New Palgrave*

Ingo Barens on Arthur August Kasper Spiethoff, vol. 4, pp. 438–39; R. J. Bigg on Ralph George Hawtrey, vol. 2, pp. 605–8: Michael Bleaney on overinvestment, vol. 3, pp. 766–67; Hans Brems on Bertil Gotthard Ohlin, vol. 3, pp. 697–99; Peter Bohm on Lindahl on public finance, vol. 3, pp. 200–1; M. Anyadike Danes on Dennis Robertson. vol. 4, pp. 208–10; Michael Dotsey and Robert G. King on business cycles, vol. 1, pp. 302–9; C. Freeman on innovation, vol. 2, pp. 858–60; Roger W. Garrison and Israel M. Kirzner on Friedrich August von Hayek. vol. 2, pp. 609–14; Bo Gustafsson on Gustav Cassel, vol. 1, pp. 375–76; Bjorn Hansson on Stockholm School, vol. 4, pp. 503–5; Arnold Heertje on Joseph Alois Schumpeter, vol. 4, pp. 263–66; Assar Lindbreck on Erik Filip Lundberg, vol. 3, p. 252; A. Medio on trade cycle, vol. 4, pp. 666–71; John Roberts on Lindahl equilibrium, vol. 3, pp. 198–200; Murray N. Rothbard on Ludwig Edler von Mises, vol. 3, pp. 479–80; Michael Schneider on underconsumption, vol. 4, pp. 741–44; Otto Steiger on *ex ante* and *ex post*, vol. 2, pp. 199–201, and on Erik Robert Lindahl, vol. 3, pp. 194–97.

See also Christopher Bliss on distribution theories: neoclassical, vol. 1, p. 883; Edwin Burmeister on Wicksell effects, vol. 4, pp. 910–12; Donald Dewey on John Bates Clark, vol. 1, pp. 429–31; John Eatwell on returns to scale, vol. 4, pp. 165–66; K. H. Hennings on capital as a factor of production, vol. 1, pp. 327–32; Peter Newman on Euler's theorem, vol. 2, p. 196; Massimo Pivetti on Wicksell's theory of capital, vol. 4, pp. 912–15; Paul A. Samuelson on Wicksell and neoclassical economics, vol. 4, pp. 908–10; Ian Steedman on the adding up problem, vol. 1, pp. 21–22; and on Philip Henry Wicksteed, vol. 4, pp. 915–19; James Tobin on Irving Fisher, vol. 2, pp. 369–76; C. G. Uhr on Johan Gustav Knut Wicksell, vol. 4, pp. 901–7.

Selected references and suggestions for further reading

Cassel, Gustav. *Theory of Social Economy*. 2 vols, Revised edn, translated by S. L. Barron (London: Ernest Benn, 1932).

Fisher, Irving. *The Purchasing Power of Money* (New York: Macmillan, 1911, revised 1922).

Haberler, Gottfried. *Prosperity and Depression*, Harvard Economic Studies no. 105 (Cambridge, Mass.: Harvard University Press, 1958).

Hansen, Bent. 'Unemployment, Keynes and the

Stockholm School.' *History of Political Economy*, 13, no. 2 (Summer, 1981), pp. 256–77.

Hawtrey, Ralph. 'The monetary theory of the trade cycle and its statistical test.' *Quarterly Journal of Economics*, 41 (1926–1927), pp. 471–86.

Hayek, Frederich. *Prices and Production*. 2nd edn (London: Macmillan, 1934).

Ohlin, Bertril. 'Some notes on the Stockholm Theory of saving and investment.' *Economic Journal*, 47 (1937) Part I, pp. 53–69; Part II, pp. 221–40.

Robbins, Lionel. Lecture 33, 'Money: Fisher, Marshall, Wicksell,' in *A History of Economic Thought*, edited by S. Medema and W. Samuels (Princeton, NJ: Princeton University Press, 1998), pp. 312–20.

Schumpeter, J. A. 'The instability of capitalism.' *Economic Journal*, 38 (1928), pp. 361–86.

Schumpeter, J. A. *The Theory of Economic Development*. 2nd edn, translated by R. Opie (Cambridge: Harvard University Press, 1934).

Schumpeter, J. A. *Business Cycles* (New York: McGraw-Hill, 1939).

Schumpeter, J. A. *Capitalism, Socialism, and Democracy*. 3rd edn (New York: Harper & Row, 1950).

Part V

The Dissent from Neoclassicism, 1890–1945

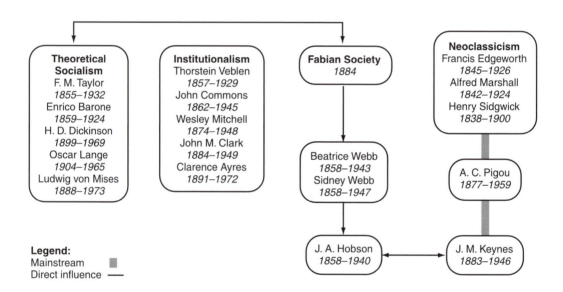

Theoretical Socialism
F. M. Taylor
1855–1932
Enrico Barone
1859–1924
H. D. Dickinson
1899–1969
Oscar Lange
1904–1965
Ludwig von Mises
1888–1973

Institutionalism
Thorstein Veblen
1857–1929
John Commons
1862–1945
Wesley Mitchell
1874–1948
John M. Clark
1884–1949
Clarence Ayres
1891–1972

Fabian Society
1884

Neoclassicism
Francis Edgeworth
1845–1926
Alfred Marshall
1842–1924
Henry Sidgwick
1838–1900

Beatrice Webb
1858–1943
Sidney Webb
1858–1947

A. C. Pigou
1877–1959

J. A. Hobson
1858–1940

J. M. Keynes
1883–1946

Legend:
Mainstream
Direct influence —

Key dates

1898	Thorstein Veblen	'Why is economics not an evolutionary science?'
1899	Thorstein Veblen	Theory of the Leisure Class
1913	Wesley Clair Mitchell	Business Cycles
1922	Thorstein Veblen	The Engineers and the Price System
1922	John A. Hobson	Economics of Unemployment
1923	John Maurice Clark	Studies in the Economics of Overhead Cost
1923	J. M. Keynes	Tract on Monetary Reform
1930	J. M. Keynes	The Treatise on Money
1933	H. D. Dickinson	Price Formation in a Socialist Community
1935	Enrico Barone	The Ministry of Production in a Socialist State
1935	Ludwig von Mises	Economic Calculation in a Socialist Commonwealth
1935	G. D. H. Cole	Principles of Economic Planning
1936	J. M. Keynes	The General Theory of Employment, Interest and Money
1938	F. M. Taylor	The Guidance of Production in a Socialist State

An overview of the dissent from neoclassicism

The dissent from orthodox thinking in economics after 1890 and into the twentieth century is essentially a critique of the written and oral tradition of neoclassicism that Alfred Marshall originated at Cambridge University. The dissent from this tradition was the product of multiple forces, the most obvious of which was the transformation of the capitalistic system itself. The system's institution of private property, under which market forces direct production, exchange, and distribution, held firm, as did the right of inheritance and enforceability of contracts to use property to earn profit. But important changes were under way. Specifically, both England and America experienced a decline in the number of small business enterprises. Capitalist owners participated less actively as business became institutionalized under the aegis of large corporations owned by stockholders and run by a professional managerial class.

The emergence of the corporation as the dominant form of economic organization changed consumer behavior and the process of saving and investment in ways that traditional theory did not appear to take into account. These institutional changes sparked a literature that was critical of the neoclassical paradigm to which most thinkers adhered. Later, there was an effort to develop alternative theories intended to replace the neoclassical paradigm.

The criticisms directed at neoclassical economics can be conveniently classified under several major headings.

1 The continuing controversy about the use of the deductive method to establish general laws about the behavior of the economic system and those who participate in the economic process. Members of the historical school continued to raise the issue of method, and their arguments were echoed by those who became associated with the American Institutionalist school.

2 The appropriateness of the concept of equilibrium, which the economist borrowed from the science of physics, to describe the behavior of the economic system was re-examined.

3 The validity of the assumption that sovereign consumers and producers behave rationally to maximize the outcome of their choices became a hotly debated issue. The relevance of marginal utility in guiding consumer choice was a related matter of controversy.

4 The possibility of achieving an efficient allocation of resources in a socialist state, in which a planning board, rather than the price system, directs production and distribution, was presented as an alternative to capitalism.

5 The possible occurrence of involuntary unemployment in a capitalistic economy was examined on the premise that, because this system is typically characterized by a high propensity to save, it may be incapable of generating sufficient aggregate demand to employ its labor resources fully.

Understandably, those who dissented from neoclassicism did not all focus on precisely the same challenges or pursue the same intellectual alternatives. American scholars were critical of both the deductive method of Neoclassicism and the assumptions on which its laws were based. But, their chief objective was to pursue institutionally oriented studies of people functioning as *social groups*, in corporations, unions, schools, churches, and other organizations, rather than as atomistic individuals.

Many American scholars had studied at German universities, where they came under the influence of the historical school. Not only did they appreciate historicism as an alternative to deductive analysis as a method of study, they also became influenced by German *sozialpolitik* and its concern with social reform. Many were also receptive to Herbert Spencer's philosophy of social evolution, which rejects the view that the universe functions in accordance with a preordained natural order. Human beings and their institutions are increasingly interpreted as subject to Darwinian change; both must adapt to suit newly emerging conditions. Spencer's goal, therefore, was to apply the methods of the emerging life sciences, biology in particular, to the study of social phenomena.

While Spencer's system postulated that social institutions are inherently beneficent, the evolutionary approach of social Darwinism raises the intellectual possibility of challenging the orthodox conclusion of social harmony. John Dewey, the philosopher, thus argued that the process of change poses questions and problems that require pragmatic solutions. He emphasized the necessity for developing an analytical, or instrumentalist, framework within which pragmatic or problem-solving answers can be derived. The intellectual influences of Spencer and Dewey are reflected in the evolutionary approach adopted by the Institutionalists for understanding the functioning of the economic process. These influences also led them in the direction of developing a theory of 'social value' and to propose various social engineering measures to serve the common interest.

The dissent from the neoclassical paradigm, which builds on the Spencer–Dewey evolutionary approach, is presented in Chap-

ter 18, which examines the contribution of the Institutionalist school. Its focus is on the work of four of its most representative proponents: Thorstein Veblen, who is the founder of the Institutionalist tradition; Wesley Clair Mitchell, founder of the National Bureau of Economic Research, who built his empirical approach to economics on the Institutionalist credo; John Maurice Clark, who is remembered chiefly for his theory of overhead cost; and Clarence E. Ayres. Ayres was the leading American institutional economist of the post-World War II era. However, he was a leading critic of economic orthodoxy well before 1945. The essentials of his criticism are therefore addressed in Chapter 18, while his theory of economic progress and his related efforts to develop a theory of social value are part of his post-1945 contribution. These topics are thus postponed until Chapter 22, which examines the work of several contemporary iconoclasts.

A different kind of dissent from the neoclassical paradigm came from thinkers who undertook to answer the question: is a rational allocation of resources possible under socialism? Some, like Oskar Lange of the Austrian school and Frederick M. Taylor, a past president of the American Economic Association, approached the question as a scientific problem to be answered on its own merits. Others were Fabian socialists whose interest in the question was part of the broader goal of achieving socialism without resorting either to Marxian theory or the revolutionary methods that Marxian socialists regarded as necessary. Their dissent from economic orthodoxy is examined in Chapter 19, which also addresses the Fabians' analysis of the phenomenon of economic depression.

The Fabian concern about analyzing the causes of economic depression was shared by others, among whom John Maynard Keynes became most influential. Keynes questioned the capability of private-enterprise economies to restore full employment through the operation of market forces. Thus, he interpreted persistent unemployment as a phenomenon that the prevailing paradigm could not explain. His *General Theory of Employment, Money and Interest* (1936) challenged the validity of the neoclassical conclusion that an economy characterized by flexible wages and prices will have strong equilibrium tendencies.

Chapter 20 examines this argument and Keynes's theory of aggregate effective demand, which he developed as an alternative to the prevailing neoclassical paradigm. His message was hailed as a major analytical breakthrough and was widely interpreted as an intellectual revolution from which we would all emerge as Keynesians. The provocative question of whether we are, indeed, all Keynesians now, is left to our concluding Part Six.

Chapter 18

The dissent of American institutionalists

•••

Economic thought, circa 1890, on the American side of the Atlantic Ocean was different in a number of ways from what developed in England and on the Continent. The seemingly boundless supply of resources in an economy that was on the verge of full-blown industrial revolution seemed to promise everlasting prosperity for the nation and for hard-working, thrifty individuals. This philosophical perspective is consistent with what is sometimes called *clerical economics*. Clerical economics maintained that there is a divine link between ethical behavior and favorable economic outcomes; capitalism is the natural system for guiding production, exchange, and distribution activities to achieve optimal results. Interference with the free operation of market forces is not only inefficient, it is immoral in the sense that it interferes with natural law. The virtue of hard work promotes production and saving without which there will be poverty for at least some members of society. In America, clerical economics was thus the counterpart of Victorian moralizing in England.

Although the predominant economic philosophy in America, as in England, was conservative, it is relevant that the reaction against conservative thinking and policy in America had different roots from England's. During the very short span of years from the Civil War to the end of the century, America experienced the turbulence of several important movements that reflected economic and political unrest.[1] There was the labor movement, which culminated in the American Federation of Labor; the Greenback and Populist movements, which promoted cheap paper and silver currency; the Granger movement, which aimed to raise farm prices; the antitrust movement that culminated in the passage of the Sherman Anti-Trust Act (1890) and The Interstate Commerce Act (1887); and the Progressive movement, spearheaded by the General Federation of Women's Clubs, whose aim was to achieve legislative changes to reform the system.

The dissenting spirit of the thinkers who are grouped under the umbrella term *Institutionalism* is best understood, not only as a reaction against clerical economics, but also against the background of the changing scene of American business and society and the growing influence of Dewey's pragmatic philosophy. Pragmatism begins with the observations of current experience, followed by hypothesis formulation and, finally, the testing of those hypotheses. This is an essentially different methodology from that used to establish classical (and neoclassical) generalizations or laws. These are derived by deductive logic from a group of postulates or premises (recall, for example, Senior's four postulates). Whereas Senior's postulates and the reluctance of the logical positivists to make value judgments precluded policy prescriptions by economists, the philosophy of pragmatism provides the basis for proposing action. It leads directly to the view that the concern of a social scientist is, quite properly, social engineering; that is, the achievement of social objectives.

A whole group of American thinkers reached intellectual maturity during the turbulent period between the Civil War and America's entry into World War I. To list them without identifying their contributions would be to offer a useless parade of names; to present enough detail to make individual contributions stand out goes beyond our objective of focusing chiefly on the development of analytical economics. We will, therefore, focus our attention on four institutionalist luminaries: Thorstein Veblen, Wesley Clair Mitchell, John Maurice Clark, and Clarence Ayres. Together, they were the leaders of a distinctively American school, which still flourishes today. Individually, each made a unique contribution that laid the foundation for further work in a still-flourishing tradition.[2]

The Veblenian Challenge

Introduction

Thorstein Veblen (1857–1929) grew up in a predominantly Norwegian farming community of rural Wisconsin. In this somewhat isolated setting, he learned first-hand the problems of farming as a way of life, which he left behind when he entered Carleton College at age 17. His life-long predilection for unorthodox attitudes and viewpoints was already much in evidence during his under-

graduate days. The vigor and originality of Veblen's antiestablishment behavior, on a personal as well as a professional level, have left an unmatched legacy of anecdotes and stories, many relating to his prowess as a 'ladies' man.'[3]

At Carleton, Veblen was introduced to economics by John Bates Clark, whose marginal productivity theory of factor prices earned him his reputation as America's foremost neoclassicist. Graduation from Carleton took Veblen briefly to Johns Hopkins where he studied philosophy and political economy. His sojourn at Johns Hopkins, where he was a classmate of John Dewey, was significant in the development of Veblen's later thinking and writing. His transfer to Yale a year later, where he earned his Ph.D. degree, opened no academic doors for him, the recommendation of John Bates Clark notwithstanding. He spent the next seven years reading on his own before becoming a student once more, this time at Cornell University, where he studied anthropology, sociology, and economics under still another proponent of neoclassicism, J. L. Laughlin. It was in this environment that Veblen's long years of study in multiple disciplines came to fruition in his first published work, *The Theory of the Leisure Class* (1899). Although this was followed by many other works, those Veblenesque expressions remembered best, such as 'conspicuous consumption' and 'captains of industry,' were introduced in *The Theory of the Leisure Class*. His unique knack for descriptive phrases, his sharp antiestablishment wit, and unorthodox appearance and behavior are even better remembered than the ideas, which his disciples perpetuated and elaborated into a school of thought that became known as *Institutionalism.*[4]

Veblen maintained that the chief failing of the neoclassicists and marginal utility theorists is their failure to comprehend the innate drives of human beings and the basis of their often irrational behavior. These are not captured by the neutral logic of Marshall's mechanical laws of human beings nor is the cultural environment reflected within which humans live and work, and which changes over time. As long as economists regard the physical sciences as the prototype of their discipline, they will fall short in coming to grips with economic issues. Thus, Veblen exhorted economists to seek their prototype in the humanities and the social sciences, for these offer the basis for developing economics as an evolutionary science.

Issues and Answers from the Masterworks 18.1

Issue

Why are biology and anthropology better prototypes than the natural order classical model for the development of economics as a science?

Veblen's answer

From 'Why is economics not an evolutionary science?' (1898).

M. G. de Lapouge recently said, 'Anthropology is destined to revolutionise the political and the social sciences as radically as bacteriology has revolutionised the science of medicine.' In so far as he speaks of economics, the eminent anthropologist is not alone in his conviction that the science stands in need of rehabilitation. His words convey a rebuke and an admonition, and in both respects he speaks the sense of many scientists in his own and related lines of inquiry. It may be taken as the consensus of those men who are doing the serious work of modern anthropology, ethnology, and psychology, as well as of those in the biological sciences proper, that economics is helplessly behind the times, and unable to handle its subject-matter in a way to entitle it to standing as a modern science. The other political and social sciences come in for their share of this obloquy, and perhaps on equally cogent grounds. Nor are the economists themselves buoyantly indifferent to the rebuke. Probably no economist today has either the hardihood or the inclination to say that the science has now reached a definitive formulation, either in the detail of results' or as regards the fundamental features of theory. The nearest recent approach to such a position on the part of an economist of accredited standing is perhaps to be found in Professor Marshall's Cambridge address of a year and a half ago. But these utterances are so far from the jaunty confidence shown by the classical economists of half a century ago that what most forcibly strikes the reader of Professor Marshall's address is the exceeding modesty and the uncalled-for humility of the spokesman for the 'old generation.' With the economists who are most attentively looked to for guidance, uncertainty as to the definitive value of what has been and is being done, and as to what we may, with effect, take to next, is so common as to suggest that indecision is a meritorious work. Even the Historical School, who made their innovation with so much home-grown applause some time back, have been unable to settle down contentedly to the pace which they set themselves.

The men of the sciences that are proud to own themselves 'modern' find fault with the economists for being still content to occupy themselves with repairing a structure and doctrines and maxims resting on natural rights, utilitarianism, and administrative expediency. This aspersion is not altogether merited, but is near enough to the mark to carry a sting. These modern sciences are evolutionary sciences, and their adepts contemplate that characteristic of their work with some complacency. Economics is not an evolutionary science – by the confession of its spokesmen; and the economists turn their eyes with something of envy and some sense of baffled emulation to these rivals that make broad their phylacteries with the legend, 'Up to date.'

Precisely wherein the social and political sciences, including economics, fall short of being evolutionary sciences, is not so plain. At least, it has not been satisfactorily pointed out by their critics. Their successful rivals in this matter – the sciences that deal with human nature among the rest – claim as their substantial distinction that they are realistic: they deal with facts. But economics, too, is realistic in this sense: it deals with facts, often in the most painstaking way, and latterly with an increasingly strenuous insistence on the sole efficacy of data. But this 'realism' does not make economics an evolutionary science. The insistence on data could scarcely be carried to a higher pitch than it was carried by the first generation of the Historical School; and yet no economics is farther from being an evolutionary science than the received economics of the Historical School. The whole broad range of erudition and research that engaged the energies of that school commonly falls short of being science, in that, when consistent, they have contented themselves with an enumeration of data and a narrative account of industrial development, and have not presumed to offer a theory of anything or to elaborate their results into a consistent body of knowledge.

Any evolutionary science, on the other hand, is a close-knit body of theory. It is a theory of a process, of an unfolding sequence. But here, again, economics seems to meet the test in a fair measure, without satisfying its critics that its credentials are good. It must be admitted, e.g. that J. S. Mill's doctrines of production, distribution, and exchange, are a theory of certain economic processes, and that he deals in a consistent and *effective* fashion with the sequences of fact that make up his subject-matter. So, also, Cairnes's discussion of normal value, of the rate of wages, and of international trade, are excellent instances of a theoretical handling of economic processes of sequence and the orderly unfolding development of fact. But an attempt to cite Mill and Cairnes as exponents of an evolutionary economics will produce no better effect than perplexity, and not a great deal of that. Very much of monetary theory might be cited to the same purpose and with the like effect. Something similar is true even of late writers who have avowed some penchant for the evolutionary point of view; as, e.g. Professor Hadley – to cite a work of unquestioned merit and unusual reach. Measurably, he keeps the word of promise to the ear; but any one who may cite his *Economics* as having brought political economy into line as an evolutionary science will convince neither himself nor his interlocutor. Something to the like effect may fairly be said of the published work of that later English strain of economists represented by Professors Cunningham and Ashley, and Mr. Cannan, to name but a few of the more eminent figures in the group.

Of the achievements of the classical economists, recent and living, the science may justly be proud; but they fall short of the evolutionist's standard of adequacy, not in failing to offer a theory of a process or of a developmental relation, but through conceiving their theory in terms alien to the evolutionist's habits of thought. The difference between the evolutionary and the pre-evolutionary sciences lies not in the insistence on facts. There was a great and fruitful activity in the natural sciences in collecting and collating facts before these sciences took on the character that marks them as evolutionary. Nor does the difference lie in the absence of efforts to formulate and explain schemes of process, sequence, growth, and development in the pre-evolutionary days. Efforts of this kind abounded, in number and diversity; and many schemes of development, of great subtlety and beauty, gained a vogue both as theories of organic and inorganic development and as schemes of the life history of nations and societies. It will not even hold true that our elders overlooked the presence of cause and effect in formulating their theories and reducing their data to a body of knowledge. But the terms which were accepted as the definitive terms of knowledge were in some degree different in the early days from what they are now. The terms of thought in which the investigators of some two or three generations back definitively formulated their knowledge of facts, in their last analyses, were different in kind from the terms in which the modern evolutionist is content to formulate his results. The analysis does not run back to the same ground, or appeal to the same standard of finality or adequacy, in the one case as in the other.

The difference is a difference of spiritual attitude or point of view in the two contrasted generations of scientists. To put the matter in other words, it is a difference in the basis of valuation of the facts for the scientific purpose, or in the interest from which the facts are appreciated. With the earlier as with the later generation, the basis of valuation of the facts handled is, in matters of detail, the causal relation that is apprehended to subsist between them. This is true to the greatest extent for the natural sciences. But in their handling of the more comprehensive schemes of sequence and relation – in their definitive formulation of the results – the two generations differ. The modern scientist is unwilling to depart from the test of causal relation or quantitative sequence. When he asks the question, Why? He insists on an answer in terms of cause and effect. He wants to reduce his solution of all problems to terms of the conservation of energy or the persistence of quantity. This is his last recourse. And this last recourse has in our time been made available for the handling of schemes of development and theories of a comprehensive process by the notion of a cumulative causation. The great deserts of the evolutionist leaders – if they have great deserts as leaders – lie, on the one hand, in their refusal to go back to the colorless sequence of phenomena and seek higher ground for their ultimate syntheses, and, on the other hand, in their having shown how this colorless impersonal sequence of cause and effect can be made use of for theory proper, by virtue of its cumulative character.

For the earlier natural scientists, as for the classical economists, this ground of cause and effect is not definitive. Their sense of truth and substantiality is not satisfied with a formulation of mechanical sequence. The ultimate term in their systematisation of knowledge is a 'natural law.' This natural law is felt to exercise some sort of a coercive surveillance over the sequence of events, and to give a spiritual stability and consistence to the causal relation at any given juncture. To meet the high classical requirement, a sequence – and a developmental process especially – must be apprehended in terms of a consistent propensity tending to some spiritually legitimate end. When facts and events have been reduced to these terms of fundamental truth and have been made to square with the requirements of definitive normality, the investigator rests his case. Any causal sequence which is apprehended to traverse the imputed propensity in events is a 'disturbing factor.' Logical congruity with the apprehended propensity is, in this view, adequate ground of procedure in building up a scheme of knowledge or of development. The objective point of the efforts of the scientists working under the guidance of this classical tradition, is to formulate knowledge in terms of absolute truth; and this absolute truth is a spiritual fact. It means a coincidence of facts with the deliverances of an enlightened and deliberate common sense.

The development and the attenuation of this preconception of normality or of a propensity in events might be traced in detail from primitive animism down through the elaborate discipline of faith and metaphysics, overruling Providence, order of nature, natural rights, natural law, underlying principles. But all that may be necessary here is to point out that, by descent and by psychological content, this constraining normality is of a spiritual kind. It is for the scientific purpose an imputation of spiritual coherence to the facts dealt with. The question of interest is how this preconception of normality has fared at the hands of modern science, and how it has come to be superseded in the intellectual primacy by the latter-day preconception of a non-spiritual sequence. This question is of interest because its answer may throw light on the question as to what chance there is for the indefinite persistence of this archaic habit of thought in the methods of economic science . . . The economists of the classical trend have made no serious attempt to depart from the standpoint of taxonomy and make their science a genetic account of the economic life process. As has just been said, much the same is true for the Historical School. The latter have attempted an account of developmental sequence, but they have followed the lines of pre-Darwinian speculations on development rather than lines which modern science would recognise as evolutionary. They have given a narrative survey of phenomena, not a genetic account of an unfolding process. In this work they have, no doubt, achieved results of permanent value; but the results achieved are scarcely to be classed as economic theory. On the other hand, the Austrians and their precursors and their coadjutors in the value discussion have taken up a detached portion of economic theory, and have inquired with great nicety into the process by which the phenomena within their limited field are worked out. The entire discussion of marginal utility and subjective value as the outcome of a valuation process must be taken as a genetic study of this range of facts. But here, again, nothing further has come of the inquiry, so far as regards a rehabilitation of economic theory as a whole. Accepting Menger as their spokesman on this head, it must be said that the Austrians have on the whole showed themselves unable to break with the classical tradition that economics is a taxonomic science.

The reason for the Austrian failure seems to lie in a faulty conception of human nature, faulty for the present purpose, however adequate it may be for any other. In all the received formulations of economic theory, whether at the hands of English economists or those of the Continent, the human material with which the inquiry is concerned is conceived in hedonistic terms; that is to say, in terms of a passive and substantially inert and immutably given human nature. The psychological and anthropological preconceptions of the economists have been those which were accepted by the psychological and social sciences some generations ago. The hedonistic conception of man is that of a lightning calculator of pleasures and pains, who oscillates like a homogeneous globule of desire of happiness under the impulse of stimuli that shift him about the area, but leave him intact . . . The later psychology, reenforced by modern anthropological research, gives a different conception of human nature. According to this conception, it is the characteristic of man to do something, not simply to suffer pleasures and pains through the impact of suitable forces. He is not simply a bundle of desires that are to be saturated by being placed in the path of the forces of the environment, but rather a coherent structure of propensities and habits which seeks realisation and expression in an unfolding activity. According to this view, human activity, and economic activity among the rest, is not apprehended as something incidental to the process of saturating given desires. The activity is itself the substantial fact of the process, and the desires under whose guidance the action takes place are circumstances of temperament which determine the specific direction in which the activity will unfold itself in the given case . . . From what has been said it appears that an evolutionary economics must be the theory of a process of cultural growth as determined by the economic interest, a theory of a cumulative sequence of economic institutions stated in terms of the process itself. Except for the want of space to do here what should be done in some detail if it is done at all, many efforts by the later economists in this direction might be cited to show the trend of economic discussion in this direction. There is not a little evidence to this effect, and much of the work done must be rated as effective work for this purpose. Much of the work of the Historical School, for instance, and that of its later exponents especially, is too noteworthy to be passed over in silence, even with all due regard to the limitations of space.

We are now ready to return to the question of why economics is not an evolutionary science. It is necessarily the aim of such an economics to trace the cumulative working-out of the economic interest in the cultural sequence. It must be a theory of the economic life process of the race or the community. The economists have accepted the hedonistic preconceptions concerning human nature and human action, and the conception of the economic interest which a hedonistic psychology gives does not afford material for a theory of the development of human nature. Under hedonism the economic interest is not conceived in terms of action. It is therefore not readily apprehended or appreciated in terms of a cumulative growth of habits of thought, and does not provoke, even if it did lend itself to, treatment by the evolutionary method. At the same time the anthropological preconceptions current in that common-sense apprehension of human nature to which economists have habitually turned has not enforced the formulation of human nature in terms of a cumulative growth of habits of life. These received anthropological preconceptions are such as have made possible the normalized con-jectural accounts of primitive barter with which all economic readers are familiar, and the no less normalized conventional derivation of landed property and its rent, or the sociological–philosophical discussions of the 'function' of this or that class in the life of society or of the nation.

The premises and the point of view required for an evolutionary economics have been want-ing. The economists have not had the materials for such a science ready to their hand, and the provocation to strike out in such a direction has been absent. Even if it has been possible at any time to turn to the evolutionary line of speculation in economics, the possibility of a departure is not enough to bring it about. So long as the habitual view taken of a given range of facts is of the taxonomic kind and the material lends itself to treatment by that method, the taxonomic method is the easiest, gives the most gratifying immediate results, and best fits into the accepted body of knowledge of the range of facts in question. This has been the situation in economics. Provided the practical exigencies of modern industrial life continue of the same character as they now are, and so continue to enforce the impersonal method of knowledge, it is only a question of time when that (substantially animistic) habit of mind which proceeds on the notion of a definitive normality shall be displaced in the field of economic inquiry by that (substantially materialistic) habit of mind which seeks a comprehension of facts in terms of a cumulative sequence.

The later method of apprehending and assimilating facts and handling them for the purposes of knowledge may be better or worse, more or less worthy or adequate, than the earlier; it may be of greater or less ceremonial or aesthetic effect; we may be moved to regret the incursion of underbred habits of thought into the scholar's domain. But all that is beside the present point. Under the stress of modern technological exigencies, men's everyday habits of thought are falling into the lines that in the sciences constitute the evolutionary method; and knowledge which proceeds on a higher, more archaic plane is becoming alien and meaningless to them. The social and political sciences must follow the drift, for they are already caught in it.

Source: Adapted from Thorstein Veblen, 'Why is economics not an evolutionary science?' *Quarterly Journal of Economics*, 12 (July, 1898), pp. 373–426.

Summing up: Veblen's key points

Veblen questioned the hedonistic conception of human behavior that envisions people as having an inherent ability to calculate the gains and losses inherent in choosing among available alternatives. This conception of behavior totally neglects the cultural setting within which economic activity takes place. Behavior is dictated by institutions such as the family, the church, the school system, and the corporation. While institutions are relatively static in the short run, they invariably evolve over time. Veblen's own studies of anthropology and the influence of Darwin's theory of evolution, as set forth in his *Origin of Species*, led Veblen to reject both reliance on the deductive method and the concept of equilibrium that economists imported into their discipline from physics. His contention was that the study of economics must reflect the dynamic or life-process aspects of the culture. These can be studied only within a framework derived from an evolutionary discipline like biology, which Veblen regarded as an inherently better prototype for studying economic behavior than physics. Although Veblen worked under Clark and Laughlin, two of the most respected neoclassical scholars of his day, his studies of human behavior within the broader framework of anthropology and biology became his basis for rejecting the assumption (fundamental to neoclassical economics) that behavior in the economic sphere is rationally directed.

Economics as an evolutionary science

Veblen sees the chief dynamic influences on human behavior as deriving from changes in technology, that is, changes in the methods of dealing with the material means of life. Technological activities reflect the inherently human 'instinct for workmanship,' 'idle curiosity,' and 'parental bent.' It is the latter instinct that, Veblen maintains, inclines people to direct their efforts toward improvement. These dynamic influences on human behavior conflict with those that derive from social institutions. The latter are 'ceremonial' and 'taboo determined' and change only slowly, if at all, from generation to generation. The individual's conduct is hedged about and directed by habitual relations to other individuals in the group. This is particularly evident in consumption patterns that are less the result of rational calculation of marginal gains and losses than of habit, and the consumption patterns of others in the society that encourage 'emulative display' and 'conspicuous consumption.' All classes in society seek to emulate the standards for consumer behavior set by a wealthy leisure class by acquiring commodities sometimes called 'Veblen goods.' The latter are goods whose utilities are derived both from the 'conspicuous consumption' implicit in the high price paid for it as from the actual use of the good.[5]

But these standards do not satisfy basic human needs – derived from the 'instinct for workmanship' – to engage in useful, welfare-serving activities. Human technological bent is thus perverted by a culture that is oriented toward wasteful, ostentatious consumption. 'The effect of conspicuous waste upon the serious activities of men is therefore to direct them with great singleness of purpose to the largest possible acquisition of wealth, and to discountenance work that brings no pecuniary gain.'[6] Thus, Veblen saw an essential dichotomy, or contradiction, in human behavior because, on the one hand, it is reacting to the impact of a dynamic technology while also being influenced, on the other, by unchanging ceremonial patterns derived from prevailing institutions.

An important implication of Veblen's observations is that a policy of *laissez-faire* does not automatically maximize consumer welfare. The functioning of the price system cannot, in his view, be equated with human well-being when the instinct for workmanship is perverted by patterns of consumption that emulate a wealthy leisure class. Thus, he suggested that the state might do well to mitigate these undesirable influences by taxing items intended for conspicuous consumption to compensate persons who experience psychological losses in consequence of their display.

Veblen's subsequent attack on the market system went even further. In *The Theory of Business Enterprise*, he distinguished between making goods and making money as a basis for the observation that the monetary returns from investments are often directly proportionate to their negative effect on the life process of the society. The community is abused via the 'advised idleness' of industrial plants and the 'capitalization of inefficiency,' which reduced output in order to maintain prices. Waste from this source is compounded by advertising directed at the sale of fashionable goods, which contribute to 'the making of money' for business enterprise rather than 'the making of goods' for consumer satisfaction.

The pervasiveness of institutional influences notwithstanding, Veblen saw their predominant role shaping contemporary life as temporary. Eventually, their influence will be destroyed by the machine process. His expectation was that individuals reared in the precise, orderly environment of a technocratic culture would eventually discard the ceremonies, taboos, and superstitions of yesteryear. Engineers and technologists, who make up the indispensable general staff of the industrial system, will develop a 'class consciousness' and take countermeasures against the wastes and inefficiencies of the present system. Financial managers and absentee owners will then be rendered powerless through a 'soviet of technicians,' even if this group constitutes only a small fraction of the population.[7] If the technological specialists engage in a general strike, a collapse of the old order will follow.

Veblenian observations about the conflicting influence on human behavior of ceremonial institutions and the machine process and his expectation that the machine process would eventually come to dominate, has implications for economic science. It implies that human experiences in the economic sphere, as elsewhere, are best thought of as an ongoing process. These observations are the basis for the Institutionalist view that economic science should be recast in a Darwinian framework, to accommodate the essentially evolutionary character of human behavior and experience.[8]

Wesley Mitchell's institutionalism

Mitchell's critique of orthodox theory

Wesley Clair Mitchell (1874–1948), Veblen's pupil, also registered his dissent from orthodox economics by criticizing the method of deductive logic to arrive at conclusions derived from greatly simplified assumptions about the real world. In particular, Mitchell riled against the inability of orthodox theorists to verify their laws and propositions empirically, while attributing their failures to 'disturbing causes,' in order not to discredit their theories.

Mitchell's criticism of deductive analysis became the basis for a lifetime of empirical work, highlighted by the founding of the National Bureau of Economic Research (NBER), which pioneered the development of statistical business-cycle indicators. These indicators are currently maintained by the US Department of Commerce, and the NBER has considerably broadened its research concerns from what they were in Mitchell's day.

The initial link between Mitchell's empiricism and his dissent from orthodox theory was his investigation of data relating to the statistical verification of the quantity theory of money. The version of the quantity theory that Mitchell tested was the straightforward proposition that the general price level is determined by the relationship between the supply of money and the work to be done by money to serve the needs of trade. His statistical data showed that, between 1860 and 1891, the amount of currency (greenbacks) in circulation (his definition of the money supply) had increased in excess of the needs of trade (in modern terms, the transactions demand for cash). On this basis, the quantity theory would have predicted that prices would rise; but the price level, in fact, fell – from which Mitchell concluded that the quantity theory was empirically invalid, chiefly because it was an excessively simplistic hypothesis to begin with.

Conceivably, Mitchell could have proceeded to construct a more complex theory of price change. For example, he could have developed a theory that includes changes in the velocity with which the currency supply circulates, which could account for the experience of falling prices in the presence of a rising supply of money. However, this would have been to follow in the footsteps of the deductive theorists of whom he was so critical. Mitchell's goal was to establish *empirical theories.*[9]

Mitchell as an empirical theorist

The terms *theoretical* and *empirical* are often used to distinguish between two alternative methods of investigation. The term *theory* is typically used in reference to generalizations about relationships that are arrived at by making logical inferences from premises to conclusions (and from causes to consequences). The role of empiricism, then, is to verify the proposition (or, according to certain contemporary philosophers, to examine whether a proposition of pure theory is falsifiable).[10] Wesley Mitchell, however, was a pioneer in trying to establish empirical theories. The term theory in this connection means inductive generalization.

The role of empiricism is quite different when its object is inductive generalization rather than verification. It then seeks to use factual data to discover empirical correlations that can then serve in the construction of theories that will be able to serve as a basis for prediction. Mitchell's work thus involved the search for the empirical relationships inherent in the data he studied so that the facts of experience are able to serve as a basis for inductive generalization or empirical theorizing.

Mitchell's business indicators: measurement without theory?

Together with Arthur F. Burns, Mitchell undertook to identify the behavior of a large number of business indicators, which they tracked over time for the purpose of measuring sequential changes in aggregate economic activity. They were able, on the basis of these indicators, to identify reference cycles from which they established the duration of business cycles from peak to peak (i.e. from one prosperity to the next) or trough to trough (i.e. from one depression to the next).

They were also able, on the basis of the speed with which certain leading indicators responded to changing conditions, to establish *turning points*, that is, the critical change in aggregate activity that signalled an upturn from depression or a downturn or crisis that precipitated a recession. Thus, Burns and Mitchell established empirically that there are continuous and sequential changes in aggregate activity in modern economies because they organize production mainly under the direction of business enterprises. According to the Burns–Mitchell definition:

> A cycle consists of expansions occurring at about the same time in many economic activities, followed by similarly general recessions, contractions and revivals which merge into the expansion phase of the next cycle; this sequence of change is recurrent, but not periodic; in duration business cycles vary from more than one year to ten or twelve years; they are not divisible into shorter cycles with amplitudes approximating their own.[11]

Clearly, the Burns–Mitchell system of indicators does not offer a business cycle *theory* analogous to those considered in Chapter 17. The theories examined there hypothesized the presence of a uniquely critical factor that has an impact on a sensitive sector of a highly interdependent sector of the economy, from which the disturbance is transmitted to all other sectors. Thus, the Burns–Mitchell approach does not hypothesize causality in the usual sense, which has provoked the comment that their work constitutes 'measurement without theory.'[12]

One response to this charge may be expressed as a question: can a single hypothesis explain all cycles? If the answer to this question is negative, then Mitchell's approach to business cycle analysis is not a rejection of theory *per se*. Rather, it is a rejection of the monocausal analyses of mainstream theorists, who view the cycle as a disturbance of economic equilibrium rather than as the outcome of an ongoing process. A contemporary student of Mitchell's work maintains that 'far from constituting measurement without theory,' Mitchell's work corroborates the possibility of understanding the real economy 'with an adequately complex theory rather than the simplified abstractions so dear to the hearts of mainstream theorists.'[13] This comprehensive perspective led him to study and collect data on wholesale and retail prices, wages, profits, interest rates, currencies and gold movements. All were recorded as part of a statistical series later included in his *Business Cycles*, a huge tome in excess of 600 pages, published in 1913.

The 'social control economics' of John Maurice Clark

Introduction

John Maurice Clark (1884–1963) was the son of John Bates Clark, the American counterpart of Alfred Marshall. He spent his undergraduate days at Amherst, in his native Massachusetts, before going on to Columbia University to study the social sciences, specializing in economics. Although he was steeped in the static laws propounded by his father, he became persuaded by many of the ideas put forward by Veblen and Mitchell. He became especially dubious about marginal utility theory as a basis for explaining consumer behavior and also questioned the profit-maximizing assumption on which the theory of business behavior was predicated. Completion of his graduate studies in 1908 led to a teaching post at Colorado College. The World War I years were spent in Chicago, which was soon to become embroiled in a clothing workers strike. His observations during this period convinced him of the potential gains to be achieved by social cooperation. By 1926, he had returned to Columbia University to take up the chair vacated by his father. However, his Chicago experience – during which he witnessed the major strike by workers in the men's clothing industry that gave rise to the Amalgamated Clothing Workers Union, and also provided the opportunity to study first hand the operation of big business – influenced his professional thinking throughout his life. This experience no doubt strengthened Clark's urge to achieve social improvements, and to push out the borders of economic inquiry in order to provide a theoretical framework for social control. Clark's ethical strain, no doubt, reflects the influence of his father, John Bates Clark. While the elder Clark created a static analysis of competitive equilibrium, complete in and of itself, there was, nevertheless, the implicit premise of social purpose and the expectation that a future generation of economists would take up the work of developing dynamic economics. The younger Clark's theory of social control is anchored in this intellectual framework.

Clark's rejection of marginal utility theory

Like Veblen, John Maurice Clark was concerned with emphasizing the shortcoming of the psychology implicit in neoclassical theory. Clark maintained that much human behavior reflects impulse and 'monetary interests' rather than rational estimates of increments of marginal satisfaction. The human mind is subjected to a myriad of outside influences and is readily influenced, particularly by advertising, largely geared to generating wants. Clark interprets this response as providing evidence that 'what every man brings into the world of markets and trading is not merely the raw material out of which economic wants for particular objects are manufactured.'[14]

Clark further criticizes marginal utility theory for its implicit assumption that the choice process is psychologically costless. Following the psychologist William James, Clark maintained that the process of decision making involves so much effort that people tend to limit the extent to which they exercise their freedom to choose. They tend to rely on habitual modes of behavior in order to avoid the psychological cost of choice. Behavior is thus less the result of continuous rational calculation, in the manner perceived by orthodox theorists, than it is circumscribed by habit and routine. Thus, Clark argues that it is necessary for economists to extend their inquiries beyond the satisfaction of existing wants. The theory of production ought to be developed to explain how businesses *create* human wants and the reasons why individual and social utilities are not always maximized.[15] This analysis underlies Clark's argument in favor of a new type of economics, which he designates as social economics.

The concern of social economics is to examine the efficiency of the whole economic system in relation to achieving the economic aims of society rather than the efficiency of the individual entrepreneur in relation to maximizing business profits. Instead of proceeding in the traditional mode of neoclassical economics, which assumes that individual efficiency leads inevitably to collective efficiency, Clark maintained that 'narrow commercial efficiency does not promote economic efficiency in the large.'[16]

Clark's economics of overhead costs

J. M. Clark's concern with social economics also led him to pursue the question of the efficiency of the price mechanism in allocating resources from a different perspective. He argued that a basic reason for the dichotomy between efficiency at the level of the firm and efficiency at the level of the economy in the aggregate derives from the unique and largely unrecognized role of overhead or fixed costs in a modern industrial economy. He maintained that the prevailing view of cost of production dates back to the domestic system and is not really relevant for any later stage of industrial development. J. S. Mill, Robert Torrens, and William Nassau Senior gave some attention to the theory of fixed cost. However, the general body of classical thought focused chiefly on the variable expenses of labor and raw material associated with specific units of output. Overhead costs, which are chargeable to output as a whole, were not of great consequence to classical thinkers.

The growth of the railroad and other public-utility industries that experienced great variations in demand focused Clark's attention on the importance of overhead expenses. The business-cycle investigations of Wesley Mitchell, who was Clark's close associate, provided detailed data about the ebb and flow of business activity from one phase of the business cycle to the next. These data supported Clark's contention that the nineteenth-century view of the economy's productive activity was totally outmoded. Productive capacity does not consist of a highly elastic capital fund easily reallocated from one economic activity to another. It is highly specific to particular industries and even the most efficient firms find themselves unable to use all their producing capacity during depression periods. Their problems are exacerbated because of the peculiar response of the durable goods industries to changes in consumer demand. This was the beginning of Clark's concern with 'magnified demand' or what present-day economists term 'the acceleration principle.'[17]

The demand for capital goods is derived from increases in the demand for consumer goods. Sometimes production turns up without waiting for a change in consumer demand. Producers expand their production of capital equipment in response to rising prices. If, subsequently, the rate of growth in the demand for consumer goods declines, it is accompanied by a *larger* percentage decline in the demand for new capital equipment. Thus, the principle of acceleration intensifies the expansion of investment in fixed capital during the upturn of the cycle. It similarly intensifies its contraction during the downturn, thus increasing the size of the capital stock that becomes idle overhead during the period of depression.

The concept of overhead cost is, in Clark's view, as applicable to labor and raw material as it is to industrial equipment. Even though business owners hire labor by the day or week when they adjust their labor supplies to the demands of output, it does not follow that labor is not an overhead cost to society. The true nature of labor as an overhead cost is obscured by contracts that make workers responsible for their own maintenance. The business owners' efforts to preserve profit margins and reduce output and jobs during a depression is evidence of the conflict between private and social welfare. This is a time when the social interest requires that production and jobs be preserved. The maintenance of labor income during a depression is a collective social or overhead cost, which business owners have passed on to the community when they lay off workers.

The phenomenon of unemployment raises questions relating to social value.[18] Clark recognizes that 'the search for standards of social value in the economics realm is a baffling task . . . for we shall presumably never discover a definite yardstick of social value comparable to the dollar yardstick of exchange values; but we may find standards by which those of the market may be revised or in some instances replaced.' Clark thus shares Veblen's doubts about the ability of the price mechanism to ensure the well-being of society as a whole. This is the basis for his urging that economists devise ways to achieve the social control of business.[19]

Clarence Ayres's critique of orthodox economics

Clarence Ayres (1891–1972) is remembered as the leading institutional economist of the post-World War II period. His long intellectual life, which began as an undergraduate at Brown University, coincided with the heady era of Dewey's pragmatism, Freudian psychology, and Veblenian ideas about cultural relativism. With a major in philosophy and minor in economics, Ayres moved briefly to Harvard University and then on to the University of Chicago, where Dewey's Chicago school of philosophy set an intellectual tone in which new modes of thought were eagerly explored. Like Chicago's philosophy department, its economics department had taken on a similarly heterodox character during the 1920s, having attracted such non-orthodox thinkers as Thorstein

Veblen, Robert Hoxie, Wesley Mitchell, Walton Hamilton, and J. M. Clark.[20] It is perhaps relevant to mention, in passing, that Frank Knight, then a young instructor in economics, was also part of Chicago's intellectual scene.[21] Although Knight's anti-pragmatic approach was the basis of an intellectual conflict between them, Ayres and Knight enjoyed a personal relationship that lasted a lifetime. All of these associations were a prelude to a teaching career that began at Amherst and culminated in the intellectually congenial environment of the University of Texas at Austin. What is sometimes referred to as the Texas School of Institutionalist Economics derived its inspiration from the intellectual legacy Ayres left there through his writing and research.

Ayres's critique of orthodox economics was launched with his attack on the neoclassical concept of equilibrium and the related notion that strong market forces drive prices to equilibrium levels that are consistent with moral justice.[22] At issue here is the whole traditional theory of a market-oriented economy.

On a more fundamental level, and in anticipation of his subsequent inquiry into technological progress, Ayres maintained that orthodox theory of capital and savings is central to the error and confusion he detected in neoclassical thinking. He argues that orthodox thinkers have the mistaken view that capital is created via savings, thereby imputing a creative function to savers and financial institutions that mobilize resources through the agency of money. In fact, Ayres maintained, it is the physical production that originates in the economy's factories that underlies economic progress. Progress is a technological, not a financial, phenomenon. Capital accumulation and real capital growth are essentially different processes that may occur separately from one another. Ayres's critique thus challenges the idea, based on Böhm-Bawerk's theory of the roundabout nature of production, that it is necessary to accumulate wage goods to make 'advances' in order to sustain capital goods workers until the gestation period is over and capital goods are able to yield their products. In this view, the sacrifice of present goods (i.e. consumption) is essential to the process of capital accumulation.

Ayres's counter-argument was that Austrian capital theory is contradicted by the facts of economic growth. Not only has the quantity of consumer and producer goods increased simultaneously, but the process of investment does not require resources to be directed away from the consumption goods industries – as is envisioned by the Austrian lengthening concept in relation to the production period.[23] Instead of being roundabout, industrial production is prodigiously direct; no more than a few days are required to convert iron ore into an automobile.[24] Real capital results not from abstinence or sacrificing time preference but from invention, discovery, science, and technology.

Ayres's critique of neoclassical capital theory led him to the conclusion that instead of aiding economic growth, the institutions of capitalism are, in fact, impediments to the accumulation of real capital. His theory of underconsumption, which, like Hobson, he linked to the inequitable distribution of income, maintains that savings accumulate simply because some people are richer than others. Anticipating Keynes's critique of Say's law, Ayres argued that savings tend to accumulate in idle balances because a sufficient number of investment outlets do not exist.[25] The basic problem of the capitalistic system is the inability of consumers, who are, in the main, wage-workers, to purchase the vast output that technology has made it pos-sible to produce. The income distributed to workers, as distinct from the incomes of property owners, is (in Ayres's view) determined by institutional factors, and changes in that division depend on changes in the economy's growth rate. Ayres is thus among the critics of the marginal productivity theory of distribution and also anticipated the contemporary post-Keynesian view of the distribution process.[26]

Concluding remarks

The objective of this chapter has been to investigate the heterodoxy of Veblen, Mitchell, J. M. Clark, and Ayres. It was Veblen who focused on the critical issue: why is it necessary for economists to adopt an evolutionary approach if economics is to become a science? The institutionalist approach, which he and his followers pioneered, is now carried forward by The Association for Evolutionary Economics, and its publication, *The Journal of Economic Issues*. Veblenian nuances are also evident in the writings of such social critics as John Kenneth Galbraith. However, the specifics of Veblen's legacy fall short of his objective to reconstruct economic science. As a compromise, many modern Institutionalists have followed Wesley Mitchell and rely on quantitative empirical work.[27] They have also recognized the complementarity of their empirical work and pure theory. It is acknowledged that a successful empiricist needs to be able to formulate economic concepts and give precise expression to economic relationships. Thus, quantitative economics follows Mitchell in working toward generalizations comparable to those that neoclassicists arrived at by deductive analysis. This objective is not, of course, shared by all modern Institutionalists, some of whom are working chiefly in the tradition of Clark and Ayres in their efforts to pursue the goal of developing a theory of social value.[28] A few even look toward a system of economic sociology, such as was visualized by Veblen or Max Weber.[29]

Notes

1 Stow Parsons, *American Minds: A History of Ideas* (New York: Holt, Rinehart, & Winston, 1959), Chapter 10.
2 Allan Gruchy's classic work, *Modern Economic Thought* (New York: Prentice-Hall, 1947), provides an in-depth study of the leading members of the Institutionalist tradition.
3 Joseph Dorfman, *Thorstein Veblen and His America* (New York: The Viking Press, 1934).
4 The first use of the term *institutionalism* was by Walton Hamilton whose famous course at the University of Chicago, in the World War I period, was entitled, 'Social and Economic Institutions.'
5 Harvey Leibenstein, 'Bandwagon, snob, and Veblen effects in the theory of consumers' demand,' *The Quarterly Journal of Economics*, 62 (May, 1950), pp. 183–207.
6 Thorstein Veblen, *The Theory of the Leisure Class* (New York: Modern Library, 1934), p. 112.
7 Thorstein Veblen, *The Engineers and The Price System* (New York: The Viking Press, 1921).
8 Veblen, 'Why is economics not an evolutionary science?'
9 The basis for Mitchell's criticism of Irving Fisher's claim that he had verified the quantity theory statistically is examined by Abraham Hirsh in 'Mitchell, Laughlin and the quantity theory of money,' *The Journal of Political Economy*, 75 (February–December, 1975), pp. 813–22.
10 The shift from verification to falsification is associated with Karl Popper's *The Logic of Scientific Discovery* (1934, translated and reprinted, London: Hutchinson, 1959).
11 Burns and Mitchell, *Measuring Business Cycles* (National Bureau of Economic Research, Studies in Business Cycles, 1946) p. 3.
12 Tjalling Koopman's 'Measurement without theory,' *Review of Economics and Statistics*

(August, 1947), reprinted in R. A. Gordon and L. A. Klein, (eds) *Readings in Business Cycle Theory*, American Economic Association (Homewood, Ill: Richard D. Irwin. 1965), pp. 161–72.
13 Philip A. Klein, 'The neglected institutionalism of Wesley Clair Mitchell's theoretical bases for business cycle indicators,' *Journal of Economic Issues* (December, 1983) pp. 867–99.
14 J. M. Clark, 'Economics and modern psychology,' preface to *Social Economics* (New York: Farrar and Rinehart, 1936) pp. 100–2.
15 John Kenneth Galbraith subsequently developed this idea as the 'dependence effect,' which maintains that because of the greater production potential of the modern techno-structure it has become essential to the survival of the modern corporation to manipulate consumer demands via advertising and other techniques to 'create' new wants. *The New Industrial State* (Boston: Houghton Mifflin, 1967), p. 128 and pp. 547–8.
16 J. M. Clark, 'The socializing of theoretical economics' in R. G. Tugwell, *The Trend of Economics* (New York: A. A. Knopf, 1924), p. 85.
17 Clark's earliest interest is expressed in his essay, 'Business acceleration and the law of demand: a technical factor in economic cycles,' *The Journal of Political Economy*, 21 (March, 1917), pp. 217–35. The problem is further investigated in *Studies in the Economics of Overhead Cost* (Chicago: University of Chicago Press, 1923), pp. 389–96.
18 J. M. Clark, 'Toward a concept of social value,' preface to *Social Economics*, p. 44.
19 For a sympathetic but well-balanced description of Clark's social cost-keeping and social-liberal planning, see Allan Gruchy, *Modern Economic Thought* (Englewood Cliffs, NJ: Prentice-Hall, 1947), Chapter 5.
20 Further details about Ayres's life are available in the chapter entitled 'Clarence Edwin Ayres: an intellectual portrait,' by William Breit and William Patton Culbertson, Jr. in their book on Ayres's institutional economics, *Science and Ceremony* (Austin: University of Texas Press, 1976).
21 See Chapter 15 for Knight's contributions.
22 C. E. Ayres 'Moral confusion in economics,'

International Journal of Ethics, 45 (1943–45), pp. 170–99. Promptly forthcoming was a rebuttal by Frank Knight, 'Intellectual confusion of morals and economics,' *International Journal of Ethics*, 46, pp. 200–20.

23 See Chapter 17. The notion of the lengthening of the production period is an integral part of Austrian business-cycle theory.

24 This apt recollection of Ayres's point is attributable to Donald A. Walker's paper 'Clarence Ayres' critique of orthodox economic theory,' *Journal of Economic Issues*, 9 (3) (September, 1980), pp. 649–80.

25 See Chapter 20.

26 Clarence Ayres, 'Capitalism in retrospect,' *Southern Economic Journal*, 9 (April, 1943), pp. 649–80, and 'Twilight of the price system,' *Antioch Review*, 3 (Summer, 1943).

27 Wesley Mitchell, 'Quantitative analysis in economic theory,' reprinted in *The Backward Art of Spending Money* (New York: Augustus Kelley, 1937), pp. 22–36.

28 See, for example, Philip Klein, 'Economics: allocation or valuation,' *Journal of Economic Issues*, no. 4 (December, 1974), and Marc R. Tool, 'A social value theory,' *Journal of Economic Issues*, no. 5 (March, 1977).

29 Karl Mannheim has attempted to establish the sociology of knowledge as an integrated system of analysis in his *Ideology and Utopia* (New York: Harcourt Brace Jovanovich, 1936).

Questions for discussion and further research

1 What were the chief issues of dissent against the tradition associated with neoclassical economics that emerged during the first part of the twentieth century? Identify who the participants of dispute were and explain what was the issue (or issues) with which they concerned themselves.

2 Select any participant from among those writers you identified above and summarize their contribution. In what way does their contribution reflect their dissent (or criticism) of mainstream thinking?

Glossary of terms and concepts

Acceleration principle (principle of magnified demand)
Changes in the demand for consumer goods generate proportionately greater changes in the demand for capital goods, including inventories. A decline in the demand for a consumer good causes excess capacity and therefore reduces the demand for new capital equipment to zero.

Conspicuous consumption
A term introduced by Veblen to describe the kind of consumption behavior associated with a wealthy leisure class.

Empirical theorizing
Inductive generalization; (*a posteriori*) theorizing.

Institutionalism
A distinctively American school of economics, largely inspired by the work of Veblen, that emphasizes the necessity of studying economics as an evolutionary discipline.

Overhead cost
The fixed costs of equipment and other capital that are associated with output as a whole.

Social economics
This tradition has matured on the basis of the work of J. M. Clark and Clarence Ayres. It is concerned with examining the efficiency of the economic system with a view to its capability of achieving social welfare in terms of human well-being that may be quite unrelated to the profit maximizing goals of private entrepreneurs.

Notes for further reading

From *The New Palgrave*

Geoffrey H. Moore on Arthur Frank Burns, vol. 1, p. 300, and on Wesley Clair Mitchell, vol. 3, pp. 481–82; Warren J. Samuels on Clarence Edwin Ayres, vol. 1, p. 165, and on John Maurice Clark, vol. 1, pp. 431–32; Thomas Sowell on Thorstein Veblen, vol. 4. pp. 799–800; E. Stankovic on conspicuous consumption, vol. 1, pp. 579–80; Basil S. Yamey on overhead costs, vol. 3. pp. 764–66.

Selected references and suggestions for further reading

Burns, A. F. and Mitchell, W. *Measuring Business Cycles* (National Bureau of Economic Research Studies in Business Cycles, 1946).

Dorfman, Joseph. *Thorstein Veblen and His America* (New York: The Viking Press, 1934).

Edgell, S. and Tilman, R. 'The intellectual antecedents of Thorstein Veblen: a reappraisal.' *Journal of Economic Issues*, 23 (December, 1989), pp. 1003–26.

Gruchy, Allen. *Modern Economic Thought* (New York: Prentice-Hall, 1947).

Hirsh, Abraham. 'Mitchell, Laughlin and the quantity theory of money.' *The Journal of Political Economy*, 75 (February–December, 1975), pp. 813–22.

Hodgson, G. 'Thorstein Veblen and post-Darwinian economics.' *Cambridge Journal of Economics*, 16 (September, 1992).

Jones, L. B. 'The institutionalists on the Origin of Species: a case of mistaken identity.' *Southern Economic Journal*, 52 (April, 1986), pp. 1043–55.

Mitchell, Wesley C. 'The German historical school: Gustav von Schmoller.' In Types of Economic Theory, II (New York: Kelley, 1969).

Mitchell, Wesley C. 'Quantitative analysis in economic theory.' Reprinted in *The Backward Art of Spending Money* (New York: Augustus Kelley, 1937), pp. 22–36.

Mitchell, Wesley C. *What Veblen Taught: Selected Writings of Thorstein Veblen* (New York: A. M. Kelley, 1964).

Raines, J. P. and Leathers, C. G. 'Evolving financial institutions in Veblen's business enterprise system,' *Journal of the History of Economic Thought*, 15 (1993), pp. 249–64.

Rutherford, Malcolm. *Institutes in Economics: The Old and New Institutionalists* (London: Cambridge University Press, 1994).

Tugwell, R. G. *The Trend of Economics* (New York: A. A. Knopf, 1924).

Veblen, Thorstein. 'Why is economics not an evolutionary science?' *Quarterly Journal of Economics*, 12 (July, 1898), pp. 373–426; vol. 14 (February, 1900), pp. 240–69.

Veblen, Thorstein. 'The preconceptions of economic science.' *Quarterly Journal of Economics* (January 1899), pp. 121–50, (July, 1899), pp. 396–426; vol. 14 (February, 1900), pp. 240–69.

Veblen, Thorstein. *The Theory of the Leisure Class* (New York: Modern Library, 1934 [1899]).

Veblen, Thorstein. *The Vested Interests and the Common Man* (New York: Capricorn Books, 1919).

Veblen, Thorstein. *The Engineers and the Price System* (New York: Viking, 1921).

Chapter 19

The economics of planning; socialism without Marxism

Introduction

Marx's *Capital* was concerned with identifying the laws of motion that brought the capitalistic system into existence and that he expected would, in time, bring about its ultimate destruction by revolution. The question of the nature of the socialist society that would come into being after the revolution was not addressed by Marx. These considerations were thought premature, and anticipation of planning for the new socialist society was viewed as an exercise in utopianism. Nevertheless, Marx clearly understood that *resource allocation* would be a basic problem under socialism.[1] Resource allocation, as has already been examined in Chapter 16, is precisely the problem that welfare theory undertook to address. There is, therefore, an important parallel in the development of welfare theory and the economics of socialism. Specifically, welfare theorists used neoclassical price theory to identify the criteria for an optimum allocation of resources and to demonstrate that such an allocation would, in fact, tend to be realized through the operation of the competitive price system. Since the pure theory of welfare economics is unrelated to any particular institutionalist structure of society, it is equally applicable to any type of economic system. It is precisely this aspect of the *theory of resource allocation* that led to its adoption as a basis for examining the possibility of rational planning under socialism.

Although the works of Jevons and the Austrians were available during Marx's lifetime, he was apparently unaware of the marginalist method of analysis. He was, however, convinced that recurring capitalist crises provide evidence that, under capitalism, the price system does not achieve an effective allocation of resources. Thus, it never occurred to him that marginal analysis might hold the key to precisely the problem that he had failed to address; namely, the problem of resource allocation. It is, therefore, something of an intellectual irony that Jevonian and Austrian subjectivism became the wellspring for the theory of rational planning under socialism.

The participants

The first economist to examine the conditions necessary for achieving an optimum allocation of resources under socialism was Enrico Barone, an Italian follower of Vilfredo Pareto.[2] His inquiry is the first to identify the parallel between socialism and the conditions that lead to maximum welfare in a capitalistic system operating with a competitive market. The logic of his arguments was pitted against the counter-argument by Ludwig von Mises

(1881–1973) who, over his long lifetime, established himself as a leading proponent of the efficiency of the free market and its compatibility with political *laissez–faire*.

The argument that social planning is incompatible with political freedom was challenged by thinkers on both sides of the ocean; the list includes American Frederick M. Taylor, President of the American Economic Association in 1928, his co-author Oskar Lange and Abba Lerner who arrived in England from Russia before coming to the USA, and 'New Deal' economists interested in planning. In the UK it includes the group of thinkers who, in 1884, organized The Fabian Society with the objective of addressing social problems through legislative reforms, such as gradual nationalization of key industries. They called themselves after Fabus, the ancient Roman general, who struck down Hannibal by waiting patiently for the right moment. The Fabians, who counted among their membership such luminaries as Sidney and Beatrice Webb (founders of the London School of Economics), as well as authors H. G. Wells and George Bernard Shaw, were also prepared to wait for socialism to be achieved without revolution. Their most effective spokespersons among economists were Hugh Gaitskell, Hugh Dalton, G. D. H. Cole, H. D. Dickson, and Evan Durban. Following the period during which marginalism developed in England, they were among the extremely intelligent and articulate group of thinkers who became committed to the principle that hope for society lay in the destruction of capitalism. They were socialists from a political perspective as well as from the standpoint of economic theory. However, they rejected Marx's view that revolution – bloody, if necessary – is the only way to achieve this goal: it was their belief that social problems are best addressed by peaceful means.

Abba Lerner, who grew up in London's East End where he was able to study at the London School, eventually became a founder and editor of the *Review of Economic Studies*. However, unlike the Fabians, he was a 'socialist of the chair,' i.e. he was not involved in politics.[3] He made his entrée into the American economics profession by earning a Harvard fellowship in 1934–35. After a sojourn at the London School, in 1937 he returned to the US, holding teaching positions at Columbia, Johns Hopkins, The New School for Social Research, Michigan State and several others. He produced numerous articles furthering the themes of his most important book *The Economics of Control* (1944) based on his Ph.D. dissertation at the London School, and extending and refining the details of his concept of 'functional finance.' The latter idea became the basis for leading intellectual roles in promoting Keynesian fiscal policy. Mention must also be made of the work of John Hobson and, the Americans, Major Paul Douglas, and Foster and Catchings. They are less well known than others included in this chapter, but are nevertheless effective critics of the efficiency of the price system.

Barone's seminal work on collective planning

The little-known Italian economist Enrico Barone built a model of a collective system in which all resources (other than labor) are socially owned and directed by a Ministry of Production. His conclusion is that if the Ministry plans for producing output so that all costs reach their minima and then sets product prices equal to these minimum costs of production, these directives will achieve an optimum allocation of resources and, in that sense, will achieve maximum welfare. Thus, on a technical level, Barone successfully identified the problem of resource allocation that confronts planners in the absence of a price system, and demonstrated that it is mathematically solvable. That is, in principle, the planning board can substitute its authority for the marketplace and achieve economic efficiency.

Yet, this demonstration did not put the matter to rest. Several respected economists argued that, in spite of Barone's mathematical demonstration, if resources are not directed by a freely operating price mechanism they cannot be used efficiently. A particularly vehement statement of this position was presented by the Austrian thinker Ludwig von Mises.

Issues and Answers from the Masterworks 19.1

Issue

Why is it that a rational allocation of resources cannot be accomplished under socialism?

Mises's answer

From 'Economic calculation in a socialist commonwealth' (translated from the German version for inclusion in *Collectivist Economic Planning*, edited by F. A. Hayek, 1935).

Introduction

There are many socialists who have never come to grips in any way with the problems of economics, and who have made no attempt at all to form for themselves any clear conception of the conditions which determine the character of human society. There are others, who have probed deeply into the economic history of the past and present, and striven, on this basis, to construct a theory of economics of the 'bourgeois' society. They have criticized freely enough the economic structure of 'free' society, but have consistently neglected to apply to the economics of the disputed socialist state the same caustic acumen, which they have revealed elsewhere, not always with success. Economics, as such, figures all too sparsely in the glamorous pictures painted by the Utopians. They invariably explain how, in the cloud-cuckoo lands of their fancy, roast pigeons will in some way fly into the mouths of the comrades, but they omit to show how this miracle is to take place. Wherever they do in fact commence to be more explicit in the domain of economics, they soon find themselves at a loss – one remembers, for instance, Proudhon's fantastic dreams of an 'exchange-bank' – so that it is not difficult to point out their logical fallacies. When Marxism solemnly forbids its adherents to concern themselves with economic problems beyond the expropriation of the expropriators, it adopts no new principle, since the Utopians throughout their descriptions have also neglected all economic considerations, and concentrated attention solely upon painting lurid pictures of existing conditions and glowing pictures of that golden age which is the natural consequence of the New Dispensation.

Whether one regards the coming of socialism as an unavoidable result of human evolution, or considers the socialization of the means of production as the greatest blessing or the worst disaster that can befall mankind, one must at least concede, that investigation into the conditions of society organized upon a socialist basis is of value as something more than 'a good mental exercise, and a means of promoting political clearness and consistency of thought.'[4] In an age in which we are approaching nearer and nearer to socialism, and even, in a certain sense, are dominated by it, research into the problems of the socialist state acquires added significance for the explanation of what is going on around us. Previous analyses of the exchange economy no longer suffice for a proper understanding of social phenomena in Germany and its eastern neighbours today. Our task in this connection is to embrace within a fairly wide range the elements of socialistic society. Attempts to achieve clarity on this subject need no further justification.

I. The distribution of consumption-goods in the socialist commonwealth

Under socialism, all the means of production are the property of the community. It is the community alone which can dispose of them and which determines their use in production. It goes without saying that the community will only be in a position to employ its powers of disposal through the setting up of a special body for the purpose. The structure of this body and the question of how it will articulate and represent the communal will is for us of subsidiary importance. One may assume that this last will depend upon the choice of personnel, and in cases where the power is not vested in a dictatorship, upon the majority vote of the members of the corporation.

The owner of production-goods, who has manufactured consumption-goods and thus becomes their owner, now has the choice of either consuming them himself or of having them consumed by others. But where the community becomes the owner of consumption-goods, which it has acquired in production, such a choice will no longer obtain. It cannot itself consume; it has perforce to allow others to do so. Who is to do the consuming and what is to be consumed by each is the crux of the problem of socialist distribution.

It is characteristic of socialism that the distribution of consumption-goods must be independent of the question of production and of its economic conditions . . . Moreover, just because no production-good will ever become the object of exchange, it will be impossible to determine its monetary value. Money could never fill in a socialist state the role it fills in a competitive society in determining the value of production goods. Calculation in terms of money will here be impossible . . . Only under simple conditions can economics dispense with monetary calculation. Within the narrow confines of household economy, for instance, where the father can supervise the entire economic management, it is possible to determine the significance of changes in the processes of production, without such aids to the mind, and yet with more or less of accuracy. In such a case, the process develops under a relatively limited use of capital. Few of the capitalistic roundabout processes of production are here introduced: what is manufactured is, as a rule, consumption-goods or at least such goods of a higher order as stand very near to consumption-goods. The division of labour is in its rudimentary stages: one and the same labourer controls the labour of what is in effect, a complete process of production of goods ready for consumption, from beginning to end.

Without economic calculation there can be no economy. Hence, in a socialist state wherein the pursuit of economic calculation is impossible, there can be – in our sense of the term – no economy whatsoever. In trivial and secondary matters rational conduct might still be possible, but in general it would be impossible to speak of rational production any more. There would be no means of determining what was rational, and hence it is obvious that production could never be directed by economic considerations. What this means is clear enough, apart from its effects on the supply of commodities. Rational conduct would be divorced from the very ground which is its proper domain . . . But then we have the spectacle of a socialist economic order floundering in the ocean of possible and conceivable economic combinations without the compass of economic calculation.

Thus, in the socialist commonwealth every economic change becomes an undertaking whose success can be neither appraised in advance nor later retrospectively determined. There is only groping in the dark. Socialism is the abolition of rational economy.

Source: *Collectivist Economic Planning*, edited by F. A. Hayek (London: Routledge, 1935). [This article appeared originally under the title 'Die Wirtschaftsrechnung im sozialistischen Gemeinwesen' in the *Archiv für Sozialewissenschaften*, vol. 47 (1920) – Ed.]

Summing up: Mises's key point

Mises argued that rational economic decisions are impossible in the absence of a price directed system. The key role played by factor markets is critical to his argument. Specifically, Mises argued that the prices that prevail in factor markets are the basis for the decisions producers make concerning the proportion in which factors will be employed to produce various products consumers wish to purchase. Since a socialist economy owns all of its factors communally (except, of course, for labor), there is no objective evaluation of their values, such as is established by the price mechanism. Therefore, according to Mises, rational decision making about resource allocation is a logical impossibility in spite of Barone's proof that, in principle, the problem of rational resource allocation can be solved. Thus, the debate about resource allocation without the intervention of a free-price mechanism was effectively initiated as a result of Mises's charge.

The debate continues

Mises's argument was eventually challenged by Frederick M. Taylor when he addressed the American Economic Association as its president in 1928.[5] His argument was, essentially, a restatement of Barone's. He begins from the premise that the state can distribute income according to whatever objectives society deems appropriate, and permit households to spend in any way they choose. Production would be planned by state-owned firms with a view to clearing all markets of the goods produced. This would, of course, require a planning board to set both commodity and resource prices. Resource prices would first be imputed from consumer demands to guide output and would then be reflected forward as commodity prices to guide consumer choices. These prices would, of course, only be *shadow prices* rather than market prices, but from the consumers' perspective, they would serve exactly the same purpose of allocating or rationing goods. Mistakes would, of course, be made, just as is often the case with market-set prices (i.e. there might be shortages of some goods and gluts of others). Trial-and-error procedures could be used to grope toward a system of prices that would effectively clear markets of already produced goods and also serve as a basis for guiding future production.

The next phase of the debate proceeded along somewhat different lines and involved two other personalities, F. A. Hayek, also a follower of the Austrian tradition who became a Nobel Prize laureate in 1974 (jointly with Gunnar Myrdal), and Lionel Robbins, of England. The issue now became whether it is a practical possibility, first, for a planning board to collect the astronomical quantity of data needed for decision making and, second, whether it is possible to establish a mathematical equation for each of the vast number of commodities demanded by households and supplied by state-directed producers, as a basis for determining the set of mutually compatible prices that will simultaneously solve the system of equations.[6]

Oskar Lange and F. M. Taylor brought an effective end to their debate with their response in *On the Economic Theory of Socialism* (1966) to Mises's original argument as well as to those of Hayek, Robbins, and Lerner. The essence of their counter-argument was, first, that rational resource allocation only requires the *existence of prices*; it matters not in the least whether these are free-market prices or shadow prices set by state planners. Trial-and-error processes are fully capable of identifying what set of prices is compatible with market clearing. As Lerner put it, all that is necessary is that the planning board require producers to follow two rules; the first is that they expand output to achieve the lowest possible average cost, and second, that they choose that scale of output at which average cost equals marginal cost.[7]

Consumer goods prices would be set freely by consumer preferences, which would thereby serve as a basis for imputing factor values by a trial-and-error process such as had already been suggested by Lange and Taylor. Thus, the problems of massive equation solutions, against which Hayek and Mises warned, were intended to be circumvented by the Lange–Taylor solution to the pricing problem. They effectively laid to rest the problem that Mises's argument raised about the impossibility of rational resource allocation under socialism. The profession was virtually unanimous about accepting his

conclusion; rational use of resources is fully possible without a free-price mechanism. Whatever the problems of socialism as a system, they do not lie in the impossibility of making rational production decisions.

One well-known scholar has argued that the chief problem of socialism is likely to be the bureaucracy inherent in the requirement for a large number of administrators. None other than Joseph Schumpeter inferred that socialism has the potential for being superior to big-business capitalism precisely because much of the capitalists' requirements to respond on an ongoing basis to the uncertainties of economic rivalry will be eliminated by economic planning.[8] Yet the events of the so-called 'Velvet Revolution' of 1989, which – without military action – brought down the Soviet Union, causing former satellites including the former East Germany, to unify with the West to pursue market driven economies, suggest a new significance for Mises's original argument.

Rent in Fabian economics

Fabian studies also undertook the collection of factual data, especially as it related to the extreme disparities in personal income distribution. Studies of this sort paved the way for Sidney Webb's book *Capital and Land* (1888), which argued that capital is essentially like land in its capability to yield rent as an unearned increment. Sidney Webb argued that modern capitalism is chiefly characterized by the Ricardian law that conceives of rent as a differential surplus. This surplus emerges not only on agricultural land, according to Webb, but also in industrial establishments. Economic growth and social development yield an unearned increment to capitalists that is in no way attributable to their efforts or services as capitalists. The source of these differential rents is community effort and it is to the community that these rents should be returned through the relatively simple reform of transferring ownership of all land to local councils. Industries should be similarly owned, Webb argued, while natural monopolies like railroads, bridges, and canals should be owned by the state. The objective of these recommendations was that, whatever surplus is earned by the means of production, should benefit society as a whole, rather than individual owners.

There are some obvious problems that would arise in implementing Webb's recommendation. First, there is the problem of identifying the unearned rental component from that portion of the resource cost that is earned. Is there a distinction between earnings on property that is purchased rather than inherited? Hugh Gaitskell criticized Webb and other early Fabians, who argued that all surpluses be interpreted as technically 'unearned', as presenting a weak argument for socialism.[9]

By the early 1920s, E. Hugh Dalton, a Cambridge-educated Fabian, who became an assistant lecturer at the London School of Economics, undertook to use marginal analysis to examine income inequality. He wrote two books, *Some Economic Aspects of the Inequality of Incomes in Modern Communities* (1920) and *Principles of Public Finance* (1922). The first was the more ambitious and scholarly and aimed chiefly at presenting evidence about the distribution of personal income. It criticized neoclassical distribution theory because it ignored the role of inheritance and the influence of opportunity, custom, and property in determining income shares. The goals that democratic socialists hoped to achieve on the basis of Dalton's work were greater income equality through improved access to education by the working class and tax reforms to limit inherited

wealth. Nationalization of industry continued to be a socialist goal, but it was no longer viewed as the sole method of advance toward greater equality.

The New Fabian Research Bureau (NFRB)

The New Fabian Research Bureau (NFRB) was organized in 1935 by G. D. H. Cole to explore the theory and practice of socialism. Besides Cole and Gaitskell, two other important participants in the work of the Fabians were Evan Durban and H. D. Dickinson, from the University of Leeds – the latter's name was mentioned above in connection with the problem of the possibility of rational resource allocation under socialism. Dickinson's paper 'Price formation in a socialist community,' has been credited with introducing the principle that pricing on the basis of marginal cost is the instrument through which a socialist economy can duplicate the efficiency of a price-directed competitive economy.[10] The same logic also led him to the conclusion that decreasing-cost industries should be subsidized while increasing-cost industries should be taxed. The timing of this exchange, which preceded Hayek's important book *Collectivist Economic Planning* (1935) by just a year, thus became part of the larger intellectual controversy about the competitive solution to the economic problem of socialist states. The conclusion is that a planned economy is not only capable of replicating the efficiency of the price system in the production of goods by adopting the marginal cost pricing rule, but it has the potential for even greater efficiency because planning avoids the economic and social losses inherent in the breakdown of competition. In short, planning under democratic socialism is held to be capable of an even more rational performance than *laissez-faire*.

The problem of unemployment

The microeconomic problem of the rational allocation of resources under socialism was by no means the only theoretical concern of the Fabians. They were also concerned with the macroeconomic problem of unemployed resources, labor in particular. An important analytical contribution towards understanding this problem came from John A. Hobson (1858–1940). Hobson had a rather undistinguished teaching career, but wrote more than 50 books, all of which not only expressed his concern with the ethical aspects of business behavior but also recorded his dissent from neoclassical economic theory and *laissez-faire* policy. His economic heresy not only gave him much in common with American institutionalists, but also earned him plaudits from none other than John Maynard Keynes, who described Hobson's first book as one 'which marks in a sense, an epoch in economic thought.'[11]

Hobson's underconsumption theory

Hobson and his co-author, A. F. Mummary, began their underconsumptionist argument with a challenge to the conventional and generally accepted premise, from the time of Adam Smith, that production imbalances are not possible. But there was a new twist to his argument: Smith, and those who followed him, maintained that this balance is assured because the market directs savings into investment, so that purchasing power cannot be destroyed. Hobson argued that investment, and therefore the production of consumer goods in excess of the capacity of consumers in the aggregate to purchase them, is a potential source of imbalance.

Specifically, Hobson argued that the amounts paid out in wages, rent, profit, and interest are generally sufficient to buy back the product of industry. However, in economies characterized by great inequalities in the distribution of income, many persons are so wealthy they are unable to spend their incomes. The lag of wages behind prices during prosperity limits the expenditures of workers as a class and transfers disproportionate amounts of income to non-wage earners. The additional flow of savings supports new investment, which eventually adds to the volume of output available for sale. Overproduction is thus inevitable in the sense that the increased stream of consumer goods, which is produced as increased saving supports new investment, cannot be absorbed at prices that are profitable for producers. The cure, in Hobson's view, is to be found in greater equality of income.[12] This proposal is certainly in accord with the arguments of Dalton and Gaitskell about the relevance for the economic well-being of society of placing stringent limits on inherited wealth and for expanding the opportunities for employment by the lower classes.

The concern of the Fabians about the problem of unemployment became the basis of the intellectual empathy that they shared with John Maynard Keynes. Keynes regarded the so-called Treasury view, which undertook to alleviate England's 1920s depression with monetary measures, as untenable policy. He argued for public works and budget deficits along with cheap money to encourage domestic expansion. It was not, however, until 1936 that the theoretical basis for these policy suggestions was systematically developed by Keynes.

Keynes's ideas about how to manage aggregate economic activity were introduced into socialist economic policy by a new generation of Fabian socialists.[13] Colin Clark, Evan Durban, and James Meade were among those who introduced Keynes's principles of macroeconomic management into socialist planning recommendations.[14] G. D. H. Cole also applauded Keynes's *General Theory* as being sympathetic to underconsumptionist views about the need to increase the spending power of the masses to alleviate unemployment. However, he also warned that while 'the Keynesian revolution in economic thought is to be welcomed and accepted by Socialists up to a point, it cannot be taken as a substitute for Socialism, or for a socialist economic theory which goes a long way beyond it.'[15] Nevertheless, the revolutionary system of thought that Keynes introduced to the world in his *General Theory of Employment, Interest and Money* (1936) also left its mark on thinkers who were committed to achieving a non-violent transition to a planned economy. Keynes's message provided an analytical basis for many socialist objectives. Specifically, Keynes's theory provided a rationale for the socialist objective of large-scale income redistribution while also indicating ways in which full employment might be achieved without large-scale nationalization. Given their pragmatic perspective that full socialism was, in all likelihood, a long way off for Great Britain, the Fabians embraced Keynes's analysis as providing a workable interim answer to the problem of capitalist collapse that was so greatly worsened in England by the worldwide depression of the 1930s. The policy imperatives confronting Great Britain at this critical time were not without impact on Keynes's formulation of his message and on the Western world, which took it to mind and heart.

A + *B* theorem

There are various versions of the *A* + *B* theorem which differ in detail, but share the common feature of attributing crises and depressions to the inability of consumers to buy industry's products at prices that will cover their production costs. One popular version is the *A* + *B* theorem, offered by another English writer, Major C. H. Douglas, to explain the source of purchasing-power insufficiency.[16] According to Douglas's explanation, the payments made by businesses consist of:

A payments made to individuals in the form of wages, salaries, and dividends.
B payments made into reserves for depreciation and payments to other businesses for raw material and equipment and interest on bank loans.

A payments provide a flow of purchasing power while *B* payments do not. Yet both *A* and *B* payments become part of the price. Thus, there is a deficiency of purchasing power equal to *B*, which must be replaced in some way if production is not to be interrupted. This logic provides the basis for various schemes for sharing the wealth.

Social welfare

The Lerner argument

The Lerner argument about the conduct of rational planning was straightforward: the planning board uses the price mechanism by establishing a set of 'shadow prices' and then instructs its managers to follow simple rules. The first is to confront all individuals with exactly the same price for each good, thereby avoiding price discrimination among them. This rule would achieve the first set of maximizing conditions. Analogously, the planning board establishes factor prices for all establishments and instructs managers to minimize production costs. Given those instructions, the second set of maximizing conditions stipulates that prices must equal marginal costs. Managers are further instructed to *expand* output if market prices are higher than marginal costs and, conversely, to contract output if marginal cost exceeds market price. Thus, Lerner's plan for rational economic control is designed to eliminate the deviations from perfect competition that free enterprise might generate. The role of authority (i.e. the planning board) in a Socialist state is to act in the manner of the Walrasian auctioneer, which Walras himself never demonstrated but only implied.

In *Economics of Control* (1944) Lerner went beyond the three sets of optimality criteria established by Hicks to include full employment among the basic welfare requirements. This led him to his important concept of 'functional finance' or the use of fiscal policies to 'steer' the economy by appropriate programs of taxing and spending, borrowing, or lending by the Treasury. The latter programs subsequently became the centerpiece for Keynesian fiscal policy.

Another important contribution to welfare economics came from Abram Bergson who, continuing the Barone tradition, restated the planning problem as being one of maximizing a social welfare function.[17] A social welfare function envisions an aggregation of the individual welfares of different individuals.

What is the best method for aggregating individual choices? The problem of aggregating individual preferences in order to arrive at a summation of all individual choices stems from the old argument going back to Robbins (1932) that individual utilities are strictly subjective so that they can neither be compared nor aggregated. As was shown in Chapter 16, it is precisely this argument that led to the Pareto ordinal ranking system along with the criteria that a given social change can be

regarded as an improvement in welfare as long as it enables at least one person to be better off; i.e. able to achieve a higher indifference curve without anyone else being pushed to a lower one.

The Pareto principle, in itself, does not go very far towards designing policies to accomplish improvements in human welfare. One attempt at achieving a forward step proceeded from the incontrovertible point that there are some 'winners' from any proposed change in policy and some prospective 'losers.' This truism suggested the possibility of the compensation principle to Nicholas Kaldor.[18] The essentials of his proposed approach was to introduce hypothetical compensation payments by the winners to the losers.

A conceptually different approach was undertaken by Abram Bergson who tried to establish a theoretical basis for circumventing the inherent non-additivity of individual preferences by proceeding in terms of individual utility functions that are inferred on the basis of an ethical belief that the preference orderings of individuals are consistent with alternative social states, such that it is possible to identify at least one social state that is 'equally good' for all members of society. Beginning from a profile of individual preference orderings, if it can be ethically shown that it is not *inconsistent* with their preferences, then ordinal utility ranking can serve as a basis for transforming them into a numerical representation of individual utility functions. These, in the aggregate, represent the social utility function.

As a practical matter, the identification of a social welfare function to be associated with alternative prospective policies is a Herculean task, as Kenneth Arrow's *Impossibility Principle* has shown. His important book *Social Choice and Individual Values* (1951) relied on the mathematics of set theory rather than calculus to enable him to reach his conclusions. His argument proceeded from the premise that the problem of choice involves the selection of one from among three possible projects, identified as A, B, and C. The one which is chosen is to represent the vote of the majority. The problem of identifying the majority choice is not as clear cut as it may seem. Consider the following: say that a three-person selection committee must choose amongst projects A, B, and C. The vote of member 1 is that A is preferred to B which is also preferred to C; the vote of member number 2 ranks B as preferred to C which is preferred to A; the third member votes C is preferred to A which is preferred to B. Thus, the third vote ranks C better than A. In short, there is a voting paradox that implies that the choice is necessarily arbitrary in the sense of requiring a dictator to choose among alternatives, causing the paradox to be referred to as Arrow's 'impossibility theorem.' Despite this negative finding, Arrow – together with Gerard Debreu (born 1921) a French mathematical economist – was able to prove mathematically that a competitive equilibrium can be shown to exist within the framework of a Walrasian equilibrium model. Debreu received the Nobel Prize in Economics for this finding – an award that Arrow had already received in 1972 jointly with J. R. Hicks.

Concluding remarks

The dilemma inherent in Marx's dialectic relating to the inevitability of social revolution produced two quite differently grounded rebuttals. One was inspired by Pareto's welfare analysis, as revitalized and reinterpreted by J. R. Hicks and subsequently given mathematical proof by Samuelson and Debreu. They undertook to establish the 'existence' of a welfare maximizing equilibrium in a com-

petitive price directed economy. The alternative intellectual approach was taken by several thinkers from many different countries. The list includes, among others, the Italian Enrico Barone, a whole group of Fabian Socialists, Abba Lerner, and several 'New Deal' economists. Their energies were directed at demonstrating the practical possibilities of achieving socially desired outcomes, ranging from marginal cost pricing to full employment by means of planning. Theirs was intended to be the intellectual rebuttal to the argument deriving largely from the Austrian tradition that it is not possible for a planning board, given the responsibility for choosing the outputs to be produced and the methods by which they will be produced by deploying factors of production, to accomplish a rational outcome because they do not have market prices to guide them. The rebuttal variously articulated by a whole spectrum of 'theoretical' socialists was that, with the assignment of 'shadow' prices, it is possible by a process of trial and error (which is much like the fluctuations in the day-to-day prices generated by the price system) to accomplish the best of all possible worlds. This includes achievement of the competitive ideal of optimum output and, with the aid of functional finance, 'full' employment when market conditions are unable to generate these socially desired outcomes. Thus, the theoretical and practical concerns the proponents of planning offer, provide a perception and mind-set that leads to the less than full employment analysis of J. M. Keynes, which is the subject matter of Chapter 20.

Notes

1 Karl Marx, *Das Kapital*, vol. III, Parts IV–V, reflect the awareness that resource allocation problems would exist.

2 Enrico Barone, 'The ministry of production in a socialist state,' in *Collective Economic Planning*, edited by F. A. Hayek (London: Routledge, 1935).

3 Peter Clarke, *Liberals and Social Democrats* (Cambridge: Cambridge University Press, 1978), p. 32.

4 V. Kautsky, *The Social Revolution and on the Morrow of the Social Revolution* (London, 1907), Part II, p. 1.

5 F. M. Taylor, 'The guidance of production in a socialist state,' in B. Lippincott, *On the Economic Theory of Socialism* (Minneapolis: University of Minnesota Press, 1938).

6 F. A. Hayek, *Individualism and Economic Order* (Chicago: University of Chicago Press, 1948), especially Chapter IV.

7 Abba Lerner, 'Economic theory and socialist economy,' *The Review of Economic Statistics* 2, (March, 1934) pp. 51–61; Oskar Lange, 'Mr. Lerner's note on socialist economics,' *Review of Economic Studies* (1936/37), pp. 143–44.

8 Joseph A. Schumpeter, *Capitalism, Socialism and Democracy* (New York: Harper & Bros., 1942), p. 167.

9 Hugh Gaitskell, 'The ideological development of democratic socialism in Great Britain,' *Socialist International Information*, 5 (52–53), (1955), p. 926.

10 Nancy Ruggles, 'The welfare basis of the marginal cost pricing principle,' *Review of Economic Studies* 17, 42 (1949–50), p. 43.

11 J. M. Keynes. *The General Theory of Employment, Interest and Money* (New York: Harcourt Brace Jovanovich, 1936), p. 365.

12 See, for example, J. A. Hobson, *Economics of Unemployment* (London: Macmillan, 1922).

13 The history and perspective of the Fabian movement, and the several dynamic individuals who provided its inspiration and momentum, are fully detailed by Elizabeth Durban, daughter of E. F. M. Durban, in *New Jerusalems: The Labour Party and the Economics of Democratic Socialism* (London: Routledge & Kegan Paul, 1985). An earlier assessment is Peter Clarke, *Liberals and Social Democrats* (Cambridge: Cambridge University Press. 1978).

14 An alternative and somewhat more complicated solution is proposed by H. D. Dickinson, 'Price formation in a socialist community,' *Economic Journal*, 43 (June, 1933), pp. 237–50.

15 G. D. H Cole, *Socialist Economics* (London: Victor Gollancz. 1950) Chapter 2, pp. 53–54. An important posthumous book by E. F. M. Durban, *Problems of Economic Planning* (London: Routledge & Kegan Paul, 1949), includes two articles on socialist economics and Durban's review of Hayek's *Road to Serfdom*, which are reprinted from *Economic Journal*, 1935, 1936, and 1945, respectively.

16 C. H. Douglas, *Credit-Power and Democracy* (London: Stanley Nott, 1935).

17 A. Bergson, 'The reformation of certain aspects of welfare economics,' *Quarterly Journal of Economics*, 52, pp. 310–34.

18 'Welfare propositions in economics and interpersonal comparisons of utility,' *Economic Journal*, 49 (September) pp. 549–52.

Questions for discussion and further research

1 Why is the question about rational economic decision making so central to the controversy about socialism as an effective alternative to capitalism?

2 What was the essence of Barone's argument (in *Collective Economic Planning*) that rational decisions are possible under socialism even though there are no market prices?

3 What are 'shadow prices'? How would they facilitate rational decision making under socialism?

4 What relevance does the rule of marginal cost pricing have for a socialist economy?

Notes for further reading

From *The New Palgrave*

M. Anyadike-Danes on Hugh Todd Naylor Gaitskell, vol. 2, pp. 454–55; W. Brus on market socialism, vol. 3, pp. 337–42; David Clark on Clifford Hugh Douglas, vol. 1, p. 920; Peter Clarke on John Atkinson Hobson, vol. 2, pp. 664–66; David Collard on Henry Douglas Dickinson, vol. 1, p. 836; B. A. Corry on

Glossary of terms and concepts

A + B theorem

A principle suggested by C. H. Douglas for explaining purchasing power insufficiencies. It attributes the deficiency to the presence of interbusiness payments, which, unlike payments to individuals, are not used for the purchase of consumer goods.

Arrow's impossibility principle

Maintains that there is a paradox inherent in attempting to establish the choice of the majority, which is arbitrary. Subsequently, he and Gerard Debreu established mathematically that a competitive equilibrium can be shown to exist in a Walrasian equilibrium model.

Fabian socialism

An English movement, organized by Sidney and Beatrice Webb in 1884, which aimed to achieve socialism by legislative means rather than by revolution.

Functional finance

Abba Lerner's tool to 'steer' the economy towards full employment by using governmental taxing, spending, borrowing and lending activities to 'manage' aggregate demand.

Impossibility theorem (Austrian)

As part of their objections to collectivist planning, the Austrians, in particular von Mises, maintained that rational allocation of resources is impossible in the absence of the price system.

Shadow prices

Prices set by a planning board in a socialist economy for the purpose of guiding consumer purchases. These can, at least theoretically, serve as a basis for imputing factor prices, which can then be used to allocate labor and other resources. The possibility of rational allocation without a price system was also maintained by the Italian, Enrico Barone, and E. M. Taylor, an American.

Social welfare function

The aggregation of individual welfares. The inherent problem stems from the Robbins's argument that the subjectivity of individual utilities implies that they cannot be measured or aggregated. The argument led to Pareto's system of ordinal ranking (Chapter 15). Accordingly, a change in social welfare can be interpreted as an improvement in social welfare if it enables at least one person to achieve a higher indifference curve.

Underconsumption (oversaving) theories of the cycle

Theories based on the premise that 'workers cannot buy their own product.' The insufficiency of purchasing power is usually attributed to inequalities in the distribution of income. The excessive savings of capitalists and landowners are viewed by underconsumption theorists as the cause of cyclical disturbances.

Lionel Charles Robbins, vol. 4, pp. 206–8; Elizabeth Durbin on Evan Frank Mottram Durbin, vol. 1, p. 945, and on Fabian economics, vol. 2, pp. 266–69; Daniel R. Fusfield on Fred Manville Taylor, vol. 4, p. 611; Ravi Kanbur on shadow pricing, vol. 4, pp. 316–17; Tadeusz Kowalik on the Lange–Lerner mechanism, vol. 3, pp. 129–31, and on Oskar Ryszard Lange, vol. 3, pp. 123–28; Michael Schneider on under consumption, vol. 4, pp. 741–44; T. Scitivsky on Abba Ptachya Lerner, vol. 3, pp. 167–68; S. C. Stimson on social democracy, vol. 4, pp. 395–98; J. M. Winter on Beatrice and Sidney Webb, vol. 4, pp. 885–86; Anthony Wright on George Douglas Howard Cole, vol. 1, p. 473.

Selected references and suggestions for further reading

Barone, Enrico. 'The ministry of production in a socialist state.' In *Collectivist Economic Planning*, edited by E. A. Hayek (London: Routledge, 1935).

Cole, G. D. H. *Socialist Economics* (London: Victor Gollancz, 1950).

Durban, Elizabeth. *New Jerusalems: The Labour Party and the Economics of Democratic Socialism* (London: Routledge & Kegan Paul, 1985).

Gaitskill, Hugh. 'The ideological development of democratic socialism in Great Britain.' *Socialist International Information*, 5, no. 52–53 (1955), p. 926.

Hayek, E. A. *Individualism and Economic Order* (Chicago: University of Chicago Press, 1948).

Lange, Oskar. 'Mr. Lerner's note on socialist economics.' *Review of Economic Studies*, 1936/37, pp. 143–44.

Lerner, Abba. 'Economic theory and socialist economy.' *The Review of Economic Statistics*, 2 (March, 1934) pp. 51–61.

Schumpeter, Joseph A. *Capitalism, Socialism and Democracy* (New York: Harper & Bros., 1942).

Taylor, E. M. 'The guidance of production in a socialist state.' In B. Lippincott, *On the Economic Theory of Socialism* (Minneapolis: University of Minnesota Press, 1938).

Vaughn, K. I. 'Economic calculation under socialism: the Austrian contribution.' *Economic Inquiry*, 18 (October, 1980), pp. 535–54.

Von Mises, Ludwig. *Economic Calculation in a Socialist Commonwealth*. Translated from the German version for inclusion in *Collectivist Economic Planning*. Edited by E A. Hayek, (London: Routledge, 1935).

Chapter 20

J. M. Keynes's critique of the mainstream tradition

Introduction

Life and times (1883–1946)

The impact of *The General Theory of Employment, Interest and Money* on the profession and in the realm of public policy has exceeded that which could reasonably have been expected from even such a distinguished and influential thinker as John Maynard Keynes. The reason for its sweeping success, in the face of received doctrine and a generally negative reception in non-academic circles at the time of its publication in 1936, is that it had something for everyone. One would have to go back to Adam Smith to find a comparable degree of persuasiveness with respect to public policy, to David Ricardo for the kind of rigorous analysis that inspires the deductive thinker, and to Karl Marx for someone who attracted sufficiently zealous and able followers to carry his message to the world.

Keynes appears to have been destined, by family circumstance and great natural ability, to make a distinguished contribution to the world.[1] His father was John Neville Keynes, registrar of the University of Cambridge, whose *Scope and Method of Political Economy* (1891) is not only a classic in its field, but remains an eminently useful treatise on the subject of methodology to this day. His mother served as mayor of Cambridge as recently as 1932. The Keyneses educated their son at Eton and King's College, where he excelled in mathematics, besides studying the classics, philosophy, and economics – the latter under Henry Sidgwick and Alfred Marshall.

In 1906, having passed the civil service examination, he went into the India Office for two years before returning once more to King's College, where he specialized in teaching Marshall's *Principles of Economics*. The academic life – broadened, especially through his marriage to Russian ballerina Lydia Lopokova, to include the arts as well as business interests, which provided a handsome additional income – suited him well.

However, Keynes was always involved in public affairs in one capacity or another, particularly with respect to matters of trade and finance. This aspect of his career was in perfect keeping with his predominantly pragmatic approach; economics as a pure science interested him far less than economics in the service of policy. Indeed, Keynes's contribution to the theory and practice of political economy must be seen in perspective against the war and interwar years in order to be fully understood and appreciated. These years were marked by the breakdown of trade relations and the gold standard during World War I, followed first by inflation, exchange rate instability, balance-of-payments disequilibria, and later by deflation and mass unemployment on an international scale. Theoretical examination of these catastrophic phenomena and, more important from Keynes's point of view, practical solutions to the problems they created, were therefore the order of the day.

With the outbreak of World War II, Keynes devoted himself to questions concerning war finance and the ultimate re-establishment of international trade and stable currencies. His ideas on these matters were offered in a pamphlet, *How to Pay for the War* (1940), and in the Keynes plan for the establishment of an international monetary authority, which he proposed in 1943. Although Keynes's plan was rejected, the proposal that was adopted at the 1944 Bretton Woods Conference, which Keynes attended as the leading British delegate, clearly reflected the influence of his thinking.

At the time of his death, early in 1946, shortly after working out the American loan agreement, he was the leading economist not only of England but also of the world. He was a brilliant theorist, but he valued theory primarily as a guide to policy. Thus, Keynes, perhaps more than any other individual, is responsible for the return to what once was known as 'political economy.'

The evolution of The General Theory

The Marshallian background: Say's Law

Because Keynes was schooled in the Marshallian tradition, and it was this background that underlay his 'long struggle to escape,' it is here one must begin to understand the origins of the paradigm shift which many think of as the Keynesian revolution. Marshall's analysis was almost wholly microeconomic in character and was little concerned with the behavior of the economy as a whole. This focus stemmed largely from the Ricardo–Mill legacy of Say's Law, from which they derived their conclusion that overproduction for the economy as a whole is an impossibility as is an over-accumulation of capital. Marshall also concluded, at least implicitly, that the labor resources of the economy would tend to be fully employed and receive a real wage equivalent to the value of its marginal product. Full employment is assured because, under competition, money wages tend to fall when there are unemployed workers, which brings about corresponding reductions in *real* wages. Neoclassical thinkers regarded wage rate reductions as a reliable mechanism for assuring full employment because they believed that money and real wages would decline together. The relationship envisioned between the behavior of money and real wages is closely related to their conception of the behavior of the general price level, which is examined next.

The Marshallian background: the quantity theory

The best known hypothesis about the behavior of the general price level is Irving Fisher's transactions version of the quantity theory of money, which emphasized changes in M, the quantity of money, as the causal factor in bringing about changes in the general price level.[2] Unlike Fisher's, Marshall's formulation emphasized changes in the use of money. The public holds some portion of the annual money value of goods and services in its cash balances at any moment of time.

Marshall thought the essential reason why people demand cash or, in modern terminology, have a preference for liquidity, is to bridge the time gap between the receipt of money income and its disbursement. If the demand for money for transactions purposes (i.e. as a medium of exchange) is such that the money stock turns over, say, at a rate of four times a year, the equivalent of one quarter of the annual money value of output will be in cash balances at any moment of time. Thus the demand for cash, which Marshall represented by the letter k, is equivalent to $1/V$, which is the reciprocal of V, the velocity of circulation. By substituting k for $1/V$ velocity in the equation $MV = PT$ and rearranging, Marshall's equation of exchange becomes $M = PTk$, where M is the quantity of money at any instant of time and PTk is the average level of prices, given the volume of trade and the demand for cash to satisfy transaction needs.

Marshall's introduction of cash balances into the equation of exchange facilitated examination of changes in the price level initiated by changes in the speed with which the public uses the stock of money, as well as changes in the quantity of money itself. Marshall's introduction of k (to represent the demand for money) did not lead to different conclusions than those associated with Fisher's quantity theory. Because k in the Marshallian formulation, like V in the Fisher formulation, is a stable factor that reflects such institutionally determined influences as the frequency with which people are paid, the demand for money for transaction purposes is a stable function of the level of income, and is not subject to autonomous variations that will affect the general price level independently of the quantity of money.

Marshall recognized that, besides wanting money as a medium of exchange, people *might* have a demand *for money as an asset*, but he regarded the holding of cash as irrational behavior. His logic was that if people find themselves with excess cash balances, perhaps because of wage and price reductions resulting from unemployment somewhere in the economy, they would simply increase their expenditures on other goods (perhaps indirectly through investments in capital goods). This would maintain the constancy of the general price level even if there are reductions in money–wage rates. A stable price level with falling money wages would reduce wages and promote the re-employment of labor if there were layoffs anywhere in the economy. Thus, for Marshall, the problem of explaining levels of unemployment and reductions in levels of resource use was considerably less challenging than the problem of explaining individual commodity and factor prices.[3]

Marshall also left to others the examination of the relationship between changes in the general price level and the demand for money as an asset. His approach was to *dichotomize* the pricing process, meaning that the forces operating in the money market were seen as operating separately from those operating in the commodity markets, as though there were no relationship between them. This is, of course, the case if there is no demand for money as an asset. In effect, this assumption has it that a money economy functions like a barter economy. The demand for cash balances is then zero, and the money market is always in a state of equilibrium. This implies that the money received from the sale of commodities is always used to purchase other commodities, which is to say, the requirements for Say's identity are fulfilled in Marshall's analysis as they were in the classical analysis which preceded his. It also allowed Marshall to compartmentalize monetary theory from the theory of income, output, and employment, and substantially limit its content to the quantity theory.

Early writings

Alhough Keynes was schooled in the traditional theories of Say's Law and the 'Quantity of Money–Price Level' link, his examination of the relationship between depression and monetary deflation after World War I led him to question whether price-directed economies tend to operate automatically at full-employment levels. The train of thought that ultimately developed out of this question later became the essence of Keynes's message.[4] His first publication, *Indian Currency and Finance* (1913), which is regarded as an outstanding examination of the functioning of the gold exchange standard, already anticipated his later view on the need for wise monetary policy to achieve economic stability. This message first emerged clearly in *The Economic Consequences of the Peace* (1919), which won him international fame. In it, he presented, in addition to his vigorous polemic against reparations payments, a vivid examination of the breakdown of what he called 'that extraordinary episode of laissez-faire capitalism.' The picture he sketched was of a system made economically moribund by the passing of the conditions necessary to entrepreneurial success: a rapidly growing population and plentiful investment opportunities born of innovation and scientific progress. Thus, Keynes's *Weltanschauung* in the period after World War I was that the system was plagued by tendencies toward economic stagnation. The theoretical schema of *The General Theory*, which was to be published more than a decade later during the worldwide depression of the 1930s, had not yet emerged. But there are few better examples in the history of economic thought of the relationship

between the germination of an economic analysis and its crystallization into theoretical propositions than we find in *The Economic Consequences of the Peace* and *The General Theory of Employment, Interest and Money*.

Keynes's *Tract on Monetary Reform* (1923) was another stepping stone to *The General Theory*. In it, he advocated that the volume of note issue be controlled by the central bank independently of the gold reserve as a means of achieving economic stabilization via price-level stabilization. Two aspects of this work are significant as regards the ultimate development of Keynes's thinking: the first is its unmistakably prescriptive nature; the second is its conception of money as an active agent in the economic process. Both are important signposts along the way to *The General Theory*.

The economics-as-a-guide-for-policy character of Keynes's work is somewhat obscured in his *Treatise on Money* (1930). But that work contributed at least one other important principle, which ultimately became embodied in *The General Theory*. This is the principle that decisions to save and decisions to invest are *unrelated* to one another. Their separateness was, however, glossed over – or better still, lost sight of – by those who conceived of the interest rate as a device to equilibrate savings and investment. It was in order to emphasize the separateness of these decisions and the idea that private thrift is not a virtue when investment opportunities are lacking, that Keynes adopted definitions of saving and investment in the *Treatise* that recognized the possibility of their diverging from each other. Gunnar Myrdal, who followed the teachings of Wicksell, had essentially the same distinction in mind when he identified savings and investment in terms of *ex ante* and *ex post* magnitudes.[5] Thus if $S > I$ (or, in Myrdal's terminology, saving *ex ante* exceeds investment *ex ante*), there will be a cumulative contraction, while $I > S$ will bring about a cumulative expansion. This formulation was intended not only as a tool for monetary theory, but also as a guide for monetary policy, the obvious goal of which is to keep $S = I$, without destructive fluctuations in income levels.[6] It proved to be one of the more successful of Keynes's many terminological innovations, though the *Treatise* as a whole was received with less applause than any among his previous works. While the definitions of savings and investment introduced in the *Treatise* were abandoned in *The General Theory*, the idea of savings and investment as separate phenomena and as magnitudes that are not equated by the interest rate is another of the foundation stones of *The General Theory*.

The completion of *The General Theory*, only five years after the *Treatise*, represents Keynes's crowning achievement. It is his magnum opus, not only as a cumulation of his previous efforts, but also as his last major publication. It brought him so enthusiastic a following that there emerged a whole school that adopted and proliferated his ideas. Among those who carried Keynes's message to the world are a remarkable number who are notable, and possibly even outstanding, thinkers in their own right. Roy F. Harrod, Joan Robinson, and Richard F. Kahn were among the leading English economists whose thinking appeared to be progressing in the same general direction as Keynes's when *The General Theory* appeared. Alvin Hansen and Abba P. Lerner were among the leading Keynesians in the United States.[7] Together with Paul A. Samuelson, now Professor emeritus at the Massachusetts Institute of Technology, all have the distinction of having added in an original way to the body of theory that Keynes presented in *The*

General Theory of Employment, Interest and Money.

The revival of macroeconomic analysis

With the publication of *The General Theory*, macroeconomic analysis once more claimed center stage. It was not the allocation of resources among alternative uses, but rather whether resources would be employed *at all* that became the primary question for economic theory to answer. This is the question to which Keynes addressed himself and that he made the basis for his disagreement with the classics. Keynes thoughtfully provides us with a footnote explaining his use of that term to include 'the followers of Ricardo, those, that is to say, who adopted and perfected the theory of the Ricardian economics, including (for example) J. S. Mill, Marshall, Edgeworth and Pigou.'[8]

Neoclassical theorists, that is, those who follow in the Marshallian tradition, were mainly concerned with pricing problems and their relation to the maximizing activities of individuals and firms. The general view that the economic problem is one of scarcity persisted into the depression. Only prolonged unemployment on a mass scale such as England experienced in the late 1920s and 1930s eventually made it apparent that scarcity is not the only dimension of the economic problem.[9] The rational allocation of resources is the economy's sole problem only when all the resources seeking employment can be absorbed into the production process. Thus, the persistence of unemployment, especially in the face of downward pressure to reduce money–wage rates and policy to reduce interest rates, led Keynes to focus on the issue of the ability of modern capitalistic economies to restore the equilibrium at which their workers are 'fully employed,' that is, they are able to find jobs at prevailing money wage rates if they wish to have them. If they are able to do so, the only kinds of unemployment to which workers will be subject are those of a frictional and voluntary nature, which are not serious. The central issue of Keynes's *General Theory* is, precisely, to address this matter.

Issues and Answers from the Masterworks 20.1

Issue

Is there a third category of unemployment, specifically involuntary *unemployment, of which classical theory does not admit and that is serious because it cannot be remedied by means of the operation of the price mechanism?*

Keynes's answer

From *The General Theory* (1936), Chapter 2.

The postulates of the classical economics

Most treatises on the theory of Value and Production are primarily concerned with the distribution of a *given* volume of employed resources between different uses and with the conditions which, assuming the employment of this quantity of resources, determine their relative rewards and the relative values of their products.[10]

The question, also, of the volume of the *available* resources, in the sense of the size of the employable population, the extent of natural wealth and the accumulated capital equipment, has often been treated descriptively. However, the pure theory of what determines the *actual employment* of the available resources has seldom been examined in great detail. To say that it has not been examined at all would, of course, be absurd, for every discussion concerning fluctuations of employment, of which there have been many, has been concerned with it. I mean, not that the topic has been overlooked, but that the fundamental theory underlying it has been deemed so simple and obvious that it has received, at the most, a bare mention.[11]

I

The classical theory of employment – supposedly simple and obvious – has been based, I think, on two fundamental postulates, though practically without discussion, namely:

I. *The wage is equal to the marginal product of labour.*

That is to say, the wage of an employed person is equal to the value which would be lost if employment were to be reduced by one unit (after deducting any other costs which this reduction of output would avoid); subject, however, to the qualification that the equality may be disturbed, in accordance with certain principles, if competition and markets are imperfect.

II. *The utility of the wage when a given volume of labour is employed is equal to the marginal disutility of that amount of employment.*

That is to say, the real wage of an employed person is that which is just sufficient (in the estimation of the employed persons themselves) to induce the volume of labour actually employed to be forthcoming; subject to the qualification that the equality for each individual unit of labour may be disturbed by combination between employable units analogous to the imperfections of competition which qualify the first postulate. Disutility must be here understood to cover every kind of reason which might lead a man, or a body of men, to withhold their labour rather than accept a wage which had to them a utility below a certain minimum.

This postulate is compatible with what may be called 'frictional' unemployment. For a realistic interpretation of it legitimately allows for various inexactnesses of adjustment which stand in the way of continuous full employment: for example, unemployment due to a temporary want of balance between the relative quantities of specialised resources as a result of miscalculation or intermittent demand; or to time-lags consequent on unforeseen changes; or to the fact that the change-over from one employment to another cannot be effected without a certain delay, so that there will always exist in a non-static society a proportion of resources unemployed 'between jobs.' In addition to 'frictional' unemployment, the postulate is also compatible with 'voluntary' unemployment due to the refusal or inability of a unit of labour, as a result of legislation or social practices or of a combination for collective bargaining or of a slow response to change or of mere human obstinacy, to accept a reward corresponding to the value of the product attributable to its marginal productivity. But these two categories of 'frictional' unemployment and 'voluntary' unemployment are comprehensive. The classical postulates do not admit of the possibility of the third category, which I shall define below as 'involuntary' unemployment.

Subject to these qualifications, the volume of employed resources is duly determined, according to the classical theory, by the two postulates. The first gives us the demand schedule for employment, the second gives us the supply schedule; and the amount of employment is fixed at the point where the utility of the marginal product balances the disutility of the marginal employment.

It would follow from this that there are only four possible means of increasing employment:

(a) an improvement of organisation or in foresight which diminishes 'frictional' unemployment;

(b) a decrease in the marginal disutility of labour, as expressed by the real wage for which additional labour is available, so as to diminish 'voluntary'' unemployment;

(c) an increase in the marginal physical productivity of labour in the wage-goods industries (to use Professor Pigou's convenient term for goods upon the price of which the utility of the money-wage depends);

or (d) an increase in the price of non-wage-goods compared with the price of wage-goods, associated with a shift in the expenditure of non-wage-earners from wage-goods to non-wage-goods .

This, to the best of my understanding, is the substance of Professor Pigou's *Theory of Unemployment* – the only detailed account of the classical theory of employment which exists.

. . .

III

Though the struggle over money-wages between individuals and groups is often believed to determine the general level of real wages, it is, in fact, concerned with a different object. Since there is imperfect mobility of labour, and wages do not tend to an exact equality of net advantage in different occupations, any individual or group of individuals, who consent to a reduction of money-wages relatively to others, will suffer a *relative* reduction in real wages, which is a sufficient justification for them to resist it. On the other hand it would be impracticable to resist every reduction of real wages, due to a change in the purchasing-power of money which affects all workers alike; and in fact reductions of real wages arising in this way are not, as a rule, resisted unless they proceed to an extreme degree. Moreover, a resistance to reductions in money-wages applying to particular industries does not raise the same insuperable bar to an increase in aggregate employment which would result from a similar resistance to every reduction in real wages.

In other words, the struggle about money-wages primarily affects the *distribution* of the aggregate real wage between different labour-groups, and not its average amount per unit of employment, which depends, as we shall see, on a different set of forces. The effect of combination on the part of a group of workers is to protect their *relative* real wage. The *general* level of real wages depends on the other forces of the economic system.

Thus it is fortunate that the workers, though unconsciously, are instinctively more reasonable economists than the classical school, inasmuch as they resist reductions of money-wages, which are seldom or never of an all-round character, even though the existing real equivalent of these wages exceeds the marginal disutility of the existing employment; whereas they do not resist reductions of real wages, which are associated with increases in aggregate employment and leave relative money-wages unchanged, unless the reduction proceeds so far as to threaten a reduction of the real wage below the marginal disutility of the existing volume of employment. Every trade union will put up some resistance to a cut in money-wages, however small. But since no trade union would dream of striking on every occasion of a rise in the cost of living, they do not raise the obstacle to any increase in aggregate employment which is attributed to them by the classical school.

IV

We must now define the third category of unemployment, namely 'involuntary' unemployment in the strict sense, the possibility of which the classical theory does not admit.

Clearly we do not mean by 'involuntary' unemployment the mere existence of an unexhausted capacity to work. An eight-hour day does not constitute unemployment because it is not beyond human capacity to work ten hours. Nor should we regard as 'involuntary' unemployment the withdrawal of their labour by a body of workers because they do not choose to work for less than a certain real reward. Furthermore, it will be convenient to exclude 'frictional' unemployment from our definition of 'involuntary' unemployment. My definition is, therefore, as follows: *Men are involuntarily unemployed if, in the event of a small rise in the price of wage-goods relatively to the money-wage, both the aggregate supply of labour willing to work for the current money-wage and the aggregate demand for it at that wage would be greater than the existing volume of employment* . . . It follows from this definition that the equality of the real wage to the marginal disutility of employment presupposed by the second postulate, realistically interpreted, corresponds to the absence of 'involuntary' unemployment. This state of affairs we shall describe in the general level of money-wages will be accompanied, at any rate in the short period and subject only to minor qualifications, by some, though not always a proportionate, reduction in real wages.

Now the assumption that the general level of real wages depends on the money-wage bargains between the employers and the workers is not obviously true. Indeed it is strange that so little attempt should have been made to prove or to refute it. For it is far from being consistent with the general tenor of the classical theory, which has taught us to believe that prices are governed by marginal prime cost in terms of money and that money-wages largely govern marginal prime cost. Thus if money-wages change, one would have expected the classical school to argue that prices would change in almost the same proportion, leaving the real wage and the level of unemployment practically the same as before, any small gain or loss to labour being at the expense or profit of other elements of marginal cost which have been left unaltered.[12] They seem, however, to have been diverted from this line of thought, partly by the settled conviction that labor is in a position to determine its own real wage and partly, perhaps, by preoccupation with the idea that prices depend on the quantity of money. And the belief in the proposition that labour is always in a position to determine its own real wage, once adopted, has been maintained by its being confused with the proposition that labour is always in a position to determine what real wage shall correspond to *full* employment, i.e. the *maximum* quantity of employment which is compatible with a given real wage.

To sum up: there are two objections to the second postulate of the classical theory. The first relates to the actual behaviour of labour. A fall in real wages due to a rise in prices, with money-wages unaltered, does not, as a rule, cause the supply of available labour on offer at the current wage to fall below the amount actually employed prior to the rise of prices. To suppose that it does is to suppose that all those who are now unemployed though willing to work at the current wage will withdraw the offer of their labour in the event of even a small rise in the cost of living. Yet this strange supposition apparently underlies Professor Pigou's *Theory of Unemployment*, and it is what all members of the orthodox school are tacitly assuming.

But the other, more fundamental, objection, which we shall develop in the ensuing chapters, flows from our disputing the assumption that the general level of real wages is directly determined by the character of the wage bargain. In assuming that the wage bargain determines the real wage the classical school have slipped in an illicit assumption, for there may be *no* method available to labour as a whole whereby it can bring the wage-goods equivalent of the general level of money-wages into conformity with the marginal disutility of the current volume of employment. There may exist no expedient by which labour as a whole can reduce its *real* wage to a given figure by making revised *money* bargains with the entrepreneurs. This will be our contention. We shall endeavour to show that, primarily, it is certain other forces which determine the general level of real wages. The attempt to elucidate this problem will be one of our main themes. We shall argue that there has been a fundamental misunderstanding of how in this respect the economy in which we live actually works.

Source: Reprinted from J. M. Keynes, *The General Theory of Employment, Interest, and Money* (New York: Harcourt Brace Jovanovich, 1936) chapter 2.

Summing up: Keynes's key points

Keynes's criticism of the neoclassical theory is its central premise that an economy with flexible wages and prices tends automatically to generate full employment. This theory was *implicit* rather than explicit in neoclassical thinking, which was concerned primarily with the problem of value and distribution and the allocation of resources among alternative uses. Its microeconomic bias is particularly evident in the postulates on which its wage theory is based. These postulates are (1) that the marginal product of labor tends to fall as employment increases, (2) that the real wage of labor tends to equal its marginal product and to reflect the psychic disutility of employment at the margin, and (3) that the money-wage bargains made by workers and their employers also determine the level of real wages. Neoclassical thinkers concluded, on the basis of these postulates, that if there is unemployment, it must be due to workers' unwillingness to accept a real wage that corresponds to their marginal productivity. It follows that an increase in employment can be brought about only by reducing money wages until they are equal, in real terms, to labor's marginal product.

Keynes, however, rejected this conclusion. Money wages are generally bargained or, at least, set by cultural and perhaps legal forces. But given the state of the art, the level of employment and output determine the marginal product of labor and, therefore, the level of real wages. Thus, the level of real wages is not determined independently of the level of employment. Moreover, the level of real wages cannot be reduced simply by reducing the level of money wages. Money-wage cuts are not an effective way to reduce real-wage rates because the total demand for consumer goods is dependent mainly on labor income. The wage bargain determines only money-wage rates and not real-wage rates. 'There may exist no expedient by which labor as a whole can reduce its real wage to a given figure by making revised money bargains with entrepreneurs.'[13]

This brings to the foreground the postulate concerning the response of workers to wage cuts. Neoclassical theorists maintained that money wages tend to equal real wages and that the latter reflect the psychic disutility of employment at the margin. Workers reject offers of additional employment at lower money wages. Neoclassical thinkers regard their unemployment as voluntary, in the sense that workers are presumed to reject job offers at reduced money wages.

The mechanism by which mainstream thinkers thought *real-wage* levels adjusted to make them compatible with full employment is important because employer incentive to expand employment requires a reduction in *real wages*. Competition among workers for jobs tends to depress money-wage rates. In certain sectors of the economy, in which production costs become lower along with wages, prices may also decline. The expectation, however, is that the *general* price level, which was thought to be determined by the relationship between the quantity of money and the volume of transactions, would *not* change. Therefore, reductions in money-wage rates in response to unemployment were regarded as a reliable (though admittedly painful) mechanism for reducing *real* wages and stimulating offers of employment. Neoclassical economists thus interpreted persistent unemployment (as distinct from the frictional unemployment experienced by workers who are between jobs) as being *voluntary.*

Keynes rejected the notion that workers who are unemployed and unwilling to accept reduced money wages are voluntarily unemployed. He agreed that workers generally *are* reluctant to accept cuts in their money wages. They will, however, *not* refuse to work at current money-wage rates, if real wages are reduced as a result of an increase in the general price level. Keynes therefore maintained that workers are voluntarily unemployed only if they refuse to work in consequence of a rise in consumer prices (i.e. a cut in real wages). Worker unwillingness to accept a cut in money wages was not regarded as a major impediment to increasing employment because he thought it is generally not possible to decrease workers' real wages via money-wage reductions.

Real wages and employment: Keynes vs the Classics

The difference between the classical analysis and Keynes's of the relationship between real wages and employment is demonstrated in Figure 20.1. Keynes accepted the neoclassicists' principle that the demand for labor is a function of the real wage which is the ratio between the money wage and price level. The supply of labor is also a function of real wages. In Keynes's view, the supply of labor is perfectly elastic at the prevailing level of real wages up to full employment. Thus, in Figure 20.1 at a real wage of W the relevant labor supply curve is $WqS' = f(W/P)$ when the demand curve for labor is $DD = f(W/P)$, and the level of employment is ON.

The difference between Keynes's view of the functioning of the labor market, and that of the classics, hinges on their perceptions about the ability of markets to restore full employment subsequent to economy-wide reductions in the demand for labor. Figure 20.1 represents a reduction in the demand for labor by the displacement of the demand curve from

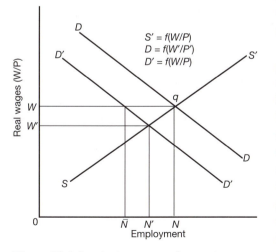

Figure 20.1 Involuntary unemployment: money wage cuts do not cut real wages

its original position to $D'D'$. The effect on employment depends on the behavior of real wages, i.e. it is necessary for money-wages to fall while prices remain constant.

If the level of real wages remains at W instead of being pushed downward, the level of employment will be reduced to $O\bar{N}$. The traditional view, which Keynes rejected, is that the downward pressure that unemployment puts on money wage rates also causes real wages to fall, say to W', so that employment can be restored to, say, ON'. The implicit premise of the traditional argument is that real wages can be reduced by simply allowing the labor market to establish a lower rate of money wages. Keynes disagreed with this analysis on two grounds: First, workers *resist* money-wage cuts; second, even if they are willing to accept reduced money wages, these reductions are *not* a mechanism for achieving a cut in *real* wages.

Experience, Keynes observed, shows that workers reject money-wage reductions even in the face of unemployment. They are, however, likely to continue to supply labor at prevailing money wages even if rising commodity prices reduce their real wages. This kind of worker behavior is sometimes identified as reacting to *money illusion*.

Money illusion is said to exist whenever people respond to a monetary magnitude, such as money wages, rather than its equivalent in real, or purchasing power, terms. This behavior is not the result of labor's lack of sophistication; on the contrary, workers are quite well informed about the wage rates of other wage earning households but *know* that they have no control over the prices of the goods they purchase. By resisting cuts in their own money wage rates, workers preserve their *relative position* with respect to other wage-earning households. The amount of labor workers offer to supply at wage rate W

therefore remains at ON; it does not decline to ON', as the classical analysis assumes it will. Since the number of workers seeking employment is represented by the horizontal distance Wq while the effective demand for labor at wage rate W is only for $O\bar{N}$, the horizontal distance between ON and $O\bar{N}$ represents *involuntary unemployment*.

Involuntary unemployment, according to Keynes's analysis, is the consequence of what Keynes termed 'insufficient aggregate demand.'[14] Forcing workers to accept 'across-the-board' wage cuts impairs their spending and so becomes self-defeating (in the sense that they further reduce aggregate demand). Moreover, in a competitive economy, wage cuts tend to be followed by price cuts. If this occurs the real wage effect of cutting money wages is eliminated. Thus, Keynes argued *against* cutting wages in the hope of stimulating aggregate demand.

The only circumstances under which Keynes agreed that falling money wages and prices *might* have favorable effects on employment would be if they helped to push interest rates downward. The probable mechanism of this favorable effect, which has since become known as the *Keynes effect*, is that the *transactions* demand for money would fall along with money wages and prices. If the monetary authority keeps the total money stock unchanged, the smaller cash requirement for transactions needs will free cash balances for the purchase of securities. This will raise security prices and reduce interest rates. Given the schedule of the marginal efficiency of capital, additional investments will then be profitable; thus, the level of aggregate demand *may* increase until full employment is reached.

While this favorable scenario is a theoretical possibility, Keynes hardly regarded it as a likely occurrence because, in a severe depression, the prices of long-term financial assets are likely to be low relative to money-wage rates. Keynes was inclined to interpret a downturn in activity as indicating that asset values are too low, rather than that wage rates are too high. This aspect of his diagnosis is clearly evidenced by his policy recommendation that, in the event of unemployment, the central bank should operate to force asset prices back up to a level at which investment would be large enough to generate full employment at going wage rates. In other words, it is *long-term interest rates*, rather than wage rates, that should be brought down.

The theory of the interest rate

Classical and neoclassical thinkers recognized that any economy can experience gluts and lapses from full employment as a result of cyclical fluctuation. However, they argued, flexible commodity prices, wage rates, and interest rates that assure that any income that is saved will be automatically invested to prevent long run overproduction and unemployment.

Neoclassical thinkers thought of the interest rate as determined by the intersection of a positively sloped schedule of the supply of loanable funds and a negatively sloped schedule of the demand for funds, as shown in Figure 20.2. Assuming that people prefer spending to saving, the normal shape of the supply curve is upward sloping. Analogously, a downward sloping demand schedule may be deduced from the declining marginal productivity of capital. If, now, competition exists on both sides of the market, so that the interest rate is free to fluctuate, it will settle at a level that equilibrates savings and investment.

Challenging this received explanation of interest rate determination, Keynes maintained that the interest rate does not automatically channel savings into investment.

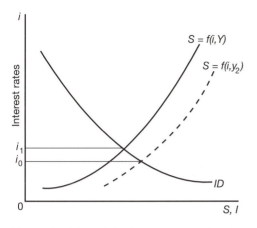

Figure 20.2 The interdependency of savings supply curves and investment demand curves renders the interest rate indeterminate

The main reason why the interest rate does not function in the manner that classical theory assumes, is that individuals have *an asset demand for money* as well as a transactions demand. People demand money for its *liquidity* rather than as an exchange medium because it satisfies the psychological need to hedge uncertainty. It is the hazard inherent in predicting the future that leads people to hold cash balances. Thus, Keynes maintained interest is the price for parting with *liquidity* (cash) rather than a reward for abstinence. Interest can reward abstinence only in a full-employment economy, for this is the only circumstance in which additional investment necessarily curtails consumption. Accordingly, he regarded the neoclassical conception of interest as inappropriate to any but a full-employment economy.

Keynes further attacked the neoclassical theory of interest on the ground that the rate is *indeterminate*. The representation in Figure 20.2, Keynes maintained, makes it clear that it is impossible to establish the savings schedule until the level of income is known. There is a different savings schedule associated with every level of income. Yet, we cannot know

the income level without first knowing the level of investment; the latter depends on the marginal efficiency of new capital at the margin and the rate of interest. Changes in the investment-demand schedule and the savings-supply schedule are therefore *interdependent* so that the interest rate is indeterminate within the neoclassical framework. What is needed, Keynes maintained, is a new approach that explains interest as a *monetary phenomenon* and to integrate monetary theory into the general theory of income, output, and employment. His theory of aggregate effective demand, which is examined in the following chapter, was intended to provide such an approach.

Concluding comments

John Maynard Keynes wrote to George Bernard Shaw in 1935 that the book he was writing on economic theory would revolutionize the way the world thinks about economic problems. His prophecy has been amply fulfilled, for *The General Theory* has changed our conception of the essential nature of the economic problem. From the time of the classics, the economic problem had been thought of in terms of the unending struggle between scarcity and unlimited human wants. In the era of Malthus and Ricardo, this struggle was given expression in the controversy over the Corn Laws. John Stuart Mill wrote that the Corn Laws were no longer at issue, but his vision of the stationary state was nevertheless premised on the solution of the scarcity problem via the intercession of human wisdom, especially as it relates to population growth. Marshall and the marginalists changed the focus of the problem to the level of the individual economic entity, that is, the consumer, the employer, and the industry; but they did not change the conception of the economic problem as being inherently one of scarcity. Their concern was with the allocation of resources among alternative uses, and continued the classical conception of the economic problem as having its origin in the scarcity of resources.

The awareness that the economic problem had another aspect, namely 'poverty in the midst of plenty,' came to Keynes after World War I. But it was not until 1936 and *The General Theory* that he formalized his criticism of the Marshallian tradition. Unlike the business-cycle theorists who believed that the economy tends toward a full-employment equilibrium through an internal mechanism that enables it to adjust even to strong exogenous shocks, Keynes emphasized the possibility of endogenous *instability*. It is his perspective about the possibility of systematic instability that manifests itself in involuntary unemployment and, thus, in a less-than-full-employment equilibrium that sets his analysis apart from the neoclassical view that the unfettered functioning of labor and capital markets imparts strong tendencies toward market clearing.

Keynes's emphasis on the inability of the system to make automatic adjustments because of imbalances between consumption and production is reminiscent of the Marxian analysis. Marx, too, emphasized the inherent instability of the capitalistic system and, like Keynes, found investment to be the crucial factor. Marx attributed the declining rate of profit to the inability of capitalists to realize surplus value from investment. This, in turn, meant that the ability to accumulate capital inhibited investment and therefore delayed revival. Keynes, on the other hand, saw the problem as being rooted, not in impediments to accumulation, but in impediments to *investment*, which then underlay an insufficiency of aggregate demand.

Notes

1 Biographical details are readily available in the *London Times*, 'Obituary,' April 22, 1946; and in the biography by Roy E. Harrod, *The Life of John Maynard Keynes* (New York: Harcourt Brace Jovanovich, 1952). A bibliography of Keynes's extensive writings is appended to *The New Economics*, edited by Seymour Harris (New York: Alfred Knopf, 1947).

2 Irving Fisher, *The Purchasing Power of Money* (New York: Macmillan, 1911, revised 1922).

3 It was consequently left to the proponents of the under-consumption doctrine, such as John A. Hobson and Thorstein Veblen, and the proponents of the disproportionate investment doctrine, such as Michael Tugan-Baranowsky, Arthur Spietoff, and Joseph A. Schumpeter, to challenge Say's law and give the problem of crisis its place in the economic theory of the period between 1870 and 1914.

4 Don Patinkin has given a most lucid account of its gradual unfolding in 'John Maynard Keynes, 1883–1946,' *The New Palgrave Dictionary*, vol. 3, pp. 19–41.

5 The possibility of a divergence between saving and investment was also given early consideration by Dennis Robertson, *Banking Policy and the Price Level* (1926), revised edition (New York: Augustus Kelley, 1949).

6 A still useful examination of the nature and usefulness of the savings and investment terminology of the *Treatise on Money* is Frederick A. Lutz, 'The outcome of the savings–investment discussion,' *Quarterly Journal of Economics*, 52 (August, 1938), pp. 588–614; reprinted in American Economic Association, *Readings in Business Cycle Theory* (Philadelphia: The Blakiston Company, 1944).

7 It is important to note, however, that there are major differences between the economics of Keynes and what is generally perceived of as 'Keynesian economics.' These differences are examined in depth in Chapter 23.

8 John Maynard Keynes, *The General Theory of Employment, Interest and Money* (New York: Harcourt Brace Jovanovich, 1936), p. 3.

9 John A. Hobson deserves recognition as being one among only a few writers who, even before Keynes wrote, recognized the failure to address

the possibility of mass unemployment as a major failure of neoclassical economics. His critique of neoclassical economics is eloquently set forth in J. A. Hobson, *Confessions of an Economic Heretic* (London: Allen & Unwin, 1938).

10 This is in the Ricardian tradition. For Ricardo expressly repudiated any interest in the *amount* of the national dividend, as distinct from its distribution. In this he was assessing correctly the character of his own theory. But his successors, less clear-sighted, have used the classical theory in discussions concerning the causes of wealth. *Vide* Ricardo's letter to Malthus of October 9, 1820: 'Political Economy you think is an enquiry into the nature and causes of wealth – I think it should be called an enquiry into the laws which determine the division of the produce of industry amongst the classes who concur in its formation. No law can be laid down respecting quantity, but a tolerably correct one can be laid down respecting proportions. Every day I am more satisfied that the former enquiry is vain and delusive, and the latter only the true objects of the science.'

11 For example, Prof. Pigou in the *Economics of Welfare* (4th edn, p. 127) writes (my italics): 'Throughout this discussion, except when the contrary is expressly stated, the fact that some resources are generally unemployed against the will of the owners is ignored. *This does not affect the substance of the argument*, while it simplifies its exposition.' Thus, whilst Ricardo expressly disclaimed any attempt to deal with the amount of the national dividend as a whole, Pigou, in a book which is specifically directed to the problem of the national dividend, maintains that the same theory holds good when there is some involuntary unemployment as in the case of full employment.

12 This argument would, indeed, contain, to my thinking, a large element of truth, though the complete results of a change in money-wages are more complex . . .

13 Keynes, *The General Theory*, p. 13.

14 Keynes, *The General Theory*, Chapter 2, p. 16

Glossary of terms and concepts

Frictional unemployment
The type of joblessness that reflects the imperfect mobility of workers and jobs and the imperfect knowledge about job vacancies for workers and the availability of desired types of workers by employers.

Interest payment
A reward for giving up *liquidity*; this contrasts with the classical view of interest as a reward for *abstinence*.

Involuntary unemployment
Joblessness over which workers are without control because they are unable to lower the level of *real* wages which determine the profitability of hiring them. Unemployment that exists despite worker willingness to accept a lower real wage. Real wages reflect the relationship between money wages and the general price level. Many wage rate levels are reduced by inflation.

Postulates of the 'classical' theory of unemployment
Keynes identified the two postulates of classical theory as: (1) that the wage of workers will tend to be determined by and equal to the value of the workers' marginal product, and (2) that the utility of wages that workers receive at a given level of employment is equal to the marginal disutility of that amount of employment. Together they imply that the level of employment that tends to come into existence is the most profitable to employers while also offering workers the best balance between work and leisure.

Questions for discussion and further research

1 While Marshall's analysis was almost wholly concerned with price theory, there are macroeconomic implications that derive from

his acceptance of Say's Law and the quantity theory of money. Explain how each of these relates to the neoclassical conclusion that commodity factor markets tend towards outcomes in which there are no outputs that go unsold or workers who cannot find employment at prevailing wage rates.

2 What is meant by the expression 'holding money as an asset'? Why did Marshall consider this use of money (as opposed to using it as a medium of exchange) as generally irrational? How does Marshall's view on this 'compartmentalize' monetary theory from the theory of income, output and employment?

3 In his *Treatise on Money* (1930) Keynes adopted definitions of saving and investment which recognized the possibility of their divergence. Why is this formulation analytically important in Keynes's objective of separating himself from 'the classics,' i.e. the Marshallian tradition? How does it relate to his concern about monetary policy, i.e. using interest rate changes as a tool to guide the economy?

4 What did Keynes mean by involuntary unemployment? How does it differ from 'frictional' and voluntary unemployment?

5 What, according to Keynes, are the 'postulates' of classical theory? Why does Keynes argue they are incompatible with involuntary unemployment? With what sort of unemployment are they compatible?

6 Why are 'across the board' wage cuts generally ineffective in promoting substantial increases in employment during a deep depression? Why, according to Keynes, can this measure not increase aggregate effective demand?

7 What is the classical theory of interest rate determination and on what basis did Keynes reject it? Why does Keynes maintain that the interest rate is 'indeterminate' according to classical theory?

Notes for further reading

From *The New Palgrave*

Edward J. Amadeo on multiplier analysis, vol. 3, pp. 566–68; Marro Baranzini on distribution theories: Keynesian, vol. 1, pp. 876–78; P. Bridal on saving equals investment, vol. 4, pp. 246–48: Michael R. Darby on consumption function, vol. 1, pp. 614–16; Paul Davidson on aggregate supply function, vol. 1, pp. 50–52; John Eatwell on Keynesianism, vol. 3, pp. 46–47, and on marginal efficiency of capital, vol. 3, pp. 318–19; Murray Milgate on Keynes's *General Theory*, vol. 3. pp. 42–46; Carlo Panico on liquidity preference, vol. 3, pp. 213–16; Don Patinkin on John Maynard Keynes, vol. 3, pp. 19–39; H. Sonnenschein on aggregate demand theory, vol. 1, pp. 47–50; L. Tarshis on Keynesian Revolution, vol. 3, pp. 47–50; John B. Taylor on involuntary unemployment, vol. 2, pp. 999–1001.

Selected references and suggestions for further reading

Bateman, B. W. and Davis, J. B. (eds). *Keynes and Philosophy: Essays on the Origin of Keynes's Thought* (Brookfield, Vt: Edward Elgar, 1991).

Clark, P. *The Keynesian Revolution in the Making 1924–1936* (Oxford: Oxford University Press, 1989).

Davis, J. D. 'Keynes's philosophical thinking,' in *The State of Interpretation of Keynes*, edited by J. B. Davis (Boston, Mass.: Kluwer Academic Publishers, 1994).

Davis, J. Ronnie. *The New Economics and the Old Economists* (Ames: The Iowa State University Press, 1971).

Dimand, R. W. *The Origins of the Keynesian Revolution: The Development of Keynes's Theory of Employment and Output* (Aldershot UK: Edward Elgar, 1988).

Harcourt, G. C. and Sardoni, C. 'Keynes's vision: method, analysis and tactics' in *The State of Interpretation of Keynes*, edited by J. D. Davis (Boston, Mass.: Kluwer Academic Publishers, 1994).

Keynes, John Maynard. *Treatise on Money* (London: Macmillan, 1930).

Keynes, John Maynard. *The General Theory of Employment, Interest and Money* (London: Macmillan, 1936).

Keynes, John Maynard. 'The general theory of employment.' *Quarterly Journal of Economics*, 1937, pp. 212–23.

Keynes, John Maynard. 'Essays in persuasion,' *Collected Writing of John Maynard Keynes* (London and New York: Macmillan and St. Martin's Press for the Royal Economic Society, 1972) vol. 9, p. 151.

Klein, Lawrence. *The Keynesian Revolution* (New York: Macmillan, 1947).

Minsky, Hyman. *John Maynard Keynes* (New York: Columbia U. Press, 1975).

Moggeridge, D. E. 'From the Treatise to the General Theory; an exercise in chronology.' *History of Political Economy*, vol. 5 (Spring, 1973).

Pigou, A. C. *The Theory of Unemployment* (London: Macmillan, 1933).

Robinson, Joan. *Introduction to the Theory of Employment* (London: Macmillan, 1937).

Skidelsky, R. *John Maynard Keynes Volume I, Hopes Betrayed 1883–1920* (London: Macmillan, 1983).

Walker, D. A. 'Keynes as an historian of economic thought: the biographical essays on neoclassical economics.' *History of Political Economy*, vol. 17 (Summer, 1985), pp. 159–86.

Chapter 21

Keynes's theory of employment, output, and income; Harrod's dynamic interpretation

In *The General Theory of Employment, Interest and Money*, Keynes introduced a radically new theoretical structure accompanied by an essentially new vocabulary to accomplish his 'struggle of escape from habitual modes of thought and expression.' His vocabulary has become incorporated even into introductory economics texts in spite of early difficulties. His theoretical structure, however, is significantly different from the income–expenditure models popularly thought of as Keynesian economics, particularly in America. These are not Keynes's models but rather are the product of several highly successful efforts at popularization.[1] There are important differences between Keynes's original work and the body of thought generally identified as *Keynesian*. This suggests the usefulness of presenting Keynes's theory of employment, output, and income by returning to *The General Theory* itself.

The principle of aggregate effective demand

Macroeconomic analysis, it will be recalled, began with the Physiocrats. *The Tableau Économique* was concerned not only with the allocation of resources but also with the size of the net product. While the Physiocratic theory of the unique productivity of land and

the prime importance of consumption in maintaining the circular flow was subsequently found unacceptable, it is nevertheless to the Physiocrats that we are indebted for a fundamental concept of macroeconomic analysis. This is the concept that production creates incomes which constitute the source from which the circular flow is maintained, while expenditure streams are the mechanism through which the aggregate demand for output and resources is maintained.

Keynes notes that one of the main problems encountered in presenting an aggregate analysis is the *choice of units*. That is, aggregate analysis requires a way of expressing both physical magnitudes (e.g. output and employment) and monetary magnitudes (e.g. income). To simplify his analysis, Keynes restricted it to the short run in which organization, technique, and equipment can be assumed as given. Changes in output and employment will then closely parallel each other. Accordingly, he chose to express the physical aspects of changes in the level of economic activity in terms of *labor units of employment*. He expressed the monetary aspects of change in the level of economic activity in terms of a constant wage unit and conducted his analysis in money, rather than in real, terms.[2] His analytical reliance on a constant wage unit is consistent with his view that changes in the average rate of money wages alter the price level proportionately and in the same direction as money wages.[3]

Keynes taught that the economy's level of the economic activity is determined by the interaction of aggregate demand and supply schedules and that this level will *not necessarily* coincide with an employment level that provides jobs for all who are seeking them. He did not undertake to draw aggregate demand and supply schedules, but his discussion indicates that, had he done so, his aggregate demand schedule would have related expected sales proceeds from consumption and investment spending to the employment levels associated with the production of varying amounts of output. The aggregate supply schedule, which Keynes called the *Z* function, is a schedule of the proceeds required to cover factor costs, including normal profit. It is a function of *N*, the level of employment and is given in the short run. Thus $Z = \varphi(N)$. Normally, the aggregate supply function is expected to rise to the right and, at some point does so at an increasing rate as does *OZ* in Figure 21.1. This shape reflects the increasing significance of diminishing returns in individual production functions as employ-

ment increases while capital stock remains unchanged. Because diminishing returns increase marginal costs and, therefore, the revenue required to make increased employment profitable, the upward slope of *OZ* implies that prices rise with employment. Every point on the aggregate-supply function reflects the relationship between employment and money outlays, and thus has an *implicit price level*. That is, the *Z* function is represented in *money terms* rather than real terms to capture Keynes's unique view of the role of money.[4] This view will be examined in more detail below, but it is relevant to note at this point that Keynes did *not* consider money to be merely one commodity among many that happens to serve as a *numéraire*. (Recall that this is the function of money in a general equilibrium system.)[5] As will be explained shortly, in a modern credit economy, money is generated in the finance process and is an active factor in determining the level of income and employment through its impact on the interest rate.[6]

Aggregate demand is generated by the spending units of the domestic economy (households, business firms, and government) and, in a global economy, by the foreign expenditure on domestic goods and services. Thus, the sales proceeds that businesses can expect to realize depend on the level of consumption and investment, including net foreign expenditures.

The aggregate (money)-demand function in Figure 21.1 shows the expenditures expected from consumption and investment (i.e. *C + I*) as the level of employment increases. The intersection of the aggregate demand-and-supply functions at *D = Z* determines the equilibrium level of employment *ON*, but it is not necessarily a *full* employment equilibrium that clears the labor market of all who wish to work at current wages.[7]

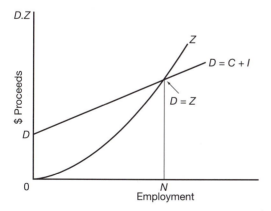

Figure 21.1 Keynes's aggregate demand and supply schedules

Paul Samuelson in 'The simple mathematics of income determination' interpreted the interaction or 'Keynesian cross' as providing a guide for fiscal policy, i.e. the use of government power to tax and spend, to borrow, and to retire portions of the federal debt for the purpose of managing the level of aggregate effective demand to achieve desired levels of employment and prices.[8] It is possible, within limits, to stimulate an economy that is not fully employing its resources via lower taxes and increased government spending, financed, if necessary, by borrowing. Conversely, within limits, it is possible to cool down inflationary pressures by reduced spending by government, higher tax collections, and repaying of some portion of the national debt. It is worth noting that Keynes would have regarded failure to reduce deficits during periods of prosperity as fiscal irresponsibility.

The determination of consumption expenditures

Keynes's focus on the level of aggregate demand requires examination of the behavior of its component parts (i.e. consumption expenditures and investment expenditures). He undoubtedly gained some appreciation of consumption behavior from Alfred Marshall, who recognized that saving is related to income. J. M. Clark may have had some pre-Keynesian insight when he presented the idea of a 'tendency toward saving a progressively larger proportion of our income as our income itself gets larger.'[9] But it remained for Keynes to hypothesize that consumption is a stable function of real income.[10]

Keynes formulated his hypothesis about consumption behavior in terms of a relationship between consumption and real income (i.e. money income corrected by a constant wage unit). His hypothesis is that, other things being equal, expenditures vary with real income. This generalization is offered as an *a priori*, rather than as an empirical proposition. People accustom themselves to certain living standards, and practices that govern the frequency of wage, receipts and dividend, and other payments. These factors change so gradually that the slope and position of the consumption function are likely to be quite stable. The expectation is that other factors that might affect consumption expenditures are exogenous and remain unchanged. Windfall gains or losses that occur in a stockmarket boom or crash, major changes in expectation about the availability and prices of goods such as are experienced in wartime and changes in fiscal and monetary policies are among the objective factors that are unlikely to change rapidly. Thus, Keynes maintained that, in the absence of unusual events, the propensity to consume out of a given income is a highly stable function of income because the subjective, or endogenous, factors that determine consumer behavior change only very slowly.

Changes in consumption expenditures are thus normally represented as movements *along* a consumption function rather than as shifts either upward or downward. This is the basis for Keynes's formulation of a 'fundamental psychological law' with respect to determining the normal slope of the consumption function. This law is that 'as a rule, and on the average, consumption will increase as income increases but not by as much as the increase in income.'[11] Thus the value of the marginal propensity to consume, $\Delta C/\Delta Y$, which is the slope of the consumption curve, is less than unity. The consumption function will therefore cut through a 45-degree line at which $C = Y$, as in Figure 21.2.

The consumption function has a positive

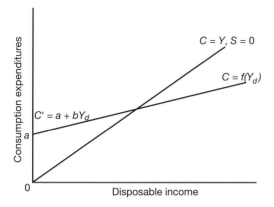

Figure 21.2 Keynes's consumption function

intercept (that is, the function starts above zero on the vertical axis) as *a* in Figure 21.2 because, at low levels of national income, consumption expenditures typically exceed income (i.e. $C > Y_d$). At income levels above some culturally set minimum, each dollar increase in disposable income, Y_d (i.e. personal income after income tax liability) causes an increase in consumption expenditures that can be represented by the equation:

$$c = a + by \qquad (21.1)$$

in which *a* is the level at which society would consume, even if income were zero, and *b* is the *marginal* propensity to consume that is represented by the slope of the consumption function. Consumption expenditures are thus an increasing function of income, but increase more slowly than income, that is, $\Delta C < \Delta Y$. The implication is that, as the income level of an economy rises, consumption expenditures become a smaller component of aggregate demand.

This far-reaching hypothesis has invited all manner of empirical testing. When properly interpreted, Keynes's proposition has stood up remarkably well. US Department of Commerce data show that, for the economy as a whole, excluding abnormal periods such as the war and early postwar years, the marginal propensity to consume is empirically less than one, just as Keynes maintained.[12] However, there eventually developed a considerable controversy about the nature of the long-run consumption function.

The marginal propensity to consume and the multiplier

Richard F. Kahn, one of Keynes's colleagues, has the distinction of having fathered the concept of the multiplier.[13] Kahn formulated the principle that an increase in investment has an expansionary effect greater than the increase in investment itself. Keynes subsequently recast the principle from its original form as a tool for analyzing the employment effects of public investment into a tool for analyzing the income effect of investment.

The importance of increments of new investment to generate new income had, of course, already been stressed by business-cycle theorists such as Wicksell, Hayek, Cassel, and Ohlin. But it was the formulation of the *multiplier principle* that revealed two fundamentals concerning the relationship between investment and income that were not clearly understood before. The first is that the expenditure of new money can have an expansionary effect on an economy with unemployed resources that is *larger* than the size of the expenditure itself. The second is that any expansionary process is necessarily limited and loses vitality because of *leakages* from the expenditure stream, i.e. new increments of income are not fully spent. Some proportions are saved or 'leaked.' Both of these insights raised intensely practical issues during the Great Depression of the 1930s, when there was considerable interest in proposals to stimulate economic activity by the introduction of scrip money. Thus, the theory of the multiplier made a very timely appearance.

Keynes reasoned that an increment of investment can initiate an expansionary process because it increases income and also consumption expenditures (unless the marginal propensity to consume is zero). This, in turn, eventually increases the demands for the factors of production and their incomes. Since a zero marginal propensity to consume is most unlikely, Keynes thought that an increment of investment would be certain to raise the income level by more than its own amount. Precisely how great the leverage will be depends on the marginal propensity to save. Any portion of an increment of new investment that leaks away from the current expenditure stream cannot generate additional new income. Since the value of the marginal propensity to consume (i.e. consumption expenditures out of an additional dollar of income) is somewhere between zero and 100 percent, the marginal propensity to save is the unspent margin of income, i.e.

$$S = Y - C \tag{21.2}$$

Thus, the multiplier is the reciprocal of the marginal propensity to save, and necessarily takes on a value that lies between 1 and infinity.[14] The mulitiplier is usually represented as a constant k, and may be derived as follows:

$$M = \frac{\Delta Y}{\Delta I} = \frac{\Delta Y}{\Delta S} = \frac{1}{\frac{\Delta S}{\Delta Y}} \tag{21.3}$$

$$\Delta Y = \Delta C + \Delta S$$

$$\frac{\Delta Y}{\Delta Y} = \frac{\Delta C}{\Delta Y} + \frac{\Delta S}{\Delta Y} - 1$$

$$\frac{\Delta S}{\Delta Y} = 1 - \frac{\Delta C}{\Delta Y}$$

$$\therefore \ M = \frac{1}{1 - \frac{\Delta C}{\Delta Y}} = \frac{1}{1 - 6}$$

where b represents the slope of the consumption function.

The increase in income associated with the operation of the multiplier principle can obviously only take place with a time lag. Thus, the operational significance of the multiplier is that, other things being equal, an expansion in national income is likely to follow from any income-creating expenditure in consequence of its effect on consumption.

Keynes chose not to emphasize the dynamic aspects of the multiplier and worked within a framework of a static conception. Thus, the new equilibrium income level is conceived as occurring without a time lag and is determined by the increment of new investment times a multiplier derived from some normal marginal propensity to consume.

Investment expenditures: the role of expectations and uncertainty

Since increases in consumption expenditures are, in general, dependent on prior increases in income, Keynes emphasized the *volume of investment* as the crucial economic magnitude. In so doing, he followed in the tradition of business-cycle theorists who pointed to investment as the key variable in the economy. Keynes's central question was: what determines the willingness of entrepreneurs to purchase new capital goods? His answer to this question is that it depends on the relationship among three elements: the cost of the capital goods, the expected dollar yield, and the market rate of interest.

The inducement to invest in a capital asset will be strong if the prospective yield a purchaser expects it to produce compares favorably with its supply price. The prospective yield of a capital good is a series of annuities, $R_1, R_2, \ldots R_n$, which are expected after deducting expenses from the revenue the sale of its output is expected to yield. Its supply price is its replacement cost, which is the price that would just induce a manufacturer to produce an additional unit of such assets. Thus, the marginal efficiency of a particular type of capital is the relationship between the prospective added income from one more unit of that type of capital and the cost of producing it. More specifically, Keynes defines the marginal efficiency of capital as 'the rate of discount which will make the present value of the series of annuities given by the returns expected from the capital asset during its life just equal to its supply price.'[15] If SP represents the supply price of a particular type of capital good that is expected to yield return R over n years, the marginal efficiency of capital can be calculated by solving for r in the equation

$$SP = \frac{R_1}{(1+r)} + \frac{R_2}{(1+r)^2} + \cdots \frac{R_n}{(1+r)^n} \qquad (21.4)$$

Each successive return in the series will be received by the prospective purchaser only after the time between the beginning of the production process and the final sale of the product elapses. Returns must, therefore, be discounted over a period of time; the marginal efficiency of capital is the internal rate of return that equates the expected income stream and the supply price of the asset.[16]

It is important to note that while the marginal efficiency of capital is a rate, it is not the same thing as the rate of interest on money.[17] It is the relationship between r, the marginal efficiency of capital, and i, the rate of interest at which money can be borrowed, that determines whether a particular investment will be made or not. An investment will be made if $r > i$; the inducement to invest comes to an end when $r = i$, as it eventually will, because of the tendency for the marginal efficiency of capital to fall.

Once a new capital asset has been produced its value (apart from its value as scrap) reflects its ability to yield an income flow. The income from capital is dependent on the *scarcity*, rather than on the productivity, of capital assets.[18] Thus, Keynes lays much stress on the role of *expectations* in governing the investment–demand schedule.

Expectations that a particular asset will continue to yield the same net return are revised downward as the physical quantity of a particular capital asset increases because the price at which output can be sold will be reduced. Then, too, a capital good with a long service life may eventually have to compete with equipment whose costs are lower per unit of product, or that can be satisfied with a lower rate of return if the money rate of interest has become lower. Thus, anticipations play a major role in determining the inducement to invest.

It is not only the expected current yield of an asset that a prospective purchaser of new capital will take into account, but also the *future* yield, which confronts an even greater degree of uncertainty and risk. The effect these factors have on the state of long-term expectations is vividly described in Chapter 12 of *The General Theory*, which observes that the ability of entrepreneurs to estimate prospective yields is especially precarious because they are usually influenced by the expectations of those who deal in the stock market, no less than they are guided by the expectations of entrepreneurs themselves.[19]

A change in expectations will make itself fully felt on the level of employment only over a period of time. Thus, Keynes speaks of 'long period employment,' which corresponds to a state of expectations that has prevailed for a sufficient length of time for its effect on employment to have worked itself out completely. The state of expectations is subject to constant change; new expectations crystallize even before previous changes have fully worked themselves out. 'The actually realized results of the production and sale of output will only be relevant to employment insofar as they cause a modification of subsequent expectations.'[20] The latter 'may change so frequently that the actual level of employment' will not coincide with the full employment. Keynes's theory is, clearly, a *less-than-full-employment theory of employment and output*. He is viewing changes in expectations and unrealized expectations as generating a response process in which employment and output adjustments do not necessarily produce full employment and its corresponding full employment output. Even more to the point, Keynes maintains that it is impossible to predict with much accuracy the outcome that will be forthcoming. This is because the future is *uncertain* and *uncertainty is not amenable to the calculus of probability*. In making this observation, Keynes articulated the issue of *uncertainty*. It has ongoing central importance, particularly as it relates to the ability of entrepreneurs to plan investment and the ability of econometricians to make useful forecasts about economic activity.

Issues and Answers from the Masterworks 21.1

Issue
What is the meaning of uncertainty with respect to knowledge of the future, especially as it relates to business matters, and how do rational individuals confront it?

Keynes's answer
From 'The General Theory of Employment' (1937).

It is generally recognized that the Ricardian analysis was concerned with what we now call long-period equilibrium. Marshall's contribution mainly consisted in grafting on to this the marginal principle and the principle of substitution, together with some discussion of the passage from one position of long-period equilibrium to another. But he assumed, as Ricardo did, that the amounts of the factors of production in use were given and that the problem was to determine the way in which they would be used and their relative rewards. Edgeworth and Professor Pigou and other later and contemporary writers have embroidered and improved this theory by considering how different peculiarities in the shapes of the supply functions of the factors of production would affect matters, what will happen in conditions of monopoly and imperfect competition, how far social and individual advantage coincide, what are the special problems of exchange in an open system and the like. But these more recent writers like their predecessors were still dealing with a system in which the amount of the factors employed was given and the other relevant facts were known more or less for certain. This does not mean that they were dealing with a system in which change was ruled out, or even one in which the disappointment of expectation was ruled out. But at any given time facts and expectations were assumed to be given in a definite and calculable form; and risks, of which, tho admitted, not much notice was taken, were supposed to be capable of an exact actuarial computation. The calculus of probability, tho mention of it was kept in the background, was supposed to be capable of reducing uncertainty to the same calculable status as that of certainty itself; just as in the Benthamite calculus of pains and pleasures or of advantage and disadvantage, by which the Benthamite philosophy assumed men to be influenced in their general ethical behavior.

Actually, however, we have, as a rule, only the vaguest idea of any but the most direct consequences of our acts. Sometimes we are not much concerned with their remoter consequences, even tho time and chance may make much of them. But sometimes we are intensely concerned with them, more so, occasionally, than with the immediate consequences. Now of all human activities which are affected by this remoter preoccupation, it happens that one of the most important is economic in character, namely, Wealth. The whole object of the accumulation of Wealth is to produce results, or potential results, at a comparatively distant, and sometimes at an *indefinitely* distant, date. Thus the fact that our knowledge of the future is fluctuating, vague and uncertain, renders Wealth a peculiarly unsuitable subject for the methods of the classical economic theory. This theory might work very well in a world in which economic goods were necessarily consumed within a short interval of their being produced. But it requires, I suggest, considerable amendment if it is to be applied to a world in which the accumulation of wealth for an indefinitely postponed future is an important factor; and the greater the proportionate part played by such wealth-accumulation the more essential does such amendment become.

By 'uncertain' knowledge, let me explain, I do not mean merely to distinguish what is known for certain from what is only probable. The game of roulette is not subject, in this sense, to uncertainty; nor is the prospect of a Victory bond being drawn. Or, again, the expectation of life is only slightly uncertain. Even the weather is only moderately uncertain. The sense in which I am using the term is that in which the prospect of a European war is uncertain, or the price of copper and the rate of interest twenty years hence, or the obsolescence of a new invention, or the position of private wealth-owners in the social system in 1970. About these matters there is no scientific basis on which to form any calculable probability whatever. We simply do not know. Nevertheless, the necessity for action and for decision compels us as practical men to do our best to overlook this awkward fact and to behave exactly as we should if we had behind us a good Benthamite calculation of a series of prospective advantages and disadvantages, each multiplied by its appropriate probability, waiting to be summed.

How do we manage in such circumstances to behave in a manner which saves our faces as rational economic men? We have devised for the purpose a variety of techniques, of which much the most important are the three following:

(1) We assume that the present is a much more serviceable guide to the future than a candid examination of past experience would show it to have been hitherto. In other words we largely ignore the prospect of future changes about the actual character of which we know nothing.
(2) We assume that the *existing* state of opinion as expressed in prices and the character of existing output is based on a *correct* summing up of future prospects, so that we can accept it as such unless and until something new and relevant comes into the picture.
(3) Knowing that our own individual judgment is worthless, we endeavor to fall back on the judgment of the rest of the world, which is perhaps better informed. That is, we endeavor to conform with the behavior of the majority or the average. The psychology of a society of individuals each of whom is endeavoring to copy the others leads to what we may strictly term a *conventional* judgment.

Now a practical theory of the future based on these three principles has certain marked characteristics. In particular, being based on so flimsy a foundation, it is subject to sudden and violent changes. The practice of calmness and immobility, of certainty and security, suddenly breaks down. New fears and hopes will, without warning, take charge of human conduct. The forces of disillusion may suddenly impose a new conventional basis of valuation. All these pretty polite techniques, made for a well-panelled Board Room and a nicely regulated market, are liable to collapse. At all times the vague panic fears and equally vague and unreasoned hopes are not really lulled, and lie but a little way below the surface.

Perhaps the reader feels that this general, philosophical disquisition on the behavior of mankind is somewhat remote from the economic theory under discussion. But I think not. Tho this is how we behave in the market place, the theory we devise in the study of how we behave in the market place should not itself submit to marketplace idols. I accuse the classical economic theory of being itself one of these pretty, polite techniques which tries to deal with the present by abstracting from the fact that we know very little about the future. I daresay that a classical economist would readily admit this. But, even so, I think he has overlooked the precise nature of the difference which his abstraction makes between theory and practice, and the character of the fallacies into which he is likely to be led.

This is particularly the case in his treatment of Money and Interest. And our first step must be to elucidate more clearly the functions of Money.

Money, it is well known, serves two principal purposes. By acting as a money of account it facilitates exchanges without it being necessary that it should ever itself come into the picture as a substantive object. In this respect it is a convenience which is devoid of significance or real influence. In the second place, it is a store of wealth. So we are told, without a smile on the face. But in the world of the classical economy, what an insane use to which to put it! For it is a recognized characteristic of money as a store of wealth that it is barren; whereas practically every other form of storing wealth yields some interest or profit. Why should anyone outside a lunatic asylum wish to use money as a store of wealth?

Because, partly on reasonable and partly on instinctive grounds, our desire to hold Money as a store of wealth is a barometer of the degree of our distrust of our own calculations and conventions concerning the future. Even tho this feeling about Money is itself conventional or instinctive, it operates, so to speak, at a deeper level of our motivation. It takes charge at the moments when the higher, more precarious conventions have weakened. The possession of actual money lulls our disquietude; and the premium which we require to make us part with money is the measure of the degree of our disquietude.

The significance of this characteristic of money has usually been overlooked; and in so far as it has been noticed, the essential nature of the phenomenon has been misdescribed. For what has attracted attention has been the *quantity* of money which has been hoarded; and importance has been attached to this because it has been supposed to have a direct proportionate effect on the price-level through affecting the velocity of circulation. But the *quantity* of hoards can only be altered either if the total quantity of money is changed or if the quantity of current money-income (I speak broadly) is changed; whereas fluctuations in the degree of confidence are capable of having quite a different effect, namely, in modifying not the amount that is actually hoarded, but the amount of the premium which has to be offered to induce people not to hoard. And changes in the propensity to hoard, or in the state of liquidity-preference as I have called it, primarily affect, not prices, but the rate of interest; any effect on prices being produced by repercussion as an ultimate consequence of a change in the rate of interest.

This, expressed in a very general way, is my theory of the rate of interest. The rate of interest obviously measures – just as the books on arithmetic say it does – the premium which has to be offered to induce people to hold their wealth in some form other than hoarded money. The quantity of money and the amount of it required in the active circulation for the transaction of current business (mainly depending on the level of money-income) determine how much is available for inactive balances, i.e. for hoards. The rate of interest is the factor which adjusts at the margin the demand for hoards to the supply of hoards.

Source: Adapted from John Maynard Keynes 'The general theory of employment,' *Quarterly Journal of Economics*, 1937, pp. 212–23. Keynes intended this article to clarify some key points of his 1935 book published under the same title.

Summing up: Keynes's key points about the uncertainty and decision making

In many ways, Keynes's vision of the real world in which decision making is unavoidably made under conditions of uncertainty is among his central points of departure from the classics and the mainstream view that builds on their teaching. What Keynes meant to convey is that the future is not simply unknown – it is *unknowable* in the sense that it cannot be inferred by using the calculus of probability as can be done when addressing problems of risk. From the standpoint of economic behavior, uncertainty regarding the future affects not only the marginal efficiency of capital and investment but also our willingness to part with our cash resources. To hold cash, says Keynes, 'lulls our disquietude,' and the rate of interest we demand for parting with liquid assets in exchange for earning assets measures the 'degree of our disquietude.' He therefore regarded interest as compensation for illiquidity and the determination of its rate as a monetary phenomenon arising out of the store-of-value function of money.[21]

Keynes's emphasis on the desire to hold money as a store of wealth represents a sharp break with his predecessors, who assumed that the only demand for money is

for transactions purposes. Keynes maintains that money is demanded to satisfy three motives: the transactions motive, the precautionary motive, and the speculative motive. The amount of cash needed to carry on personal and business transactions and the additional amount desired to meet possible future contingencies vary directly with the economy's level of output. Since expenditures normally increase as business activity expands, the transactions demand for money increases with national output and income. The precautionary demand for money also increases as the volume of business activity expands and is therefore functionally related to output. The amount of cash wanted for transactions and precautionary reasons is generally interest inelastic, although conceivably there may be some motivation for economizing the cash balances held for these purposes if interest rates become very high. The aggregate demand for money to satisfy the speculative motive, however, usually shows a continuous response to gradual changes in the rate of interest; that is, there is a continuous curve relating changes in the demand for money to satisfy the speculative motive and changes in the rate of interest reflected in changes in the prices of bonds and debts of different maturities.[22]

Keynes's monetary theory

The money supply: its origin in the finance process

Keynes's monetary theory – that is, his conception of the origin of the money supply, the demand for it and the structure of interest rates – is the logical counterpart of his view of the relationship between the pricing of capital assets and the flow of investment output. Money 'comes into existence along with debts, which are contracts for deferred payment.'[23] The prospect of financial gain induces foreign and domestic business firms (and individuals) to enter into debt contracts. A considerable part of this financing takes place through the banking system, which interposes its guarantee between depositors who lend it money and borrowing customers to whom it loans money to finance the purchase of real assets.[24] Government may also initiate the demand process, which generates an *endogenous* increase in the money supply. Thus, Keynes's perception of a modern capitalistic economy characterized by a sophisticated banking system, which functions on the basis of fractional reserves, conceives of the money supply as originating in the finance process. This contrasts with the mainstream view that the money supply is an *exogenous* magnitude established by the monetary authority.

Keynes' contrary view is that the money supply will increase as long as investors expect the marginal efficiency of capital (relative to the interest rate) to keep the purchase of new capital goods profitable, and banks are willing to finance their debts. The resulting change in the money supply affects *the level of interest rates* rather than the level of prices. The latter is the impact that would be expected on the basis of the quantity theory

of money, which Keynes, in contrast with traditional theorists, rejected as an explanation of the general price level.

Liquidity preference: the demand for money

Keynes's explanation of the demand for money as a store of value under uncertainty is easily understood in terms of the behavior of bond yields. Where there is an organized market, fixed-income bonds are not greatly inferior to money itself as highly liquid assets even though, technically, they are not exchange mediums. They do, however, have the risk of price change, which is a disadvantage because it correspondingly alters their yield. If the market price of a bond rises, the ratio of its fixed dollar income to the bond price falls. Its yield, which is the income to be earned by illiquidity, is therefore falling. Low interest rates and bond yields may be less attractive to a wealth holder than cash itself, even though the latter earns no income at all. This is so because when bonds are bought at a relatively high price (low yield), a subsequent small drop in price may be sufficient to wipe out the income earned from illiquidity. Cash is then a relatively more attractive asset than a bond. Thus, the preference for liquidity for speculative purposes is virtually unlimited if the market is convinced that bond prices cannot rise further.

The relationship between various possible interest rates and the demand for money (i.e. liquidity) at a given level of income may be represented as

$$L = f(i, Y) \tag{21.5}$$

graphically by the *L* curve in Part A of Figure 21.3. Since some cash balances will be required at every income level, irrespective of the interest rate, the segment of the curve representing the sum of the transactions and

(a)

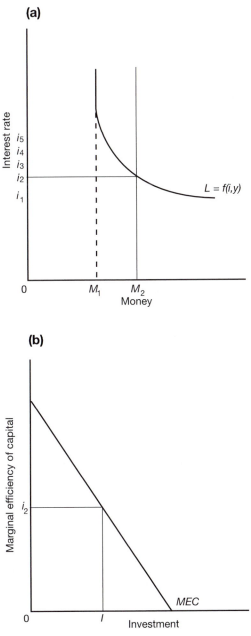

(b)

Figure 21.3 Liquidity preference and investment demand schedules

is sensitive to small changes in the interest rate and approaches perfect elasticity when the rate is very low, for example, at a level corresponding to i_1 in Part A of Figure 21.3. Thus, the total demand for money, as represented by the L curve, is the sum of the transactions, precautionary, and speculative demands and is a function of the income level and the rate of interest, as follows:

$$L = L_t + L_p + L_s = f(i, Y) \tag{21.6}$$

According to Keynes's liquidity preference theory, the interest rate is a monetary phenomenon that results from the interaction of the total demand for money and its supply. The supply of money depends primarily on the actions of the monetary authority and the commercial banks in response to the demand of individuals, businesses, and government. Thus, if the money supply is OM_1, as in Part A of Figure 21.3, the interest rate is i_2; OM_1 is the proportion of the money supply held for transactions and precautionary purposes, while M_1M_2 satisfies the speculative motive.

Part A of Figure 21.3 makes it apparent that, in Keynes's analysis, the interest rate equates the demand for, and the supply of, *money*. It does not, *as in the neoclassical analysis*, equate savings and investment. Rather, it is the interest rate which, together with the schedule of the marginal efficiency of capital, determines the level of investment, as shown in Part B of Figure 21.3.

The marginal efficiency of capital is the schedule relating the demand for new capital goods to the expected rate of return. For simplicity, the curve has been assumed to be linear (although it is not possible, *a priori*, to know what its shape is). Its slope is necessarily negative because the net income stream that can be expected from additional units of a given capital good is certain to fall and its supply price is likely to increase. As long as

precautionary demands is shown in Part A of Figure 21.3 as interest-inelastic at rates above i_5. The speculative demand for cash, however, the expected return from investment is higher than the rate of interest it will be profitable to invest. Thus, when the interest rate is at i_2 and the investment-demand curve is as given in Part B of Figure 21.3, the volume of investment will be OI.

The central bank is generally able to exert pressure on interest rates because it can usually buy or sell bonds by bidding their prices up or down. This induces the public to hold either more or less cash, which causes an *inverse* change in interest rates. There is, however, a floor below which the interest rate is not likely to fall even when the monetary authority is seeking a policy of extreme monetary ease. Liquidity preference may become 'virtually absolute in the sense that almost everybody prefers cash to holding a debt which yields so low a rate of interest' that the earnings from illiquidity do not offset the risk of loss on capital account.[25] It is evident from Part A of Figure 21.3 that an enlarged money supply could not reduce the rate of interest below i_1. The additional stock would simply be absorbed into hoards. This 'liquidity trap' presents the main impediment to the effective use of monetary policy as an anti-depression device. From an analytical point of view, it is the basis of Keynes's rejection of Say's identity.

It is evident that, in Keynes's analysis, money is far from being the passive medium of exchange and unit of account that classical and neoclassical thinkers assumed it to be. It is an active determinant of the level of income, output, and employment because its relationship to the marginal efficiency of capital determines the worthwhileness of investment. Given the schedule of the marginal efficiency of capital, it is the rate of interest that determines the volume of real investment. Given the level of income and the quantity of money decided upon by the monetary authority, wealth owners determine whether they will profit most from holding money or from holding bonds or other assets. The relative advantage of each alternative becomes equal at the margin because wealth holders will shift from one alternative to another whenever one appears to offer a superior opportunity for gain. Thus, the state of expectations, the preference for liquidity, the rate of interest, and the prospective yield on capital assets are all interrelated.[26]

The relationship between value theory and monetary theory

Keynes lamented what he called the 'false division' between the theory of value and distribution on the one hand, and the theory of the general level of prices, on the other. The dichotomy, already evident in the crudest statements of the quantity theory dating back to the preclassical economists, was perpetuated even in the refined presentations of Marshall and Fisher. Money was regarded as determining only the absolute level of prices, whereas relative prices were thought to be determined by a set of equations that were independent of the absolute level of prices. One of Keynes's objectives was 'to bring the theory of prices as a whole back to close contact with the theory of value.'[27] He conceived of his theory of employment and output as providing the necessary link between them.

In pursuit of his objective of linking the theory of employment and output to that of the general price level, Keynes begins with some brief observations about price determination in single industries and then proceeds to the industry as a whole and the general price level. He reminds us that commodity prices reflect the marginal cost of producing output. In the short run, when the stock of capital is fixed, so that labor is the only variable input in the production process, the marginal cost of producing output, which the competitive price must cover, is set by the wage cost. This part of Keynes's analysis has already been utilized above to derive the aggregate supply schedule (Keynes's Z function) from the supply curves of the individual firms.[28] A firm's supply curve indicates the output it is willing to sell at each price; thus, its supply curve is that portion of its marginal cost curve that lies above average variable cost. The short-run supply curve of an industry is derived by the lateral summation of the marginal cost curves of its firms in order to relate industry output with expected market prices. Since employment is correlated with output, an aggregate-supply function for the economy as a whole (i.e. a function relating employment with required sales revenues) can be built up by aggregating the required revenue-employment functions for all industries. As has already been shown in Figure 21.1, the aggregate supply function slopes upward and does so at an increasing rate as diminishing returns assert themselves.

An alternative way of explaining the shape of the aggregate supply (or Z) function is to say that it relates each level of employment to the money proceeds (i.e. GNP) level required to support it. Keynes's insights about the analytical route for bringing 'the theory of prices as a whole back to close contact with the theory of value' thus anticipate the link between his theory of employment and output (macroeconomics) and the theory of microeconomic behavior (i.e. of business firms and households).[29]

The dynamic aspects of Keynes's analysis

Keynes's model, relating as it did to the short run, assumed the stock of capital to be a con-stant magnitude. His concern with the investment process concentrated on whether savings would, in fact, become invested to create new income (and employment). It did not consider that there would also be a capital-creating effect of investment or ask: what is the requirement for the growth of demand if the new capital resulting from the investment of savings is to be utilized? Will additions to the capital stock be utilized in production, or will they simply pose the problem of excess capacity?

Roy F. Harrod's 'Essay in dynamic theory' emphasized that investment which results in a net addition to the stock of capital makes it necessary for the economy either to grow at an increasing or geometrical rate or confront the problem of unemployed capital resources. Accordingly, he outlined a dynamic theory based on the marriage of the acceleration principle and the multiplier.[30] Whereas Keynes's static approach concerns itself with an instantaneous or timeless examination of economic variables, a dynamic analysis is concerned with their *rate of change*. The essential characteristic of a dynamic process (or system) is that it is self-generating over time, much like a servomechanism. Its motion through time is the result of its 'built-in' response to an initial internal condition or its response to changing external conditions.[31]

The American economist Evsey Domar also formulated a growth equation which expressed the principle that the very existence of a growth problem derives from the stability of the saving function and a fixed capital coefficient.[32] If a reduction in investment tends to be automatically offset by an increase in consumption, the problem of maintaining the necessary rate of growth to give full employment to a growing capital stock would not exist. Similarly, if investment were accompanied by technological changes associated with the deepening of capital, productive capacity would grow less rapidly than if the capital coefficient remained constant or reflected technological changes of a capital-saving variety. Steady growth requires that the relationship between the savings and capital ratios be such that there will be continuous full employment of an accumulating stock of capital. This condition is automatically assured when a constant proportion of income is added to capital every year and capital bears a constant ratio to income, for income will then expand continuously at a constant proportional rate. Domar has the distinction of having formulated this principle in specific terms, and of recognizing productive capacity as a key element in the growth problem, even though he was anticipated in its perception by Harrod.

Harrod's 'Essay' proceeded from the observation that 'once the mind is accustomed to thinking in terms of trends of increase, the old static formulation of problems seems stale, flat and unprofitable.'[33] He reasoned that the necessary growth rate of income required in order fully to employ a growing capital stock depends on the long-run savings function and the productivity of the additional increments of capital which result from net investment. The larger the volume of investment and the more each additional dollar of investment adds to productive capacity, the greater the rate at which income and investment will have to increase in order to give full employment to the growing capital stock. Specifically, the required rate of growth is the product of the marginal propensity to save, or the saving ratio, and the productivity ratio. Therefore, with a constant marginal propensity to save and a given productivity ratio, and full employment in year t, in order that full employment continues to occur in year $t + 1$, investment and income will have to grow at an exponential or compound interest rate. That is, they will have to grow at a rate that is the product of the productivity ratio and the savings ratio.

Harrod's warranted rate of growth and its perpetuation

The most important concept in Harrod's analysis is the 'warranted rate of growth.' It is defined as 'that rate of growth which, if it occurs will leave all parties satisfied that they have produced neither more nor less than the right amount. Or, to state the matter otherwise, it will put them into a frame of mind which will cause them to give such orders as will maintain the same rate of growth.'[34] The concept is also expressed symbolically as $G_w = s/v$, where G_w is the warranted growth rate, or $\Delta Y/Y$; s is the long-run constant average and marginal savings ratio; and $v = \Delta K/\Delta Y$ is the *desired* ratio between an increment of induced investment and new output (income). This formulation reveals that Harrod's theory of growth is essentially a capital stock adjustment theory, i.e. the growth process is viewed as one that manifests itself in addition to capital stock, which in turn increases income. Its Keynesian origins are plainly in evidence, paralleling the equilibrium requirement that desired savings must equal desired investment in the static Keynesian model; therefore, in Harrod's growth form of the model, the equilibrium requirement is that the desired ratio be maintained between the capital stock and the rate of output. If, now, the propensity to save is given, and the relationship between capital and output is a technological constant, it follows that the capacity to produce output will grow at a constant percentage rate determined by the productivity of additions to capital stock and the proportion of the increase in output devoted to the creation of new capital. It is plain, therefore, that Harrod's G_w is an exponential growth rate. Harrod has given us, in addition, however, a hypothesis concerning the origin of the forces which propel the economy along its steady upward path of growth and of the manner in which divergences may take place from the equilibrium path. This hypothesis is essentially a theory of entrepreneurial investment behavior in which the key role is played by the effect of expectations and hence desires on induced investment.

Harrod, like many other business-cycle theorists, reasons that the psychology of human behavior suggests that, in the absence of evidence to the contrary, the business community expects economic conditions in the foreseeable future to be similar to those of the immediate past. Business people generally assume that they can safely project current economic events into the future. Thus, Harrod's conception of the warranted rate of growth implies that the rate of growth of income in period t will be followed by an equal rate of growth in period $t+1$, i.e. $G_t = G_{t+1}$. The formula implicitly assumes that the anticipations of period G_t were, in fact, realized so that in projecting satisfactory output and investment decisions into the following period, business firms expect a similar rate of growth in the following period. This outcome, in turn, tends to perpetuate itself precisely because businessmen behave in such a way that expectations are realized.

It is worth noting that Harrod's theory envisions businessmen as repeating in period $t+1$ not the *amount* of output and capital outlays of period t, but their *rate of growth*. This is essential to the whole concept of the warranted rate of growth, for the latter is the growth rate which ensures the full utilization of the productive capacity represented by the new capital stock of the period.

In addition to the warranted growth rate there is another growth rate which Harrod identifies as 'the natural growth rate,' or G_n. When the economy is growing at its natural rate, the ratio of an increment of induced investment to output is the maximum consistent with the full employment of is resources and the rate of technological progress. Contrary to what one might expect, there is no inherent tendency for this rate to be realized. The warranted growth rate *may* coincide with the natural growth rate; the desired ratio of induced investment to new output. $\Delta K/\Delta Y$ is then equal to the actual ratio $\Delta K^*/\Delta Y^*$, and the warranted growth rate coincides with the natural growth rate. However, the warranted growth rate may diverge from the natural growth rate; according to Harrod's theory, divergences are the source of cyclical fluctuations.

If G_w exceeds G_n, the *desired* ratio of induced investment to new output, $\Delta K/\Delta Y$, will exceed $\Delta K^*/\Delta Y^*$, the actual ratio. The economy will experience a tendency toward stagnation because the growth rate of savings and investment, and thus the capital stock, is greater than that associated with the full employment of labor resources. Excess capacity will therefore appear and dampen business expectations. Investment will decline further, so that the actual growth rate will be still further below the warranted growth rate. Only more investment could have avoided this decline. Thus, we are confronted with a seemingly paradoxical situation in which the only way the capacity resulting from some previous level of investment can be fully utilized is by investing even more. If $G_n > G_w$, the *actual* ratio, $\Delta K^*/\Delta Y^*$, will exceed $\Delta K/\Delta Y$, the desired ratio, and the economy will experience a state of secular exhilaration; actual investment is less than acceleration-induced planned investment. Existing capital stocks will be utilized intensively and provide high rates of return, so that there is a continuous stimulus to new investment. Harrod's warranted rate of growth is thus seen as being inherently unstable. Divergences from G_w are not associated with the development of corrective counterbalancing forces. On the contrary, any divergence from G_w leads to an even greater divergence.

The unstable character of Harrod's warranted rate of growth derives from the assumption that there is no lag between the receipt and the spending of income. The absence of an investment lag is evident in its formulation as $G_w = s/v$. With respect to the volume of induced investment, this means that changes in income are instantaneously followed by investment outlays. Because the model does not assume an investment lag, induced investment is treated as a function of the current income, of which it is itself a component. Thus, if income increases between period t and t_1 acceleration-induced investment will take place which increases income and induces still more investment, and thus income. The change thus perpetuates itself in the same period. Conversely, a reduction in income is instantaneously reflected in a self-perpetuating reduction of the income level. Harrod's system is, therefore, one which will either 'explode' and produce an astronomically large income or else break down. It is thus a disequilibrium model which is conceptually consistent with Keynes's static equilibrium model.

Concluding remarks

Awareness that the economic problem had another aspect besides scarcity, namely 'poverty in the midst of plenty,' came to Keynes after World War I. But it was not until 1936 and *The General Theory* that he offered his formal argument that the level of employment depends on the level of aggregate demand. He showed that even an economy with flexible wages, prices, and interest rates may not be restored automatically to full employment. A full-employment equilibrium is only one of many possible equilibria.

Keynes considered the theory of aggregate effective demand as an anchor for his policy recommendations to England during the 1930s. There is no question that *The General Theory* contributed in a significant way to the acceptance by modern governments of the responsibility for maintaining the level of employment at satisfactory levels. Fiscal policy has come into its own since the time of *The General Theory*.[35] There is also no doubt that the popularity of *The General Theory* in the pre-World War II period derived in no small measure from the fact that it took a positive approach to the problems of its day.

That is not to say, however, that *The General Theory* cannot be divorced from the specific problems of the 1930s. The principle of aggregate effective demand, which is the core of Keynes's theory, is *independent* of this particular institutional setting and is *neutral* as far as policy is concerned. The introduction of the principle of aggregate effective demand in *The General Theory* marks a milestone in the history of economic analysis because it is the culmination of a number of earlier efforts to develop an alternative to the quantity-theory approach to aggregate demand.

The difference between the quantity-theory approach and Keynes's approach is that the latter conceives of aggregate demand as the sum of consumption and investment expenditures rather than as the money stock times its velocity of circulation. The expenditure stream is separated in order to take account of the factors affecting these two independently determined magnitudes. The quantity-theory approach, by way of contrast, makes no analytical distinction between consumer demand and investment demand but simply assumes that income not used for consumer goods purchases will be used for capital goods purchases as long as the interest rate is flexible. The proportions in which consumer goods and capital goods are bought may become altered as their relative prices and utilities change, but all will find a market at some price. In short, the theory of aggregate demand implicit in the quantity theory is precisely the same as that in Say's law. Thus, Keynes avoids the neoclassical conclusion that sales proceeds will necessarily cover the cost of producing the full-employment output because the money value of that output is associated with the creation of an equivalent money income. The notion that money is demanded as an asset to offset the uncertainty of the future and the view that the supply of money is an exogenous variable that responds, via the lending activities of financial institutions, to the 'animal spirits' that determine investor behavior, are companion ideas to the principle of aggregate demand. The investment expenditures of business owners and the consumption expenditures of households are the chief components of aggregate demand in a closed economy.

Finally, there is the view that aggregate demand and employment cannot be raised by a reduction in money wages. Workers cannot reduce their real wages by simply accepting reduced money wages. If unemployment is accompanied by an asset demand for money, because interest rates are low, there may be no mechanism for recovery from an unemployment disequilibrium.

In the years that followed the publication of *The General Theory*, concern with the macroeconomic behavior of the economy almost eclipsed the economists' earlier concern with the allocation of resources. The accumulation of data to quantify aggregates like employment, GNP, and various related income categories, consumer spending, savings and investment, combined with the development of econometric techniques made it possible to test Keynes's macroeconomic relationships empirically. Not only did the terminology of the *General Theory* become incorporated into the general language of the profession, but the policy implications of his analysis were widely adopted to provide the tax, expenditure, and debt management agendas of most Western economies. Thus, it could truly be said that, as the post-World War II era began, we had, in a sense, all become Keynesians.

Yet, the years that followed the publication of the *General Theory* also brought an intellectual counterrevolution. Many of the ideas and analytical tools that Keynes initiated were challenged or reinterpreted in such a fundamental way that they appear to have lost much of their original intent. Interest in growth theory that was sparked by Roy Harrod was shifted to focus on the problems of stable or steady state growth. The emergence of econometrics as the sister discipline of economics has, as will be examined in Chapter 22, become central to the intellectual counterrevolution which some scholars interpret as substantially undermining the message of Keynes's *General Theory*. Their rebuttal has been joined (though frequently on other grounds) by other critics of mainstream economics. The vigor of their theoretical and methodological arguments is the reason why contemporary economics is a discipline that is characterized by *competing paradigms* rather than by a single paradigm, as is the case in the natural sciences. Thus, the task of Part VI is to examine the theoretical and methodological contributions that have been made since approximately 1945.

Notes

1 We particularly note among these Alvin H. Hansen, *A Guide to Keynes* (New York: McGraw-Hill, 1953); Dudley Dillard, *The Economics of John Maynard Keynes* (Englewood Cliffs, NJ: Prentice-Hall, 1948); and Lawrence Klein, *The Keynesian Revolution* (New York: Macmillan, 1961). Paul Samuelson has perhaps been the leading disseminator of popular Keynesianism by virtue of his highly successful test *Economics* (New York: McGraw-Hill, 1st edn, 1948; 10th edn, 1976).

2 This approach is one of the features that distinguishes the economics of Keynes himself from Keynesian economics. The income expenditure models in textbook presentations of aggregate economic activity are typically conducted in real terms. The modern convention now is to substitute output on the horizontal axis for employment. The logic is, of course, that output is a function of employment. This is precisely the way in which Keynes expressed his aggregate supply or Z function. It is also consistent with the empirical finding, established for the US economy, that each 3 percent increase in output (or GDP) is associated with a 1 percent increase in employment. This generalization is known as 'Okun's law' – after the late Arthur Okun, a well-known government economist who was at one time chairperson of the President's Council of Economic Advisors.

3 J. R. Hicks. *Crisis in Keynesian Economics* (New York: Basic Books, 1974).

4 The derivation of the Z function on the basis of Keynes's work is attributable to Sidney Weintraub, 'A macroeconomic approach to the theory of wages,' *The American Economic Review*, 46(5) (December, 1956), pp. 835–56.

5 It is relevant to note that had Keynes preferred to present his analysis in real terms, he would have used an index of wage costs rather than commodity prices.

6 For further treatment of this topic, see the section entitled 'Keynes's Monetary Theory,' later in this chapter.

7 Victoria Chick, *Macroeconomics after Keynes* (Cambridge MA, 1983), p. 21.

8 Paul Samuelson, 'The simple mathematics of income determination,' in *Income, Employment and Policy: Essays in Honor of Alvin Hansen* (New York: W. W. Norton, 1948), p. 635.

9 J. M. Clark, *Economic Reconstruction* (New York: Columbia University Press, 1934), p. 109.

10 Keynes, *The General Theory*, Chapters 8–10.

11 Keynes, *The General Theory*, p. 114.

12 For an account of efforts at empirical testing, see Ronald Bodkin, Chapter 4, 'Keynesian econometric concepts' in *Modern Economic Thought* edited by Sidney Weintraub (Philadelphia: University of Pennsylvania Press, 1976).

13 R. F. Kahn, 'The relation of home investment to unemployment,' *Economic Journal*, 41 (June, 1931), pp. 173–98.

14 For example, if one third of a new investment of $100,000 is saved rather than spent to finance new consumption, only $66,666.66 generates new income in the next period. If the propensity to save causes one third of this amount to again be drained into cash balances in the next period, national income will increase by an additional $44,444.44. Each successive round of expenditures will add an additional amount to national income. Given a marginal propensity to save of 0.33 (i.e. a marginal propensity to consume of two thirds), a new investment of $100,000 will eventually, other things being equal, raise national income by three times the original amount, or $300,000.

15 Keynes, *The General Theory*, p. 133.

16 Keynes himself pointed out that his marginal efficiency of capital is the same concept as Irving Fisher's 'rate of return over cost' (*The General Theory*, p. 140).

17 Keynes, *The General Theory*, p. 165.

18 Keynes, *The General Theory*, p. 213.

19 Keynes regarded the relationship between the stock market and investment decisions as one of the least-desirable features of *laissez-faire* capitalism. He remarks, 'When the capital development of a country becomes the by-product of the activities of a casino, the job is

likely to be ill-done' (*The General Theory*, p. 159).

20 Keynes, *The General Theory*, p. 47.

21 Keynes, *The General Theory*, pp. 166–72.

22 Keynes, *The General Theory*, p. 197.

23 J. M. Keynes, *Treatise on Money* (London: Macmillan, 1930), vol. 1, p. 3.

24 J. M. Keynes, 'Essays in persuasion.' *Collected Writing of John Maynard Keynes* (London and New York: Macmillan and St. Martin's Press for the Royal Economic Society, 1972), vol. 9, p. 151.

25 Keynes, *The General Theory*, p. 207.

26 Keynes examines these interrelationships much more precisely in 'The general theory,' *Quarterly Journal of Economics*, 51 (February, 1937), pp. 212–23, than in *The General Theory* (excerpted above) itself.

27 Keynes, *The General Theory*, p. 29.

28 Sidney Weintraub, *Classical Keynesianism, Monetary Theory and the Price Level* (Philadelphia: Chilton, 1961) pp. 41–64.

29 Keynes, *The General Theory*, Preface, vi.

30 A multiplier–accelerator model envisions a sequence of the behavior of income over time which is constructed on the basis of the values of the multiplier $(1/\Delta S/\Delta Y)$ and the acceleration coefficient $\Delta K/\Delta Y$. See Paul A. Samuelson, 'Dynamic process analysis,' in *A Survey of Contemporary Economics*, vol. 1, edited by Howard Ellis (Philadelphia: Blakiston, 1949).

31 The pattern which a particular process will generate over successive periods depends on the numerical value of its determining variables. If this value is a positive number greater than one, the process is one that increases at a geometric rate. The compound-interest problem is a classic economic illustration of the operation of this type of process. The value of a principal invested at a certain rate of interest increases at a geometric rate. Its value at the end of period t is determined according to the formula

$$X_{(t)} = (1 + r)^t X_o \qquad (21.7)$$

where X_o is the principal initially invested and r is the interest rate. This formula may be rewritten in a simpler form as

$$X(t) = X_o a^t \qquad (21.8)$$

where $a = (1 + r)$. Any dynamic process that is characterized by growth, whether or not it is in the realm of economics, will behave according to the same principle as a sum of money invested at compound interest. That is, $X_{(t)}$ will increase exponentially as i increases and will, when shown graphically, result in a curve that is sloping upward at an increasing rate. If the product of an initial magnitude, X_o, and the exponential value of the variables which determine its value in time, t, is a positive number greater than one, the process is one of growth. If, for example, $X_o = 3$ and $a = 2$ the numerical values of the process are 3, 6, 12, 24, 48, . . . for $t = 0$, 1, 2, 3, 4, which produce the upward sloping curve associated with the growth process.

32 See Evsey Domar, 'Capital expansion, rate of growth and employment,' *Essays in the Theory of Economic Growth* (New York: Oxford University Press, 1957).

33 Harrod, 'An essay in dynamic theory,' *Economic Journal*, vol. 49 (March, 1939), p. 14.

34 Harrod, 'An essay in dynamic theory,' p. 16.

35 What does seem strange, however, is that *The General Theory* has so frequently been interpreted as being a polemic against monetary policy. To anyone familiar with Keynes as a monetary theorist, the importance of monetary policy is implicit in *The General Theory*.

Questions for discussion and further research

1 Define and/or explain:

(a) frictional unemployment,

(b) involuntary unemployment.

2 The traditional or classical 'cure' for unemployment is to allow the market to drive the wage rate down until employers find it profitable to increase the level of employment. Keynes argued that the widespread unemployment that characterizes a depression cannot be cured by across the board wage cuts. Explain carefully why not.

3 According to Keynes, the level of aggregate demand is the most critical factor in

Glossary of terms and concepts

Aggregate demand function

The relationship between the proceeds employers expect from consumption and investment expenditures (or the sale of output) to different levels of employment. Keynes represented this function as $D = f(N)$ where N is employment.

Aggregate effective demand

The total demand for output based on consumption and investment expenditures.

Aggregate supply schedule

The relationship between the proceeds employers consider necessary to earn from the sale of the outputs produced at different levels of employment in order to make it profitable to provide each level, that is, $Z = \Phi(N)$.

Capital stock adjustment growth models

Dynamic models inspired by *The General Theory* (but not created by Keynes himself) in which the growth process is visualized as consisting of additions to capital stock which, in turn, increase income and employment levels. Harrod's growth equation specifies that to avoid excess capacity (and unemployed labor) the stock of capital must increase at a rate which is the product of the savings ratio and the productivity ratio.

Consumption function

Relates consumption expenditures to *real* income. Conceptually, this implies that consumers are not subject to money illusion.

Demand for money

People wish to hold cash (currency) in order to facilitate purchases; i.e. they have a 'transactions' demand for money. Keynes recognized they may also have a 'precautionary' demand which encourages them to hold higher balances depending upon their incomes to meet unexpected needs. While Marshall did not think in terms of a 'speculative' demand for money which causes people

to hold money as an asset in order potentially to profit from unexpected opportunities, Keynes regarded this as the most important reason for money demand. Larger amounts are held at lower rates of interest because the 'price' of liquidity is lower.

Demand insufficiency

A level of consumption and investment expenditures that is inadequate for full employment. Government expenditures, and/ or net imports, may fill the gap.

Interest payment

A reward for giving up *liquidity*; this contrasts with the classical view of interest as a reward for *abstinence*.

Keynesian cross

The intersection of the aggregate demand and supply functions, which some thinkers interpreted as providing a guide to fiscal policy. The 'inflationary gap' can, in principle, be offset by increased tax collection and less government spending while a 'deflationary gap' may be offset by lower tax collections and increased government expenditures.

Keynes effect

The possible stimulative effect of a wage–price reduction on employment that operates if interest rates fall relative to the marginal efficiency of capital, in response to a reduced transactions demand for money at a lower income level.

Keynes's equilibrium

A balance between aggregate demand and aggregate supply which is not necessarily market clearing but only represents a 'state of rest' from which forces of change may be absent. This unique concept of equilibrium is *central* to Keynes's view that forces restoring full employment do not automatically come into play.

Keynes's fundamental psychological law

Keynes suggested that 'as a rule, and on the

average, consumption expenditures will increase as income increases but not by as much as the increase in income.' It follows that the *marginal propensity to consume, ΔC/ΔY* < 1.

Liquidity trap

An accumulation of idle balances at very low rates of interest. It is represented graphically by an infinitely elastic liquidity preference curve.

Marginal efficiency of capital

The rate of discount at which an expected series of earnings from a capital good is equal to its supply price.

Money illusion

The response of persons to nominal magnitudes, like money wages, rather than to their *real* or 'purchasing power' value, which requires taking account of the price level.

Multiplier effect

The expansion in national income that may be expected from an increase in consumption expenditures. Mathematically, the multiplier is the reciprocal of the marginal propensity to save, or

$k = 1/(1 - \Delta C/\Delta Y)$.

Savings equal investment

In Keynes's system $S = I$ in the sense that both saving and investment are defined as the portion of total output that is 'unconsumed.' $S = I$ is also an equilibrium relationship that results from *income* adjustments that cause the level of savings to come into equality with the level of investment. This contrasts with the neoclassical perception, which views the interest rate as the equilibrating mechanism between quantities of savings and investment.

Static versus dynamic analysis

The static approach concerns itself with an instantaneous or timeless examination of economic variables. A dynamic analysis is concerned with the rate of change in economic variables. The motion of a dynamic process through time results from its 'built-in' response to an initial internal condition.

Static state growth

The rate of growth at which the total output of the economy and its stock of capital grow together at a constant proportionate rate which reflects the rate of increase of the population and the rate of increase in output per man.

Warranted rate of growth

That rate of growth which maintains the same rate of growth as was previously achieved. This rate is to be distinguished from the *natural rate*, which is the maximum rate of growth consistent with the full employment of all resources and the rate of technological progress.

---

3 According to Keynes, the level of aggregate demand is the most critical factor in determining the level of employment in the short run.

  (a) What determines the aggregate demand schedule?

  (b) Why, according to Weintraub's interpretation, is the *Z* function not properly shown as a 45° line?

  (c) Show aggregate demand and supply on a graph. Label carefully. Is there a price level implicit in the diagram?

  (d) In what way can it be said that Keynes's concept of equilibrium is 'unique'? How is it related to Keynes's perception of the General Theory as 'a struggle to escape' from traditional thinking?

4 (a) What is the nature of Keynes's consumption function? What are its implications with respect to the problem of maintaining the economy at full employment levels?

(b) The hypothesis has been advanced that the true long-run relationship between consumption and income is a proportional one. If this is the case, would it invalidate, alter or modify the conclusions which derive from Keynes's original formulation of the consumption function? How?

5 Discuss Keynes's contribution to the theory of the interest rate. To what extent does the interest rate play a fundamentally different role in the Keynesian system than in the classical analysis? How does Keynes integrate monetary theory into the theory of employment and output?

6 How did Harrod's equation of economic growth go beyond Keynes's central question: will saving be invested?

7 What are the requirements for achieving the warrented rate of growth?

8 Has the emphasis which contemporary growth theorists put on the concept of the 'stable' or 'equilibrium' rate of growth, changed the focus of the question Harrod was undertaking to answer?

Notes for further reading

From *The New Palgrave*

Edward J. Amadeo on multiplier analysis, vol. 3, pp. 566–68; Marro Baranzini on distribution theories: Keynesian, vol. 1, pp. 876–78; P. Bridal on saving equals investment, vol. 4, pp. 246–48; Michael R. Darby on consumption function, vol. 1, pp. 614–16; Paul Davidson on aggregate supply function, vol. 1, pp. 50–52; John Eatwell on Keynesianism, vol. 3, pp. 46–47, and on marginal efficiency of capital, vol. 3, pp. 318–19; Murray Milgate on Keynes's *General Theory*, vol. 3. pp. 42–46; Carlo Panico on liquidity preference, vol. 3, pp. 213–16; Don Patinkin on John Maynard Keynes, vol. 3, pp. 19–39; H. Sonnenschein on aggregate demand theory, vol. 1, pp. 47–50; L. Tarshis on the Keynesian Revolution, vol. 3, pp. 47–50; John B. Taylor on involuntary unemployment, vol. 2, pp. 999–1001.

Selected references and suggestions for further reading

Chick, Victoria. *Macroeconomics After Keynes* (Cambridge Mass: MIT, 1983).

Clark, Peter. *The Keynesian Revolution in the Making 1924–1936* (Oxford: Oxford University Press, 1989).

Hansen, Alvin H. *A Guide to Keynes* (New York: McGraw-Hill, 1953).

Harris, Seymour E. (ed.) *The New Economics* (New York: Alfred A. Knopf: 1947).

Harrod, R. E. *The Life of John Maynard Keynes* (New York: Harcourt Brace, 1951).

Johnson, H. 'Keynes's general theory: a revolution of a war of independence?' *Canadian Journal of Economics*, vol. 9 (November, 1976), pp. 580–94.

Kahn, R. E. 'The relation of home investment to unemployment.' *Economic Journal*, 41 (June, 1931), pp. 173–98.

Keynes, J. M. *The Collected Writing of John Maynard Keynes, Vols. I–XXX*, edited by Don Moggridge (London: Macmillan).

Leijonhufvud, Axel. *On Keynesian Economics and the Economics of Keynes* (New York: Oxford University Press, 1968).

Lekachman, Robert (ed.) *Keynes' General Theory Reports of Three Decades* (New York: St. Martin's Press, 1964).

Minsky, Hyman. *John Maynard Keynes* (New York: Columbia University Press, 1975).

Patinkin, Don. *Money, Interest and Prices*, 2nd edn (New York: Harper & Row).

Shackle, G. L. S. *The Years of High Theory* (Cambridge: Cambridge University Press, 1967).

Skidelsky, R. *John Maynard Keynes*, Vol. II, *The Economist As Savior* (London: Macmillan).

Weintraub, Sidney. *Classical Keynesianism, Monetary Theory and the Price Level* (Philadelphia: Chilton, 1961).

Young, Warren. *Interpreting Mr. Keynes: The ISLM Enigma* (London: Polity, 1987).

Part VI

Beyond High Theory

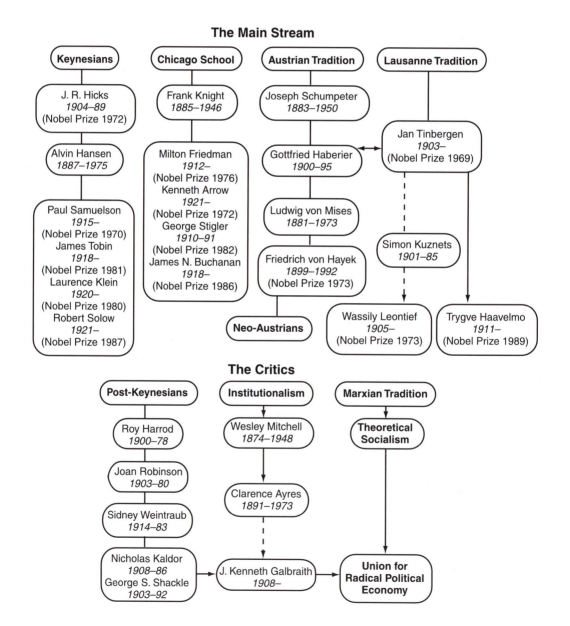

The Main Stream

| Keynesians | Chicago School | Austrian Tradition | Lausanne Tradition |

J. R. Hicks
1904–89
(Nobel Prize 1972)

Frank Knight
1885–1946

Joseph Schumpeter
1883–1950

Jan Tinbergen
1903–
(Nobel Prize 1969)

Alvin Hansen
1887–1975

Milton Friedman
1912–
(Nobel Prize 1976)
Kenneth Arrow
1921–
(Nobel Prize 1972)
George Stigler
1910–91
(Nobel Prize 1982)
James N. Buchanan
1918–
(Nobel Prize 1986)

Gottfried Haberier
1900–95

Paul Samuelson
1915–
(Nobel Prize 1970)
James Tobin
1918–
(Nobel Prize 1981)
Laurence Klein
1920–
(Nobel Prize 1980)
Robert Solow
1921–
(Nobel Prize 1987)

Ludwig von Mises
1881–1973

Simon Kuznets
1901–85

Friedrich von Hayek
1899–1992
(Nobel Prize 1973)

Neo-Austrians

Wassily Leontief
1905–
(Nobel Prize 1973)

Trygve Haavelmo
1911–
(Nobel Prize 1989)

The Critics

| Post-Keynesians | Institutionalism | Marxian Tradition |

Roy Harrod
1900–78

Wesley Mitchell
1874–1948

**Theoretical
Socialism**

Joan Robinson
1903–80

Sidney Weintraub
1914–83

Clarence Ayres
1891–1973

Nicholas Kaldor
1908–86
George S. Shackle
1903–92

J. Kenneth Galbraith
1908–

**Union for
Radical Political
Economy**

Key dates

1921	J. M. Keynes	A Treatise on Probability
1935	Frank Knight	The Ethics of Competition
1935	Friedrich Hayek	Prices and Production
1937	J. R. Hicks	Mr. Keynes and the Classics
1939	Gunnar Myrdal	Monetary Equilibrium
1939	Paul A. Samuelson	Interactions between the Multiplier Analysis and the Principle of Acceleration
1941	Friedrich Hayek	The Pure Theory of Capital
1942	Joseph A. Schumpeter	Capitalism, Socialism, and Democracy
1944	T. Haavelmo	The Probability Approach in Econometrics
1947	Paul Samuelson	Foundations of Economic Analysis
1948	F. A. Hayek	Individualism and Economic Order
1949	Ludwig V. Mises	Human Action: A Treatise on Economics
1949	Friedrich A. Hayek	Individualism and Economic Order
1950	L. R. Klein	Economic Fluctuations in the United States
1951	Kenneth Arrow	Social Choice and Individual Values
1953	Alvin Hansen	A Guide to Keynes
1956	Milton Friedman	Studies in the Quality Theory of Money
1958	John Kenneth Galbraith	The Affluent Society

1960	Piero Sraffa	The Production of Commodities By Means of Commodities
1961	Clarence Ayres	Toward a Reasonable Society: The Values of Industrial Civilization
1961	Sidney Weintraub	Classical Keynesianism, Monetary Theory and the Price Level
1962	Harry Johnson	Money, Trade, and Economic Growth
1962	Milton Friedman	Capitalism and Freedom
1963	Joan Robinson	Essays in the Theory of Economic Growth
1963	Milton Friedman and Anna Schwartz	A Monetary History of the United States 1867–1960
1964	John Kenneth Galbraith	The Affluent Society
1965	Don Patinkin	Money Interest and Prices, 2nd edn.
1966	Axel Leijonhufvud	On Economics and the Economics of Keynes
1967	John Kenneth Galbraith	The New Industrial State
1967	George L. S. Shackle	The Years of High Theory
1968	Gunnar Myrdal	Asian Drama: An Inquiry into the Poverty of Nations
1970	Amartya K. Sen	Collective Choice and Social Welfare
1971	Gary S. Becker	The Economics of Discrimination
1971	George J. Stigler	The Theory of Economic Regulation
1972	David M. Gordon	Theories of Poverty and Underemployment
1972	George L. S. Shackle	Epistemics and Economics: A Critique of Economic Doctrines
1975	Hyman Minsky	John Maynard Keynes
1975	Piero Sraffa	The Production of Commodities by Means of Commodities
1976	Gary S. Becker	The Economic Approach to Human Behavior
1980	Amartya K. Sen	Poverty and Famines: An Essay on Entitlement and Deprivation

Overview of contemporary theoretical economics

The era of contemporary theoretical economics was ushered in during the period George L. S. Shackle has so eloquently called 'the years of high theory.' Writing in the mid-1960s, and looking back, he tells us that 'there began in the mid-1920's an immense creative spasm which completely altered the orientation and character of economics.'[1] The most substantial among the major innovations of theoretical economics was J. M. Keynes's *General Theory*, which was clearly intended to reflect Keynes's rejection of the critical 'second postulate' of neoclassical theory with its implicit conclusion that labor markets tend to achieve full employment equilibrium. When Keynes wrote to George Bernard Shaw that he expected his *General Theory of Employment, Interest and Money* to change the way people think about economics he was, in effect, expressing the view that his work would lay the foundation for a new paradigm in the discipline. To qualify as a paradigm, a particular scientific achievement must attract an enduring group of adherents away from competing modes of scientific activity.[2] It must also be sufficiently open-ended to leave all sorts of problems for the redefined group of practitioners to resolve. There are many examples of paradigmatic breakthroughs in the natural sciences. The works of Ptolemy, Newton, and Lavoisier brought about whole new modes of thought in their respective fields of astronomy, physics, and chemistry.

To some extent the field of economics underwent such a paradigmatic shift with the development of the marginal utility theory of value in the closing decade of the nineteenth century and, somewhat later, the marginal productivity theory of distribution. The almost simultaneous but completely independent discovery of the principle of diminishing marginal utility in the 1870s by Jevons, Menger, and Walras, which was examined in Chapter 13, is often referred to as constituting a *marginalist revolution* in economics in the sense of providing the building block for the new kind of static microeconomics that matured into the *neoclassical paradigm.* As we have seen, this paradigm was fully anticipated by Alfred Marshall and his American counterpart John Bates Clark, both of whom used the marginal principle to fashion a theory of value and distribution. Marshall's efforts were the more successful in the sense that he attracted and trained a school of followers among whom, in Chapters 15 and 16, we singled out Pigou, Robinson, and J. R. Hicks as those who undertook to refine and extend Marshall's work. J. M. Keynes was, of course, also Marshallian until the break he undertook in *The General Theory.*

Before we examine whether Keynes's efforts to disassociate himself from the neoclassical mainstream have, indeed, brought about a paradigmatic shift that has caused his fellow economists to disassociate themselves from a previously accepted theory that has now been found inadequate for 'puzzle solving,' it is relevant to recognize that intellectual revolutions in economics appear to be different from those that characterize the natural sciences. The works of Jevons, Menger, Walras, Wicksell, and John Bates Clark were anticipated, in varying degrees, by Gossen, von Thünen, Cournot, Dupuit, and even Ricardo. Similarly, Marshall always maintained that the essential elements of classical analysis were, in no respect, affected by his analysis, which he viewed as harmonizing the work of Ricardo with the newer marginal utility analysis. The critical change wrought by the Marshallian synthesis was to bring about a redefinition of the economic problem. Whereas the classicists were concerned with analyzing the causes of the increase in a nation's wealth and the distribution of this wealth among landowners, laborers, and capitalists, the marginalist or neoclassical approach made pricing and the allocation of a fixed supply of resources *the* economic problem. In brief, the accepted mode of reasoning became 'constrained maximization,' which is an approach that leaves aside all questions relating to changes in the quantity and quality of resources through time. Yet, the Marshallian system preserved the essential insights of the classical cost-of-production theorists. These examples suggest that, in economics, unlike the natural sciences, intellectual revolution apparently does not sweep away prevailing modes of thought so that a new paradigm can take over as a basis for guiding future work.

The reinterpretation of the economics of John Maynard Keynes in terms of the Marshallian and Walrasian paradigms represented, in effect, a *counter-revolution* against Keynesian principles. Equally important from the standpoint of understanding the development of contemporary theory is recognizing that the counter-revolution coincided with a technical revolution that launched econometrics as a sister discipline to economics.[3] The long-term legacy of high theory for economics can only be fully understood in relation to the computer revolution and the emergence of econometrics. Both substantially affected the way in which the analytical tools and concepts that originated during the years of high theory would become harnessed into service in the task of model building. Thus, the task of Chapter 22, 'The emergence of econometrics as the sister discipline of economics,' is to provide an account of these developments, several of

which were subsequently recognized with Nobel Prizes in Economics.

Table VI.1 summarizes the complete list of awards, the first of which was conferred jointly on Ragnar Frisch and Jan Tinbergen in 1969, both of whom were recognized for statistical/quantitative contributions to economics. It is relevant to note that, with few exceptions, the awards have gone to thinkers who are working in econometrics or are mathematical and mainstream oriented, Friedrich Hayek, Gunnar Myrdal, and Douglass North are among the relatively few exceptions. Hayek (1890–1990) focused on 'coordination' failures as part of ongoing market processes. Working in the Austrian tradition, his interpretation of price theory, capital theory, and monetary theory integrated nineteenth and twentieth century economic phenomena as reflecting instances of spontaneous order in the framework of a price system.

Gunnar Myrdal (1898–1987) wrote in the Swedish tradition of Wicksell, Heckscher, and Cassel. He is remembered for facilitating a transition in economics from static to dynamic analysis. By introducing the role of expectations using the concepts of the *ex ante* and *ex post* to distinguish between intentions and actual outcomes in key aggregates like savings and investment, he was able to clarify the effects of unexpected price changes. He was also a political economist *par excellence* focusing on the need for value premises (justice, liberty and equality of economic opportunity) to purge conventional economic theory of biases, especially when applied to underdeveloped countries. For his monumental *Asian Drama* (1968) he was awarded the Nobel Prize in 1974. Hayek was honored the same year for his contribution.

Chapter 23 examines the efforts of some of the profession's most highly regarded

Table VI.1 Nobel Laureates in economics

1969	Ragnar Frisch, Oslo University
	Jan Tinbergen, The Netherlands School of Economics
1970	Paul Samuelson, Massachusetts Institute of Technology
1971	Simon Kuznets, Harvard University
1972	John R. Hicks, Oxford University
	Kenneth Arrow, Harvard University
1973	Wassily Leontieff, Harvard University
1974	Gunnar Myrdal, University of Stockholm
	Friedrich A. Hayek, University of Freiburg
1975	Leonid Kantorovich, Moscow Academy of Sciences
	Tjalling Koopmans, Yale University
1976	Milton Friedman, University of Chicago
1977	Bertil Ohlin, Stockholm School of Economics
	James E. Meade, Cambridge University
1978	Herbert A. Simon, Carnegie-Mellon University
1979	Theodore W. Schultz, University of Chicago
	W. Arthur Lewis, Princeton University
1980	Lawrence Klein, University of Pennsylvania
1981	James Tobin, Yale University
1982	George J. Stigler, University of Chicago
1983	Gerard Debreu, University of California, Berkeley
1984	J. Richard Stone, Cambridge University
1985	Franco Modigliani, Massachusetts Institute of Technology
1986	James M. Buchanan, George Mason University
1987	Robert Solow, Massachusetts Institute of Technology
1988	Maurice Allais, Ecole Nationale des Mines de Paris
1989	Trygve Hamvelmo, Oslo University
1990	Harry Markowitz, City University of New York
	Merton H. Miller, University of Chicago
	William F. Sharpe, Stanford University
1991	Ronald Coase, University of Chicago
1992	Gary S. Becker, University of Chicago
1993	Robert W. Fogel, University of Chicago
	Douglass C. North, Washington University
1994	John C. Harsinyi, University of California
	John F. Nash, Princeton University
	Reinhard Selten, Reinische Friedrich-Wilhelms University, Bonn
1995	Robert E. Lucas, University of Chicago
1996	James A. Mirrlees, Cambridge University
	William Vickrey, Columbia University
1997	Robert C. Merton, Harvard University
	Myron S. Scholes, Stanford University
1998	Amartya K. Sen, Trinity College, Cambridge University
1999	Robert Mundell, Columbia University

members, John R. Hicks among them, to fashion a body of macroeconomic principles by marrying the economics of J. M. Keynes to Marshallian and Walrasian paradigms. It is premature to identify any of these reinterpretations as masterworks in the same sense as those that were identified in Parts I through V. Economics at the present time, as was suggested in the introduction to Part I, has become a quite controversial discipline, especially as it relates to the several contemporary interpretations of Keynes's work. It would thus be inappropriate to tout a particular contemporary selection as more seminal than another, with respect to its anticipated effect on future economic thought. This concluding part of the book will therefore opt not to choose which among the very large number of post-World War II contributions to economic thought is likely to survive into the next century as a masterwork. The most prudent course is to identify the leading contenders while directing the interested reader to specific sources in the references and endnotes.

The most persuasive reinterpretation of Keynesian principles, to the majority of the profession, has become identified as *monetarism*. Led by 1976 Nobel Prize winner Milton Friedman of the University of Chicago, monetarists have focused chiefly on explaining the difficulties of achieving the dual goals of full employment and price level stability. The perceived trade-off between unemployment and inflation, as implied by the Phillips curve apparatus, is a matter of special concern and is the basis for the monetary policy recommendations of Friedman and his associates. Much of this analysis is predicated on what has come to be known as a *rational expectations* view of individual decision making. The essence of this view of behavior is that individuals behave in accordance with

their expectations about economic outcomes, especially in relation to changes in wage and interest rates and price level changes. This view of the behavior of market participants has guided much of the econometric research and policy analysis of economic thinkers, who are collectively known as *new classicals*.

The microeconomic aspects of the work of Chicago School economists have also been of major importance in shaping the research and teaching of the majority of the economics profession. As is examined in Chapter 24, this work is rooted in the Austrian tradition of Menger and was intellectually transported to Chicago under the leadership of Frank Knight. These efforts extended the theory of individual choice to study households as 'production' units that seek to maximize utility, much as firms seek to maximize profits. They have also pioneered in promoting law and economics as the chief interdisciplinary fields of the social sciences by studying the effects of the assignment of property rights.

Chicago school interests have been further extended toward the analysis of growth in underdeveloped economies via the agency of the market mechanism. Economists adhering to the libertarian philosophy of the efficiency of the market mechanism regard economic freedom as the most effective way of allocating resources in developing economies as well as in already advanced economies. Mainstream academic economists have considerable faith in the positive role of the market mechanism and the limited need for government intervention. This policy view appears to be as widely accepted by the American electorate as it has been by British voters. The latter supported the Conservative Government, led by Margaret Thatcher, which reversed the nationalization of industry undertaken by the previous Labour Government. Although the Labour Government of Tony Blair has now displaced Mrs. Thatcher, many elements of *laissez-faire* policy remain in place. It is thus clear, whether viewed in terms of prevailing economic policy or the underlying theoretical structure, that we are *not* all Keynesians now. Contemporary mainstream economics is more neoclassical, neo-Walrasian and neo-Austrian than it is a refinement and extension of the economics of J. M. Keynes's *General Theory*.

However, criticisms of mainstream economics, and the related efforts to develop alternatives to the mainstream paradigm, are by no means dead. Thus, the focus of Chapter 25 is on the ideas of the leading critics, some of whom – like John Kenneth Galbraith – are extremely persuasive. The writers of the New Left also command a following. Their criticisms are sounding a note of discord on the contemporary scene that cannot be neglected in assessing the present state of economics as a discipline. Whether or not the magnitude of the discord is such that it can be judged as indicative of intellectual crisis, it is a certainty that this dissent will leave its mark on future economic thought.

The critics of orthodox economics also include Keynes's contemporary followers, among them American post-Keynesians originally led by Sidney Weintraub. Their English counterparts include Joan Robinson and Nicholas Kaldor (both now deceased). Both had strong classical associations derived from the late Piero Sraffa's reinterpretation of Ricardo's economics.

Finally, the modern Austrian School has emerged as an intellectual group that, although it has its roots in the Austrian tradition of Menger and his followers, is today intellectually distinct in the criticism it levels against mainstream theories of market behavior and price determination. As will be explained below, they have articulated an anti-equilibrium perspective that has something in common with that of the post-Keynesians, with whom they share reservations about the place of econometrics as the sister discipline of economics. Since that development has been so central to contemporary economic theorizing, the chapter that follows presents a brief examination of the origins of econometrics and how it came to its present primacy as the sister discipline of economics.

Notes

1   G. L. S. Shackle, *The Years of High Theory* (Cambridge: Cambridge University Press, 1967), p. 5.

2   Thomas Kuhn, *The Structure of Scientific Revolutions* (Princeton, NJ: Princeton University Press, 1970).

3   Hans Brems has recently likened the setting of the period between the end of World War II and the great inflation as coinciding with the 'third industrial revolution,' which was set in motion by the advent of nuclear fission and the microchip. See Hans Brems, *Pioneering Economic Theory 1630–1980* (Baltimore and London: The Johns Hopkins Press, 1986) pp. 225–27. The former breakthrough launched the nuclear power industry with its multiplicity of military and civilian applications; the second is the foundation of high-speed electronic computation.

Chapter 22

The emergence of econometrics as the sister discipline of economics

The 'second stage' in the development of numeracy in economics, which hales from the founding in 1883 of the Statistical Section (F) of the British Association for the Advancement of Science and the Statistical Society of London, focused on data collection and statistics for the purpose of establishing 'correct views' about the moral sciences and their relationship to the physical sciences. Some thinkers, William Stanley Jevons among them, believed that the science of Political Economy 'might gradually be erected into an exact science.' He became an avid student of commercial fluctuations in search of laws that governed seasonal and cyclical variations by linking them to meteorological changes, but his enthusiasms were not widely shared. This was partly because the construction of an hedonic balance sheet for the guidance of policy makers was recognized as insoluble, so that British economists disassociated themselves from the notion of utility as a measurable magnitude. As was noted in Chapter 12, Jevons' views on the prospective role of inductive research in economics failed to dominate, because many contemporaries, among them John Elliot Cairnes, were of the opinion that, as a moral science, economics is inherently deductive. This was, of course, also Marshall's view.

By the mid-1920s, the deductive method had long since become the accepted mode of inquiry for discovering laws relating to the behavior of market phenomena. There was little concern about reinforcing deductive analysis with empiricism beyond the casual sort that used actual (or conjectural) data for purposes of example and illustration. Wesley Mitchell's work at Columbia University, and at the National Bureau of Economic Research, on business cycles, along with Irving Fisher's development at Yale of index numbers to measure price level changes, were exceptions to the preference in the United States toward deductive economics. Marshall's *Principles* and his strong reservations about the application of mathematical methods to economics influenced most economists to teach deductive analysis to their students and relied on it for their own work. Thus, mathematics and statistics existed as disciplines that remained quite separate from economics.

The creative spasm of theoretical innovation known as 'high theory,' which dates from the mid-1920s, also encouraged new methods for studying the behavior of the economy, although these were not primarily mathematical or statistical. Concern about cyclical phenomena and the usefulness of the *ex ante–ex post* construct of the Stockholm School are among the intellectual breakthroughs of the period. Unlike the neoclassical concept of equilibrium, which focused on the requisites for an economy's return to stability, the *ex ante–ex post* construct offered a way of conceiving of an economy in the *process* of changing from one phase of the business cycle to another.[1] Once suggested, this idea implied the need to invent a method to evaluate the relative merits of one plausible cycle theory as opposed to another equally plausible theory. The challenge was taken up by the League of Nations, which commissioned Jan Tinbergen, a Dutch scholar, to evaluate their relative merits empirically. Jointly, with the Norwegian Ragnar Frisch, he became the 1969 recipient of the Nobel prize in economics. Tinbergen's 1939 statistical verification of alternative business cycle theories, which pioneered the method of least squares and regression analysis, marks the beginning of econometrics as the sister discipline of economics. It also marks the beginning of the third and present stage of numeracy, in which economics has emerged as a *predictive* rather than as a moral science.

Econometrics is the branch of economics that is concerned with establishing empirical content into economic relations. The term, which is a combination of the words economics and metrics (from the Greek *metron*, which means 'measurement') was apparently coined by Ragnar Frisch, one of the founders of the Econometrics Society in 1930.[2] More precisely, econometrics is concerned with 'the quantitative analysis of actual economic phenomena based on the concurrent development of theory and observation, related by appropriate methods of inference.'[3]

Modern-day quantitative analysis is clearly dependent on computer technology. The information storage and processing capability of the microchip is truly awesome. A computer chip can now execute more than one million instructions per second, which is more than 200 times faster than the capability of the first high-speed electronic computer installed at the University of Pennsylvania in 1946. Early practitioners must have been considerably handicapped by having to rely on manual calculators. The computer technology advances since the 1950s are thus among the reasons why econometrics has not only flourished as a separate discipline, but has in fact become 'the existing methodology of economics, tailored for the subject, and taught as such to graduate students almost everywhere.'[4]

While the lack of technology for processing large quantities of data was a central reason why econometrics as a separate field dates only from the 1950s, there are other reasons, especially in view of the fact that many nineteenth- and early twentieth-century contributors to economics were in command of the mathematical and statistical tools that are an integral part of econometrics. They understood probability distributions, least squares, simultaneous equations, and matrix algebra. Yet they were fearful that the very precision of mathematics and statistics would give the impression of exactness to economic conclusions, which they regarded as unwarranted. Alfred Marshall more than anyone, although he was anxious to establish economics as a science, argued that the results of economic forces are not quantifiable.[5] Doubt concerning the relevance of the laws of statistical probability to economics were also expressed by J. M. Keynes, among others, when he reviewed Jan Tinbergen's empirical work on business cycles.[6] Thus, the early development of econometric techniques that will be reviewed in this chapter was very largely inspired by European scholars and transplanted to the United States and England during the late 1930s and early 1940s. It is also relevant to note that this development became a central influence in shifting the dominance of the economics profession from English universities, principally Cambridge and Oxford, to such leading American centers of learning as the University of Chicago, Yale, the Massachusetts Institute of Technology, and Harvard, among others. Previously, many American scholars were lured to the great centers for economic research and teaching at Cambridge, Vienna, and several cities in Germany and France.

European influences

The anticipations of Ragnar Frisch

Ragnar Frisch (1895–1973) came into economics via the University of Oslo where he earned a degree in mathematical statistics in 1926. Accordingly, his particular interest became the quantification of economics; the years that followed the Great Depression encouraged his interest in social planning and economic dynamics. The latter interests led him to propose that economists use the terms *static* and *dynamic* to describe the relationships among variables; specifically, he described a relation as *static* if the variables it includes relate to a single point in time. Analogously, a relation whose variables relate to different points in time is *dynamic*.[7]

This set of interests led Frisch to examine the *acceleration principle* (already pioneered by J. B. Clark). He concluded that, in and of itself, the acceleration principle is unable to explain the turning points of business cycles and demonstrated that, by including a replacement demand for investment goods into the relation, it is possible to develop a fully determined model. What he found is that the interaction of consumption and investment magnitudes could simulate vari-

ous 'paths' for the economy: monotonic oscillatory, damped or explosive. Thus, he inferred that the phenomenon of the business cycles requires an exogenous impulse mechanism to put it into motion and sustain it. The impulse might derive from technological and entrepreneurial innovations such as those Schumpeter envisioned as entering the system, and perpetuate business fluctuations that would die out in their absence. The economy thus appeared to Frisch as responding to exogenous factors that generate endogenous swings within the economy that eventually become damped until another exogenous stimulus comes along.[8]

Ragnar Frisch's formulation of mathematical laws of the economy's cyclical behavior represents something of a 'bridge' between the second and third stages of the development of measurement and quantification techniques in economics. It stands apart from the business cycle theories, which are described in Chapter 17, as well as Wesley Mitchell's collection of statistical data to establish reference cycles and to arrive at an inductively established generalization about business cycle causality. Frisch thus envisioned the possibility of establishing economics as a *predictive* science, thereby anticipating the subsequent marriage of regression analysis and general equilibrium theory as the essential building blocks for the present stage of econometric model building and mathematical formalism.

Tinbergen's business-cycle research

The statistical evaluation of business-cycle theories undertaken by Jan Tinbergen under the sponsorship of the League of Nations has already been noted. Tinbergen's first volume, published in 1939 under the title *A Method and Its Application to Investment Activity*, was a harbinger of future technique in its formulation of a multi-equation system defined by constant coefficients, lags, and shocks that obey the laws of probability. The essentials of his approach are captured in a summary paper that outlined a scheme for representing the logical structure of the business cycle mechanism to explain how a change in variable *A* at moment *t* acts on other variables *B*, *C*, . . . *X* at moments *t* + 1, *t* + 2, . . .[9] This scheme, represented in Figure 22.1, identifies a list of phenomena *A*, *B*, *C* . . . (variables) in vertical columns. Horizontal rows display 'dots' A_1, A_2, A_3 to represent the consecutive time intervals of separate phenomena. Tinbergen represented these hypothetical impacts over time by arrows that mapped out relationships.

These relationships may also be represented as a system of equations in which each equation expresses how changes in one variable cause changes in other variables. In its complete form a system of equations contains both constant coefficients and lags to represent the structure of the model. As many equations will be written as there are unknown variables, and there will be add-itional unsystematic terms to represent accidental causes, or shocks, which may be unexpected and sudden but, nevertheless, obey the laws of probability. Tinbergen maintained that it is possible, in principle, to predict changes in the system on the basis of the equations that describe its logical structure. He also claimed that his method is sufficiently flexible to test virtually any theory that relates to the behavior of interdependent variables.

Keynes on the laws of probability and Tinbergen's study

J. M. Keynes's reservations about Tinbergen's efforts at empiricism merit further consideration, especially because they also relate to contemporary controversy about the role of econometrics. Long before he was asked to review Tinbergen's statistical analysis of business cycles, Keynes had already studied the usefulness of mathematical probabilities for addressing questions arising in the so-called moral sciences, economics and psychology among them. Even before he published his *Treatise on Money* (1930) and *The General*

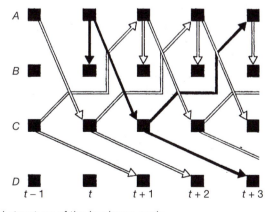

Figure 22.1 The logical structure of the business cycle

Source: Jan Tinbergen 'Econometric business cycle research', *The Review of Economic Studies*, 7 (1940), Chart I.

Theory (1936), Keynes had reached the conclusion that

where our experience is incomplete, we cannot hope to derive from it judgments of probability without the aid of intuition or of some further *a priori* principle. Experience, as opposed to intuition, cannot possibly afford us a criterion by which to judge whether on given evidence the probabilities of two propositions are or are not equal.[10]

Keynes had thus taken the position that prediction of human behavior and events *cannot be successfully addressed by means of the principles of probability*. This perspective bears directly on his later evaluation of Tinbergen's work and his understanding of the conceptual difficulties inherent in the econometric method and thus its usefulness as an adjunct to economic theory.[11]

The issue that Keynes was addressing resurfaced in another form when the possibility of predicting business crises and revivals became a research agenda. Among those who also addressed the problem of business-cycle prediction, no one came closer than Oskar Morgenstern to sharing Keynes's view. His 1928 book *Wertsschaftsprognose*, written at his Vienna Institute as part of his business-cycle research, specifically addressed the problem of predicting the behavior of economic variables that derives from the interdependence among market participants. He recognized that economics is concerned with live variables rather than with dead variables such as are encountered in nature. He argued that prediction is only possible when 'dead' variables are involved. When live variables are in operation, the matter is conceptually different, because these represent the wills of other persons that may impact on another's behavior and thereby influence predicted events. His famous 'Sherlock Holmes–Moriarty' example (inspired by the exploits of Conan Doyle's fictional detective and his equally clever, but criminal, arch rival) illustrated why the premise that either man would outthink the other is untenable and made it clear that the problem posed when human beings interact is, necessarily, one of *strategy*. That is, a new action by either party not only changes the outcome, but also the scenario for future actions. Morgenstern was, therefore, doubtful about the possibility for successful forecasting. He argued (1) that the use of economic theory and statistics for the purpose of forecasting is *impossible* in principle and (2) that even if a technique for forecasting can be developed, it would not be applicable in actual situations (i.e. the forecast would itself alter the outcome).

John von Neumann and game theory

Morgenstern's perception of the mathematical problem inherent in prediction as a result of behavioral interdependencies persisted despite his awareness, as a participant of Menger's famed Vienna Circle, of John von Neumann's 1921 paper on the theory of games.[12] That paper identified, in principle, the possibility that interacting parties can achieve mutually compatible maxima (or minima). The winner-take-all outcome of a two-person game is not the only outcome if the possibilities envisioned are allowed to be more complex than the either/or outcome of 'Holmes arrests Moriarity' or 'Moriarity escapes.' Such games as 'Treasure Hunt' or 'Bridge' readily envision outcomes in which the skill (and luck) of the participants result in a 'saddle point,' or a division of treasure or tricks; that is, a minimax (least loss) or a maximin (least gain) outcome. Von Neumann's approach was thus the key to solving the puzzle of the indeterminate two-person game and led to the later collaboration on *The Theory of Games and Economic Behavior* (1944).

Keynes's early reservations about the relevance of mathematical probability to economic phenomena were also shared by Chicago's Frank Knight. Knight's opposition to empiricism in economics reflected both his philosophical aversion to quantification in the social sciences and his fear about its use as a basis for policy.[13] Joseph Schumpeter, on the other hand, saw no reason to be opposed to quantification, and was quite willing to confront and evaluate theoretical hypotheses (specifically, theories of the business cycle) with descriptive and historical tests. However, he did maintain that statistical concepts and their associated techniques are considered as appropriate for use in testing procedures only if meaning, in the sense of distinct corresponding phenomena, can be established.[14]

The Haavelmo contribution: stochastic models

Although systems of equations can be used to express interdependencies among variables, identification of causal relationships is complicated by the fact that while certain elements are constant throughout the period of observation, others are changing. The changing element reflects the influence of unknown variables whose precise effect is, as Morgenstern and Keynes both argued, *unpredictable*. Trygve Haavelmo, who was Tinbergen's colleague in Oslo during the 1930s, countered this argument by suggesting that it is possible to make an empirically significant statement about how a random variable will affect an outcome by adopting probability theory. In his view, a theoretical model 'will have an economic meaning only when associated with a design of an actual experiment that describes and indicates how to measure a system of true variables (or objects) $x_1, x_2 \ldots x_n$ that are to be identified with the corresponding variables in the theory.'[15] His argument was that the gap between the exactness of a theory and the necessarily compromised accuracy of observational fact can be bridged by evaluating measurement errors in terms of probability laws. By properly specifying a stochastic (or probabilistic) model, the admissible set of values can be identified and weighted. This technique, known as the maximum likelihood method of parameter estimation, makes it possible to simultaneously maximize a joint likelihood function with respect to all parameters. In essence, what Haavelmo proposed is thus the statistical counterpart of simultaneous equations of the Walras–Pareto type.[16] His method, for which he was honored as a Nobel laureate in economics in 1989, lent itself to becoming incorporated into the empirical research that the computer revolution made possible. As will be elaborated next, the research institution known as the Cowles Commission, more than any other research institution in America, adopted the method he recommended and thus played a major role in encouraging the economics profession's reliance on mathematics and econometrics that has characterized the discipline for the last three decades.

The Cowles Commission

Alfred Cowles founded the research institution bearing his name in 1932 after the stock market crash of 1929 and the depression that followed called attention to the information gap as it relates to stock prices. Shortly afterward, the Cowles Commission became associated with the Econometric Society, which was organized in 1930 by a small group of academics – among them Irving Fisher, who was the Society's first president, Ragnar

Frisch and Charles Roos, then research director of the National Recovery Administration (NRA) of the United States government. Roos became the Commission's first director of research and, simultaneously, professor of econometrics at Colorado College. Summer conferences, held at Colorado Springs, and which attracted a virtual who's who among statisticians, mathematicians, and economists oriented toward mathematical and statistical approaches, were among the highlights of the Commission's activities. The international character of these meetings, which Trygve Haavelmo, from the University of Oslo, and Abraham Wald attended between 1937 and 1939, and the quality of their research work, established a base for a 'university in exile' as refugee scholars fled the Nazis.[17]

After Cowles moved his business headquarters to Chicago in 1939, the Commission sought a new affiliation, ultimately with the University of Chicago. The move to Chicago marked the beginning of financial support by the Rockefeller Foundation, the National Bureau of Economic Research, the Social Science Research Committee of the University of Chicago, and various sponsors in Canada and Europe. In 1949, it entered into a contract with the Rand Corporation to conduct research relating to the theory of allocation; two years later the US Office of Naval Research contracted it to conduct a project identified as 'Decision making under uncertainty.' Thus, the stage was set for the Cowles Commission to undertake a leading role in the American knowledge industry.[18]

Activity analysis (linear programming)

The theory and practice of resource allocation became an important research focus of the Cowles Commission during the war years.

A major part of this effort reflects the direction of Tjallings Koopmans, a physicist who was also a former Tinbergen student, who had worked with the British–American Combined Shipping Adjustment Board, studying merchant shipping problems during World War II. This work provided the foundation for the subsequent development of activity analysis, or linear programming, after he joined the Cowles Commission in 1944. Economists had long been concerned with the optimizing behaviors of individuals and business firms, which they addressed in terms of equating marginal (or infinitely small) magnitudes. Differential calculus was the only mathematical tool needed. However, the problem Koopmans was called upon to solve was far more complicated. The question of how to conduct ocean shipping with a minimum number of empty ship miles was not one that could be solved with differential calculus. The solution to this problem involves the formulation of a program in which vessels are (hypothetically) rerouted among (a limited number) of ports at different (hypothetical) prices until an overall optimum is reached. This is the basic idea that was subsequently developed as the Simplex algorithm.[19]

There was remarkable similarity between the formal structure of Koopman's model and the Air Force procurement and deployment models. Its insights, which were derived from the von Neumann–Morgenstern theory of games, led to the recognition that a two-person zero-sum game is the mathematical equivalent of a linear programming problem, which solves input–output models that relate to alternative production processes (activities). This work was a prelude to the Cowles Commission's Monograph 13, edited by Koopmans and published under the title *Activity Analysis of Production and Allocation*

(1951). Work along these lines, which also became known as *operations research* or *program management*, was not a large part of the work of the Cowles Commission, but it became the expanding applied field of management science. In economics, these linear models also became useful in the solution of planning and welfare problems. On the other hand, work that built on the Walrasian general equilibrium model assumed increasing importance as the dominant Cowles research concern.

With the appointment of Jacob Marshak as research director, and of Haavelmo, in 1943, and Lawrence Klein, in 1944, as research associates, a substantial reorientation in the Cowles Commission research program was undertaken. Its agenda is sketched in the following passage from the Annual Report for 1943:

> The method of the studies planned . . . is conditioned by the following four characteristics of economic data and economic theory: a) the theory is a system of simultaneous equations, not a single equation; b) some or all of these equations include 'random' terms . . .; c) many data are given in the form of time series . . .; d) many published data refer to aggregates . . . To develop and improve suitable methods seems, at the present state of our knowledge, at least as important as to obtain immediate results. Accordingly, the Commission has planned the publication of studies on the general theory of economic measurements . . . It is planned to continue these methodological studies systematically.[20]

This credo makes it clear that the general equilibrium approach to problem perception and the probability approach to problem solution were to become dominant in the Commission's future research. The proposed method is the statistical counterpart of the Walras–Pareto simultaneous equation approach.[21]

The alternative approach of the National Bureau

The orientation of the Cowles Commission associated with the multi-equation probability methodology for doing macroeconomic research proved highly controversial and pitted the commission against other quantitative researchers at the University of Chicago and The National Bureau of Economic Research. It also provoked a more philosophically grounded disagreement with the Chicagoans, Frank Knight in particular. The controversy with the National Bureau over the method was provoked by the empirical work of Arthur Burns and Wesley Mitchell in their 1946 book *Measuring Business Cycles*. The latter became the prototype for the Bureau's research program of collecting statistical data and developing statistical techniques. It was profoundly influenced by Mitchell's institutionalist perspective, which looked to empirical research to provide the basis for economic theory. Together with Arthur Burns, he undertook to identify the behavior of a large number of business indicators, which they tracked over time for the purpose of measuring sequential changes in aggregate economic activity. They were able, on the basis of these indicators, to identify reference cycles from which they established the duration and turning points of cycles. The role of empiricism in their work was thus to provide a basis for generalizations that had been arrived at inductively rather than by the Cowles method of seeking statistical verification for generalizations arrived at deductively. The Bureau's approach, which was very different philosophically as well as technically from that of the Cowles Commission, led Koopmans, writing under the provocative title 'Measurement without theory' (1947), to argue that Burns and Mitchell cannot know what variables to study and, further, that in the absence of theory, relevant policy conclusions cannot be drawn.[22]

Without defending the particular methodological procedure of the National Bureau, Rutledge Vining in 1949 suggested that the methodological controversy between the two sides related less to the 'existence or absence of a hypothetical framework than the nature of the entity the behavior of which is to be accounted for.'[23] Implicitly, Koopmans' argument was predicated on the formal economic theory of aggregating a dual maximizing decision, which Vining (and other institutionalists) rejected. Vining regarded the Cowles Commission's 'Walrasian conception . . . [as] . . . a pretty skinny fellow of untested capacity on which to load the burden of a general theory accounting for the events in space and time.' Economic research, in Vining's view, is still at the 'Kepler stage' of seeking hypotheses and is not yet ready for the 'Newton stage' of testing and the applications that follow from the methodology Koopmans proposed.[24]

The second area of controversy in which the Cowles Commission found itself involved was the Chicago School's philosophical opposition to the premise that prediction of human behavior and events is possible; Knight, in particular, was opposed to empiricism in the social sciences, economics included, at least partly because of his fear that it might serve as the basis for policy. It is perhaps relevant to recall that Adam Smith rejected Petty's *Political Arithmetick* on essentially the same grounds. Theodore Shultz (department chair from 1946 to 1961), Milton Friedman, and Fredrich Hayek, all Nobel Prize winners, were also among Chicagoans critical of the Cowles approach.[25] The outcome of the rift was that the Cowles Commission relocated from the University of Chicago to Yale University in 1953. While its research methodology was seriously questioned by economics department colleagues at Chicago, its reception elsewhere was positive to a degree that its general equilibrium–probability methodology became *the* accepted method for doing macroeconometric research. That is, the profession largely came to accept the view that theoretical models require empirical support that is derived from a properly specified stochastic model from which a set of values can be identified. Clearly, both the availability of computers and the necessity for solving large numbers of equations largely account for the emergence of econometrics as the sister discipline of economics.

Concluding comments

Empirical work relating to the consumption function, the multiplier, the investment demand function, and the liquidity preference function is obviously of Keynesian inspiration. In spite of Keynes's reservations about Tinbergen's work and, more generally, about the relevance of probability theory for interpreting economic reality, shortly before World War II Keynes became associated with the 'Cambridge Research Scheme' of the National Institute of Social and Economic Research. He also accepted the invitation of Alfred Cowles to become the first president of the Econometric Association. Thus, the inference may be made that Keynes did not reject *per se* all econometric work.[26]

Keynes's *General Theory* itself gave substantial impetus to multi-equation macro models – of the sort pioneered by the Cowles Commission – for prediction purposes and to serve as a basis for policy formulation. There are now many simultaneous-equation models that have undertaken to represent the economy as a whole. The relatively small 1955 Klein–Goldberger model of the United States, which contained 15 stochastic and 15 non-stochastic equations with 20 endogenous and 18 exogenous variables, has been replaced by the Wharton group of models, whose original version consisted of 118 variables. The Data Resources Inc. (DRI) model of the United States had 718 endogenous and 170 exogenous variables in its original version.[27] These models have chiefly been used for short-term forecasts that relate to the likely state of the economy in the next year or so. They have also been used for simulations that undertake to evaluate the likely effects of different policy scenarios.

The macroeconometric modeling that derived from Keynes's *General Theory* substantially coincided with the theoretical developments that are the subject matter of Chapter 23 which follows. They were, however, greatly enhanced and perhaps even redirected by the advent of the computer revolution that extended from the late 1930s to 1960, the period that overlapped World War II and the so-called 'Cold War' that followed. This was a period during which the government and that part of the American industrial complex that was concerned with the production and development of military hardware were confronted with the political agenda of 'winning the war' and, afterward, 'winning the peace.' Accordingly, there was a massive inflow of financial support from governmental sources to the military and government contractors to develop tools for strategic decision making. While the private sector did not regard the prospects of producing and marketing computers as promising profits, military problems required new computational equipment and new techniques for defining and solving problems relating to ballistics, defense systems, flight training,

code breaking, and rocket launches. Clearly, the perceived needs of the military–industrial complex were the driving force in the problem selection and resource allocation to develop computational equipments and techniques for their effective use.[28] This perspective is clearly encapsulated in the following brief quote taken from a recent historical account of computing in the twentieth century.

in historical honesty we have to realize that it was dedication to the struggle against Hitlerism, and later to other problems of national defense, that provided the main driving force behind the development of the computer in the 1940s. It is absolutely impossible to understand it except in that context.[29]

This driving force required astronomical funding to harness the talent of physicists, engineers, mathematicians and economists working at a variety of 'think tanks,' among them the Rand Corporation, the Cowles Foundation, the Hudson Institute and the Radio Corporation of America, several of which interfaced with such leading universities as the University of Pennsylvania, Massachusetts Institute of Technology, Princeton University, California Institute of Technology and the University of Illinois. Academicians thus participated in the exploration of potential business applications for electronic equipment and software that 'ranged from planning crop rotation to planning large scale military actions, from the routing of ships between harbors to the assessment of the flow of commodities between industries of the economy.'[30] As these applications became case studies, linear programming became incorporated into the core of graduate economics education because it offers an approach to studying optimizing behavior that is considerably more sophisticated than that reachable with differential calculus.[31]

Notes

1 See Chapter 17.

2 See M. Hashem Peseran on econometrics in *The New Palgrave Dictionary*, vol. 2, p. 8.

3 Paul Samuelson, Tjallings Koopmans, and Richard Stone, 'Report of the Evaluation Committee for Econometrics,' *Econometrica*, 22 (1954), pp. 141–46.

4 Terence Gorman, 'Towards a better economic methodology' in Peter Wiles and Guy Rauth (eds), *Economics in Disarray* (Oxford: Basil Blackwell, 1984), p. 261.

5 Marshall wrote: ''In my view every economic fact, whether or not it is of such a nature as to be expressed in numbers, stands in relation as cause and effect to many other facts: and since it never happens that all of them can be expressed in numbers, the application of exact mathematical methods to those which can is nearly always a waste of time, while in the large majority of cases it is positively misleading; and the world would have been further on its way forward if the work had never been done at all.' See letter to Bowley, dated 3 March, 1901 in A. C. Pigou, (ed.), Memorials of Alfred Marshall (London: Macmillan, 1925), p. 422.

6 J. M. Keynes, 'Statistical testing of business cycle theories,' *Economic Journal*, 49, (1939), pp. 558–68.

7 Ragnar Frisch 'On the notion of equilibrium and disequilibrium,' *Review of Economic Studies*, 3(2) pp. 100–105.

8 Ragnar Frisch, 'Propagation problems and impulse problems in dynamic economics' in *Essays in Honor of Gustav Cassel*, pp. 171–205. (London: Allen and Unwin, 1933).

9 Jan Tinbergen, 'Econometric business cycle research,'' *The Review of Economic Studies*, 7 (1940), pp. 73–90.

10 J. M. Keynes, *Collected Works*, vol. 8, edited by Elizabeth Johnson, Donald Moggridge and Sir Austin Robinson for the Royal Economic Society (Macmillan, Cambridge University Press), p. 94.

11 This topic is examined further by Ingrid H. Rima in ''Keynes's vision and economic analysis' and by Robin Rowley in 'The Keynes–Tinbergen exchange in retrospect,' both included in O. F Hamouda and J. H. Smithin (eds), *Keynes and Public Policy after Fifty Years*, vol. 2 (Hertfordshire, UK: Edward Elgar, 1988).

12 Oskar Morgenstern, 'Collaborating with von Neumann,' *Journal of Economic Literature*, 14, pp. 805–16.

13 On this point see Melvin Reder, 'Chicago economics: performance and change,' *Journal of Economic Literature*, 20, pp. 1–38.

14 J. A. Schumpeter, *A History of Economic Analysis* (New York: Oxford University Press, 1938) p. 908.

15 T. Haavelmo, 'The probability approach in econometrics,' *Econometrica*, Supplement (1944), p. 8.

16 T. Haavelmo, 'The probability approach in econometrics,' *Econometrica*, Supplement (1944), pp. 910–14.

17 L. Szilard, 'Reminiscences,' in O. Flemming and B. Barlyn (eds), *The Intellectual Migration* (Cambridge, Mass.: Harvard University Press 1969), pp. 94–145.

18 Carl Christ, 'History of the Cowles Commission, 1932–1952,' in *Economic Theory and Measurement* (Chicago: Cowles Commission, 1952), pp. 3–67.

19 C. Hildreth, *The Cowles Commission in Chicago, 1939–1955* (Vienna: Springer-Verlag, 1986), p. 74.

20 Christ, 'History of the Cowles Commission,' pp. 30–31.

21 The specific problem encountered in the construction of early macroeconomic models is put into historical perspective by Laurence Klein in 'Developments and prospects in macroeconomic modeling,' *Eastern Economic Journal*, 16 (October–December, 1989).

22 T. Koopmans, 'Measurement without theory,' *Review of Economic Studies*, 29 (1947), pp. 161–72.

23 R. Vining, 'Koopmans on the choice of variables to be studied and of methods of measurement,' *Review of Economic Studies*, 31 (1949), pp. 77–86.

24 Reply by Koopmans *Review of Economic Studies*, 31 (1949), pp. 86–91; Reply by Vining, *Review of Economic Studies*, 31 (1949), 91–94.

25 *Review of Economic Studies*, 31 (1949).

26 Ronald Bodkin, Laurence Klein, and Kanta Marwah, 'Keynes and the origins of macro-

economic modeling,' in O. F. Hamouda and J. Smithin (eds), *Keynes and Public Policy*, p. 3–11.

27 These developments are neatly encapsulated by Laurence R. Klein in 'Developments and prospects in macroeconomic modeling,' in *Eastern Economic Journal*, 15(4) (October–December, 1989), pp. 287–304.

28 This section is indebted to Robin Rowley's unpublished paper (1998) 'Normative microeconomics and the creation of a revised North American taxation: the transformation of management science 1935–1960.'

29 G. Birkhoff (1980) 'Computing Developments 1935–1955 as seen from Cambridge, USA,' in Metropolis *et al.* (eds), *A History of Computing in the Twentieth Century* (New York: Academic Press, 1980), pp. 21–30.

30 Dantzig, G. B. *Linear Programming and Extensions* (Princeton, NJ: Princeton University Press, 1963).

31 Dorfman, Samuelson and Solow, *Linear Programming and Economic Analysis* (New York: McGraw-Hill, 1958) p. vii.

Questions for discussion and further research

1 What was the basis for Keynes's criticism of Tinbergen's empirical studies of the business cycle?

2 The Cowles Commission and the National Bureau of Economic Research are leaders in empirical research. However they reflect very different approaches toward empiricism. In what way are they different? What are some of their most important studies and why is there ongoing controversy about their methods?

3 How did the game theory approach of von Neumann and Morgenstern contribute to the probabilistic methodology of the Cowles Commission?

Glossary of terms and concepts

Activity analysis (linear programming)

A technique for choosing among alternative production processes (activities), in order to identify an optimal product mix, given the constraint of available resources.

Econometrics

The application of mathematical and statistical methods to the analysis of economic data.

Game theory

The interactive behavior of decision makers (players) whose decisions affect one another. The major applications of game theory are to economic decisions but the technique applies equally to non-human players (i.e. strategies, military decisions, interfirm competition for markets).

Probability theory

A tool for deciding what to do when confronted with the need to predict the relative frequency with which possible outcomes will occur.

Notes for further reading

From *The New Palgrave*

M. Hashem Pesaran on econometrics, vol. 2, pp. 8–22; H. M. Polemarchakis on decision theory, vol. 1, pp. 755–56; R. J. Aumam on game theory, vol. 2, pp. 460–79; George B. Danzig on Linear Programming, vol. 3, pp. 203–6. Martin Shubik on Oskar Morgenstern, vol. 3, pp. 556–57; Gerald R. Thompson on John von Neumann, vol. 4, pp. 818–22.

Selected references and suggestions for further reading

Burns, A. E. and Mitchell, W. C. *Measuring Business Cycles* (New York: Columbia University Press for the National Bureau of Economic Research, 1947).

Bodkin, R. G., Klein, L. R. and Marwah, K. 'Keynes and the origins of macroeconomic modeling.' In *Keynes and Public Policy After 50 Years*, edited by Omar F. Hamouda and John Smithin (Hertfordshire, UK: Edward Elgar, 1988).

Christ, Carl. 'History of the Cowles Commission, 1932–1952.' In *Economic Theory and Measurement* (Chicago: Cowles Commission, 1952), pp. 3–67.

Haavelmo, T. 'The probability approach in econometrics.' *Econometrica*, supplement, 12 (1944), pp. 1–118.

Hildreth, C. *The Cowles Commission in Chicago, 1939–1955* (Vienna: Springer-Verlag, 1986).

Keynes, J. M. *A Treatise on Probability* (London: Macmillan, 1921).

Keynes, J. M. 'The statistical testing of business cycle theories.' *Economic Journal*, 49 (1939), pp. 558–68.

Klein, L. R. *Economic Fluctuations in the United States, 1921–1941*. Cowles Commission Monograph No. 11 (New York: John Wiley, 1950).

Marshak, Jacob. 'Economic measurements for policy and prediction.' In *Studies in Econometric Method*, edited by W. C. Hood and T. C. Koopmans (Cowles Commission for Research in Economics, 1953).

Morgenstern, Oskar. 'Collaborating with von Neumann.' *Journal of Economic Literature*, 14, pp. 805–16 (Monograph No. 14, New York: John Wiley).

Rima, I. H. 'Keynes's vision and economic analysis.' In *Keynes and Public Policy After 50 Years*, vol. 2, edited by Omar F. Hamouda and John H. Smithin (Hertfordshire, UK: Edward Elgar, 1988).

Rowley, J. C. R. 'The Keynes–Tinbergen exchange in retrospect.' In *Keynes and Public Policy After 50 Years*, vol. 2, edited by Omar F. Hamouda and J. H. Smithin (Hertfordshire, UK: Edward Elgar, 1988).

Tinbergen, Jan. 'Econometric business cycle research.' *The Review of Economic Studies*, 7 (1940), pp. 73–90.

Chapter 23

Keynesians, neo-Walrasians, and monetarists

• •

The 'economics of Keynes,' as distinct from 'Keynesian economics,' has passed into history.[1] The *Treatise on Money* and *The General Theory* have become classics and share the common fate of being known largely through secondary sources. The 50 years that have elapsed since publication of *The General Theory* have witnessed a phenomenal amount of empirical and theoretical work built on Keynesian foundations. The main thrust of the empirical work has been to try to verify Keynes's theoretical constructs.[2] The most important of these early empirical findings concerned the consumption function.[3]

Important work has also estimated the numerical value of the multiplier and the responsiveness of investment demand to interest rates. Empirical research also attempted to establish the demand for money to test Keynes's concept of liquidity preference and its related liquidity trap hypothesis. More recently, macroeconomic models of the economy as a whole have been developed, the best known among them being the St. Louis Model of the Federal Reserve Bank of St. Louis and the larger Wharton Model of the University of Pennsylvania's Wharton School under the direction of Lawrence Klein.

While these efforts at empirical research have yielded important results, our interests here are more specifically focused on the developments in theoretical economics that came after *The General Theory*. Several are of particular interest because they reflect a counter-revolution against Keynes's economics. The 'Keynesian cross' and the ISLM (investment, savings, liquidity-preference, money) apparatus, which have become mainstays of contemporary macroeconomics even at the textbook level, are products of the counter-revolution. In conjunction with the 'real-balance effect,' the ISLM apparatus has been used to demonstrate the possibility of a general equilibrium among commodity, money, and labor markets. A major concern of this chapter is to explain these developments as reflecting a return to the neoclassical tradition Keynes rejected, despite the frequent observation that 'we are all Keynesians now.'

A second concern of this chapter is to examine the body of doctrine and policy prescriptions that have come to be known as Monetarism. The third is to examine the hypothesis that there is a trade-off between inflation and unemployment that is associated with an apparatus known as the Phillips curve. The Phillips curve trade-off has been interpreted to represent the policy choice that, according to some economists, must inevitably be made between lower rates of unemployment and low inflationary pressure. The ideal of low rates of unemployment and low rates of inflation is an unattainable combination, when viewed from this perspective.

Keynesian economics

Keynesian economics, as distinct from the economics of Keynes, began its development scarcely a year after the publication of *The General Theory*. In 1937, J. R. Hicks, of the London School of Economics, undertook a neoclassical reinterpretation of Keynes's message in his article 'Mr. Keynes and the classics, a suggested reinterpretation.'[4] Its impact was delayed temporarily by a general equilibrium interpretation of Keynes's system that MIT's Paul Samuelson has dubbed the 'Keynesian cross.' Its textbook popularity was enhanced by its use of a geometric representation (as in Part A of Figure 23.1). This Keynesian cross shows real expenditures on the vertical axis and output on the horizontal. The aggregate-supply curve is expressed as a 45° line. This line represents the $C + I = Y$ output combinations compatible with the condition $C = Y$, $S = 0$.[5]

Aggregate demand, which is represented by $C + I$, represents (real) expenditures on consumption and investment. It will be recalled from Chapter 21 that is vertical intercept is positive because consumption expenditures

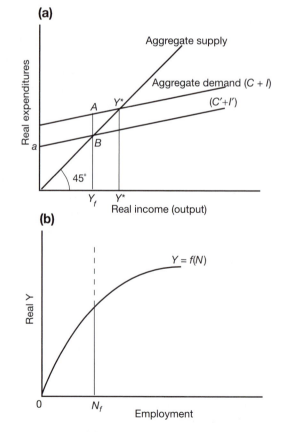

Figure 23.1 (a) The Keynesian cross; (b) The production function

exceed disposable income when income is at levels below $C = Y$. The intersection of aggregate demand with the aggregate-supply curve determines the equilibrium level of output. Part B of Figure 23.1 displays the production function $Y = f(N)$ relating output to employment. If, as in Figure 23.1 (A), the equilibrium level of real income established by aggregate demand and supply is Y^*, which exceeds the income needed to support full employment of labor resources at N_f (as in Part B of Figure 23.1), there will be an *inflationary* gap equivalent to AB. This excess of purchasing power has been interpreted as providing a reason for higher tax collections and/or reduced government expenditures to lower aggregate demand so that it is represented by the broken line $C' + I'$. This intersects with aggregate supply at B and generates income Y_f, which is consistent with full employment N_f.

Conversely, if $C + I$ were to intersect aggregate demand so that equilibrium output is less than the full employment income Y_f, a *deflationary* gap would exist. This problem might be amenable to expansionary fiscal policy instruments, such as reduced tax collections and greater government expenditures, which would generate a multiplier and perhaps even an acceleration effect.'[6]

The Hicks–Hansen ISLM apparatus

Despite the attractive simplicity of the Keynesian cross model, it was eventually displaced by a new apparatus made up of two composite curves, *IS* and *LM*. The logic of the *ISLM* apparatus will be easily seen in relation to Keynes's views of the neoclassical theory of the interest rate. As noted in Chapter 20, Keynes maintained that neoclassical theory did not provide a determinate solution of the interest rate because the saving-supply schedule, which together with the investment-

demand schedule are supposed to determine the interest rate, is itself dependent on the income level.[7] Yet the income level is not known until the volume of investment is known, and the latter itself depends on the interest rate. In other words, the interest rate is *indeterminate* in the neoclassical framework because the savings-supply schedule and the investment-demand schedule are *interdependent*.

Hicks countered that Keynes's criticism of indeterminacy is equally applicable to his own theory of the interest rate. The liquidity–preference schedule and the supply schedule of money also do not yield a determinate rate of interest because there is a different liquidity–preference schedule for every level of income. Even though the schedule of liquidity preference for speculative purposes is independent of the level of income, it is necessary to know the income level in order to know what the transactions and precautionary demands for money will be. Thus, the criticism of indeterminancy of interest rate determination that Keynes leveled against the neoclassical theory was held by Hicks to be equally applicable to his own.

Hicks's suggested reinterpretation demonstrated that, by joining Keynes's theory and the neoclassical theory, it is possible to establish a determinate solution because together they include all of the variables of the interest rate problem.[8] These variables are (1) the savings function, (2) the investment–demand function, (3) the liquidity–preference function, and (4) the quantity of money. They can be combined to construct two new curves, the *IS* curve and *LM* curve.

The *IS* curve is derived from the relationship between the investment–demand curve and a family of curves showing savings as a function of *both* income and the interest rate. Figure 23.2 shows a different savings schedule

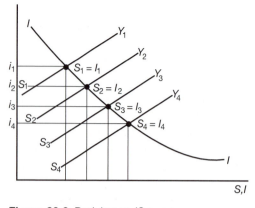

Figure 23.2 Deriving an *IS* curve

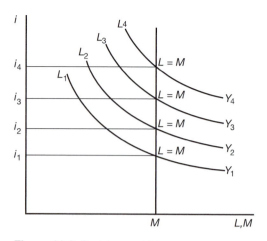

Figure 23.3 Deriving an *LM* curve

for every possible combination of interest rate and income levels. Thus, when income is Y_1, the savings schedule is $S_1 Y_1$ and, given the investment demand curve, savings will equal investment at interest rate i_1. Similarly, when income is Y_2, savings will equal investment at i_2. The locus of all the points at which savings and investment are equal yields what Hansen and Hicks have called the *IS* schedule. The *IS* function expresses interest as a function of three variables: savings, investment, and the income level. It is the *IS* function that, together with a curve that has become known as the *LM* function, determines the rate of interest, as shown in Figure 23.3.

The *LM* curve is derived from the relationship between a family of liquidity–preference curves and the schedule of the money supply. There is a different liquidity–preference schedule at every income level. These curves, together with *M*, the money supply made available by the monetary authority, show the various combinations of income levels and interest rates consistent with the willingness of the public to hold the money supply in its balances. The upward slope and increasing inelasticity of the *LM* curve show that, with a given quantity of money (say *M*, as in Figure 23.3), a greater preference for liquidity will

result in a higher interest rate rather than additional hoarding. It should also be observed that higher income levels are associated with higher interest rates because the transactions and precautionary demands for money increase at higher income levels so that, given the money stock, there is less left to satisfy the speculative motive. This puts an upward pressure on the interest rate and accounts for the increasing inelasticity of the *LM* curve.

Figure 23.4 shows the *IS* curve, derived from Figure 23.2, and the *LM* curve, derived from Figure 23.3, on the same graph. The interest rate may then be thought of as determined by the intersection of *LM* and *IS* curves, which bring together the four variables of the problem. The intersection of the two curves was interpreted by Hicks as representing a stable monetary equilibrium in the sense that (a) *realized* savings and investment are equal to *planned* savings and investment and (b) the amount of money people wish to hold is equal to the actual money stock. If this representation is indeed relevant to the real world, as Hicks and Hansen maintained it is, the implication is that markets *do* tend to come to equilibria consistent with market clearing.

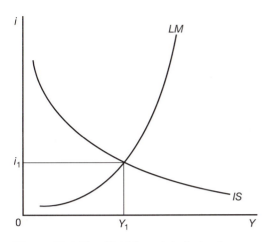

Figure 23.4 The *IS-LM* model of simultaneous determination of the interest rate and income level

The real-balance effect and general equilibrium

Keynes rejected the notion of the simultaneous clearing of markets on the grounds that there is no mechanism for achieving a general equilibrium among the commodity, labor, and financial markets, and that labor markets have special difficulties that often result in involuntary unemployment. The rebuttal to his view represents an anti-Keynes counter-revolution that proceeded under the leadership of Cambridge's A. C. Pigou, J. R. Hicks, then of the London School of Economics, and University of Chicago-trained Don Patinkin. Their complete model conceives of the economy as consisting of four aggregate markets that tend, in a way reminiscent of Walras's general equilibrium model, to achieve a simultaneous clearing. They argued that Keynes did not adequately recognize the impact and significance of price changes on the real value of money balances and wealth as a mechanism for restoring equilibrium.[9] The *real-balance effect* reflects the effect of the real value of money balances (i.e.

of M/P, where M represents stock of money and P is the price level) on expenditures for consumption and investment. Patinkin argued that, *in principle*, flexible prices and wage rates can restore commodity, bond, and labor markets to equilibria consistent with full employment.

The relationships Patinkin believes exist may be illustrated in terms of the diagrams in Figure 23.5. In Part A, aggregate demand is represented by the IS_1 curve (which is equivalent to $C + I$ in Figure 23.1). Given M, the stock of money, LM represents the demand for cash balances at different interest rates and income levels. LM and IS_1 establish that the commodity market is willing to absorb Y_f, that firms desire to produce at the real wage rate W/P. As shown in Figure 23.5(B), W/P is consistent with employment for ON_f workers, when $N_s = f(W/P)$ and $N_d = f(W/P, \bar{K})$ are the supply and demand curves for labor at various real-wage rates, and $\bar{K}$, the stock of capital, is constant.

What is the nature of the forces that operate if aggregate demand falls to IS_2? Recall Keynes's argument that a deficiency of aggregate demand results in involuntary unemployment that is not automatically corrected even if the wage-price structure is flexible downward. Thus, he would not expect the aggregate demand-curve to be restored to the IS_1 level. Patinkin, however, argues that Keynes's view 'overlooks the direct influence of the real balance effect on aggregate demand. Similarly it overlooks the supply side of the commodity market which, by its excess demand, generates this effect.'[10] Patinkin reasoned that a decrease in commodity-demand will create an excess supply of commodities, in the sense that supply exceeds what the market is willing to absorb at a given price. As commodity prices are bid down there is a repercussion in the labor market

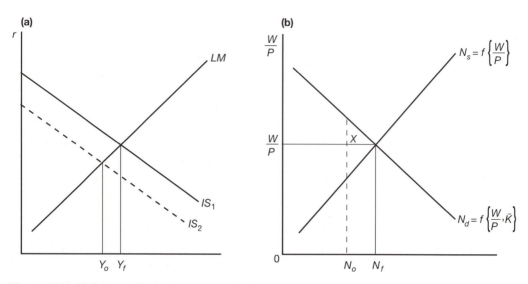

Figure 23.5 (a) Commodity and money markets. (b) The labor market

because it raises real wage levels. This causes a reduction in the demand for labor, say, to ON_o). Patinkin thus describes employment ON_o, which is represented by point x in Figure 23.5(B), as reflecting the 'involuntary departure of firms from their labor demand curves.'[11] He sees it as the counterpart, from the employers' point of view, of involuntary unemployment from labor's point of view.

However Patinkin's analysis suggests that the economy will not languish indefinitely in a disequilibrium state. The decrease in commodity demand results in a price fall that sets a dynamic process into motion. This process will first increase the value of net liquid assets, which stimulates consumption expenditures in the same way as an increase in income.[12] The rise in consumption expenditures, Patinkin argues, acts to restore the IS curve back to IS_1 from IS_2. The commodity market is then again willing to purchase the full employment output Y_f.

Concurrently, the demand for labor is pulled up to a level appropriate to the unchanged real-wage rate. When firms are again able to sell the full employment level of output, Y_f, they will be able to return to their labor-demand curves and hire ON_f workers as before. This equilibrium position differs from the original only in having lower nominal levels (i.e. in money terms) of wages, prices, and interest rates. Patinkin contends that even if wages and prices do not initially fall in the same proportion, this does not change the equilibrating process although there may be a 'prolongation of the dynamic process into which the economy is thrown by an initial decrease in demand.'[13]

In what way does this analysis narrow the analytical distance which Keynes tried to identify between himself and the classics? Patinkin agrees with Keynes that the source of involuntary unemployment or its persistence is not to be found in worker unwillingness to accept money-wage cuts. His reasoning reinforces Keynes's contention that involuntary unemployment is the result of inadequate aggregate demand in the commodity market and need not, as the classicists contended, have its origin in wage rigidities.

Patinkin identifies the 'offending rigidities' as 'the rigidities of sovereign consumers and investors unwilling to modify their expenditure habits on short notice.'[14] Thus, the wealth effect may not be immediately operative in the equilibrating process. Patinkin's essential conclusion, therefore, is that involuntary unemployment is a phenomenon of economic dynamics: 'granted full flexibility of prices, it is still highly possible that a deflationary process will not work, due to the dynamic factors involved.'[15] As interpreted by Patinkin, 'the Keynesian position [as distinct from that of Keynes] . . . states that even with uncertainty full employment would eventually be generated by a policy of price flexibility; but the length of time that might be necessary for the adjustment makes the policy impractical.'[16] Nevertheless, Patinkin's analysis, as well as that of J. R. Hicks, adapted the logic of Walras's general equilibrium model, which they grafted onto a neoclassical demand and supply analysis. Thus, these economists were led back to the pre-Keynes conclusion that the labor and money markets of the economy have essentially the same *equilibrating tendencies* that Alfred Marshall taught us to expect in commodity markets.

Keynesianism and the Phillips curve

One of the limitations of the *ISLM* apparatus is that it does not link real output (or GDP) and employment to the monetary magnitudes of price and wage levels. The necessity for establishing this link became evident as the difficulties of achieving the dual goals of full-employment and price level stability without wage and price controls became apparent.[17] It is in this connection that Keynesian economists pressed into service the results of a 1958 study by A. W. Phillips that employed British data to relate the rate of wage increases to the percentage of unemployment of the civilian labor force.

The convex, downward-sloping curve plotted by Phillips for Great Britain, for the period 1861 to 1913, is reproduced in Figure 23.6 from the original study.[18] This study shows a fairly close relationship between the percentage change in wage rates and the percentage of the unemployed civilian labor force studied, for each of three periods, 1861 to 1913, 1913 to 1948, and 1948 to 1957. Omitting the years largely associated with wars, during which import prices rose rapidly enough to generate a wage–price spiral, and assuming a productivity increase of 2 percent per year, Phillips's conclusion for the United Kingdom was that the money–wage level could become stabilized with a 5.5 percent rate of unemployment. An alternative interpretation is that the rate of increase of money wages could be held down to the 2 to 3 percent consistent with the historical increase in productivity rates with about 2.5 percent of the labor force unemployed.

It is important to note that the relationships between money–wage rate changes and unemployment exhibited by the Phillips curve do not, in and of themselves, support any hypothesis about the cause of inflation. The Phillips curve tells us only that the tighter the labor market, the greater the upward pressure on wage rates.

However, the correlation between wage changes $\Delta w/w$ and U, the rate of unemployment, has been interpreted as providing a basis for *inferences* about increases in the general price level by linking them to changes in money wage rates.[19] That is, money–wage rate changes have been taken as a proxy for price-level changes on the premise that market prices reflect a fairly stable mark-up over wage costs.

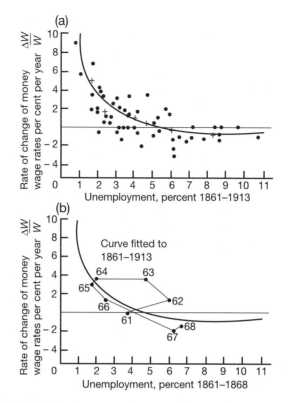

Figure 23.6 Rate of change of money wage rates, percent per year

Source: A. W Phillips, 'The relation between unemployment and the rate of change in money wage rates in the United Kingdom, 1862–1957,' *Economica*, 25 (1958), p. 285.

A convenient way of representing this relationship is in terms of a mark-up price equation that has been found useful in econometric research:

$$P = kw/A,$$

in which P is the price level, k is the average price mark-up over unit labor costs, w is average wages and salaries in money terms, and A is the average productivity of labor. The price mark-up equation implies that wage increases that exceed productivity increases tend to become associated with inflationary price increases and higher unemployment.[20] If the relationship between average prices and the mark-up on unit labor costs is reliable, then,

according to the Phillips curve, the tighter the labor market at given productivity levels, the greater the upward pressure on wage rates and prices. Conversely, lower rates of inflation tend to accompany higher rates of unemployment. The trade-off between rates of unemployment and rates of inflation is reflected in the convex shape of the Phillips curve.

The Phillips curve relationship is the basis for the belief, which has persisted up to the recent past, that policy makers can choose among alternative combinations of rates of unemployment and rates of inflation. Thus, it was thought possible to reduce the rate of inflation, but then higher rates of unemployment will have to be tolerated, even in a generally prosperous economy. However, the notion that there is a trade-off between inflation and unemployment was shaken by the puzzle of the simultaneous increases in unemployment and rates of inflation that existed during the 1970s and early 1980s. This puzzle eventually led a group of thinkers, who have become known as *New Classicals*, to the notion that the Phillips curve might be *vertical* at a rate of unemployment which they thought of as *natural*. Their rational expectations hypothesis is the basis for their argument that there is a level of unemployment that is *natural* in the sense that it tends to *persist* in spite of monetary or fiscal policies to reduce unemployment to a lower level.

The New Classical Economics: rational expectations

The thinking that underlies the concept of a vertical Phillips curve is attributable chiefly to Milton Friedman who provided the essential foundation for what is today identified as the *New Classical Economics*. Its starting point, as it relates to the behavior of the labor market, is that workers (and employers) respond to *expected* (rather than current) *real wages*. The premise is that workers have 'rational expectations' about what wage and price levels are likely to be. While individual workers are likely to err in their expectations about rising or falling future price levels, these errors are likely to cancel out; it can thus be assumed that workers in the aggregate are able to anticipate inflation or deflation. Within this framework of inquiry, the phenomenon of unemployment (i.e. joblessness among persons who want to work at prevailing real wage levels) is attributable to the failure of the unemployed to forecast the rate of inflation correctly, which leads them to refuse jobs they would normally accept.

The scenario is the following: assume that, in response to a level of unemployment that is considered excessive, monetary and/or fiscal policy (e.g. interest rate and/or tax reductions) are used to encourage employers to increase their demand for workers. Without a sufficient number of unemployed workers with suitable job skills, employers will have to offer higher nominal (or money) wages. New Classical theory argues that workers will interpret higher wage offers as representing higher *real* wages, not having a reason to anticipate a rise in commodity prices over the period of their wage contracts. Yet, employers will pass the costs of rising wages along to consumers as higher commodity prices so that, in fact, workers are not receiving higher *real wages*. Nor will they be 'fooled' into thinking they are better off.

For some, the work–leisure trade-off is reassessed in favor of leisure. The unemployment level thus tends to return to the 'natural rate' as workers voluntarily choose leisure. However, the price level remains at the level that stimulative policy brought into being. The short-run trade-off between unemployment rates and inflation rates that is reflected in the convex Phillips curve is thus not the long-run experience.

Economists who accept the notion that advanced economies such as the United States are inherently prone to some *natural rate of unemployment*, represent the long-run experience by a *vertical Phillips curve*, such as is represented in Figure 23.7, on which inflation rates (i.e. price levels) are represented on the vertical axis, and the rate of unemployment on the horizontal. Let us assume that the prevailing 'trade-off' between inflation and unemployment is represented by Phillips curve SPC_1, and that the amount of unemployment coincides with U_n, which is the 'natural rate' in the sense that any attempt

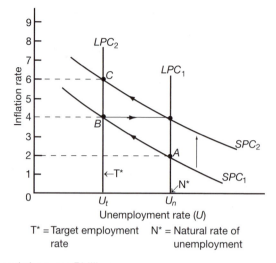

Figure 23.7 Long-run and short-run Phillips curves

to reduce the unemployment rate (say by means of monetary or fiscal policy) will tend to be 'offset' by workers themselves as soon as they realize that the higher money wages they earn when unemployment is reduced are offset by rising prices (i.e. higher rates of inflation). Thus in Figure 23.7 workers are initially at point A, the original price level–unemployment combination. Policy to reduce the unemployment rate provides funding to increase the demand for labor and therefore worker wages. Thus, workers move along the Phillips curve from point A to point B, at which the unemployment rate has been reduced to U_t. But they soon realize that their higher wages have been followed by higher commodity prices: 2 percent inflation has risen to 4 percent. Since real wages are now no higher than previously (only nominal wages have risen), workers now alter the work–leisure 'trade-off' that they make. This is represented on Figure 23.7 by their movement to point C on the higher short-run Phillips curve SPC_2, which passes through the long-run Phillips curve, LPC_2, that is consistent with the natural rate of unemployment U_n.

Proponents of the natural rate hypothesis believe that the Phillips curve is resistant to policy measures to reduce the unemployment rate, except in the short run. Such measures are viewed as self-defeating, because they are anticipated by workers and by the public generally, which acts to circumvent policy outcomes. The view that the Phillips curve is vertical in the long-run pertains to thinkers who favor *laissez-faire* free market outcomes.

Monetarism

Reaffirmation of the importance of money

The Keynesian cross model and the *ISLM* model are both presented in *real* terms; i.e. they do not include an explicit price level. This characteristic made them suspect as analytical tools for analyzing the phenomenon of inflation. This lack gave impetus to a modern version of the quantity theory as an alternative analytical and policy tool. The essence of monetarist views, which can be dated back to David Hume, is that changes in the price level are attributable to changes in the quantity of money. Following Irving Fisher, modern theorists discounted the likelihood of autonomous changes in *v*, the velocity of circulation, except during transition periods, because of the unchanging nature of spending habits and the institutional factors governing them.

The concern of modern economists with the role of money and the potential of monetary policy to achieve employment and price level goals has changed over time. It was accorded little interest during the 1930s and 1940s. Thus, the publication of Milton Friedman's *Studies in the Quantity Theory of Money* in 1956 reflects a reassessment that has been in progress in more recent decades about the role of money and the place of monetary policy.[21] The essence of its message, and of the research it stimulated, is that 'money matters.' Unlike the Keynesians, whose ISLM apparatus reduces money to a *numéraire* (common denominator) in a general equilibrium-model, the monetarists, led by Milton Friedman, focused on the importance of specifically analyzing the demand for money and formulating a 'positive theory' for the guidance of policy.[22]

The modern quantity theory

The fundamental question that the theory of the demand for money seeks to answer is: why do people hold money that is not an income-earning asset, rather than productive goods or interest-bearing securities? In Friedman's view, the demand for money by the wealth-owners of society can be examined within the framework of the theory of consumer choice.[23] Thus, the demand for money depends on (a) the total wealth to be held in various forms (which is analogous to the budget constraint); (b) the price of, and the return on, this (and alternative) forms of wealth; and (c) the tastes and preferences of wealth-owning units.

Total wealth includes all sources of what Friedman terms *permanent* income.[24] It includes (a) money identified as *claims* that are acceptable for making payments at a fixed nominal value, (b) bonds, (c) equities, (d) physical goods, and (e) human capital. Wealth owners are conceived to convert one form of wealth into another in order to maximize utility.

There is utility in holding part of one's wealth in the form of money; thus, the holder of money alters his money holdings 'until the value to him of the addition to the total flow of services produced by adding a dollar to his money stock is equal to the reduction in the flow of services produced by subtracting a dollar from each of the other forms in which he holds assets.'[25] As in all demand analyses predicated on maximizing a utility function, the demand for money is independent of the nominal unit used to measure money variables. Thus, the demand for money is a demand for *real* balances as a function of *real* variables.

Quantity theorists maintain that the demand for money (in real terms) is highly stable and are satisfied that there is empirical evidence to verify this hypothesis. Philip Cagan's study, in particular, identified the stability of the *real* demand for money with his finding that changes in the rate of change of prices affect the *nominal* quantity of money demanded.[26] The higher the rate of change of prices, the lower will be the nominal quantity of money held because it makes alternative forms of holding wealth more attractive. Friedman regards the stability of the money-demand function (in terms of real balances) to be one of the few constants that economists have been able to identify.

Friedman's permanent income hypothesis

Keynes thought it a reasonable proposition that, as a general rule, consumption will increase less than proportionally to an increase in income. There was much debate about this view after his work was published. Three sets of facts have been utilized by various investigators to test this proposition empirically. There are data on aggregate savings and income for the period 1869 to 1958 collected by the 1971 Nobel Prize winner in economics, the late Professor Simon Kuznets; budget studies for 1935–36 and 1941–42 by the National Resources Committee and the US Bureau of Labor Statistics; and, finally, Department of Commerce data showing decade by decade that, in the US, there has been a *long-run constant ratio* between consumption and income of about 88 percent. These data do not show any tendency for the proportion of income saved to rise with income.

Budget studies, however, suggest that the savings ratio *increases* with income. Department of Commerce data support the thesis that the ratio of savings to income varies over the trade cycle. Of course, such evidence does not necessarily mean that the *long-run relationship* between consumption and income may not be a proportional one. Friedman is among those advancing the hypothesis that the true long-run relationship between consumption and income is proportional.[27]

Friedman's view that consumption behavior depends on permanent income – that is, on the resources an individual expects to have over a lifetime – is closely related to his finding that the demand for real-money balances is stable. His theory seeks to extend Keynes's initial inquiry to consumption behavior.

His approach is to distinguish between the permanent and transitory components of income and consumption. Thus, income includes a permanent component, Y_p, and a transitory component, Y_t. Similarly, for consumption there is a permanent component, C_p, and a component that is transitory, C_t. Permanent income, in the Friedman sense, is determined by two factors: the wealth of the consumer unit expressed as the present value of a stream of expected future receipts, and the rate at which the receipts are discounted.

The ratio (k) between permanent income (Y_p) and permanent consumption (C_p) depends on the rate of interest (r), the ratio of non-human wealth to income (w), and a composite variable (u) whose value reflects the propensity to consume of consuming units that are different with respect to age and taste. The ratio k is, however, independent of permanent income, and Friedman asserts that transitory consumption (C_t) is unrelated to transitory income (Y_t). The measured consumption established from cross-section data as the sum of permanent and transitory consumption depends on permanent income rather than measured income. That is, consuming units are considered as determining their consumption on the basis of the returns from resources *they expect to receive* over a lifetime. Their expenditures are a constant proportion (k) of their permanent-income level. The various transitory factors, such as unexpected bills or income losses, that produce deviations between observed income and expenditures and their permanent levels are random factors. Symbolically:

$$Y = Y_p + Y_t$$
$$C = C_p + C_t$$
$$C_p = k Y_p$$
$$k = f(r, w, u)$$

While the difficulty of measuring permanent income and consumption makes the permanent-income hypothesis difficult to test, Friedman has established some empirical support for it. Using time-series aggregates, he has established that (1) after allowances are made for transitory components of consumption and income, the ratio k of permanent consumption to permanent income seems to have been constant since 1897, and (2) the income elasticity of consumption rises as the period of observation to which a consumption function is fitted increases, which suggests that transitory components become less important over a longer time period. Thus, the theory predicts a long-run consumption function in which consumer expenditures are a constant proportion of income. This relationship is the basis for the expectation that the demand for real-cash balances to facilitate consumption expenditures is going to be stable.

Arthur Smithies also supports the view that the long-run relationship between consumption and income is a proportional one. His explanation emphasizes the tendency toward upward drift of the consumption function. He has suggested several reasons why such an upward secular shift of the consumption function – that is, an increase in consumption relative to income and essentially independent of its growth – has taken place in the United States. One is that population has become increasingly urbanized. Since a rural population typically saves more and spends less than an urban one, the shift of population to cities is probably a factor that has contributed to the upward drift of the consumption function. The constant stream of new consumer goods that have become available, along with the emergence of various financial institutions catering to satisfying demands for consumer credit, is also a factor. So too is the change in the age composition of the population. With the increase in the size of the retired, a larger percentage of the population are

consumers without being current income earners.[28]

The perverse effect of monetary expansion on interest rates

In Friedman's view, the stability of the demand for cash balances, in real terms, underlies the perverse effects that monetarists believe changes in the quantity of money have on long-term interest rates. The growth of the money supply is expected to stimulate spending and raise income. This will tend to raise the liquidity–preference schedule and the demand for loans.[29] It may also raise prices, which will have the effect of reducing the *real* quantity of money. These effects, Friedman maintains, tend to *reverse* the initial downward pressure that money expansion has on interest rates and return them to their previous level. 'The *initial* impact of increasing the quantity of money at a faster rate is to make interest rates lower for a time than they would otherwise have been. But this is only the beginning of the process, not the end.'[30] Indeed, monetarists argue that a higher rate of monetary expansion will ultimately correspond to a *higher*, not lower, level of interest rates than would otherwise have prevailed, because it will generate the *expectation* of further increases in the price level. Since the demand for real balances is stable, the nominal demand for money increases, which increases, rather than decreases, the rate of interest. Thus, Friedman argues, in practice, interest rates cannot be pegged.[31]

Nor is it possible for the monetary authority to adopt a target for unemployment. Their belief is, generally, that at any moment there is a level of unemployment that is consistent with the structure of *real* wage rates. Real wage rates are tending, on average, to increase at a normal secular rate that is compatible with the rate of capital formation and technological improvements, and there is a natural rate of unemployment consistent with them. It is the relationship between real-wage and money-wage changes that explains why the trade-off postulated by the Phillips curve between money-wage changes and the unemployment rate is a short-run trade-off.[32] Thus, Friedman argues that the Phillips curve is vertical in the long run. The trade-off between inflation and unemployment is the temporary result of unanticipated (i.e. a rising rate of) inflation.

Friedman's recommendations for monetary policy

Friedman's recommendations for controlling the money supply are predicated on his identification of what monetary policy can and cannot accomplish. The monetary authority can control the *nominal* quantity of money (i.e. its own liabilities) and thereby control *nominal* magnitudes such as the price level, exchange rates, and the nominal level of national income. But it cannot use control over nominal quantities to peg real quantities such as the rate of unemployment, the real rate of interest, the real quantity of money, or the level of real national income.[33]

The chief objective of monetary policy should, in Friedman's view, be to prevent money itself from becoming a source of major disturbance. What is required is to provide a 'stable environment' within which consumers, producers, employees, and employers are reasonably assured that the average level of prices will behave in a known (preferably stable) way in the future.

This is a function which, in an earlier era, was performed by the gold standard. There are persuasive reasons for the demise of the gold standard but, according to Friedman, the monetary authority could operate as a surrogate for the gold standard. To this end he recommends that the monetary authority adopt a policy of increasing the money supply (however defined) at some specified and unchanging rate. If the money supply is defined as consisting of currency and commercial bank deposits, the rate of increase that he has estimated would be suitable is between 3 to 5 percent per year.[34] A publicly stated policy of *a steady rate of monetary growth* is, he believes, the most important contribution the monetary authority can provide to facilitate economic stability.

Keynes versus the monetarists

What separates modern monetarists from the Keynes of *The General Theory* (and contemporary followers of Keynes)? Clearly, it cannot be said that the view that 'money matters' is attributable to the monetarists and not to Keynes. Keynes's particular concern with the nature and role of money has been emphasized at several junctures. It is incorrect, in view of this emphasis, to construe his limited faith in monetary policy during severe depression to mean that he thought money did not matter.

What separates Keynes from the monetarists thus turns, in simplest terms, on the question of whether the key *endogenous variable* of the system is the quantity of money or money–wage rates. In viewing money as an asset that is demanded to circumvent uncertainty, and which comes into existence as a result of the debt-creating activities of commercial banks, Keynes identified money as being *endogenously* generated within the system (and explainable in terms of the economist's tools). Money wages, on the other hand, are the outcome of institutional arrangements, and are therefore *exogenous* to the system. According to Keynes's view, the collective bargaining activities of unions, legal wage minima, and wage customs of various kinds impinge on demand and supply forces to a degree that makes it impossible to explain wage behavior in terms of the market mechanism.

Monetarists and Keynesians, however, conceive of the quantity of money as being generated by policy and is therefore *exogenous* to the system, while real wages are established *endogenously* via the operation of the price mechanism. These differences, as will be seen in Chapter 25, are also fundamental to the *counter* counter-revolution that contemporary followers of Keynes are now conducting against monetarists, Keynesians and new classicals whose work has been reviewed in this chapter.

Neoclassical growth models

The reaffirmation of the neoclassical tradition in the period of counter-revolution that followed the publication of *The General Theory* manifested itself in a variety of ways. Chief among these are the development of the ISLM apparatus examined above and the general-equilibrium approach it implies, together with the restatement of the quantity-theory and its related view of monetary policy and positive economics. A further aspect of the ongoing influence of neoclassical conceptions is concerned with the problem of economic growth.

Roy Harrod's contribution, described in Chapter 21, not only revitalized concern with the problem of growth, but served to focus attention on the question of stability. A model in which growth is conceived to proceed at a constant rate is one which has a 'steady-state' growth. Analytically speaking, steady-state growth is the counterpart of long-period equilibrium in static theory.

An economy may be identified as exhibiting stable growth if a divergence from the equilibrium or steady-state path causes reactions that tend to bring the system back to equilibrium. In Harrod's model, movement along the steady-state path is possible only if warranted growth G_w is equal to G_n, the natural rate of growth, i.e. the highest rate of growth that can be achieved, given the parameters of the system. Harrod concluded that equality between G_w and G_n is possible only in the special case in which all business expectations are fulfilled. Any divergence between G_w and G_n, instead of resulting in self-correction, only serves to accentuate the departure from the steady-state path. Harrod concluded, therefore, that full-employment steady-state growth is, in general, not possible. Harrod's model is thus in the tradition of Keynes's economics of less than full employment.

Writers who construct growth-models that depict an economy in which steady-state growth is possible reject the assumptions on which Harrod's model is based. The critical assumptions of his model are that the propensity to save is constant, and that production-functions are characterized by fixed coefficients, so that substitution between labor and capital is not possible. Writers of neoclassical persuasion, whose work is discussed in the next section, developed models in which these assumptions have been relaxed. For example, Harrod's assumption of fixed factor coefficients may be relaxed to allow substitutability between labor and capital in the production function. Another way is to construct a model in which the savings–income ratio is assumed to be flexible. A third way is to introduce economically induced changes in the rate of population-growth instead of assuming that population and the labor force are determined by the operation of non-economic demographic forces. Making one or the other of these changes in the original Harrod model affects either the warranted-rate growth or the natural rate of growth and serves to bring them into equality with each other. These approaches, which are examined below, are *neoclassical* in the sense that divergences of the system from equilibrium cause factor-price changes that bring the system back to the steady-state path.

Neoclassical models

The variable capital–output ratio model

Models in which the capital–output ratio is variable rather than fixed in response to changes in factor-prices occupy an important place in the most recent literature on growth-theory. Robert Solow of Harvard and Paul T. Samuelson of Massachusetts Institute of Technology are among the US economists who are closely associated with the construction of such neoclassical models, as are the Englishmen, T. W. Swan and James E. Meade. Solow has characterized the Harrod model as 'balanced on the knife-edge of equilibrium-growth.' This balance depends on the assumption that production takes place under conditions of fixed proportions. 'If this assumption is abandoned, the knife-edge notion of unstable balance seems to go with it.'[35]

The model developed by Robert Solow is designed to demonstrate this proposition. It is predicated on the assumption that output consists of a single composite commodity produced by labor and capital. It assumes that the labor force increases as a result of population growth, which reflects the operation of non-economic exogenous factors. It assumes technological change to be absent, so that the rate of increase in the labor force is, in effect, equivalent to Harrod's natural rate of growth. The problem, then, is to determine whether there is a rate of increase in the stock of capital which is consistent with the rate of growth of the labor force. If there is, the warranted rate is equal to the natural rate; i.e. the knife-edge conditions of the Harrod model are satisfied. However, even if these two rates are not initially equal, Solow demonstrates that the inherent instability of the Harrod model is not inevitable.

Models of the Solow variety are *neoclassical* in that the rate of growth is determined by decisions made in response to price adjustments on the supply side. Their crucial difference from the Harrod model is that they are characterized by a production–function which has alternative capital–labor and, therefore, capital–output ratios. The Harrod problem of divergence between the natural rate and the warranted rate is avoided by the choice of a production method with a capital-intensity which checks any tendency for capital stock to grow at a rate different from the rate of population growth.

For example, if the savings associated with full employment are in excess of what is required to enable the capital stock to grow at the same rate as the labor force, the warranted rate of growth will be above the natural rate. The real rate of interest will tend to fall in this situation. As a result, a deepening of capital, which increases the capital–labor ratio and therefore the capital–output ratio, tends to take place. This serves to reduce the warranted rate of growth as well as the savings ratio. The deepening process continues as long as the warranted rate is above the natural rate. When the warranted rate has fallen to the level of the natural rate, growth takes place along the steady-state path. Saving will then have been reduced to a level at which the capital stock grows at the same rate as the labor force.

Conversely, if the size of the initial capital stock is such that the warranted rate is below the natural rate, capital and output will grow at a faster rate than the labor force until the warranted rate of growth is equal to the natural rate. In short, the model shows that the natural rate of growth and the warranted rate of growth are not inherently divergent from each other if a method of production is chosen in which the capital intensity is appropriate to the size of the capital stock. If the interest rate is flexible, the neoclassical model envisions growth occurring at the long-run natural rate, by virtue of the variability of the equilibrium or warranted rate of growth. An important implication of this model, in contrast with the Harrod model, is that it downgrades the significance of savings and capital accumulation as the 'engine' of economic growth.[36]

The variable population growth model

The adjustment needed to bring about equality between the natural and warranted rates of growth may, theoretically, take place via a change in the natural rate instead of through a change in the warranted rate. It will be recalled that the natural rate is the maximum growth-rate consistent with the full employment of resources and the rate of technological progress. Given the labor requirements per unit of output, the natural rate of growth cannot be greater than the rate of growth of the labor supply.

A model in which the warranted growth-rate and the natural growth-rate are brought to equality via a change in the natural rate can be constructed by dropping the assumption that the rate of population growth is

determined by non-economic forces. Growth-models typically assume the rate of growth of the labor supply is an exogenous constant. In principle, however, economically induced changes in the rate of growth of population, as has been demonstrated by the late Simon Kuznets, can be incorporated into growth-models.[37]

There are various ways of doing this. But all are Malthusian in inspiration in the sense that they conceive of birth and death rates as resulting from the operation of economic forces. The Malthusian hypothesis has it that the supply of labor is perfectly elastic at a real wage that corresponds to subsistence. Given a fixed supply of land and no technical progress, the growth of population and hence total output is presumed to depend on the capitalists' propensity to save out of profits. That is, a relationship between income (output) and population and between population and the real wage is postulated. A high real wage is presumed to induce a high rate of population growth and output. Increases in population, in turn, reduce the capital-to-labor ratio, which adversely affects income and real wages. If the rate of growth of population responds to real wages, the natural growth rate may be envisioned as being reduced until it coincides with the warranted rate.

The technological change

While there are growth models of Malthusian inspiration, there is only limited interest in models incorporating changes in the rate of growth of the labor supply. Demography, which is the study of population behavior, remains a specialized area of inquiry in spite of pioneering efforts to examine population behavior in response to economic stimuli. There has been relatively greater interest among economists in those aspects of growth that are associated with changes in technique and technological progress.[38] Neoclassical models have been constructed in which investment is associated with capital of different 'vintages,' which are associated with technologies that prevailed at various points of time. The nature and role of 'human capital' as distinct from physical capital has also challenged the interest of neoclassical economists. Part of this interest was originally sparked by the growth problem and evidenced by an effort to estimate the proportion of growth associated with the quality of the labor force as distinct from its size.[39] On a more theoretical level, Kenneth Arrow has worked out a growth model in which 'experience,' i.e. improvements in human capital that are the product of learning, is the engine of progress.[40] Experience is seen as facilitating improvements in the design of new machines, which serve to reduce the labor requirements per unit of output. Investment does not increase the productivity of labor employed on existing machines, but it does increase the productivity of labor working on machines subsequently designed and built.[41]

While the growth phenomenon is closely related to the quality of the labor force, the economists' interest in investment in human capital is only peripherally related to problems of growth. The most important theoretical and empirical work has taken place within the context of decision-making by the household. As such, human capital analysis is of limited importance in connection with the macroeconomic topics explored in this chapter.

Concluding remarks

This chapter began in the context of the distinction between Keynesian economics and the economics of Keynes. Keynes's revolution was hardly underway before it was countered by J. R. Hicks's suggested neo-Walrasian reinterpretation. While Hicks's ISLM apparatus is an analytical tool, it also reflects a different perception of reality than does the economics of Keynes. It conceives of an economic system in which commodity, factor, and financial markets tend toward a *general equilibrium* via the functioning of the price mechanism. From an analytical perspective, these thinkers have mounted a *counter-revolution* against Keynes's own argument that advanced capitalistic economies, like the United Kingdom, the United States, and those of Western Europe, have an inherent tendency toward less-than-full-employment equilibria. Both Pigou and Patinkin maintained that *in principle*, the real-balance effect can bring about cuts in real wages and interest rates that are compatible with simultaneous equilibriums in the commodity, labor, and financial markets. The counter-revolution represented by their ideas is thus *neo-Walrasian* quite as much as it is neoclassical.

The ISLM apparatus, originally developed by J. R. Hicks and Alvin Hansen, has become the conventional way of representing the behavior of the macroeconomy, although the Keynesian cross remains popular, particularly in introductory textbooks. The ISLM apparatus is, however, at a particular disadvantage when focus shifts to examining the behavior of *money magnitudes*, because the price level is abstracted from the *ISLM* model. The role of money in this general equilibrium model is to serve as a numéraire – one commodity among many that serves as an exchange medium. Thus, the Phillips curve that relates changes in unemployment rates and wage rates – the latter serving as a proxy for changes in the general price level – has been pressed into service in order to explain the relationship between unemployment and prices.

To confront the problem of explaining *simultaneous* increases in the price level and unemployment rates, monetarists have focused on the relationship between changes in the money supply, the nominal income level, and the price level. The monetarist position is that inflation cannot take place without the acquiesence of the monetary authority. They interpret the demand for money by households as a highly stable demand for *real* balances. Changes in the quantity of money can therefore affect interest rates perversely; increases in the quantity of money *initially* reduce interest rates and stimulate the economy. However, as rising prices reduce the *real* quantity of money, interest rates become higher because of unanticipated changes in either interest rates or the money supply. In practice, central bankers in the United States and elsewhere have taken a more active role in altering interest rates and money supplies. This is the monetarist interpretation of Keynesian principles. It provides the basis for Milton Friedman's policy recommendation that the Federal Reserve System ought to provide a stable monetary environment within which consumers, producers, workers, and employers can make choices without the persistent threat that their expectations are likely to be disappointed because of *unanticipated* monetary disturbances.

Notes

1 The distinction between Keynesian economics and the economics of Keynes was made by Axel Leijonhufvud in *On Economics and The Economics of Keynes* (New York: Oxford University Press, 1966).
2 Keynes himself attempted some empiricism. See *The General Theory of Employment, Interest and Money* (New York: Harcourt Brace Jovanovich, 1936), pp. 102–4.
3 A particularly useful summary of this empirical work is in Ronald Bodkin. 'Keynesian econometric concepts: consumption functions, investment functions, and the multiplier,' in *Modern Economic Thought*, edited by Sidney Weintraub (Philadelphia: University of Pennsylvania Press, 1976), Chapter 4.
4 *Econometrica*, 5 (1937), pp. 147–59. For a more extensive review of Keynesianism than is given here, see the various contributions to Sidney Weintraub's *Modern Economic Thought*, Part 1, especially his own Chapter 3, 'Hicksian Keynesianism: dominance and decline.'
5 Algebraically the model is usually represented in terms of five equations. The first two represent the real, or commodity, sectors of the economy. In the consumption function which is written

$$C = C(Y,r) \tag{23.1}$$

C represents consumption expenditures, *Y* is real income, and *r* represents the interest rate structure. The investment relationship in which *I* is real investment is represented as

$$I = I(r) \tag{23.2}$$

The next two equations represent the money, or bond, market. The liquidity preference function in which *L* is the money demand function is written

$$L = L(Y,r) \tag{23.3}$$

The fourth equation

$$M = M^* \tag{23.4}$$

represents the money supply created by the monetary authority; it is assumed to be an exogenous constant set by the policy of the monetary authority. The final equation

$$C + I = Y \tag{23.5}$$

completes the system.

This system may be simplified by substituting equations (23.1) and (23.2) into (23.5) to derive a single equation with two unknowns.

$$C(Y,r) + I(r) = Y \tag{23.6}$$

which can be equated with $M = L(Y,r)$, which expresses equality between the money supply and the demand for it. The model is thus determinate.

6   Paul A. Samuelson, 'Interactions between the multiplier analysis and the principle of acceleration,' *Review of Economics and Statistics*, 21(2) (May 1939), pp. 75–78. In *Crisis in Keynesian Economics*, Hicks observed that 'Keynesianism became fiscalism because interest-rate reductions came to be viewed as unreliable for expanding investment expenditures' (Oxford: Basil Blackwell, 1974), p. 33.

7   Hicks, *Crisis in Keynsian Economics*, pp. 398–99.

8   Alvin Hansen also provides a demonstration in *A Guide to Keynes* (New York: McGraw Hill, 1953), Chapter 7.

9   Their interpretation perhaps, gained some degree of support from the fact that Keynes himself appears to have appreciated the possibility of constructing an *IS* curve. He specifically noted that the level *of* income and the interest rate must be 'uniquely correlated' (*The General Theory*, pp. 178–81). The rebuttal to this interpretation is considered in Chapter 24.

10 Don Patinkin, *Money, Interest, and Prices*, 2nd edn (New York: Harper & Row, 1965), p. 325.

11 Don Patinkin, *Money, Interest, and Prices*, p. 324.

12 The net liquid assets of the private sector are the sum of 'outside' money, that is, money for which there is no corresponding private liability (which excludes most commercial bank deposits) and the interest-bearing government debt.

13 Patinkin, *Money, Interest, and Prices*.

14 Don Patinkin, *Money, Interest, and Prices*, p. 343; Patinkin maintains that the evidence on the real-balance effect is inconclusive. His model assumes outside money is an asset without a corresponding debt. But if there is also inside money, the price level has no effect on real wealth. A price reduction makes an asset holder richer in real terms and a debtor poorer; that is, the new effect of a price change is zero if there is inside money.

15 Don Patinkin, 'Price flexibility and full employment.' *Readings in Monetary Theory* (New York: The Blakeston Company, 1951).

16 Patinkin, *Readings in Monetary Theory*.

17 Both Keynes and Joan Robinson anticipated this problem. See J. M. Keynes, *The General Theory*, pp. 298–302, and Joan Robinson, *Essays in the Theory of Employment* (New York: Macmillan, 1937), chapter 1.

18 A. W. Phillips, 'The relation between unemployment and the rate of change of money wage rates in the United Kingdom, 1862–1957,' *Economica*, 25 (1958), pp. 283–99.

19 Paul Samuelson and Robert Solow made the first empirical estimate of the Phillips curve for the United States in 'Analytical aspects of anti-inflation policy,' *American Economic Review, Papers and Proceedings* I (1960), pp. 177–94. They conclude that if wage increases do exceed productivity increases, an unemployment rate of 5 to 6 percent of the labor force would persist. Alternatively, to maintain unemployment at the 3 percent level, the price index would have to rise by as much as 48.5 percent each year. Studies by Bhatia and France indicate even more pessimistic curves, the latter indicating approximately 10 percent unemployment when the annual wage inflation rate is 2.4 percent. See R. J. Bhatia, 'Unemployment and rate of change in money earnings in the United States, 1900–1959,' *Economica*, 28 (August, 1961), pp. 285–96.

20 It is relevant to note that this conception of the relationship among money, wages, labor productivity, and inflation is consistent with Keynes's own view. See R. E. Harrod, *Reforming the World's Money* (London: Macmillan, 1965). See also Sidney Weintraub, *Keynes and the Monetarists* (New Brunswick: Rutgers University Press, 1959), pp. 24–25.

21 *Studies in the Quantity Theory of Money* (Chicago: The University of Chicago Press, 1956). Friedman was honored with the Nobel Prize (1976) for his contribution to economics.

22 See, for example, Robert Lucas, 'Unemployment policy,' *American Economic Review, Papers and Proceedings*, 68, (1978), pp. 353–557.

23 Friedman, *Studies*, p. 4.

24 Friedman's permanent income concept is examined in the section that follows.

25 Friedman, *Studies*, p. 14.

26 Philip Cagan, 'The monetary dynamics of hyperinflation,' in Friedman, *Studies*, pp. 25–111.

27 This is also the view of Franco Modigliani and Richard Brumberg. See their 'Utility analysis

and the consumption function: an interpretation of cross-section data,' reprinted in *Macroeconomic Theory: Selected Readings*, edited by H. R. Williams and J. D. Hufnagle (New York: Appleton-Century-Crofts, 1969), p. 102.

28 See Arthur Smithies, 'Forecasting postwar demand,' *Econometrica*, 13 (January, 1945), pp. 1–14. Many non-monetarists have also advanced hypotheses to explain why the long-term relationship between consumption expenditures and income is proportional. James Duessenberry (in *Income, Savings, and the Theory of Consumer Behavior*, Harvard Economic Study, no. 87, 1959) has advanced the view that consumption depends not only on the absolute level of current income, but more particularly on the level of current income relative to the income peak previously achieved. This hypothesis reflects his disagreement with two of Keynes's fundamental assumptions. These are (1) that every individual's consumption behavior is independent of that of every other individual and (2) that consumption relations are reversible in time. Given the distribution of income, there are strong psychological and sociological reasons that cause an individual's desire to increase consumption expenditures to be functionally related to the percentile position in the income distribution pattern. It follows that the proportion of income saved is a function of the same variable. Duessenberry is, therefore, led to the following conclusions.

(1) At any one moment, the proportion of income saved will be higher for the higher income groups than for low-income groups.

(2) If income increases while the proportional distribution remains constant, the ratio of savings to income will be constant.

29 Milton Friedman, 'The role of monetary policy,' *American Economic Review*, 58 (March 1961), pp. 1–17.

30 It is relevant to point out that much of the ongoing controversy between the monetarists and writers who profess to be working in the tradition of Keynes (as distinct from the Keynesians) turns on their analysis of the demand for money. See Chapter 20.

31 Friedman, 'The role of monetary policy,' p. 7.

32 Friedman, 'The role of monetary policy,' p. 8.

33 Friedman, 'The role of monetary policy,' pp. 10–11.

34 Friedman, 'The role of monetary policy,' pp. 1–17.

35 Robert M. Solow, 'A contribution to the theory of economic growth,' *Quarterly Journal of Economics*, 70 (February, 1956).

36 J. R. Hicks has shown that one way of constructing a model that will not 'explode' in the Harrodian manner is to introduce lags in consumption and investment. See John R. Hicks, 'Mr. Harrod's dynamic theory,' *Economica*, 16(62) (May, 1949) pp. 106–21.

37 Simon Kuznets, 'Long swings in the growth of population and related economic variables,' *Proceedings of the American Philosophical Society*, 102(1) (February, 1958). Also Richard Easterlin, *Population, Labor Force and Long Savings in Economic Growth* (New York: Natural Bureau of Economic Research, 1968).

38 Edwin Mansfield, *The Economics of Technological Change* (New York: W. W. Norton, 1968).

39 Theodore W. Schultz, 'Rise in the capital stock represented by education in the United States 1900–1957' in *Economics of Higher Education* edited by S. Mushkin (Washington, Department of Health, Education and Welfare, 1962).

40 Kenneth Arrow, 'The economic implications of learning by doing,' *Review of Economic Studies*, 29 (June, 1962).

41 N. Kaldor and J. Mirrlee in 'A new model of economic growth,' *Review of Economic Studies*, 29 (June, 1962) have presented a more complex model of growth which incorporates both the learning process and rates of increase in gross investment. That is, learning is viewed as a function of the rate of increase of gross investment. In the Kaldor–Mirrlee model, investment enhances productivity because it generates opportunity of learning new methods.

Questions for discussion and further research

1 J. R. Hicks and Alvin Hansen have demonstrated that Keynes's liquidity preference theory and neoclassical interest rate theory can together provide a determinate solution of both the interest rate

Glossary of terms and concepts

General equilibrium system

A representation of the economy by equations relating to commodity, labor, and financial markets that tend toward simultaneous clearing through the functioning of the price mechanism. These relationships have also been shown graphically with the aid of the Hicks–Hansen ISLM apparatus.

Modern quantity theory

Modern quantity theorists (e.g. Milton Friedman) maintain that the demand for cash balances is stable in real terms. The process of increasing the nominal quantity of money at a faster rate reduces interest rates only temporarily. The exception of further increases in the price level reduces the real value of the balances held. Since the demand for real balances is stable, the nominal demand for money increases, which increases rather than decreases the rate of interest. Because this adversely affects the level of income and employment, the monetarist position is to advocate a policy of increasing the money supply at a steady, unchanging rate.

Permanent income

Friedman's term for the resources an individual expects to have over a lifetime. His interpretation of long-run consumption behavior is that expenditures are proportional to expected lifetime income. This interpretation is consistent with Kuznets's empirical evidence that there is a long-run constant ratio between consumption and income of about 88 percent.

Real-balance effect

An increase in the real value of cash balances that might operate to increase the volume of real spending and shift the consumption function upward.

Vertical Phillips curve

A graphic representation of the natural rate of unemployment consistent with a zero expectation of price change. It has been hypothesized (by Friedman and his followers) that the trade-off between employment and wage increases is observable only in the short run. Policy measures to reduce unemployment below the natural rate raise wage rates and generate inflationary expectations. Short-run Phillips curves therefore shift upward and restore unemployment to its natural level. This logic is associated with the accelerationist view of unemployment and inflation.

and the level of income, because they include all the variables of the interest rate problem. What are these? How are they the basis for generating IS and LM curves? Show these graphically and explain in what sense they reflect a reconciliation of Keynesian and neoclassical approaches to explaining interest rate determination.

2 What is the Phillips curve apparatus? How has it been used to explain the phenomenon of inflation and the perceived 'trade off' between levels of unemployment and the price level?

What, in the view of the 'new classicals,' is the role of rational expectations in causing the level of unemployment to converge toward what they term a 'natural rate,' which they represent by a vertical Phillips curve?

3 Studies of consumption behavior support Keynes's interpretation that the slope of the consumption function is less than one only in the short run. In the long run the evidence is that the relationship between consumption and income is proportional. How does Keynes's data indirectly support this

interpretation? Others, specifically Friedman and Duesenberry, have also argued the case for proportionality. What theoretical argument have they offered?

4   Monetarists agree with Keynes's argument in *The General Theory* that 'money matters.' Yet, there is deep disagreement about the proper role of monetary policy. Explain their differing views and how they are rooted in their differing interpretations about the money supply as an exogenous or endogenous variable.

Notes for further reading

From *The New Palgrave*

Philip Cagan on Monetarism, vol. 3, pp. 492–96; Edmund S. Phelps on the Phillips Curve, vol. 3, pp. 855–60; Axel Leijonhvud on *IS-LM* analysis, vol. 2, pp. 1002–4; Stanley Fisher on New Classical macroeconomics, vol. 3, pp. 647–50; Thomas I. Sargent on rational expectations, vol. 4, pp. 76–79; Milton Friedman on quantity theory of money, vol. 4, pp. 3–19; Don Patinkin on real balances, vol. 4, pp. 99–101; Stanley Fischer on New Classical Macroeconomics, vol. 3, pp. 647–51.

Selected references and suggestions for further reading and research

Clark, K. B. and Summers, L. H. 'Labor force participation: timing and persistence.' *Review of Economic Studies*, 49 (1982), pp. 825–44.

Duessenberry, James. *Income, Savings, and the Theory of Consumer Behavior*. Harvard Economic Study, no. 87, 1959.

Friedman, Milton. *Capitalism and Freedom* (Chicago: University of Chicago Press, 1962).

Friedman, Milton. *Essays in Positive Economics*. (Chicago: University of Chicago Press, 1953).

Friedman, Milton. *The Optimum Quantity of Money and Other Essays* (Chicago: Aldine, 1969).

Friedman, Milton (ed). *Studies in the Quantity Theory of Money* (Chicago: University of Chicago Press, 1956).

Friedman, Milton. *A Theory of the Consumption Function* (Princeton, NJ: Princeton University Press, 1957).

Friedman, Milton. 'The role of monetary policy.' *American Economic Review*, 58 (March 1961), pp. 1–17.

Friedman, Milton and Schwartz, Anna J. *A Monetary History of the United States 1867–1960* (Princeton, Princeton University Press, 1963).

Harrod, R. F. *Reforming the World's Money* (London: Macmillan, 1965).

Hansen, Alvin. *A Guide to Keynes* (New York: McGraw Hill, 1953) Chapter 7.

Hansen, Alvin. *Crisis in Keynesian Economics* (New York: Basic Books, 1974).

Hicks, J. A. 'Mr. Keynes and the classics: a suggested reinterpretation.' *Econometrica*, 5 (1937), pp. 147–59.

Leijonhufvud, Axel. *On Economics and The Economics of Keynes* (New York: Oxford University Press, 1966).

Lucas, Robert. 'Unemployment policy.' *American Economic Review, Papers and Proceedings*, 68 (1978), pp. 353–557.

Muth, John E. 'Rational expectations and the theory of price movements.' *Econometrica*, 29 (1961), pp. 315–35.

Patinkin, Don. *Money, Interest and Prices*. Revised edition (New York: Harper & Row, 1963).

Patinkin, Don. 'Price flexibility and full employment.' *Readings in Monetary Theory* (New York: The Blakeston Company, 1951).

Phillips, A. W. 'The relation between unemployment and the rate of change of money wage rates in the United Kingdom, 1862–1957.' *Economica*, 25 (1958), pp. 283–99.

Samuelson, Paul A. 'Interactions between the multiplier analysis and the principle of acceleration.' *Review of Economics and Statistics*, 21(2), (May, 1939) pp. 75–78.

Samuelson, Paul A. and Solow, Robert. 'Analytical aspects of anti-inflation policy.' *American Economic Review, Papers and Proceedings*, 1, (1960), pp. 177–194.

Smithies, Arthur. 'Forecasting postwar demand.' *Econometrica*, 13 (1945) pp. 1–14.

Chapter 24

The analytics of economic liberalism: the Chicago tradition

••

Introduction

The premise that individuals are capable of maximizing behavior in the markets in which they operate, whether as consumers, producers, savers, investors, workers, and/or employers, is the *leitmotif* of the tradition that has become associated with the Chicago School of economics. Members of this group of academic economists, who have taught or studied at the University of Chicago or other institutions (among them The University of California at Berkeley, Stanford, and MIT) where they have come under the energizing influence of the Chicago view, share an identifiable intellectual bond. Although their professional association is very loose and they disagree about many specifics, they are, nevertheless, relatively homogeneous with respect to their methodology, philosophy, and policy preferences. Chicago economists are, first and foremost, advocates of an individualistic market economy. Indeed, they are sometimes referred to as 'the Chicago school of libertarian economists.'[1] It is the *degree* of this advocacy that sets the Chicagoans apart from other economists, who may also prefer a predominantly market-oriented economy, but who do not necessarily believe that individual liberty (political as well as economic) cannot exist outside a free enterprise system, or that a free-enterprise system is more productive than any other.[2]

A related difference between Chicagoans and many other economists is their belief that the market economy is characterized by commodity prices and wage rates that are, by and large, flexible. This view, as was pointed out in the preceding chapter, with particular reference to the concept of the natural rate of unemployment, is an integral part of monetarist macroeconomic analysis. Chicago economists tend to be less concerned with, and give less weight than others to, the implications of oligopoly and labor unions largely because they maintain that these do not significantly alter the essentially competitive nature of the economy. Their concern with questions relating to the distribution of income and wealth is similarly limited.

On the positive side, Chicagoans are committed to the usefulness and relevance of a theory of individual choice based on the assumption that sovereign consumers are capable of engaging in 'maximizing behavior' in their economic activity. With the aid of empirical tests, they have brought an impressive range of problems within the purview of the economist. Among those, particular mention may be made of the economics of education, of crime, marriage contracts, birth rates, and the behavior of voters, which have traditionally been viewed as lying outside the scope of economics. There are thus substantial differences in focus among individual Chicagoans.[3]

Milton Friedman and others concerned chiefly with the price level and monetary economics should be identified separately from Gary Becker, Jacob Mincer, Ronald Coase, and others who are chiefly concerned with problems of *allocative efficiency*. The latter are chiefly responsible for the development of the new microeconomics. Since the monetarist concerns of Friedman and others were examined in the preceding chapter, this chapter will focus chiefly on the concerns of Becker, Mincer, Coase, *et al*. That is, (1) the problem of allocative efficiency with respect to using the time and income resources of the individual household, (2) allocative efficiency in market activities that involve common property, (3) the role of the market mechanism in promoting economic growth in less developed countries and (4) the nature and role of property rights. The interests of Chicagoans are thus very diverse. But there is a *leitmotif* that will become apparent as the highlights of their concerns are examined. Their common intellectual debt to Frank Knight and the Austrians is a useful starting point.

The Menger–Knight heritage

The utility principle

The microeconomic propositions formulated and subjected to empirical testing by modern Chicagoans build chiefly on the work of Carl Menger as interpreted and transmitted by Frank Knight. Their analyses proceed from the premise that choice is governed by individual perceptions of the utility associated with alternative courses of action. Following

Menger, Knight maintained that the relevant cost of any economic decision is the utility of the alternatives sacrificed. No resource has any value other than that imputed to it by the consumer, who seeks to maximize the returns a given supply of resources can yield. Knight credits Menger for establishing this principle as the basis of human behavior:

> It is to the everlasting credit and renown of Menger . . . that he not only grasped the utility principle but extended and applied it in two directions: in the field of complementary goods and in that of indirect goods. He reiterated . . . the principle that costs are simply the values of cost goods, which values are *derived from* or reflect the value of some final consumption good, and that this value, in turn, is that of the 'need satisfaction' dependent upon a small portion or increment (*Teilquatität*) of the final good in question. This is perhaps as accurate a statement as can be put into words . . . of the general principle that explains, as far as it goes, all valuation.[4]

Knight's commitment to Menger's utility principle became the basis for his defense of the concept of 'economic man' which, in turn, became fundamental to his defense of neoclassicism. Both concepts brought him into intellectual conflict with the institutionalist interpretation of human behavior espoused by Clarence Ayres on the basis of Veblen's teachings.

Knight on consumer sovereignty and the methodology of economics

It will be recalled, from Chapter 18, that Veblen's rejection of the concept and *modus operandi* of economic man was basic to his disassociation from the neoclassical tradition. Frank Knight's effort to clarify the nature and role of economic man may thus be viewed as fundamental to his defense of neoclassicism. Knight agreed with Veblen that the determinants of human behavior are multifaceted. However, instead of insisting that all these aspects be incorporated and reflected in the behavioral assumptions made by the economist, Knight maintained that it is not only proper but necessary to abstract from reality and focus on those aspects that are relevant to explaining *economic* behavior. Its assumption is that the material aspects of an individual's life conditions behavior so as to maximize gains, both as a consumer of goods and services and as a producer. In making this abstraction, the economist is following precisely the same procedure as the natural scientist who also excludes the influence of those variables whose operation is either irrelevant or prejudicial to the conclusion he or she is seeking to establish.

The 'economic' individual does not and, indeed, cannot approximate the person of the real world. Nevertheless, the abstraction is useful for helping us understand the purely economic dimension of behavior. What the economist is seeking to explain is *pecuniary behavior*. Knight therefore questions the distinctions Veblen makes between industrial and pecuniary employment and between 'conspicuous' consumption and that which is not conspicuous. He reasons that economic activity is simply a matter of maximizing producer and consumer gains. Technological efficiency supports rather than thwarts pecuniary gain, and all consumption, beyond that essential to mere subsistence, is emulative in some degree. Knight therefore rejected Veblen's argument that consumer sovereignty is destroyed because people are conditioned to imitate the consumption patterns of the financially well-to-do, and saw it simply as an expression of Veblen's personal disapproval of certain types of consumer behavior.

Not only is the consumer sovereign, but, according to Knight, the producer who, in an uncertain world, correctly anticipates what forms of production are most likely to find favor with consumers will be rewarded with profits that arise as a residual after contractual obligations have been met. Profit is the return for bearing uncertainty: there is no assurance that sovereign consumers will actually purchase what has been produced. Thus, Knight's contribution to the theory of profits is directly related to his rebuttal against Veblen's attack on consumer sovereignty.[5]

Modern writers in the Chicago tradition have built on this Menger–Knight perspective of the relationship between utility and cost (i.e. the cost of any choice is the utility lost in choosing one alternative rather than another) to explore the behavior of the household in managing its time and income resources. An impressive range of topics traditionally examined by sociologists or psychologists has come within their scope of analysis. Using the framework provided by economic theory, the 'new microeconomics' has examined such topics as the allocation of time to education and training as investment in human capital, the rearing of children, criminal behavior as an alternative to market behavior, and choice among sexual partners.[6] These inquiries represent contemporary efforts to explore Knight's classic observation: 'To live, in the human plane, is to choose.'[7] The modern microeconomists' emphasis on time as a scarce allocable input reflects, it should be noted, a different conception of time than the Marshallian one that relates to processes maturing through time.

Courtship and marriage

Studies of the family and the relationships among its members are generally considered to lie in the intellectual domain of sociologists and social psychologists. Chicagoans have chosen to ignore this traditional division of intellectual labor and made the family unit the focal point of analysis. Viewed in this light, the family is a producing unit. It is, in effect, a firm, which utilizes time and other resources at its disposal to produce the utilities desired by family members.[8] Within this analytical framework, marriage is identified as a contract in which the parties have made commitments with respect to the time each will allocate to market and non-market activity, including housework, further schooling and training, leisure, and the bearing and rearing of children. Thus, Becker conceives of dating and engagement as providing opportunities for couples to work out 'the rules of the game' and arrive at the contractual arrangement under which they will live their life together.[9] According to this line of reasoning, the search for a marriage partner is extended until the expected marginal benefit is equal to the marginal cost. Courtship is, in this sense, an investment process expected to eventuate into the flow of returns associated with marriage. It produces a flow of returns or benefits in the form of goods and services that the family desires and that 'mature out' over the expected life of the marriage contract. Some economists include children among these goods.

The net benefit of the marriage relationship reflects the difference between the flow of the benefits it yields and the costs it imposes. Improved efficiency in the production of wanted goods and services as a result of specialization and division of labor in the household and trade among family members is a major benefit. A chief cost, which is among several that must be evaluated in order to assess the net return from a family relationship, is that associated with joint decision making. In general, it is more costly to make a decision when the preferences of both parties

need to be taken into account. From this, Chicagoans infer that agreements between the partners about the part of the relationship in which each has autonomy (e.g. wives typically assume the responsibility for meal planning), minimize the costs of decision making. These costs tend to increase directly with the number of family members (i.e. older children) and the extent of their participation in the process of decision making and production. Family arrangements requiring members to assume a share of responsibility for the performance of household tasks is, in effect, akin to a tax imposed to pay for a collective good that is not necessarily shared equally.

The analytical framework of the family unit has also been used to examine the allocation of time by family members between work in the home and work in the market. One of its implications is that the traditional female role of homemaking and caring for children is not wholly dictated by socially determined values. These do play a role, but the chief determinant is the relative value of the labor time of men and women in the market place.[10] The cost of a woman's time in the performance of household and child-care duties is the wage she loses by remaining outside the market. Since men typically command higher wages than their partners (either because they are more productive or they experience less discrimination), having men engage in market activity while women work in the home minimizes the household's cost of producing the goods it wants.

Child production

Essentially the same analytical apparatus used to study female labor force participation has been extended to examine the decision-making process with respect to the production of children. These inquiries reflect a renewed interest by economists in population problems, which were very much in the purview of classical economists but were subsequently neglected by their modern counterparts. Extensive work by Gary Becker, and others at the National Bureau of Economic Research, has contributed significantly toward reaffirming the economists' interest in demographic questions.[11] Becker has undertaken to examine questions relating to population behavior using conventional tools of microeconomic analysis. Thus, he has suggested that, from the standpoint of economics, children might be considered as consumer goods that, in common with other commodities, yield satisfactions but can be acquired only at a price. The price of children consists of the time and goods sacrificed in bearing and rearing them. There are direct costs congealed in the prices of goods and services associated with their birth and nurture, and the additional indirect cost of the time parents spend with their children.

Assuming that the care of children falls largely on the mother, the price of the mother's time is a major component of the overall price of children. From this, it may be inferred that an increase in female wage rates or fringe benefits raises the price of children and thus potentially reduces the demand for them. By the same reasoning, and assuming that children are not inferior goods, the demand for them is, presumably, positively related to income.[12] This logic has provided a basis for the hypothesis that each level of satisfaction a household can achieve, given its income, is compatible with various combinations of children and other goods among which the household is indifferent.

Attitudes about having children are so traditional that the very suggestion of a trade-off between children and goods is unfamiliar and perhaps even repugnant. However, it is precisely the objective of the new microeconomics to demonstrate that the usual assumption of rationality with respect to household decision making applies to *all aspects* of household behavior, including family planning. It is the view of the new microeconomists that the rationality assumption implies nothing more than that children may be viewed as sources of satisfaction (or psychic income) and that the household responds to economic variables (i.e. prices and incomes) in making its choices.

R. A. Easterlin has extended this logic in an attempt to explain the reversal of the long-run trend of declining fertility rates after 1940.[13] He offered the hypothesis that, after 1940, couples planning their families were typically earning average real incomes that exceeded those of their parents at a comparable stage in their lives. The increase in their incomes, relative to that of their parents, encouraged them to enjoy higher standards of consumption – including more children.

By 1957, rates of population growth began to decline in spite of continued high income levels. According to Easterlin, this can be explained by much the same logic as the earlier period of increasing rates. Couples planning their families in the 1960s had grown up as dependent members of households in which the average income was above that which they were then achieving for themselves. Thus, their actual income was low relative to their desired income, based on their parents' earnings. The decline in fertility rates that became apparent in 1957 is interpreted by Easterlin as reflecting the decline in the ratio of actual to desired income during this period. His hypothesis is consistent with the work of those associated with the Chicago school and is of particular interest to us because it exemplifies the effort to extend the economists' conventional range.[14]

The Chicago view of developing economies

The perspective

Chicago economists have also had a particular interest in the economics of underdeveloped countries. A major influence in shaping their perspective was the recognition that economic growth cannot be wholly explained in terms of additions to an economy's stock of physical capital and number of workers.[15] The *residual*, which is the name given to that portion of growth not accounted for by increases in the stock of physical capital and increases in the labor force, has been attributed in part to technical progress and in part to improvements in human capital.

Chicagoans, as already noted, have had a particular interest in the process and significance of investment in human capital which they have examined in many different connections, one of which is the matter of economic development. A major study undertaken by Theodore W. Schultz focused on identifying the portion of investment in human capital represented by education.[16] Numerous studies examine the requisites for labor development in particular countries with a view also to identifying alternative strategies for developing human resources.[17]

Complementing their concern with the role of human capital in the development process is the Chicago school's view of human nature as being universally responsive to market incentives.[18] Many economists take the position that market-oriented behavior is limited to capitalistic economies in which work habits and entrepreneurial activity have traditionally experienced the spur of monetary rewards. Chicagoans, however, maintain that while people in underdeveloped countries are often viewed as strangers to the idea of maximizing gains, there is evidence that the supply of effort is responsive to the incentive of improved rates of remuneration and that wants are elastic through time in large parts of the underdeveloped world.[19]

Their belief that this behavior pattern prevails is the basis for the Chicago view that the market mechanism can stimulate efficiency and growth in an underdeveloped economy more effectively than the alternative policy of governmental planning as an instrument of economic development.[20] 'What is required in underdeveloped countries is the release of the energies of millions of able, active, and vigorous people . . . an atmosphere of freedom, of maximum opportunity for people to experiment, and of incentive for them to do so in an environment in which there are objective tests of success and failure – in short a vigorous, free capitalistic market.'[21]

The necessity for encouraging the emergence of 'entrepreneurial personalities' in underdeveloped countries is a matter of special concern to Chicagoans. Assuming the distribution of entrepreneurially talented people is approximately the same in developed and in underdeveloped countries, they emphasize the need for underdeveloped countries to provide a social environment that does not militate against development and contributes in a positive way to its realization. Thus, they urge government to facilitate private investment by supplying information and data not generally available to individual entrepreneurs. Education, free elections, and nationwide communication services are regarded as especially useful for opening up an otherwise closed society.[22] These measures are expected to contribute to a social environment of economic opportunity that encourages the mobility and adaptability of economic agents. This is the kind of environment in which economic development requires minimal administration and very little policing other than the provision of a legal system for the enforcement of contracts.

It is recognized that there are objections to relying on the market mechanism as an instrument of growth. The late Harry Johnson specifically noted that the pattern of income distribution produced by the market may be unjust and socially undesirable. But in his view, it is 'unwise for a country anxious to enjoy rapid growth to invest too strongly in policies aimed at ensuring economic equality and a just income distribution.'[23]

A second objection to relying on the market mechanism as the instrument of growth is that it may not produce as high a rate of growth as is desirable because it may not sufficiently stimulate saving and investment. The counter-argument offered by the Chicago school is that it is preferable to stimulate saving by offering high market rates of interest and to stimulate investment by tax concessions, subsidies, and cheap credit. As they see matters, it is dangerous to have government underwrite investment because it contributes to the creation of vested industrial interests that hinder further development, especially by resisting technical change.

Trade versus inflation as an instrument of development

Most underdeveloped countries have a strong orientation to foreign trade. Typically, they are characterized by a high ratio of export production to total output in the cash sector of the economy, a high proportion of foreign owned enterprises, and an inflow of long-term capital. In the early stages of development, the foreign trade sector tends to grow faster than the rest of the economy.[24] Economists concerned with studying developing countries have, therefore, examined their problems within the context of their external environment.

Trade doctrine as developed by Ricardo and Mill asserted that comparative differences in labor costs determine in what products nations will specialize and, consequently, what they will export and import. Since factors of production are typically not mobile internationally, trade itself becomes the alternative to factor movements as a mechanism for adapting productive activity to natural and population resources. The expectation is that factor prices and incomes will tend toward equality as a result of international trade.

Contrary to the prediction of the theory of international trade, the interplay of market forces has not resulted in equalizing tendencies among countries. In the underdeveloped countries of the Third World, international trade has stimulated the production of primary products that employ mostly unskilled labor. The demand for these products is often inelastic, with the result that technological improvement in their production tends to transfer the advantages of cheapening production to the importing countries. The question of what is appropriate policy in the face of the worsening of the terms of trade experienced by underdeveloped countries is a matter of considerable controversy. Chicago economists continue to put their faith in the positive contribution that free trade will make to growth and urge the necessity of working towards the elimination of trade impediments.

The counter-argument is that it is necessary for the underdeveloped countries to cut themselves off from those that are more developed and mobilize the capital resources they require for industrialization via the route of the forced saving that accompanies inflation and other policy measures.[25] Inflation in

Third World countries is expected to promote development in two ways: first, it redistributes income from workers and peasants, who typically have a low propensity to save, to capitalist entrepreneurs, who have a high propensity to save and invest. Second, it is expected to promote investment by raising the nominal rate of return from investment relative to the rate of interest. Both arguments are rejected by members of the Chicago school.

The basis for Harry Johnson's rejection of the 'forced savings' argument is that all income groups tend to adjust to inflationary expectations as the process becomes sustained. As a result, the effect of inflation is not to redistribute income from workers and savers to capitalist entrepreneurs, but to redistribute it from holders of money balances to the monetary authority. The *real* value of the money the central bank issues will steadily depreciate. That is, there is an 'inflationary tax' on the money balances the public holds, which it tries to evade by reallocating resources to consumption. Thus, the reduction of saving may outweigh the positive contribution inflation makes to development and growth.[26] In short, Chicagoans argue that inflation may well discourage rather than encourage saving. In their view, inflation has a further adverse effect because it encourages the allocation of resources into forecasting and searching for alternatives that hedge against uncertainty. This distorts the allocation of resources and encourages the waste of inflation-gathered resources on consumption because it encourages policies of protectionism and exchange control. The Chicago position is, thus, to urge against economic nationalism and in favor of free international trade. They consider it the responsibility of the more advanced nations to facilitate the development process by reducing barriers to trade that handicap their less developed neighbors.[27]

Law and economics: the property rights approach to pricing

The Chicago school's concern with allocational efficiency has still another dimension. It is among its concerns to analyze how the assignment of property rights affects the choices of decision makers and, through them, the allocation of society's resources. Property rights are the legally sanctioned relations among persons (and businesses) that arise from the existence and utilization of scarce resources. Knight's disagreement with Pigou about the usefulness of using taxes and subsidies to correct divergences between private and social marginal products turned on the alternative of a proper identification of property rights in order to achieve the social welfare idea Pigou sought.

Frank Knight's paper 'Fallacies in the interpretation of social cost' asserted that Pigou's demonstration of the failure of the market mechanism is, in fact, indicative of the failure of government to establish and protect private property rights.[28] The results Pigou anticipates with respect to the example of highway use, described earlier, follow only if it is assumed that the owner of the narrow road fails to set a toll equivalent to the difference in value to the user between it and the wider, but otherwise inferior, road. As a profit-maximizing entrepreneur, the owner of the better road will charge a toll equivalent to the differential surplus or rent associated with the service of the good road. A toll that recaptures this differential surplus, which is rent in the Ricardian sense of the term, will be exactly equal to the tax prescribed by Pigou. Furthermore, it will cause traffic to adjust itself in such a way that social interests are not abused by private decisions to use alternative transportation routes. Thus, Knight maintains, Pigou's conclusion is not evidence of market failure calling for government interference, but rather evidence of the failure of government to identify and protect property rights.[29]

A leading modern proponent of the property rights approach conceives of economics as 'the study of property rights over scarce resources. The question of economics, or of how prices should be determined, is the question of how property rights should be defined and exchanged, and on what terms.'[30] Chicagoans thus promote law and economics as the leading interdisciplinary field of the social sciences. R. H. Coase's now classic article, 'The problem of social costs,' has given this interdisciplinary effort direction, and *The Journal of Law and Economics*, which is published at the University of Chicago, provides a forum for research emanating from Coase's article.

The Coase theorem

The problem of externalities, which was addressed by the Pigou–Knight controversy, has been a matter of continuing concern to economists. It will be recalled that externalities arise in production or consumption when the activities of one party generate costs (or benefits) for a second party for which the first party is not compensated (or for which there is no payment). The problem involved is readily apparent if the impact of externalities – unpriced costs and benefits – is explored in terms of production and/or consumption functions. Virtually every firm that produces goods utilizes not only the inputs that it purchases or leases at a market price but also some inputs for which it pays nothing at all.

Consider, for example, a production function such as $q = f(x_1 \ldots x_n; y_1 \ldots y_n)$ in which q represents output (or consumption if the function is an individual welfare function), the xs represent the priced inputs, and the ys the unpriced inputs. Since y inputs have a zero price, their allocation among alternative uses is not price directed.

The service provided by the assimilative capacity of the environment is a major category of unpriced inputs. In a free market, producers use the waste receptor capabilities of water, air, and land resources *without charge*. Pigou would have argued that in the absence of regulation (e.g. waste emission standards, or pollution charges) there will be no incentive for either producers or consumers to limit their utilization of what appears to them to be a free good or service, although it is obviously not free when viewed from the standpoint of society as a whole.

Coase examined the possibility that individual action, as opposed to authority, might suffice as an instrument for dealing with externalities in a context that differs from the Pigou–Knight inquiry. He notes that the courts have been called on many times to determine what is an appropriate action in particular cases in which damages have been inflicted as a result of what the economists call *externalities*. In Coase's view, their findings have an implication for the economists' concept of factors of production.

Productive factors are generally thought of as physical entities. Coase suggested that the concept might usefully be given a *legal definition*; that is, factors of production may be thought of as *property rights* to engage in certain physical acts. Thus, the concept of land as a factor of production implies that the owner of land has the 'right to carry out a circumscribed list of actions. The rights of the landowner are not unlimited ... For example, some people may have the right to cross his land. Furthermore, it may or may not be possible to erect certain types of buildings or to grow certain crops or to use particular drainage systems on the land.'[31] If factors of production are thought of as *property rights*, then the 'cost of exercising a right (to use a factor of production) is always the loss suffered elsewhere in consequence of that right – the inability to cross land, to park a car, to build a house, to enjoy a view, to have peace and quiet, or to breathe clean air.'[32] In short, when property rights are assigned, there is necessarily a *reciprocal denial*.

The reciprocal relationship inherent in the assignment of property rights is interpreted by Coase as providing insight into the way in which parties engaged in conflicting activities can resolve their differences without outside intervention. There are several arrangements by which externalities can be 'internalized.' For example, the parties might make an agreement according to which the damaged party (A) pays the party inflicting the damage (B) to modify its activities. Or, if B has a legal right against A, A might pay B for putting up with an optimal amount of the loss it is causing B to experience. Thus, the Coase theorem proceeds from the rational two-party bargain, which is shown as capable of capturing economic efficiency without social interference.[33]

Coase recognizes that the market has its limits because the transactions costs of setting matters right may be prohibitively high. If this is the case, the legal system may be called on to decide the proper allocation of resources.[34] If the costs of allowing the market to function are in excess of the costs of allocating the resources by means of a legal decision, it is the function of the court to apply the test of 'which party's interest has the greatest market value.'[35] That is, in cases

in which the functioning of the market is precluded because of transactions' costs, Chicagoans identify the function of the courts to make the correct decision based on the principle of opportunity cost. The premise is that resources tend always to gravitate toward their highest valued uses in a free market. Legal decisions that affect the use of resources will thus be consistent with economic principle if the courts invoke the principle of opportunity price in their decisions.[36]

The Chicago view of public utility regulation

In the light of their inquiries into the relationship between law and economics, it is not surprising that members of the Chicago school also have a special interest in the institution of public regulation and its effects. Early members of the Chicago school, among them Henry Simons and Frank Knight, were opposed to social control of monopoly through regulation and recommended public ownership of such natural monopolies as railroads and power industries. This was the dominant Chicago view throughout the 1930s and 1940s, which was a period during which public regulation was greatly extended in the United States.

The stance of the Chicago school on public regulation underwent a drastic change in the late 1950s and early 1960s, when Stigler, Friedman, Coase, and others re-examined the economic effects of regulation and proposed a new solution to the natural monopoly problem. The essence of this solution was that private monopoly can result in a competitive level of profits without regulation. Friedman expressed the view that 'the conditions making for technical monopoly frequently change and I suspect that both public regulation and public monopoly are likely to be less responsive to such changes in conditions, to be less readily capable of elimination than private monopoly.'[37] The present Chicago view is that private monopoly is superior to government regulation and public ownership is attributable, in some measure at least, to the support it has had from Milton Friedman, although the theoretical basis for this position is more specifically associated with Harold Demsetz's *competitive bidding principle.*

How can private monopoly be reconciled with a competitive level of profits in the absence of direct price-earning regulation? Demsetz has argued that a competitive level of profits can be achieved indirectly via an auctioning process.[38] Government can award a franchise or operating license to the highest bidder who offers to serve consumers at the lowest price. Competition among bidders for a franchise award would force earnings down to the level a competitive market would generate. The competitive auctioning process has been particularly urged in connection with the development of off-shore gas and oil development as an alternative to the existing system of discretionary licenses.[39] The aim of competitive bidding for royalties is to reconcile natural monopoly with competitive profit levels without resort to government regulation.

In recent years, the Chicago school has extended its arguments against direct governmental control to support its view that the free market offers solutions to the energy crisis. The essence of their position is that demand and supply forces are capable of establishing a proper balance between lower and higher valued uses of energy. For example, if the OPEC cartel of oil producers again restricts its supply, A. A. Alchian recommends the use of the bidding process to bring down their monopoly price.[40] He argues that this technique for promoting a market

solution under oligopoly will promote access to the US market and thereby limit the economic rents the cartel can enjoy. This recommendation reflects the Chicago school's present preference for market solutions even in the case of natural monopoly, which, historically, they would have subjected to public ownership.

Public choice

Modern public choice economics consists of the application of the maximizing propositions and analytical tools to problems that are thought of as belonging to the field of political science. Its concern is with the allocation of public monies to provide public goods, i.e. goods to which everyone has equal access at the same price (which may be zero) and whose supply is not (in general) lessened when, like a public beach, park or museum, it is made available for public use.

While the study of public choice is on the periphery of economics, its concern with voters and the voting process is of some interest, for it relates to the kind of social choice problems considered by Kenneth Arrow, although with the difference that it relates to voter behavior with respect to supporting particular causes or the politicians likely to support them. The public is linked to politicians and policy outcomes by the voting process. Recognizing that voters are generally poorly informed, although they know what is in their best interests, there is likely to be some conflict between their interests and the views that officials have about how the interests of the public are likely to be best served.

While the writers who are concerned with the above and related issues are *not* part of the so-called Chicago tradition, they share the mindset of the underlying importance of public decision making that approximates as close as possible the wishes of the individuals involved. James Buchanan and Gordon Tulloch, who are the foremost writers in this area, have argued quite persuasively in the *Calculus of Consent* (1962) that a simple majority vote in legislative bodies is unlikely to be in accord with the preferences of the common man. They have argued the case for bicameral legislatures as a way of circumventing the skewed outcomes that may be inherent in simple majority voting.

One efficiency type argument that has been put into practice with greater frequency in recent years is the argument that certain government activities be 'contracted out' to the private sector so that they are brought under the decision rules of the price system. A private profit making firm can produce a public good or services and exclude anyone who is unwilling to pay for access to them. This is, of course, not possible with a pure public good which may be over-produced. What is required is a way of determining how much of a public good should be produced and how the cost is to be defrayed in the form of taxes. This is precisely the problem which Jules Dupuit addressed (Chapter 11 above) when he drew up demand curves for public goods in order to choose the 'socially best' quantity of a public good (e.g. a tax road) to produce and how best to establish the tax rate required to pay for it. Contemporary writers have demonstrated that the 'price' of the public good, i.e. the tax levied to pay for it, will tend to equal the marginal utility of the good to each voter who expects to consume the good in question. A possible problem, of course, is that of the 'free rider' who may find a way to enjoy a public good without contributing to the taxes out of which it is funded, as might be the case when out-of-towners visit a public museum on a 'free

day.'[41] This type of analysis may be thought of as the 'new' political economy in the sense that it is using the concept of individual trade-offs of marginal utilities and marginal costs as a basis for explaining how rational individual choice governs the decision to produce public goods. This 'new political economy' thus utilizes standard microeconomic principles to explain decisions to produce public goods.

There is also an emerging area of public choice research relating to various aspects of the political process. Among these is the possibility that political manipulation might thwart publicly desired outcomes in ways that could redistribute society's surplus among groups that may be inconsistent with individual preferences.[42] While this literature is important in its own right, its concern is the political process, and is thus tangential to our concerns, except to recognize that it represents an extension of the economic principles of maximizing behavior to the realm of the political process.[43]

Concluding remarks

Considering the extraordinarily wide range of the intellectual concerns of Chicago economists, it seems useful to return to the question posed at the beginning of this chapter: to wit, is there a group of economists associated with the University of Chicago whose work has been relatively homogeneous with respect to their methodology, philosophy, and policy preferences, and who are in a position to reach and persuade a sufficiently sizable segment of the economics profession to ensure the extension and further proliferation of their ideas? The diversity of their interests would, at the very outset, be adverse to identifying a unifying theme. Besides the Monetarism (and the various macroeconomic concerns it implies) of Friedman and his associates, various aspects of family life have become the focus of a number of writers, among whom Becker and Mincer are the most prolific, in terms of both their own writing and research and the number of doctoral students they have trained. Their work has helped to close the gap between economics, sociology, and psychology. Another identifiable group has undertaken to explore the relationship between economics and the law, with Coase as a leading figure. The work of the late Harry Johnson and Peter T. Bauer is devoted to development economics and various aspects of international trade.

The common thread linking these diverse inquiries is that they have built on the work of Frank Knight as an economic theorist, as a methodologist, and as a social philosopher. These 'three hats' of Frank Knight are scarcely separable from each other, and they are similarly blended into the work of most of his followers. From the standpoint of economic principle, the starting point of Knight's analysis, which is clearly reflected in the present Chicago tradition, is his commitment to the principle that sovereign consumers are capable of maximizing behavior. Given freedom, each individual uses the available means to achieve his or her own ends and each transaction reflects a choice among alternatives. Expressed in the language of the economist, the choices of the autonomous individual are thought of as governed by the universal principle of opportunity cost. Thus, the objective of the economist is to arrive at a body of scientific (i.e. value-free) truths predicated on individual freedom to choose among alternatives.

Most of Knight's teaching as a theorist and as a methodologist reflects his commit-ment as a philosopher to the dictum that 'to live on the human plane is to choose.' The essence of freedom is *possibility*, as distinct from coercion, which implies denial of possibility. For Knight, *economic freedom* is the essential freedom, because he saw it as underlying all other forms of freedom – religious, political, and intellectual.[44] The perfect market, which is the embodiment of complete freedom, is identified as ideal in the sense that human capability for maximizing behavior is most completely realized under these conditions. Efficient resource allocation thus became inextricably interwoven with the perfect market in Knight's thinking and teaching.

The 30 years that Knight spent at Chicago, from 1927 to 1957, were dedicated to articulating the utility principle and extolling economic *laissez-faire*, although he was not blind to the necessity for 'extensive legislation to prevent intolerable divergences from free market conditions.'[45] His commitment is very much in evidence in the *Journal of Political Economy* during the years when he shared its editorship with Jacob Viner. Approximately three quarters of the articles published by that journal from 1930 to 1946 were the product of the Chicago faculty or former students.[46] In more recent years, this journal, together with *The Journal of Law and Economics*, continued the tradition that crystallized during the tenure of Knight, Viner, and Henry Simons.[47] Their work reflects an ongoing search to identify the operation of the market system of rewards and penalties.[48] Their concerns are reflected in the doctoral dissertations of their graduate students, which are largely empirical and heavily concentrated in the fields of land economics, labor economics (a classification that includes the economics of the household), and monetary economics.[49] Within these areas, the Chicago approach is characterized by efforts to reaffirm (typically with the aid of empirical work) the efficacy of the individualistic market economy. This is accompanied by a fear of power aggregates, whether these are concentrated in the hands of big business or big government, and a preference for a competitive market structure.

It is precisely at this juncture that the Chicago school invites the most rousing criticism. Critics argue that Chicagoans (especially the present generation) are prone to blur the distinction between the actual market and the ideal market represented by perfect competition. This presents a strong contrast with Chicagoans who strongly favored *laissez-faire* but did not hesitate to advocate the socialization of industries in which the market performed poorly.[50]

Modern Chicagoans, as already noted, fear government interference as the greater evil and look to the market to restrain monopoly. Many others in the profession are skeptical of this policy stance. Large segments of the profession, unlike members of the Chicago School, identify the discrepancy between actual market conditions and perfect competition as being significantly greater than Chicagoans believe it to be. Nor do they have the faith most Chicagoans seem to have in the ability of competitive capitalism to separate economic and political power to a degree that will enable them to offset one another. They emphasize that the market system has, in fact, produced large inequities in the distribution of income. Chicagoans are wont to interpret these inequalities as reflecting the free choices of rich and poor alike.

Against this view, many non-Chicagoans interpret income inequalities as reflecting the failure of competition, which they charge Chicagoans with failing to identify because they neglect the specifics of the institutional environment of modern capitalism. This critique is an essential part of the ongoing controversy between traditional economists and those who have rejected mainstream views about economic theory and its methods. Just as Marx, Veblen, Roscher, and their followers dissented from the traditional economics of their day, so modern writers – among them John Kenneth Galbraith and other Neo-Institutionalists, New Radicals, American post-Keynesians, along with those associated with Cambridge (UK) University and Neo-Austrians – are re-examining the tenets of contemporary macro- and microeconomics that were developed in this chapter and the one that preceded it. The problems of contemporary society – especially the conundrum of inflation and unemployment, but also the unhappy results of numerous programs of social reform – have become so pressing that the critics of mainstream economics are being heard even in the academic circles of professional societies. It therefore seems increasingly appropriate to bring our inquiry into the development of economic analysis to a close with a brief survey in our concluding chapter of the main thrust of contemporary criticism and the nature of competing paradigms.

Notes

1 See Duncan J. Foley, 'Problems vs. conflicts? Economic theory and ideology,' *American Economic Review, Papers and Proceedings*, 65 (May, 1975), pp. 231–36.
2 Martin Bronfenbrenner, 'Observations on the Chicago School(s),' *Journal of Political Economy*, 70 (1962), pp. 72–75.
3 It is also important to recognize the non-monolithic character of those associated with Chicago. Paul Douglas and Harry Millis, both outstanding labor economists, and Oscar Lange, who was a socialist, were among the Chicagoans who held dissenting views during

the 1930s. More currently, Tjallings Koopmans and Jacob Marshak, who were at the University of Chicago until 1954, cannot be identified as committed to the propositions that have come to be associated with the Chicago school. This observation also applies to Lloyd Meltzer.

4 Frank Knight, *Introduction to Carl Menger's Principles of Economics*, translated and edited by James Dingwall and Bert Hoselitz (New York: The Free Press, 1950), p. 15.

5 Frank Knight, *Risk, Uncertainty and Profit* (Boston: Houghton Mifflin, 1921).

6 For a popular exposition of application of the theory of choice to problems generally not treated by economists, see Richard B. McKenzie and Gordon Tullock, *The New World of Economics* (Homewood, Ill.: Richard D. Irwin, 1975).

7 Frank Knight, 'Economic psychology and the value problem,' reprinted in *The Ethics of Competition and other Essays* (New York: Augustus Kelley, 1951), p. 88.

8 Gary Becker, 'A theory of the allocation of time,' *The Economic Journal* (September, 1965) pp. 493–517.

9 Gary Becker, 'A theory of marriage: Part I,' *Journal of Political Economy*, 81 (July–August, 1973), pp. 813–46, and 'A theory of marriage: Part II,' *Journal of Political Economy*, 82, Supplement (March–April, 1974), pp. 511–26.

10 Jacob Mincer has undertaken to test the hypothesis that female labor force participation reflects the net benefit from market activity as compared with work in the home. See 'Labor force participation of married women, a study of labor supply,' in *An Anthology of Labor Economics*, edited by R. Marshall and R. Perlman (New York: John Wiley & Sons, 1972).

11 Gary Becker, 'An Economic Analysis of Fertility,' in *Demographic and Economic Change in Developed Countries* (Princeton, NJ: Princeton University Press, 1960), pp. 209–31.

12 If a good is inferior, the demand for it declines as income rises.

13 R. A. Easterlin, 'Population' in *Contemporary Economic Issues*, edited by N. Chamberlin (Homewood, Ill.: Richard D. Irwin, 1973). See also Richard A. Easterlin, *Population, Labor Force and Long Swings in Economic Growth*

(New York: National Bureau of Economic Research, 1968), chapter 5.

14 Easterlin's hypothesis has provoked considerable controversy among demographers. Some of this literature is reviewed in Harvey Leibenstein, 'An interpretation of the economic theory of fertility: promising path or blind alley?' *Journal of Economic Literature*, 12 (June, 1974), pp. 457–70.

15 Simon Kuznets, *Modern Economic Growth* (New Haven, Conn.: Yale University Press, 1966).

16 T. W. Schultz, 'Rise in the capital stock represented by education in U.S., 1900–1957,' in *Economics of Higher Education*, edited by S. H. Muskin (Washington, DC: GPO, 1962).

17 See, for example, F H. Harbison and C. A. Myers, *Education, Manpower and Economic Growth: Strategies of Human Resource Development* (New York: McGraw-Hill, 1964).

18 For this point of view, see Harry G. Johnson, *Money, Trade and Economic Growth* (London: George Allen and Unwin, 1962). This view also underlies the approach to economic development of some prominent textbooks. See, for example, Henry Bruton, *Principles of Economic Development* (Englewood Cliffs, NJ: Prentice-Hall, 1965).

19 Writers who have studied the economies of Southeast Asia and Africa have especially noted the readiness with which these populations accept consumer and capital goods brought to their notice and within their means. Bauer and Yancey maintain there are also many examples that 'the inhabitants of poor countries (e.g. Cyprus and Uganda) generally are well informed as producers *and* consumers, and that they are responsive to changes in the alternatives open to them.' See P. T. Bauer and Basil S. Yancey, *The Economics of Underdeveloped Countries* (Chicago: The University of Chicago Press, 1957), p. 88.

20 Harry G. Johnson, *Money, Trade, and Economic Growth*, especially pp. 152–53, 156–59, 160–63.

21 Milton Friedman, 'Foreign economic aid: means and objectives,' *Yale Review* (Summer, 1958) p. 509.

22 Bruton, *Principles*, pp. 258–59.

23 Johnson, *Money, Trade, and Economic Growth*, especially Chapter 7.

24 W. A. Lewis, *The Theory of Economic Growth* (London: Allen and Unwin, 1955), p. 342.

25 See Gunnar Myrdal, 'Development and underdevelopment,' National Bank of Egypt, fifteenth Anniversary Commensuration Lectures, Cairo, 1956.

26 Harry G. Johnson, 'Is inflation the inevitable price of rapid development?' in *Economic Policies toward Less Developed Countries* (Washington, DC: The Brookings Institution, 1967).

27 Johnson, 'Is inflation the inevitable price of rapid development?' *Economic Policies toward Less Developed Countries.*

28 *Quarterly Journal of Economics*, 38 (May, 1924), pp. 582–606; reprinted in *Readings in Welfare Economics*, edited by Kenneth B. Arrow and Tibor Scitovsky (Homewood, Ill.: Richard D. Irwin, 1969), pp. 213–27.

29 Pigou eliminated this example from subsequent editions of *The Economics of Welfare* as a result of Knight's refutation.

30 The best contemporary statement of this position is in Ronald Coase's 'The problem of social costs,' *The Journal of Law and Economics*, 3 (October, 1960), pp. 1–44.

31 Coase, 'The problem of social costs,' pp. 43–44.

32 Coase, 'The problem of social costs,' pp. 44.

33 Coase notes the case of *Sturgis v. Bridgeman* (1879). Sturgis, a physician, bought a property next door to a candy factory, which had been in operation for several decades. The doctor had been practicing at his location without complaint for eight years when he constructed a new consulting room on that part of the property located near the confectioner's machinery. When he experienced difficulty in examining his patients, he brought suit to enjoin the candy factory from making noise and vibrations. In ruling in favor of the physician, the court observed that any other decision would have had a prejudicial effect upon the development of land for residential purposes. The court believed it was determining how the land was used. In Coase's interpretation, the court was, in fact, assigning a right to the physician and imposing a loss on the confectioner by forcing him to relocate his factory. He concludes that resort to the courts was unnecessary in this type of situation and that the parties could have struck a bargain which would have internalized the externality.

34 R. A. Posner, *Economic Analyses of Law* (Boston, Mass.: Little, Brown, 1972), p. 320.

35 Posner, *Economic Analyses of Law.*

36 Critics of this view maintain that it serves chiefly to make law the instrument of existing social order. See, for example, H. H. Liebhafsky, 'Price theory as jurisprudence,' *Journal of Economic Issues*, 10 (March, 1976) pp. 23–44. Liebhafsky argues that price theory as jurisprudence is an exercise in logical positivism suspended in mystical natural law philosophy.

37 Milton Friedman, *Capitalism and Freedom* (Chicago: University of Chicago Press, 1962), p. 28.

38 Harold Demsetz, 'Why regulate public utilities?' *Journal of Law and Economics*, 11 (April, 1968), pp. 55–66.

39 Kenneth Dam, 'The evolution of North Sea licensing policy in Britain and Norway,' *Journal of Law and Economics*, 17 (October, 1974), pp. 213–63.

40 A. A. Alchian, 'No time to confuse,' *Institute of Contemporary Studies*, 9 (1972), p. 15.

41 Paul A. Samuelson, 'The pure theory of public expenditure', *Review of Economics and Statistics*, 36 (November, 1954), pp. 387–89.

42 See, for example, W. Mark Crain and Robert D. Tolleson, 'Campaign expenditures and political competition,' *Journal of Law and Economics*, 19 (April, 1976), pp. 177–88, and Richard E. Wagner 'Economic manipulation for political profit: macroeconomic consequences and constitutional limitations', *Kyklos*, 30 (1977), pp. 395–410.

43 Dennis Mueller's paper 'Public choice: a survey,' in the *Journal of Economic Literature*, 14 (June, 1976), pp. 395–433, remains a useful compendium of the literature that has largely directed current discussions.

44 Frank Knight, 'Ethics and economic interpretation,' in *The Ethics of Competition* (New York: Harper & Row, 1935), pp. 19–43.

45 Frank Knight, 'Abstract economics as absolute ethics,' *Ethics*, 76 (April, 1966), pp. 163–77.

46 The status of the *Journal of Political Economy* as a house organ is not unique. *The Economic Journal*, published at Cambridge University (UK), and the *Quarterly Journal*, published at Harvard University (Cambridge, Mass.), have exhibited a similar preference for publishing articles written by faculty and former students.

47 Martin Bronfenbrenner in 'Observations on the Chicago school(s)' suggests that there are *two* Chicago Schools; 'the departure of Jacob Viner and the passing of Henry Simons marks a 'dividing line' between the pre-war school and the post-war school. The pre-war school, which included Knight, Viner, and Simons, exhibited more concern about the price level and was less concerned about the money supply than the post-war school. It also had more concern about economic freedom and allocative efficiency.'

48 See, for example, R. Kessel, 'Price discrimination in medicine,' *Journal of Law and Economics*, 1 (October 1958), pp. 20–53, and S. Rottenberg, 'The baseball players labor market,' *Journal of Political Economy*, 64 (June, 1956), pp. 242–58.

49 This is in significant contrast with the greater concern at Harvard and Columbia Universities with economic history and development, public finance, fiscal policy, international economics, and industrial organization. See the report for the year 1959–60 in *American Economic Review*, 50 (September, 1960), pp. 864–91.

50 See Henry Simons, 'A positive program for laissez-faire: some proposals for a liberal economic policy,' reprinted in *Economic Policies toward Less Developed Countries*, pp. 40–77.

Glossary of terms and concepts

Coase theorem
Economic efficiency can be achieved without resorting to legal action by various arrangements that internalize externalities; for example, there is an optimal amount a damaged party may pay the party inflicting damage to modify its activities. Legal intervention is available unless transactions costs are so high that the costs of allocating resources via the market mechanism exceed those of legal determination.

Human capital investment
The allocation of resources for education, training, and moving for the purpose of increasing the expected future income stream. Chicagoans explain these allocations in terms of the principle of rational household behavior.

Property rights
Relations established by law among persons (and businesses) that involve the use of scarce resources.

Questions for discussion and further research

1 Are there distinctive attributes or a common set of beliefs on the basis of which it is meaningful to maintain that the economists affiliated with the University of Chicago are identifiable as representing a 'school' of thought? Identify such specific contributors and the topics about which they write to substantiate your interpretation.

2 What are the essentials of Gary Becker's theory of household choice? How does it build on the Menger–Knight heritage? What are some of the aspects of human behavior, which that are not usually conceived to be topics, that are investigated by economists that Becker's approach has encouraged economists to investigate?

3 How has Richard Easterlin extended the theory of household choice to explain long-run trends in population growth?

4 Frank Knight and A. C. Pigou disagreed fundamentally about the reasons why market outcomes might reflect market failure. How does Pigou's explanation and suggested policy approach reflect his Marshallian origins? Knight's argument, on the other hand was that divergences between private and social welfare reflect an improper identification of property rights. Explain Knight's argument and show why its policy orientation is different from Pigou's.

5 What is the 'Coase theorem'? How can a market be created in property rights? How does such a market help solve the Knight–Pigou problem?

6 How has the Chicago view manifested itself in explaining and making policy toward third world economies?

7 What is the focus of contemporary 'public choice' literature? How does it enlighten us about the role of political processes in relation to economic outcomes?

Notes for further reading

From *The New Palgrave*

M. W. Reder on the Chicago School, vol. 1, pp. 413–17; Robert D. Cooter on the Coase theorem, vol. 1, pp. 457–59; Stanley Reiter on efficient allocation, vol. 2, pp. 107–18; George Stigler on Frank Knight, vol. 3, pp. 55–59; Sherwin Rosen on human capital, vol. 2, pp. 681–89; Richard A. Berk on household production, vol. 2, pp. 675–77; Gary S. Becker on family, vol. 2, pp. 281–85; R. Gronau on value of time, vol. 4, pp. 796–97; Arman A. Alchian on property rights, vol. 3, pp. 1031–34.

Selected references and suggestions for further reading

Arrow, Kenneth. *Social Choice and Individual Values* (New York: Wiley, 1951).

Becker, Gary S. *The Economic Approach to Human Behavior* (Chicago: University of Chicago Press, 1976).

Becker, Gary S. *The Economics of Discrimination.* 2nd edn (Chicago: University of Chicago Press, 1971). [Originally published in 1957.]

Becker, Gary S. *Human Capital: A Theoretical and Empirical Analysis with Special Reference to Education* (New York: National Bureau of Economic Research, 1964).

Becker, Gary S. *A Treatise on the Family* (Cambridge, Mass.: Harvard University Press, 1981).

Ben-Porath, Yoram. 'Economics and the family–match or mismatch? A review of Becker's *A Treatise on the Family.*' *Journal of Economic Literature*, 20 (March, 1982), pp. 52–64.

Bronfenbrenner, Martin. 'Observations on the Chicago School(s).' *Journal of Political Economy*, 70 (1962), pp. 72–75.

Buchanan, J. M. 'The pure theory of government finance: a suggested approach.' *Journal of Political Economy*, 57 (December, 1949), pp. 496–505.

Coase, Ronald. 'The problem of social cost.' *Journal of Law and Economics*, 3 (October, 1960), pp. 1–44.

Easterlin, Richard A. *Population, Labor Force and Long Swings in Economic Growth* (New York: National Bureau of Economic Research, 1968).

Foley, Duncan J. 'Problem vs. Conflicts? Economic theory and ideology.' *American Economic Review, Papers and Proceedings*, 65 (May, 1975), pp. 231–36.

Gronau, Reuben. 'Leisure, home production, and work – the theory of the allocation of time revisited.' *Journal of Political Economy*, 85 (December, 1977), pp. 1099–1123.

Johnson, Harry G. *Money, Trade, and Economic Growth* (London: George Allen and Unwin, 1962).

Hannan, Michael T. 'Families, markets, and social structures: an essay on Becker's *A Treatise on the Family.*' *Journal of Economic Literature*, 20 (March, 1982), pp. 65–72.

Knight, Frank. *Introduction to Carl Menger's Principles of Economics.* Translated and edited by James Dingwall and Bert Hoselitz (New York: The Free Press, 1950).

Lancaster, Kelvin J. 'A new approach to consumer theory.' *Journal of Political Economy*, 74 (April, 1966), pp. 132–57.

Nelson, Phillip. 'Advertising as information.' *Journal of Political Economy*, 82 (1974), pp. 729–54.

Peltzman, Sam. 'Toward a more general theory of regulation.' *The Journal of Law & Economics*, 9 (August, 1976), pp. 211–40.

Posner, Richard A. 'The social costs of monopoly and regulation.' *Journal of Political Economy*, 83 (August, 1975), pp. 807–27.

Reder, Melvin W. 'Chicago economics: permanence and change.' *Journal of Economic Literature*, 20 (March, 1982): pp. 1–38.

Samuelson, Paul A. 'The pure theory of public expenditures,' *Review of Economics and Statistics*, 36 (November, 1954), pp. 387–89.

Schumpeter, J. A. *Capitalism, Socialism, and Democracy* (New York: Harper & Row, 1942).

Simons, Henry. *A Positive Program for Laissez-Faire*. In Public Policy Pamphlet no. 15, edited by Harry D. Gideonse (Chicago: The University of Chicago Press, 1934).

Stigler, George J. 'The economics of information.' *Journal of Political Economy*, 69 (June, 1961), pp. 213–25.

Stigler, George J. 'Information in the labor market.' *Journal of Political Economy*, 70, supplement (October, 1962) 94–105.

Stigler, George J. 'The theory of economic regulation.' *The Bell Journal of Economics and Management Science* 2 (Spring, 1971), pp. 3–21.

Stigler, George J. and Friedland, Claire. 'What can regulators regulate? The case of electricity.' *Journal of Law & Economics*, 5 (October, 1962), pp. 1–16.

Stigler, George J. and Becker, Gary S. 'De Gustibus Non Est Disputandum.' *American Economic Review*, 67 (March, 1977), pp. 76–90.

'Symposium on the Chicago school.' *Journal of Economic Issues*, 9 (December, 1975) and 10 (March, 1976).

Chapter 25

Competing paradigms in contemporary economics

....

Reflections about the history of economics and its method

The first chapter of this book suggested that human minds undoubtedly entertained thoughts and ideas about the material aspects of life from the beginning of mankind. However, it was not until the eighteenth century that speculation about economic phenomena developed as economic *analysis* rather than economic thought. In previous centuries ideas relating to the material aspects of human life were simply incorporated into religious, philosophical, ethical, political and legal thought forms to which economic questions, while certainly not irrelevant, were nevertheless peripheral. The kinds of activities and events which gave individuals control over the material aspects of their lives were so limited that there was neither a basis or a need for systematic explanation. It was not until the latter part of the seventeenth century that the then rising merchant class was able to gain sufficient economic and political power to wrest away a portion of the economy's increasing surplus (or rent) from the Tudor kings and their fellow aristocrats. It was only then that individuals were able to engage in activities which reflected what John Locke expressed as 'the right to life, liberty and property.'

The tracts and pamphlets written by merchants during the seventeenth century are the source of interesting and even important ideas on production, wealth, trade, rent, interest and money. Yet, *analytical* economics extends no further back in time than Richard Cantillon's *Essai* (1755) and the writings of Quesnay and his fellow French reformist intellectuals who called themselves *les economists*. Although Physiocratic writings were voluminous, and James Steuart published the first systematic treatise on the *Principles of Political Economy* in 1767, their subject matter failed to emerge as a separate discipline until Adam Smith's *Wealth of Nations* was published in 1776. Even so, *Wealth of Nations* failed to stir up substantial intellectual energy in the pursuit of analytical economics. Smith was a professor of moral philosophy; in retrospect *Wealth of Nations* is a great contribution because he was a master at synthesizing (though without attribution) the insights and positive knowledge derived from the scholastics, the mercantilists and many of the Physiocrats. His great insight was that the force of competition that Smith saw as implicit in the laws of nature directs an economy's resources into employments which maximize social welfare, even though individuals are seeking out their own selfish interests. Smith thus helped lay the foundation for

545

the body of principles now known as 'mainstream' economics. The writings of J. B. Say, Robert Malthus, David Ricardo, John Stuart Mill and other less well known nineteenth century classicals were essentially engaged in refining, extending and elaborating the themes set forth in *Wealth of Nations*. Philosophy, history, and jurisprudence continued to provide the essential intellectual background for their thinking. However, the usefulness of political arithmetic for establishing empirical arguments had not been forgotten, despite Adam Smith's negative assessment of its possible abuse because of overconfidence in the quality of data, especially as a basis for formulating policy.

While Smith had reservations about the quantitative reasoning of political arithmeticians such as Sir William Petty, John Graunt and William King, he was, nevertheless, concerned with policy quite as much as he was with analysis. It was the appropriateness of policy concerns that became a point of difference between classicists like Smith, Malthus, Ricardo and J. S. Mill and people such as William Nassau Senior who took the position that, if economics is to be a science, it must restrict itself to analyzing the functioning of the economy and not intrude into policy making, where value judgments are a significant consideration. Thus, nineteenth century thinkers were chiefly concerned with articulating the 'laws' of classical economics, i.e. laws which operate as impersonally as physical laws to direct the economy's human and physical resources among alternative uses and propel it along its growth path. While nineteenth century contributors, unlike Adam Smith, were generally *political economists* rather than moral philosophers, the number of individual scholars who identified themselves with this field remained very small when compared with the number of professionals in other intellectual fields such as theology, medicine and law.

The establishment of The Statistical Section of the British Association for the Advancement of Science (later Section F) in 1833 and the Statistical Society of London (later the Royal Statistical Society) in 1834, mark the beginning of the collection and classification of data relating to all branches of knowledge. Richard Jones identified the object of the Statistical Section to be the accumulation of all 'classes of facts relating to communities of men which promise when sufficiently multiplied to indicate general laws.'[1] While there was no unanimity at first that 'the moral, political and metaphysical, as well as the physical portions of knowledge' were equally deserving of inclusion, statistics and economics were the first *non-physical* subjects accorded recognition as belonging to science.[2]

Once data became available they provided a basis for challenging the traditional deductive method of classical economics. Bentham, Mill and Jevons were among nineteenth century British thinkers who understood that the classification of branches of knowledge lays the foundation for arriving at scientific truths. They particularly anticipated that data collection and classification would be useful for the hedonic analysis in which they were interested. The work they undertook in this direction marks the beginning of the 'second stage' in the development of numeracy in economics.

When hedonic analysis ultimately proved impractical, the techniques of graphs, rate charts, averages and, later, an understanding of calculus as a tool for rigorous thought and expression, paved the way for marginalism, not only in the UK, but also in Austria, France, Sweden, America and Italy. By the end of the nineteenth century a rising proportion of intellectual talent was being devoted to economics. Indeed, there was substantial, although isolated, progress on the Continent in the writings of Gossen, Thünen, Cournot, Dupuit and Menger. Except for Menger, these thinkers were pioneers in the use of mathematics as a tool for establishing rigorous analysis that developed into contemporary microeconomics. Marshall also had mathematical training, although he almost disdained its use in furthering the largely oral tradition of neoclassicism that flourished in Cambridge. That tradition neatly incorporated the diminishing marginal utility principle which Jevons had hoped would constitute the basis for a marginal revolution into its analysis of demand. Yet, the introduction of diminishing marginal utility failed to produce a paradigm shift, since Marshall's eclecticism effectively preserved the Ricardo–Mill attribution of exchange value to cost of production. It did, however, facilitate a renaming of the discipline from its earlier 'political economy' to 'economics,' although Marshall's first edition defined the terms synonymously as a 'study of mankind in the ordinary business of life; it examines that part of individual and social action which is most closely connected with the attainment and use of the material requisites of well-being'[3]

The theories of monopolistic and imperfect competition articulated by Edward Chamberlin and Joan Robinson during the years of 'high theory' were clear extensions of Marshall's particular equilibrium analysis. However, Keynes's principle of aggregate demand was without question a paradigmatic challenge to Marshall's particular equilibrium analysis. Its repudiation of Say's Law and the quantity theory of money, along with its perception that economic outcomes are inherently uncertain, negates the mainstream view,

which implies that commodity, labor, and money markets have strong equilibrium tendencies. Yet, Keynes's message has since been compromised by neo-Walrasian, Monetarist, and new classical principles that have convinced a very large segment of the economics profession that the economy is, indeed, characterized by equilibrium tendencies in the short run and by 'steady state growth' in the long run. This body of macroeconomic principles is complemented by the body of microeconomic principles that explain the 'allocative efficiency' of the maximizing behaviors of households and business firms. These have been extended to incorporate a property rights approach to circumvent possible 'market failure.' Together these macro- and microeconomic principles comprise what has been termed 'normal science,' i.e. the core of ideas which 'prepare[s] the student for membership in the particular scientific community with which he will later practice.'[4] For many, given the sophistication of its empirical tools, econometrics has become the 'sister discipline' of economics. Its development has also been accompanied by a professionalization of economics that has been accompanied by a level of mathematical competence that rivals that of natural scientists; in particular, physicists. Nevertheless, mainstream thinkers are confronting challenges that relate both to their micro- and macroeconomic analyses and their heavy reliance on mathematics and econometrics.

Four clear cut alternative paradigms have been articulated by mainstream critics. These are: Neo-Institutionalism, Radical or 'New Left' Economics, Modern Austrian Economics, and Post-Keynesian Economics in which the American post-Keynesian approach identifies itself as separate from the Cambridge tradition. Clearly, in economics, intellectual crises that signal a deep inconsistency or misfit between the puzzle solving capabilities of practitioners within the framework of the paradigm do *not* result in scientific revolutions which bring about the replacement of the existing paradigm, as is the case in the natural sciences. Every science has its dissenters who engage in what Thomas Kuhn describes as *extraordinary research* directed against traditional tenets and beliefs. Except for Marx, Veblen and Keynes, the critics of the mainstream are accorded little space in textbooks on the history of economics. Yet, dissent now reflects such a substantial volume of contemporary writing in economics that it seems appropriate to conclude this volume with a sufficiently detailed survey of writings directed against mainstream theorizing and its methodology to provide an appreciation of the possible future direction of economics.

The Neo-Institutionalist challenge

Clarence Ayres: towards a theory of social value

Clarence Ayres, until his death in 1972, was the leading academic proponent of the Dewey–Veblen tradition and contributed to the positive development of Institutionalism by addressing the problem of social value.

While the pioneers of Institutionalism, especially J. M. Clark, had an appreciation of the link between the social-engineering proposals and the development of a theory of social value, it was Clarence Ayres who made progress towards identifying a criterion to provide guidance for relating means to ends. His starting point was an attack on the neoclassical premise that price (i.e. value in exchange) is a suitable surrogate for, and measure of, utility (i.e. value in use). His argument was that market phenomena are not a basis for evaluating social value.

By utilizing Dewey's instrumental logic and Veblen's evolutionary view of the economic process, Ayres advanced the argument that social values and the criteria according to which they are evaluated are themselves an aspect of the social process or, more particularly, the 'technological continuum' of that process. The continuity of society provides the basis for an objective definition or standard for social value and welfare. 'When we judge a theory to be good or bad, or an action to be right or wrong, what we mean is that, in our opinion the thing or act in question will, or will not, serve to *advance the life process* insofar as we can envision it.'[5] Thus, for Ayres, the essential criterion of social value is the furtherance of the life process of humanity.

When this process is impeded by 'ceremonial' behavior (to use Veblen's term), which tends to 'distort' the production and distribution of real income, the principle of social value is violated. The clear requirement, then, is for *social engineering* to alter the institutions from which adverse ceremonial behavior patterns derive. He chides Western social scientists for having accepted the view that, 'we must trust the conduct of our affairs to the operation of the market, cheerfully accepting whatever anomalies of wealth and poverty may then ensue, because no other social instrumentality is equal to the task of allocating resources.'[6] Ayres maintained that prices are not the only data about which rational decisions can be made and, influenced in considerable measure by Keynes's analysis, emphasized the relevance of the macroeconomic objective of full employment. He thus tried to incorporate macroeconomic analysis into institutionalist economics. 'Macroeconomics is Veblenian precisely in the sense that it turns away from the sterilities of price equilibrium theory to the realities of the community's efforts to feed and clothe and house itself.'[7] Thus, Ayres advocated the redistribution of income in order to increase consumption until the full employment output made possible by modern technology can be absorbed. He believed this policy would eliminate recessions and provide the basis for a new age of economic progress. He recommended that redistribution be achieved via a sharply progressive system of direct taxation of income and estates. He thought tax policy, which he regarded as 'the perfect instrument' for achieving income redistribution, could be coupled with a guaranteed income proposal whose general outline he had formulated as early as 1952.[8]

Galbraith's new industrial state

While Ayres is known to few outside academic circles, John Kenneth Galbraith, Professor Emeritus of Harvard University, is very much in the public eye and, no doubt, commands the largest readership among those who are currently disassociating themselves from mainstream economics. He has also established himself as a popular lecturer and TV personality besides having the distinction of being a recent past president of The American Economic Association. In Galbraith's 1972 address to this national association, he observed that contemporary theory has no 'useful handle for grasping the economic problems that now beset … modern society,' which leaves a 'whole galaxy of … urgent economic issues largely untouched.'[9]

In common with the pioneers of institutional economics, Galbraith recognizes the dominant role of technology in shaping the present American economy. But he conceptualizes the impact of technology in terms of the management principle of firm viability

rather than on the philosophical level implicit in the Clark–Ayres notion of social value. Much of his thinking builds on the requirement of today's giant corporations for minimum levels of earnings to assure their survival, growth, and technical virtuosity. Galbraith sees these needs as negating the conventional assumption that firms seek to maximize profits. In the present industrial state, power is no longer associated with capitalists and entrepreneurs, but resides in a technostructure that includes salaried managers who 'must eschew personal profit making.' In Galbraith's view, the assumption that managers will do for stockholders what they are forbidden to do for themselves weakens the tenability of the profit-maximizing assumption on which mainstream analysis is predicated.

Galbraith's observations about the high-powered advertising and merchandising that characterize most markets have also raised anew the Veblenian question of consumer sovereignty. Firms that are able to manipulate consumer demand through advertising and related techniques have an impact on the ability of the consumer to make rational choices among alternatives.[10] Galbraith, therefore, regards the traditional view that the consumer is sovereign as being untenable in the affluent society that modern technology makes possible. The creation of new wants is essential to the survival and growth of the modern corporation because the productive capacity of today's technostructure is so vast.

There has thus emerged what Galbraith calls the *dependence effect*; a higher level of want creation – generated by advertising and other techniques designed to manipulate consumer demands – has become essential because of the greater production potential of the production technostructure.[11] The implications of these observations about consumption go considerably beyond those of the theories of imperfect competition. They are also different from Veblen's view of 'pecuniary emulation' as a cultural phenomenon. Galbraith would, however, agree with Veblen that the relationship between consumption and production cannot be explained in neoclassical terms. Orthodox economics cannot explain either the emergence of the technostructure or how consumer sovereignty became supplanted, via the dependence effect, by *producer* sovereignty.

In his *Economics and the Public Purpose* (1973), Galbraith's argument concerning the dependence effect and the creation of 'contrived' wants is modified somewhat to make selling efforts compatible with some level of actual want satisfaction at the consumer level. However, his more important insight is that producer efforts at want creation is a safe form of competition among ostensibly rival producers. Instead of competing for larger shares of each other's markets, they are concerned with promoting the growth of the entire industry. The survival requirements of giant corporate enterprises thus present a different perspective on the phenomena of growth than is inherent in the mainstream view.

The planning system

Galbraith interprets the development of giant corporations as organizational entities as the outcome of extensive planning at the level of the firm. His inquiry also explores the relationship between corporate planning systems and the state. Government, especially the Department of Defense, is a major customer of business enterprise. Congress and governmental and public regulatory agencies typically have a symbiotic relationship with big business; their interests are mutually compatible. Witness the classic phrase, 'What's good for General Motors is good for the country.' Galbraith's institutionalism is thus fully cognizant of the role of the political process in the generation of changing institutions, legal and otherwise, which shape economic behavior and outcomes.

The goals of organized labor are also interpreted by Galbraith as being essentially compatible with those of the corporate structure. In his view the historical enmity between labor and industry has become reconciled within the framework of the technostructure. Labor unions have shown themselves capable of exerting what Galbraith termed 'countervailing power.' The extent to which this will continue in the US now that substantial segments of manufacturing industry (where unions have historically been the strongest) have declined, remains to be seen. It is possible, that while consumers are gaining from the availability of cheaper imports, these benefits are offset, in some degree at least, by job losses. Because giant corporations may become less able to pass on wage increases in the form of higher prices because of increased global competition, their interests may become less compatible with those of workers. Thus, 'social imbalance' which Galbraith recognized as a negative aspect of an affluent society may become exacerbated by still more pronounced income inequality. Income inequality 'distorts' the use of resources because 'it diverts them from the wants of the many to the esoteric desire of the few . . .' While Galbraith's social criticism has invited its share of adverse comment, many highly respected economists agree that the questions Galbraith raises concerning the quality of life, as it is shaped by the modern technostructure, are relevant.

The challenge of radical economics

The radical paradigm

Modern radical economists are considerably to the left of Galbraith in terms of their politics and their economics. The rapidity with which their ideas have gained currency since 1969, when a group of young rebels demanded to be heard at the convention of the American Economic Association, is due, at least in part, to the intellectual sympathy displayed by Galbraith and other well-established economists, among them Kenneth Boulding, the late Martin Bronfenbrenner, Robert Heilbroner, and Daniel Fusfeld. During 1971, when Galbraith was president of the American Economic Association, the radical contingent from Harvard University was well represented at the annual convention. Their organization originated when a group of Harvard graduate students and faculty tried (unsuccessfully at first) to add a course to the economics curriculum that aimed at examining and resolving a host of controversial issues, among them poverty, discrimination, pollution, the Vietnam War, inflation, and unemployment.

The modern radical school – sometimes referred to as the *new left* – emerged during the 1960s. It owes a considerable intellectual debt to the economics of Karl Marx, although it is by no means wholly Marxian. Its Marxist aspect is evident chiefly in its historical perspective and its view that society is an integrated system whose economic, political, and social aspects are interrelated and inseparable. These interrelationships are interpreted as reflecting the mode of production, which modern radical economists construe in the Marxian sense of referring not simply to the technology embodied in production processes, but also to the ownership of the means of production and, therefore, the social relationships among classes.[12] 'The most important and most distinctive feature of the mode of production in capitalist societies is its organization of labor by means of the wage contract.'[13] The governance of labor's economic status by the wage contract reflects its propertyless state. Workers have no alternative but to work for wages and have their surplus products appropriated by those owning the means of production.

Modern radicals have added a number of new insights of a sociological nature to their Marxian interpretation of the economic relationships among classes. Particular interest attaches to the problem of worker alienation and the role of various institutions, specifically the school and the family unit, in supporting and perpetuating the capitalistic system. Those who own capital and control the work process nurture the development and maintenance of institutions – in particular public schools – that are compatible with the kinds of work habits and attitudes (e.g. punctuality and regular attendance) that are supportive of capitalism.

The characteristics of the working class have become substantially changed in the system's present phase of monopoly capitalism. Radicals note that when the factory system first emerged, the handicraft workers of the preceding age became obsolete; the worker thus became alienated as separate skills and crafts gradually became obliterated by the requirements of the factory system for 'labor pure and simple.' Raw labor power required only the most general skills that are quickly learned on the job.

With the continued technological advance that characterizes the present phase of capitalism, the requirement for more specific work skills emerged again for many workers. These are typically learned via on-the-job training.

Since the training process is expensive, today's capitalists, unlike those of past decades, have an interest in retaining the workers they have trained as 'quasi-fixed' factors, and tend to encourage uninterrupted job tenure. Their requirements promote what radical economists refer to as *stratified* labor markets.

Depending on their race, sex, and class, certain workers are identified as likely to exhibit the kind of stable work habits essential to capitalist production. Minorities – including women, who traditionally have had unstable work patterns – are thus shunted into the lower strata of the labor market. Here they are confronted with entry jobs that are not only low paying but provide neither job training nor benefits. These workers are alienated by their work experiences and tend to have high turnover rates. Because employees have little or nothing invested in their training, they typically bear the brunt of the unemployment that accompanies a decline in aggregate demand. Their unstable employment experiences, in turn, are likely to be associated with poverty levels of living, typically in urban slums.[14] Poverty, sexism, and racism are thus inherent, in the view of the radical economists, in the functioning of capitalism. Even the political process operates to serve the interests of the capitalist class. The primary function of the state is to protect private property; in a mature system like that of the US or the UK, the degree of state action required to preserve the interests of the capitalists is minimal; capitalists 'do not need the state to enhance their position, only to assure it.'[15]

A further aspect of the radical paradigm, which also reflects its Marxian heritage, is its interpretation of the competitive forces of capitalism as functioning 'inevitably [to] spur owners of capital to protect themselves against their competitors by producing more goods and accumulating more and more profit.'[16] The drive toward capital accumulation and productive capacity underlies the great internal contradictions that characterize capitalism. On the one hand, the necessity for division of labor creates an interdependence among people as producers; at the same time, capitalist production requires ruthless competition to ensure individual survival. A further contradiction of capitalism is that conflict about the sharing of the surplus product persists in spite of the fact that the system has the productive capability to provide adequately for all members of society.

Can capitalism survive? The radical view

Unlike some of the more moderate critics of mainstream economics and the capitalist system, modern radical economists do not envision the possibility of correcting capitalism's faults. No amount of social engineering in the form of equal opportunity legislation, desegregated schools, Head Start, and government sponsored worker training and retraining programs can remedy the basic fault of the capitalistic system. The relationship between the state and the capitalist class is such that measures threatening the relative share of the capitalist class preclude any really meaningful program to redistribute income. The only effective cure for the ills of capitalism is the destruction of the system itself.

The challenge of modern Austrian economics

The tradition of which Menger was the founding father was, as noted in Chapter 12, transmitted to the University of Chicago largely through the efforts of Frank Knight. The emphasis of Chicago scholars on subjectivism, marginal analysis, opportunity cost, and libertarianism became so fully absorbed into the economics of the mainstream that some historians of economic thought view Austrian economics as a school whose separate identity came to an end in the 1930s.[17] There are, however, important differences that set modern Austrian thinking (as distinct from the Austrian tradition that continued chiefly in Vienna into the 1930s) apart from the mainstream. Thus, the term *Austrian* has come to have different meanings among contemporary practitioners.

One important variant builds on Böhm-Bawerk's capital and interest theory. It will be recalled from Chapter 13 that the concept of roundabout production and the time dimension inherent in the production process was a key feature of Böhm-Bawerk's contribution. It became the foundation for Friedrich Hayek's examination of *information* as an overlooked dimension of the process of producing and pricing goods.[18] Hayek's argument was that the discovery and mobilization of information is the essential characteristic of the production process. The competitive market process is, in essence, a discovery procedure. In place of the neoclassical view of the mechanistic maximizing individual. Hayek and other Austrians are concerned to address the formation of individual tastes and, above all, knowledge and expectations about available opportunities. What drives the market, in their view, is thus not the somewhat anemic atomistic individuals whose maximizing behaviors are a response to given price parameters, but the interaction of blood-and-guts rivals whose individual plans become coordinated in the market. The role of the market is thus to mobilize and transmit knowledge.

Neo-Austrians therefore have a particular interest, as did Schumpeter, in the role of the entrepreneur. Indeed, Schumpeter's theory of the innovating entrepreneur as the key agent in bringing about both cyclical and secular changes is a critical building block toward furthering this variant of the neo-Austrian paradigm. Harkening back to Böhm-Bawerk's view of the capitalist's agio as a payment for the creation of 'near goods,' modern Austrians view profits as rewarding entrepreneurs for the discovery of new knowledge that coordinates markets.

The neo-Austrian concern about the process of knowledge acquisition has also led in another important direction, which has brought about an interesting and intellectually important overlap with the strand of post-Keynesian thought that emphasizes uncertainty about the knowledge process. Ludwig von Mises and J. R. Hicks examined decision making in a world characterized by events and circumstances that mathematical probabilities cannot render knowable, i.e. by uncertainty.[19] A substantial literature has resulted, which includes, in particular, the work of Murray N. Rothbard and Israel Kirzner.[20] Both criticize the equilibrium-oriented thinking of the mainstream and offer an alternative view that repudiates the focus the mainstream has accorded econometrics as the sister-discipline of economics. Together with the post-Keynesians, modern Austrians reject the premise that economic outcomes can be successfully predicted by assuming that the variables on which they depend behave according to the laws of probability. The methodological criticisms these economists direct against the mainstream thus reflect a considerable consensus, which will be examined immediately after the challenge being directed against the mainstream by post-Keynesian thinkers.

The challenge of post-Keynesian theory

A very large and diverse 'after-Keynes' litera-ture, which is critical of the mainstream, has developed and lends itself to being categor-ized under four main headings. The first and most influential of these challenges under-took to counter the influence of J. R. Hicks's 'suggested reinterpretation' of Keynes's work. It was initiated by the late American economist Sidney Weintraub (1914–83) with extensive support and substantial original contributions from Joan Robinson (1903–80). Its impetus was the phenomenon of inflation whose rapid acceleration in the 1960s and 1970s led them to undertake a major intel-lectual battle with the Monetarist analysis and policy recommendations examined in Chapter 23.

A second strand of post-Keynesian analy-sis explores the tendency that capitalist econ-omies exhibit toward endogenous instability in consequence of the uncertain relationship between the pricing of capital assets and the flow of investment.

The third strand of post Keynesian eco-nomic analysis pursues the theme of uncertainty to examine the phenomenon of change over time. This focus is traceable to the influence of Roy Harrod's growth for-mula $G = s/v$ in which s is the long-run aver-age savings ratio and $v = \Delta K/\Delta Y$ the *desired* ratio between an increment of induced investment and new output and income. The chief concern of this capital stock adjustment model is to explain the erratic expansion path of capitalist economies as being related to the financing of investment out of profits in an economy dominated by large corporate enterprise.

There is also a fourth strand of post-Keynesian economics that is focused on chal-lenging the marginal productivity theory of factor income distribution. It is associated primarily, though not exclusively, with scholars at Cambridge University, UK, who are engaged in pursuing the theme that wages and other income shares are determined chiefly by social and political institutions. In the sections which follow each of these will be reviewed in turn.

Weintraub's 'classical' Keynesianism

An early effort to counter the influence of Hicks's 'suggested reinterpretation' of Key-nes's work was initiated by Sidney Weintraub, who undertook to link the theory of employment and output with the theory of value and distribution via the aggregate-supply function. It will be recalled that the aggregate-supply schedule (the Z function) was not explicitly stated in the Keynes system and was popularly represented simply as a 45° line. Because this simplification obscures the cost and productivity conditions of the econ-omy, Weintraub undertook to show that the aggregate-supply function can be derived from the supply curve of the firm. The firm's supply curve, it will be recalled, is the segment of its marginal cost curve lying above average variable cost. It indicates the output the firm is willing to sell at each price and is upward sloping because, for a given stock of capital, additional inputs of labor eventually yield diminishing returns. The industry short-run supply function, which is the lateral summa-tion of the marginal cost curves of the firms, relates industry output to expected market prices. Since employment is correlated with output, an employment function (i.e. a func-tion relating employment with required sales revenues) can be generated for each industry. The aggregate supply schedule for the economy as a whole can then be built up by aggregating the revenue–employment values required as a condition for providing various levels of employment for the economy as a whole. An alternative way of expressing this is to say that the aggregate money-supply function relates each level of employment to the GDP level (in current dollars) required to support it.[21]

The aggregate-supply function thus derived is in *money*, not real, terms. It is normally expected to rise to the right at an increasing rate, as does *OZ* in Figure 25.1. This shape reflects the increasing significance of diminishing returns in individual production functions when capital stock remains unchanged while employment increases. Its upward slope implies that prices rise with employment because diminishing returns increase marginal costs and, therefore, the revenues required to make increased employment profitable. Every point on the aggregate-supply function reflects the relationship between employment and money outlays, and has an implicit price level.[22]

The aggregate (money) demand function in Figure 25.1 shows the expenditures *expected* from consumption and investment as the level of employment increases. Every point on the

DD function, therefore, also has a price level implicit in it that corresponds to a point on the aggregate supply curve. For example, in Figure 25.2, the price level implicit in Z_2 is also implicit in D_2 while the (lower) price level implicit in Z_1 is also implicit in D_1. The intersection of the aggregate-demand and supply functions determines the equilibrium level of employment ON_1, which is consistent with price level P_1.

Post-Keynesian inflation analysis

By presenting aggregate-supply and aggregate-demand functions in money terms, Weintraub's apparatus is specifically designed to treat the problem of inflation. Following him, post-Keynesians reject the theory of inflation inherent in the Phillips curve linkage of wage-rate and price-level increases and also its implied trade-off between inflation and unemployment. His alternative theory focuses on the relationship between money wage rate changes and productivity changes to explain inflation. His reasoning is that a change in the money wage will produce a shift in both the aggregate-demand curve, via its influence on consumer spending, and the aggregate-supply function via its effect on

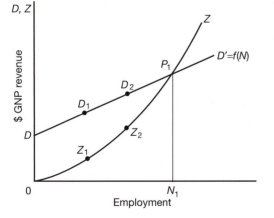

Figure 25.1 A post-Keynesian view of inflation and reduced employment

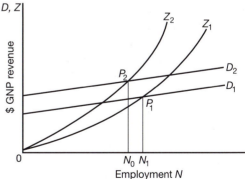

Figure 25.2 The employment–price level relationship

industry supply curves. The aggregate-supply function, Z_1, in Figures 25.1 and 25.2 reflects a given rate of money wages, w_1, and a constant mark-up, k, over the wage bill. If the average wage rate in the economy increases to w_2, there will be related changes in both the aggregate-demand and aggregate-supply functions to D_2 and Z_2. Aggregate demand shifts upward via the effect of the higher wage on income and consumption; aggregate supply, Z_1, rotates leftward via higher wages on cost of production, to Z_2.

The position of the Z function reflects the relationship between wage rates and labor productivity and is critical, according to post-Keynesians, for understanding inflation. If average money wages rise while labor productivity remains constant, or rises proportionately less than wages, the leftward movement of the Z function from Z_1 to Z_2 will be greater than the upward shift of aggregate demand from D_1 to D_2. The result is that the higher average money wage is associated with the *smaller* volume of employment N_0 and the *higher* price level P_2. Weintraub thus hypothesized that, depending on their relationship to labor productivity, higher money wages can be associated not only with *less employment* but also with a *higher price level*. Microtheory and macro-theory are joined in a manner which, in Weintraub's view, satisfies more closely Keynes's own objective of bringing the theory of prices as a whole into closer contact with the theory of value.[23]

Instability, uncertainty, and finance

The arguments of the (neoclassical) Keynesians, as discussed in Chapter 23, imply that, in the absence of strong exogenous shocks, the economy tends toward equilibrium. Keynes himself was, however, more inclined to emphasize the possibility of the economy's endogenous instability which he attributed to the uncertain relationship between the pricing of capital assets and the flow in investment.

The economy's instability reflects the uncertainty that characterizes the real world. The post-Keynesian view, following in the tradition of J. M. Keynes, is that it is *conceptually inappropriate* to 'transform' uncertainty into certainty via the calculus of probability as though there is no distinction between uncertainty and risk.[24]

The effect of uncertainty surrounding the financing decisions of individual firms is compounded in sophisticated capital-using economies by the practice of financing long-term capital assets via 'speculative financing,' that is, via the issuance of new debt.[25] Since the future is unknowable, such financing takes place amidst environments of alternating (and unpredictable) euphoria or despair. A fundamentally unstable environment is thus generated. Instability with respect to asset values, income, prices, and employment are inherent characteristics of capitalistic economies. Employment and income disequilibria are the consequence of the unstable investment environment that is generated by uncertainty.

The Cambridge post-Keynesians

Post-Keynesians who are affiliated with the modern Cambridge tradition repudiate much of Marshall's theoretical legacy, especially as it relates to income distribution. Whereas mainstream thinkers believe that the distribution of income is explainable in terms of the marginal productivity of variable factor inputs, Cambridge post-Keynesians contend that the price system does *not* determine either the prices of factor inputs or the distributive shares. Factor prices and, thus, the distributive shares flowing to the income recipients of the economy, are the outcome of institutional forces. This view of distribution is a return to the classical Ricardo–Mill conception. Contrary to neoclassical theory, which teaches that factor prices (and thus income shares) are to be understood in terms of essentially the same demand and supply principles that explain commodity prices, Ricardo maintained:

> In different stages of society, the proportions of the whole produce of the earth which will be allotted to each of these classes (landowners, capitalists and workers) under the names of rent, profit, and wages will be essentially different ... To determine the laws which regulate this distribution is the principal problem in Political Economy.[26]

Later, John Stuart Mill, reaffirming Ricardo's view that the problem of distribution is distinct from the problem of production, wrote: 'The laws or conditions of the Production of Wealth partake of the character of physical truths. There is nothing optional or arbitrary in them ... It is not so with the Distribution of Wealth. This is a matter of human institution solely.'[27]

Cambridge post-Keynesian economists who follow Piero Sraffa's rendering of Ricardo's theory of distribution interpret these well-known passages from classical political economy to mean that, on a macroeconomic level, the problem of explaining the distributive shares is *independent* of the value problem.

Sraffa's general equilibrium model, which he set out in his brief, but extremely influential, book *The Production of Commodities by Means of Commodities* (1950), is the basis for much of the post-Keynesian analysis emanating from Cambridge. Sraffa's full-employment general equilibrium model has n commodity outputs, which are known. It also has $n - 1$ unknown prices to be determined and given expression in terms of one of the commodities (possibly gold) that serves as a numéraire or common denominator of value. Outputs are assumed to have been produced by a given number of homogeneous labor units, which receive an unknown average wage rate w. Non-labor units receive a rate of return (or gross profit) r, which is also an algebraic unknown. Inputs and outputs are linked by technologically given production coefficients so that there are n equations relating each output to its input(s). Finally, there is an equation expressing the sum of the outputs, which is equal to national income. Assuming the presence of a competitive market, Sraffa's system establishes uniform wage and profit rates as the equilibrium condition.

Since commodities are both outputs and means of production, the price of each commodity is linked to every other commodity so that it is necessary to determine their relative prices simultaneously. If prices are assumed as given, the rate of profit is identifiable as a residual distributive variable. Conversely, if the rate of profit is given, then wages emerge as the distributive variable. Differently expressed, Sraffa's system is intended to demonstrate that the problem of distribution cannot be theoretically solved unless the system of equations, which represent the relationships between output values and the values of the factor inputs (i.e. r and w), is somehow closed by means of an institutionally established wage determinant. The observations of the late Joan Robinson are particularly relevant in making this point.

> Technical conditions and the rate of profit determine the pattern of normal prices, including the price of labor time ... but what determines the rate of profit? Marx closes his system (sometimes following Ricardo) by postulating a real wage governed by the conventional standard of life, and sometimes by taking as given

the share of the net profit in the value of the net output. Marshall conceals the problem behind the smoke-screen of moral sentiments. The latter-day neoclassicals are forever chasing definitions around a circular argument . . . The question of what determines the rate of profit, when the wage rate is not to be taken as given is the huge blank in traditional economic teaching.[28]

Joan Robinson's observations are a clear indictment of neoclassical distribution theory, and an implicit recommendation for the classical view that prevailed before the marginal revolution. Her intent was to make the point that it is not possible to accept Keynes's macroeconomics and at the same time maintain a neoclassical approach to microeconomic theory, especially as it relates to the theory of distribution.[29]

Sraffa's analysis is also concerned with identifying the conditions which assure the reproduction of a capitalist economy. His 'reproducibility approach' was also the approach of the Physiocrats who, as will be recalled from Chapter 4, were concerned with the maintainability of the 'net product.' It differs from the so-called 'scarcity' approach which interprets prices as reflecting the relative scarcity of goods. Sraffa thus rejects the 'circular flow' perspective of production and consumption, substituting for it a 'one-way' view that leads from the factors of production (i.e. land and labor) to consumption goods. Capital, in this view, is not an 'original' factor of production, but the product of one stage of production that is on its way to the next stage.

Post-Keynesian growth and dynamics

The dynamic aspects of post-Keynesian theory can be traced to the influence of Roy Harrod's growth formula $G = s/v$, in which G is the rate of national income, s is the average propensity to save, and v is the capital/output ratio.[30] Nicholas Kaldor's post-Keynesian models hypothesize a savings–income ratio that depends on the distribution of income.[31] Savings by wage earners and profit receivers are postulated to be functionally related to their incomes, with the propensity to save out of profit being greater than the propensity to save out of wages. In the special classical case in which the propensity to save out of wages is zero, all saving comes out of profits. If, as in Kaldor's model, the capital–output ratio is assumed given, which implies that the coefficients of production are fixed, it follows that the equality of saving and investment is brought about through changes in the *distribution of income* rather than changes in its level, as is the case of the static Keynesian model described in Chapter 21.

The chief objective of post-Keynesian growth theory is to explain why, in fact, the expansion path of a free enterprise economy is so erratic. The analysis conceives the rate of expansion to be related to the distribution of income. Recalling the world of the classical economists, income from wages is presumed to be wholly spent on consumption. Savings out of wages are thus zero, while the savings out of the profits of capitalists (i.e. non-wage earners), who receive profits through their ownership of the means of production, are 100 percent. Profit is therefore the only source for financing investment, and the expenditures of capitalists control the rate of investment.

In an economic system dominated by large corporations, the economy's propensity to save is equivalent to that of the corporate sector. These savings are the prime source of the discretionary expenditures (investment) that are critical to determining the level of economic activity. This analysis suggests that, if the rate of growth of discretionary expenditures is not equal to the investments that 'animal-spirited' business owners are willing to make in an uncertain world, the economy will move off the growth path necessary to maintain a steady state.[32] The economy will then experience a cyclical pattern around the trend line. Thus, Cambridge post-Keynesians concern themselves chiefly with the problem of short-period cyclical movements, while neoclassical growth theorists, as was explained in Chapter 21, are chiefly concerned with the analysis of long-run, steady-state expansion.

Summing up the post-Keynesian paradigm

The important differences between the prevailing neoclassical position and the challenge that is being leveled against it by post-Keynesian thinkers is conveniently summarized under the headings presented in Table 25.1. It restates in an easily read format the differences that post-Keynesians maintain set their work apart from orthodox economics. Its emphasis on the key role of the megacorp is consistent with many of Galbraith's observations in *The New Industrial State*; its

Table 25.1 A comparison of neoclassical and post-Keynesian theories

Aspect	Post-Keynesian Theory	Neoclassical Theory
Dynamic properties	Assumes pronounced cyclical pattern on top of a clearly discernible secular growth rate	Either no growth or steady expansion with market mechanisms assumed to preclude any but a temporary deviation from that growth path
Explanation of how income is distributed	Institutional factors determine a historical division of income between residual shareholders, with changes in this distribution depending on changes in the growth rate	The distribution of income explained solely by variable factor inputs and the marginal productivity of those variable factor inputs
Amount of information assumed to be available	Only the past is known, the future is uncertain	Complete foresight exists as to all possible events
Conditions that must be met before the analysis is considered complete	Discretionary income must be equal to discretionary expenditures	All markets cleared with supply equal to demand in each of those markets
Microeconomic base	Imperfect markets with significant monopolistic elements	Perfect markets with all micro units operating as price takers
Purpose of the theory	To explain the real word as observed empirically	To demonstrate the social optimality if the real world were to resemble the model

Source: Alfred Eichner and J. A. Kregel, 'An Essay on Post-Keynesian Theory: A New Paradigm in Economics,' *Journal of Economic Literature* 13 (December 1975), p. 1309.

emphasis on the institutional aspects of the income distribution process is consistent with the perception held by modern radicals, and its emphasis on the critical role of information under uncertainty is shared by modern Austrians. The question of the nature and process of knowledge acquisition has brought about an interesting and intellectually important overlap between post-Keynesian and Austrian thought. Both criticize the equilibrium oriented thinking of the mainstream and repudiate its focus on econometrics as the sister discipline of economics. Together with modern Austrians, post-Keynesians reject the premise that economic outcomes can be successfully predicted by assuming that the variables on which they depend behave according to the laws of probability.

Concluding comments

Speculation about how the issues raised by paradigmatic controversy are likely to be addressed is necessarily beyond the scope of a book about the development of economic analysis. One thing, however, appears certain: the political and economic restructuring of the world at the beginning of the twenty-first century is likely to focus once again the attention of economic theorists on the grand old questions of political economy – the wealth of nations, the sources of their growth, the distribution of gross domestic product among income claimants, levels of employment, and market gluts. These questions are less relevant to the neoclassical and new classical theories of self-regulating markets than they are to the non-market clearing, anti-equilibrium theories of the critics of the mainstream. There are, as yet, no firm answers; however, the great masterworks of economics provide insight into the kinds of questions that are likely to be confronted in

the future and without which there can be no answers.

Induction versus deduction

What is certain is that the criticisms aimed at those who espouse the allocative efficiency and market clearing views of the mainstream reflect both a methodological disagreement about how to study economic questions and philosophical disagreement about the appropriate role of authority in delineating individual and business behaviors. The mainstream position represents what is essentially a triumph of individualism, i.e. the economic problem is seen essentially as the science of analyzing household and business choices which are envisioned as culminating in a general equilibrium type of market clearing. Most economists believe that the development and refinement of the statistical/mathematical method enabled them to join these techniques with general equilibrium theory to generate econometrics as something of a 'super' tool, making it possible for economics finally to achieve status as a science. Their perception is that contemporary economics is deductive at the theoretical level, as it has been historically, while, at the empirical level, econometric techniques utilize data to quantify the values of parameters and substantiate or reject the relationships established deductively. It is precisely this perspective on which regression-based empirical work has been established as the counterpart of pure theory. Their view, as was set out in Chapter 21, is that the probabilistic approach can *circumvent* uncertainty by treating it as if it were a problem of risk.

Advocates of the use of probabilistic methods are, broadly speaking, encountering criticism from two directions. One is from other empiricists who favor Bayesean methods of statistical inference.[33] Their arguments are technically focused and are, in that sense, different from the more philosophically grounded arguments of neo-Austrians and post-Keynesians, who have rejected the premise that the laws of probability can somehow tame unknown information about the future to render it knowable. It is the latter argument that is of special concern to post-Keynesian and neo-Austrian economists. Their thinking draws heavily on the ideas of George L. S. Shackle.[34] The essence of Shackle's argument is that economic theory does not have the power to predict future economic outcomes.

> Looking into the future is analogous to looking through a kaleidoscope – a constantly altering landscape of shapes and pieces. Theories which tell us what will happen are claiming too much: too much independence from their turbulent surroundings; too much capacity to remain upright in the gale of politics, diplomacy and technical choice and change. Kaleidic theories give insight; preparedness for what cannot, in its nature, be known for sure . . . but which need not spring from total surprise. Classification is no second-rate technique. It is the method of medicine . . . of the law . . . of the organization of libraries . . . of astronomy . . . of botanical and zoological organization . . . Even the procedure on finding solutions for differential equations is a question of groping in a catalog of possibilities.[35]

What follows, especially for post-Keynesians and neo-Austrians, is the conclusion that because economic processes move forward in historical (or calendar) time, past observations cannot produce knowledge about current and/or future events. Economic science must therefore be *explanatory* and its efforts to predict should not depend on probabilistic methods. The counter-argument of the large majority (i.e. the 'mainstream') is that 'the question is not whether probabilities exist or not, but whether – if we proceed as if they existed – we are able to make statements about real phenomena that are correct for practical purposes.'[36]

To those whose concern is whether the 'real phenomena' the mainstream chooses to study are chiefly those that lend themselves to being studied with probabilistic regression techniques applied to the data sets that are at hand, this is not an appropriate rebuttal. The very nature of a social science, addressing as it does human behavior, renders exact formalization not only impossible but inappropriate for 'capturing' the 'animal spirits' which Keynes so vividly depicted as ruling investors and entrepreneurs. Thus econometric techniques are most appropriate when data samples are large, which is unfortunately often not the case; furthermore, the deficiencies of inadequate data are generally too expensive to be remedied by econometricians who are better trained at *using* data than collecting it. Most data sets are produced by government as part of the activities of taxing and regulation and their usability by econometricians is often fortuitous.

There is the further problem that economists who have been trained during the last quarter century, during which econometrics has become the sister science of economics, have made such heavy investments in learning the techniques of the discipline that they are naturally inclined to focus on the kinds of problems that lend themselves to being studied with the aid of the tools of which they have become masters. However, when the techniques are no longer suitable to address the problems, it becomes impossible for the discipline to progress towards discerning new 'truths.' It is relevant that even some of the most highly respected mathematical economists have strong reservations about reliance on mathematics and econometrics as the chief vehicles for research in a social science such as economics. Oskar Morgenstern, for example, made it clear that prediction is possible in nature because the variables are 'dead.'[37] However, the matter is conceptually different when 'live' variables are at issue, for these represent other 'wills' that impact on the behavior of others in ways that cannot be rendered 'predictable' when relying on probability theory.[38]

Individualism versus authoritarianism

It is also relevant to note that the grand old questions posed by the Masterworks of Economics are, in principle, ideologically neutral. That is, they are supposed to lead to a body of self-contained generalizations that are universal in the sense of being independent of the socio-political frameworks of alternative economic systems. Yet, it is a fact that the laws of classical economics, which are the economics 'knowledge base' from which much of the economic inquiry of the nineteenth and twentieth centuries proceeded, were articulated within the context of a price directed economy conceived to operate under a system of 'natural liberty.' In it individuals rely largely on their own self-interest, and count on the leavening influence of the 'invisible hand' to provide for the public good. Thus, *laissez-faire* is the logical policy derivative of natural law philosophy that has shaped economic theory, and has been well nigh inseparable in the history of economics.

In terms of philosophy, the opposing views about individual capabilities and responsibilities versus the need for authority are, as has been seen, traceable to the ancient Greeks and, after them, the Scholastics of the medieval era who incorporated their thinking into church doctrine during the Renaissance. However, from the standpoint of the history of economics, the opposition of views about the role of authority first becomes apparent in Physiocratic thinking. Their ideal was to achieve the natural order by prevailing on the King and his ministers to moderate the harsh restrictions of Colbertism. The Physiocrats failed politically, as was seen in Chapter 4, because they were unable to achieve the reforms needed to revitalize the agricultural sector while also satisfying the objectives of the peasant class. The primary long-term effect of Turgot's position as Finance Minister was that his deregulation of the corn trade and his introduction of tax reforms matured as belief in the 'invisible hand.'

Smith valued physiocracy as the most perfect system ever devised. He thought monopoly harmful and interpreted the competitive price as the 'just' price. Contrary to today's conventional wisdom, Smith was not a great champion of businessmen, though he was a great advocate of free competition. 'People in the same trade seldom meet together, even for merriment and diversion, but the conversation ends in conspiracy against the publick, or in some contrivance to raise prices'.[39] Accordingly, Smith championed free markets and maintained that it is the responsibility of government to erect and maintain 'those publick institutions and publick works which, though they may be in the highest degree advantageous to a great society, are however of such a nature that the profit could never repay the expense to any individual or a small number of individuals'.[40]

The great social consciousness of the Utilitarians (including Malthus, Mills, and Jevons) led them to favor policy measures to maximize 'the greatest good for the greatest number.' Although they had important differences, they supported data collection and the development of statistical methods, ultimately to achieve a hedonic calculus, precisely because of its potential to provide a rationale for policy measures. Particularly for J. S. Mill, a positive role for government was balanced by an equally strong commitment to individual liberty. Thus, as was seen in Chapter 8, he rejected socialism as the best system for alleviating poverty.

More or less contemporaneously, the contrary view of the Utopian socialists held that private property is an unmitigated evil. Together with Marx's even stronger argument that private property rights will inevitably be destroyed by the contradictions of the capitalistic system, these nineteenth century negative expressions about the reliability of individual property rights as opposed to the actions of government to achieve the public good, anticipate the twentieth-century views that are certain to be reprised in the twenty-first century.

The return to confidence in the effectiveness of competition that characterized the Marshallian era again came to an end with the mass unemployment problems of the 1920s and 1930s and Keynes's challenge to the mainstream tradition of his generation. Like Marx, Keynes emphasized the inherent instability of the capitalistic system. Marx attributed the declining rate of profit to the inability of capitalists to realize surplus value from investment, which generated breakdowns that are the prelude to the destruction of capitalism. For Keynes, the main factors causing breakdowns are derived from basic human propensities. He thus saw a necessity for government intervention to 'socialize' investment in order to offset the tendency under capitalism for aggregate demand to be inadequate for creating satisfactory employment levels. But he regarded the destruction of capitalism as being neither desirable nor

inevitable. On the contrary, he felt that the essentials of the capitalistic system could be preserved without sacrificing full employment if government exercises the proper controls. Precisely what the nature of this intervention should be, Keynes did not examine in detail. However, the social philosophy that underlies the concluding chapter of *The General Theory* is that there are certain areas that should not be left to individual initiative. Keynes suggests that:

> The state will have to exercise a guiding influence on the propensity to consume, partly through its scheme of taxation, partly by fixing the rate of interest, and partly, perhaps, in other ways. Furthermore, it seems unlikely that the influence of banking policy on the rate of interest will be sufficient by itself to determine the optimum rate of investment . . . [But it] is not the ownership of the instruments of production which it is important for the state to assume. If the state is able to determine the aggregate amount of resources devoted to augmenting the instruments and the basic rate of reward to those who own them, it will have accomplished all that is necessary.[41]

Thus, what Keynes proposed is essentially a mixed economy in which investment is socialized but in which private self-interests will continue to function in all areas in which it is compatible with full employment. He regarded this as 'the only practicable means of avoiding the destruction of existing economic firms in their entirety and as the condition of the successful functioning of individual initiative.'[42]

After Keynes

The credibility of Keynes's analysis was undermined by the advent of the dual problem of inflation and unemployment. Commitment to the policy of demand management to control the level of employment came to a concomitant end. The neoclassical synthesis is an amalgam of Keynesian principles and Walrasian general equilibrium, which is accompanied by the view that the predilection of the economy to a 'natural' rate of unemployment undermines the usefulness and necessity for government interventions in most markets because the public anticipates them so that they become counterproductive.

The microeconomic counterpart of the macroeconomic paradigm is similarly predicated on individual choice principles that are extended to a whole range of questions that are relatively new to economics as a discipline: the economics of education, of crime, of marriage, of public choice. The role of government within the framework of this paradigm is chiefly to define property rights to facilitate market solutions. Yet, if history is any guide, the present era of assigning as many activities as possible to the private sector is unlikely to rule indefinitely. The selfsame competitive forces that have caused the leading industrial economies to become 'post industrial' are certain again to call forth what J. K. Galbraith has so eloquently termed 'countervailing power.' The documented decline in real wages during the last decade is likely to refocus attention on wage and employment issues, and rekindle an interest in the study of the institutions that determine the distribution of income.

Employment issues, in particular, have moved center stage again, partly in consequence of technological changes which are not only substituting capital for labor, but require greater investments in 'human' capital to complement new investments in physical capital.[43] The capability of industrial countries, which now include the 'newly emerged' industrial economies of Asia and Eastern Europe, are posing a world-wide competition

for markets. In short, the phenomenon of potentially deficient aggregate demand, which was of such great concern to Keynes, has relevance beyond the Western economies and the era of history to which they were originally thought to apply.

The globalization of markets, i.e. the relatively free movement of goods, services, financial assets and, to some extent, the international mobility of labor, especially skilled labor, implies increasing interaction between Western economies and the rest of the world. Much of this world comprises economies with long histories of state management to which the principles of capitalist economies do not apply. Yet, the quest for profitable markets and rising standards of living is equally relevant to all. Economists who undertake to address these joint problems of their respective economies will almost necessarily find themselves drawing not only on neoclassical principles, but on the several other paradigms we have examined. What is likely to emerge is a new multi-dimensionalism or pluralism in economic theory which offers a broader range of analytical tools and a richer perspective than that of the present tradition. Indeed, there is, even now, an ongoing evolution within neoclassical theory that is too recent for inclusion in a text such as this but, nevertheless, suggests that the next generation of professionally trained economists will be able to expand on the traditional models of current mainstream thought to generate propositions that relate more clearly to the questions of a global economy.[44]

Individuals who have studied the history of economic thought are likely to have a far greater appreciation than those who have not, to understand what kinds of questions are likely to arise in different circumstances, and how the answers given to these questions are likely to become reflected in policy. Thus, we end as we began. We study the history of economics for its own sake; but more importantly, we study it to better understand and address the economic questions that arise in our lifetimes and in those of our children.

Notes

1 Cited by James P. Henderson in 'Ordering society,' in *Measurement, Quantification and Economic Analysis*, edited by Ingrid H. Rima (London: Routledge, 1993, p. 54)

2 In 'Ordering society,' in *Measurement, Quantification and Economic Analysis*.

3 The relevance of clearly defining the nature of the discipline is clearly understood by J. S. Mill who defined his subject matter as the study of 'the laws of production and distribution and some of the practical consequences deducible from them' (J. S. Mill, 1848, p. 21). John Cairnes expressed matters more briefly, writing that 'Political economy' espouses the laws of the phenomena of wealth' (1875, p. 35). Friedrich Engels (along with Karl Marx) conceived of political economy as 'the theoretical analysis of modern bourgeois society' (1959, p. 218). Thus the very descriptions of the nature of the discipline suggested that a name change might be appropriate. One suggestion was that it be renamed *Plutology* (Hearn, 1863), to convey that the discipline is concerned with human wants. Ultimately, however, as urged by William Stanley Jevons, the discipline's new name became economics; his last published book in 1905 adopted the title *Principles of Economics*. (See Peter Groenewegen 'Political economics and economics,' *The New Palgrave*, 3, pp. 905–6).

4 Thomas Kuhn, *The Structure of Scientific Revolutions* (Princeton, NJ: Princeton University Press, 1970), p. 176.

5 Clarence Ayres, *Toward a Reasonable Society: The Values of Industrial Civilization* (Austin, Tex.: The University of Texas Press, 1961), p. 113; italics added.

6 Clarence Ayres, 'The impact of the Great Depression on economic thinking,' *American Economic Review, Papers and Proceedings* (May, 1964), p. 122.

7 Clarence Ayres, 'The legacy of Thorstein Veblen,' in *Institutional Economics: Veblen, Commons and Mitchell Reconsidered*, edited by Joseph Dorfman *et al.* (Berkeley, Calif.: University of California Press, 1964), p. 61.

8 See Donald A. Walker, 'The economic policy proposals of Clarence Ayres,' *Southern Economic Journal*, 44(3) (January, 1978), p. 622.

9 John Kenneth Galbraith, 'Power and the useful economist,' *American Economic Review*, 63 (March, 1973), pp. 2–3.

10 John Kenneth Galbraith, *The Affluent Society* (Boston, Mass.: Houghton-Mifflin, 1958), p. 158.

11 John Kenneth Galbraith, *The New Industrial State* (Boston, Mass.: Houghton Mifflin, 1967), p. 128.

12 David M. Gordon, *Theories of Poverty and Underemployment* (Lexington, Mass.: D.C. Heath, 1972), pp. 56ff.

13 Gordon, *Theories of Poverty and Underemployment*, p. 3.

14 Gordon, *Theories of Poverty and Underemployment*, pp. 66–81.

15 Richard C. Edwards and Arthur MacEwan, 'Radical approach to economics,' *American Economic Review, Papers and Proceedings*, 60 (1970), p. 350.

16 Gordon, *Theories of Poverty*, p. 60.

17 See for example, Israel Kirzner on Austrian School of Economics, *The New Palgrave*, vol. 1, p. 149.

18 F. A. Hayek, *Individualism and Economic Order* (London: Routledge and Kegan Paul, 1949).

19 L. von Mises, *Human Action, A Treatise on Economics* (New Haven: Yale University Press, 1949); and John Hicks, *Capital and Time: A Neo-Austrian Theory* (Oxford, UK: Clarendon Press, 1973).

20 I. M. Kirzner, *Competition and Entrepreneurship* (Chicago: University of Chicago Press, 1973); M. N. Rothbard, *Man, Economy and State: A Treatise on Economic Principles* (Princeton, NJ: Von Nostrand, 1962).

21 Sidney Weintraub, 'A macroeconomic approach to the theory of wages,' *American Economic Review*, 46(5) (December, 1956), pp. 835–56.

22 Modern writers working in the tradition of Keynes view their emphasis on monetary magnitudes as a hallmark of their approach.

23 For a readable exposition see his Chapter 3, 'Hicksian Keynesianism,' in *Modern Economic Thought* (Philadelphia, Pa.: University of Pennsylvania Press, 1977). Earlier expositions include *An Approach to the Theory of Income Distribution* (Philadelphia: Chilton Press, 1958) and *A Keynesian Theory of Employment, Growth and Income Distribution* (Philadelphia: Chilton Press, 1965). Weintraub's wage-cost mark-up hypothesis of inflation may also be represented in terms of the equation $P = kw/A$, in which w = the average money wage, A the average productivity of labor, and k the average mark-up of unit prices over unit-labor costs. In his view of the economic process, the price level is resolved once the money-wage rate is given. See *Classical Keynesianism, Monetary Theory and the Price Level* (Philadelphia, Pa.: Chilton Press, 1961), pp. 41–64.

24 See, in particular, George L. S. Shackle, *Epistemics and Economics: A Critique of Economic Doctrines* (Cambridge, UK: Cambridge University Press, 1972); Paul Davidson, *Money and the Real World* (London: Macmillan, 1972); and Douglas Vickers, *Financial Markets in the Capitalist Process* (Philadelphia, Pa.: University of Pennsylvania Press, 1978).

25 Hyman Minsky, *John Maynard Keynes* (New York: Columbia University Press, 1975).

26 David Ricardo, *Principles of Political Economy and Taxation*, vol. 1, Preface (reprint from London, 1817; Cambridge University Press, 1951).

27 John Stuart Mill, *Principles of Political Economy* (London: Longmans, Green).

28 Joan Robinson, 'The basic theory of normal prices,' in *Essays in the Theory of Economic Growth* (Oxford, UK: Blackwell, 1963), p. 11.

29 Thus, Robinson anticipated that there would eventually be 'a second half' to Keynes's revolution, whose implications would be even more far-reaching than the first. This anticipation is explored by Ingrid H. Rima in 'Robinson and the 'second half' of the Keynesian Revolution' in *The Joan Robinson Legacy*, edited by Ingrid Rima (Armonk, NY: M. E. Sharpe, 1991).

30 Roy Harrod, 'An essay in dynamic theory,' *Economic Journal*, 49 (March, 1939), pp. 14–33. Errata (June, 1939), p. 379.

31 Nicholas Kaldor, 'Alternative theories of distribution,' *Review of Economics Studies*, 23 (1956), pp. 83–100.

32 In this connection, Alfred S. Eichner focuses on the pricing policy of the megacorp as a determinant of its rate of saving. Alfred S. Eichner, 'A theory of the determination of the mark-up under oligopoly,' *Economic Journal*, 83 (December, 1973), pp. 1184–200.

33 These are reviewed by Roy J. Epstein, 'The fall of OLS in structural estimation,' *Oxford Economic Papers*, 41 (1989), pp. 94–107.

34 George L. S. Shackle, *Epistemics and Economics: A Critique of Economic Doctrines* (Cambridge, UK: Cambridge University Press, 1972).

35 Shackle, *Epistemics and Economics*, p. 72.

36 T. Haavelmo, 'The probability approach to econometrics,' *Econometrica*, 12, (Supplement, 1944), p. 43.

37 Morgenstern (1928), p. 806

38 See Ingrid Rima 'The place of econometrics in economic analysis,' in *Measurement, Quantification and Economic Analysis* (London: Routledge, 1995), pp. 212–229.

39 Smith, 1976, *The Wealth of Nations*, New York: Modern Library, 1957, vol. 2, p. 145.

40 Smith, 1976–83, p. 723.

41 Keynes, *The General Theory*, p. 378.

42 Keynes, *The General Theory*, p. 380.

43 Ingrid H. Rima 'Sectoral changes in employment: an eclectic interpretation of "good" jobs and "poor" jobs. *Review of Political Economy*, 12 (April 2000), pp. 171–90.

44 We especially wish to call the reader's attention to the eloquence with which the late Sir Lionel Robbins (1890–1984) expressed the view that the history of economic thought is a foundation for a sophisticated, as opposed to a naïve, understanding of what goes on in both the contemporary world and intelligent conversation about it (*A History of Economic Thought: The London School of Economics Lectures 1979–80 and 1980–81*, Lecture 1, p. 6, edited by Steven Medema and Warren Samuels, Princeton, Pa.: Princeton University Press, 1998).

Questions for discussion and further research

1 What are the chief issues of contemporary controversy in economics? Who are the main participants and what are their important works that bear on the controversy?

2 How has the 'new left'' drawn on the economics of Karl Marx? What are some of the new issues of their concern that Marx had no reason to address?

3 Cambridge post-Keynesians are particularly critical of neoclassical distribution theory. In what way have they drawn on classical distribution theory as being an essential complement to Keynes's macroeconomic analysis?

4 American post-Keynesians have been especially concerned with explaining the phenomenon of inflation. What is the nature of Weintraub's aggregate money supply function? How is it related to diminishing returns and the increasing marginal cost of offering additional employment?

5 Post-Keynesian writers (both British and American) have recently focused on Keynes's early writing on the irrelevance of mathematical probability theory to economics and finance. How do Keynes's insights relate to his conception of uncertainty (as opposed to risk) and the tendency of capitalistic systems to be inherently unstable?

6 Neo-Austrians share the post-Keynesian concern about the implications of uncertainty for economic decision-making. This concern has made both schools skeptical about the high place which has been accorded to econometrics as the sister-discipline of economics. What are the essentials of their respective arguments?

7 How is Piero Sraffa's interpretation of classical economics anticipated by the Physiocrats?

8 Is there a basis for anticipating that in its future development economic theory might become increasingly pluralistic?

Suggestions for further reading

From *The New Palgrave*

Warren T. Samuels on Clarence Edwin Ayres, vol. 1, p. 165; Lester C. Thurow on John Kenneth Galbraith, vol. 2, p. 455; I. A. Kregel on Sidney Weintraub, vol. 4, p. 888; Anatol Rapoport on Kenneth E. Boulding, vol. 1, pp. 265–66; Diane Flaherty on radical political Economy, vol. 4, pp. 36–38; G. C. Harcourt on post-Keynesian economics, vol. 3, pp. 924–27: Israel Kirzner on the Austrians, vol. 1, pp. 149–51.

Selected references and suggestions for further research

Austrian economics

Mises, Ludwig von. *The Theory of Money and Credit*. Translated by H. E. Batson (New York: The Foundation of Economic Education, 1971 [1912]).

Mises, Ludwig von. *Human Action: A Treatise on Economics* (New Haven: Yale University Press, 1949).

Rothbard, M. N. 'The Austrian theory of money.' In *The Foundations of Modern Austrian Economics*, edited by E. G. Dolan (Kansas City: Sheed & Ward, 1976).

Shackle, George L. S. *Epistemics and Economics: A Critique of Economic Doctrines* (Cambridge, UK: Cambridge University Press, 1972).

Neo-Austrian economics

Kirzner, I. M. *Competition and Entrepreneurship* (Chicago: The University of Chicago Press, 1973).

Institutional economics

Ayres, Clarence. *Toward a Reasonable Society: The Values of Industrial Civilization* (Austin, Tex.: The University of Texas Press, 1961), p. 113.

Ayres, Clarence. 'The impact of the Great Depression on economic thinking.' *American Economic Review, Papers and Proceedings* (May, 1964), p. 122.

Ayres, Clarence. 'The legacy of Thorstein Veblen.' In *Institutional Economics: Veblen, Commons and Mitchell Reconsidered*, edited by Joseph Dorfman *et al.* (Berkeley, Calif.: University of California Press, 1964).

Galbraith, J. K. *The Affluent Society* (Boston, Mass.: Houghton Mifflin, 1964).

Galbraith, J. K. *Economics and Public Purpose* (Boston, Mass.: Houghton Mifflin, 1973).

Galbraith, J. K. 'Power and the useful economists.' *American Economic Review*, 63 (March, 1973).

Rutherford, Malcolm. 'American institutionalism and the history of economics.' *Journal of the History of Economic Thought*, 19(2), (1997).

Walker, Donald A. 'The economic policy proposals of Clarence Ayres.' *Southern Economic Journal* 44(3) (January, 1978).

Post-Keynesian and Sraffian economics

Applebaum, Eileen. 'Radical economics,' in *Modern Economic Thought*, edited by Sidney Weintraub (Philadelphia, Pa.: University of Pennsylvania Press, 1977), pp. 559–74.

Paul Davidson. *Money and the Real World* (London: Macmillan, 1972).

Eichner, Alfred S. and Kregel, J. A. 'An essay in post-Keynesian theory: a new paradigm in economics.' *Journal of Economic Literature*, 13 (December, 1975), pp. 1293–314.

Garegnani, P. 'Piero Sraffa,' in *The Elgar Companion to Classical Economics*, vol. II, edited by H. D. Kurz and N. Salvadori (Cheltenham, UK: Edward Elgar), pp. 391–98.

Gram, Harvey, and Walsh, Vivian. 'Joan Robinson's economics in retrospect.' *Journal of Economic Literature*, 25(2) (June, 1983) pp. 518–50.

Kaldor, Nicholas. 'Alternative theories of distribution.' *Review of Economics Studies*, 23 (1956), pp. 83–100.

Minsky, Hyman. *John Maynard Keynes* (New York: Columbia University Press, 1975).

Rima, Ingrid H. 'Involuntary unemployment and the respecified labor supply curve.' *Journal of Post-Keynesian Economics*, 6(4) (Summer, 1984).

Rima, Ingrid H. *The Joan Robinson Legacy* (Armonk, NY: M. E. Sharpe, 1991).

Rima, Ingrid H. 'Sectoral changes in employment: an eclectic perspective on "good" jobs and "poor" jobs' in *Review of Political Economy*, 12 (2) (April 2000) pp. 171–90.

Roncaglia, A. 'Piero Sraffa as an interpreter of the classical economists,' in *The Elgar Companion to Classical Economics*, vol. II, edited by H. D. Kurz and N. Salvadori (Cheltenham UK: Edward Elgar), pp. 391–98.

Weintraub, Sidney. 'A macroeconomic approach to the theory of wages.' *The American Economic Review*, 46(5) (December, 1956), pp. 835–56.

Weintraub, Sidney. 'Hicksian Keynesianism.' In *Modern Economic Thought* (Philadelphia, Pa.: University of Pennsylvania Press, 1977).

Weintraub, Sidney. *An Approach to the Theory of Income Distribution* (Philadelphia, Pa.: Chilton Press, 1958).

Weintraub, Sidney. *A Keynesian Theory of Employment, Growth and Income Distribution.* (Philadelphia, Pa.: Chilton Press, 1965).

Radical economics

Edwards, Richard C., and MacEwen, Arthur. 'A radical approach to economics.' *American Economic Review, Papers and Proceedings*, 60 (1970), pp. 352–63.

Franklin, Raymond S., and Tabb, William P. 'The challenge of radical political economics.' *Journal of Economic Issues*, 8 (1974), pp. 124–50.

Fusfeld, Daniel P. 'Types of radicalism in American economics.' *American Economic Association, Papers and Proceedings* (May, 1973), pp. 145–51.

Gordon, Donald. *Theories of Poverty and Underemployment* (Lexington, Mass.: D. C. Heath, 1972).

Gordon, Donald, (ed.) *Problems in a Political Economy: An Urban Perspective* (Lexington, Mass.: D. C. Heath, 1971).

The methodology of economics

Blaug, Mark. *The Methodology of Economics* (Cambridge, UK: Cambridge University Press, 1992).

Kirzner, I. M. *The Economic Point of View* (Kansas City, Kans.: Sheed & Ward, 1960).

Kirzner, I. M. 'On the method of Austrian economics,' in Dolan, E. G. (ed.) *The Foundation of Modern Austrian Economics* (Kansas City, Kans.: Sheed & Ward, 1976).

Lange, O. 'The scope and method of economics.' *Review of Economic Studies*, reprinted in *Kamerschen* (1967), pp. 3–22.

Index of names

Index of subjects

Chapter III

Historical development of the conception

It will be most convenient to open the discussion by a historical survey of the development of the conception.

Originally the word Capital (*Capitale* from *Caput*) was used to signify the Principal of a money loan (*Capitalis pars debiti*) in opposition to Interest. This usage, already foreshadowed in the Greek formation ΚΦραλαιον, became firmly established in medival Latin, and appears to have remained the prevailing one for a very long time, even pretty far down in the new era. Here, therefore, Capital meant the same thing as 'an interest-bearing sum of money.'

In the meantime, the disputes which had arisen over the legitimacy or illegitimacy of loan interest brought about an essential deepening and widening of the conception. It had become apparent that the interest-bearing power of 'barren' money was at bottom a borrowed one – borrowed from the productive power of things that the money could buy. Money only gave the exchange form – to a certain extent the outward garb – in which the interest-bearing things passed from hand to hand. The true 'stock' or parent stem which bore interest was not money but the goods that were acquired for it. In these circumstances the obvious course was to change the conception that, besides embracing the representative thing, money, it would embrace the represented thing, goods.

Thus, Turgot gave the second reading in historical succession to the conception of capital.

It was very soon superseded by a third. For when Turgot designated all saved goods indiscriminately as Capital, he seemed to have gone too far in broadening the conception. To replace the word 'money' in the definition by the word 'goods' only reflected, indeed, the more thorough grasp, which was now taken of the subject. But to give the name of Capital, without any further discrimination, to stocks of goods, was to give up, without sufficient reason, the second feature in the old conception ... It was no less a man than Adam Smith who changed and rectified Turgot's definition. The 'saved' stocks, he said, must be distinguished as containing two parts. One portion is destined for immediate consumption, and gives off no kind of income; the other portion is destined to bring in an income to its owner, and this part alone rightly bears the name of Capital.

With this distinction, however, Adam Smith connected another consideration, that was destined to have very serious consequences on the development of the conception. He remarked that his use of the term was applicable as well to the case of individuals as to that of a whole community; only, with this shifting of the standpoint, the group of things embraced by the conception was also somewhat changed. Individuals, that is to say, can make a gain, not only by the production of goods, but also by lending to other individuals for a consideration goods which are destined in themselves to immediate consumption, such as houses, masquerade dresses, furniture, etc. But the community, as a whole, cannot enrich itself otherwise than by the production of new goods.

But all the time, in virtue of the old parent conception – that known later as Private Capital – the term capital remained connected with the phenomenon of interest, which belonged to the theory of distribution or income. Thus, from that time onward appeared the peculiar phenomenon, which was to be the source of so many errors and complications, that two series of fundamentally different phenomena and fundamentally different problems were treated under the same name. Capital, as National Capital, became the central figure of the

Chapter III

Historical development of the conception

It will be most convenient to open the discussion by a historical survey of the development of the conception.

Originally the word Capital (*Capitale* from *Caput*) was used to signify the Principal of a money loan (*Capitalis pars debiti*) in opposition to Interest. This usage, already foreshadowed in the Greek formation ΚΦραλαιον, became firmly established in medival Latin, and appears to have remained the prevailing one for a very long time, even pretty far down in the new era. Here, therefore, Capital meant the same thing as 'an interest-bearing sum of money.'

In the meantime, the disputes which had arisen over the legitimacy or illegitimacy of loan interest brought about an essential deepening and widening of the conception. It had become apparent that the interest-bearing power of 'barren' money was at bottom a borrowed one – borrowed from the productive power of things that the money could buy. Money only gave the exchange form – to a certain extent the outward garb – in which the interest-bearing things passed from hand to hand. The true 'stock' or parent stem which bore interest was not money but the goods that were acquired for it. In these circumstances the obvious course was to change the conception that, besides embracing the representative thing, money, it would embrace the represented thing, goods.

Thus, Turgot gave the second reading in historical succession to the conception of capital.

It was very soon superseded by a third. For when Turgot designated all saved goods indiscriminately as Capital, he seemed to have gone too far in broadening the conception. To replace the word 'money' in the definition by the word 'goods' only reflected, indeed, the more thorough grasp, which was now taken of the subject. But to give the name of Capital, without any further discrimination, to stocks of goods, was to give up, without sufficient reason, the second feature in the old conception . . . It was no less a man than Adam Smith who changed and rectified Turgot's definition. The 'saved' stocks, he said, must be distinguished as containing two parts. One portion is destined for immediate consumption, and gives off no kind of income; the other portion is destined to bring in an income to its owner, and this part alone rightly bears the name of Capital.

With this distinction, however, Adam Smith connected another consideration, that was destined to have very serious consequences on the development of the conception. He remarked that his use of the term was applicable as well to the case of individuals as to that of a whole community; only, with this shifting of the standpoint, the group of things embraced by the conception was also somewhat changed. Individuals, that is to say, can make a gain, not only by the production of goods, but also by lending to other individuals for a consideration goods which are destined in themselves to immediate consumption, such as houses, masquerade dresses, furniture, etc. But the community, as a whole, cannot enrich itself otherwise than by the production of new goods.

But all the time, in virtue of the old parent conception – that known later as Private Capital – the term capital remained connected with the phenomenon of interest, which belonged to the theory of distribution or income. Thus, from that time onward appeared the peculiar phenomenon, which was to be the source of so many errors and complications, that two series of fundamentally different phenomena and fundamentally different problems were treated under the same name. Capital, as National Capital, became the central figure of the